Therapist's Guide to Substance Abuse Intervention

Therapist's Guide to Substance Abuse Intervention

SHARON L. JOHNSON

ACADEMIC PRESS

An imprint of Elsevier Science

Amsterdam   Boston   London   New York   Oxford   Paris
San Diego   San Francisco   Singapore   Sydney   Tokyo

Academic Press
An imprint of Elsevier Science
525 B Street, Suite 1900, San Diego, California 92101-4495, USA
http://www.academicpress.com

Academic Press
84 Theobald's Road, London WC1X 8RR, UK
http://www.academicpress.com

Library of Congress Catalog Card Number: 2003104115

International Standard Book Number: 0-12-387581-1

PRINTED IN THE UNITED STATES OF AMERICA
03 04 05 06 07   8 7 6 5 4 3 2 1

CONTENTS

Introduction   xvii

Part I

Chapter 1

DEFINING SUBSTANCE ABUSE AND DEPENDENCE   3

Continuum of Substance Use Behaviors   5
DSM IV Criteria   6
   Substance Abuse   6   •   Substance Dependence   7   •   Specifiers   7
Additional Considerations   8
   Dual Diagnosis   8   •   Codependents   8   •   References   9

Chapter 2

CHARACTERISTICS AND CLASSIFICATION OF SUBSTANCES   11

Characteristics of Substances   11
   Drug Dosage   12   •   Potency   12   •   Therapeutic Ratio   12
   Drug Equivalence   12   •   Frequency of Use   12   •   Route of Admission   12
   Drug Interactions   13   •   Types of Drug Effects   13
Substance Use and Conditioning   13
Physiological Functioning   14
   Pharmacokinetics   14   •   Pharmacodynamics   16
Physiological Characteristics or Factors of
   the Substance User   17
Psychological Characteristics of the User   18
Sociocultural Environment   19

Classification of Substances   19

    Depressants   19   •   Cannabinoids   22
    Opioids   23   •   Hallucinogens   26
    Stimulants   29   •   Nicotine   31
    Anabolic Steroids   31   •   Club Drugs   32
    References   38

Chapter 3

DEVELOPMENT OF SUBSTANCE ABUSE AND DEPENDENCE   39

Models of Substance Dependence   40
Causal Factors of Substance Abuse and Dependence   41
Biological Mechanisms   42
Early Onset Variables   50
Late Onset Variables   51

    References   51

Chapter 4

STAGES OF SUBSTANCE DEPENDENCE AND RECOVERY   53

A Causal Model for Substance Abuse   54
Problematic Behavior and Thought Patterns   54
Patterns of Use   55
Developmental Stages of Dependence   56

    Preaddictive–Early Stage   56   •   Addictive–Middle Stage   57
    Chronic–Late Stage   58

Recovery stages   58
Experience of Object Loss   59
Relapse Symptoms   60
Relapse Autopsy   61
Process of Relapse   62
Special Issues of Substance Dependence   62

    Dry Drunk   62   •   Family System Response to Substance Dependency   64
    Codependency   65   •   Common Symptomatology of Substance-Dependent and
    Codependent Individuals   66   •   References   70

Part II

Chapter 5

ASSESSMENT   75

Purpose of Assessment   76
Motivational Interviewing   76
Individualized Treatment Plan   77
Assessment Questions   78
Multivariate Treatment Planning   79

Important Components of a Substance Abuse History   79

Objective Assessment   81

Psychological and Neuropsychological Assessment   82

Substance-Related Assessment Inventories   83

Mnemonic Screening Devices   86

> *CAGE (Ewing, 1984)   86   •   TWEAK (Russel et al., 1991)   86*

Functional Importance of Substance Use   86

Follow-up Assessment   87

Conceptual Assessment of Substance Abuse   87

Questionnaires   89

> *The Johnson Substance Use Psychological Questionnaire (Adapted From Johnson, 1997)   89   •   Adult Psychosocial (Adapted from Johnson, 1997)   100 The Johnson Brief Initial Assessment (Adapted from Johnson, 1997)   104 Substance Use Survey   108   •   Chemical Dependency Assessment (Adapted from Johnson, 1997)   113   •   Chemical Dependency Psychological Assessment   114 Substance Use History   117   •   Substance Use History: A Phase Review   118 Family Substance Use History   122   •   Chemical Dependency Psychosocial Assessment: Brief Form   123   •   Alcohol Involvement Scale   127   •   Substance Abuse–Dependence Personal Evaluation   128   •   Outline for Diagnostic Summary   129   •   Withdrawal Symptoms Checklist (Adapted from Johnson, 1997)   131*

Factors Indicating a Need for Adolescent Substance Use Assessment   132

> *Psychological–Social Factors   132   •   Substance Use Associated Factors   132*

Adolescent Screening and Assessment   132

> *Screening   132   •   Assessment   133*

Diagnostic Criteria for Codependency   133

Special Topic: Employment Setting   134

> *Employer and Supervisory Training   134   •   How to Constructively Confront the Employee   135   •   Summary Outline of How to Constructively Confront an Employee with a Problem   136   •   Supervisors as Enablers   137   •   Defensive Strategies of Employees   138   •   Warning Sign Checklist   139*

Prevention   142

> *Prevention Models   143   •   Prevention Programs   145   •   Model for Effective Health Education (Adapted from Green et al., 1980)   146   •   References   146*

Part III

Chapter 6
TREATMENT GUIDELINES   153

Biopsychosocial Perspective   154

A Simple Comparison of Recovery and Mental Health Models   155

Theoretical Orientation   157

The Role of 12-Step and Other Self-Help Programs   157

Resistance and Other Problems   158   •   Increasing Engagement   158
Alternatives to 12-Step Groups   159

Harm Reduction   159

Principles of Harm Reduction   160   •   Integration of Harm Reduction and
Substance Abuse Treatment   160   •   Clinical Rationale for Harm
Reduction   161

Special Considerations for Dual Diagnosis   161

Models of Treatment   162

The Individual Entering Treatment   162
Treatment Concerns   163
Rational Emotive Therapy Philosophy   164
Therapist Guidelines   165

Professional Codependent Versus Helper   166

Preparation of Individuals, Couples, and Families for
   Recovery   166
Treatment Prioritization   169
Course of Treatment   170
Agents of Change   170
Areas of Personal Vulnerability for those in Treatment   172
Obstacles to Change   172
Overcoming Obstacles to Change   173
Individualized Treatment Planning   174

Formulating the Treatment Plan   175   •   Record Keeping   176
The Johnson Independent Treatment Plan—Short Form   177   •   The Johnson
Individualized Treatment Plan   178   •   Basic Treatment Plan Format
Sample   180   •   Understanding Your Experience of Treatment   181
Treatment Rules   182   •   Treatment Contract   182

Guidelines for an Intervention   183

Criteria for an Intervention   183   •   Guidelines for those Participating in an
Intervention   184

Legal Issues Associated with Screening and Assessing
   Adolescent Substance Use   185
Role of Americans with Disabilities Act   185

Substance Abuse Services in Practice   186
References   186

Chapter 7
CONTINUUM OF CARE   191

Key Aspects of Treatment   191
Substance Abuse–Dependence Continuum of
   Care Services   192

Outpatient Treatment Program   192   •   Intensive Outpatient Treatment
Program   193   •   Partial Hospitalization Substance Dependency Program   194
Residential Treatment Program   195   •   Inpatient Detoxification   195
Treatment Groups   196

ASAM-PPC-2 Assessment Criteria   196

    Assessment Dimensions   197   •   Diagnostic Criteria for Determining
    Level of Care   198

Specific Substance Class Treatment Considerations
  Associated with Continuum of Care   201

    Depressants   201   •   Stimulants   205   •   Polysubstance Abuse   205

Community Reinforcement   206

Controlled Drinking: A Treatment Alternative   207

    References   212

Part IV

Chapter 8
SOLUTION-FOCUSED THERAPY   219

Potential Problems   221

Strategies for Improving Motivation (Miller &
  Rollnick, 1991)   222

Predictive Measures of Outcome   222

Therapist Responses to Slips   222

Decreasing Treatment Dropout Rate   223

Role of Family Treatment   223

Inpatient Treatment   224

Patient–Treatment Matching   224

Discharge and Aftercare   225

Treatment Interventions Supported by Research   226

Treatment Models   227

    Cognitive Restructuring   227   •   Behavior Modification   228
    Psychodynamic Therapy   231

Medical Treatment for Substance Dependence   234

    Pharmacotherapy   234

Integration of Psychotherapy and Pharmacotherapy   235

Evidence for Effectiveness of Combined Treatment   236

Individual Therapy   237

Importance and Usefulness of the Support Group
  Forum   238

Benefits of Support Groups   239

Therapeutic Group   240

Basic Areas of Education   241

Stages of Solution-Focussed, Outcome-Oriented
  Treatment   242

Group Topics   245

    Substance Use–Abuse Group   245   •   Codependency   247   •   Shyness   249
    Anger Management   250   •   Assertiveness Training   252   •   Skills
    Acquisition   253   •   Social Skills Training   254   •   Anxiety and Stress
    Management   255   •   Adult Children of Alcoholics (Dysfunctional Families)   256

Domestic Violence (Offender Group) 257 • *Domestic Violence (Victim Group)* 260 • *Adults Molested as Children* 261
Understanding the Impact on Children 263

Marital and Family Therapy 264
Family Therapy 266
Family Patterns of Substance Dependency 267
Stages of Family Intervention 267
Relapse 271

Relapse Prevention Techniques 272 • *Dealing with a Slip, Lapse, or Relapse* 278

Aversion Therapy for Alcohol Dependence 279
Moderation of Use 280

Behavioral Self-Control Training (Hester & Miller, 1989) 281
Setting Limits or Guidelines for Moderate Drinking 281

Recommendations for Improving Substance Abuse
Treatment 282

References 282

Chapter 9
SPECIAL POPULATIONS AND DUAL DIAGNOSIS 289

Key Issues for Treating Dual Diagnosis Individuals 292

Short-Term Treatment Plan 293 • *Long-Term Treatment Plan* 294

Dual Diagnosis 295

Nonchronic Versus Chronic Symptoms 295 • *Mood Disorders* 296
Anxiety Disorders 297 • *Personality Disorders* 297 • *Psychotic Disorders* 301

Adolescents 303

Overview of Adolescent Substance Abuse 305
Family Education and Intervention 310
Pregnancy and Substance Use 311
Intervention 311 • *Intervention with Parents* 313

Geriatrics 316

Assessment 317 • *Continuum of Use to Abuse of Prescribed Psychoactive Medications* 322 • *Effects of Aging on Response to Substance Effects* 323 • *Treatment Considerations* 323 • *Substance-Alcohol Interactions* 331

AIDS–HIV 331

Overview 331 • *Assessment of the Substance Abusing HIV–AIDS-Infected Individual* 333 • *Treatment* 337 • *Harm Reduction: Understanding the Risks* 339 • *Continuum of Care with Associated Treatment* 339
HIV–AIDS and Pain Management 341 • *Assessment of Needs in Addition to Substance Abuse Treatment* 342

Adults Molested as Children 342

Dissociative Experiences Scale 344

Women and Minorities 344

       Intervention Considerations 345 • Women 346 • Minorities 353

  Court-Mandated Treatment 359

    References 361

Part V

Chapter 10

SKILL BUILDING RESOURCES 375

    Risk Factors for Substance Abuse 376

    Consequences of Substance Abuse 377

    Six Cardinal Signs Indicating Substance Dependence 378

    Symptoms of Alcoholism 379

    Do I Have a Drinking Problem? 380

    Problem Drinker 382

    Substance Use or Abuse: Diagnosing Dependency 383

    Self-Diagnosis: Do You Have a Problem with
      Substance Use? 384

    Relationship Addiction 386

    Compulsive Gambling 387

    Sexual Addiction 388

    Substance Dependency: A Family Illness 389

    Understanding the Dynamics of the Chemically
      Dependent Family 390

    Recovery Needs of Family Members 391

    Identifying Patterns of Codependency 393

    Does Someone You Know Have a Problem
      with Substances? 394

    Stages of Recovery 395

    Recovery is a Choice 396

    Your Choice 397

    Why is Substance Abstinence Important? 398

    How has Substance Abuse Affected Your Life? 399

    How to Cut Down on Your Drinking 400

    An Overview of Where I am and Where I am Going 401

    Recovery Inventory 403

    My Recovery Plan 404

    Reviewing Your Recovery Program 405

    Preparation for Attending a 12-Step Meeting 406

        What is a 12-Step Program? 406 • What Does a 12-Step Program Do? 406

    The 12 Traditions of Alcoholics Anonymous 407

    Twelve Steps Outline 408

    Ten Steps (Modification of 12 Steps) 409

    Twelve Steps 410

    Twelve Steps to Recovery 413

        Step 1 413 • Step 2 414 • Step 3 415 • Step 4 416
        Step 5 417 • Step 6 418 • Step 7 419 • Step 8 420
        Step 9 421 • Step 10 423 • Step 11 424 • Step 12 425

Taking Inventory   426

An Outline for Making Amends   427

The Five S's of Recovery   429

Understanding Craving   430

Coping with Craving   431

Assessing High-Risk Situations   432

Self-Monitoring Journal   433

Daily Log   434

  Part I   434   •   *Part II   435*

Experience Log   436

Daily Recovery Schedule   437

Journal Writing as Part of Your Recovery   438

  Part I   438

Evening and Weekend Schedule and Journal   440

  Evening Journal   440   •   *Journal   440*

Consequences   441

  Consequence Journal   441

Relapse Prevention   443

  Part I   443   •   *Part II   444*   •   *Part III   446*   •   *Part IV   447*

Maintaining Progress   448

Interrupting Potential Relapse   449

Choices—Learning More About Yourself   450

Practicing Change   452

Increasing Self-Understanding   453

Lingering Withdrawal   454

What to do When Confronted with the Urge to Use   455

Points to Consider When Confronted with the Urge to Use
  Substances   456

Planning How to Cope with a Lapse   457

Dealing with a Slip, Lapse, or Relapse   458

Anticipating How to Cope with an Emergency   459

Getting Unstuck   460

Beast   461

Help Me   462

Refusal Skills   463

  What to Do   463

Substance Use Aggravates Stress   464

Self-Care Plan   465

Relaxing Without Substances   466

  Rest   466   •   *Sleep   466*

Excitement without Substances   468

Deep Breathing: A Relaxation Skill   469

  How it Works   469   •   *Results of Deep Breathing   469*

Monitoring Use of Relaxation   470

  Relaxation   470

Self-Control   471

Modified Drinking   472

>*Drinking Journal*   472

What is Responsibility?   473

Coping with Disappointment   475

>*The Meaning and Value of Disappointment*   475   •   *How to Decrease Disappointment*   475

Surviving the Holiday Blues   476

Stinking Thinking   477

Understanding the Role of Thinking and Relapse   479

Coping with Negative Thinking   480

Managing Thoughts about Using Substances   481

List of Symptoms Leading to Relapse   482

Symptoms of Relapse   483

Early Warning Signs   486

Reviewing Personal Risks of Relapse   486

Feeling Like Your Life is Out of Control   488

Dealing With Feeling Emotionally Overwhelmed   489

Prevention   490

>*Adults*   490

Developing and Utilizing Social Support   491

>*Characteristics of a Supportive Relationship*   491

How to Build a Recovery Support System   493

Maintaining a Support System   495

Factors that Interfere with Developing a Social Support System   498

The Role of Relationships and Substance Use   500

>*Questionnaire for Potential Social Support Member*   500

Defense Mechanism Definitions   501

Defense Mechanisms   502

Dealing with Fear   504

Breaking Through the Negative Thoughts Cycle   506

Thought Stopping   507

Fifteen Rules for Emotional Health   508

Dealing with Difficult People   509

Surviving the Loss of a relationship   510

The Art of Negotiation   511

Self-Confidence   512

Coping with Confrontations   514

Dealing with Embarrassment or Being Self-Conscious   515

Coping with Embarrassment   516

Emotional First Steps for Dual Diagnosis   518

>*Anxiety Disorders Symptoms*   519   •   *Mood Disorder Symptoms*   520
>*Personality Disorder Symptoms*   520   •   *Thought Disorder Symptoms*   522
>*Accepting Your Illness*   523

The Twelve Steps and Dual Diagnosis   529

The First Step   529   •   The Second Step   532   •   The Third Step   533
The Fourth Step   534   •   The Fifth Step   536   •   The Sixth Step   537
The Seventh Step   538   •   The Eighth Step   539   •   The Ninth Step   540
The Tenth Step   541   •   The Eleventh Step   542   •   The Twelfth Step   543

Identifying Depression   544
Managing Depression   545
Understanding Grief   546
Daily Activity Schedule   547
Identifying Anxiety   548
Managing Anxiety   549

     Management Skills   549

Anxiety Relapse   550
Identifying Feelings   551
Understanding Your Feelings   552
Self-Honesty   553
Communication   554
Communicating Difficult Feelings   555

     How to Deal with Uncomfortable Feelings   555

Constructively Expressing Angry Feelings   556
Dealing With Criticism and Giving Feedback   557

     Dealing with Criticism   557   •   Ten Steps for Giving Feedback   557

Understanding Anger   558
Managing Anger   559
Ways of Dealing with Anger   561
The Steps for Letting Go of Anger   562
Goal Setting   563
Goal Development   564

     Steps for Developing Goals   564

Setting Priorities   565

     Steps for Setting Priorities   565

Problem Solving   566
Decision Making   567

     Steps for Decision Making   567

Time Management   568

     *Four Central Steps to Effective Time Management   568   •   How to Start Your
Time Management Program   568*

How to Budget   569
Your Personal Budget   570
Applying for a Job   571
How to Give a Good Job Interview   572
Setting Career Goals   573

     Potential Career Goals and How to Reach Them   573

Work Ethics   574
Survey of Personal Strengths   575
Writing a Thank you Letter   576

Sample Letter   577

Coping Skills for Caregivers   578

Guidelines for Family Members–Significant Others of the
    Alcoholic–Chemically Dependent Individual   579

Detaching with Love Versus Controlling   580

The Enabler—The Companion to the
    Dysfunctional–Substance Abusing Person   581

Healing for the Substance Abusing Family: From Enabling
    to Recovery   583

No Talk Rule   584

> *Family Lessons and Rules Learned in Substance Dependency and
> Dysfunctional Homes   584*

Stages of Family Adjustment to Substance
    Dependence   585

Ten Steps to Feeling Better if You are an Adolescent Living
    with Someone Who Uses Substances   586

First Step for Family Members and Significant Other   587

Functional Vs. Dysfunctional Families   589

Parenting Style and Adolescent Substance Use   590

Healthy Parenting, Healthy Family   591

The Healthy Family is a Parent-Centered Family   592

Parents Helping Children   593

Summary of Substances   594

I Think My Child may be Using Substances   595

A Parent's Checklist about Adolescent Substance Use   596

Adolescent Substance Abuse Quiz   597

Actions to take if Your Child is Using Substances   600

Dealing with Peer Pressure   601

> *Part I   601*

Dealing with Peer Pressure   603

> *Part II   603*

Dealing with Peer Pressure   605

> *Part III   605*

Dealing with Peer Pressure   607

> *Part IV: Making Your Own Decisions   607*

Family Rules and Expectations   609

Tips for Parents   610

Keeping Children Drug-Free   611

How Substance Abuse Harms an Unborn Child or
    Nursing Child   613

Fetal Alcohol Syndrome (FAS)   615

Identifying Children of Substance Abusing Parents   616

Self-Esteem and Mentoring   618

Characteristics Often Found in Members of Substance-
    Dependent Families   620

How to Help Children Through a Crisis   622

A Parents' Pledge   623

The House with the Pink Elephant   624

Parents, Teenagers, and Honest Communication   625
Skills for Positive Parenting   627
Understanding the Experience of the Significant Other   628
Twelve Things You can do if Your Loved One is a Substance
     Abuser   630
Eight Steps for Feeling Better if You Live with Someone
     Who Abuses Substances   631
Breaking the Codependency Cycle   632
Signs of an Unhealthy Relationship   635
Ten Ways to Improve Your Marriage   636
Working Together   637

     Relationship Self-Monitoring   637

Being a Healthy Couple   638
Self-Acceptance   639
Stop the Rescuing   640
Adult Children of Alcoholics   641
Children of Alcoholics   642
The Consequences of Codependency   643
Feelings   644
Behaviors of the Codependent   645
How to Deal with Codependency   646
Couples Homework   647
Couples Learning to Solve Problems   648
Relationship Challenges   649
Improving Relationships by Using Clear
     Communication   650
Communication Guidelines   651
A Senior's Guide for Using Medications Wisely   653

     Do   653   •   Do Not   653

Nail in the Fence   654
Information Sheets   655

     Alcohol   655   •   Central Nervous System (CNS) Depressants   656
     Cannabis   657   •   Narcotics   658   •   Hallucinogens   659
     Central Nervous System (CNS) Stimulants   660   •   Steroids   661

National Helplines   662

INTRODUCTION

THE *Therapist's Guide* strives to convey the immense complexity of substance abuse and substance dependence disorders woven through biological, psychological, and social environmental roots. This understanding is necessary for the development of comprehensive individualized treatment, which encompasses behavioral, psychological, social and pharmacological interventions. To gain a perspective of the prevalence and impact upon society by the abuse and dependence on one substance, review the consequences of alcohol. There are approximately 14 million American alcoholics with about 10 million children (1 in 4 children) being exposed to familial alcohol problems (*The Fresno Bee*, Associated Press, December 31, 1999). Likewise, the Community Epidemiology Work Group (1999) states that 14.8 million Americans used illicit drugs, with 3.5 million dependent on illicit drugs and 8.2 million people dependent on alcohol.

This book will serve as a useful resource manual for all therapists. Information ranges from the needs of the specialist in the area of substance abuse to those of the therapist in general practice requiring the knowledge to identify, assess, diagnose, and intervene with appropriate treatment and/or refer those presenting with a diagnosis of substance abuse or dependence. Substance abuse is one of the most prevalent and costly health care problems facing the United States today. It is important to note that, even if one lacks the necessary experience, education, and training in this area, knowledge is still required for a level of assessment that results in appropriate referrals for substance abusers, addicts, or family members of someone experiencing difficulties associated with substances. The goal is not to promote a single theory, but to offer basic and effective tools for appropriately intervening with individuals and families struggling with substance abuse issues. Every therapist is obligated to familiarize himself or herself with prevention strategies and the resources in his or her community so that he or she can complete the necessary interventions and referrals.

Over the years there has been a significant shift in treatment with the focus being on outpatient care. As this change has evolved, so have the philosophy and acceptance that here is no single treatment approach that stands out as being superior to others. In fact, being rigid in one's treatment approach immediately limits the range of individuals who will be successfully treated and impedes the maintenance and progress of the recovery process as well. Unfortunately, availability and an appropriate continuum of treatment choices to fit individualized needs are often not to be found in many communities. Therefore, regardless of the setting, this book is intended to provide a broad conceptualization of basic information.

A comprehensive treatment plan is required that includes identified factors that facilitate and maintain change through the combination and integration of cognitive–behavioral interventions and dynamic understanding and processing. The process of recovery is multileveled and multidimensional, requiring that individual presentation and associated complexities be a focal point of consideration in developing an effective treatment plan (Stephanie Brown, 1895).

Regardless of one's discipline, the therapist can learn to recognize the abuse of alcohol and other substances so that he or she may effectively assess, intervene, and refer. The information in this book should help the clinician to better understand substance abuse disorders and deliver more effective treatment. Additionally, the use of the information in this book should help to increase clinician accountability and effectiveness in working with managed care, case review, and peer review. Research does not support a narrow theoretical perspective or limited interventions. Optimal outcome must take into consideration clinician skills, resources, and the individualized needs of those in treatment. Therefore, a central theme of this book is to increase therapist understanding of symptoms, dynamics, and interventions to enable the blending of the therapist's own clinical strengths and preferences with approaches demonstrated to be effective. The users of this text must consider their own expertise in providing any services. Professional and ethical guidelines require that any therapist providing clinical service be competent and have appropriate education, training, supervision, and experience. This includes a knowledge of current scientific and professional standards of practice and familiarity with associated legal standards and procedures. Additionally, it is the responsibility of the provider of psychological services to have a thorough appreciation and understanding of the influence of ethnic and cultural differences on case conceptualization and treatment and to assure that such sensitivity is always utilized.

This book is organized into five parts: (1) definition, (2) assessment, (3) treatment guidelines and continuum of care, (4) solution-focused therapy and special populations, and (5) skill building resources. The first part introduces the reader to a summary of substance classification and diagnostic criteria. Somehow most education and training neglect psychopharmacology at a level that offers a mechanistic understanding. This is beneficial for understanding the experience of substance use, the selection of substances, and the combination of substances as well as enhancing treatment team effectiveness. Although it is not necessary to immerse oneself in the knowledge base of a treatment team colleague, it is important that members of the treatment team have a minimal knowledge base that facilitates effective consultation and thorough treatment. Therapists must be prepared to interact with all disciplines. In other words, the more they understand the perspective of those with whom they collaborate and are able to effectively communicate in the varied terminology associated with substance abuse, the greater the likelihood of effective teamwork and treatment planning.

The second part, assessment, is a broad-based section reviewing the central areas associated with assessment, which is an initial stage of intervention. Therefore, it offers information on a range of available diagnostic instruments, samples of biopsychosocial questionnaires, guidelines on motivational interviewing, information specific to the workplace, and prevention. The assessment is an opportunity to facilitate "thinking" about choices and consequences, which can result in increased self-responsibility, positive health choices, and personal growth. Through this episode of facilitated self-awareness comes an opportunity for improved health and quality of life.

The third part covers treatment guidelines and continuum of care. The purpose of the treatment guidelines chapter is to clarify the diversity of presenting issues in consideration of applied theoretical orientation, the role of self-help groups, the integration of harm reduction, special considerations for dual diagnosis, the importance of collaborative treatment planning, systems issues, what facilitates versus impedes change, and treatment planning. Continuum of care attempts to take this expansive information and formulate it into steps or stages of treatment directly associated with level of functioning and individual needs.

The fourth part, solution-focused therapy and special populations, is self-explanatory. Solution-focused therapy is designed to offer a thorough review of structured treatment that is individualized to meet the needs of the person. This facilitates staying on task, acts to facilitate an increased self-awareness and self-responsibility, provides adequate support, and measures change. It reviews the continuum of treatment modalities and setting specific to individualized and system needs. Additionally, it offers a brief review of general pharmacotherapy along with information on combining pharmacotherapy and psychotherapy. It also challenges the therapist to consider or at least familiarize himself or herself with moderation of use and behavioral self-control training when the goal of abstinence is not desired by the substance-abusing/dependent individual as a means of reducing harm. There are outlines on individual, group, and systems interventions. The second half of this part includes a review on special populations to increase the awareness of the therapist to the issues of human diversity.

The fifth and final part, skill building resources, offers numerous tools that a therapist can use directly or reformulate and personalize for any individual to increase treatment effectiveness. Early in my training on a dual diagnosis unit of a hospital there was often evidence of treatment positively influencing those that relapsed and were readmitted. Use of substances, in lieu of what they had learned about themself and the consequences of substance use, often created an increase in cognitive dissonance. Therefore, every opportunity to share information or increase self-understanding in terms the person in treatment can grasp and identify with is fertile ground that demands to be sown. Any therapist who neglects such opportunities must acknowledge his or her potential role in the unnecessary extension of various treatment phases. Skill building resources is one way to educate, increase awareness, and discover choices and associated consequences, and thereby increase self-responsibility and treatment effectiveness.

Part I

Chapter 1

Defining Substance Abuse and Dependence

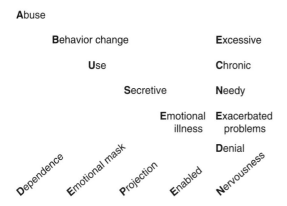

Abuse

Behavior change   **E**xcessive

Use   **C**hronic

Secretive   **N**eedy

Emotional illness   **E**xacerbated problems

Denial

Dependence   **E**motional mask   **P**rojection   **E**nabled   **N**ervousness

Substance abuse and substance dependence are major social problems in our culture. According to the National Institute on Drug Abuse (1999), the estimated total cost of alcohol and drug abuse in 1992 was $245.7 billion, up 50% from the 1985 data. Of this estimated cost, $97.7 billion was due to drug abuse. The primary contributors to this increase were the cocaine epidemic, the HIV epidemic, and the 8-fold increase in incarceration rate for substance-related offenses (<3-fold increase in substance-related crimes). The study determined the primary costs (46%) were governmental in nature, whereas the remaining costs (44%) were associated with substance abusers and members of their households: (1) prevention, (2) substance abuse treatment, (3) health care costs, (4) reduced job productivity–lost earnings, and (5) costs to society (crime–social welfare).

For many, substance abuse is difficult to define, other than it being excessive, mind altering, and/or mood altering. On the other hand, substance dependence refers to the psychological or physical compulsion to use substances in order to experience an altered state. Psychological and physical substance dependence often occurs in conjunction, requiring comprehensive treatment that deals with both aspects of dependence. Physiological dependence can be described as repeated substance use that results in a consistent pattern of tolerance and withdrawal. The pattern of tolerance and withdrawal implies that the physiological homeostatic mechanisms have adjusted to the substance effects. As a result, without the substance(s) the system becomes destabilized, or out of balance, and withdrawal symptoms are experienced. Factors that contribute to or determine patterns of substance use include the following:

1. Availability of substances
2. The experience of substances

a. fast acting, which render their effects relatively quickly
b. sedating or relaxation
c. feelings of power or grandiosity
d. energized

3. Development of tolerance and physical dependence: avoidance of withdrawal symptoms
4. Genetic background: appearance of some genetic predisposition to alcoholism
5. Culture
   a. limits set by some religious sects that prohibit the use of substances or substance use in certain religious or spiritual rituals
   b. recreational substance practices, i.e., social drinking

6. Family systems experience–environment
   a. substance use habits handed down from one generation to another
   b. experience of abuse leading to a desire to mask emotional pain
   c. compulsive behavioral patterns (also possibly rooted genetically)
   d. general dynamics

7. Socioeconomic status (SES): all backgrounds and SES groups are represented; professionals, nonconformists, etc.
8. Social
   a. setting
   b. peer relationships (influences and pressures)
   c. societal messages

9. Psychological
   a. trauma
   b. skill level for coping, problem solving, conflict resolution, etc.
   c. external locus of control

10. Mental illness
    a. medicating of preexisting emotional disorders (depression, anxiety, psychosis)
    b. disorders that commonly underlie substance abuse include
       i. mood disorders
       ii. anxiety disorder
       iii. psychotic disorders
       iv. somatoform disorders
       v. personality disorders

11. Medical illness
    a. chronic pain
    b. sleep disturbance
    c. loss of functioning

There is no single cause of substance dependence. In general, addicted individuals often experience:

1. Confusion
   a. search for distraction, pleasure, or excitement (recreational use)
   b. identity issues (who am I, individual feels changed when using substances)

2. Overwhelming feelings: remorse, guilt, shame, self-hatred, and mood disturbance
3. Ineffective coping mechanisms
   a. rationalization (irrational–emotional thinking, rationalizing needing a substance to cope)
   b. projection of blame on everyone and everything as the basis of problems instead of lack of effective coping and the impact of substance abuse
   c. denial through self-deception or by the denial of others close to the addict (codependents are drawn into the system of denial, sustain it, and perpetuate it)

CONTINUUM OF SUBSTANCE USE BEHAVIORS

The view of dependence as a syndrome implies that multidimensional criteria are necessary for assessment. Nondependent as well as dependent substance abusers may experience substance-related disabilities and functional impairments.
Observation of the symptoms associated with level of use demonstrate that

1. Integrated use presents little to no appreciable negative impact on functioning.
2. Abuse leads to a range from mild to significant impact on biopsychosocial problems.
3. Dependence is indicative of continued use despite negative consequences, loss of control, and obsessive–compulsive behavior. Dependence becomes a lifestyle.

According to Leshner (1997), clinical relevance to the distinction between physical and psychological dependence is insignificant. For example, cocaine and methamphetamine use results in little or no physical dependence, but they are two of the most highly addictive substances. The involuntary (out of control) nature of dependency is a function of fundamental brain changes created by the use of the substances. The Center for Substance Abuse Prevention (2001) cites a "direct connection to the use of methamphetamine and the American work Ethic. As many as 9.4 million Americans have used the drug at least once. Many users are workers, high school students and truck drivers." Therefore, the most useful characterization of dependency can be set forth as being based upon

1. Physical control systems
2. Motivational control systems
3. Associative memory systems

Nonuse	Mild use	Moderate use	Heavy use
Nonuse	Integrated substance use	Abuse	Dependence
Continuum of impact	Little to no impact on functioning	Interferes but consequences are not significant	"Crossing the wall"(AA) biobehavioral Increasing functional impairment
		Voluntary	Involuntary

Zinberg (1974) offers a model for organizing the variables associated with substance using behaviors: "substance, set, and setting."

Substance	Set	Setting
pharmacological properties	attitudes	social
physiological effects	personality	physical
consequences of the substance use	intrapsychic processes	cultural environment (where use takes place)

According to the *DSM IV* (1994), substance use disorders encompass a constellation of cognitive, behavioral, and psychological symptoms associated with continued use of a substance. Generally, there is a pattern of use resulting in tolerance, withdrawal, and compulsive use. Intoxication and withdrawal are the most prevalent substance-related disorders. Intoxication is a reversible, substance-specific syndrome that often influences or disturbs perception, wakefulness, sleep, attention, judgment, emotionality, and movement. Withdrawal is a substance-specific disorder that results when the chronic intake of a substance has abruptly decreased significantly or ceased. Symptoms of withdrawal include restlessness, anxiety, irritability, insomnia, impaired concentration, and numerous other physiological symptoms that can be quite serious, requiring medical monitoring and treatment. Tolerance is described as the need for increased amounts of a substance to achieve a previous high or intoxication. Tolerance levels vary across substances and individuals. Tolerance levels for amphetamines and opioids can be substantial, especially with heavy use. In fact, the tolerance level for a user may be a lethal dose for a nonuser. In the *DSM IV*, Table 1 (p. 177) offers an overview of the various diagnoses associated with each class of substances.

DSM IV CRITERIA

SUBSTANCE ABUSE

According to the *DSM IV*, the criteria for diagnosing substance abuse require that there be a maladaptive pattern of substance use resulting in significant impairment–distress demonstrated by one or more of the following factors occurring in a 12-month time frame:

1. Recurrent substance use resulting in a failure to fulfill responsibilities associated with work, school, and home.
2. Recurrent substance use in situations that could be physically hazardous (driving or use of machinery or heavy equipment).
3. Recurrent substance-related legal issues.
4. Continued substance use despite persistent or recurrent social–interpersonal problems that are either caused or exacerbated by substance use.

It is important to note, when making a diagnosis of abuse whether the individual has never met the criteria for substance dependence.

SUBSTANCE DEPENDENCE

The *DSM IV* defines substance dependence as a constellation of three or more of the following symptoms occurring within a 12-month time frame:

1. Tolerance, defined as the need for increasing amounts of a substance needed to achieve the desired effect *or* a markedly diminished effect.
2. Withdrawal, as demonstrated by the negative characteristics associated with not using more substance as its effects wear off *or* the intake–use of a substance to alleviate and avoid withdrawal symptoms.
3. Using increasingly larger amounts of a substance over time *or* over a longer period of time than was previously practiced or intended.
4. Persistent desire or unsuccessful efforts to reduce *or* control substance use.
5. Significant time spent on obtaining, using, or recovering from substances.
6. Significant negative impact upon social, occupational, or recreational activities because of substance use.
7. Continued use of a substance even though the individual has knowledge of recurrent–persistent physical and/or psychological problems that are likely caused or exacerbated by substance use.

SPECIFIERS

Specifiers refer to the attempt by the *DSM IV* to clarify the diagnosis, differentiate the continuum of dependency, and clarify the spectrum of abstinence:

1. With Physiological Dependence: must present with evidence of either tolerance or withdrawal
2. Without Physiological Dependence: there is no evidence of tolerance or withdrawal
3. Early Full Remission
4. Early Partial Remission
5. Sustained Full Remission
6. Sustained Partial Remission
7. On Agonist Therapy
8. In a Controlled Environment

Once an individual is diagnosed as dependent the diagnosis cannot change, but it can be modified using specifiers.

Psychological dependence is characterized by the compulsive abuse of a substance, taking it longer than planned, intense craving, unsuccessful efforts to cut down, and a preoccupation with obtaining the substance. Physiological dependence is the repeated use of a substance to avoid physical withdrawal reactions or taking larger amounts of a substance to get the same tolerance effect. Physiological and psychological dependence often coexists. In general, substances that do not demonstrate a withdrawal syndrome are likely to only elicit psychological dependence. There are numerous substance-related phenomena of which the therapist should be aware. Such information plays a significant role in an increased understanding of the appropriate education, treatment, and risk factors to which a substance abuser is exposed. Two examples are cross tolerance and reverse tolerance. Heroin and methadone offer an example of cross tolerance. Cross tolerance refers to the tolerance to substance effect intensity demonstrated after repeated and sustained dosing not only with the substance used but with other substances in the same pharmacological class. With substances such as alcohol, barbiturates, opiates, phenylcyclidine, solvents, and inhalants there can be reverse tolerance, which greatly increases the risk of death by overdose.

Self-medication is not the random use of substances to alleviate distress, but rather the choice of a specific substance (or class of substances) to alleviate specific symptoms. Substance abuse treatment must consider the underlying cause of abuse and treat the original motive as well as the dependency if treatment is to be effective and sustaining. Some examples include the following.

1. Narcotics: mask pain
2. Hypnotics: induce sleep
3. Cocaine: mask depression
4. Amphetamines: energy and experience enhancement
5. Marijuana: relax

Caffeine is listed under stimulants; however, it is the only substance in its classification for which a diagnosis of substance dependence is not made.

ADDITIONAL CONSIDERATIONS

DUAL DIAGNOSIS

Substance abusing individuals are often difficult to detect and evaluate. This dilemma is complicated by the coexistence of substance abuse–dependence with other psychiatric disorders. Substance abuse is often associated with personality disorders (particularly antisocial, borderline, and narcissistic) and those who self-medicate as an effort to cope with distress associated with the experience of depression, anxiety, and psychosis. An even more complicated diagnostic picture occurs when a concomitant medical condition exists, which may maintain the focus of health care and result in minimizing the mental health needs of the individual versus the development of a more comprehensive and accurate diagnostic formulation. A medical condition may be causing physical or emotional pain, which is being medicated, or the substance use may be the root cause of or exacerbate the medical condition. The most effective treatment will view the individual as a whole system instead of segmented, and a treatment team approach will facilitate the development of a comprehensive individualized treatment plan.

CODEPENDENTS

Although this is not of diagnostic relevance, it rarely is absent from the clinical picture. Those who abuse or are dependent on substances often experience intertwined relationships with individuals referred to as codependents. Whereas codependence is not a formal diagnostic category, it is defined in this section because of the equally detrimental impact of their behavioral patterns in maintaining substance abuse and dependence. Codependence may be viewed as a normal reaction to substance abuse and dependence. Often, those in a relationship with someone abusing or dependent on substances seek to control or change the abuser's behavior. High stress, chaos, and powerlessness are part of the home environment. To avoid mood disturbance (anxiety–depression), family members deny reality with efforts to control addictive behavior. The result of this intertwined personal association leads to a constellation of symptoms, which includes:

1. Confusion regarding what normal behavior is
2. Difficulty remaining on task and completing projects
3. Do not know how to have fun (or not allowing themselves to have fun)
4. Low self-esteem and harsh self-judgment
5. Relationship problems (both developing and sustaining)
6. Difficulty coping with change
7. Overreacting
8. Continuously seeking approval of others
9. Lack of self-identity
10. Feeling of being different (an outsider–do not fit in)
11. Confusion
12. Feeling inadequate
13. Extremes of being overresponsible or irresponsible
14. Lack of self-confidence
15. Difficulty making decisions
16. Feelings of fear, insecurity, guilt, hurt, and shame (often denied versus being validated)
17. Lack of problem solving skills and development of alternative perspectives or resolutions
18. Impulsivity
19. Social withdrawal and isolation
20. Fear of emotions
21. Difficulty managing criticism
22. Addicted to excitement and chaos
23. Dependency upon others
24. Fear of abandonment
25. Confusion between sympathy and love
26. Rigid and inflexible
27. Need to control
28. Lying

When an individual enters treatment, his or her family system must be integrated into the treatment plan to achieve optimal recovery success. Substance abuse treatment of the individual without system intervention will increase stress, neglect necessary healing and personal growth of system members, and prolong recovery. Family members in a substance abusing home often feel isolated, ashamed, guilty, and unable to confront the problems affecting them. The feelings and needs of each individual in the family system must be recognized, accepted, and validated.

REFERENCES

American Psychiatric Association (1994). "Diagnostic and Statistical Manual of Mental Disorders," 4th ed. Washington, DC: American Psychiatric Association.

Leshner, A. I. (1997). Drug abuse and addiction: Blending scientific and public interest psychology. Casette Recording No. APA97-2276. Washington, DC: American Psychological Association.

Miller, N. S., Belken, B. M., & Gibbons, R. (1994). Clinical diagnosis of substance use disorders in private practice populations. *J. Substance Abuse Treatment* 2(4):387–392.

National Institute on Drug Abuse (1999). Cost to society. NIDA INFOFAX No. 038. Ph. No. 1-888-644-6432 or online http://www.nida.nih.gov/.

Waldinger, R. J. (1986). "Fundamentals of Psychiatry." Washington, DC: American Psychiatric Press, Inc.

World Health Organization (1982). Nomenclature and classification of drug and alcohol related problems: A shortened version of a WHO memorandum. *Br. J. Addiction* 77:3–20.

Zinberg, N. E. (1974). "High States: A Beginning Study." Washington, DC: National Drug Abuse Council.

Zinberg, N. E., & Harding, W. M. (1982). "Control over Intoxicant Use." New York: Human Sciences Press.

Chapter 2

Characteristics and Classification of Substances

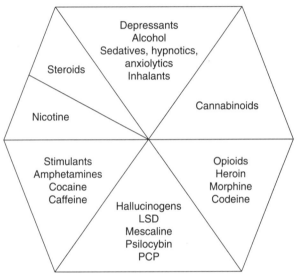

Psychotherapeutics (antidepressants, antipsychotics, and mood stabilizers) are not discussed.

The classes of substances discussed in this chapter include (1) depressants, (2) stimulants, (3) cannabinoids, (4) nicotine, (5) opioids, (6) steroids, and (7) hallucinogens. The substances are identified under each class later in this chapter in a manner to convey the breadth of information to be considered clinically. The substance list under each class is not exhaustive.

CHARACTERISTICS OF SUBSTANCES

The effect of a drug depends on dosage, potency, composition, frequency of use, method of use, the presence of other substances, and physiology. Because legal and illicit substances are both abused, basic evaluation factors of psychopharmacology also need to be considered, such as therapeutic effect, adverse reactions, allergic reaction, idiosyncratic reactions, and toxic effects. The following definitions were adapted from Lewis *et al.* (1994).

DRUG DOSAGE

The dose–response relationship is understood in terms of an adequate dose required for threshold or experienced effect. Below the threshold dose there is no noticeable effect. As dosage is increased, there is a commensurate effect until a maximum effect is reached. The maximum effect is physiologically determined.

POTENCY

Drug potency determines the amount of the drug necessary to produce a certain effect. There is an inverse relationship between potency and dosage regarding desired effect, i.e., the more potent the drug, the lower the dose required for the desired effect. Potency is determined by affinity and efficacy. Affinity refers to the drug's ability to bind to the receptor–site of action. Higher affinity results in better receptor binding. Efficacy refers to the drug's power to stimulate the receptor. This means that drugs with high efficacy significantly stimulate the associated receptors. The greater the affinity and efficacy, the stronger or more potent the drug. Both affinity and efficacy are necessary to produce an effect.

THERAPEUTIC RATIO

This is also referred to as the "safety margin." This ratio comprises two representative dosages of a drug: the effective dose and the lethal dose. *Effective dose* is the dose required for a specific effect in a percentage of the population (ED). For example, ED_{50} symbolizes that a certain dose is effective for 50% of the population. *Lethal dose* is the lethal dose for a percentage of the population (LD). LD_{50} symbolizes a certain dose at a level of lethality for 50% of the population. The lethal dose has not been determined for many drugs.

DRUG EQUIVALENCE

There are three different ways to determine drug equivalence. (1) *Chemical equivalence* means that the active ingredient in two or more drugs is identical. (2) *Biological equivalent* (bioavailability) refers to drug compounds offering the same "equivalent" amount of the active ingredient. (3) *Clinical equivalence* refers to the observable effects of the compound. If two drug compounds produce identical effects, they have clinical equivalence. Bioavailability may differ even when drugs have the same clinical effect.

FREQUENCY OF USE

Frequency of use significantly impacts drug effects in two main ways. (1) Frequent use of a drug increases physiological and psychological changes. Therefore, the drug user's effects change from one episode of use to the next. (2) Accumulation of a drug or its metabolic byproducts can take place if there is a high frequency of drug use.

ROUTE OF ADMISSION

Also referred to as "method of use" is the manner in which a drug is administered. The method of use will affect the onset of effect(s), peak effects, and duration of effects. The most common methods of use include

1. Oral: generally takes at least 15 min to produce effects. This will be influenced by stomach contents and drug composition. This method of use produces a **load** or maximum effect but generally has a longer duration of effect than other methods of use.
2. Intranasal–snorting: absorbed through nasal membranes.

3. Injection: rapid onset (few seconds to a few minutes), very high peaks, and relatively short duration.
4. Inhalation: similar to injection in that this method of use results in quick onset (within seconds) and a relatively short duration.

DRUG INTERACTIONS

The interaction of substances varies along a continuum of intensifying effects, countering effects, or resulting in an unexpected response. These responses are described as follows.

1. Additive: Additive drug interactions occur when various drugs combine to increase the number, intensity, or duration of all the separate drug effects. For example, alcohol or marijuana may be used to enhance the effects of a second drug.
2. Synergistic: Synergistic drug interactions refer to unexpected interactions.
3. Antagonistic: Antagonistic drug interactions happen when drugs counter each other's effects.
   a. *Pharmacologic antagonism* happens when separate drugs compete for the same receptor, for example, naltrexone and morphine. Naltrexone has greater bindability or affinity, but no apparent efficacy (stimulating power).
   b. *Physiological antagonism* is when separate drugs stimulate opposing physiological reactions, for example, speedballs or goofballs, which are a combination of an opiate and a depressant. Together the extremes of stimulation and coming down (depressant effect) take the edge off.
   c. *Chemical antagonism* is where the chemical combination of substances acts to neutralize each other. An example that is common and affects nonsubstance abusers is the combination of dairy products and tetracycline.
4. Agonistic: Agonistic drug interactions refer to a drug or other substance aiding another drug.

TYPES OF DRUG EFFECTS

Types of drug effects include (1) therapeutic effects or desired effects, (2) adverse effects–reactions, also known as side effects (not all side effects are adverse; some drugs are selected from a drug formulary because they offer two or more simultaneous effects), (3) allergic effects (e.g., skin rash), (4) idiosyncratic effects–reactions, (which are unusual effects that are unanticipated and unreliable (e.g., excitation–stimulation), and (5) toxic effects or overdose, which is the result of ingesting a near-lethal or lethal dose (e.g., respiratory depression, coma, death). The emotional state and environmental factors (atmosphere, air quality, people in the room, numerous forms of stimuli) at the time of substance use can also influence substance effect.

SUBSTANCE USE AND CONDITIONING

Substance effects tend to be smaller when individuals take substances in the context of the usual substance administration environment than when taken in an environment not usually paired with substance use. For example, an individual may experience an increased sense of intoxication when alcohol is consumed in an unusual setting or at an unusual time or when an unfamiliar alcoholic beverage is consumed. This conditioning or internal self-administration cues are paired with substance effect. In other words, the pairing of the internal cues and substance effects results in a conditioned response that decreases the effect of the substance.

PHYSIOLOGICAL FUNCTIONING

Individual physiology will impact the differential experience of each substance used by each substance user. One of the fundamental principles of physiological functioning is the striving to maintain a homeostatic balance. Homeostasis refers to a dynamic equilibrium. This means that for every change that takes place, compensation is made in another area. Substance-induced changes in neural transmission can lead to homeostatic changes in other neurological processes. The result of such compensatory changes can be tolerance to the effect(s) of a substance. Such a change is referred to as psychodynamic or neurological balance. To maintain homeostasis at this new homeostatic level requires the presence of the substance. As the substance is metabolized and excreted from the body, a disequilibrium results that leads to continuing physiological adjustments. Associated with compensatory physiological changes are the experience of rebound and withdrawal. Dynamic compensation from occasional use results in rebound or the state opposite of intoxication. In the long-term chronic use of a substance, the compensatory process for the absense of the substance can require more time and be more difficult to achieve. This situation is referred to as withdrawal and can be viewed as a protracted (longer extent of time) rebound effect. The withdrawal of a substance can also require a substantial period of time to achieve a normal state. In order to highlight the impact and interaction of substances and physiological functioning, it is necessary to have a general overview of pharmacokinetics and pharmacodynamics.

PHARMACOKINETICS

Pharmacokinetics refers to the action of drugs in the body such as absorption, distribution, metabolism and excretion.

Absorption

Absorption refers to the passage of substances into tissue. The condition at the site of administration will affect the user's absorption of the substance.

1. Oral
    a. Liquids are more readily absorbed than pills.
    b. Drugs are more readily absorbed in the intestines than in the stomach, and food in the stomach may delay absorption as well.
    c. Acidity–alkalinity of the stomach and intestines affects solubility.
    d. Higher doses result in higher drug concentrations, and high concentrations are absorbed more readily than low concentrations.
    e. Blood level also has an association to lipid solubility and protein binding properties.

2. Intranasal: Not inhaled through the lungs; absorption is through nasal membranes.
3. Injection:
    a. Main factor with injections is the volume of blood flow in the area of injection.
    b. Intravenous (IV) and intraarterial (IA) are most readily absorbed.
    c. For intramuscular (IM) and subcutaneous (SQ) injections, the speed of absorption depends on the blood flow in the areas.

4. Inhalation: Absorption varies with disease or damage to nasal and oral cavities, trachea, and lungs (generally the most rapid rate of absorption).

$$oral \rightarrow intranasal \rightarrow injection \rightarrow inhalation$$

Factors that affect the speed of absorption aside from route of administration include the following.

1. Lipid solubility
   a. How rapidly a substance can move out of the bloodstream to the nerve cell.
   b. Lipid solubility versus water solubility. The more lipid soluble, the more rapidly it is absorbed (out of blood to site of action). In other words, the more lipid soluble a substance is, the faster that it gets to the brain receptors.
   c. pH level affects the chemical property of substances in solution because it affects lipid solubility.
   d. Chemical structure. An example is methamphetamine, which is more potent than amphetamine due to the methylation, which makes it more lipid soluble. Therefore, the more lipid soluble the structure, the more rapid the absorption.

2. Protein binding
   a. Affinity: Some substances have more of an affinity to bind to proteins.
   b. Size: Some molecules are too large to move across a membrane. Alcohol has a low affinity, so it exists in the bloodstream primarily in an unbound form.

Distribution

Distribution is the distance that a substance must travel to the site of action from the site of administration. Distribution is systemic: the substance is distributed through the body as it travels with the blood. Substances must have an affinity (attraction) for elements in blood chemistry or move by hydraulic pressure (fluid pressure). Cardiac efficiency determines the speed at which a substance is distributed. Dose and affinity of the substance for various biological components determine whether enough drug reaches the site of action.

Metabolism

Metabolism is the liver process of chemical detoxification. It is the chief method by which a drug's actions are terminated. The liver chemically alters the substance by performing oxidation, hydrolysis, reduction and conjugation. As the liver metabolizes the substance, it is redistributed from other tissue back into the bloodstream to maintain relative equilibrium. As this redistribution results in a substance leaving the site of action, the effects are terminated. The rate of metabolism will be inhibited by liver disease or damage, malnutrition, cardiovascular functioning, and storage of the substance in body tissue (sequestration). On the other hand, metabolism is enhanced by the substance or a related substance having been used previously. The four metabolic routes for substances are oxidation, hydrolysis, reduction, and conjugation. The liver is the primary site of metabolism, and bile, feces, and urine are the major routes of excretion. Psychoactive substances are also excreted in sweat, saliva, tears, and milk.

Excretion

The final stage of pharmacokinetics is excretion of the substance and its byproducts. For most substances the primary method of excretion is urination. The kidneys change the substance molecules to decrease lipid solubility and increase water solubility, resulting in the excretion via urine. Other methods of excretion include defecation, respiration, or perspiration. Any delays in excretion associated with cardiovascular and liver function or impairment of the kidneys or bladder can result in significant reabsorption of the active substance. The amount of time it takes to metabolize and excrete one-half of the original dose is referred to as the half-life of that substance. The half-life measures the substance's duration of action.

PHARMACODYNAMICS

Pharmacodynamics refers to the location and method of action associated with the manner in which a substance produces its effects. The nervous system is generally the site where psychoactive substance effects are produced.

The central nervous system (CNS) consists of the brain and spinal cord. It is these areas of the nervous system that form the regions for integration, thought, and transmission of messages to and from the periphery. The peripheral nervous system (PNS) consists of all of the nervous tissue lying outside the brain and spinal cord. It is the PNS that provides a means of detection of changes in the internal and external environments of the body. This information is transmitted to the CNS for action, and the PNS then delivers messages to muscles and glands for response. The PNS is composed of somatic fibers (somatic nervous system) that stimulate skeletal muscle and special skin receptors and autonomic fibers (autonomic nervous system, ANS) that are involved in the processes of reflexes that control breathing, heart rate, blood pressure, digestion, and other body functions in an automatic and continuous manner. The ANS is divided into the parasympathetic and sympathetic divisions of function. The parasympathetic division of the ANS acts to conserve body resources and maintain normal levels of function. The sympathetic division of the ANS provides impulses that act to stimulate body activity, by acceleration or deceleration, in order to tolerate or resist stressful or dangerous situations as needed for survival or tolerance (McClintic, 1978).

The nerve cell or neuron is the basic component of the nervous system. Electrochemical processes conduct messages throughout the nervous system. The neurotransmitters stimulate (excite or inhibit) this electrochemical process, which allows the message to travel from one neuron to the successor neuron (excited) or impede (inhibit) conduction of the message. Neurotransmitters that are of particular importance with regard to psychoactive substances include the following:

1. Acetylcholine: Neurotransmitter found in the PNS, ANS, and CNS. It can act to excite or to inhibit impulses. It is involved in sleep and arousal, food and water intake, motor activity, learning, and memory.
2. Catecholamines: A group of neurotransmitters with similar chemical composition.
   a. *adrenaline* is involved in the fright–fight–flight arousal mechanism.
   b. *noradrenaline* is involved in the mechanisms controlling arousal, body temperature, and intake of food and water.
   c. *dopamine* is involved in motor activity.
3. Endorphins: Morphine-like compounds produced by the body that have strong pain-relief (analgesic) action.
4. γ-Aminobutyric acid (GABA): The major inhibitory neurotransmitter in the brain.
5. Serotonin: Involved in arousal and mood modification processes; also referred to as 5-hydroxytryptamine.

Neurotransmission can be altered by substances in a variety of ways (Leavitt, 1982). Some substances that interfere with neural transmission in one or a combination of the methods mentioned next have a well-understood method of action, whereas for others the method of action is not clear.

1. Destruction of neurons.
2. Alteration of neuron membranes: When the permeability of the neuron membrane is altered, a substance can act to stimulate or inhibit impulses along the neuron.

3. Effect of enzymes: Enzymes synthesize neurotransmitters. When substances affect these enzymes, it also affects the synthesis of neurotransmitters.

4. Release of neurotransmitters: Once synthesized, neurotransmitters are stored. A substance may stimulate neural stimulation, thereby causing the release of neurotransmitters.

5. Destruction of neurotransmitters: A substance may facilitate or inhibit the breakdown of neurotransmitters (which is required for termination of action), resulting in either increased or decreased stimulation of the postsynaptic neuron.

6. Uptake inhibition: Neurotransmitter activity is also terminated through the process of reabsorption or uptake of the transmitter chemical. This reabsorption can be facilitated or inhibited by a substance that results in decreasing or increasing the action of the transmitter.

7. Neurotransmitter competition: A substance can mimic a neurotransmitter by having both receptor affinity and efficacy, resulting in a false transmission.

8. Judas neurotransmitter: A substance can be absorbed by the neuron and utilized to produce a neurotransmitter that lacks either affinity or efficacy.

9. Blocking of the receptor: A substance that has receptor affinity but lacks efficacy can occupy the receptor and block transmission.

10. Alteration of receptor sensitivity: When a substance attaches to the postsynaptic receptor, it can result in altering the sensitivity of the receptor, either stimulating or inhibiting the neurotransmitter's action on the receptor.

PHYSIOLOGICAL CHARACTERISTICS OR FACTORS OF THE SUBSTANCE USER

According to NIDA (1996), Babor (1994), Thompson and Pratto (1992), and Galizio and Maistro (1985), the following individual physiological characteristics of the substance user play a role in drug dosage and effects.

Age is an important variable in determining substance dosages and effects. This factor exhibits a relative correspondence to weight. In other words, adolescents, young adults, and middle-aged individuals are at the greatest weights across the developmental range (versus infants, children, and the elderly). Additional age-related issues include

1. Physiological functions (for example, gradual slowing of cardiovascular, metabolic and excretory functions associated with aging)
2. Age-associated neurological development
3. Age-associated variations in proportions of body fat, protein, and water
4. Age-associated social factors

Body mass or weight is an indicator of variants such as volume of blood, cardiovascular function, body fat, and protein proportions. Generally, the more an individual weighs, the more of a substance he or she can consume without experiencing undesirable effects of the substance.

Damage and disease can negatively affect absorption, distribution, metabolism, or excretion of a substance. Damage and disease to the nervous system can alter the type and extent of effects normally produced by a substance.

Food–drug interactions take place when the presence of food in the stomach delays the onset of swallowed substances by interfering with absorption. Also, foods may contain certain chemicals that can inactivate a substance, such as the interaction between the calcium in dairy products with tetracycline, or stimulate a serious negative reaction like the interaction of an MAO inhibitor and certain products contained in foods.

Gender factors include body weight, lean (muscle-to-fat ratio), greater muscle mass, hormonal differences, and psychosocial issues.

Genetics can result in predisposition toward sensitivity to a substance(s), as has been demonstrated by alcohol sensitivity in Asian and Native American populations, and the increased risk of children of alcoholics to abuse alcohol themselves.

Nutrition–diet, if not adequate, can alter the course of a substance's effects as a function of the required carbohydrates, proteins, vitamins, and minerals for physiological functioning, such as the enzymes necessary for the metabolism of substances.

Race–ethnicity offers such factors as direct effects related to blood chemistry and other physiological characteristics. Indirectly there are psychosocial influences.

Biorhythms is an area that continues to be explored but has not, to this date, been able to offer consistent quantified predictions.

PSYCHOLOGICAL CHARACTERISTICS OF THE USER

NIDA (2001) Frances and Miller (1998), Galizio and Maistro (1985), and Leavitt (1982) set forth psychological characteristics of the substance user and the relationship to substance use experience.

Prior substance experience can influence expectation about effects with reuse of the same or a similar substance. Some aspects of learning that take place that are associated with prior use include the following:

1. How to maintain the appearance of control
2. Contribution to tolerance
3. How to adjust behavior to compensate for substance-induced changes in mood, thinking processes, and voluntary behavioral control
4. Effects will wear off

Expectations of effects can have a considerable impact on the experience of a substance. Expectations are developed from information via personal experience, friends'–associates' experiences, media, education–training, and professional descriptions. This has been demonstrated with the use of placebos, information provided, method of administration, and physical characteristics (size, color, taste). Therefore, the substance user's beliefs about a substance often determine the experience.

Mood: According to Wilter's law (Leavitt, 1982), a substance cannot make a user exceed their capability behaviorally, emotionally, or cognitively and the substance's effects depend on the user's pre-substance-administration emotional state. Therefore, if a person is already stimulated, the use of a substance will have relatively little effect, but when in a fatigued state, the same substance and dose will have a considerable impact. Wilder's law suggests a paradoxical effect whereby the response is opposite of what is expected when the user is already at or near his or her maximum and he or she ingests a substance to further enhance his or her state. An example is the use of a stimulant for managing hyperactive children.

Psychopathology is a predictor of increased risk presenting a negative feedback loop.

Behavior(s) is considered among four major areas of variation: complexity, abstractness, time frame of acquisition, and the degree of performance motivation. Behavioral impairment is directly related to complexity, abstractness, time frame of acquisition, and motivation to perform.

SOCIOCULTURAL ENVIRONMENT

According to McCarty(1985), the physical environment and social environment influence one another. *Physical environment* acts to either encourage and facilitate or inhibit substance use. The physical environment offers an important determinant of a substance's effects and the user's behavior. *Social environment* or other people and their behavior impact the relationship between an individual and the use of a substance. Other people and their behavior

1. Provide an atmosphere that establishes mood (pleasant/unpleasant).
2. Offer modeling and information used to establish rules and rituals associated with the use of a substance.
3. Offer a comparison for evaluating their own experience.
4. Act as the source for identifying and defining the effects of a substance.
5. Provide social support and reinforcement for both appropriate and inappropriate behavior associated with substance use.

CLASSIFICATION OF SUBSTANCES

The following is a summarization of information from Frances and Miller (1988), Kaplan and Sadock (1990), Bezchlibnyk-Butler and Jeffries (1998), and Maxman and Ward (1995). This brief overview of the properties of substances and the individual factors that play a role in the resulting experience of substance use demonstrates the complexity of substance use, abuse, and dependence across the population in general. Combined with issues of cultural diversity and dual diagnosis, one can see how entangled the clinical picture can become.

DEPRESSANTS

Alcohol

Alcohol is abused more than any other substance. Ethyl alcohol is produced by a fermentation process whereby yeast cells act upon the carbohydrates in fruits and grains. The three types of alcoholic beverages include beer, wine and distilled liquor. A person under the influence of alcohol may look drowsy and sedated and may demonstrate decreased inhibition. Alcohol is a central nervous system depressant, which means that it acts on the brain like an anesthetic. Alcohol is the most commonly used depressant. The effects are based upon the amount ingested and the ability of the body to metabolize it. Alcohol acts like an analgesic, tranquilizer, sedative, hypnotic, and soporific. The more alcohol ingested, the stronger the anesthetizing effect. One of the most important effects of alcohol is the potential for personality change, such as depressed, angry, violent, or just talkative. People who abuse substances often mix depressants (tranquilizer with alcohol). The result is an added effect. Their heart rate, pulse rate, and breathing slow down. They could be at risk for coma or death. Mortality rates of male alcoholics are about twice as high as they are for their nonalcoholic counterparts. The predominant causes of death in alcoholics are arteriosclerotic heart disease, pneumonia, cirrhosis, ulcers, cancer of the upper digestive and respiratory organs, accidents, and suicide. Basically, alcoholism is an assault on every organ system. Poor nutrition and alcoholism can result in Wernicke–Korsakoff syndrome manifested by eye movement disturbance, ataxia, confusion, and impaired short-term memory. If the syndrome is treated quickly with high doses of thiamine, the symptoms are alleviated and eliminated. In the case where treatment is not given within several days Korsakoff's psychosis may develop, which is a potentially permanent dementia that is characterized by impaired cognitive ability, impaired short-term memory, disorientation, and confabulation. Severe cases can result in serious memory deficits. Various characteristics play a role in the individual experience of alcohol abuse. For instance, tolerance level is decreased if the individual is young, female, slender, hungry, tired, or depressed.

Street names	Booze, moonshine, highballs, white lightning, firewater homebrew, hooch (street names and terms vary over time)
Method of use	Oral
Acute effects	Relaxation, loss of inhibitions, lack of concentration, agitation, euphoria, drowsiness, impaired judgement, impaired cognition, slowed heart rate and respiration, slowed reaction time, impaired memory, motor dysfunction such as staggering, slurred speech, unsteady gait, nystagmus, impaired attention, sedation, sleep, coma, death. May be changes such as aggressive–violent behavior
Chronic use effects	Physiological: destroyed nerve cells, impaired liver function, metabolism decreases with cirrhosis, hand tremors, diarrhea, morning nausea–vomiting, impotence, headaches, polyuria, hepatomegaly, peripheral neuropathy, increased CNS tolerance, dependence
	Psychological: blackouts, insomnia, nightmares, intellectual–cognitive impairment, impaired judgement, hallucinations, organic mental disorders (Wernicke–Korsakoff syndrome), dependence
Overdose	Nausea, vomiting, cold–clammy skin, weak–rapid pulse, shallow respiration, coma, possible death
Withdrawal	Agitation, irritability, anxiety, tremors, hallucinations, insomnia, shakes, chills, convulsions, delirium tremens, tachycardia, psychosis, seizures (delirium tremens generally occur 2–3 days after drinking stops and can be fatal if untreated)
Related problems	Major depression, dysthymia, deterioration in job performance, deterioration in health, increased risk of accident-related death
Drug interactions	Concerns related to hepatotoxicity, additive CNS effects, potentiation of CNS effects, acetaminophen (risk of hepatotoxicity), some antibiotics (disulfiram type reaction), anticonvulsants (additive CNS), antidepressants, cocaine (hepatotoxicity), neuroleptics (additive CNS), salicylates (increased gastric bleeding), benzodiazepines (additive CNS)
Period of detection	6–10 hours
Duration of effects	1–4 hours

Sedatives, Hypnotics, and Anxiolytics

Sedatives, hypnotics, and anxiolytics (traquilizers and antianxiety drugs), also known as depressants or "downers" along with alcohol, which was discussed previously, depress the central nervous system. These drugs are highly addictive and are used medically for sedation tranquilization, and sleep. A person under the influence of one of these drugs will have a presentation similar to someone who has been ingesting alcohol. A demonstration of symptoms such as loss of inhibition, lack of coordination, slurred speech, and sleepiness are likely to be seen. Some barbiturates have sedative and hypnotic effects, whereas others only have sedative effects. Sedatives are prescribed for calming and do not necessarily cause sleep. Hypnotic drugs cause sleep. In the substance abuse culture, sedative–hypnotics are used for their euphorant effect, to potentiate the effects of CNS depressants, or to temper the excitatory effects of stimulants.

Barbiturates
Barbiturates include seconal, nembutal, amytal, butisol, tuinol, phenobarbitol, and mebaral.

Street names	Downers, barbs, reds, goofballs, yellows, yellow jackets, pinks, devils, phennies
Method of use	Oral, injection
Acute effects	Diaphoresis, ataxia, hypotension, sedation, drowsiness, slurred speech, impaired memory, unsteady gait, dysphoria, delirium, incoordination, miosis, seizures
Chronic use effects	Physiological: incoordination, unsteady gait, slurred speech, impairs erection and ejaculation, tolerance, dependence
	Psychological: confusion, inattentiveness, impaired memory, impaired judgment, dependence
Overdose	Low margin of safety, therapeutic dose is close to toxic dose
Withdrawal	Withdrawal can be fatal, never abruptly withdraw; nausea, weakness, irritability, insomnia, anxiety, autonomic hyperactivity, increased sensitivity to light and sound, hallucination–delusions, seizures
Related problems	Involved in many drug interactions; can evoke hyperactivity and conduct disorders in children and depression in adults; increased risk of overdose and death, excess sedation, retrograde amnesia, hypotension, respiratory depression
Drug interactions	Potentiation with CNS depressants, tricyclic antidepressants (accelerated metabolism makes the antidepressant ineffective)
Period of detection	2–10 days
Duration effects	1–16 hours

Nonbarbiturates

With nonbarbiturates there is the possibility of dependence. The effects are much like those of alcohol, with the result of the person looking and acting drunk.

Choral hydrate:

Street names	Mickey Finn, knockout drops
Method of use	Oral
Acute effects	Sedation, hypnotic (sleep), disinibition, amnesic disorder
Chronic use effects	Physiological: ataxia, drowsiness, seizure, tolerance, dependence
	Psychological: confusion, inattention, delirium, impaired judgment, dependence
Overdose	Stomach distress, hypotension, hypothermia, respiratory depression, cardiac arrhythmias, coma, potentially life threatening
Withdrawal	Potentially life threatening, delirium, seizures
Related problems	Amnestic disorder
Drug interactions	Cross tolerance with other sedatives, hypnotics, and alcohol
Period of detection	2 weeks
Duration of effects	5–8 hours

Methaqualone or quaalude:

Street names	Ludes
Method of use	Oral
Acute effects	Ataxia, hypotension, delirium, seizures, tolerance, dependence
Chronic use effects	Physiological: euphoria, sedation, disinhibition, tolerance, dependence
	Psychological: drowsiness, confusion, inattentiveness, impaired judgment, dependence
Overdose	Potentially life threatening
Withdrawal	Potentially life threatening, delirium, seizures
Related problems	Amnestic disorder
Drug interactions	Cross tolerance with other sedatives, hypnotics, and alcohol
Period of detection	2 weeks
Duration of effects	4–8 hours

Benzodiazepines

Benzodiazepine brand names include the following: Ativan, Halcion, Librium, Rohypnol, Valium, Xanax, Tranxene, Restoril, Clonipin, Serax, Dalmame, and Centrax.

Street names	Roofles, tranks
Method of use	Oral–injected
Acute effects	Euphoria, relaxation, drowsiness, lack of concentration, disorientation, sleep, hypotension, miosis, nystagmus, incoordination, muscle weakness, blurred vision, delirium, coma

Chronic use effects	Physiological: relaxation, drowsiness, diaphoresis, sexual dysfunction, fatigue, muscle weakness, dry mouth, increased tolerance, dependence.
	Psychological: confusion, inattentiveness, decreased concentration, insomnia, hallucinaions, nightmares, rage reaction, memory impairment, impaired judgment, depression, dependence
Overdose	Rarely if ever fatal when taken alone, may be lethal in combination with other CNS depressants, hypotension, depressed respiration, coma
Withdrawal effects	Anxiety, insomnia, sensitivity to light and sound, tachycardia, mild systolic hypertension, tremor, headache, sweating, abdominal distress, craving, seizures
Related problems	Lowers tolerance to other CNS depressants, depression, increased risk of accidents (falls–injuries), rebound anxiety
Drug interactions	Lowers the tolerance to alcohol, can diminish the therapeutic efficacy of ECT (raising seizure threshold), antihistamines (increased CNS depressant)
Period of detection	1–6 weeks
Duration of effect	4–8 hours

Inhalants

Inhalants are considered the "poor man's" drug of abuse. They are also often used by children and adolescents because of availability. In fact, according to the National Inhalant Prevention Coalition (2001), "Inhalant use is most prevalent among young children and usually entails inhaling or huffing such household items as shoe polish or paint thinner. More than 1000 products widely available in households can be used as inhalants. Inhalants are volatile substances that vaporize as they are exposed to the air and are drawn into the lungs. Most inhalants contain additives that are more poisonous than the volatile substance. Inhalants depress the CNS from mild intoxication to unconsciousness, depending on the dosage and individual experience to the substance. The immediate effect lasts from a few minutes to hours. There is found to be high rate of psychopathology associated with individuals who engage in inhalant use. Those with a history of inhalant use often demonstrate comorbidity with alcoholism, depression, and antisocial personality disorder.

Street names	Sniffing, chemo, glue
Methods of use	Torching = inhaling fumes discharged from a cigarette lighter
	Bagging = pouring volatile organic compounds into a plastic bag or balloon
	Sniffing = holding mouth over a container as gas is discharged
	Huffing = holding a soaked rag over mouth or nose
Acute effects	Drowsiness, impaired judgment, fluctuating levels of awareness, impaired memory, euphoria, hallucinations, feelings of invincibility, delirium, vivid fantasies, dizziness, slurred speech, impaired motor function, nausea, salivation, sneezing, coughing, blurred vision, hypotension, stupor, coma, decreased respiration, decreased heart rate effects differ somewhat depending on the type of drug inhaled
Chronic use effects	Psysiological: encephalopathy, hearing loss, visual impairment, sinusitis, rhinitis, laryngitis, chronic lung disease, kidney and liver damage, bone marrow damage, cardiac arrhythmias ataxia, analgesia, respiratory depression, hypotension, hypoxia, peripheral neuropathy, brain damage, death; may be used during sex to intensify orgasm
	Psychological: inability to think clearly, memory disturbance, irritability, hostility, belligerence, paranoia, depression, euphoria, impaired judgment
Overdose	Unconsciousness, coma, seizures, liver, kidney and brain damage, possible death
Withdrawal	As per *DSM IV* no diagnosis for withdrawal
Related problems	Brain damage, liver damage, bone marrow depression, peripheral neuropathies, immunosuppression, bronchitis, asthma (chronic respiratory conditions)
Drug interactions	Concerns related to CNS depressants

CANNABINOIDS

Cannabionoids are categorized independently because they possess characteristics of both central nervous system depressants and hallucinogens. There is evidence of tolerance if high levels are used regularly over a sustained period of time. Learning plays an important role in the psychological reactions to cannabinoids especially at low doses. When cannabinoids are smoked, there is rapid absorption to the brain and other tissues. Effects are sustained within 5–10 minutes. Peak effects take place at about 30 minutes, diminishing at 90 minutes to 72 hours. Cannabinoids have high lipid solubility, so that they are taken up and stored in fatty tissues and released slowly. High doses can product toxic delirium with confusion, agitation, disorientation, loss of coordination, and hallucinations. The most common adverse reaction is acute anxiety or panic, sometimes accompanied by paranoid thoughts. Under these conditions, an individual may become fearful of dying or going insane. He or she may misinterpret what is happening around him or her (delusional). Possible harmful physical effects include bronchitis, emphysema, and lung cancer.

Cannabis		
	Street names	
	Marijuana	Weed, pot, dope, Mary Jane, reefer, ganga, joint, hemp
	Hashish	Hash, black, weed oil, tea (stronger than marijuana), grass, columbian, sinsemilla (most potent marijuana)
	Method of use	Smoked or cooked, swallowed in solid form
	Acute effect	Euphoria, relaxation, positive sense of self–confidence, slow reaction time, altered sense of time, enhanced senses, increased cravings for sweets, loss of interest and motivation, response may be agitated, anxious, and suspicious–paranoid, tachycardia
	Chronic use effects	Physiological: bloodshot eyes, impaired hand–eye coordination, weight gain, bronchitis, possible damage to lungs, heart, fatigue
		Psychological: impaired memory perception, apathy, interferes with motivation, possible deterioration of learned behaviors, chronic high doses can lead to psychotic episode if there is genetic predisposition (they may not recover from psychosis), lack of cognitive clarity
	Withdrawal	As per *DSM IV* no diagnosis of withdrawal
	Related problems	Possible decreased testosterone in males, retards fetal growth during pregnancy, and causes withdrawal symptoms in infants
	Drug interactions	Tricyclic antidepressants (desipramine, cardiac complications), MAOIs (serotonin syndrome), barbiturates (additive), disulfiram (synergistic CNS, hypomanic)
	Combined with other drugs	With PCP: "killer weed"
		With heroin: "A-bomb"
		With opium: "o.j."
	Period of detection	1 day to 5 weeks; half-life of approximately 72 hours THC in blood has a half-life of approximately 19 hours
	Duration of effect	2–4 hours

OPIOIDS

Opioids, also known as narcotics, are CNS depressants. Most people are familiar with them as pain killers (analgesics). Narcotics are inhibitory compounds referred to as neuromodulators because they stop the brain from receiving signal about pain. The source of pain does not go away, but the person does not feel it. After a while the substance wears off and the pain signal starts being received by the brain. Narcotics are powerfully addictive, which translates to a high potential for abuse and addiction. A person under the influence of an opiate will experience a state of euphoria and sedation. After they have been taken for a while, larger doses are required to achieve the same effect. This is generally accompanied by a loss of energy and ambition. There are numerous opiates, and they differ somewhat depending on the drug and the method of use. Narcotics purchased from street dealers offer significant risk. Illegal narcotics may be mixed with strychnine or other poisons as well as other ingredients. The amount of narcotic in the mixture will never be exactly same. This contributes to death from overdose. The likelihood of addiction varies with individual personal characteristics, substance, dose, route of administration, frequency, and duration of use. Addicts who take it regularly develop tolerance and, therefore, are unable to experience the effects when taken for medicinal purposes. However, they continue to take it because a lack of the substance produces (in addicts) a withdrawal syndrome that is severe and can be fatal. Because of the numerous drugs in this class, the major ones will be identified along with their street names and a brief differentiating dialog.

Method of use	Oral, injected, smoked, sniffed
Acute effects	Analgesic "rush" sensation resulting in a state of relaxation, euphoria, slowed pulse, slowed respiration, increased body temperature, decreased GI motility, constricted pupils, dry mouth drowsiness, slurred speech, impaired memory, coma
Chronic use effects	Physiological: lethargy, loss of appetite with overall poor health, dependence
	Psychological: euphoria, sense of well-being, good mood, happy, lethargy, lack of motivation, drowsiness
Overdose	Shallow breathing, slowed pulse, pulmonary edema, clammy skin, respiratory depression, convulsions, coma, possible death
Withdrawal	Anxiety, dysphoria, muscle aches, irritability, runny nose, teary eyes, sneezing, goose bumps, dilated pupils, tachycardia, vasodilation, hypertension, vomiting, diarrhea, restlessness; withdrawal can be painful and create intense feelings of being sick

Post addiction syndrome involves anxiety, depression, and craving for the substance. Relapse results not from striving for pleasure, but from the need for release from the postaddiction syndrome. Methadone alleviates–eliminates these symptoms. Other agonist treatments are ineffective because they do not "replace" the narcotic. Ironically, methadone is successful because it is addictive, unlike other agonists that are not addictive and allow the individual to quit using the agonist and return to narcotic use.

Medical effects of narcotics include

1. analgesic
2. tranquilization
3. sense of well-being (euphoria)
4. sedation
5. sleep
6. relief of coughing–diarrhea

Opium

Street names	"O"
Method of use	Oral, smoked
Acute effects	Euphoria, lethargy, drowsiness, lack of motivation, slowed pulse, analgesia, constricted pupils, nausea, constipation, respiratory depression, cardiovascular complications, coma, death
Chronic use effects	Physiological: general loss of energy, tolerance, dependence
	Psychological: loss of ambition and drive, dependence
Overdose	Respiratory depression, cardiovascular complications, coma, death; always consider polyoverdose
Withdrawal	Anxiety, irritability, dilated pupils, vasodilation, tachycardia, elevated blood pressure, vomiting, diarrhea, restlessness, tremors, chills, piloerection, bone pain, abdominal pain, cramps, loss of appetite
Drug interactions	Overdose is often caused by combined use with other substances; cimetadine (enhanced narcotic effect), some antihistamines (opiate high); cross tolerance occurs with other narcotics
Period of detection	1–2 days
Duration of effects	3–6 hours

Heroin

Street names	Horse, junk, snow, stuff, Harry, H, white horse, horse, joy powder, scag, smack, black tar, Jane
Method of use	Injected, smoked, inhaled
Acute effects	Euphoria, sense of well-being, happy, rush (strong analgesic effects), lethargy, drowsiness, lack of motivation, slowed pulse, hypoactive; effects last for a short period of time, then more of the substance is required; frequently cut with quinine, which produces a rush
Chronic use effects	Physiological: general loss of energy, lethargic, tolerance, dependence
	Psychological: loss of ambition, drive, dependence
Overdose	Respiratory depression, cardiovascular complications, coma, death

	Withdrawal	Runny nose, sneezing, dilated pupils, vasodilation, tachycardia, elevated blood pressure, vomiting, diarrhea, restlessness, tremors, chills, piloerection, bone pain, abdominal pain, cramps, loss of appetite, anxiety, irritability
	Related problems	Increased rate of spontaneous abortion and premature labor–stillbirths; withdrawal symptoms experienced by newborns, who are born smaller than average and demonstrate an increased risk of death; addicts share needles, which results in spreading HIV–AIDS, hepatitis, and endocarditis; many die as a result of overdose; very expensive drug and addicts often turn to illegal behavior to support their habit
	Drug interactions	Cross tolerance occurs with other narcotics; Doxepin
	Period of detection	1–2 days
	Duration of effects	3–6 hours
Morphine	Street names	Morpho, Miss Emma, "M", unkie, hocus, dreamer, sweet Jesus, junk
	Method of use	Oral–capsule, tablet, liquid, injected
	Acute and chronic use effects	Effects parallel heroin, but is slower and longer acting; high dependence liability (second to heroin) due to powerful analgesic and euphoric effects
	Overdose	Parallels heroin
	Withdrawal	Parallels heroin
	Period of detection	1–2 days
	Duration of effects	3–6 hours
Codeine, Oxycodone, and Hydrocodone	Street names	Schoolboy, 3 s, 4 s
	Method of use	Oral, liquid, capsule–tablet (combined prescriptions of tylenol with codeine, empirin with codeine, and with cough syrup)
	Acute effects	Analgesic effect, drowsiness, euphoria, lack of motivation; also helps to stop coughing spasms and is often added to prescription cough syrup; used by dentists and physicians following surgery
	Chronic use effects	Physiological: loss of energy, tolerance develops gradually, dependence
		Psychological: relaxed, lack of ambition and drive, dependence
	Overdose	Drowsiness, restlessness, agitation, nausea, vomiting, vertigo, weakness, lethargy, stupor, coma, seizures
	Withdrawal	Irritability, agitation
	Related problems	May result in birth defects and infant withdrawal symptoms
	Drug interactions	Alcohol (intensifies effect), sedatives (increase effect); combined with glutethimide = "loads" or "pacs," tolerance develops gradually
	Period of detection	1–2 days
	Duration of effects	3–6 hours

Over the last several years the abuse of this drug has often been the focus of concern. According to the U.S. Department of Justice Drug Enforcement Agency (2001), "The estimated number of emergency department episodes involving oxycodone was stable from 1990–1996. Emergency episodes doubled from 3190 episodes in 1996 to 6429 in 1999".

Meperidine and Demerol	Street name	Doctors
	Method of use	Oral, injected
	Acute effects	Analgesic, euphoria, relaxed, affects concentration; high doses result in disorientation, hallucinations, respiratory depression, stupor, coma
	Chronic use effects	Physiological: highly toxic metabolite responsible for convulsions with chronic use, drowsiness, lightheadedness, impaired concentration, tolerance, dependence
		Psychological: relaxed, lack of ambition and drive, dependence
	Overdose	Marked drowsiness, confusion, tremors, convulsions, stupor, coma, disorientation, hallucinations, respiratory depression
	Withdrawal	Irritability, anxiety, tremors, restlessness, vasodilation, tachycardia, elevated blood pressure, vomiting, diarrhea
	Related problems	Avoid breast feeding, do not use during pregnancy
	Drug interactions	MAOIs
	Period of detection	1–2 days
	Duration of effects	3–6 hours

Methadone	Street names	Dollies, dolly meth, methadose, kick pill
	Method of use	Oral, injected
		Drug used in detoxification and withdrawal from opiates; synthetic narcotic; subject to abuse and dependence, but tolerance unlikely (also psychological dependence); methadone works directly on the CNS, stopping the brain from receiving pain signals; generally used to help people who are addicted to narcotics when they are withdrawing; the goal is to prescribe it in a stepwise, decreasing dosage so that at the end point the addict is not receiving methadone; it is also prescribed at times for pain management
	Related problems	Newborns reported to experience withdrawal effects; it also crosses the barrier into breast milk (nurse prior to dosing or 2–6 hr postdosing)
	Period of detection	1 day to 1 week
	Duration of effects	12–24 hr

Advantages of methadone in the treatment of heroin addiction:

1. Taken orally (risk of infection eliminated)
2. Long acting substance
3. Unnecessary to increase dose for desired benefit
4. Blocks effects of heroin

HALLUCINOGENS

Hallucinogens are also known as psychedelic, phantastica, or psychotomimetic. They are mind-altering drugs that impact perception, comprehension, sensation, self-awareness, and emotion. The effects of hallucinogens are very unpredictable; they alter perceptions of reality. A person under the influence of a hallucinogen may think that he or she hears and sees things that are not there. They may hurt themselves and be unaware of it because hallucinogens block the nerves that communicate the experience and sensation of pain. Because these substances are stored in the fatty tissue, the effects may last a long time and even return at a later time. The more dangerous effects of hallucinogens include unpredictable behavior, permanent and irreversible liver and brain damage, damage to genes, paranoia, suicide, and sudden death. There are numerous hallucinogens, and they differ somewhat depending on the drug and the method of use. Psychological effects are highly influenced by personality, previous experience, expectations, attitudes, environment, use of other substances, and their interactions. Because of the numerous drugs in this class, the major ones will be identified along with their street names and a brief differentiating dialog.

	General effects of use	Physiological: hypertension, tachycardia, pupil dilation, sweating, chills, nausea, hyperventilation, lack of coordination, muscle weakness to extreme of super strength, trembling, numbness
		Psychological: perceptual disturbance, altered body awareness, impaired attention and concentration, distorted sense of time, depersonalization, derealization, euphoria, mystic experiences, religious experiences, anxiety, panic, grandiosity, visual hallucinations and distortions, erratic behavior, aggressive and violent behavior
	General effects of overdose	Extreme hyperactivity, agitation, irritability, violent behavior directed toward self and others, hallucinations, psychosis, convulsions, possible death
	Withdrawal	As per *DSM IV* no diagnosis of withdrawal
Lysergic Acid Diethylamide (LSD)	Street names	Acid, Lucy in the sky with diamonds, pearly gates, wedding bells, microdot, cube, purple haze, tabs, hits, heavenly blue
	Method of use	Oral–tablet, capsule, liquid, snorted, smoked, inhaled, licked off paper, injected; the gelatin–liquid can be put in the ears; usually taken orally
	Acute effects	Perceptual disturbances, confusion, restlessness, emotional lability, paranoia, mania, bad trip, cardiac depression, hypotension

Chronic use effects	Physiological: tolerance, reverse tolerance	
	Psychological: anxiety, depression, personality changes	
Overdose	Psychosis, longer or more intense trips, possible death	
Related problems	Increased risk of spontaneous abortions and birth defects associated with pregnancy; flashbacks and recurrent psychotic symptoms may reoccur even years after use	
Drug interactions	Combined with cocaine, amphetamines, and mescaline to achieve prolonged effects, SSRI– fluoxitine (grand mal seizures)	
Period of detection	8 hours; no addiction of physical dependence	

Phases of LSD experience

1. Somatic phase: substance is absorbed, causing changes in CNS
2. Sensory phase: indicative of sensory distortions
3. Psychic phase: at peak effect there are changes in mood, thought distortions, experience of altered time, depersonalization, hallucinations, and/or psychotic episode

Adverse reaction or toxicity is demonstrated by (1) negative impact on the psychological state of the user and (2) flashbacks. A failure of normal defenses results in increased vulnerability. For example, flooded with images, inability to cope, or psychosis. The effects may be transient, long lasting, or permanent.

Psilocybin		
	Street names	Shroom, sacred mushrooms, magic mushrooms
	Method of use	Oral–capsule, injection, eaten raw, cooked, steeped in tea
	Acute effects	Chemically related to LSD and DMT, with similar reactions
	Chronic use effects	Tolerance develops rapidly, cross tolerance with LSD, physical or psychological dependence not reported
	Overdose	Confusion, emotional lability, panic, paranoia, mania, cardiac depression
	Related problems	Mistaken identity with deathcap mushrooms can result in accidental poisoning
	Period of detection	8 hours
	Duration of effects	Variable

Peyote *(Mescaline)*		
	Street names	Mescal buttons, mesc, huatari
	Method of use	Oral–capsules, dried, chewed, swallowed
	Acute effects	Hallucinogen used by Native Americans for heightened spiritual experience; experience varies, with panic, anxiety, nausea, vomiting, dizziness, convulsions, weightlessness, time distortion, break from reality, bright geometric colors
	Chronic use effects	Physiological: pupillary dilation, tachycardia, palpitations, sweating, blurred vision
		Psychological: anxiety, depression personality changes
	Overdose	Fast pulse, tachycardia, nausea, vomiting, chills, trembling, convulsions, cardiac depression, respiratory depression
	Related problems	Can cause genetic damage and possibly result in fetal deformities
	Period of detection	2–3 days
	Duration of effects	8–12 hours

Mescaline is the active substance in peyote. There are over 30 psychoactive alkaloids in peyote. Many naturally occurring substances have a synthetic that has been developed to mimic their effects. The following are examples.

Trimethoxyamphetamine (TMA)	TMA is a synthetic drug similar to mescaline. Reactions are similar to those of mescaline, but with greater potency. The period of detection is 1–2 days.

Phenylcyclidine (PCP)	Street names	Angel dust, dust, hog, super grass, crystal, animal tranquilizer, peace pill, killer, rocket fuel, "CJ"
	Method of use	Oral, injected, smoked
	Acute effects	Belligerence, assaultiveness, agitation, impulsiveness, unpredictability, increased blood pressure and heart rate, diminished response to pain, ataxia, dysarthria, muscle rigidity, seizures; rapid cycling of intense anxiety, euphoria, and fear; violent actions are common when intoxicated
	Chronic use effects	Physiological: agitation, hypertension, dysarthria, ataxia, increased muscle tone, hyperactive reflexes; at low doses PCP acts as a CNS depressant, producing nystagmus, blurred vision, numbness, incoordination
		Psychological: apathy, feelings of isolation, confusion, depersonalization, unreality, detachment–estrangement, persecutory delusions, psychosis, dependence
	Overdose	Can cause seizures, severe hypertension, diaphoresis, hypersalivation, cardiac depression, respiratory depression, stupor, coma, death
	Related problems	Death has occurred secondary to seizures and intercranial hemorrhage resulting from hypertension; posthallucination perception disorder
	Period of detection	2–8 days

PCP and ketamine are psychedelic anesthetic substances. PCP was originally developed for use as an anesthetic, but reactions were unpredictable. Patients demonstrated unmanageable manic-like behavior and psychosis lasting up to 4 days after administration. Paranoia and unpredictable violence are often experienced while under the influence. Resembles schizophrenia more than LSD.

Ketamine (ketalar)	Street names	K, special K
	Method of use	Oral–capsules, tablets, solution snorted, injected; general anesthetic used in day surgery
	Acute effects	Disorientation, delusion, hallucinations, euphoria, confusion, flashbacks; bad trips can occur ("K-hole")
	Chronic use effects	Physiological: tolerance can occur with regular use
		Psychological: anxiety, depression, delusions, hallucinations, personality changes
	Overdose	Confusion, emotional lability, panic, mania, paranoia, cardiac depression, hypotension, convulsions
	Related problems	Posthallucination perception disorder
	Period of detection	1–2 days
	Duration of effects	2–4 hours

Methylenedioxy-methamphetamine (MDMA)	Street names	Ecstasy, XTC, E, love drug, M&M, Adam
	Method of use	Oral
	Acute effects	Excitement, energized, panic, paranoid psychosis, flashbacks, depression
	Chronic use effects	Physiological: tolerance can occur with regular use
		Psychological: anxiety, depression, personality changes, delusions, hallucinations
	Overdose	Confusion, emotional lability, panic, paranoia, mania
	Related problems	Physical reactions can be severe; tachycardia, hypotension, hyperthermia, seizures, coma; death can result from raves (excessive physical activity), which may lead to disseminated intravascular coagulation, rhabdomyolysis, and renal failure; posthallucination perception disorder; risk of brain damage
	Period of detection	1–2 days

Dimethoxymeth-amphetamine (STP)	Street names	Serenity, peace, tranquility
	Method of use	Oral
	Acute effects	Excitement, delirium, exhaustion, convulsions, psychosis, "bad trips;" more potent than mescaline
	Chronic use effects	Physiological: tolerance can occur with regular use
		Psychological: anxiety, depression, personality changes, delusions, hallucinations
	Overdose	Confusion, emotional lability, paranoia, mania
	Related problems	Posthallucination perception disorder
	Period of detection	1–2 days

STIMULANTS

Cocaine

STIMULANTS, known as "uppers," describe a classification of drugs that stimulate the central nervous system. The most commonly used stimulant is caffeine. Nicotine is also a stimulant. Initially, they can make one feel sharp and energetic, but they can also result in feeling anxious, nervous, and fatigued after the rush. Most people relate the initial positive evaluation of their experience as an increase in activity and mental alertness. The effect is similar to that caused by adrenalin or epinephrine produced by the body, which hormonally plays a role in the survival mechanism and allows a person to function beyond his or her normal limits under unusual and stressful circumstances. There are numerous stimulants, and they differ somewhat depending on the drug and the method of use. This category also includes look-alike drugs resembling amphetamines, which contain caffeine, phenyl-propanolamine (PPA), and ephedrine. Because of the numerous drugs in this class, the major ones will be identified along with their street names and a brief differentiating dialog.

General effects of use	Physiological: tachycardia, hypertension, hyperthermia, increased respiration, dry mouth and lips, bad breath, sweating, tremors, decreased appetite, pupil dilation, anorexia, increased energy, insomnia, increased sensory awareness, increased libido, ejaculatory delay
	Psychological: euphoria, exhilaration, alertness, enhanced task performance, talkativeness, escalation of obsessive–compulsive symptoms, anxiety, panic attacks, grandiosity, delusions, hallucinations, agitation, mania, paranoia, enhanced sense of power, restlessness, irritability, violence, flashbacks
General effects of overdose	Headaches, hypertension, rapid heart rate, cardiac arrhythmias, coma, possible death
Withdrawal	Anxiety, irritability, social withdrawal, depression, disorientation, apathy, difficulty concentrating, voracious hunger, anorexia, nausea, diarrhea, abdominal pain, chills, tremors, craving, exhaustion, excess sleep, paranoid psychosis, suicidal ideation, homicidal ideation, myalgia, diaphoresis, convulsions, stroke, intense vasospasm resulting in retinal damage
Chronic effects	Intense psychological dependence, sleeplessness, anxiety, nasal passage damage, lung damage, death from overdose

Amphetamines

Dextroamphetamine

Street names	Uppers, pep pills, bennies, benn, jelly beans, dex, dexies, black beauties, truck drivers, hearts, sky rockets, ice, crank, eye-openers
Method of use	Injected, oral, smoked, sniffed
Acute effects	Excess activity, euphoria, rapid pulse, alert, hypertension, tremors, loss of appetite, increased libido, argumentativeness, anxiety, paranoia, delirium, psychosis, violence
Chronic use effects	Physiological: decreased appetite, insomnia, increased sexual arousal, reduced fatigue, agitation, increased risk for stroke, high blood pressure, irregular heart rate, impotence, headaches, anxiety, difficulty urinating, violence, tolerance, dependence
	Psychological: exacerbation of OCD symptoms, anxiety, delusions of persecution, easily agitated–angered, dependence
Overdose	Panic, delusions, hallucinations, paranoia, delirium, violence, hyperactivity, cardiac arrhythmias, respiratory failure, cerebral hemorrhage, coma, convulsions, death
Withdrawal	Anxiety, sleep disturbance, chronic fatigue, irritability, depression, difficulty concentrating, craving suicidal–homicidal ideation, paranoid psychosis
Related problems	Premature births, withdrawal effects and hyperexcitability in offspring
Overdose	Severe palpitations, headaches, hypertension, tachycarida, agitation, seizures
Drug interactions	Tricyclic antidepressants (enhanced antidepressant effect), phenothiazines (increased plasma level of amphetamine), many interactions
Period of detection	1–2 days
Duration of effects	2–4 hours

Methamphetamine (Desoxyn)

The most potent amphetamine substance (related to amphetamine and ephedrine synthetic). It is sold legally under the brand name Desoxyn. Street dealers sell it in the form of "rock," which looks like a rock of wax, and the user shaves off powder for use. The effect is like that of cocaine. It is expensive, addictive, and deadly. It is easy to become addicted.

Street names	Speed, crystal, meth, crank, crosses, uppers, moth, glass, ice
Method of use	Oral, injected, smoked, snorted
Acute effects	Rush, euphoria, rapid pulse, hypertension, alert, loss of appetite, argumentativeness, psychosis, paranoia, increased aggression–violence, visual and tactile hallucinations, tremors agitation
Chronic use effects	Physiological: weight loss, tremors, agitation, mydriasis, dry mouth, bad breath, tachycardia, hypertension, weight loss, arrhythmias, tolerance, dependence
	Psychological: anxiety, irritability, aggressiveness, paranoid tendency, visual and tactile hallucinations, dependence
Overdose	Severe palpitations, headache, hypertension, tachycardia, agitation, seizures, cerebral hemorrhage, death
Withdrawal	Anxiety, sleep disturbance, chronic fatigue, irritability, depression, difficulty concentrating, craving, suicidal–homicidal ideation, paranoid psychosis
Period of detection	1–2 days
Duration of effects	2–4 hours

Cocaine

This substance has no acceptable medical uses and is highly addictive. Cocaine users become frightened and paranoid after experiencing ideas of reference that everyone wants to hurt them in some way. Cocaine is a significant stimulant whose effects last only a few minutes. Physiologically there is a surge of dopamine, resulting in the experience of euphoria. As the new receptor sites are emptied, craving is initiated to refill the sites. The tolerance–withdrawal cycle is acute, which often means no use during the week and binging on the weekends. The experience of "coming down" is miserable, which can lead to severe depression and increased risk of suicide. The user's main focus is to use cocaine—the substance becomes the most important thing to him or her.

Cocaine is such a powerful stimulant that it leaves people tense and unable to sleep. When they crash they can be very agitated, irritable, and depressed. Because of the mood extremes associated with cocaine use, coke addicts often use other substances to mediate these extremes, i.e., amphetamines to mediate depression and alcohol–sleeping pills to mediate coming down. Other significant effects are tremors, hallucinations, nosebleeds, paranoia, irritability, insomnia, weight loss, and stuffy–runny nose. Street dealers cut cocaine with other substances such as amphetamine, sugar, or quinine. These mixtures can be dangerous and highlights the fact that a person never knows what he or she is buying.

Street names	Snow, coke, blow, big C, candy dust, stardust, crack, rock, nose, toot, happy dust
Method of use	Snorted, injected, smoked (smoking is ineffective—almost instantly vaporizes)
Acute effects	Powerful dependence (risk of dependence after one dose); euphoria, excitability, lack of appetite, restlessness, talkativeness, anxiety, panic, depression, paranoia, irritability, increased aggressive behavior, sexual dysfunction, delirium, hallucinations, feels like skin is crawling, psychosis, dilated pupils, tachycardia, elevated–lowered blood pressure, psychomotor agitation–retardation, cardiac arrhythmias, convulsions, pulmonary edema, respiratory failure, coma, cardiac arrest, possible death
Chronic use effects	Physiological: weight loss, abdominal pain, vomiting, difficulty urinating, high blood pressure, increased risk for stroke, irregular heart rate, impotence, headaches, tolerance, dependence nosebleeds–other nasal problems
	Psychological: anxiety, irritability, agressiveness, exacerbation of OCD symptoms, psychosis
Overdose	Convulsions, pulmonary edema, respiratory failure, coma, cardiac arrest, possible death
Withdrawal	Fatigue, vivid–unpleasant dreams, insomnia–hypersomnia, increased appetite, psychomotor retardation–agitation
Related problems	Associated with spontaneous labor–abortion, prematuare birth, infants experiencing withdrawal symptoms, lower than average birth weight, length, and head circumference, seizures, EEG abnormalities, genitourinary tract abnormalities
Period of detection	1–4 days
Duration of effects	1–2 hours

Crack or Freebase Cocaine

Cocaine with increased potency. Crack is the strongest and most dangerous form of cocaine. It is also the most addictive form of cocaine. The substance gets to the brain in 6 sec, and the effect lasts for 6–8 min. Some people become addicted after one use. The substance can take over their lives and become the only thing that they want to do. Freebase is a process used to burn out the other ingredients in cocaine. Freebase is also a form of cocaine that is smoked. It often results in fatal burning accidents. The period of detection is 1–4 days, and the duration of effects is 4–14 hours.

A subcategory referred to as sympathomimetics is sometimes misrepresented as amphetamine because they produce a similar effect if abused. Two examples are ephedrine and phenylpropanolamine.

Caffeine

Caffeine is safe in small quantities, but can be dangerous in large dosages with associated dependency. A dose of 240 mg can cause headaches, irritability, and stomach nervousness. A dose of 200 mg is generally viewed as the ceiling dose to avoid those symptoms. Numerous beverages, foods, and over-the-counter preparations contain caffeine. If an individual is dependent on caffeine, he or she can feel sleepy and lethargic without it. When using any of these products, it is advisable to avoid other products that include caffeine as an ingredient. The immediate effects of caffeine are reduction in fatigue, improved alertness, decreased appetite, mild diuretic, constricted blood vessels (relieves headache pain), and a subjective sense of well-being. *A Diagnosis of substance dependence is not applied to caffeine in the DSM IV.*

Acute effect	Improved alertness, increased energy, decreased appetite, sense of well-being, mild diuretic, constricts brain blood vessels acting to relieve headaches (except for those who have sensitivity to caffeine; they may experience migraine-type headaches and other symptoms)
Chronic effects	A daily intake of 500 mg/day or more can result in insomnia, nervousness, restlessness, anxiety, stomach aches, headaches, diarrhea, and rapid heartbeat
Withdrawal	The following symptoms may be experienced: headache, drowsiness, fatigue; symptoms should subside after a few days

NICOTINE

Nicotine is a stimulant and sedative to the CNS. It contributes to feelings of stimulation, agitation, and nervousness (energy), which are then followed by depression and fatigue, leading the abuser to seek more nicotine. Nicotine is an addictive stimulant, which means that there can be both physical and psychological symptoms of withdrawal, initially resulting in fatigue and nervousness.

Acute effects	Stimulation (discharge of epinephrine from the adrenal cortex)
Chronic effects	Dependence, cancer, heart disease, emphysema, death
Withdrawal	Craving, agitation, low frustration tolerance, insomnia, anxiety, difficulty concentrating, restlessness, decreased heart rate, increased appetite for weight gain
Period of detection	1–2 days

ANABOLIC STEROIDS

Common anabolic steroids include maxibolin, anadrol 50, teslac, winstrol, methyltestosterone, dianabol, and nandrolone. Andronergic anabolic steroids are derivatives of testosterone that promote the growth of skeletal muscle and increase lean body mass. They are generally used to improve physical appearance and enhance performance. Because of the hormone's masculinizing action, it is not suitable for prolonged use in women or children. It is typically taken in cycles of weeks or months versus continuous use. Users may combine several different types of steroids in an effort to maximize effectiveness and minimize negative effects. This process is referred to as "stacking." Steroids are usually taken orally or injected.

Many of the negative health issues of *short-term* effects are reversible. Major side effects include increased incidence of liver tumors, jaundice, hypertension, stroke, fluid retention, severe acne, and trembling. Age and gender also offer additional side effects profiles for consideration.

1. Men: shrinking of the testicles, decreased production of male hormone, decreased sperm count, infertility, changes in libido, balding, gynomastia, decrease in high-density lipids, which may increase development of hardening of the arteries
2. Women: growth of facial hair, changes in cessation of menstrual cycle, enlargement of clitoris, deepened voice, baldness, increased libido
3. Adolescents: premature halting of growth via premature skeletal maturation, accelerated pubertal changes

Psychiatric symptoms include increased aggression, mood swings, rages, paranoid jealousy, extreme irritability, delusions, and impaired judgment associated with feeling invincible. Effects last for days to weeks.

CLUB DRUGS

According to the NIDA (2001), while club drugs or "date rape" drugs continue to expand, four drugs have been prevalent in the press that they have received: Ecstasy, Rohypnol, GHB, and ketamine. Their use on the dance scene (raves) of teenagers and young adults is well-known. However, their use is not limited to the stated age groups or activities. The so-called "date rape" drugs have been used to exploit and assault those at all ages. The low reporting rate is associated with fear and embarrassment.

The individuals using these drugs for clubbing are aiming to enhance their experience. They are attractive because of the low cost, intoxicating highs that enhance the sought-after experience, and increased energy or stamina. Unfortunately, these individuals lack the knowledge of the potential harmful side effects of these drugs, such as mood alternation, brain damage, sharp increases in body temperature with associated muscle breakdown, kidney failure, and cardiovascular failure.

Ecstasy *(MDMA)*	Ecstasy is a synthetic drug possessing both stimulant and hallucinogenic properties. Although it is usually taken in pill form, it can be injected, snorted, or used in suppository form.
Rohypnol	Rohypnol is the trade name for the benzodiazepine flunitrazepam. When mixed with alcohol this drug can incapacitate a victim, preventing him or her from resisting a sexual assault. Additionally, anterograde amnesia is experienced. The use of other benzodiazepines for the purpose of date rape is also being noted.
GHB	GHB or γ-hydroxybutyrate has been abused for its euphoric, sedative, and anabolic effects. It is commonly mixed with alcohol, and its overdose appears higher when compared to the use of other club drugs. When GHB is combined with methamphetamine, coma and seizures can occur. When combined with alcohol, nausea and difficulty breathing can occur.
Ketamine	Ketamine was developed as an anesthetic approved for both human and animal use. It can be injected or snorted. At certain doses it can cause dreamlike states and hallucinations. At high doses, side effects can be delirium, amnesia, impaired motor function, hypertension, and potentially fatal respiratory problems.

TABLE 2.1   Substances of Abuse: Class Examples[a]

Depressants
  Alcohol
  Barbituates
    Seconal
    Nembutal
    Amytal
    Butisol
    Tuinol
    Phenobarbital
    Mebaral
  Benzodiazepines
    Ativan
    Halcion
    Librium
    Rohypnol
    Valium
    Xanax
    Tranxene
    Restoril
    Clonipin
    Sexax
    Dalmane
    Centrax

Cannabinoids
  Marijuana
  Hashish

Hallucinogens
  LSD
  Mushrooms
  Mescaline
  PCP
  Ecstasy

Stimulants
  Amphetamine
  Methamphetamine
  Cocaine
  Crack (freebase cocaine)

Opioids
  Opium
  Heroin
  Morphine (and derivatives)
  Codeine
  Meperidine (Demerol)
  Methadone (Synthetic)

[a]For a thorough list of drug street names, publication no. (ADP) 97-2534, contact: Resource Center, State of California, Alcohol and Drug Programs, 1700 K Street, Sacramento, CA 95813; telephone (916) 327-3728, fax (916) 323-1270.

TABLE 2.2   Substance Abuse Testing Retention Times[a]

Substance class	Approximate detection time
Depressants	
Alcohol	6–10 hours
Barbiturates	Short acting, 1–3 days
	Long acting, 2–10 days
Benzodiazepines	1–6 weeks
Methaqualone	1–14 days
Cannabinoids	Occasional use, 1–7 days
	Chronic use, 1–5 weeks
Opioids	
Opium	1–2 days
Heroin	1–2 days
Morphine	1–2 days
Codeine	1–2 days
Meperidine	1–2 days
Methadone (synthetic)	1–7 days
Hallucinogens	
LSD	8 hr
Mushrooms	8 hr

(Continues)

TABLE 2.2 (*Continued*)

Substance class	Approximate detection time
Mescaline	2–3 days
PCP	2–8 days
Ecstasy	1–2 days
Stimulants	
Amphetamine	1–2 days
Methamphetamine	1–2 days
Cocaine	1–4 days
Crack (freebase cocaine)	1–4 days

[a]Many factors have an effect on retention time. The following factors should be considered: (1) the frequency and duration of substance use; (2) the differences in metabolic rates from one individual to the next; and (3) the acknowledgement that illicit substances are not monitored or regulated. Therefore, there are no controls over substance derivation, purity, or potency.

TABLE 2.3 Symptoms Indicating Specific Substance Abuse[a]

Marijuana
  Sleepiness or, at times, stuporous behavoir
  Loud talking, often rapid, with bursts of laughter
  Forgetting train of thought in midconversation
  Whites of eyes may appear inflamed, pupils will be dilated
  Strong odor on breath or on clothing
  Tendency to drive slowly, often below the speed limit
  Distorted sense of time, often overestimating its passage
  Possession of paraphernalia
  Slow reaction time
  Decreased motivation
  Impaired memory
  Apathy

Alcohol
  Odor on the breath or body (through sweat)
  Difficulty focusing, glazed appearance of the eyes
  Either very passive behavior or very argumentative behavior
  Sudden deterioration in personal hygiene or appearance
  Unexplained accidents or bruises
  Irritability
  Blackouts
  Preoccupation with drinking, protection of supply
  Loss of inhibition
  Impaired thinking
  Slurred speech
  Relaxed sedated
  Insomnia

Stimulants
  Dilated pupils
  Dry mouth and nose, bad breath, lip licking
  Irritability, argumentative behavior
  Conversations lack continuity
  Difficulty staying still, excessive activity
  Lack of sleep and appetite
  Runny nose, chronic sinus problems, nose bleeds
  Use of paraphernalia
  Violence
  Anxiety
  Social withdrawal
  Difficulty with concentration
  Mania

(*Continues*)

TABLE 2.3 (*Continued*)

Paranoia
Enhanced sense of power

Depressants
Seems intoxicated (as with alcohol), but without odor
Slurred speech
No animation or expressiveness in face
Slowed reaction time
Motor dysfunction
Drowsiness
Confusion
Euphoria
Inattention
Impaired judgement

Narcotics
Drowsiness, lethargy
Constricted pupils
Scars on inner arms or other places from injecting
Possession of paraphernalia
Euphoria–good mood
Slurred speech
Loss of appetite
Lack of motivation
Sense of well-being,
'Rush' analgesic affect

Inhalants
Odor of paint, glue, etc. on breath and clothes
Runny nose and watering eyes
Poor muscle control
Drowsiness or unconsciousness
Preference for group activities, not being alone
Possession of bags or rags with dried solvents
Discarded whipped cream or similar dispensers
Impaired memory
Impaired motor function
Sneezing-coughing
Euphoria
Feeling of invincibility

Hallucinogens
Extremely dilated pupils
Warm skin, excessive perspiration, and body odor
Mood and behavior changes
Distorted senses of sight, hearing, and touch
Distorted image of self and concept of time
Unpredictable flashback episodes long after withdrawal
Depersonalization–derealization
Euphoria
Paramour
Lack of coordination
Muscle weakness to extreme of super strength

PCP
Unpredictable behavior, swings between passivity and violence
Symptoms of intoxication
Disoriented behavior, agitation–violence if overly stimulated
Fear and terror
Rigid muscles and strange gait
Deadened sensory perception
Pupils appear dilated
Pupils float and appear to follow a moving object
Masklike facial appearance

[a]Aside from social indicators of changes in friends (peer group), alienation from family and dysfunction in job or school performance, other symptoms that indicate the abuse of a substance may include, but are not limited to, the list in this table.

TABLE 2.4 Common Drugs of Abuse

| Substance | Prescription brands or street names | Medical uses | Dependence potential | | Tolerance | Duration of effects | Period of detection | Method of use | Possible general effects of class | General effects of overdose | General effects of withdrawal |
			Physical	Psychological							
Depressants											
Alcohol	Beer, wine, spirits	None	Yes	Yes	Yes	Hours	6–10 hr	Oral			Anxiety, insomnia, tremors, delirium, convulsions, possible death
Inhalants	Gas, give, cleaning fluids	None	No	Yes, moderate	Yes	24–48 hr	2–10 days	Oral–injected	Slurred speech, disorientation, drunken behavior, relaxed inhibitions	Shallow respiration, cold and clammy skin, dilated pupils, weak and rapid pulse, coma, possible death	
Sedative–Hypnotics[a]	Seconal, Nembutal, Amytal, Butisol, Tuinol, phenobarbitol	Anesthetic, anti convulsant, sleep, sedation	Yes	Yes	Yes	1–16 hr					
Anxiolytics[a]	Atiran, Halcion, Librium, Rohypnol, Valium, Xanax, etc.	Antianxiety, sleep, sedation	Yes	Yes	Yes	4–8 hr	1–6 weeks	Oral–injected			
Some overlap between sedative hypnotics and anxiolytics											
Cannabinoids											
Marijuana	Pot, grass, joint	Nausea	Degree unknown	Yes	Yes	2–4 hr	1 day to 5 weeks	Oral–smoked	Euphoria, disinhibition, increased appetite	Fatigue, parasomnia, possible psychosis	Insomnia, hyperactivity, decreased appetite
Hashish	Hash, black, weed oil, Columbian					2–4 hr		Oral–smoked			
Opioids											
Opium	"O"	Analgesic–antidiarrheal	Yes	Yes	Yes	3–6 hr	1–2 days	Oral–smoked	Euphoria, drowsiness,	Slow and shallow breathing,	
Heroin	Horse, junk, stuff, "H"	None	Yes	Yes	Yes	3–6 hr	1–2 days	injected–sniffed	Depression, constricted pupils, nausea,	Clammy skin, convulsions, coma, possible death	
Morphine	Morpho, "M," dreamer	Analgesic	Yes	Yes	Yes	3–6 hr	1–2 days	Injected–smoked	Euphoria, drowsiness, deppression,	Slow and shallow breathing, clammy skin,	

Drug	Street names	Medical uses	Physical dependence	Psychological dependence	Duration	Duration	Methods of administration	Possible effects	Effects of overdose	Withdrawal syndrome
Codeine	School boys, 3's, 4's	Analgesic–antitussive	Yes	Yes	3–6 hr	1–2 days	Oral–injected	constricted pupils, nausea,	convulsions coma, possible, death	
Methadone	Dollies, methadose, kick	Analgesic–heroin substitute	Yes	Yes	12–24 hr	1 day to 2 weeks	Oral–injected			Withdrawal syndrome, not reported
Hallucinogens										
LSD	Acid, purple, haze, tabs	None	No	Degree unknown	Variable	8 hr	Oral			
Psilocybin	Shrooms, magic mushrooms	None	No	Degree unknown	Variable	8 hr	Oral	Illusions, hallucinations, poor perception of time	Longer, more intense trips, episodes of psychosis and possible death	
Mescaline	Mese, huatari, mescal buttons	None	No	Degree unknown	Variable	2–3 days	Oral			
Phenylcyclidine (PCP)	Angel dust, "CJ," killer	Veterinary anesthetic	No	Degree unknown	Variable	2–8 days	Oral–injected, smoked			
Stimulants										
Amphetamines	Uppers, pep pills, dex, bennies, ice	Hyperkinesis, weight control, narcolepsy	Possible	Yes	2 hr	1–2 days	Oral–injected	Increased alertness, excitation, euphoria, dilated pupils, increased pulse, increased blood pressure, insomnia, loss of appetite	Agitation, increase in body temperature, hallucination, convulsions, possible death	Apathy, long periods of sleep, irritability, depression, disorientation
Cocaine	Snow, coke, blow, toot, big "C"	None	Possible	Yes	2–4 hr	1–4 days	Injected, sniffed, smoked			
Caffeine	Numerous diet products and soft drink	None	No	Yes	2–6 hr			Increased blood pressure, increased alertness, insomnia, headache	Shakiness, agitation, insomnia, nausea	Headache, irritability, fatigue
Nicotine	Cigarettes	None	Yes	Yes	1–2 days		Oral, smoked	Increased blood pressure	Shakiness, agitation	Craving, anger, anxiety, irritability, restlessness, bradescardia, increased appetite
Anabolic steroids: Maxibolin Anadrol 50 Winstrol Methyl-tetosterone							Oral–injected			

There is some overlap between sedative–hypnotics and anxiolytics.

REFERENCES

Babor, T. F. (1994). Method and theory in the classification of alcoholics. *In* "Type of Alcoholics: Research" (T. Babor, V. Hasselbrock, R. Meyer, & W. Shoemaker, Eds.), pp. 1–6. New York: Annals of the New York Academy of Science.

Best, S. E., Oliveto, A. H., & Kosten, T. R. (1996). Opioid Addiction: Recent advances in detoxification and maintenance therapy. *CND Drugs* **6**(4):301–314.

Bezchlibnyk-Butler, K. Z., & Jeffries, J. J. (1998). "Clinical Handbook of Psychotropic Drugs." Seattle: Hogrefe & Huber Publishers.

Blum, K. (1984). "Handbook of Abusable Drugs." New York: Gardner Press.

Frances, R. J., & Miller, S. I. (1998). "Clinical Textbook of Addictive Disorders," 2nd ed. New York: Guilford Press.

Galizio, M., & Maistro, S. A. (1985). "Determinants of Substance Abuse." New York: Plenum.

Gilman, G. A., Goodman, L. S., & Gilman, A. (1980). "Goodman and Gilman's The Pharmacological Basis of Therapuetics," 6th ed. New York: Macmillan.

Gilman, A.G., Mayer, S. E., & Melmon, K. L. (1980). Pharmacodynamics: Mechanisms of drug action and the relationship between drug concentration and effect. *In* "Goodman and Gilman's The Pharmacological Basis of Therapeutics" (A. G. Gilman & A Gilman, Eds.), 6th ed. New York: Macmillan.

Kaplan, H., & Sadock, B. (1990). "Pocket Handbook of Clinical Psychiatry." Baltimore, MD: Williams & Wilkin.

Lader, M. (1980). "Introduction to Psychopharmacology." Kalamazoo, MI: Upjohn Co.

Leavitt, F. (1982). "Drugs and Behavior," 2nd ed. New York: Wiley.

Lewis, J. A., Dana, R. Q., & Blevins, G. A. (1994). "Substance Abuse Counseling: An Individual Approach." Pacific Grove, CA: Brooks/Cole Publishing.

Maxman, J., & Ward, N. (1995). "Psychotropic Drugs Fast Fact." New York: W. M. Norton & Company.

Mayer, S. E., Melmon, K. L., & Gilman, A. G. (1980). Introduction: The dynamics of drug absorption, distribution, and elimination. *In* "Goodman and Gilman's The Pharmacological Basis of Therapeutics" (A. G. Gilman, L. S. Goodman, & A. Gilman, Eds.), 6th ed. New York: Macmillan.

McCarty, D. (1985). Environmental factors in substance abuse. *In* "Determinants of Substance Abuse" (M. Galizio & S. A. Maistro, Eds.). New York: Plenum.

McClintic, J. R. (1978). "Physiology of the Human Body." New York: John Wiley & Sons.

National Inhalant Prevention Coalition (2001). *APA Monitor*, June 11.

National Institute on Drug Abuse (2001). NIDA INFOFAX, Club Drugs. Telephone no. 1-888-644-6432 or online http://www.nida.nih.gov/.

National Institute on Drug Abuse (1996). Research Monograph Series 159, 5600 Fisher Lane, Rockville, MD 20857.

Schatzberg, A. E., & Cole, J. (1986). "Manual of Clinical Psychopharmacology." Washington, DC: American Psychiatric Press.

Thompson, A. D., & Pratto, E. (1992). Interaction of nutrients and alcohol: Absorption, transport, utilization, and metabolism. *In* "Nutrition and Alcohol" (R. R. Watson & B. Watzl, Eds.), pp. 75–100 Boca Raton, FL: CRC Press.

Wilford, B. B. (1981). "Drug Abuse: A Guide for the Primary Care Physician." Chicago: American Medical Association.

Chapter 3

The Development of Substance Abuse and Dependence

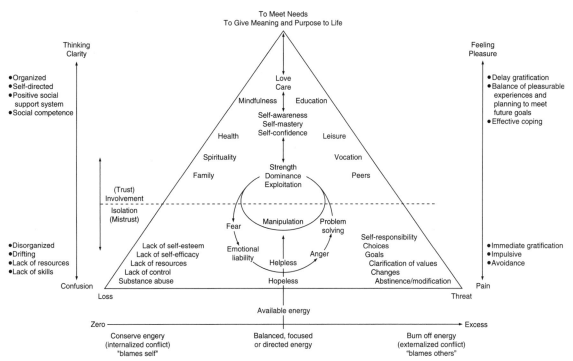

To Meet Needs
To Give Meaning and Purpose to Life

Thinking
Clarity

●Organized
●Self-directed
●Positive social
 support system
●Social competence

Love
Care

Mindfulness   Education

Self-awareness
Self-mastery
Self-confidence

Health   Leisure

Spirituality   Vocation

Family

Strength
Dominance
Exploitation

Peers

Feeling
Pleasure

●Delay gratification
●Balance of pleasurable
 experiences and
 planning to meet
 future goals
●Effective coping

(Trust)
Involvement

Isolation
(Mistrust)

Manipulation

Fear   Problem
                             solving

●Disorganized
●Drifting
●Lack of resources
●Lack of skills

Lack of self-esteem
Lack of self-efficacy
Lack of resources
Lack of control
Substance abuse

Emotional
liability

Helpless

Hopeless

Anger

Self-responsibility
Choices
Goals
Clarification of values
Changes
Abstinence/modification

●Immediate gratification
●Impulsive
●Avoidance

Confusion   Pain

Loss   Threat

Available energy

Zero   Excess

Conserve engery
(internalized conflict)
"blames self"

Balanced, focused
or directed energy

Burn off energy
(externalized conflict)
"blames others"

Adapted from David Schwartz, M. D.

Entire books have been dedicated to the identification and discussion of the various models of addiction (substance abuse–dependence). There is variability in thinking and uncertainty regarding the nature and etiology of problems associated with substance abuse. The more thorough the acknowledged possibilities for substance dependence, the more informed a therapist is in working with a client to develop an appropriate and effective treatment plan. According to Hester and Miller (1989), "inappropriate (treatment) matching can result in wasted money, treatment, and staff time, even lost families and lives." A resounding outcome of a literature review is that substance abuse and dependence are a complex issue that requires a thorough assessment with a clinical focus on matching the individual with the appropriate treatment. This is in contrast to traditional intervention offering all individuals seeking substance abuse treatment the same or similar treatment plan and program.

MODELS OF SUBSTANCE DEPENDENCE

Although a review of the literature offers numerous theories on abuse and addiction over the years, it appears that the history of the models of addiction can be divided into three main areas due to similar themes of etiology. The three basic models of dependence development are as follows:

1. Medical Model: Based on disease concept, genetics, and physiology. This model has been a dominant influence on treatment approach since the 1970s. Disease concept states that substance use disorders are a primary disorder. It also views dependence as being similar to other disease states. The key concepts are loss of control, denial, and continued use despite negative consequences. This model fails to adequately address how environmental and genetic factors interact. However, this does not diminish the information offered by this model. For example, Wallace (1996) points out the possibility that these individuals may have damaged neurotransmitter or neuropeptide systems through years of substance abuse, and it cannot be determined who was born with a genetic predisposition versus those damaged by abuse.

2. Psychosocial Model: Any theoretical orientation that can be applied to explain behavior; sociocultural, systems theory, social learning, conditioning, characterological, educational, temperament, and morality. All of these theories are based upon the premise that all behavior is learned and can be modified by the same learning processes, including thoughts, feelings, and physiological changes. Important treatment contributions have resulted from these theories' analysis of the consequences of substance abuse.

3. Biopsychosocial Model: The most comprehensive model, which integrates all factors that may play a role in the development of addiction. Comprehensive, multifaceted, and interdisciplinary model from which to understand substance abuse and addiction. According to NIAAA (1993), the strongest evidence for the genetic transmission of a predisposition to substance dependence disorder exists for alcohol. However, research data exist that suggest a biochemical, if not genetic, basis for dependence on other substances.

Regardless of the substance class with which an individual has an issue of substance dependency, a common if not prevalent treatment perspective includes the following:

1. The dependence is the primary disease (not a symptom of an underlying disease) with the associated factorial relationships
   a. genetic
   b. psychosocial
   c. environment

2. Substance dependence may be progressive and can be fatal. The cumulative impact physically, emotionally, and socially often contributes to premature death.

3. Substance dependence is a phenomenon associated with a common constellation of characteristics, which places the individual at a disadvantage and outside of mainstream functioning.

4. Impaired control (or loss of control) as evidenced by an inability to limit the amount of substance consumed, the time frame during which an episode takes place, or heed the consequences of use.

5. Preoccupation with obtaining and using substances. It becomes the primary object. The result is a disengagement from all other life concerns.

6. Experience of numerous adverse consequences associated with substance use:
   a. physical health (e.g., alcohol: withdrawal, liver damage, gastritis, pancreatitis, heart problems, anemia, neurological disorders)
   b. psychological functioning (cognitive impairment, mood changes with associated behavioral changes)
   c. interpersonal functioning (relationship problems, social problems, child abuse–neglect)
   d. occupational functioning (school–job problems)
   e. legal problems (DUI, bad checks, ignoring responsibilities)
   f. financial problems
   g. spiritual problems

7. Denial of the significance of all of the aforementioned events and issues.

8. Losses.

CAUSAL FACTORS OF SUBSTANCE ABUSE AND DEPENDENCE

Another way of viewing the development of abuse and dependence is to consider the causal factors that contribute to an individual's abuse of substances and the pattern of substance abuse (Crabbe *et al.*, 1985; Mc Carthy, 1985; Washton, 1995).

1. Availability of substances: Substances being readily accessible is a necessary condition for substance abuse; however, it is not a factor, in and of itself, that results in an individual using substances.

2. Onset of action: Substances that act quickly to mask symptoms and alter mood are more prone to abuse. Additionally, the benefit being sought by using a specific substance plays a role in the choice of the substance used.

3. Biological predisposition: There appears to be some genetic predisposition to alcoholism. There may be numerous biological factors involved in the development of substance dependence.

4. Childhood experiences and environment: Learning theory states that behaviors are handed down from one generation to another. The issue of "identification" may be at work when children unconsciously adopt behaviors or learn through modeling the various characteristics of their caretakers and other role models while growing up. Other factors playing a role under the rubric of experiences would be neglect and various forms of abuse and the impact on coping, etc.

5. Culture: Socially sanctioned versus prohibition based upon cultural, familial, peer, and spiritual–religious beliefs.

6. Socio economic status: No barriers.

7. Development of tolerance, psychological dependence, and physical dependence

8. Mental illness: Disorders that commonly underlie substance abuse include affective disorders, mood disorders, somatoform disorders, and personality disorders.

Therefore, biological, psychological, and social experience factors are integrated in the initiation and maintenance of substance use problems. It is possible that neurochemical imbalance creates a primary drive (craving) for substance use, which overwhelms or overrides the cognitive factors of judgment, insight, and impulse control, thus, propelling an individual into a substance-dependent lifestyle where the substance(s) is the central object. Regarding sociocultural factors, environment, socioeconomic status, culture, and availability of substances are all key. Among psychological factors, expectations of the effects of a given substance contribute to the desire to use. According to Burkstein (1995) and Rotgers (1996), expectancy studies reveal that an individual is more likely to use substances if he or she expects greater effects from a substance to feel good, decrease tension, or avoid negative affect states. Numerous social messages reinforce the positive expectations associated with substance use, which particularly impacts adolescents when combined with adult role models and their peer group affiliations, which normalize such thinking and behaviors.

BIOLOGICAL MECHANISMS

The Harvard Mental Health Letter (June 1998) states that, contrary to most psychiatric disorders, substance dependence can be reliably produced in animals. Addictive substances achieve their effect by intensified activity of dopamine (in the medial forebrain bundle), but they take different routes:

1. Cocaine blocks the mechanism by which dopamine is reabsorbed into the cells that produce it.
2. Amphetamines provoke the release of dopamine.
3. Nicotine acts on a receptor for the neurotransmitter acetylcholine in the reward system and may prevent the enzyme monoamine oxidase from breaking up the dopamine molecule.
4. Opiates indirectly affect the dopamine system by acting on the receptors for endorphins and enkephalins (the brain's own morphine-like substance).
5. Alcohol, barbiturates, and benzodiazepines indirectly affect the dopamine system by acting on the neurons that release GABA (an inhibiting transmitter).

By enhancing dopamine transmission, addictive substances disturb the natural control system of the cell and cause changes in functioning. Some of these changes are long lasting. As a result, there is a decrease in dopamine production, which leads to a decrease in receptors and an increase in sensitivity. As tolerance increases, pleasure associated with use decreases and may actually become absent. At this point, individuals need the substance "just to feel normal." An example experienced by many therapists is the individual who uses stimulants to medicate their depression. What the individual does not understand is that chronic use of stimulants exacerbates depression by depleting neurotransmitters (Gold, 1992). Another example cites that low brain serotonin levels have been linked with alcohol consumption, and serotonin uptake inhibitors have been associated with decreased alcohol consumption (Gill & Amit, 1989).

When the issue of dual diagnosis is added to the clinical picture, there appears to be increased risk. *The Harvard Mental Health Letter* (July 1998), it states that depression, chronic anxiety, ADD, and other psychiatric disorders that demonstrate a genetic influence may also increase the risk for substance abuse–dependence because these disorders decrease the capacity for rewarding experiences.

One view of treatment has been that substance dependence causes long-lasting changes in the brain, is a chronic condition, and sometimes requires long-term care and treatment. This would also indicate that repeated relapses would be an expected part of recovery. According to the NIAAA (2000), brain autopsies of men with a history of chronic alcohol consumption in comparison to the brains of nonalcoholic adults demonstrate the following.

1. Smaller and lighter brains
2. Brain shrinkage: Extensive shrinkage of the frontal lobe cortex (intellectual function), deeper brain regions associated with memory, and the cerebellum (helps to regulate coordination and balance).
3. The amount of brain shrinkage approximately correlated with the amount of alcohol consumed. Current studies will demonstrate if the same effect occurs in women. At this point, research has suggested that women may be more vulnerable or susceptible to brain shrinkage.

The use of positron emission tomography (PET) and single photon emission computed tomography (SPECT) identified decreased blood flow and metabolic rates in certain brain regions, even without evidence of measurable shrinkage in the brains of chronic heavy drinkers as compared to nonalcoholics. Magnetic resonance spectroscopy (MRS) and PET scans reflected a decrease in the number or size of neurons or a decrease in the density of communication sites between adjacent neurons. Both of these results are complimentary to anatomical changes noted in brain autopsies. Research efforts will continue to focus on identifying changes in specific brain regions that can be correlated with alcohol-related behaviors. An example of such findings includes the imaging of the cerebellum, which linked shrinkage and decreased blood flow to impaired balance and gait. Such information not only has predictive value but helps to clarify different points of information that may be presented upon assessment, i.e., impaired balance and gait may lead to falls by older alcoholics, resulting in head trauma and other injuries. Some evidence has been found for a possible correlation between the shrinkage of memory-related brain regions and degree of memory impairment. However, no consistent relationship has been found between shrinkage of the frontal cortex and short-term memory and problem solving.

With even brief periods of abstinence (3–4 weeks), there may be partial improvement in cognitive functions, motor coordination, reversal of brain shrinkage, and some recovery of metabolic functions in the frontal lobes and cerebellum. Additionally, frontal lobe blood flow continues to increase with abstinence, with a return to near normal levels within about 4 years. Relapse to drinking will lead to all of the changes and deficits previously outlined. According to Enoch Gordis director of NIAAA, researchers are beginning to measure the effects of alcohol on mood, affect, emotional states, craving, and cognition while at the same time evaluating metabolic, physiologic, and neurochemical functioning. All of the advances with continuing research will hopefully lead to a scientific understanding of the development of substance dependence and the recovery process at the biological and genetic level.

To reinforce the strides that have been made in how substance dependence is conceptualized, Table 3.1 offers a historical overview. Clearly, whereas the manifestations of abuse demonstrate great diversity, treatment was traditionally based upon a single theoretical model at any given time. Unfortunately, the treatment limitations with associated limitations in positive outcome have contributed to the negative social stereotyping and often lack of empathy for the substance-dependent individual and the difficulties confronting him or her in recovery.

The National House Survey on Drug Abuse (NHSDA) offers statistical trends for annual prevalence (grades 8–12) and long-term trends of substance use. Refer to Tables 3.2–3.5.

TABLE 3.1

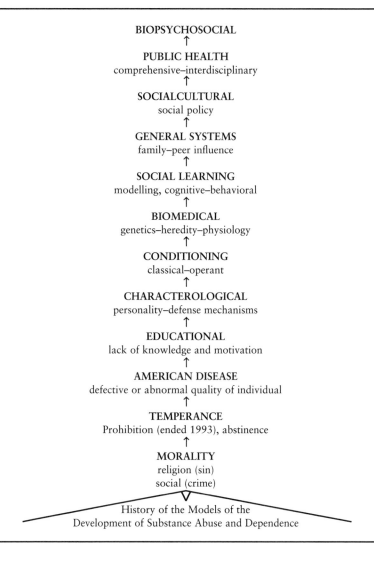

BIOPSYCHOSOCIAL
↑
PUBLIC HEALTH
comprehensive–interdisciplinary
↑
SOCIALCULTURAL
social policy
↑
GENERAL SYSTEMS
family–peer influence
↑
SOCIAL LEARNING
modelling, cognitive–behavioral
↑
BIOMEDICAL
genetics–heredity–physiology
↑
CONDITIONING
classical–operant
↑
CHARACTEROLOGICAL
personality–defense mechanisms
↑
EDUCATIONAL
lack of knowledge and motivation
↑
AMERICAN DISEASE
defective or abnormal quality of individual
↑
TEMPERANCE
Prohibition (ended 1993), abstinence
↑
MORALITY
religion (sin)
social (crime)

History of the Models of the
Development of Substance Abuse and Dependence

TABLE 3.2   Trends in Lifetime Prevalence of Use of Various Drugs for Eighth, Tenth, and Twelfth Graders[a]

	Lifetime[b]								
	1991	1992	1993	1994	1995	1996	1997	1998	1997–1998 change
Any illicit drug									
8th grade	18.7	20.6	22.5	25.7	28.5	31.2	29.4	29.0	−0.4
10th grade	30.6	29.8	32.8	37.4	40.9	45.4	47.3	44.9	−2.4
12th grade	44.1	40.7	42.9	45.6	48.4	50.8	54.3	54.1	−0.2
Any illicit drug other than marijuana									
8th grade	14.3	15.6	16.8	17.5	18.8	19.2	17.7	16.9	−0.8
10th grade	19.1	19.2	20.9	21.7	24.3	25.5	25.0	23.6	−1.4
12th grade	26.9	25.1	26.7	27.6	28.1	28.5	30.0	29.4	−0.6

(Continues)

TABLE 3.2 (*Continued*)

	Lifetime[b]								1997–1998 change
	1991	1992	1993	1994	1995	1996	1997	1998	
Any illicit drug including inhalants									
8th grade	28.5	29.6	32.3	35.1	38.1	39.4	38.1	37.8	−0.3
10th grade	36.1	36.2	38.7	42.7	45.9	49.8	50.9	49.3	−1.6
12th grade	47.6	44.4	46.6	49.1	51.5	53.5	56.3	56.1	−0.2
Marijuana–hashish									
8th grade	10.2	11.2	12.6	16.7	19.9	23.1	22.6	22.2	−0.4
10th grade	23.4	21.4	24.4	30.7	34.1	39.8	42.3	39.6	−2.7s
12th grade	36.7	32.6	35.3	38.2	41.7	44.9	49.6	49.1	−0.5
Inhalants									
8th grade	17.6	17.4	19.4	19.9	21.6	21.2	21.0	20.5	−0.5
10th grade	15.7	16.6	17.5	18.0	19.0	19.3	18.3	18.3	0.0
12th grade	17.6	16.6	17.4	17.7	17.4	16.6	16.1	15.2	−0.9
Nitrites									
8th grade									
10th grade									
12th grade	1.6	1.5	1.4	1.7	1.5	1.8	2.0	2.7	+0.7
Hallucinogens									
8th grade	3.2	3.8	3.9	4.3	5.2	5.9	5.4	4.9	−0.5
10th grade	6.1	6.4	6.8	8.1	9.3	10.5	10.5	9.8	−0.7
12th grade	9.6	9.2	10.9	11.4	12.7	14.0	15.1	14.1	−1.0
LSD									
8th grade	2.7	3.2	3.5	3.7	4.4	5.1	4.7	4.1	−0.6
10th grade	5.6	5.8	6.2	7.2	8.4	9.4	9.5	8.5	−1.0
12th grade	8.8	8.6	10.3	10.5	11.7	12.6	13.6	12.6	−1.0
Hallucinogens other than LSD									
8th grade	1.4	1.7	1.7	2.2	2.5	3.0	2.6	2.5	−0.1
10th grade	2.2	2.5	2.8	3.8	3.9	4.7	4.8	5.0	+0.2
12th grade	3.7	3.3	3.9	4.9	5.4	6.8	7.5	7.1	−0.4
PCP									
8th grade									
10th grade									
12th grade	2.9	2.4	2.9	2.8	2.7	4.0	3.9	3.9	0.0
MDMA (Ecstasy)									
8th grade						3.4	3.2	2.7	−0.5
10th grade						5.6	5.7	5.1	−0.6
12th grade						6.1	6.9	5.8	−1.1
Cocaine									
8th grade	2.3	2.9	2.9	3.6	4.2	4.5	4.4	4.6	+0.2
10th grade	4.1	3.3	3.6	4.3	5.0	6.5	7.1	7.2	+0.1
12th grade	7.8	6.1	6.1	5.9	6.0	7.1	8.7	9.3	+0.6
Crack									
8th grade	1.3	1.6	1.7	2.4	2.7	2.9	2.7	3.2	+0.5s
10th grade	1.7	1.5	1.8	2.1	2.8	3.3	3.6	3.9	+0.3
12th grade	3.1	2.6	2.6	3.0	3.0	3.3	3.9	4.4	+0.5
Other cocaine									
8th grade	2.0	2.4	2.4	3.0	3.4	3.8	3.5	3.7	+0.2
10th grade	3.8	3.0	3.3	3.8	4.4	5.5	6.1	6.4	+0.3
12th grade	7.0	5.3	5.4	5.2	5.1	6.4	8.2	8.4	+0.2

(*Continues*)

TABLE 3.2 (*Continued*)

	Lifetime[b]								
	1991	1992	1993	1994	1995	1996	1997	1998	1997–1998 change
Heroin									
8th grade	1.2	1.4	1.4	2.0	2.3	2.4	2.1	2.3	+0.2
10th grade	1.2	1.2	1.3	1.5	1.7	2.1	2.1	2.3	+0.2
12th grade	0.9	1.2	1.1	1.2	1.6	1.8	2.1	2.0	−0.1
Other opiates									
8th grade									
10th grade									
12th grade	6.6	6.1	6.4	6.6	7.2	8.2	9.7	9.8	+0.1
Stimulants									
8th grade	10.5	10.8	11.8	12.3	13.1	13.5	12.3	11.3	−1.0
10th grade	13.2	13.1	14.9	15.1	17.4	17.7	17.0	16.0	−1.0
12th grade	15.4	13.9	15.1	15.7	15.3	15.3	16.5	16.4	−0.1
Ice									
8th grade									
10th grade									
12th grade	3.3	2.9	3.1	3.4	3.9	4.4	4.4	5.3	+0.9
Barbiturates									
8th grade									
10th grade									
12th grade	6.2	5.5	6.3	7.0	7.4	7.6	8.1	8.7	+0.6
Tranquilizers									
8th grade	3.8	4.1	4.4	4.6	4.5	5.3	4.8	4.6	−0.2
10th grade	5.8	5.9	5.7	5.4	6.0	7.1	7.3	7.8	+0.5
12th grade	7.2	6.0	6.4	6.6	7.1	7.2	7.8	8.5	+0.7
Alcohol									
Any use									
8th grade	70.1	69.3	67.1						
			55.7	55.8	54.5	55.3	53.8	52.5	−1.3
10th grade	83.8	82.3	80.8						
			71.6	71.1	70.5	71.8	72.0	69.8	−2.2s
12th grade	88.0	87.5	87.0						
			80.0	80.4	80.7	79.2	81.7	81.4	−0.3
Been drunk									
8th grade	26.7	26.8	26.4	25.9	25.3	26.8	25.2	24.8	−0.4
10th grade	50.0	47.7	47.9	47.2	46.9	48.5	49.4	46.7	−2.7s
12th grade	65.4	63.4	62.5	62.9	63.2	61.8	64.2	62.4	−1.8
Cigarettes									
Any use									
8th grade	44.0	45.2	45.3	46.1	46.4	49.2	47.3	45.7	−1.6
10th grade	55.1	53.5	56.3	56.9	57.6	61.2	60.2	57.7	−2.5s
12th grade	63.1	61.8	61.9	62.0	64.2	63.5	65.4	65.3	−0.1
Smokeless tobacco									
8th grade	22.2	20.7	18.7	19.9	20.0	20.4	16.8	15.0	−1.8
10th grade	28.2	26.6	28.1	29.2	27.6	27.4	26.3	22.7	−3.6ss
12th grade		32.4	31.0	30.7	30.9	29.8	25.3	26.2	+0.9
Steroids									
8th grade	1.9	1.7	1.6	2.0	2.0	1.8	1.8	2.3	+0.5s
10th grade	1.8	1.7	1.7	1.8	2.0	1.8	2.0	2.0	0.0
12th grade	2.1	2.1	2.0	2.4	2.3	1.9	2.4	2.7	+0.3

[a]National House Survey on Drug Abuse (NHSDA), courtesy of the National Clearinghouse for alcohol and Drug Information (NCADI).
[b]Entries are percentages.

TABLE 3.3 Trends in Annual and 30-Day Prevalence of Use of Various Drugs for Eighth, Tenth, and Twelfth Graders[a]

	Annual[b]									30-day[b]								
	1991	1992	1993	1994	1995	1996	1997	1998	1997–1998 change	1991	1992	1993	1994	1995	1996	1997	1998	1997–1998 change
Any illicit drug																		
8th grade	11.3	12.9	15.1	18.5	21.4	23.6	22.1	21.0	-1.1	5.7	6.8	8.4	10.9	12.4	14.6	12.9	12.1	-0.8
10th grade	21.4	20.4	24.7	30.0	33.3	37.5	38.5	35.0	-3.5ss	11.6	11.0	14.0	18.5	20.2	23.2	23.0	21.5	-1.5
12th grade	29.4	27.1	31.0	35.8	39.0	40.2	42.4	41.4	-1.0	16.4	14.4	18.3	21.9	23.8	24.6	26.2	25.6	-0.6
Any illicit drug																		
Other than marijuana																		
8th grade	8.4	9.3	10.4	11.3	12.6	13.1	11.8	11.0	-0.8	3.8	4.7	5.3	5.6	6.5	6.9	6.0	5.5	-0.5
10th grade	12.2	12.3	13.9	15.2	17.5	18.4	18.2	16.6	-1.6	5.5	5.7	6.5	7.1	8.9	8.9	8.8	8.6	-0.2
12th grade	16.2	14.9	17.1	18.0	19.4	19.8	20.7	20.2	-0.5	7.1	6.3	7.9	8.8	10.0	9.5	10.7	10.7	0.0
Any illicit drug																		
Including inhalants																		
8th grade	16.7	18.2	21.1	24.2	27.1	28.7	27.2	26.2	-1.0	8.8	10.0	12.0	14.3	16.1	17.5	16.0	14.9	-1.1
10th grade	23.9	23.5	27.4	32.5	35.6	39.6	40.3	37.1	-3.2ss	13.1	12.6	15.5	20.0	21.6	24.5	24.1	22.5	-1.6
12th grade	31.2	28.8	32.5	37.6	40.2	41.9	43.3	42.4	-0.9	17.8	15.5	19.3	23.0	24.8	25.5	26.9	26.6	-0.3
Marijuana–hashish																		
8th grade	6.2	7.2	9.2	13.0	15.8	18.3	17.7	16.9	-0.8	3.2	3.7	5.1	7.8	9.1	11.3	10.2	9.7	-0.5
10th grade	16.5	15.2	19.2	25.2	28.7	33.6	34.8	31.1	-3.7sss	8.7	8.1	10.9	15.8	17.2	20.4	20.5	18.7	-1.8s
12th grade	23.9	21.9	26.0	30.7	34.7	35.8	38.5	37.5	-1.0	13.8	11.9	15.5	19.0	21.2	21.9	23.7	22.8	-0.9
Inhalants																		
8th grade	9.0	9.5	11.0	11.7	12.8	12.2	11.8	11.1	-0.7	4.4	4.7	5.4	5.6	6.1	5.8	5.6	4.8	-0.8s
10th grade	7.1	7.5	8.4	9.1	9.6	9.5	8.7	8.0	-0.7	2.7	2.7	3.3	3.6	3.5	3.3	3.0	2.9	-0.1
12th grade	6.6	6.2	7.0	7.7	8.0	7.6	6.7	6.2	-0.5	2.4	2.3	2.5	2.7	3.2	2.5	2.5	2.3	-0.2
Nitrites																		
8th grade																		
10th grade																		
12th grade	0.9	0.5	0.9	1.1	1.1	1.6	1.2	1.4	+0.2	0.4	0.3	0.6	0.4	0.4	0.7	0.7	1.0	+0.3
Hallucinogens																		
8th grade	1.9	2.5	2.6	2.7	3.6	4.1	3.7	3.4	-0.3	0.8	1.1	1.2	1.3	1.7	1.9	1.8	1.4	-0.4
10th grade	4.0	4.3	4.7	5.8	7.2	7.8	7.6	6.9	-0.7	1.6	1.8	1.9	2.4	3.3	2.8	3.3	3.2	-0.1
12th grade	5.8	5.9	7.4	7.6	9.3	10.1	9.8	9.0	-0.8	2.2	2.1	2.7	3.1	4.4	3.5	3.9	3.8	-0.1
LSD																		
8th grade	1.7	2.1	2.3	2.4	3.2	3.5	3.2	2.8	-0.4	0.6	0.9	1.0	1.1	1.4	1.5	1.5	1.1	-0.4s
10th grade	3.7	4.0	4.2	5.2	6.5	6.9	6.7	5.9	-0.8	1.5	1.6	1.6	2.0	3.0	2.4	2.8	2.7	-0.1
12th grade	5.2	5.6	6.8	6.9	8.4	8.8	8.4	7.6	-0.8	1.9	2.0	2.4	2.6	4.0	2.5	3.1	3.2	+0.1

(Continues)

TABLE 3.3 (Continued)

	Annual[b]									30-day[b]								
	1991	1992	1993	1994	1995	1996	1997	1998	1997–1998 change	1991	1992	1993	1994	1995	1996	1997	1998	1997–1998 change
Hallucinogens																		
Other than LSD																		
8th grade	0.7	1.1	1.0	1.3	1.7	2.0	1.8	1.6	−0.2	0.3	0.4	0.5	0.7	0.8	0.9	0.7	0.7	0.0
10th grade	1.3	1.4	1.9	2.4	2.8	3.3	3.3	3.4	+0.1	0.4	0.5	0.7	1.0	1.0	1.0	1.2	1.4	+0.2
12th grade	2.0	1.7	2.2	3.1	3.8	4.4	4.6	4.6	0.0	0.7	0.5	0.8	1.2	1.3	1.6	1.7	1.6	−0.1
PCP																		
8th grade																		
10th grade																		
12th grade	1.4	1.4	1.4	1.6	1.8	2.6	2.3	2.1	−0.2	0.5	0.6	1.0	0.7	0.6	1.3	0.7	1.0	+0.3
MDMA (Ecstasy)																		
8th grade						2.3	2.3	1.8	−0.5						1.0	1.0	0.9	−0.1
10th grade						4.6	3.9	3.3	−0.6						1.8	1.3	1.3	0.0
12th grade						4.6	4.0	3.6	−0.4						2.0	1.6	1.5	−0.1
Cocaine																		
8th grade	1.1	1.5	1.7	2.1	2.6	3.0	2.8	3.1	+0.3	0.5	0.7	0.7	1.0	1.2	1.3	1.1	1.4	+0.3
10th grade	2.2	1.9	2.1	2.8	3.5	4.2	4.7	4.7	0.0	0.7	0.7	0.9	1.2	1.7	1.7	2.0	2.1	+0.1
12th grade	3.5	3.1	3.3	3.6	4.0	4.9	5.5	5.7	+0.2	1.4	1.3	1.3	1.5	1.8	2.0	2.3	2.4	+0.1
Crack																		
8th grade	0.7	0.9	1.0	1.3	1.6	1.8	1.7	2.1	+0.4s	0.3	0.5	0.4	0.7	0.7	0.8	0.7	0.9	+0.2
10th grade	0.9	0.9	1.1	1.4	1.8	2.1	2.2	2.5	+0.3	0.3	0.4	0.5	0.6	0.9	0.8	0.9	1.1	+0.2
12th grade	1.5	1.5	1.5	1.9	2.1	2.1	2.4	2.5	+0.1	0.7	0.6	0.7	0.8	1.0	1.0	0.9	1.0	+0.1
Other cocaine																		
8th grade	1.0	1.2	1.3	1.7	2.1	2.5	2.2	2.4	+0.2	0.5	0.5	0.6	0.9	1.0	1.0	0.8	1.0	+0.2
10th grade	2.1	1.7	1.8	2.4	3.0	3.5	4.1	4.0	−0.1	0.6	0.6	0.7	1.0	1.4	1.3	1.6	1.8	+0.2
12th grade	3.2	2.6	2.9	3.0	3.4	4.2	5.0	4.9	−0.1	1.2	1.0	1.2	1.3	1.3	1.6	2.0	2.0	0.0
Heroine																		
8th grade	0.7	0.7	0.7	1.2	1.4	1.6	1.3	1.3	0.0	0.3	0.4	0.4	0.6	0.6	0.7	0.6	0.6	0.0
10th grade	0.5	0.6	0.7	0.9	1.1	1.2	1.4	1.4	0.0	0.2	0.2	0.3	0.4	0.6	0.5	0.6	0.7	+0.1
12th grade	0.4	0.6	0.5	0.6	1.1	1.0	1.2	1.0	−0.2	0.2	0.3	0.2	0.3	0.6	0.5	0.5	0.5	0.0
Other opiates																		
8th grade																		
10th grade																		
12th grade	3.5	3.3	3.6	3.8	4.7	5.4	6.2	6.3	+0.1	1.1	1.2	1.3	1.5	1.8	2.0	2.3	2.4	+0.1
Stimulants																		
8th grade	6.2	6.5	7.2	7.9	8.7	9.1	8.1	7.2	−0.9	2.6	3.3	3.6	3.6	4.2	4.6	3.8	3.3	−0.5
10th grade	8.2	8.2	9.6	10.2	11.9	12.4	12.1	10.7	−1.4s	3.3	3.6	4.3	4.5	5.3	5.5	5.1	5.1	0.0
12th grade	8.2	7.1	8.4	9.4	9.3	9.5	10.2	10.1	−0.1	3.2	2.8	3.7	4.0	4.0	4.1	4.8	4.6	−0.2

									Change									Change
Ice																		
8th grade																		
10th grade																		
12th grade	1.4	1.3	1.7	1.8	2.4	2.8	2.3	3.0	+0.7	0.6	0.5	0.6	0.7	1.1	1.1	0.8	1.2	+0.4
Barbiturates																		
8th grade																		
10th grade																		
12th grade	3.4	2.8	3.4	4.1	4.7	4.9	5.1	5.5	+0.4	1.4	1.1	1.3	1.7	2.2	2.1	2.1	2.6	+0.5s
Tranquilizers																		
8th grade	1.8	2.0	2.1	2.4	2.7	3.3	2.9	2.6	−0.3	0.8	0.8	0.9	1.1	1.2	1.5	1.2	1.2	0.0
10th grade	3.2	3.5	3.3	3.3	4.0	4.6	4.9	5.1	+0.2	1.2	1.5	1.1	1.5	1.7	1.7	2.2	2.2	0.0
12th grade	3.6	2.8	3.5	3.7	4.4	4.6	4.7	5.5	+0.8s	1.4	1.0	1.2	1.4	1.8	2.0	1.8	2.4	+0.6ss
Alcohol																		
Any use																		
8th grade	54.0	53.7	51.6 / 45.4	46.8	45.3	46.5	45.5	43.7	−1.8	25.1	26.1	26.2 / 24.3	25.5	24.6	26.2	24.5	23.0	−1.5
10th grade	72.3	70.2	69.3 / 63.4	63.9	63.5	65.0	65.2	62.7	−2.5s	42.8	39.9	41.5 / 38.2	39.2	38.8	40.4	40.1	38.8	−1.3
12th grade	77.7	76.8	76.0 / 72.7	73.0	73.7	72.5	74.8	74.3	−0.5	54.0	51.3	51.0 / 48.6	50.1	51.3	50.8	52.7	52.0	−0.7
Been drunk																		
8th grade	17.5	18.3	18.2	18.2	18.4	19.8	18.4	17.9	−0.5	7.6	7.5	7.8	8.7	8.3	9.6	8.2	8.4	+0.2
10th grade	40.1	37.0	37.8	38.0	38.5	40.1	40.7	38.3	−2.4s	20.5	18.1	19.8	20.3	20.8	21.3	22.4	21.1	−1.3
12th grade	52.7	50.3	49.6	51.7	52.5	51.9	53.2	52.0	−1.2	31.6	29.9	28.9	30.8	33.2	31.3	34.2	32.9	−1.3
Cigarettes																		
Any use																		
8th grade										14.3	15.5	16.7	18.6	19.1	21.0	19.4	19.1	−0.3
10th grade										20.8	21.5	24.7	25.4	27.9	30.4	29.8	27.6	−2.2s
12th grade										28.3	27.8	29.9	31.2	33.5	34.0	36.5	35.1	−1.4
Smokeless tobacco																		
8th grade										6.9	7.0	6.6	7.7	7.1	7.1	5.5	4.8	−0.7
10th grade										10.0	9.6	10.4	10.5	9.7	8.6	8.9	7.5	−1.4
12th grade											11.4	10.7	11.1	12.2	9.8	9.7	8.8	−0.9
Steroids																		
8th grade	1.0	1.1	0.9	1.2	1.0	0.9	1.0	1.2	+0.2	0.4	0.5	0.5	0.5	0.6	0.4	0.5	0.5	0.0
10th grade	1.1	1.1	1.0	1.1	1.2	1.2	1.2	1.2	0.0	0.6	0.6	0.5	0.6	0.6	0.5	0.7	0.6	−0.1
12th grade	1.4	1.1	1.2	1.3	1.5	1.4	1.4	1.7	+0.3	0.8	0.6	0.7	0.9	0.7	0.7	1.0	1.1	+0.1

[a] National House Survey on Drug Abuse (NHSDA), courtesy of the National Clearinghouse for alcohol and Drug Information (NCADI).
[b] Entries are percentages.

TABLE 3.4   Trends in 30-Day Prevalence of Daily Use of Various Drugs for Eighth, Tenth, and Twelfth Graders[a]

	Daily[b]								
	1991	1992	1993	1994	1995	1996	1997	1998	1997–1998 change
Marijuana–hashish									
8th grade	0.2	0.2	0.4	0.7	0.8	1.5	1.1	1.1	0.0
10th grade	0.8	0.8	1.0	2.2	2.8	3.5	3.7	3.6	−0.1
12th grade	2.0	1.9	2.4	3.6	4.6	4.9	5.8	5.6	−0.2
Alcohol									
Any daily use									
8th grade	0.5	0.6	0.8						
			1.0	1.0	0.7	1.0	0.8	0.9	+0.1[d]
10th grade	1.3	1.2	1.6						
			1.8	1.7	1.7	1.6	1.7	1.9	+0.2[d]
12th grade	3.6	3.4	2.5						
			3.4	2.9	3.5	3.7	3.9	3.9	0.0[d]
5 + drinks in last 2 weeks									
8th grade	12.9	13.4	13.5	14.5	14.5	15.6	14.5	13.7	−0.8
10th grade	22.9	21.1	23.0	23.6	24.0	24.8	25.1	24.3	−0.8
12th grade	29.8	27.9	27.5	28.2	29.8	30.2	31.3	31.5	+0.2
Cigarettes									
Any daily use									
8th grade	7.2	7.0	8.3	8.8	9.3	10.4	9.0	8.8	−0.2
10th grade	12.6	12.3	14.2	14.6	16.3	18.3	18.0	15.8	−2.2ss
12th grade	18.5	17.2	19.0	19.4	21.6	22.2	24.6	22.4	−2.2s
>Half pack/day									
8th grade	3.1	2.9	3.5	3.6	3.4	4.3	3.5	3.6	+0.1
10th grade	6.5	6.0	7.0	7.6	8.3	9.4	8.6	7.9	−0.7
12th grade	10.7	10.0	10.9	11.2	12.4	13.0	14.3	12.6	−1.7s
Smokeless tobacco									
8th grade	1.6	1.8	1.5	1.9	1.2	1.5	1.0	1.0	+0.1
10th grade	3.3	3.0	3.3	3.0	2.7	2.2	2.2	2.2	0.0
12th grade		4.3	3.3	3.9	3.6	3.3	4.4	3.2	−1.2

[a]National House Survey on Drug Abuse (NHSDA), courtesy of the National Clearinghouse for alcohol and Drug Information (NCADI).
[b]Entries are percentages.

Aside from physiological gender differences associated with substance abuse and dependence, there are also differences in the clinical characteristics of early and late onset problem drinkers. Looking at these differences is another reinforcer for increased sensitivity to the variations in substance abuse and dependence along numerous variables (Atkinson, 1994; Atkinson & Ganzini, 1994; Atkinson et al., 1990; Beresford & Lucey, 1995; Moos et al., 1991; Schonfeld & Depree, 1991).

EARLY ONSET VARIABLES

1. Age: up to 45.
2. Gender: higher proportion of men than women.
3. SES tends to be lower.

4. Drinking to relieve stress is a common response.

5. Family history of alcohol dependence is more prevalent.

6. Severity of alcohol problems: increased severity–more psychosocial problems.

7. Alcohol-related chronic illness (pancreatitis, cirrhosis, etc.) is more common.

8. Psychiatric comorbidities are less reversible and cognitive loss is more severe.

9. Age-related medical problems exacerbated by alcohol use (hypertension, diabetes, etc.) is common.

10. Treatment compliance and outcome: relapse rates do not vary with age and possibly less compliant.

LATE ONSET VARIABLES

1. Age: from age 55.

2. Gender: higher proportion of women than men.

3. SES tends to be higher.

4. Drinking to relieve stress is common.

5. Family history of alcohol dependence is less prevalent.

6. Severity of alcohol problems: lower severity–fewer psychosocial problems.

7. Alcohol-related chronic illness (pancreatitis, cirrhosis, etc.) is less common.

8. Psychiatric comorbidities are more reversible and cognitive loss is less severe.

9. Age related medical problems exacerbated by alcohol use (hypertension, diabetes, etc.) is common.

10. Treatment compliance and outcome: relapse rates do not vary by age of onset and possibly more compliant. They may demonstrate a more positive response to brief intervention, because of fewer alcohol-related problems and they are more sensitive to informal social pressure.

REFERENCES

Atkinson, R. M. (1994). Late onset problem drinking in older adults. *Int. J. Geriatric Psychiatry* 9:321–326.

Atkinson, R. M., & Ganzini, L. (1994). Substance abuse. *In* "Textbook of Geriatric Neuropsychiatry" (C. E. Coffey & J. L. Cummings, Eds.), pp. 297–321. Washington, DC: American Psychiatric Press.

Atkinson, R. M., Tolson, R. L., & Turner, J. A. (1990). Late versus early onset problem drinking in older men. *Alcoholism: Clin. Exp. Res.* **14**:574–579.

Bacon, S. D. (1973). The process of addiction to alcohol. *Q. J. Studies Alcohol* **34**:1–27.

Bean, M., & Zinberg, N., Eds. (1981). "Dynamic Approaches to the Understanding and Treatment of Alcoholism." New York: The Free Press.

Beresford, T. P., & Lucey, M. R. (1995). Ethanol metabolism and intoxication in the elderly. *In* "Alcohol and Aging" (T. P. Beresford & E. S. Gomberg, Eds.), pp. 117–127. New York: Oxford University Press.

Bernard, L. C., & Krupat, E. (1994). "Health Psychology: Biopsychosocial Factors in Health and Illness." Orlando, FL: Harcourt Brace.

Brown, S. (1985). "Treating the Alcoholic." New York: John Wiley & sons.

Burkstein, O. G. (1995). "Adolescent Substance Use: Assessment, Prevention, and Treatment." New York: Wiley.

Crabbe, J., McSwigan, J., & Belknap, J. (1985). The role of genetics in substance abuse. *In* "Determinants of Substance Abuse" (M. Galizio & S. Maistro, Eds.). New York: Plenum.

Estes, N., & Heinemann, M. (1986). Issues in identification of alcoholism. *In* "Alcoholism: Development, Consequences, and Intervention" (N. Estes & M. Heinemann, Eds.), pp. 317–333. St. Louis, MO: C. V. Mosby.

Gill, K., & Amit, Z. (1989). Serotonin uptake blockers and voluntary alcohol consumption. A review of recent studies. *In* "Recent Developments in Alcoholism" (M. Galanter, Ed.), Vol. 7, pp. 225–248. New York: Plenum.

Gold, M. (1992). "Cocaine (and Crack) Substance Abuse: A Comprehensive Textbook," 2nd ed. Baltimmore, MD: Williams & Wilkins.

The Harvard Mental Health Letter (1998). *The Harvard Mental Health Lett.* June, **4**(12):1–3.

The Harvard Mental Health Letter (1998). *The Harvard Mental Health Lett.* July, **15**(1):1–3.

Hester, R. K., & Miller, W. R. Eds. (1989). "Handbook of Alcoholism Treatment Approaches." New York: Pergamon Press.

McCarthy, D. (1985). Environmental factors in substance abuse. *In* "Determinants of Substance Abuse" (M. Galizio & S. Maistro, Eds.). New York: Plenum.

Moos, R. H., Brennan, P. L., & Moos, B. S. (1991). Short-term processes of remission and nonremission among late life problem drinkers. *Alcoholism: Clin. Exp. Res.* **15**:948–955.

National House Survey on Drug Abuse (NHSDA) published by the National Clearinghouse for Alcohol and Drug Abuse Information (NCADI), P.O. Box 2345, Rockville, MD 20847-234.

National Institute on Alcohol Abuse and Alcoholism (2000). Alcohol alert (april) **47**:1–2.

National Institute on Alcohol Abuse and Addiction (1993). "Alcohol and Health." Eighth special report to the U.S. Congress (DHHS Publication No. ADM-281-91-0003, Rockville, MD: NIAAA.

Rotgers, F. (1996). Behavioral therapy of substance abuse treatment: Bringing science to bear on practice. *In* "Treating Substance Abuse: Theory and Techniques" (F. Rotgers, D. Keller, & J. Morgenstern, Eds.), pp. 174–201. New York: Guilford Press.

Schonfeld, L., & Depree, L. W. (1991). Antecedents of drinking for early and late onset elderly alcohol abusers. *J. Studies Alcohol* **52**:587–592.

Wallace, J. (1996). Theory of 12-step oriented treatment. In "Treating Substance Abuse: Theory and Technique" (F. Rotgers, D. Keller, & J. Morgenstern, Eds.), pp. 117–137. New York: Guilford Press.

Washton, A. M. (1995). "Psychotherapy and Substance Abuse." New York: Guilford Press.

Zinberg, N. E. (1984). "Drug, Set, and Setting." New Haven, CT: Yale University Press.

Chapter 4

Stages of Substance Dependence and Recovery

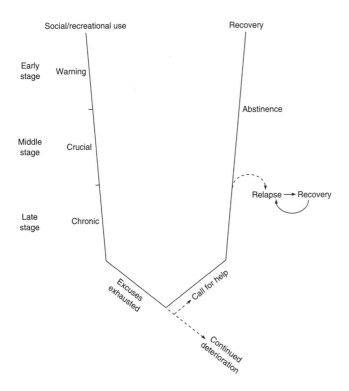

Individuals who struggle with substance dependence did not start out with that as a goal. It all started with a desire to relax, escape emotional distress, belong, or engage in experimentation. Some theories of substance dependence may suggest a hereditary predisposition to the *disease* of substance dependence, referred to as *disease concept*. One of the factors inherent in disease concept is the acknowledgment that substance dependence is a disease of relapse. It is the issue of relapse that has led to a lack of understanding of and disdain for those with substance dependency. An individual may have accepted and entered treatment, been working on a program and making associated changes, and been practicing abstinence when he or she experiences a relapse. For those that subscribe to disease concept, relapse is always a possibility with any chronic disease and is a confirmation of the need for total abstinence. Others believe that relapse is associated with ambivalence or is part of the learning process of change.

A CAUSAL MODEL FOR SUBSTANCE ABUSE

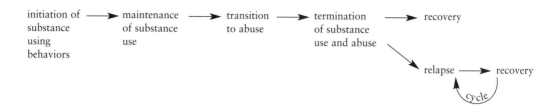

PROBLEMATIC BEHAVIOR AND THOUGHT PATTERNS

Some of the behaviors and thought patterns indicative of substance dependence are the following.

1. Increased substance use: This is related to tolerance, frequency, or duration of use.
2. Denial: The individual is deluded about his or her substance use, behavior, and related problems. Denial also plays a role in suppression, repression, and rejection.
3. Projection: Blaming others, externalizing. It is not unusual for individuals to accuse others of the behaviors they themselves are exhibiting.
4. Rigidity: Poor self-management requires an external structure of rules regulations for adequate functioning, especially for "looking normal".
5. Anger: Often seen as hostility and verbal aggression as a response that is distancing from others and controlling (most individuals will avoid an angry outburst).
6. Manipulation: Can be superficially portrayed as charm. They are genuinely nice people who have learned that this pleasing personal presentation often results in others being reluctant to confront them.
7. Perfectionism: Find fault with everything that is done. Nothing is quite good enough. Often applied to others. Easy excuse for avoidance and anger.
8. Promises: May be genuine or an effort to appease others (put them off). Eventually people stop expecting them to keep their word and loss of trust is the outcome.
9. Superiority: Defense against inadequacy and fear. Stands in the way of change because it is used to devalue the efforts of others to help the individual change his or her behavior.
10. Grandiosity: Looking for the big and easy scheme and unrealistic thinking, leading to financial difficulties.
11. Irresponsibility: Inverse relationship of substance dependence and responsible behavior.
12. Self-pity: Victim thinking. "Everyone and everything is against me." This behavior pulls for codependency and caring–nurturing people.

13. Sexually inappropriate behavior: Indiscretions and promiscuity, as well as incest and molestation.

14. Social and emotional withdrawal: Primary relationship is with substance(s).

15. Pink elephant rule: No one talks about it so it must not exist.

PATTERNS OF USE

To increase the understanding for the foundation of problematic behavior and thought patterns, a review of amphetamine use may be illuminating. With a strong stimulant like cocaine, if there is low-intensity use (occasional use), the body has time to recover from the blocking effects of normal reabsorption, which allows it to return to a level of normal energy balance. However, if the stimulant is used for prolonged periods of time, consumed in large quantities, or both, tolerance develops. Changes in thinking and behavior are clearly demonstrated.

There are three general patterns of substance use (California Narcotics Officers Association, 2000).

1. Low intensity: Although this pattern of use is related to the recreational use of substances for desired effects on an occasional basis, there are also risks associated with toxic effects such as psychological disturbance, severe weight loss, and insomnia.

2. Binge cycle (five-stage cycle)
   a. rush: This is the initial response experienced when amphetamine is injected or smoked, but not when it is snorted or ingested orally. This difference is due to the fact that when the substance is smoked or injected the adrenal glands are triggered to release adrenaline. Characteristics of rush include increases in heartbeat, metabolism, blood pressure, and pulse. The length of time for the rush stage depends on the amphetamine used (e.g., crack cocaine 2–5 min, methamphetamine as long as 20 min).
   b. high: During this stage the user often has a sense of heightened intelligence (smarter than everyone else) and becomes challenging and argumentative.
   c. binge: The binge is a continuation of the high associated with continued use. This is the well-defined attempt to recapture the original experience of the rush. Each time, for example, that cocaine is smoked, the smaller the euphoric rush that is experienced until the high is diminished to being nonexistent. Neuroadaptation requires or forces the user to increase the dose to maintain the euphoric effect. There is conscious failure of association, and, as a result, the user binges. The usual binge lasts for 12–24 hr. Intense feelings of distress include dysphoria, paranoia, agitation, and "coming down." Once binging has started, generally only the depletion of substance will end it.
   d. tweaking: Describes the end state of the binge where the user is incapable of getting rid of the emptiness and dysphoria and is very uncomfortable. At this stage a user may utilize a depressant such as alcohol to ease the distress. This is the most dangerous stage of the cycle due to the potential for violence. Two common scenarios are demonstrated: the person becomes excessively stimulated and experiences paranoid delusions or trades sex for drugs.
   e. crash: The body's adrenaline (epinephrine) has been depleted, requiring an incredible amount of sleep to replenish its supply. There is deep, lifeless sleep. The sleep deprivation associated with binging results in cognitive and behavioral consequences, such as inability to concentrate and decreased accuracy of task performance. The crash can last for 1–3 days or longer.

3. High intensity: Frequent daily use of stimulants is a less common and more lethal pattern of use. Those that are high-intensity users may stay up for days at a time. Their entire focus is on preventing the experience of a crash while they seek the initial euphoric experience. For these individuals, each successive rush offers a decrease in the euphoric experience and an increase in the amount of substance used in an effort to achieve the desired outcome.

DEVELOPMENTAL STAGES OF DEPENDENCE

When the developmental phases of substance dependence are reviewed, a series of warning signs emerge that cluster into stages (Brownell *et al.*, 1986; Hester & Miller, 1989).

PREADDICTIVE–EARLY STAGE

Substance(s) used as an effort to achieve, exaggerate, or enhance some feelings and experiences, leading to the initial stages of deterioration in functioning.

1. Popularity (especially if involved in dealing)
2. Artistic abilities
3. Sexual experience (arousal–heighten experience)
4. Self-esteem–self-confidence
5. Pain management
6. Coping
7. Relieve stressors
8. Manage excess worrying
9. Relax in social situations
10. Reduce inhibitions
11. Stimulation and excitement
12. Results in changed personality
13. Occasional memory lapses
14. Evident changes in self-care and social behaviors
15. Prepares self prior to social functions
16. Selects environments–socializing where substances are available
17. Uncomfortable in situations where substances are not available
18. Preoccupation with substances and their use
19. Rapid ingestion of substances (gulping drinks)
20. Desire to continue using substances when others cease
21. Increase in tolerance (increased use of substance to attain effect)
22. Blackouts–temporary amnesia–occasional memory lapses after heavy drinking or substance use
23. Hides use of substances from others
24. Avoids reference to substances by minimizing, lying, etc.

ADDICTIVE–MIDDLE STAGE

This developmental stage of dependence is associated with an escalation in and exacerbation of symptoms. Rationalization begins as the transition from the early stage to middle stage of addiction. Warning signs of this stage include the following:

1. Increased tolerance
2. Increased family, work, and relationship problems
3. Denial increases (defensiveness about substance use)
4. Increased use of excuses
5. Frequent blackouts
6. Increased craving and urgency to use
7. Increased physical dependency
8. Increased withdrawal symptoms–efforts to control use fail
9. Unpredictability of the amount consumed
10. Increased changes in self-care and social behaviors
11. Feels guilty about substance use and associated behaviors
12. Increased self-medication for dealing with stress, pain relief, etc.
13. Suicidal ideation–death wish
14. Family–friends complain about and confront use of substances and associated behavioral changes
15. Stays away from family–friends to avoid their confrontations
16. Changes in relationship behaviors by family–friends (their efforts to avoid substance-use-associated personality and behavioral changes in person)
17. Changes in pattern of use (trades substances, gives up substances for Lent, quits using for a period of time to prove he or she is not addicted)
18. Uses substances when alone
19. Neglects relationships and as a result loses social support
20. Loss of control associated with frequency–amount to substance used
21. Rationalizes, minimizes, blames others for problems
22. Grandiosity
23. Indulgence associated with use of money–financial problems
24. Aggressive behavior–fighting
25. Self-pity
26. Remorse
27. Periodic abstinence as an effort to control use
28. Work-related problems: look for patterns of deterioration associated with attendance, general behavior, and job performance
29. Decreased use of positive health behaviors
30. Changes in personal appearance
31. Loss of interest in healthy activities, family activities, hobbies, etc.
32. Jealousy and resentment
33. Uses substances at inappropriate times and places

34. Contemplates or attempts geographical–psychological–social escape
35. Poor nutrition (neglect of regular eating pattern–skips meals)

CHRONIC–LATE STAGE

Over time, the later developmental stage of chronic use can lead or contribute to disease and increased mental illness. Signs and symptoms of chronic use include the following:

1. Cognitive distortions
2. Irreversible physical problems
3. Decreased tolerance
4. Increased severity of withdrawal symptoms
5. Delirium tremors
6. Self-care deteriorates
7. Social changes
8. Persistent feelings of remorse
9. Legal problems (arrest(s), DWI–DUI, possession, bad checks etc.)
10. Protective to substance supply (stockpiling, etc.)
11. Withdrawal symptoms emerge earlier (tremors, cramps, etc.)
12. Medical care required (accidental injuries, detoxification, etc.)
13. Court-remanded treatment (DWI–DUI school, counseling etc.)
14. Suicidal ideation and associated self-harm behaviors
15. Job loss
16. Increased relationship deterioration
17. Divorce
18. Use of substances with individuals with whom he or she would not normally socially associate
19. Psychomotor inhibition (substance use negatively influencing walking, talking, and general presentation)
20. Paranoia, indefinable or irrational fears
21. Poor decision making
22. Impaired cognitive ability
23. Moral and ethical deterioration
24. Binges or nonstop usage in excess of 12 hr
25. Seizures
26. Severe psychiatric problems
27. Death

RECOVERY STAGES

Just as substance dependence is a developmental progression, the process of recovery is also a progression. Recovery is about learning, change, and living an improved quality of life. Once abstinence has been well-established, change must continue to occur if the gains acquired are to be sustained. In general, 90 days of continuous abstinence from all substances, though an early stage of recovery, is a frequent time frame for moving into the next phase of recovery. During this time, it is imperative that coping strategies are developed or strengthened to replace the prior substance use management of life stressors. The stepwise progression of recovery demonstrates the path generally taken for lifestyle change to be initiated and can be summarized as follows (Shaffer, 1992; Brownell *et al.*, 1986; Gorski, 1991).

1. Precontemplation: Individual does not interpret his or her use of substances as a problem, little if any awareness of the negative consequences associated with substances.
2. Contemplation: Increased awareness of the negative associations of substance abuse, beginning to think about changes and doing something about substance use. He or she has to be ready to give up substances.
3. Action: Begins to actively take responsibility for change.
4. Maintenance: Focus on the tasks associated with change, continued efforts toward personal growth and goals.

EXPERIENCE OF OBJECT LOSS

As substance abuse progresses to substance dependence, the substance(s) becomes the primary object. The individual identifies with the "positive" aspects of substance use and defends against acknowledgment of the associated consequences. Therefore, losses begin when substance abuse begins. However, the continuum of losses often is not acknowledged until an individual enters recovery and acutely experiences issues of loss. He or she has given up his or her object of security and desire.

1. Denial
   a. unconscious
   b. self-image deteriorates with development of addiction
   c. increased defensiveness and rigidity to protect ego
   d. defenses function as a wall of protection against negative feelings

2. Anger
   a. major defense often demonstrated as blame
   b. external projection of responsibility
   c. views self as a victim

3. Bargaining
   a. strives to feel in control
   b. reluctant to defer to authority (or higher power)
   c. struggles with belief that "I can do it on my own" or "I don't have a problem"

4. Depression
   a. overwhelmed by emotion
   b. struggling to develop identity and fit in
   c. feeling of being behind peers in life accomplishments

5. Acceptance
   a. acknowledges he or she has lost control

b. recognizes relationship between behavior and consequences

c. accepts the importance of change and need for support

Recovery is not a uneventful linear path. Instead, it is generally fraught with many struggles as an individual regains control over his or her life and works through issues created or exacerbated by substance abuse. Therefore, an integral part of treatment is relapse prevention, which tries to consider all of the difficulties that someone may experience that could jeopardize his or her abstinence. As a result, the individual in treatment as well as all of those participating professionally in intervening must strive to maintain awareness of what those difficulties might be and what kind of associated regressive symptoms may be evident. The following is a list of some relapse symptoms.

RELAPSE SYMPTOMS

1. Return of denial: concern about well-being—denial of the concern
2. Avoidance and defensive behavior
   a. "I'll never drink again"—worries about others instead of self
   b. defensiveness and tendency toward loneliness
   c. compulsive behavior
   d. impulsive behavior

3. Crisis building
   a. tunnel vision
   b. minor depression
   c. loss of constructive planning
   d. plans begin to fail

4. Immobilization
   a. daydreaming with wishful thinking
   b. feeling that nothing can be solved
   c. immature wish to be happy

5. Confusion and overreaction
   a. periods of confusion, may begin to tell self they can control using
   b. irritation with friends
   c. easily angered

6. Depression
   a. irregular eating habits
   b. lack of desire to take action, nagative self talk
   c. irregular sleeping habits
   d. loss of daily structure
   e. periods of deep depression

7. Behavioral loss of control
   a. irregular attendance to program meetings
   b. development of "I don't care" attitude
   c. open rejection of help
   d. dissatisfaction with life
   e. feelings of powerlessness and helplessness

8. Recognition of loss of control
   a. self-pity
   b. thoughts of social–recreational use
   c. conscious lying
   d. complete loss of self-confidence

9. Option reduction
   a. unreasonable resentment
   b. discontinuance of all treatment structure, efforts, and support
   c. overwhelming loneliness, frustration, anger, and tension

10. Acute relapse episode
    a. loss of behavioral control
    b. acute relapse episode
       i. deterioration in all areas of life
       ii. disruption of social structures
       iii. substance use
       iv. emotional collapse
       v. accident prone
       vi. physical exhaustion
       vii. stress-related illnesses
       viii. psychiatric illness (continuum includes suicide)

RELAPSE AUTOPSY

To facilitate an understanding of how all of thee factors combine and result in a relapse episode, an integrative composite or "relapse autopsy" can be used. Remember that this is one example of how these factors could be combined. Sample case history:

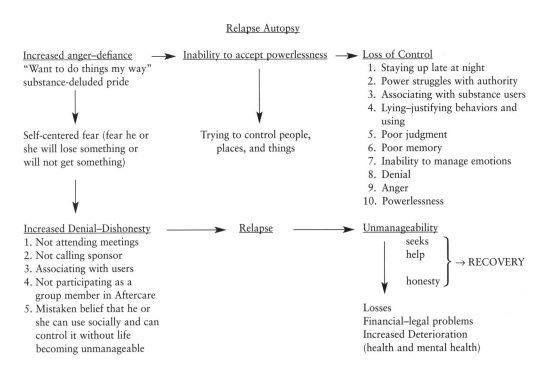

Relapse Autopsy

PROCESS OF RELAPSE

In summary, the process of relapse can be viewed as follows:

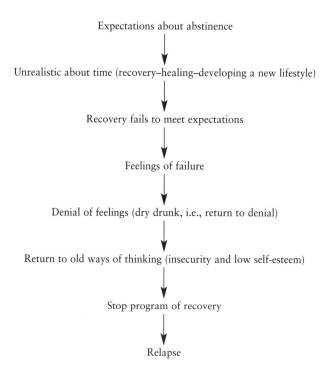

Expectations about abstinence

↓

Unrealistic about time (recovery–healing–developing a new lifestyle)

↓

Recovery fails to meet expectations

↓

Feelings of failure

↓

Denial of feelings (dry drunk, i.e., return to denial)

↓

Return to old ways of thinking (insecurity and low self-esteem)

↓

Stop program of recovery

↓

Relapse

A well-documented potential case of relapse is referred to as the "dry drunk." This phrase is used to describe the individual who may be abstinent but is not working through and resolving recovery issues. This leaves the individual vulnerable to relapse or to maintain the same dysfunctional thought patterns and behaviors experienced during his or her active use of substances.

SPECIAL ISSUES OF SUBSTANCE DEPENDENCE

DRY DRUNK

The dry drunk phenomenon is manifested in the attitudes and behaviors of a clean and sober individual, just as seen in the actively using individual. Although the term "drunk" is applied, this phenomenon is not restricted to alcoholics. Recovery is not a process that is completed with abstinence. Instead, it is the substitution of newly learned attitudes and behaviors following abstinence that offer the quality of life hoped for and often expected with abstinence. To assure that a maximum quality of life is achieved requires awareness and conscious decision making. Anytime during the course of recovery an individual may reexperience an episode of being a dry drunk. For many, abstinence is a lifelong task associated with self-responsibility, patience, honesty, new ways of coping, management of emotions, and resolution of traumas and losses. It means creating new life patterns with a consistent focus on self-care. When an individual's priorities of investing in conscious awareness, self-responsibility, and self-care begin to slip, the risk of experiencing a dry drunk episode increases and there is associated risk for further relapse.

The dry drunk is a serious condition that exceeds the highs and lows associated with day to day living. "Dry" refers to the fact of abstinence and "drunk" signifies the significant pathology that is evident (even when not using). The dry drunk may have feelings and behave as though he or she is intoxicated although no substance has been consumed. For example, an alcoholic who is 6–12 months into his or her sobriety may experience a "dry hangover." The individual will often have dreams of being high or experience "euphoric recall" accompanied by negative emotions such as irritability, depression, fatigue, resentment, self-centeredness, and overreaction. This may be due to lurking indecision about committing to a life of abstinence. Attached to this phenomenon is the consequence of using in the past. Some of the symptoms are

1. Grandiosity or exaggeration of one's own importance.
2. Judgmentalism as seen in the tendency to make inappropriate evaluations.
3. Intolerance, which makes it difficult to delay gratification, and associated confusion.
4. Impulsivity, which is also related to intolerance and difficulty delaying gratification without consideration of consequences for the self or others.
5. Indecisiveness related to impulsivity. There is a lack of realistic perspective of consequences associated with actions. When presented with more than one choice, there is a good chance that nothing will be done.

The combination of these factors results in discomfort and distress as evidenced by

1. Mood swings
2. Lack of spontaneity and difficulty expressing emotions freely
3. Lack of necessary introspection, self-awareness, and self-understanding
4. Detachment
5. Self-absorption
6. Lack of pleasure and enjoyment of activities previously enjoyed
7. Disorganization and easily distracted
8. Yearning for the past, i.e., old using buddies and other associations
9. Romanticizing via unrealistic valuing of things, lifestyle, and "character" traits that present a risk to abstinence
10. Daydreaming, fantasizing, and wishful thinking considered escapism with further removal from reality

Suggested intervention for a dry drunk episode is

1. Therapy
2. Utilization of support system (self-help group, sponsor, etc.)
3. Appropriate recreation and relaxation
4. Review program (e.g., redo 12 steps), confront old thinking or behavioral patterns identified earlier in treatment, etc.
5. Meditation, prayer, etc. (efforts to center and clear mind for redirecting healthy focus)

Dry drunks often overreact. The family can get pulled into the dry drunk syndrome just as they did to the progression of substance dependence. The dry drunk may signify codependent issues coming out. It is important to remember how these two components of a family system facilitate and sustain dysfunctional patterns. An individual in a dry drunk episode may be in a codependent crisis. Feeling distress and pain or facing it may result in relapse if he or she is not turning to recovery resources.

FAMILY SYSTEM RESPONSE TO SUBSTANCE DEPENDENCY

Just as changes in an individual can be identified as stages of progression, the family system also demonstrates changes as an adjustment to substance dependency (Shaffer, 1992; Marlatt, 1988; Steinglass *et al.*, 1987). The stages of family adjustment are as follows.

Denial

Family members, significant others, and close friends often attempt to deny the problem. Despite evidence, the family system members refuse to acknowledge the pattern of behaviors, instead choosing to explain away each incident or episode as it happens. Therefore, each episode is identified, explained, and handled as if it were an isolated incident instead of pattern.

Recognition

Generally, the significant other, but it could be other family system members as well, begins to pressure the substance abusing individual to modify his or her behavior or quit using substances because he or she recognizes that the abuser has a problem. Unfortunately, there is a concomitant effort to mask the problem outside of the system frame. It is during this stage that the negative impact upon children in the environment becomes evident.

Destabilization

Homeostasis of the family system has been broken down. It can be described in terms of chaos and disorganization. The significant other is no longer able to maintain the outward appearance that everything is fine. The feelings of being trapped and of not having choices permeate the family system.

Mobilization

The significant other takes on an increasing share of responsibility for the family system. The result is an effort to reorganize the family system by taking over more and more family system responsibilities. The substance-dependent family member has lost power and respect and is often ignored and treated as an irresponsible child. The significant other is now in control of the family system and tries to promote family life in spite of the substance dependency.

Escape

At this stage there may be attempts at separation or divorce. Often there is such distance in the central family system relationship that the only thing taking place is a sharing of the home environment. There is a lack of hope for change. Patterns of behavior and familial interaction are set.

Stabilization

Everyone in the family has accepted how things are as being normal. Therefore, it is no longer adequate to treat the substance-dependent person "as the individual with the problem." The entire family needs intervention. Intervention with the entire family system facilitates family reorganization. The family begins to stabilize even if the substance-dependent person does not participate (or is not ready to participate). If a separation or divorce has taken place, there may be reconciliation. New patterns of behavior need to be established, practiced, and reinforced. Support is necessary as the family system adjusts to changes.

CODEPENDENCY

The life partner of a substance-dependent individual presents with characteristics that allow him or her to fit the partner in a complementary way that maintains the dysfunctional behavior. The behaviors generally develop out a need for survival and often were established in response to conditions in his or her family of origin. As a parent in his or her adult life, survival of the family is a priority over self-survival. The domain of the codependent life partner includes the following:

1. Loss of individual identity: The individual's life aspirations are put on hold as he or she becomes immersed in the issues of the partner's life.

2. Denial: Denial of the problem and denial of the impact upon him or her.

3. Rigidity: Attempts to control and stabilize home through rules, regulations, and repetitious patterns. This gives the chaotic home a false perception of predictability.

4. Controlling: The codependent lives the double bind of being in control of keeping things going and at the same time being criticized for it. It is through this distorted double bind that dysfunctional family is maintained.

5. Emotional shutdown: In order to decrease the emotional pain and abuse suffered from the partner, he or she shuts down. If he or she does not shut down, the experience of pain is greater, and if he or she displayed the intensity of the emotion the experienced there is a risk of being labeled as the problem.

6. Get even: The behavior of the substance-dependent person feels punishing. The response of the codependent partner is to get even. The goal of this sarcastic and vindictive behavior is to enforce compliance (this is not limited to the home environment).

7. Separation: Over time the codependent may spend more time out of the home than in the home because he or she cannot tolerate the lack of control. As a result, the dynamic of role reversal takes place and children end up parenting children.

8. Protectiveness: The codependent is protective of the substance-dependent person often at the expense of everyone else in the family system. This behavior may be the most resistant to change.

9. Passivity: The degree of passivity or inferiority directly complements the degree of superiority and grandiosity of the substance-dependent partner.

10. Martyr: The self-righteous, self-sacrificing partner gets a lot of support for being the "good" person and is therefore reluctant to give it up. Her or she may seek to maintain the dysfunction of others in order to maintain the role of caretaker. This role may lead to more pathology than exhibited by the substance-dependent individual, and, as a result, he or she may refuse therapeutic intervention.

11. Overly responsible: The degree of responsibility on behalf of the partner is directly related to the degree of irresponsibility of the substance-dependent partner.

12. Self-pity: This is most prominently seen as attempts to manipulate the substance-dependent partner. It is generally framed as, "if you loved me...." or "if you cared...."

13. Busy bee: He or she is always busy waiting on others, caring for others, fulfilling the responsibilities of others. He or she has no time to take care of him- or herself because he or she is too busy taking care of everyone and everything else.

14. High achiever: He or she may do everything inside and outside of the family system and do all of it well. The codependent is driven. House, full-time job, school, kids in activities—all of it.

15. Pink elephant rule: This rule is initiated by the substance-dependent partner, but he or she enforces it as the protector.

COMMON SYMPTOMATOLOGY OF SUBSTANCE-DEPENDENT AND CODEPENDENT INDIVIDUALS

Substance-Dependent	Codependent
Issues of self-worth	Issues of self-worth
Shame, unsure of self, low self-esteem, feeling out of control	Shame, low self-esteem due to not being able to get dependent person to stop using
Experiences relief with substance use	Experiences relief when enamored with being in love (everything okay)
Alters mood with substances	Alters mood with external experience (new job, new relationship, etc.)
Dependent on substances	Dependent on adrenaline and chaos associated with addict relationship
Preoccupation with substances	Preoccupation with addict's use
Use of substances to deflect from self-focus	Focus concern on the addict and his or her use to deflect from self-focus
Feels disloyal hiding behind lies and excuses	Feels disloyal when angry
Increased tolerance of substances	Increased tolerance for inappropriate behavior and dysfunction
Avoids discussion about substance use	Avoids discussion about addict's behavior and own tolerance
Promises to do better	Deludes self that things will get better
Rigid feelings and behaviors to assure continued use	Rigid feelings and behaviors that maintain continued use and associated patterns
Repressed reality–blackouts	Repressed reality
Unkept promises to abstain	Mixed messages
Deterioration of values covered	Deterioration of values evidenced by behavior
Increased substance use associated with increased withdrawal from family and friends	Preoccupation with addict's use leads to withdrawal from family and friends
Sneaky behavior: hidden supply, plans ahead for use	Sneaky behavior: finding hidden supplies, dumping, watching, checking
May use alone, going against cultural and social standards	Such change in partner leads to increased social withdrawal
Increased physical symptoms associated with substance use	Increased physical symptoms associated with anxiety

Key factors identified as being similar in nature between the substance-dependent individual and the codependent fall into five major areas:

1. Changes in lifestyle
2. Tolerance
3. Psychosocial problems
4. Deterioration of value system (rules, ethics, self-worth)
5. Defensive posturing (denial, rationalization, repression, anger–aggression)

TABLE 4.1 Experience of Addiction and Recovery: An Abbreviated Review of Four Phases[a]

Stage I

Substance Abuse ⟶ Dependence

The use of substances in an effort to achieve comfort with him- or herself, mood management, and enhance positive experiences and abilities. As an individual proceeds through the stages of addiction deterioration is clearly evident.

Stage II

Preparing for Recovery

The individual has little awareness of the negative association with substances, which begins to change as he or she becomes ready to give up substance use. He or she prepares to enter treatment and take responsibility for change. He or she begins to focus on tasks associated with change.

Recovery and Maturation

Transitions of Awareness, Personal Growth, and Self-Responsibility

Stage IV

Recovery with Utilization of Program Resources

Individual has developed increased awareness coupled with self-responsibility. The result is achieving abstinence and maturing, comfort with him- or herself, appropriate mood management, and excelling at his or her abilities.

Stage III

Initial Stages of Recovery

Through the initial stages of recovery, the individual is given support and facilitated to develop necessary life skills for improved management and maintaining recovery.

[a]Stage I represents a compilation of the continuum encompassing abuse through the stages of addiction. Stage IV program resources refer to individualized treatment, which could include the more traditional interventions or a self-help program such as SMART Recovery or Rational Recovery.

TABLE 4.2 Developmental Stages of Adult Substance Dependence and Recovery[a][b]

Dependence	Recovery

Preaddiction and early stages

Social use of substances to
  enhance experience
  facilitate coping
  social lubricant
Decreased inhibitions
Changes in personality
Black outs
Preoccupation with substances
Hiding use of substances
Occasional memory lapses
Increased tolerance

Middle stages

Rationalization–denial
Increased tolerance
Increased blackouts–memory lapses
Increased craving and urgency to use (substance becomes central object)
Unpredictable amount–duration of use
Avoids confrontations regarding behavior
Increased self-medication
Uses alone
Grandiosity–jealousy–resentment
Increased problems and losses

Late stages

Increased physical problems
Decreased tolerance
Withdrawal symptoms magnified
Increased losses (family, job, relationships)
Impaired cognitions–problem solving
Legal problems–financial problems
Moral–ethical deterioration
Social affiliations change (focus on substance use)
Successive lengthy binges of use
Obsession with use

Precontemplation
1. Person does not interpret use of substance as a problem.
2. Little if any awareness of negative consequences associated with substance use.
3. Individual either enters treatment or continues on path of deterioration.

Maintenance

Focus on tasks associated with change
Work toward personal growth
Diminished fear and increased hopefulness
Increased emotional control
Continuation of support and treatment
Increased feelings of self efficacy
New interests develop
Contentment with abstinence
Continuing adjustment to substance-free lifestyle
Continuing personal growth and path of recovery

Action

Commitment to abstinence and treatment (lost object)
Actively takes responsibility for change
Honest self-appraisal
Realistic thinking
Awareness of others
Struggles with change
Vulnerable to relapse
Family system appreciates efforts—their maintenance of old patterns is reviewed and intervention takes place
Onset of new hope and renewed self-interest
Adjustment to change—working program

Contemplation

Increased awareness of negative consequences of substance use
Begins to think about change
Increased readiness to give up substances
Recognizes lack of control
Attempts to abstain
Improved personal care
Begins to affiliate with others in recovery
Begins to see how life can be different
Desire for substances continues
Honest desire for help and change

Pivotal point •

Transition into recovery

Continued deterioration, possibly death

Continued recovery

[a]Both dependence and recovery are progressive processes.
[b]Nor an exhaustive list of crieteria or symptoms.

68

TABLE 4.3 Developmental Stages of Adolescent Substance Dependence and Recovery

Stage	Dependence	Recovery
Early stages / Warning	Experimental substance use Increased amount and frequency of use Increasingly irresponsible behavior Decreased attention span Decreased frustration tolerance Decreased quality in efforts (school–home–job) Truancy and other school problems Change in peer relationships Change in lifestyle patterns Increased conflict with parents (and other authority figures) Lack of ability to control substance use	Continued participation in treatment Improved quality of life Improved responsible behavior Improved family member Improved academic performance Recognition of denial and rationalization Increasing contentment with abstinence Redeveloping trust of others Increased emotional control Confronting situations honestly Increased self-interest
Middle stages / Crucial	Changes in appearance and personal hygiene Immediate gratification need increases Increased problems associated with irresponsible behavior Decreased involvement in extracurricular activities Increased concern from family system Legal problems Increased association with substance culture Deterioration of physical, emotional, and mental status Lack of control	Increased motivation to resume extracurricular activities Clarification of values Improved physical status Increased awareness of others Realistic thinking Decreased fear and life feels increasingly manageable
Late stages / Chronic	Loss of interest in education—may lead to dropping out Extended high (similar to binging in adults) Loses sense of self Obsessed with substance use Compulsive substance use Feelings of fear and being overwhelmed (life falling apart) Increased poor judgment Vague or ambivalent desire for help	Attending treatment program Feelings of hopefulness Recognizing negative impact that substance abuse has had on life Realistic appraisal of self and need for change, which requires help Attempts to control

Pivotal point

Enter recovery

Continue downward with increased loss and decompensation

Recovery ←

Continued recovery

TABLE 4.4   Progressive Developmental Stages of Relapse[a][b]

Change in attitude and perspective	Situational change and increased risk	Emotional deterioration	Return to substance use	

Change in attitude and perspective

Adamant commitment to abstinence
Impulse attempt to impose abstinence on others
Compulsive behavior
Minimizing problems
Unrealistic expectations and limitations
Tendency toward loneliness
Mood disturbance
Loss of constructive daily planning
Denial
Tunnel vision

Emotional deterioration

Commitment present, but not as strong
Mood swings
Low frustration tolerance
Some defensiveness and dishonesty (with self and others)
Feelings of resentment building up
Becoming dissatisfied
Self-confidence and self-esteem diminishing
Begins to avoids others
Becoming confused
Feeling lonely and hopeless

Situational change and increased risk

Increasing avoidance
No longer speaking openly–honestly about substances
Irregular sleeping–eating (decreased focus on self-care)
Decreased participation in program, decreasing to little or no attendance
Increase in risk taking behavior
Reminiscing about past
Increased confusion
Lying
Rejection of program support–intervention
Escalation of problems

Return to substance use

Deterioration in positive daily structure
Negative attitude ("I don't care")
Open hostility and continued distancing (little association with healthy relationships)
Complete loss of self-confidence and self-esteem
Preoccupation with substances
Return to use of substances
Loss of control
Stops participation in treatment
Feeling powerless–hopeless
Resumes substance abuse culture lifestyle

[a]Follows a period of abstinence, treatment, return of physical–emotional health, and a desire to remain abstinent.

[b]The potential for relapse exists throughout the continuum of the recovery process. However, the longer the period of abstinence, the lower the risk of relapse. Also, a return to recovery can take place at any time. Not every symptom need be experienced for a realpse to occur, nor is this an exhaustive list of symptoms. A constellation of symptoms indicates stage of progress.

REFERENCES

Brown, S. (1983). "Treating the Alcoholic: A Developmental Model of Recovery." New York: Wiley.

Brownell, K. D., Marlatt, G. A., Lichtenstein, E., & Wilson, G. T. (1986). Understanding and preventing relapse. *Am. Psychologist* 41:765–782.

California Narcotics Officers Association (2000). Presentation at the 36th Annual Training Institute, November 2000.

Daley, D. (1988). "Relapse Prevention in the Addictions: A Biopsychosocial Approach." New York: Pergamon Press.

Daley, D. (1989). A psychoeducational approach to relapse prevention. *J. Chem. Dependency Treatment* **2**(2):105–124.

Daley, D., & Roth, L. (1992). "When Symptoms Return: A Guide to Relapse in Psychiatric Illness." Holmes Beach, FL: Learning Publications.

Galanter, M., Egelko, S., & Edwards, H. (1993). Rational recovery: Alternative to AA for addictions. *Am. J. Drug Alcohol Abuse* **19**(4):499–510.

Gorski, T. (1991). "Understanding the Twelve Steps." New York: Prentice Hall.

Gorski, T., & Miller, M. (1988). "Staying Sober Workbook." Independence, MO: Independence press.

Hester, R., & Miller, W. (1989). "Handbook of Alcoholism Treatment Approaches." New York: Pergamon Press.

Jonhson, S. L. (1997). "Therapist's Guide to Clinical Intervention." San Diego CA: Academic Press.

Kleinman, A. (1987). Culture and clinical reality: Commentary on culture-bound syndromes and international disease classification. *Culture, Medicine Psychiatry* **11**:49–52.

Kleinman, A. (1988). "The Illness Narratives: Suffering, Healing and the Human Condition. New York: Basic Books.

Marlatt, G. A. (1988). Matching clients to treatment: Treatment models and stages of change. *In* "Assessment of Addictive Behaviors" (D. M. Donovan & G. A. Marlatt, Eds.), pp. 474–484. New York: Guilford Press.

Marlatt, G. A., & Gordon, J. R., Eds. (1985). "Relapse Prevention: Maintenance Strategies in the Treatment of Addictive Behaviors." New York: Guilford Press.

Millman, J. R., & Ketchum, K. (1981). "Under the Influence: A Guide to the Myths and Realities of Alcoholism." Seattle, WA: Madrona Publication.

Olitzky, K. M., & Copans, S. A. (1991). "Twelve Jewish Steps to Recovery." Woodstock, VT: Jewish Lights.

Prochaska, J. O., & DiClemente, C. C. (1982). Transtheoretical therapy: Toward a more integrative model of change. *Psychotherapy: Theory, Res., Practice* **19**:276–288.

Shaffer, H. J. (1992). The psychology of stage change: The transition from addiction to recovery. *In* "Comprehensive Textbook of Substance Abuse" (J. H. Lowinson, P. Ruiz & R. B. Millman, Eds.), 2nd ed., pp. 100–105. Baltimore, MD: Williams & Williams.

Steinglass, P., Bennet, L. A., Wolin, S. J., & Reiss, D. (1987). "The Alcoholic Family." New York: Basic Books.

Tims, F., & Leukefeld, C. (1987). "Relapse Prevention for Addictive Behaviors." London: Blackwell Scientific Publication.

Wanigaratne, S. (1990). "Relapse Prevention for Addictive Behaviors." London: Blackwell Scientific Publication.

Zackon, F., McAuliffe, W., & Ch'ien, J. (1985). "Addict Aftercare: Recovery Training and Self-Help," DHHS Pub. No. ADM85-1341. Rockville, MD: National Institute on Drug Abuse.

Zweben, J. E. (1987). Recovery oriented psychotherapy: Facilitating the use of 12 step programs. *J. Psychoactive Drugs* **19**(3):243–251.

Part II

Assessment

Psychological

Disposition
Emotional Functioning
Self-efficacy
Self-esteem
Defense Mechanism
Character Structure
Influence of Education
Pleasure Seeking
Avoidance
Effect of Substance
Patterns of Use

Biological

Genetic predisposition
Current Biological Functioning
Bioeffects of Substance
Seeking Pleasure
Health Issues
Avoid Pain
Patterns of Use

Social

Family–Peers
Ethnicity–Culture
Socioeconomics
Education Level
Legal Issues
Religion–Spirituality
Impact of Substances
Avoidance
Patterns of Use
Availability
Advertising
Modeling
Customs
Laws

Substance
Affected
Lifestyle

Due to the prevalence of the comorbidity of substance abuse and mental health problems, obtaining an accurate substance use history is imperative. One only has to look at the *DSM IV* to recognize the interrelationship that takes place, whether it is self-medication or poor coping skills associated with a psychiatric diagnosis or the behavioral and mood symptoms associated with a central nervous system depressant or stimulant. At the very least, comorbidity results in a complicated clinical picture and the exacerbation of psychiatric symptomology (Schottenfield *et al.*, 1993; Miller *et al.*, 1994). There are frequent associations between substance abuse and personality disorders or mood and anxiety disorders in adults and attention deficit disorder and mood disorders in adolescents. In many cases substance abuse will not be diagnosed if it is not assessed as part of every mental health evaluation.

Assessment begins with a face to face interview where observation and intent listening to what is being said and not said initiate case conceptualization via numerous hypotheses. Each piece of information is like a new factor added to the equation. *Red flags* to keep in mind associated with presentation and history include the following.

Physiological	Psychological	Behavioral
Genetic predisposition	Treatment history	History of substance abuse problems
Liver problems	Chronic pain problems	Legal problems
Diabetes	Depression	Poor work history
Hypertension	Anxiety	Financial problems
Ulcers	Attention deficit disorder	Extreme talkativeness
Weight fluctuations	Drug seeking behavior	Poor judgment
Rhinorrhea	Excessive mood swings	Erratic behavior
Lip–finger burns	Loss of interest in friends	Evidence of intoxication
Dilated–pinpoint pupils	Loss of interest in activities	Frequent falls
Excess perspiration	Suicidal ideation–talk–gesture	Frequent hospitalizations
Tremors–tachycardia		Tendency to underreport substance use
Unexplained bruises		Decreased inhibition in
Track–injection marks		self-destructiveness

PURPOSE OF ASSESSMENT

Often, as the individual is presenting issues for treatment he or she does not experience or perceive his or her substance abuse as a problem in need of treatment. He or she may even mention substance abuse without identifying it as a contributing problem. Even when it is identified, many individuals will be reluctant or ambivalent to give up the use of mood altering substances. Generally, they are focused on alleviating symptoms they experience as distressing, such as depression and anxiety symptoms. The purpose of an assessment is to

1. Clearly and thoroughly identify an accurate clinical picture.
2. Initiate a therapeutic dialogue and interaction.
3. Promote increased awareness on behalf of the individual to see the broader picture (beyond the immediate feelings of distress).
4. Offer objective feedback.
5. Establish a diagnosis.
6. Collaboratively develop a treatment plan with appropriate goals and objectives.
7. Encourage positive change (by preparing them to change abusive/addictive behavior).
8. Improve motivation.

MOTIVATIONAL INTERVIEWING

Miller and Rollnick (1991) developed an alternative to the direct, and often confrontative interviewing technique generally used for substance abuse assessment, termed motivational interviewing. The purpose of motivational interviewing is to explore the client's view of the problem, encourage change by avoiding labels, and acknowledge that the responsibility for treatment goals and decision making reside with the client. The therapist carefully completes a thorough assessment, sharing the results with the client so that treatment planning can be initiated as a collaborative effort. By engaging the client in this manner, a true treatment collaboration with an increase in positive outcome is heightened. Miller and Rollnick offer the following process of motivational interviewing with a client-centered approach to assess individuals with substance abuse and addiction problems. It is a perspective that emphasizes the following.

1. The acceptance of applied labels such as addict or alcoholic is not a prerequisite for change.
2. Treatment is a personal choice.
3. The individual is responsible for change.
4. Resistance should be viewed as a relationship of influence by the therapist's attitude or behavior toward the individual.
5. Encourages collaborative treatment planning.
6. Views ambivalence versus denial as a central treatment issue.

The most basic, and sometimes the most revealing, aspect of assessment is observation of the individual and/or his or her significant other or family. During assessment, close attention is paid to verbal and nonverbal communication, behavior, and overall mental status in order to generate numerous hypotheses relevant to motivation and treatment choices.

INDIVIDUALIZED TREATMENT PLAN

Development of an individualized treatment plan (ITP) requires a thorough assessment, which includes substance use history, associated family history, and personal functioning. The personal areas to assess should include topics such as

1. Social skills
2. Communication assertiveness–appropriate expression, identification of feelings
3. Unresolved issues of loss
4. Stress management
5. Ability to self-soothe and relax
6. Coping skills
7. Depression and anxiety management
8. Self-esteem–worthiness–self-efficacy
9. Relationship issues–significant other–family–peers
10. Social support system
11. Compulsiveness
12. Impulsiveness
13. Self-defeating patterns
14. Presence of self-destructive, suicidal thoughts–behaviors
15. Academic abilities
16. Work history
17. Problem solving
18. Judgment

19. Decision making
20. Endocrine system functioning
21. General medical condition
22. Recreation activities

ASSESSMENT QUESTIONS

As with the initiation of the assessment and treatment planning process, the following types of questions serve as a good tool for engaging the individual, clarifying the desired change(s), and developing the objectives necessary to accomplish the identified goals. Locus of control is an important factor to clarify in the context of understanding the individual's desired goals and feelings of self-efficacy. This factor can play an important role in problem solving the appropriate level of support and reinforcement required for facilitating change. Does the individual believe in his or her own influence upon creating change and achieving success, i.e., the role of self-efficacy and responsibility, versus fate as the major influence, asserting that things just happen and he or she lacks control over his or her own destiny, making him or her a "victim of circumstance" and alleviating the issue of self-responsibility. Taking this into consideration, proceed with the following assessment questions.

1. What does the individual identify as the problem(s)?
2. What are the identified goals?
3. What are all of the generated choices available to help the individual achieve his or her goals?
4. What obstacles may impede progress?
5. What methods or resources could be used to prevent, minimize, or avoid these obstacles?
6. Has the individual resolved other life crises, and how did such experiences affect self-efficacy?
7. What are the strengths and internal resources that will help the individual achieve his or her goals?
8. What are the external resources that can help the individual achieve his or her goals?
9. What are the most useful ways to utilize these internal and external resources?
10. What is the individual willing to do differently?

A model for describing different motivational states associated with corresponding therapeutic tasks is presented by Prochaska and DiClemente (1986) and Davidson *et al.*, (1991). They emphasize timing as being significantly important for successful intervention. Abstinence requires many changes, and an individual may not be ready to make that choice. However, when an individual is wavering with ambivalence between being unsure and being ready, and a skilled therapist takes the time to be genuinely interested and encourages him or her to clarify "where he or she is" regarding readiness to change, it can facilitate an individual to examine his or her ambivalence, identify the reasons for concern, and present reasons for change. During the course of recovery, it is expected that many individuals will experience crises and periods of ambivalence. Therefore, motivational interviewing is a useful tool to use at any stage of change: ready to change, in the process of change, and maintenance.

MULTIVARIATE TREATMENT PLANNING

Substance abuse is multivariate in nature, which requires the assessment process to thoroughly evaluate the multiple, complex factors to be identified so that treatment is not simplistically conceptualized and developed. Different factors play a role in the complex problems of substance abuse for each individual. This demonstrates the importance of an individualized treatment plan (ITP). Therefore, if treatment is to be successful the following is required of the treatment plan:

1. Individualized.
2. Collaboratively developed with the client.
3. Issues of confidentiality should be thoroughly clarified.
4. Maintain a structure and clear focus on the agenda.
5. A broad understanding by the client of how the information obtained by the assessment–clinical interview all relates in some way to the substance abuse.
6. Avoid preconceived views and stereotypes of substance abuse clients.
7. Sensitive in consideration of issues of human diversity for both diagnosis and treatment.
8. Clarify that abstinence is not the only goal.
9. Accept that multiple variables are woven together into the complexity of substance abuse, which includes multiple patterns of abuse.
10. Multimodal.

Assessment must seek to understand the following: (1) What does the substance mean to an individual? (2) What does he or she get out of it–perceived benefit? (3) Does use create any problems? Instead of looking at substance abuse as the problem, broaden the approach to focus on goals associated with improving the quality of life.

IMPORTANT COMPONENTS OF A SUBSTANCE ABUSE HISTORY

1. Referral source
2. Presenting problem and events leading to treatment
3. History of presenting problem
4. History of substance use and abuse (including over the counter and prescription drugs)
   a. events leading to treatment
   b. age of onset of substance use (for each substance used)
   c. duration and pattern of use
      i. method of use
      ii. last time used
      iii. period of abstinence
   d. effects of substance of symptomatology and functioning

e. meaning that the chosen substance has had for the individual

f. motivation for change

5. Prior treatment history

   a. when

   b. where

   c. what type of treatment

   d. treatment completed or premature termination

   e. what was helpful–not helpful

   f. past–present 12-step participation

   g. how long abstinence maintained (why abstinence chosen and whether successful–benefit(s) of abstinence)

   h. what factors contributed to relapse

6. Current life situation

   a. living arrangement

   b. marriage–cohabitation

   c. children

   d. social life

   e. work–school

   f. level of current functioning–mental status

7. Family history of substance abuse

   a. generational genogram with identified family members

   b. patterns of use

   c. disruption–dysfunction in family life

   d. how–where raised

   e. how emotions were dealt with

   f. central values–beliefs

   g. any received treatment and when

   h. course of treatment and outcome

   i. currently abstinent or actively using

   j. health–related issues or death(s) associated with substance use

   k. current role in perpetuation of individual's use

      i. provoke

      ii. pressure

      iii. maintain–enable financial support, support in obtaining substances, sabotaging attempts to abstain, tolerate–compensate for irresponsible behavior

   l. any family member directly involved in individual's substance use

8. Religious–spiritual beliefs

9. Work history of client, siblings, parents

10. Legal history

11. Sexual history

12. History of emotional functioning

13. Multiple compulsions–dependencies (e.g., food, shopping, gambling, self-destructive behavior, sex): be alert to switching, alternating, numbing, disinhibiting values in compulsions other than using substances

14. Medical health history and physical examination

   a. previous illness(es)

   b. infectious diseases

c. medical trauma

d. pregnancies

e. sexually transmitted diseases, and (risk behavior status should also be evaluated)

Physical signs of substance abuse:

1. Signs of intoxication and withdrawal
2. Change in pupil dilation
   a. constricted–miosis with opiates and PCP
   b. dilated–mydriasis with amphetamines, hallucinogens, and anticholinergics
3. Nasal symptoms of cocaine abuse (swollen, dripping)
4. Marks such as abscesses, ulcers, needle tracks, scarring, or tattooing along a vein

OBJECTIVE ASSESSMENT

The only objective assessment of substance abuse (Frances & Miller, 1998) is thorough blood–urine testing over time. The method for body fluid testing is referred to as enzyme immunoassay (EMIT). Such testing can act as a confirmation of the individual's report of use or unreported use. Urine testing only offers information on relatively recent use and does not clarify patterns of use. Body fluid samples should test for alcohol, amphetamines, benzodiazepines, barbiturates, cannabinoids, hallucinogens, and opioids. Some examples of laboratory examinations include the following:

A. Urine Screens
   1. Thin layer chromatography (TLC) is used only for screening; it is sometimes inaccurate.
   2. Enzyme immuno-assay (EIA) is a qualitative test and Radio immuno-assay (RIA) is a quantitative test. In comparison to TLC, these two tests have a relatively high degree of specificity and sensitivity.
   3. Gas chromatography–mass spectrometry (GC–MS) is the most expensive, but it is also the most reliable.

B. Serum Levels
   1. Used when urine tests are positive or abused substances are already identified.
   2. Psychotropic medications.

C. Other Body Fluids
   1. Saliva has been analyzed but is not a standard for testing.
   2. Sweat has been analyzed but is not a standard for testing.

D. Liver and Kidney Function Tests
   1. In the case of alcoholism, the liver enzyme γ-glutamyl transferase (GGT) is often the first to demonstrate an escalation.
   2. Other medical effects: Washton (1995) states that, if the physical exam is not feasible, it is recommended, at a minimum, to do blood screening that includes the following and to be aware of other useful markers that indicate the possibility of health problems associated with drinking.
      a. blood screening that includes the enzymes serum glutamic–oxaloacetic transaminase (SGOT) and serum glutamic pyruvate transaminase (SGPT)

b. mean cellular volume

c. high-density lipoproteins–tritiglycerides (high)

d. uric acid

e. bilirubin (high)

f. anemia

Other considerations in the medical examination include the following:

1. A review of physical signs previously noted (pupil dilation, needle tracks, etc.).
2. Nasal membranes infected or eroded septum.
3. Rectal and pelvic exam because substances may be hidden in either orifice.
4. A thorough and comprehensive medical examination with appropriate lab testing.
   a. substance abuse can result in significant health problems as well as a method of masking or coping with health problems (pain, insomnia, etc.)
   b. medical complications of alcoholism (as an example) include negative impact on the following organ systems: gastrointestinal tract, pancreas, liver, cardiovascular system, nervous system, hematology, endocrine system, musculoskeletal system, immune system, skin, and fetal effects.

Over the last several years, controversy regarding the ethical issues of substance testing outside of the clinical setting, as well as how the information is to be used, has taken public stage. Additional concerns include how testing information should be used, confidentiality (who should know the results of testing and under what circumstances), and how selection for testing is made. The two largest arenas where testing has taken place is in association with business and athletics. Substance testing is a powerful tool that can have significant influence on people's lives and, therefore, is justified in raising public concern. However, it has the benefits of resulting in prevention, early intervention, and prevention of accidents and harm, which culminate in improved health and safety, and fiscal savings. These benefits are not to be taken lightly. The National Institute on Drug Abuse (NIDA, 1989) has estimated that on any given day if every worker aged 18–40 years was tested for substance abuse, 14–25% would test positive for a variety of substances. Additionally, Schwab (1997) states that workplace substance abuse costs our economy $60–100 billion per year in lost productivity.

PSYCHOLOGICAL AND NEUROPSYCHOLOGICAL ASSESSMENT

Psychological and neuropsychological evaluations are used to measure

1. Frontal lobe functioning–cognitive deficits
2. Visual–perceptual tasks
3. Psychological functioning
4. Dual diagnoses
5. Coping style–skills

A brief screen may include

1. WAIS subtest on block design–digit symbol (Wechsler, 1981).
2. Halstead–Reitan subtests on tactile performance (using time, memory, and location score) and the trail making test (parts A and B) (Halstead, 1947; Reitan & Davison, 1974).

Other testing and screening may include the following.

1. Beck Depression Inventory (BDI) yields a score descriptive of the degree–level of depression experienced (Beck, 1961).
2. Bender Gestalt yields a gross measure of brain dysfunction (Bender, 1938).
3. WAIS auditory stimulation associated with subtests of digit span, digit symbol, and block design to measure attention, concentration, short-term memory, and retention (Wechsler, 1955).
4. Memory for Design Test is a test of visual stimulation that yields information regarding the dysfunction of attention, concentration, short-term memory, and retention (Graham & Kendall, 1960).
5. Minnesota Multiphasic Personality Inventory (MMPI), Mac Andrews (MAC), and other experimental scales. The MAC scales consist of 49 items that can be used to differentiate between a person diagnosed solely with a psychiatric disorder and one with a substance abuse disorder (University of Minnesota, 1943).
6. 16 Personality Factor (16 PF): each scale reflects a basic aspect of personality structure. It places a greater emphasis on day to day personality traits than the focus on pathology seen in the MMPI (Cattell *et al.*, 1970).
7. Tennessee Self-Concept Scale (TSCS) includes descriptive statements that yield information about how an individual views–evaluates him- or herself (Fitts, 1965).
8. Shipley Institute of Living Scale (SILS) is a brief test that offers quantitative measures of verbal skills and abstract thinking, which render an inferred–estimated IQ (Shipley, 1940).
9. Locus of Control (LOC) provides information on generalized expectations for internal versus external control of reinforcement, i.e., belief in the individual's own skills versus fate (Rotter, 1966).
10. Sensation Seeking Scale (SSS) is a questionnaire describing a variety of exciting, interesting, stimulating, and risk taking activities (Zuckerman, 1979).

SUBSTANCE-RELATED ASSESSMENT INVENTORIES

It is not recommended that one rely on a single assessment instrument because of the variety and depth of information that can be gathered. Multiple instruments can be used along with a clinical interview and mental status exam. There are numerous assessment tools that focus specifically on substance use and patterns of use. These instruments offer a variety of structures and aid in clarifying the clinical picture. Some examples include the following.

1. Addiction Severity Index (ASI) assesses medical status, employment status, drug–alcohol use, legal status, family–social relationships, and psychological status. The ASI gives a severity rating for each area from 0 (no treatment necessary) to 9 (intervention needed in a life threatening situation) (McLellan *et al.*, 1980).

2. Alcohol Use Inventory (AUI) is thorough assessment tool that groups multiple dimensions into four domains: benefits of drinking, styles of drinking, consequences of drinking, and concerns associated with drinking. Research suggests that the AUI may be a resource for predicting outcomes and matching individuals to appropriate levels of care (Jacobson, 1989; Horn *et al.*, 1987).

3. Brief Drinker Profile (BDP) uses a grid that breaks down typical use over the period of a week into days of the week and time of day. Additionally, it has a section for measuring periodic or binge drinking (Marlatt & Miller, 1987).

4. Cognitive Appraisal Questionnaire (CAQ) helps clients to identify cognitive factors that interfere with self-efficacy or appraisal of success (Annis, 1982a).

5. Form 90 is a set of instruments formatted to gather drinking and drug use data, which gives a day by day picture of an individual's substance abuse (Miller, 1991).

6. Inventory of Drinking Situations (IDS) identifies situations associated with drinking: negative emotional states, negative physical states, positive emotional states, testing of personal control, urges and temptation, interpersonal conflict, social pressure to drink, and positive time with others. The composite results in a profile of high–low drinking situations, which facilitates the client's understanding of his or her drinking antecedents so that appropriate interventions and coping strategies can be developed accordingly (Annis, 1982b).

7. Michigan Alcohol Screening Test (MAST) contains 24 items that focus on drinking habits. It has some tendency toward false positive results. Short Michigan Alcohol Screening Test (SMAST) is an instrument of 17 questions derived from the MAST that more accurately diagnoses alcoholism and does not demonstrate a tendency toward false positives like the Mast (Porkonoy *et al.*, 1972).

8. Situational Confidence Questionnaire (SCQ) has clients put themselves in various situations and indicate their degree of confidence to be able to handle the situations without drinking. The result is the development of a hierarchy of drinking situations to be reinforced by handling manageable tasks about which they feel confident and gradually work through a progression of situations about which they feel less confident(Annis, 1982c).

9. Substance Abuse Problem Checklist (SAPC) is a long self-administered inventory covering problems associated with treatment motivation, health problems, personality problems, social relationship problems, job-related problems, problems associated with misuse of leisure time, religious–spiritual problems, and legal problems. The SAPC facilitates active participation by the client in the treatment planning process, along with clarification of diagnosis and treatment by the therapist (Carroll, 1984).

10. Time-Line Follow Back Assessment Method (TFBAM) gathers information about drinking behaviors over time, viewing drinking behavioral variables as being continuous (Sobell *et al.*, 1980).

11. The Obsessive Compulsive Drinking Scale (OCDS) appears to be sensitive to alcoholism severity and changes during abstinence and relapse, which could be very useful in treatment planning and the need for flexibility of the plan to meet the needs of the individual at any given time during the course of recovery (Anton *et al.*, 1996).

Numbers 12–20 are instruments that cover both drug and alcohol use as well as other life domains–problem areas such as health, psychological problems, school, social relationships, and family relationships.

12. Chemical Dependency Adolescent Assessment Project (CDAAP) addresses the special diagnostic and treatment needs of children and adolescents (Winters & Henley, 1987).

13. Adolescent Drug Abuse Diagnosis (ADAD) offers a 10-point severity rating for each of nine life problem areas. Composite scores to measure client behavioral change in each life problem area during and after treatment can be calculated (Friedman & Utada, 1989).

14. Personal Experience Inventory (PEI) is a comprehensive assessment instrument that consists of three parts. The two that are of major interest here are the Chemical Involvement Problem Severity (CIPS) and the psychosocial section Winters & Henley, 1989).

15. Assessment of Chemical Health Inventory (ACHI) contains both alcohol- and drug-related items as well as critical life items (Krotz *et al.*, 1988).

16. Drug Use Screening Inventory-Revised (DUSI-R) consists of three parts: (1) the Personal History Form for documenting the individual's background; (2) the Drug Use Screening Instrument for assessment and diagnostic evaluation, and (3) a demographic, medical, and treatment or prevention summary plan (Tarter, 1990).

17. Prevention Intervention Management and Evaluation System (PMES) is designed to be administered in a structured interview shortly after admission to treatment and provides information considered theoretically significant for adolescent drug use and related problems (Hater & Simpson, 1981).

18. Problem Oriented Screening Instrument for Teenagers (POSIT) is designed for extensive assessment and referral. It identifies problems and treatment needs in 10 life problem areas (Rahdert, 1991).

19. Adolescent Drinking Index (ADI) provides a screening index to ascertain the relative severity of substance abuse and associated behavioral and psychological problems (Harrell & Wirtz, 1989).

20. Adolescent–Parent Communication Form focuses on family communication as reported by the adolescent and parents (Friedman *et al.*, 1991).

MNEMONIC SCREENING DEVICES

CAGE (EWING, 1984)

Cut down: Has anyone ever recommended that you cut back or stop drinking?

Annoyed: Have you ever felt annoyed or angry if someone comments on your drinking?

Guilt: Have there been times when you have felt guilty about or regretted things that have occurred because of drinking?

Eye-opener: Have you ever used alcohol to help you get started in the morning to steady your nerves?

According to Jacobson (1989), this questionnaire accurately determines the presence or absence of alcoholism 90% of the time. Two or more positive responses indicate alcohol dependence.

TWEAK (RUSSEL *et al.*, 1991)

Tolerance : How many drinks can you hold or how many drinks does it take to get high?

Worried: Have close friends or relatives been worried about your drinking?

Eye-opener: Do you sometimes take a drink in the morning to wake up?

Amnesia: Has a friend or relative ever told you things you said or did while you were drinking that you could not remember?

Kut (cut): Do you sometimes feel the need to cut down on your drinking?

Measurement of motivation for change can be done by assessing the stages of change and motivation using the following assessment tools:

1. Change Readiness and Treatment Eagerness Scale (SOCRATES)(Miller, 1989).
2. University of Rhode Island Change Assessment (URICA)(DiClemente & Hughes, 1990).

FUNCTIONAL IMPORTANCE OF SUBSTANCE USE

This issue plays a role in motivation, which warrants it being addressed in conjunction with measuring motivation. Most individuals will offer a perception of positive benefits associated with substance use. Therefore, assess these perceived benefits to identify and address ambivalence regarding change, to determine motivation, and to determine specific treatment interventions available when the individual is ready to enter treatment. The combination of positive and negative consequences is a key factor associated with resistance in changing substance abuse/dependent behaviors.

FOLLOW-UP ASSESSMENT

Another component of assessment, which is discussed at the beginning of treatment, is the follow-up assessment. At predetermined intervals of time a systematic review of the continuing course of treatment and recovery is conducted, especially at high-risk time frames. Face to face contact is recommended over a mailed questionnaire. A face to face meeting allows for additional questions, increased understanding or clarification, pursuit of concerns, problem solving, and if necessary strategic organization of reentry at a particular point of treatment. The majority of relapse episodes occur within the first 6–12 months of treatment. Recognized intervals of relapse are 3, 6, 9, and 12 months.

At the end of this chapter are some basic questionnaires for assessing substance use and abuse. There is variation in the depth of information as well as specific information identified in each questionnaire. Some questionnaires have a psychosocial format in order to gather a more encompassing view of the individual and his or her history. There are also some brief questionnaires or survey instruments designed for obtaining specific focussed information.

CONCEPTUAL ASSESSMENT OF SUBSTANCE ABUSE

This four-part conceptual model strives to clarify the relationship of substance-specific symptomatology on a continuum of problematic use to late-stage substance dependency.

1. Primary substance of choice
   a. what substance(s) are being used
   b. list in decreasing order in association with frequency and quantity of use

2. Stage of the disorder (disease)
   a. continuum of non-problematic to problematic use–the disorder has progressed (early, middle, late-stage dependency).
   b. Evaluate three central areas
      i. problems in living (financial, legal, occupational, social)
      ii. physical effects: (health problems, risk, tolerance, withdrawal)
      iii. psychological and behavioral effects: ability to abstain control use, use to regulate affect, use of defenses.

3. Status of current use
   a. choice of substance (what needs being met)
   b. degree of use
   c. non using–abstaining

4. Prior treatment efforts
   a. describe program
   b. what worked-what did not
   c. understanding of recovery

5. Special features relevant to diagnose and treatment
   a. dual diagnoses
   b. medical evaluation
   c. medically supervised prescription medications

d. age of onset of problematic use
e. family history
f. legal issues
g. history of violence
h. suicide potential
i. route of administration
j. other compulsions

QUESTIONNAIRES

THE JOHNSON SUBSTANCE USE PSYCHOLOGICAL QUESTIONNAIRE (ADAPTED FROM JOHNSON, 1997)

Date: _____

Client Name: _____

Sex: _____   Date of Birth: _____   Age :_____   Marital Status: _____

Living Arrangements: _____

_____

_____

Referral Source: _____

_____

Presenting Problems and Events Leading to Treatment: _____

_____

_____

_____

1. Use of alcohol and/or drugs:

Substance Used	How Used (Route)	Age Started	Amount	Frequency	Last Use

2. Has there been any change in the pattern of alcohol–drug use in the last 6 months to 1 year?

   Yes   No

   If yes, describe:_____

   _____

   _____

3. Preferred alcohol or drugs: _____

_____

_____

4. For what medical conditions are you currently being prescribed medications, by whom, and what are you taking? _____

_____

_____

5. Do you use alcohol or drugs to get started in the morning? _____

_____

_____

6. Has your physician ever told you to cut down or stop using alcohol–drugs?_____

_____

_____

7. Have you ever been hospitalized or treated in the emergency room for substance overdose? _____

_____

_____

8. Have you ever felt the need to cut down the use of alcohol–drugs (if yes, explain): _____

_____

_____

9. What benefit or meaning do you (have you) associate with substance abuse?_____

_____

_____

10. Why have you chosen to use a particular substance? _____

_____

_____

11. Has the use of alcohol–drugs caused you to be late or miss work?_____

_____

_____

12. Has the use of alcohol–drugs affected your home life relationships?_____

_____

_____

13. How do you feel about your use of alcohol–drugs?_____

_____

_____

14. Have you ever attended an AA–NA meeting?_____

_____

_____

Treatment History

1. Number of attempts to stop alcohol–drug use and how (when, where, response, outcome):_____

_____

_____

_____

_____

_____

2. Length of time you abstained from alcohol–drug use:_____

_____

_____

_____

_____

1. Occupation: _____

2. Level of education completed: _____

3. Relationship or social problems made worse by substance use: _____

	No	Yes
arguments with partner, parents, sibling, other	_____	_____
partner threatened to leave–has left	_____	_____
thrown out of household	_____	_____
loss of family support	_____	_____
loss of friends	_____	_____
social isolation	_____	_____

Please answer the following questions:

1. Have you ever been hospitalized for substance abuse? _____ _____

2. Have you ever been treated in the emergency room for substance abuse? _____ _____

3. Have you ever been treated with medication for depression–anxiety–hearing voices? _____ _____

4. Have you ever felt suicidal or had repeated thoughts of harming yourself? _____ _____

5. Have you ever felt suicidal while using substances? _____ _____

6. Have you ever developed a plan for suicide? _____ _____

7. Have you ever attempted suicide? _____ _____

8. Have you ever been hospitalized for suicidal thoughts or attempts? _____ _____

9. Do you fear you might try to harm yourself or attempt suicide in the future? _____ _____

10. Has anyone in your family ever attempted or succeeded in committing suicide? _____ _____

11. Have you ever had thoughts of harming someone else? _____ _____

12. Have you ever been hospitalized for thoughts–attempts to harm someone else? _____ _____

13. Do you have a history of having difficulty managing anger or being violent? _____ _____

14. Has anyone in your family ever had emotional or psychotic problems? _____ _____

15. Have you ever been verbally or physically abused? _____ _____

16. Have you ever been sexually abused? _____ _____

Symptoms	Yes/No	If yes, please explain
Depression (mild–moderate–severe)	_____	_____
Fatigue–decreased activity level	_____	_____
Restlessness	_____	_____
Sleep problems	_____	_____
Teary eyes	_____	_____
Appetite problems–changes	_____	_____
Memory problems–changes	_____	_____
Suspicious, paranoid	_____	_____
Anxiety (mild–moderate–severe–panic)	_____	_____
Irritability	_____	_____
Fever, sweaty, chills	_____	_____
Shortness of breath	_____	_____
Chest pain–discomfort	_____	_____
Palpitations	_____	_____
Dizziness	_____	_____
Sinus problems (runny nose, etc.)	_____	_____
Tremors	_____	_____
Blackouts	_____	_____
Severe frequent headaches	_____	_____
Periods of confusion	_____	_____
Convulsions with loss of consciousness	_____	_____
Hallucinations	_____	_____
Staggering or balance problems	_____	_____
Tingling	_____	_____
Muscle weakness	_____	_____
Suicidal attempts–thoughts	_____	_____
Violent thoughts–thoughts of hurting others	_____	_____

Medical Problems

Has your physician ever told you that you have any of the following?

	No	Yes
Diabetes	_____	_____
Cirrhosis	_____	_____
Hepatitis	_____	_____
Anemia	_____	_____
Gout	_____	_____
High blood pressure	_____	_____
Heart disease	_____	_____
Delerium tremors	_____	_____
Gastritis	_____	_____
Pancreatitis	_____	_____
Other	_____	_____

Current medications prescribed, dosage and directions for use, how long have you been taking it, what is it prescribed for, and who has prescribed it?

_____

_____

_____

_____

Name: _____   Phone: _____

Religious–ethnic–cultural background: _____

_____

Marital Status: _____   Children: _____

Living Arrangements: _____

_____

Present Support System (family–friends): _____

_____

Chemical History: _____

Age Started Using Substances: _____

Length of Use: _____   Last Dose: _____

Chemical Used	How Used (Route)	Started	Amount	Frequency	Last Use

Description of Presenting Problems (patient's view): _____

_____

_____

Previous Counseling:

When	Where	Therapist and Title	Response

Have you ever attended 12-step or other self-help meetings (when–how long–how often did you have a sponsor)?

_____

_____

_____

Relationship and History of Chemical Use: _____

_____

_____

_____

Effects of/on Family Support System: _____

_____

_____

Daily activities that

a. support abstinence: _____

_____

_____

b. encourage usage: _____

_____

_____

History of Sexual–Physical Abuse (victim–abuser): _____

_____

_____

Sexual Orientation: _____

Education: _____

Vocational History: _____

Leisure–Social Interests: _____

_____

_____

Current Occupation: _____

_____

Current Employer: _____

Impact on job performance: _____

	No	Yes
Jeopardy of losing job–previous job loss:	_____	_____
Late to work–missed days of work:	_____	_____
Loss of productivity at work:	_____	_____
Missed appointments for promotion–raise:	_____	_____

Socioeconomic–Financial Problems: _____

_____

_____

_____

Legal problems:

    DUI: Yes   No

Court ordered: Yes   No

Preliminary Treatment Plan: List presenting problems based upon initial assessment of the client's physical, emotional, cognitive, and behavioural status.

Detox: yes _____   no _____   Explain: _____

_____

Rehab: yes _____   no _____   Explain: _____

_____

Problem #1: _____

_____

Problem #2: _____

_____

Problem #3: _____

_____

Immediate Treatment Recommendations to Address Identifying Problems:

_____

_____

_____

_____

_____

_____

Client's Presenting Treatment Goals: _____

_____

_____

Mutually Agreed upon Treatment Goals: _____

_____

_____

Client: _____   Therapist: _____

ADULT PSYCHOSOCIAL (Adapted from Johnson, 1997)

Identifying Information (age, gender, ethnicity, marital status):

_____

_____

Presenting Problem:

_____

_____

Current Social Information:

1. Describe your present living arrangements (include with whom you are living and a brief description of these relationships): _____

   _____

   _____

2. How long have you been married–dating–living together? Describe this relationship (include occupation and age of significant other): _____

   _____

   _____

3. How many children do you have (name, sex, age)? _____

   _____

   _____

4. Are there any significant problems with any of these children (describe)? _____

   _____

   _____

   _____

5. Give details of previous relationships–marriages: _____

   _____

   _____

6. Any history of abuse (emotional, physical, sexual) in current or previous relationships: _____

   _____

   _____

Family History

1. Describe your childhood and adolescence (include home atmosphere and relationship with parents): _____

_____

_____

_____

_____

2. Any history of significant life events such as death, abuse (physical, emotional, sexual) divorce, separation, or other? _____

_____

_____

_____

3. List mother and father by age, include occupations: _____

_____

_____

4. List siblings by age and describe how you relate to them (past and present):

_____

_____

_____

5. Have any family members been treated for–have emotional problems? Describe:

_____

_____

_____

Drug and Alcohol Abuse

1. Any family history of drug and/or alcohol usage? List and describe: _____

_____

_____

2. Any personal history of drug–alcohol usage? List and describe: _____

_____

_____

Educational
History

1. Describe all school experiences: high school, college, vocational school. Were there any problems with truancy, suspensions, special education, vocational training, etc.? _____

_____

_____

_____

_____

Employment
History

1. Present employment status and where (positive and negative aspects of what is going on at work): _____

_____

_____

_____

2. If on leave of absence or disability, will you return to present job? _____

_____

Socialization
Skills

1. List clubs and organizations you belong to: _____

_____

_____

2. What do you do for pleasure and relaxation? _____

_____

_____

Summary

This _____ year old (include sex, marital status, ethnicity) is currently participating in outpatient treatment for _____ (summary of reasons for treatment).

1. What–who seems to be placing the most stress on you at this time? _____

_____

2. Are there any legal issues pending? _____ No _____ Yes (describe): _____

_____

3. Are you having financial problems at this time? _____

_____

4. Describe your plans regarding any help you would like to have with your living arrangements: _____

_____

_____

Treatment
Plan and
Recommendations
_____

1. _____

2. _____

3. _____

4. _____

_____   _____
Therapist   Date

THE JOHNSON BRIEF INITIAL ASSESSMENT
(Adapted from Johnson, 1997)

Date: _____

Patient: _____

Primary Care Physician: _____

Reason for Referral: _____

_____

_____

Medications Currently Prescribed: _____

_____

Medical Problems Currently Experiencing: _____

_____

Therapist–Psychiatrist Previously Seen: _____

_____

Symptoms (circle all that apply):

Depression	Sweating–Flushes–Chills	Work Problems
Tearful	Dizziness–Nausea	Legal–Financial Problems
Sleep Disturbance	Fatigue	Relationship Problems
Difficulty	Hypervigilance	Difficulty Relaxing
Concentrating	Intrusive Thoughts	Eating Disorder
Memory Problems	Asthma–Allergies	School Problems–Truancy
Social Isolation	Mania	Hyperactivity
Headaches	Bowel Problems	Defies Rules
Abdominal Distress	Palpitations	Annoys Others
Suicidal Ideation	Hopeless–Helpless	Easily Annoyed
Sexual Abuse–Assault	Anger–Frustration	Blames Others
Homicidal Ideation	Depersonalization–Derealization	Use Obscene Language
Appetite Disturbance	Compulsive Behaviors	Drug Use
Anxiety	Obsessive Thoughts	Somatic Concerns
Fears–Phobias	Issues of Loss	Excessive Drinking
Shakiness–Trembling	Stress	Argues

History of Current Problem:

_____

_____

_____

_____

_____

Substance Use
History
_____

1. Does patient report that he or she drinks or uses drugs?   Yes _____   No _____

2. Describe the pattern of use for substances listed below, whether or not such use has been identified as a problem.

Substance	Quantity	Pattern of use	Amount and date of last use	Uptake route
Alcohol				
Stimulants				
Opiates				
Cocaine				
Cannabis				
Barbiturates				
Sedative–Hypnotic				
Other				

3. Does patient report blackouts or medical complications?
   No _____   Yes _____ (specify: _____)

4. Has the patient been able to abstain?   No _____   Yes _____

5. How long? 24 hr _____ 72 hr _____ 1 week _____ 1 month _____ More than _____

6. Has the patient had prior substance abuse treatment?   No _____   Yes _____

   When Last? 6 months _____   12 months _____   More than 12 months _____
   Inpatient_____   Detox _____   Structured Outpatient _____

7. Has patient tried to modify or stop use before?

   Yes _____   When: _____

                     Why: _____

                     How: _____

                     What Happened: _____

   No _____

8. Is patient utilizing self-help support such as AA, NA, sober living, or rational recovery?

   Yes _____   Last Meeting Date: _____

   Typical number of meetings per week: _____

   Has patient ever had a sponsor?   Yes _____   No _____

   No _____

Mental Status

Mood	_____ Normal	_____ Depressed	_____ Elevated
	_____ Euphoric	_____ Angry	_____ Anxious
Affect	_____ Normal	_____ Broad	_____ Restricted
	_____ Blunted	_____ Flat	
	_____ Inappropriate	_____ Labile	
Memory	_____ Intact	_____ Short-Term Problems	_____ Long-Term Problems
Processes	_____ Normal	_____ Blocking	_____ Loose Associations
	_____ Confabulations	_____ Flight of Ideas	_____ Ideas of Reference
	_____ Grandiosity	_____ Paranoia	
	_____ Obsession	_____ Perseverations	
	_____ Depersonalization	_____ Suicidal Ideation	
Hallucinations	_____ None	_____ Auditory	_____ Visual
	_____ Olfactory	_____ Gustatory	_____ Somatic
		_____ Tactile	
Judgment	_____ Good	_____ Fair	_____ Poor
Insight	_____ Good	_____ Fair	_____ Poor
Impulse Control	_____ Good	_____ Fair	_____ Poor

Initial Diagnosis

Impression

I. _____

II. _____

III. _____

IV. _____

V. _____

Recommended

Treatment

Plan–Level of

Care

Initial Treatment Plan–Level of Care

_____Individual Therapy

_____Group Therapy

_____Brief Psychotherapy

_____Supportive Psychotherapy

_____Cognitive Restructuring

_____Specialized Group

_____Child Protective Services

_____Chemical Dependency Treatment

_____Self-Esteem Enhancement

_____Potential Violence

_____Medical Evaluation with PCP

_____Medical Referral

_____Social Skills Training

_____Problem Solving–Conflict Resolution

_____Stress Management

_____Other

_____Behavior Modification

_____Partial Hospitalization

_____Pain Management

_____Legal Alert

_____Psychological Testing

_____Substance Abuse Treatment

_____Hospitalization/Medical Detox

_____Intensive Outpatient Rehabilitation

_____Recovery Home–Halfway House

_____Recovery Monitoring–Maintenance

_____Relapse Prevention

_____Self-Help

_____Suicide Alert

_____Parent Counseling

_____Potential Abuse

Additional Information–Recommendations

_____

_____

_____

_____

_____

_____

_____   _____

Therapist Signature   Date

SUBSTANCE USE SURVEY

Name: _____   Date: _____

In order that we may match you to the most effective treatment, please answer the following questions thoroughly and accurately about the ways in which you and your family have used alcohol, drugs, and other substances that can affect you psychologically.

1. Think about any and all substances you have used and indicate how much you have used (amount) and how often (frequency). Then indicate all of the effects it had on you (mental, physical, family, legal, etc.).

Chemical	First use		Last use		Over the last 30 days			Method of use
	Age	Amount	Date	Amount	Amount	How often	Effects–Consequences	
Caffeine								
Tobacco								
Smoked								
Chewed								
Alcohol								
Marijuana								
Cocaine–crack								
Injected								
Smoked								
Snorted								
Inhalants								
Sleeping medications								
Anxiety medications								
Heroin								
Morphine								
Codeine								
Demerol								
LSD								
PCP								
Mushrooms								
Amphetamines								
Others								

2. If you use more than one substance, number their importance to use (#1 most important).

3. For each substance you currently use, what causes you to stop?
Enter one or more of these letters in the last column of #Z:
A=the money runs out; B=I use up my supply;
C=personal choice; D=unconsciousness;
E=achieved my purpose; F=other reasons.

4. How did you get the money to buy the substances?

_____

_____

_____

5. Which of these have you had? _____ Blackouts _____ Bad reactions _____ Withdrawal symptoms _____ Overdoses _____ Detoxification in a hospital _____ Detoxification on own _____ Detoxification with help from your medical doctor _____ Other problems

6. Family patterns of Substance Use:
Please describe the substance(s) used by family members.

| | | First use | | Last use | | Over the last 30 days | | |
Name	Chemical	Age	Amount	Date	Amount	Amount	How often	Effects
Father								
Mother								
Brothers–Sisters								
Spouse								
Other relatives								

Please add any other information you think is important: _____

_____

_____

_____

_____

_____

7. Prior Treatment for Substance Use:

Dates From	To	Type of program[a]	Voluntary? (Yes or No)	Length of treatment	Participation in aftercare programs (no, yes, which one(s))	which treatment was most helpful

[a]Use these codes: AA–NA = Alcoholics–Narcotics Anonymous; OC = outpatient counseling; ID = inpatient detoxification; IT = inpatient treatment (e.g., 28 day, etc.); O = other.

8. How do you describe your use of substances? ____social drinker ____heavy drinker ____an alcoholic ____a drinking problem ____recreational drug user ____an addict ____a drug problem. Please explain: _____

9. What do you get out of substance use (benefit)? _____

10. Have there been any consequences associated with substance use? _____

CHEMICAL DEPENDENCY ASSESSMENT
(Adapted from Johnson, 1997)

Date: _____

Name: _____

1. Description of Patient (identifying information):

   _____

   _____

   _____

   _____

2. Reason for Referral:

   _____

   _____

   _____

   _____

3. Patient's Perception of Chemical Use:

   _____

   _____

   _____

   _____

4. Patient's Treatment Expectations and Goals:

   _____

   _____

   _____

   _____

5. Effects of Lifestyle–Symptomatology
   a. Family (history of family problems in original and/or present family, including chemical dependency):

   _____

   _____

b. Social (description of peer association, isolation–hypersocialization):

_____

_____

c. Occupational–scholastic (absenteeism because of chemical use, decreased performance, dismissal):

_____

_____

d. Physical (emesis, blackouts–passouts, hallucinations, tremors, convulsions, serious injury–illness, surgery, handicaps):

_____

_____

e. Psychological–emotional (cognitive functioning, emotionality, paranoia, history of treatment, behavioral problems):

_____

_____

f. Spiritual (change or conflict within belief system):

_____

_____

g. Financial:

_____

_____

h. Legal implications (underage consumption, driving while under the influence, dealing; include disposition if any):

_____

_____

6. Impressions and Recommendations:

Client's Response to Therapist: ☐ cooperative ☐ fearful ☐ suspicious
☐ hostile ☐ negative ☐ other _____

Mental Status:

Mood   ____ normal ____ depressed ____ elevated ____ euphoric
                    ____ angry ____ irritable ____ anxious

Affect   ____ normal ____ broad ____ restricted ____ blunted
                    ____ flat ____ inappropriate ____ labile

Memory   ____ intact ____ short-term problems
                    ____ long-term problems

Processes   ____ normal ____ blocking ____ loose associations
                    ____ confabulations ____ flight of ideas
                    ____ ideas of reference
                    ____ grandiosity ____ paranoia ____ obsession
                    ____ perseverations ____ depersonalization
                    ____ suicidal ideation ____ homicidal ideation

Hallucinations   ____ none ____ auditory ____ visual ____ olfactory
                    ____ gustatory ____ somatic ____ tactile

Judgment   ____ good ____ fair ____ poor

Insight   ____ good ____ fair ____ poor

Impulse Control   ____ good ____ fair ____ poor

Client's Attitude toward Treatment: ☐ accepting ☐ neutral ☐ resistant
Communication: ☐ talkative ☐ satisfactory ☐ open ☐ guarded
☐ answers questions only ☐ other _____

7. Diagnostic Impression (Multiaxial):

I. _____

II. _____

III. _____

IV. _____

V. _____

_____   _____
Therapist   Date

CHEMICAL DEPENDENCY PSYCHOLOGICAL ASSESSMENT

Date: _____ Age: _____

Name: _____

Significant Other's Name: _____ Phone: _____

Religious–Ethnic–Cultural Background: _____

_____

Marital Status: _____ Children: _____

Living with Whom: _____

Present Support System (Family–Friends): _____

Chemical History:

Substance Use	Route	Age started	Amount	Frequency	Last Used	Length of use

Description of Presenting Chemical Dependency Problems: _____

_____

Previous Counseling:

When	Where	Therapist	Response to

Family–Significant Other Relationships–History of Chemical Use: _____

_____

_____

_____

Significant Other Relationships and History of Chemical Use: _____

_____

_____

_____

Effects of Chemical Dependency on Family–Support System: _____

_____

_____

_____

Daily Activities that: 1. support abstinence: _____

             2. encourage usage: _____

History of Sexual–Physical Abuse (victim–abuser): _____

_____

Sexual Orientation: _____

Education: _____

Vocational History: _____

Leisure–Social Interests: _____

_____

Current Occupation: _____

Current Employer: _____

Impact of Chemical Use on Job Performance: _____

_____

EAP?   Yes _____ No _____ Name: _____ Phone: _____

Socioeconomic–Financial Problems: _____

_____

_____

Legal _____   DUI: Yes _____ No _____   Court Ordered: Yes _____ No _____

Patient's Perceptions of Strengths and Weaknesses: _____

_____

_____

Preliminary Treatment Plan: List presenting problems based on initial assessment
                         of the client's physical, emotional, cognitive, and
                         behavioral status

Detox: Yes_____   No_____   Explain: _____

Rehab: Yes_____   No_____   Explain: _____

Problem #1: _____

Problem #2: _____

Problem #3: _____

_____

Immediate Treatment Recommendations to Address Identifying Problems: _____

_____

_____

_____

_____

_____   _____

Therapist   Date

SUBSTANCE USE HISTORY

| Check if used | Chemical classification | Past history | | | | Current use (last 6 months) | | | Comments (cost, chemical of choice) |
		Description of substance	First use (onset)	Age of regular use	Frequency and amount	Range of frequency (include date of last use)	Range of amount	Route of administration	
	Alcohol								
	Amphetamines								
	Cannabis								
	Cocaine								
	Hallucinogens								
	Inhalants								
	Opiates								
	Phenylcyclidine (PCP)								
	Sedatives– hypnotics– anxiolytics								

SUBSTANCE USE HISTORY: A PHASE REVIEW

Name: _____ Date of Birth: _____ Age: _____

Date: _____ Social Security No.: _____

Think of your substance use history in terms of three phases.

1. Early phase: Beginning of dependence, use to decrease inhibitions, social coping.

2. Middle phase: Increased use of defenses, changes in behavior, physical problems, relationship problems.

3. Late phase: Chronic, increased physical and psychological problems, obsessed with use and losses.

Early Phase

How many years in this phase? _____

Age first started? _____

Identify the following substance(s) used:

	Depressants alcohol sedatives hypnotics anxiolytics inhalants	Cannabinoids Combinations	Opioids heroin morphine codeine	Hallucinogens LSD mescaline mushrooms PCP Ecstasy	Stimulants amphetamines cocaine	Nicotine
How often have you used each substance (never, 1–4×/yr, 5–12×/yr, 2–7×/month, 2–4×/week, 5–7×/week, several times/day)?						
What was your maximum daily dose during heaviest use?						
Any psychological disabilities associated with use?						
Any physical disabilities associated with use?						
Treatment and hospitalizations associated with use?						
Number of legal problems– experiences?						
Number of times not caught doing something illegal under the influence?						

	Depressants alcohol sedatives hypnotics anxiolytics inhalants	Cannabinoids Combinations	Opioids heroin morphine codeine	Hallucinogens LSD mescaline mushrooms PCP Ecstasy	Stimulants amphetamines cocaine	Nicotine
				Identify the following substance(s) used:		
Number of times missed school–work associated with use?						
Loss of job–kicked out of school associated with use?						
Loss of relationship associated with use?						
Has use of substances changed your lifestyle in this phase?						

How many years in this phase? _____

Age first started? _____

Identify the following substance(s) used:

	Depressants alcohol sedatives hypnotics anxiolytics inhalants	Cannabinoids Combinations	Opioids heroin morphine codeine	Hallucinogens LSD mescaline mushrooms PCP Ecstasy	Stimulants amphetamines cocaine	Nicotine
How often have you used each substance (never, 1–4×/yr, 5–12×/yr, 2–7×/month, 2–4×/week, 5–7×/week, several times/day)?						
What was your maximum daily dose during heaviest use?						
Any psychological disabilities associated with use?						
Any physical disabilities associated with use?						
Treatment and hospitalization associated with use?						
Number of legal problems–experiences?						
Number of times not caught doing something illegal under the influence?						
Number of times missed school–work associated with use?						
Loss of job–kicked out of school associated with use?						
Loss of relationship associated with use?						
Has use of substances changed your lifestyle in this phase?						

Late Phase   How many years in this phase? _____

Age first started? _____

Identify the following substance(s) used:

	Depressants / alcohol / sedatives / hypnotics / anxiolytics / inhalants	Cannabinoids / Combinations	Opioids / heroin / morphine / codeine	Hallucinogens / LSD / mescaline / mushrooms / PCP / Ecstasy	Stimulants / amphetamines / cocaine	Nicotine
How often have you used each substance (never, 1–4×/yr, 5–12×/yr, 2–7×/month, 2–4×/week, 5–7×/week, several times/day)?						
What was your maximum daily dose during heaviest use?						
Any psychological disabilities associated with use?						
Any physical disabilities associated with use?						
Treatment and hospitalizations associated with use?						
Number of legal problems– experiences?						
Number of times not caught doing something illegal under the influence?						
Number of times missed school– work associated with use?						
Loss of job–kicked out of school associated with use?						
Loss of relationship associated with use?						
Has use of substances changed your lifestyle in this phase?						

FAMILY SUBSTANCE USE HISTORY

Patient Name: _____ Date of Birth: _____ Age: _____

Date: _____ Social Security No.: _____

Chemical name	Never	1–2 times per year	3–12 times per year	2–7 times per month	2–4 times per week	5–7 times per week	Several times per day
1. Paternal grandfather Substance 1: Substance 2:							
2. Paternal grandmother Substance 1: Substance 2:							
3. Maternal grandfather Substance 1: Substance 2:							
4. Maternal grandmother Substance 1: Substance 2:							
5. Father Substance 1: Substance 2:							
6. Mother Substance 1: Substance 2:							
7. Brothers Substance 1: Substance 2:							
8. Sisters Substance 1: Substance 2:							
9. Uncles Substance 1: Substance 2:							
10. Aunts Substance 1: Substance 2:							
11. Spouse Substance 1: Substance 2:							
12. Children Child A Substance 1: Substance 2: Child B Substance 1: Substance 2:							
13. Friends Substance 1: Substance 2:							

CHEMICAL DEPENDENCY PSYCHOSOCIAL ASSESSMENT: BRIEF FORM

Date: _____

Patient Name: _____ Age: _____

Significant Other Name: _____ Phone: _____

Religious–Ethnic–Cultural Background: _____

_____

Marital Status: _____ Children: _____

Living with Whom: _____

Present Support System (Family–Friends): _____

Chemical History:

Chemical use	Route	Age started	Amount	Frequency	Last used	Length of use

Description of Presenting Chemical Dependency Problems: _____

_____

Previous Counseling:

When	Where	Therapist	Response to treatment

Family–History of Chemical Use: _____

_____

_____

_____

Significant Other Relationships and History of Chemical Use: _____

_____

_____

_____

Effects of Chemical Dependence on Family–Support System: _____

_____

_____

_____

Daily Activities That   a. support abstinence: _____

                        b. encourage usage: _____

History of Sexual–Physical Abuse (Victim–Abuser): _____

_____

Sexual Orientation: _____

Education: _____

Vocational History: _____

Leisure–Social Interests: _____

_____

Current Occupation: _____

Current Employer: _____

Impact On Chemical Use on Job Performance: _____

_____

EAP?   Yes _____ No _____ Name: _____ Phone: _____

Socioeconomic–Financial Problems: _____

_____

_____

Legal: _____   DWI: Yes _____ No _____   Court Ordered: Yes _____ No _____

Patient's Perceptions of Strengths and Weakness: _____

_____

_____

Preliminary Treatment Plan: List presenting problems based on initial assessment of the client's physical, emotional, cognitive, and behavioral status.

Detox: Yes _____   No _____   Explain: _____

Rehab: Yes _____   No _____   Explain: _____

Problem #1: _____

Problem #2: _____

Problem #3: _____

Immediate treatment recommendations to address identifying problems: _____

_____

_____

_____

_____   _____
Therapist   Date

Please rate each drinking behavior on the scale as indicated.

Never	Rarely or infrequently	Half the time	Usually-mostly	Always	
0	1	2	3	4	
					Stops drinking when effects felt
					Eats when drinking
					Drinks to safe limit
					Drinks as part of other activity
					Enjoys social occasions where few drinks
					Drinks before party
					Annoyed by low drinking
					Continues to drink after party
					Looks forward to drinking times
					Drinks more than intends
					Enjoys social occasions only if drinking
					Sneaks drinks
					Extravagant when drinking
					Drinks whatever is available
					Attends nondrinking party
					Leaves nondrinking party
					Drinks when upset
					Buys enough alcohol for holidays
					Suffers loss of memory
					Suffers hangovers
					Treats hangover with drink
					Uneasy with talk of drinking
					Worries about drinking
					Drinking is part of doing most activities
					Goes on binges
					People disapprove of drinking
					Gets drunk without intending to
					Drinks regardless of consequences
					Drinks in morning
					Drinks alone
					Needs days to recuperate from drinking
					Drunk steadily
					Ashamed of habit
					Drinks to relieve depression
					Able to control drinking

SUBSTANCE ABUSE–DEPENDENCE PERSONAL EVALUATION

1. Age of first drug use?
2. What drug did you use?
3. Who introduced you to drugs?
4. What drug(s) did you go on to use after that?
5. What was your reason for using drugs?
6. Did you ever try to stop?
7. If so, what is it like when you are not using?
8. Do your friends use?
9. Are you easily influenced by others?
10. Family history of substance abuse?
11. Do you and your significant other use together?
12. How has drug abuse affected your life?
13. What do you see as your options?
14. What do you have to do to abstain from drug abuse?
15. Have you been in a treatment program before or attended 12-step meetings?
16. What do you feel like when you are using?
17. How do you think you benefit from using or what do you get out of it?
18. How do you view drug screening in the workplace or school?

OUTLINE FOR DIAGNOSTIC SUMMARY

Date: _____

Patient Name: _____

Date of Birth: _____

Sources of Information: Including but not limited to mental status exam, history and physical, psychiatric evaluation, psychosocial, and treatment plan.

Identification of the Patient: Demographic information, including but not limited to age, race, marital status, etc.

_____

_____

_____

_____

_____

Presenting Problems: Including but not limited to why the patient was hospitalized, abuse of over the counter or prescribed drugs, drug of choice, route of admission, frequency of use, pattern of use, medical problems, mood, affect, mental status, legal problems, etc.

_____

_____

_____

_____

_____

Treatment Plan–Recommendations–Goals: Including problem list, therapeutic interventions, and goals.

_____

_____

_____

_____

_____

Discharge Plan: Including but not limited to follow-up with therapy, a physician, a sponsor, a 12-step recovery program, vocational guidance, etc.

_____

_____

_____

_____

_____

_____   _____
Therapist   Date

WITHDRAWAL SYMPTOMS CHECKLIST
(ADAPTED FROM JOHNSON, 1997)

Ratings: 0 = none   1 = mild   2 = moderate   3 = severe

Psychological

___ Drowsiness

___ Excitability (jumpiness, restlessness)

___ Unreality

___ Poor memory–concentration

___ Confusion

___ Perceptual distortion

___ Hallucinations

___ Obsessions

___ Agoraphobia–phobias

___ Panic attacks

___ Agitation

___ Depression

___ Fear

___ Paranoid thoughts

___ Rage–aggression–irritability

___ Craving

Somatic

___ Headache

___ Pain (limbs, back, neck)

___ Pain (teeth, jaw)

___ Tingling–numbness, altered sensation (limbs, face, trunk)

___ Stiffness (limbs, back, jaw)

___ Weakness ("jelly legs")

___ Tremor

___ Muscle twitches

___ Ataxia (lack of muscle coordination)

___ Dizziness–lightheadedness

___ Blurred–double vision

___ Ringing in the ears

___ Speech difficulty

___ Hypersensitivity (light, sound, taste, smell)

___ Insomnia–nightmares

___ Nausea–vomiting

___ Abdominal pain

___ Diarrhea–constipation

___ Appetite–weight change

___ Dry mouth

___ Metallic taste

___ Difficulty swallowing

___ Skin rash–itching

___ Stuffy nose–sinusitis

___ Influenza-like symptoms

___ Sore eyes

___ Flushing–sweating

___ Palpitations

___ Overbreathing

___ Thirst

___ Frequency–polyuria, pain on micturition

___ Incontinence

___ Abnormal heavy periods

___ Breast pain–swelling

___ Other symptoms (specify)_____

FACTORS INDICATING A NEED FOR ADOLESCENT SUBSTANCE USE ASSESSMENT

PSYCHOLOGICAL–SOCIAL FACTORS

1. History of physical–emotional–sexual abuse
2. Parental substance abuse
3. Delinquent behavior
4. Peer reference group involved in delinquent behavior (criminal activity)
5. Negative change in academic performance
6. Negative change in physical health
7. Negative changes in appearance
8. Changes in friends (distant, secretive attitude)
9. Indication of serious psychological problems
   a. mood swings
   b. angry, irrational, threatening
   c. severe depression, isolation
   d. suicidal ideation
10. High-risk behaviors
    a. sexual promiscuity
    b. intravenous substance use
    c. sexual activity with intravenous substance use

SUBSTANCE USE ASSOCIATED FACTORS

1. Substance use during childhood–adolescence
2. Signs of intoxication
3. Use of substances before–during school
4. Peer reference group involved in substance use–drug culture
5. Regular use of one or more substances

ADOLESCENT SCREENING AND ASSESSMENT

There are numerous screening and assessment instruments. Whatever method chosen, the evaluation of adolescent substance use should explore (1) predisposing risk factors, (2) comorbid psychiatric disorders, (3) perpetuating risk factors, and (4) distortions in accuracy (frequency, amount, faking good–bad). Sources of information include (as per ethical–legal guidelines) the individual being assessed, peers, parents, employer(s), teachers–counselors, significant other, and physician.

SCREENING

1. Sources of information
   a. individual being assessed
   b. parent(s)

2. Method
   a. brief questionnaire
   b. brief clinical interview

3. Information
   a. history of substance use and severity
   b. family–home life
   c. peer relationships
   d. school status
   e. level of psychological–emotional functioning

ASSESSMENT

1. Sources of information
   a. individual being assessed
   b. parent(s)
   c. teachers–counselors
   d. physician
   e. peers
   f. employer
   g. significant other

2. Method
   a. structured interview
   b. standardized questionnaire
   c. observation–self-report
   d. diagnostic test

3. Information
   a. history of substance use and severity
   b. family–home life
   c. peer relationships–drug culture
   d. delinguency
   e. physical–emotional–sexual abuse
   f. academic performance–learning disabilities
   g. medical status
   h. personal strengths–weaknesses
   i. environmental strengths–weaknesses
   j. family dynamics
   k. sexual development and history
   l. leisure–recreation
   m. emotional–psychological functioning

DIAGNOSTIC CRITERIA FOR CODEPENDENCY

1. Continued investment of self-esteem in the ability to influence–control feelings and behavior, both in oneself and in others, in the face of serious adverse consequences. This form of manipulation results in detrimental consequences for all involved.

2. Assumption of responsibility for meeting others' needs, to the exclusion of acknowledging one's own needs.
3. Anxiety and boundary distortions around intimacy and separation.
4. Enmeshment in relationships with personality-disordered, chemically dependent, and impulse-disordered individuals.
5. Exhibits at least three of the following:
    a. excessive reliance in denial
    b. constriction of emotions (with or without dramatic outbursts)
    c. depression
    d. hypervigilance
    e. compulsions
    f. anxiety
    g. substance abuse
    h. recurrent victim of physical or sexual abuse
    i. stress-related medical illnesses
    j. has remained in a primary relationship with an active substance abuser for a least 2 years without seeking outside support
    k. anger and resentment
    l. controlling and martyr identity

The author acknowledges that codependency is not a formal diagnosis. Therefore, it is offered as an assessment outline of characteristics often found in the partner or other significant relationships of the impulse-control-diserded individual. The dynamics of such a relationship acts to maintain dysfunctional behaviors. The brief outline has been added to this chapter highlight the importance of assessment beyond the identified patient.

SPECIAL TOPIC: EMPLOYMENT SETTING

The source for this section is Employee Assistance Professionals Association, Inc. This information is to educate regarding workplace issues and is not a substitute for CEAP Certification or legal consultation and recommendation.

EMPLOYER AND SUPERVISORY TRAINING

Unless one is an employer who also serves in a supervisory capacity, it is the supervisor who serves as the link between management and the workforce. In such a role, supervisors are key to the successful implementation of substance abuse policy. Therefore, it is helpful for supervisors to be trained in:

1. Identifying and documenting job performance and on the job behavior that may be indicative of substance abuse.
2. Identifying evidence of on the job use of substances, impairment, or work decompensation associated with substance use.
3. Constructive confrontation techniques to facilitate a positive outcome.

Additionally supervisors need to have identified professional resources and a protocol for referring troubled employees for assessment and testing those suspected of violating company policy. In association with this, an employer and supervisor should consider the following issues:

1. What interventions will trigger the desired action by the employee so that he or she will return to being a productive part of the workforce?
2. In what way do federal, state, and local regulations affect the manner in which an employer–supervisor intervenes?
3. What labor–management agreements affect the employer–supervisor options for intervention?
4. What are the available resources for addressing substance abuse problems and referral sources?
5. What disciplinary approach does the company have in place?
6. If the employee is temporarily relieved from duty, the following are necessary:
   a. evaluation documenting that the employee is ready (and when) to return to work
   b. any conditions or limitations associated with the release to return to work

A supervisor has the primary role of being an observer. They monitor job performance to ensure that all tasks are completed in accordance with specifications, quality, requirements, and deadlines. Supervisors are to document any deterioration or alteration in work performance, attendance, and/or any violation(s) of company policies and regulations. When an employee begins to show a consistent pattern of problematic behavior, it is necessary to take action. Avoiding or ignoring the situation acts to perpetuate the problem. The employee is likely to pay attention to any threat associated with his or her employment and be motivated to seek appropriate professional intervention. There are numerous warning signs, and if caught early and with the appropriate intervention, the company can maintain the employment of a good employee and the individual has been given the opportunity to get his or her life on track.

HOW TO CONSTRUCTIVELY CONFRONT THE EMPLOYEE

Once patterns of behavior have been carefully documented that demonstrate deterioration in job performance, it is time to directly confront the employee with the observed issues. It is important to avoid being accusatory during the interview. Instead, convey the goal to resolve the situation from the perspective of the impact that it is having upon the company. Remember, this issue is in the professional realm and not a personal life realm. Depending on the circumstances, there may initially be a warning to the employee regarding job performance. If this is the situation, the employee should be made aware of what criteria will be closely monitored with the anticipation of improved performance.

Obviously, specific goals and objectives should be determined for and conveyed to the employee. Short-term work goals offer feedback and reinforcement to the employee for his or her efforts and leave him or her with a feeling of accomplishment. The employee must feel valued. Additionally, the short-term goals should be linked to overall performance goals and responsible behavior(s) to be demonstrated by the employee. In the end, it is the employee who will either comply with job performance expectations and related job security or choose not to.

The information presented and decisions made during any meeting with an employee should be documented. Make sure that the employee is made aware of resources, whether there is a referral for assessment and what that means, and that he or she is a valued asset to the company, who looks forward to the issue(s) being resolved. Be sure to thoroughly document the content of all meetings. A follow-up discussion with the employee is recommended.

The following guidelines are recommended when confronting an employee:

1. Ensure a clear understanding of the nature and scope of job responsibilities.
2. Provide an expectation of the level of job performance.
3. Records should be thorough and specific in their documentation of all work-related issues.
4. Be consistent in the treatment of all employees (no exceptions).
5. Be firm.
6. Be assertive.
7. Be yourself.
8. Do not be judgmental.
9. Do not diagnose—that is what a referral for an assessment is for.
10. Focus the interview on job performance exclusively.
11. Be clear, concise, and direct.
12. Prepare your discussion based upon facts.
13. Confrontations are done respectfully and in private.
14. Do not tolerate excuses or denial of reality.
15. Stay focused, do not get derailed from the subject.
16. Stay cool, do not raise your voice or lose your temper.
17. Emphasize the employee's strengths.
18. Establish specific goals at the onset of the meeting.
19. Do not interrogate.
20. Do not negotiate.
21. Listen with understanding to what the employee has to say.
22. Follow up.
23. Keep your word.
24. Maintain confidentiality.

If the employee admits that there is a problem when assistance is offered, keep your word and work with the employee. This is not any easier for the employee than it is for the supervisor. If there are supportive measures that can be taken on behalf of the employee, then take them. This makes a positive statement about the employee's value to the company.

One of the most challenging situations for the supervisor is when the employee responds in a manner of complete denial about substance abuse when the evidence has been quite clear. Under such circumstances, it is best to use the services of a professional trained in the specific area of substance abuse for an assessment and intervention recommendations. If a supervisor is struggling with anxiety associated with confronting employees that interferes with his or her job duties or he or she takes a parental role with employees, the supervisor may be enabling those with a substance abuse problem.

SUMMARY OUTLINE OF HOW TO CONSTRUCTIVELY CONFRONT AN EMPLOYEE WITH A PROBLEM

DO:

1. Arrange for an adequate, uninterrupted period of time.
2. Meet in private.

3. Be straightforward. Stick to concrete, documented facts, observations the employee cannot refute.

4. Focus entirely on the deteriorated job performance or erratic on the job behavior.

5. Use descriptive statements.

6. Establish and maintain eye contact.

7. Show respect for the employee.

8. Maintain control of the discussion.

9. Be honest. Speak with authority.

10. Accept no excuses.

11. Explain the company's alcohol and drug abuse policy.

12. Explain the need for a drug test.

13. Explain the consequences of both positive and negative test results.

DO NOT:

1. Become angry or argumentative.

2. Lecture or talk down to.

3. Judge behavior or motives.

4. Ask why the employee does certain things; "why" serves as an excuse.

5. Be put off by sympathy provoking tactics, which could include crying.

6. Diagnose the problem.

7. Accuse the employee of alcohol or drug abuse.

8. Discuss possible disciplinary actions.

SUPERVISORS AS ENABLERS

Supervisors who may be taking the role of enabler with employees demonstrate the following characteristics:

1. Parental role.

2. Make excuses for employees' poor performance.

3. Stand in the way of employees directly taking responsibility for job performance.

4. Instead of appropriately intervening, "believe" that employees will resolve the issues on their own.

5. Allow a problem to continue, which is a detriment to the company and the employees.

6. Cover for employees.

7. Offer unwanted advice to employees.

8. Feel angry when their help is not accepted.

9. Do work for others who are capable of doing their work.

10. Overcommit themselves.

11. Want everyone to like them.

12. Try to please others instead of maintaining focus of their job.
13. Believe that other people are their problem.
14. Feel angry, used, and taken for granted.
15. Take responses in the workplace personally.
16. Feel pressured and overworked.
17. Find that "needy" employees are attracted to them.
18. Ignore problems or pretend they are not happening.
19. Focus energy on the problems of others and/or try to catch them misbehaving.
20. Try to control events and people.

DEFENSIVE STRATEGIES OF EMPLOYEES

Defense	Employee	Supervisor
Excuses and sympathy	Employee will have a good reason for everything that happens. "You'd have the same problems I do if you had a wife–husband like mine" or "if you were going through what I have been going through."	Stay focused on the work issue. "You may have problems at home. I am concerned about your performance, and my data here say you are not doing your job."
Apologies and promises	"I'm really sorry. You know that! I'll never do it that way again."	Remain focused on the problem. "I appreciate your apology, but what you did is serious."
Switching	"I know all about that, but look what a good job I've done on that job."	"You did well on that job. I want good work on all jobs. You've had more problem jobs than successful ones lately. Let's review the last 3 months."
Anger	"Dammit!! One mistake and the roof falls in after 15 years of killing myself for this place."	"I think it's important that you listen. Getting angry won't help anyone. I'm concerned about your performance and I'm not talking about one mistake. Let's review the history of issues."
Emotional: tears and helplessness	"I don't know what to do. I'll never get out of this mess" (crying).	"I appreciate and understand how you feel. I want you to know that I want to help, which is why I set up this meeting. You have been a valuable part of our organization."
Deflecting	"But everyone else is lax about that."	"Let's review this list of problems again. I'm talking with you now about your work performance."
Self-pity	"I knew this would happen. I've never been able to do anything right."	"I wouldn't be taking this time to talk with you if I didn't have faith in you. So let's move on to talk about what can be done to help you."
Innocence	"It's not my fault. You let me down. I don't get any help at all around here."	"Be realistic. You have done good work. I want more of that from your department, which is why I set up this meeting."

WARNING SIGN CHECKLIST

Physical signs or condition
___ Weariness, exhaustion
___ Unusual untidiness
___ Yawning excessively
___ Sleepiness (nodding)
___ Poor concentration
___ Easily distracted

Actions
___ Withdrawn or improperly talkative
___ Spends excessive amount of time on telephone
___ Argumentative
___ Has exaggerated sense of self-importance
___ Displays violent behavior
___ Avoids talking with supervisor regarding work issues

Work patterns
___ Inconsistency in quality of work
___ High–low periods of productivity
___ Poor judgment–more mistakes than usual and general carelessness
___ Lapses in concentration
___ Difficulty in recalling instructions
___ Difficulty in remembering own mistakes
___ Using more time to complete work–missing deadlines
___ Increased difficulty in handling complex situations
___ Difficulty in sorting out priority items from nonessential ones
___ Increased personal phone calls

Accidents
___ Taking needless risks
___ Disregard for safety of others
___ Higher than average accident rate on the job
___ Mood swings

Absenteeism
___ Acceleration of absenteeism and tardiness, especially Mondays, Fridays, and before and after holidays
___ Frequent unreported absences, later explained as "emergencies"
___ Unusual or questionable excuses for absences
___ Unusually high incidence of colds, flu, upset stomach, headaches
___ Frequent use of unscheduled vacation time
___ Leaving work area more than necessary (e.g., frequent trips to water fountain and bathroom)
___ Unexplained disappearance from the job with difficulty locating employee
___ Requesting to leave work early for various reasons

Mood
___ Appears to be depressed or extremely anxious all the time
___ Irritable
___ Suspicious
___ Complains about others
___ Emotional unsteadiness (e.g., outbursts, of crying)

Relationship to others on the job
___ Overreaction to real or imagined criticism
___ Avoiding and withdrawing from peers
___ Complaints from co-workers
___ Borrowing money from fellow employees
___ Complaints of difficulties at home, such as separation, divorce, and child discipline problems
___ Persistent job transfer requests
___ Refusal to accept authority
___ Frequent non-work-related visits by strangers or employees from other areas
___ Unauthorized meetings with employees in remote work areas

Referral for Assessment _____ Yes _____ No

_____   _____
Employee's Name   Supervisor's Name

_____   _____
Employer's Name   Supervisor's Signature

                                    _____
                                    Date

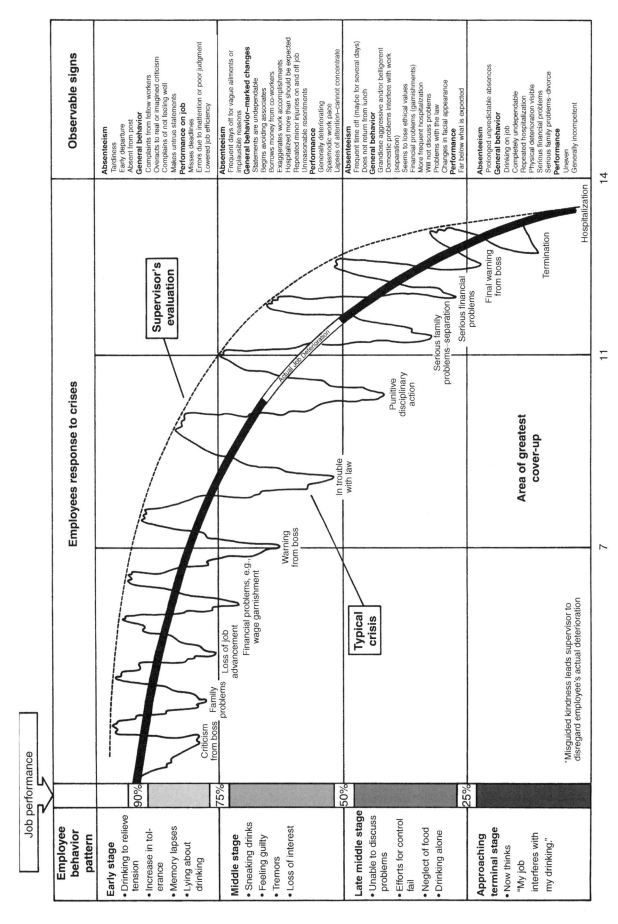

FIGURE 5.2 Behavioral Pattern of Employee with Drinking Problem

PREVENTION

Prevention refers to the activities or factors that (preferably) prevent the onset of substance use or decrease–stabilize those currently using substances. Therefore, the goal of prevention is to promote healthy behaviors, decisions, and environments that will prevent, reduce, or eliminate the problematic use of substances. There are two central components of this perspective, which aims to assist people to change:

1. Increasing positive health behaviors (protective factors).
2. Decreasing or eliminating health compromising behaviors (risk factors).

A basic description of the stages of intervention is as follows:

1. Primary prevention is a proactive effort that identifies factors that contribute to the possible development of substance abuse problems. Children and adolescents are given the highest priority in prevention planning. Basic components are information, education, and alternatives.
2. Secondary prevention involves early identification of developing problems and appropriate intervention, thus eliminating further development. Basic components are alternatives, treatment, and relapse prevention.
3. Tertiary prevention is primarily focused on decreasing the prevalence of existing problems, preventing further decompensation, and preventing relapse. Basic components are relapse prevention, aftercare, and continuing recovery.

Helping people to change old behaviors and learn new behaviors in the pursuit of health is a biopsychosocial issue. The associated education, support, and facilitation can be promoted in many different settings, such as home, school, work, church, formal programs, and community-based programs. It can take place on a 1-to-1 small group, or lecture level, ranging in intensity and cost-effectiveness. Examples of the topics for such classes might include:

1. substance use education
2. smoking cessation
3. stress management
4. relaxation, meditation
5. yoga
6. exercise–swimming
7. family wellness
8. couple's communication
9. prenatal education
10. parent effectiveness training
11. family–focused prevention efforts
12. nutrition

13. weight management
14. importance of dental health
15. critical problem solving
16. time management
17. high-risk health behaviors

A needs assessment of the population that is being targeted for prevention is necessary for the best use of resources and obtaining the best outcome. Children and adolescents get the highest priority in prevention planning, roughly corresponding to primary and secondary prevention on the prevention continuum and all three spheres of influence in the public health model. Primary prevention identifies factors that predispose or in some other way contribute to the possible development of substance use problems and the necessary changes in the individual and environment to prevent the initial occurrence of substance use. Secondary prevention strategies involve early identification of developing problems, skill development, and facilitating proactive resources. Tertiary prevention has the goal of decreasing the prevalence of existing the problems, preventing further deterioration (stabilization), and facilitating the development of appropriate environmental–societal resources.

PREVENTION MODELS

Two basic and well-known prevention models are the continuum of prevention model and the public health model. NIDA uses a continuum model of prevention, whereas NIAAA has adopted the public health approach to prevention of substance abuse. The continuum of prevention model has been traditionally initiated at three stages of problem development, offering a continuum of intervention from educative information on one end to recovery on the other end. The public health model identifies three overlapping components with numerous factors that are related to substance abuse. Like the components of this model, the causes of substance abuse and addiction are overlapping and impossible to separate.

The Continuum of Prevention Model

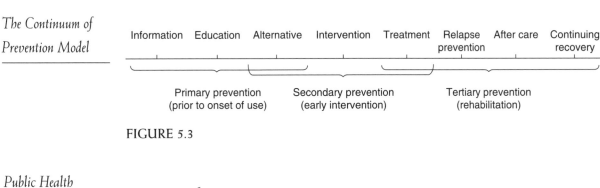

FIGURE 5.3

Public Health Model

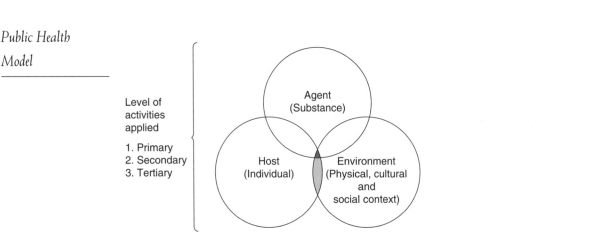

FIGURE 5.4

The risk factors associated with each component are as follows:

1. Agent (substance associations)
   a. accessibility
   b. affordability
   c. addictive properties
   d. family acceptance of use
   e. social acceptance
   f. perceived benefits
   g. harmful effects on health
   h. unenforced laws
   i. perceived benefits of use
   j. addictive properties

2. Host (individual and all relational associations)
   a. age of first use
   b. transgenerational use
   c. family use of substances
   d. family attitudes about use
   e. early antisocial behavior
   f. genetic vulnerability–predisposition
   g. inappropriate coping skills
   h. cognitive deficits
   i. lacks effective social and management skills
   j. low self-esteem
   k. mainstream alienation
   l. rejection of prosocial values–behaviors
   m. lack of involvement in social, recreational, and cultural activities
   n. psychological problems
   o. lacks close attachment to parents–family
   p. deficient skill development
   q. lacks refusal skills
   r. loss of job

3. Environment (cultural, social, physical)
   a. availability
   b. family substance-related behaviors–patterns of use
   c. family acceptance of use
   d. peer relationships (substance use culture)
   e. economic deprivation
   f. social deprivation
   g. frequent residential moves
   h. conflict between modeling and media messages
   i. condoned use by community
   j. rapid changes in neighborhood populations
   k. external stressors
   l. misleading advertising–media portrayal
   m. use of substances viewed as normal
   n. community resources

o. public policy

p. laws

According to Lewis *et al.* (1994), both models indicate that treatment and rehabilitation programs are focused on late stage–chronic substance abusers, therefore demonstrating that treatment is an incomplete and inadequate response to substance abuse problems. The logical deduction then is that treatment is unlikely to result in a significant decrease in the prevalence of substance abuse and that a comprehensive prevention model is in great need of implementation.

PREVENTION PROGRAMS

Prevention programs should be designed to enhance and encourage positive health behaviors and decrease health compromising behaviors.

1. Positive health behaviors
   a. strong, positive family relationships
   b. prosocial behaviors and values
   c. parental monitoring and involvement (children–adolescents)
   d. consistency in enforcing clear rules–limits–boundaries
   e. successful academic performance
   f. accept conventional norms associated with substance use
   g. exercise–pleasurable activities
   h. positive social support system

2. Compromising health behaviors
   a. parental use of substances
   b. family attitudes about substances
   c. experience of ineffective parenting
   d. lack of attachment and nurturing
   e. poor social skills
   f. peer group supportive of antisocial behavior
   g. perception of substance use–abuse approval
   h. negative family, peer, and community environment
   i. lacks achieving academic–professional success

Goals of
prevention
programs

Information is a prerequisite for change. However, information needs to be supplemented with techniques that increase motivation, facilitate skill development, identify resources, and change the environment. Therefore, program components must encompass family relationships, peer relationships, academic–work environment, and the community. For children and adolescents, there must be developmentally appropriate intervention methods, and caregivers must participate in order to learn appropriate parenting strategies and reinforce what is being learned about substances. The creation of interactive environments such as peer discussion groups and skill development in addition to didactic education increases and reinforces self-awareness, choices, and associated consequences. In general, prevention programs should offer:

1. General life skills training
2. Substance abuse education

3. Refusal skills training

4. Clarifying values and strengthening a positive attitude

5. Strengthening the commitment for abstinence

6. Increased social competency

7. Knowledge of community resources for appropriate referrals

8. Programming that is developmentally appropriate and culturally sensitive

9. Adaptation to address the specific nature of substance abuse in the community

10. Adequate length with repeat interventions to reinforce original prevention goals (the higher the level of risk, the more intensive the intervention)

MODEL FOR EFFECTIVE HEALTH EDUCATION (ADAPTED FROM GREEN *et al.*, 1980)

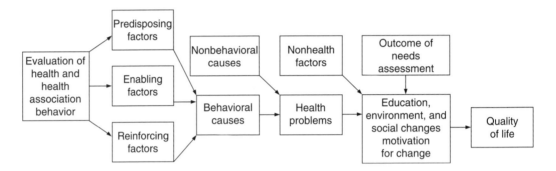

FIGURE 5.5

1. Predisposing factors
   a. involve beliefs, attitudes, and perceptions of the target population
   b. provide motivation or lack of motivation for change

2. Enabling factors
   a. availability of skills, facilities, and personal–community resources
   b. facilitate or hinder change

3. Reinforcing factors: Positive and negative consequences that encourage or discourage behavioral change

REFERENCES

Abbott, M. W. (1984). Loss of control and treatment outcome in alcoholism. *J. Studies Alcohol* 45:46–52.

Alcoholics Anonymous World Services, Inc. (1996). Membership Survey. 475 Riverside Drive, New York, NY 10115 (212) 870-3400.

American Psychiatric Association (1994). "Diagnostic and Statistical Manual of Mental Disorders," 4th ed. Washington, DC: American Psychiatric Association.

Annis, H. M. (1982a). "Cognitive Appraisal Questionnaire." Toronto: Addiction Research Foundation of Ontario.

Annis, H. M. (1982b). "Inventory of Drinking Situations." Toronto: Addiction Research Foundation of Ontario.

Annis, H. M. (1982c). "Situational Confidence Questionnaire." Toronto: Addiction Research Foundation of Ontario.

Bedi, A. (1987). Alcoholism, drug abuse, and other psychiatric disorders. *In* "Alcohol and Drug Abuse Handbook" (R. E. Herrington, G. R. Jacobson & D. G. Binzer, Eds.), pp. 346–384. St. Louis, MO: Warren H. Green, Inc.

Berg, J. K., & Miller, S. D. (1992). "Working with the Problem Drinker." New York: W. W. Norton.

Carroll, J. F. (1984). Substance abuse problem checklist: A new clinical aid for drug and/or alcohol treatment dependency. *J. Substance Abuse Treatment* 1:31–36.

Cox, W. M. (1983). "Identifying and Measuring Alcoholic Personality Characteristics." San Francisco, CA: Josey-Bass.

Dahlstrom, W. G., Welsh, G. S., & Dahlstrom, L. (1972). "An MMPI Handbook, Vol. 1, Clinical Interpretation," Minneapolis, MN: University of Minnesota Press.

Davidson, R., Rolnick, S., & MacEwan, I., Eds. (1991). "Counseling the Problem Drinker." London: Routelede.

DiClemente, C. C., & Hughes, S. O. (1990). Stages of change profiles in outpatient alcoholism treatment. *J. Substance Abuse* 2:217–235.

Donovan, M., & Mareatt, G. A., Eds. (1988). "Measurement of Addictive Behaviors." New York: Guilford Press.

Employee Assistance Professionals Association, Inc. 2101 Wilshire Blvd., #500, Srlington, VA 22201-3062.

Ewing, J. A. (1984). Detecting alcoholism: The CAGE questionnaire. *J. Am. Med. Assoc.* **252** (14): 1905–1907.

Frances R. J., & Miller S. I. (1998). "Clinical Textbook of Addictive Disorders," 2nd ed. New York: Guilford Press.

Friedman, A. S., & Utada, A. A. (1989). A method for diagnosis and planning the treatment of adolescent drug abusers (the Adolescent Drug Abuse Diagnosis (ADAD) instrument). *J. Drug Education* **19**(4):285–312.

Goldstein, S. G., & Chotlos, J. W. (1965). Dependency and brain damage in alcoholics. *Perceptual Motor Skills* **21**:135–150.

Goldstein, S. G., & Lenden J. D. (1969). Multivariate classification of alcoholics by means of the MMPI. *J. Abnormal Psychol.* **74**:661–669.

Green, L. W., Kreuter, M. W., Deeds, S. G., & Partridge, K. B., Eds. (1980). "Health Education and Planning: A Diagnostic Approach." Palo Alto, CA: Mayfield Publishing.

Harrell, A. V., & Wirtz, P. W. (1989). "Alcohol Drinking Index (ADI)." Psychological Assessment Resources, Inc. P.O. Box 998, Odessa, FL 33556.

Harrell, T. H., Honkaker, L. M., & Davis, E. (1991). Cognitive and behavioral dimensions of dysfunction in alcohol and polydrug abusers. *J. Substance Abuse* **3**:415–426.

Hater, J. J., & Simpson, D. D. (1981). "The PMES Information Form on Family, Friends, and Self: A Report on Scale Construction, Report to Drug Abuse Prevention Division and the Texas Department of Community Affairs." Fort Worth, TX: Institute of Behavioral Research, Texas Christian University.

Hay, W., & Nathan, P. (1982). "Clinical Case Studies in the Behavioral Treatment of Alcoholism." New York: Plenum.

Helzer, J. E., & Pryzbeck, T. R. (1988). The co-occurrence of alcoholism with other psychiatric disorders in the general population and its impact on treatment. *J. Studies Alcohol* **49**(3): 219–224.

Horn, J. L., Wanberg, K., & Foster, F. M. (1987). "Guide to the Alcohol Use Inventory." Minneapolis, MN: National Computer Systems.

Jacobson, G. R. (1989). A comprehensive approach to pretreatment evaluation: 1. Detection, assessment and diagnosis of alcoholism. *In* "Handbook of Alcoholism Treatment Approaches. Effective Alternatives" (R. K. Hester & W. R. Miller, Eds.), pp. 17–43 Boston: Allyn & Bacon.

Johnson, S. L. (1997). "The Therapist's Guide to Clinical Intervention," San Diego: Academic Press.

Krotz, D., Krominowski, R., Beernston, B., & Sipe, J. (1988). "ACHI: The assessment of Chemical Health Inventory (Brochure), Renovex, Inc. Strategies for Health." Minneapolis, MN: Renovex, Inc.

Krug, S. E. (1981). "Interpreting 16 PF Profile Patterns." Champaign, IL: Institute for Personality and Ability Testing.

Lewis, J. A., Dana, R. Q., & Blevins, G. A. (1994). Substance abuse counseling: An individualized approach (2nd ed.), Belmont CA: Wadsworth, Inc.

Lowinson, J. H., Ruiz, P., Millman, R. B., & Langrod, J. G., Eds. (1992). "Substance Abuse: A Comprehensive Textbook." Baltimore, MD: Williams and Wilkins.

MacAndrews, C. (1983). Alcoholic personality or personalities: Scale and profile data from the MMPI. *In* "Identifying and Measuring Alcoholic Personality Characteristics (W. M. Cox, Ed.), pp 73–85. San Francisco, CA: Josey-Bass.

Maistro, S. A., Galizio, M., & Carey, K. (1985). Individual differences in substance abuse. *In* "Determinants of Substance Abuse: Biological, Psychological, and Environmental Factors." (M. Galizio & S. A. Maistro, Eds.). New York: Plenum.

Marlatt, G. A., & Miller, W. R. (1987). "The Brief Drinker Profile." Odessa, FL: Psychological Assessment Resources.

McClellan A. T., Luborsky, L., Woody, G. E., & O'Brien, C. P. (1980). An improved diagnostic evaluation instrument for substance abuse patients: The Addiction Severity Index. *J. Nervous Mental Dis.* **168**:26–33.

Miller, N. S., Belkin, B. M., & Gibbons, R. (1994). Clinical diagnosis of substance use disorders in private psychiatric populations. *J. Substance Abuse Treatment* **2**(4):387–392.

Miller, P. M., & Mastria, M. A. (1977). "Alternatives to Alcohol Abuse: A Social Learning Model." Champaign, IL: Research Press.

Miller, W. R. (1976). Alcoholism scales and objective assessment methods: A review. *Psychol. Bull.*, **83**:649–670.

Miller, W. R. (1989). Increasing motivation for change. *In* "Handbook of Alcoholism Treatment Approaches" (R. K. Hester & W. R. Miller, Eds.), pp. 67–80. New York: Pergamon Press.

Miller, W. R., & Marlatt, G. A. (1984). "Manual for the comprehensive Drinking Profile:" Odessa, FL: Psychological Assessment Resources.

Miller, W. R., & Rollnick, S. (1991). "Motivational Interviewing: Preparing People to Change Addictive Behavior." New York: Guilford Press.

Miller, W. R., & Salcedo, C. F. (1985). Assessment of neurological impairment and brain damage in problem drinkers. *In* "Alcoholism: Theory, Research, and Treatment" (W.R. Miller, Ed.), pp. 141–195. Lexington, MA: Ginn Press.

Miller, W. R., & Taylor, C. A. (1980). Relative effectiveness of bibliotherapy, individual and group self-control training in the treatment of problem drinkers. *Addictive Behav.* **15**:13–24.

Mirin, S. M., Weiss, R. D., & Michael, J. (1990). Psychopathology in substance abusers: Diagnosis and treatment. *Am. J. Drug Alcohol Abuse* **14**:139–157.

National Institute on Drug Abuse (1989). Drug abuse curriculum for employee assistance program professionals. (DHHS Publication No. ADM 89-1587, pp. i–vi, 98). Washington DC: U.S. Government Printing Office.

Parsons, O. A., Butters, N., & Nathan, P. E. (1987). "Neuropsychology of Alcoholism: Implications for Diagnosis and Treatment." New York: Guilford Press.

Porkonoy, A. D., Miller, B. A., & Kaplan, H. B. (1972). The brief MAST: A shortened version of the Michigan Alcohol Screening Test. *Am. J. Psychol.*, **129**:342–345.

Potash, A., Gold, M., & Extein, I. (1982). The use of the clinical laboratory. *In* "Inpatient Psychiatry: Diagnosis and Treatment" (L. Sederer, Ed.), pp. 205–221. Baltimore, MD: Williams & Wilkins.

Prochaska, J., & DiClemente, C. C. (1982). Transtheoretical therapy: Toward a more integrative model of change. *Psychotherapy: Theory, Res., Practice* **19**:276–288.

Prochaska, J., & DiClemente, C. (1986). Toward a comprehensive model of change. *In* "Treating the Addictive Behaviors: Processes of Change" (W. R. Miller & N. Weather, Eds.), pp. 3–27. New York: Plenum Press.

Rahdert, E. R. (1991). The Adolescent Assessment/Referral System Manual. DHHS Publication No. (ADM) 91-1735. Rockville, MD: U.S. Department of Health and Human Services, Alcohol, Drug Abuse, and Mental Health Administration, National Institute on Drug Abuse.

Ross, H. E., Glaser, F. B., & Germanson, T. (1988). The prevalence of psychiatric disorders in patients with alcohol and other drug problems. *Arch. Gen. Psychiatry.* **45**:1023–1031).

Russel, M., Martier, S. S. Sokol, R. J., Jacobson, S., & Bottoms, S. (1991), Screening for pregnancy risk drinking . TWEAKING the tests (Abstract). *Alcoholism: Clin. Exp. Res.* **15**(2):368.

Schottenfield, R., Carroll, K., & Rounsaville, B. (1993). Comorbid psychiatric disorders and cocaine abuse. *In* "Cocaine Treatment: Research and Clinical Perspectives" (F. K. Tims & C. G. Leukefeld, Eds.), Research Monograph No. 135, pp. 31–47. Rockville, MD: National Institute on Drug Abuse.

Schwab, P. (1997). Scientific meeting on drug testing of alternative specimens and technologies: Proceedings of the DHHS/Publication Health Service Substance Abuse and Mental Health Services Administration/Drug Testing Advisory Board. Rockville, MD: National Institute on Drug Abuse.

Sobell, L. C., Cooper, A. M., Cooper, T. C., & Sanders, B. (1980). Developing a prototype for evaluating alcohol treatment effectiveness. *In* "Evaluating Alcohol and Drug Abuse Treatment Effectiveness: Recent Advances" (L. C. Sobell, M. B. Sobell, & E. Wards, Eds.), pp. 129–150. Elinsford, NY: Pergamon Press.

Tarter, R. E. (1990). Evaluation and treatment of adolescent substance abuse. A decision tree method. *Am. J. Drug Alcohol Abuse* **16** (1–2):1–46.

Verebey, K. (1992). Diagnostic laboratory screening for drug abuse. *In* "Substance Abuse: A Comprehensive Textbook" (J. H. Lowinson, R. B. Millman, & J. G. Langrod, Eds.), pp. 425–436, Baltimore, MD: Williams & Wilkins.

Winters, K. C., & Henley, G. A. (1989). "Personal Experience Inventory Test and Manual." Los Angeles, CA: Western Psychological Services.

Winters, K. C., & Henley, G. A. (1987). Advances in the assessment of adolescent chemical dependency: Development of a chemical use problem severity scale. *Psychol. of Addictive Behav.* 1:146–153.

Zivich, J. M. (1981). Alcoholic subtypes and treatment effectiveness. *J. Consulting Clin. Psychol.* **49**:72–80.

Part III

Chapter 6

Treatment Guidelines

**General Substance Abuse
Treatment Diagram**

No Intervention Needed

↓

Brief Intervention–Outpatient-treatment
has not been using for some time
has not used substances at the addictive level

↓

Self-Help Groups
12-step program
Smart Recovery, Rational Recovery, etc.

↓

Outpatient Treatment Program
medication evaluation–monitoring
individual therapy
marital–family therapy
relapse prevention
social skills training
mood–affect management
community reinforcement

↓

Intensive Outpatient

↓

Rehab–Residential

↓

Detox

According to Whircomb's (1999) review of a California study, the cost to treat a substance-dependent individual is only 10% of the expense of incarcerating him or her for possession of a substance. He also states that treatment is no less necessary than prevention, citing that prevention does not come early enough and that the root of many problems in our society is associated with addicts, which signifies that treatment is imperative.

DSM IV sets forth the diagnostic criteria for substance abuse and dependence. The most striking aspect of these criteria when applied is the range of multiple variables that have an influence on the individual's experience: gender, age, size–weight, consumption, pattern(s) of use, consequences of use, personality, ethnicity, and social–family environment. Another facet or perspective of experience includes problems associated with medical diagnoses, legal issues, occupation, and general health behaviors.

BIOPSYCHOSOCIAL PERSPECTIVE

Putting all of the information and resources into action allows for a comprehensive case formulation, which encourages movement toward a multitude of intervention strategies necessary for the development of individualized treatment planning. Substance abuse problems and the individuals who manifest them are diverse, which requires the broad-based view of the biopsychosocial treatment philosophy and individualized treatment planning. A review of the biopsychosocial components will elaborate this concept:

1. Bio: A biological system programmed to respond in a certain "individualized" manner to any given substance or combination of substances.
2. Psycho: Emotional, psychological, and cognitive factors. Characterological impairment, sensation-seeking (drive theory), adaptation, ego, and self-disturbances.
3. Social: Environmental factors associated with the initiation and maintenance of substance abuse. Social learning plays a role in developing and maintaining thoughts, beliefs, and behaviors.
   a. family system: role of abuser and family members in the maintenance of substance abuse
   b. drug subculture: comfort, familiarity, status
   c. substance using environment: comfort, familiarity, status

TABLE 6.1   The 12 Steps of Alcoholics Anonymous[a]

Step 1	We admitted we were powerless over alcohol—that our lives had become unmanageable.
Step 2	We came to believe that a power greater than ourselves could restore us to sanity.
Step 3	We made a decision to turn our will and our lives over to the care of God *as we understood Him.*
Step 4	We made a searching and fearless moral inventory of ourselves.
Step 5	We admitted to God, to ourselves, and to another human being the exact nature of our wrongs.
Step 6	We were entirely ready to have God remove all these defects of character.
Step 7	We humbly asked him to remove our shortcomings.
Step 8	We made a list of all persons we had harmed and became willing to make amends to them all.
Step 9	We made direct amends to such people wherever possible, expect when to do so would injure them or others.
Step 10	We continued to take personal inventory, and when we were wrong we promptly admitted it.
Step 11	We sought through prayer and meditation to improve our conscious contact with God *as we understood Him*, praying only for knowledge of his will for us and the power to carry that out.
Step 12	Having had a spiritual awakening as the result of these steps, we tried to carry this message to alcoholics and to practice these principles in all our affairs.

[a]Source: Alcoholics Anonymous, 1952.

TABLE 6.2   The 12 Traditions of Alcoholics Anonymous (AA)[a]

Tradition 1	Our common welfare should come first—personal recovery depends upon AA unity.
Tradition 2	For our group purpose, there is but one ultimate authority—a loving God as he may express Himself in our group conscience. Our leaders are but trusted servants; they do not govern.
Tradition 3	The only requirement for AA membership is a desire to stop drinking.
Tradition 4	Each group should be autonomous except in matters affecting other groups or AA as a whole.
Tradition 5	Each group has but one primary purpose—to carry its message to the alcoholic who still suffers.
Tradition 6	An AA group ought never endorse, finance, or lend the AA name to any related facility or outside enterprise, lest problems of money, property, and prestige divert us from our primary purpose.
Tradition 7	Every AA group ought to be fully self-supporting, declining outside contributions.
Tradition 8	Alcoholics Anonymous should remain forever nonprofessional, but our service centers may employ special workers.
Tradition 9	AA, as such, ought never be organized, but we may create service boards or committees directly responsible to those they serve.
Tradition 10	Alcoholics Anonymous has no opinion on outside issues; hence, the AA name ought never be drawn into public controversy.
Tradition 11	Our public relations policy is based on attraction rather than promotion: we need always maintain personal anonymity at the level of press, radio, and films.
Tradition 12	Anonymity is the spiritual foundation of our traditions, ever reminding us to place principles before personalities.

[a]The Twelve Steps and Twelve Traditions are reprinted with permission of Alcoholics Anonymous World Services, Inc. (A.A.W.S.) Permission to reprint the Twelve Steps and Twelve Traditions does not mean that A.A.W.S. has reviewed or approved the contents of this publication, or that A.A. necessarily agrees with the views expressed herein. A.A. is a program of recovery from alcoholism *only*-use of the Twelve Steps and Twelve Traditions in connection with programs and activities which are patterned after A.A., but which address other problems, or in any other non-A.A. context, does not imply otherwise.

A similar perspective set forth Zinberg (1974) posits the following format:

1. Substance: Individualized biochemistry in the context of each person and each substance.
2. Set: Psychology, attitudes, beliefs, personality, coping skills, ego strengths.
3. Setting: Environment, social support.

A SIMPLE COMPARISON OF RECOVERY AND MENTAL HEALTH MODELS

Recovery model[a]	Mental health model[a]
Disease process	Syndrome concept
Biopsychosocial–spiritual factors	Biopsychosocial factors and some attention to philosophical issues

Chronic condition	Chronic condition of many major disorders
Relapse issues	Relapse issues
Genetic–physiological component	Genetic–physiological component in many disorders
Chemical use primary	Psychiatric disorder primary
Out of control	Ineffective coping
Denial	Poor insight
Despair	Demoralization
Family issues	Family issues
Social stigma	Social stigma
Abstinence early goal	Stability early goal
Recovery long-term goal	Rehabilitation long-term goal
Powerlessness	Empowerment
No use of mood-altering chemicals	Psychotropic medications used
Education about illness	Education about illness
Halfway houses, ALANO clubs	Group homes, day treatment
Sponsors	Case manager–therapist
AA, Al-Anon, self-help groups	Support groups
Concrete action	Behavior change
Self-examination and acceptance	Awareness and insight
Label self as alcoholic–addict	See self as whole person with a disorder
Practice of communication and social skills	Practice of communication and social skills
Slogans, stories, affirmations	Positive self-talk, imagery
Step work	Psychotherapy
Use of spiritual concepts	Use of existential, transpersonal concepts
Family therapy	Family therapy
Group and individual work	Group and individual work
Continuum of care	Continuum of care
Nutrition, exercise, growth as value	Wellness concepts

aSource: Evans & Sullivan (1990a).

The models do not need to be mutually exclusive. The optimal use of community resources and formal treatment programs is to combine all resources to best fit the needs of individuals seeking intervention and lifestyle changes. The longer term benefit is the reinforcement of continuing successful recovery.

The concept of diversity, as experienced by the substance using individual, is most easily understood by utilizing a continuum to represent the level of functioning associated with degree of use:

Nonuse	Mild use	Moderate use	Heavy use–dependence
	No associated problem	No associated problem	No significant associated problem, but careless use
	Use of one substance	Experimental use of substances	Some biopsychosocial problems
	Experimental use of substances	Possible use as coping mechanism for Depression Anxiety Grief Social discomfort Stress	Serious problems over time Clear biopsychosocial problems Impact can be serious–severe

Treatment will vary along this continuum and in accordance with individual diversity. The treatment plan should fit the current needs of the client while considering the long-term goals as well. Traditional treatment has focused on the constellation of problems associated with the individuals at the end of the continuum where there is heavy use and dependence. More effective intervention would take place much earlier, when problems or consequences have just been experienced and intervention is far less intrusive. One last thought regarding the continuum: whereas there are general trends that flow along the continuum, there could be exceptions. For example, someone described as engaging in "mild use" might respond with a significantly more negative outcome associated with use due to genetic predisposition or a medical problem.

THEORETICAL ORIENTATION

Cognitive, behavioral, and psychodynamic interventions are viewed as being equally important. The choice of intervention is related to the stage of recovery and specific needs of the individual. In general, withdrawal, intoxication, and dependence should be addressed in this sequence. In some cases, withdrawal can be lethal or, at the very least, fraught with physical and psychological adjustment, which places it as a priority. There is the potential for behaviorially weighted treatment programs that ignore the fact that emotions, self-regulation, vulnerabilities, and disturbance play a significant role, and at times the primary role, in substance use. The meaning, cause, and consequences of substance abuse, according to psychoanalytic theory, would consider personality organization, ego, and self-regulation in accordance with how an individual interacts with distress, environmental factors, and the effects of substances. Blatt et al. (1984) as well as Treece and Khantzian (1986) propose a psychoanalytic perspective of substance dependence on ego organization, sense of self, an individual's attempts to cope, and the role that various substances play in the success or failure of attempts to cope. Khantzian et al. (1990) state that the underlying issues of emotion and self-concept are understood, accessed, and modified using psychodynamic methods of treatment. For personality problems accompanied by drinking, studies show that psychodynamic–insight-oriented therapy has a success rate ranging from 65 to 82% at 1 year (Brownell 1982), with the higher rates of success being cut in half at a 3-year follow-up (Wiens & Menustik, 1983). Cognitive–behavioral treatment interventions offer invaluable skill building recourses and have been shown to be more successful than psychodynamic therapy in individuals with more severe psychopathology and sociopathy (Cooney et al., 1991; Litt et al., 1992). Wiens and Menustik (1983) found 63% abstinence at 1-year follow-up, with success rates dropping to 31% at the 3-year follow-up for those who had been treated with cognitive–behavioral techniques.

THE ROLE OF 12-STEP AND OTHER SELF-HELP PROGRAMS

For most therapists and substance abuse programs, treatment includes the integration of Alcoholics Anonymous and/or Narcotics Anonymous. Brehm and Khantzian (1992) state that, at the beginning of recovery, when control is of chief importance, 12-step groups provide the individual with a "social family." It is with this social family that he or she learns that life is tolerable and manageable without the use of substances. According to Robinson (1979), AA maintains that two-thirds of the people who want to stop drinking have been successful in the program. Brandsma et al. (1980) conducted a well-controlled study that compared an AA group, an insight-oriented group, a cognitive-behavioral group, and no treatment group participants. The result was that AA had the highest dropout rate at 68%, and for those who did not drop out, AA did not demonstrate any higher level of success than any other type of group therapy. However, unique to AA are its availability, sponsorship, and affiliation at no cost.

Although there has been a long history of distance between AA and mental health professionals, it appears that the gap has been closing to a degree. An AA membership survey (Alcoholics Anonymous, 1996) indicates that 60% of the responding members received treatment–counseling of some sort, and of those 77% felt it played an important role in directing them to AA. Once in AA, 62% received treatment–counseling, and 85% of those individuals stated that it played an important role in their recovery.

Therapy, with its inherent view of stages of change, offers a shifting of tasks–goals associated with the individual's stage of recovery (Zweben, 1986, 1989). The concomitant participation in 12-step (and other self-help) groups challenges the individual to work and rework issues associated with all stages of recovery. The affiliation, or fellowshipping, facilitates and guides individuals toward increased self-efficacy, awareness, and self-responsibility and the resolution of difficult issues. Because of their growth in self-confidence and self-assurance, they believe that they have the ability to respond appropriately and effectively in any given situation. Obviously, the treatment goal related to self-help group meetings is not attendance but engagement.

It is through conceptual change and the group process that increased generalized application of change is seen—not just the focus on dependence patterns. Although all treatment components can increase the rate of progress in the recovery process, it should be acknowledged that, for many, it often takes a long time. Here are some examples of what self-help groups and therapy have in common and how they differ:

Self-help group	Therapy
Minimal–no cost	Financial commitment
Social support	Social support
Personal development	Personal development
Guidance for working through issues	Guidance for working through issues
Family support–intervention	Family support–intervention
Higher level of access as needed	Generally scheduled appointments
Peer affiliation	Therapeutic relationship
Potential lack of confidentiality	Confidentiality

RESISTANCE AND OTHER PROBLEMS

1. Difficulty acknowledging dependency
2. Not ready to make a commitment to abstinence
3. Feeling like an outsider when the individual first begins to attend self-help groups
4. Fear of losing identity
5. Discomfort with the emphasis on a higher power
6. Expressing a lack of time to attend meetings
7. Discomfort associated with lack of social skills

INCREASING ENGAGEMENT

Gitlow (1985) suggests the following recommendations for increasing an individual's engagement in 12-step participation:

1. Attend at least one meeting per day until one or more meetings have been selected above the others that you feel you could benefit from attending regularly.
2. Commit to regular attendance to specific meetings.
3. Consistently arrive early.
4. Sit in the first row.
5. Introduce yourself to those sitting around you or anyone with whom you have yet to become acquainted.
6. Practice participation at every meeting, even if it is only to share a brief comment.

7. Ask the meeting chairperson to assign you some task to help out, such as putting chairs away, coffee detail, etc. (qualify after 90 days of abstinence).
8. Never leave a meeting without sharing some discussion with another attendee.
9. Leave the meeting last and always invite someone to share coffee–meal–discussion.
10. Choose someone with a successful history of abstinence that can be met with socially between meetings (whether or not he or she is designated as a sponsor).

ALTERNATIVES TO 12-STEP GROUPS

Such organizations include, but are not limited to,

1. Rational Recovery
2. Smart Recovery
3. Secular Organization for Sobriety (SOS)
4. Women for Sobriety

Other self-help groups such as Smart Recovery and Rational Recovery emphasize self-responsibility, self-motivation, and self-discipline utilizing cognitive–behavioral methods of change. Some of their views are in opposition to traditional AA beliefs. Their philosophy of substance dependence and recovery is as follows:

1. Substance abuse is the result of life problems and stressors.
2. Substance abuse–dependence is how a person is choosing to cope with feelings, thoughts, and external stressors.
3. If a person learns skills to effectively cope with feelings, thoughts, and external stressors, he or she is no longer addicted.
4. Addiction is a continuum of behavior with associated consequences.
5. Problem solving with appropriate and effective skills, along with realistic expectations and limitations, is how a person learns to manage life.
6. Affiliation should be with a range of individuals, which would be considered normal.

HARM REDUCTION

Contrary to the 12-step and other traditional treatment philosophy (Riley & O'Hare, 2000) that abstinence is the goal, the public health approach of harm reduction seeks to broaden the perspective of substance abuse treatment. Harm reduction, instead of focusing on abstinence, seeks to decrease problems associated with substance use and cites that abstinence is not necessarily a realistic or desirable goal. For example, moderation management or controlled drinking. Proponents of harm reduction feel that this is especially true of the short-term treatment framework, which is currently dominant. Those professing the acceptance of harm reduction do not want it viewed as being mutually exclusive from abstinence, but note that it involves developing a hierarchy of goals where all treatment choices reside.

PRINCIPLES OF HARM REDUCTION

1. Pragmatism in accepting that there will be some use of mind-altering substances and stating that some degree of substance use is normal in society.

2. Humanistic values accept the substance user's decision to use substances to be his or her own choice, without any moralistic judgment. The rights of the substance abuser are respected.

3. Focus on harm means that the degree of the individual's substance use is secondary in importance to the harm that results from use.

4. Balancing of the cost–benefit ratio is carried out in such a way as to utilize resources for priority issues. This principle extends beyond the substance user to include the interest of community and society.

5. The hierarchy of goals structures intervention so that the most urgent needs are given immediate attention.

6. Cultural and socioeconomic sensitivity: Harm reduction accepts the impact of poverty, class, racism, social isolation, past trauma, and all social inequities upon vulnerability to substance abuse.

Coinciding with the continuum of use and associated level of functioning, some might apply the concept of harm reduction or "substance use management" versus the traditional premise of abstinence. According to Marlatt (1998), harm reduction, the clinical rationale, and its integration with traditional substance abuse treatment would result in a decrease in negative consequences of substance abuse. Harm reduction or substance use management

1. refers to programs and policies that help active users to manage their ongoing use of substances.

2. offers a choice other than abstinence or punishment (social sanctions such as mandated program attendance and jail).

3. offers a wide variety of choices for any change (not the single option of abstinence).

4. places both substance use and its risks along a continuum ranging from minimum to extreme.

5. has as a program goal the prevention of a high percentage of early dropouts.

6. offers education for reducing the harm–risk associated with safer substance use administration.
   a. decreased amounts
   b. less harmful environments–settings
   c. how to get help to cut back or quit

INTEGRATION OF HARM REDUCTION AND SUBSTANCE ABUSE TREATMENT

1. Offer a wide range of self-help groups (not limited to traditional 12 step) to improve retention. For example,
   a. Rational Recovery
   b. Smart Recovery
   c. Women for Sobriety
   d. Secular Organization for Sobriety

e. Self-Management Recovery Training

f. Moderation Management

2. Believe that individuals are more successful in treatment when given a choice of treatment than when they are assigned to treatment by someone else.

3. Offer choices on basic life skills training, including
   a. social skills
   b. coping skills
   c. stress management
   d. parenting skills
   e. nutrition and exercise
   f. job training

4. Make the overall choice of goals "client driven" and supported by the therapist. This places the responsibility on the therapist to find methods that work for the individual in terms of his or her goals.

CLINICAL RATIONALE FOR HARM REDUCTION

The clinical rationale for engaging in harm reduction as set forth includes the following.

1. The approach acknowledges the diversity of individuals who use substances.
   a. type of substance used
   b. different motivational stages of change
   c. psychiatric comorbidity

2. Benefits to the therapeutic alliance associated with shared acknowledgment of the individual's initial treatment goals.

3. Substance use is viewed as the individual's attempt to cope with life stressors.

4. Assumes that complex behaviors change incrementally.

5. The focus of harm reduction strategies is on reducing the harm incurred by substance use. Success is measured by the reduction of heavy or problematic use.

The concept and principles of harm reduction have become increasingly recognized and accepted in other parts of the world, such as the United Kingdom, Australia, and The Netherlands. North America remains ambivalent in accepting harm reduction as it pertains to substance abuse. The debate is expected to continue.

SPECIAL CONSIDERATIONS FOR DUAL DIAGNOSIS

Sometimes there are negative attitudes toward the use of psychotropic medications. This perspective comes from a less than beneficial history of treatment with mental health providers and the idea of giving "drugs" to an individual with a history of substance dependence. The issue of treatment with psychotropic medications covers a range of diagnoses. If the disorder is difficult to stabilize (rather consistently) and the individual is torn between needed treatment and philosophy, there are workbooks available that offer modified step work for individuals with dual diagnoses (Evans & Sullivan, 1990b).

MODELS OF TREATMENT

1. Sequential treatment
   a. Many substance abuse professionals feel that the individual must be abstinent prior to the treatment of psychiatric disorders.
   b. The individual is treated by one system and then by another (substance abuse then other mental health needs).
   c. Sometimes this is the best course of treatment; however, there are also instances where there must be psychiatric stability, as in the case of schizophrenia.

2. Parallel treatment
   a. The individual is simultaneously receiving substance abuse treatment and other mental health treatment.
   b. It is not uncommon for treatment providers to rarely communicate with each other.
   c. The individual may be caught between conflicting information from two treatment forums.

3. Integrated treatment
   a. Both substance abuse and mental health treatment are combined and integrated into a comprehensive treatment program.
   b. Professionals involved in integrated treatment are often cross-trained.
   c. Unified case management improves monitoring and treatment.

THE INDIVIDUAL ENTERING TREATMENT

The individual's perspective of "what works" generally is not an issue discussed in a treatment planning meeting. However, it is helpful to review how therapeutic interventions are viewed and what is important to the process of change from the individual's standpoint. He or she may be ambivalent, confused, and in need of guidance for an increased understanding of how treatment can benefit him or her. What the therapist can offer to encourage a collaborative process, promote change, and at times change or modify the client's view of things includes the following.

1. Motivational interviewing (acronym FRAMES; Miller & Rollnick, 1991)
   F: provide Feedback on drinking–drug behavior
   R: individual's Responsibility for changing behavior
   A: state Advice about changing behavior
   M: discuss a Menu of options to change behavior
   E: express Empathy for the individual
   S: support the individual's Self-efficacy

2. Active listening
   a. objective listening without personal investment
   b. validate the individual's experience (does not mean agreeing with it, simply acknowledge what he or she has shared that is useful clinically)

3. Talking through thoughts, feeling, and beliefs
   a. aids in organizing thoughts
   b. allows for ventilation and clarification

4. Use of simple questions: May promote new–alternative perspectives that facilitate engaging in situations in a more positive manner.

TREATMENT CONCERNS

To compensate for termination of self-treatment via substance use, there must be a substitution of adequate ego and social support. Empathy and nonjudgmental acceptance are imperative. Most individuals in substance abuse treatment already have well-developed negative impressions of themselves.

1. Conflict–ambivalence: "substances are harming me, but I need them."
2. Defenses, such as projection and splitting resulting from a state of discomfort.
3. Resistance:
   a. Acknowledge the individual's experience of benefit from substance use (felt good, etc.).
   b. Avoid power struggles.
   c. Joining the individual's position may result in his or her shift in position.
4. Confused motivation can be alleviated by initiating intervention where it feels most important to the individual. He or she may want to discuss losses and feelings of aloneness; listen, and as an alliance is formed, he or she can be helped to understand that it will not improve until there is abstinence and doing things differently.

It is the combination of positive and negative consequences that creates a challenging impediment to the commitment to changes associated with treatment and recovery. An individual can be confronted with the negative consequences and acknowledge their impact. However, it is the perception of and reliance on the "benefits" of substance use that are likely to provoke resistance. Therefore, the therapist must acknowledge this dilemma and be prepared to work constructively with someone in treatment to resolve this issue.

Collaborative treatment planning allows for the development of an inventory of major problems confronting the individual and how his or her life is affected by each problem. If the collaborative effort is difficult or feels strained, encourage the development of three initial goals to avoid power struggles, alienation, or feelings of being overwhelmed. Once these initial goals are identified, break down each goal into three to five objectives that demonstrate progress toward reaching a given goal. The individual can intermittently self-monitor by rating his or her progress as

1. less than expected
2. expected
3. better–more than expected.

Without a lot of effort, this process encourages continued problem solving and collaboration. Treatment goals should be

1. Realistic
2. Manageable

3. Concrete and specific
4. Behavioral and cognitive
5. Small steps that are prioritized in a progressive manner
6. Perceived as important–beneficial

RATIONAL EMOTIVE THERAPY PHILOSOPHY

Ellis and co-workers' ABCDE Model of RET (Ellis & Drydes, 1987; Ellis et al., 1988):

A: Activating event–potential trigger
B: Beliefs (helpful = rational, nonhelpful = irrational)
C: Consequences (a person's behavior, feelings, and thoughts resulting from "A")
D: Disputing–intervening (how to intervene and change, i.e., challenging irrational beliefs and dysfunctional behavior)
E: Effects–results (associated with disputing–intervening)

Rational emotive therapy (RET) and rational emotive behavior therapy (REBT; Ellis, 1994) engender many of the characteristics of substance abuse treatment. In general, treatment programs based upon rational emotive (behavior) therapy emanate from the central belief that individuals overcome addiction(s) by gaining improved control over their thinking, emotions, and behaviors, which requires the development of effective relapse prevention skills. The defining characteristics of RET–REBT relapse prevention are as follows:

1. An individual is responsible for his or her own behaviors.
2. An individual can recover and regain control over his or her addictive behaviors.
3. Lifetime participation–membership in self-help groups is not required, and many individuals are capable of recovery in 1–2 years.
4. Labeling is discouraged. An individual does not have to refer to him- or herself as an alcoholic–addict to recover.
5. Alcoholism (substance dependence) may be a disease. Regardless, an individual has to find an effective way to cope and take responsibility for his or her life.
6. An individual's value is not tied to his or her behavior–addiction. Someone who achieves abstinence may be happier, have better relationships, and be better able to maintain employment, but that does not make him or her a better person.
7. An individual is not viewed as being in denial if he or she refuses to accept the basic tenets of AA.
8. An individual can recover on his or her own with or without the help of professionals and/or self-help groups.

THERAPIST GUIDELINES

1. Be sensitive to human diversity.
2. The least intrusive treatment should be selected.
3. Have a clear understanding of the continuum of substance use, abuse, and dependence.
4. Develop treatment plans specifically to meet the needs of the individual.
5. Utilize approaches that facilitate personal growth and the acquisition of skills that positively influence self-care and self-efficacy.
6. Treatment must be multimodal to adequately deal with biopsychosocial complexities.
7. A treatment plan should be flexible to adjust to and incorporate new methods and goals as the field of substance abuse treatment continues to expand and evolve.
8. Be familiar with all treatment resources and social supports in the community.
9. Be willing to work in a collaborative manner with the individual entering treatment. When treatment is initiated, the first recommendation, if there are not any medical complications, is to educate the individual regarding the benefits or abstinence with encouragement to attempt a brief period of abstinence (30 days). If medical concerns are present, an individual is referred for a thorough medical evaluation. If the individual is not able to sustain abstinence with appropriate effort, he or she should be referred to a higher level of intervention.
10. Always be prepared to explore and resolve personal issues of countertransference.

A factor that each clinician needs to address personally is that of countertransference. Carroll (1993) studied the attitudes of professionals toward substance abusers based upon their professional role, socialization, and prior experience with substance abuse treatment. The outcome demonstrated the need for professionals trained to work with substance abusers to take responsibility for clarifying potential countertransference issues. Specifically, such clarification should be aimed at exploring attitudes that tend to be rejecting, blaming, stigmatizing, and punitive.

Regarding sensitivity to diversity, a significant additional factor that is often overlooked in treatment is religion–spirituality. Religion–spirituality offers an asset of strength and support that can be an extremely useful resource for overcoming obstacles to change.

1. Explore an individual's religious–spiritual beliefs as a source of strength and support.
2. Be respectful of his or her values and beliefs.
3. Inquire about obtaining a release for collateral contact with his or her religious leader for support or your own need for consultation and education.
4. Be aware of countertransference.

PROFESSIONAL CODEPENDENT VERSUS HELPER

Another issue important to the awareness of those working in substance abuse treatment was identified by Bell (1992) and referred to as "treatment dependence syndrome". Bell states that this phenomenon is prevalent in the substance abuse treatment community and is a demonstration of behaviors by researchers and professionals that strikingly resemble those of the alcohol dependence syndrome (defined in *DSM III*). This syndrome is indicative of research and treatment being the most important focus, resulting in displaced concern for patients and how to help them. Treatment becomes more narrow and rigid. The result is often a negative view of the patient as resistant instead of recognizing that as the professional he or she is seeking the gratification associated with providing treatment. Bell's conclusion is that substance abuse treatment professionals are at risk of becoming dependent on treatment (as a function of the difficulty in defining effective treatment goals and success). Effective identification and understanding of personal attitudinal factors influencing the treatment of substance abusing individuals require a thorough personal examination (Imhoff *et al.*, 1983). It may be helpful to examine the dichotomy of codependent versus helper at the professional level.

Professional codependent	Professional helper
Sidesteps obvious problems	Promotes self-responsibility
Avoids confrontation	Identifies and educates regarding specific behaviors that are disruptive, disturbing, and self-defeating
Separates self from others	Recognizes the limitation that he or she cannot be everything to everyone
Minimizes seriousness of events, thereby decreasing consequences	Reinforces consistent consequences associated with choices
Manipulative control via facade of protection and care	Maintains awareness to sudden changes in behavior
Defends and excuses poor choices	Seeks appropriate interventions
Frustrated due to inability to effect change	Knows when to let go
Sometimes compromises own values and professional standards	Always maintains high standards and values
Maintains the "no talk" rule	Expresses care and concern
Labels and oversimplifies	Open to a variety of possibilities as the cause of the problem and various resources for intervening

Steinglass *et al.* (1987) state that a therapist must not only meet individuals where they are in their preparedness for change but also conceptualize for them realistic expectations and limitations. It is from this point of initiation that they are facilitated to learn more about themselves and the use–abstinence cycle in which they (in their family and social systems) engage. In others words, the therapist is preparing them through education to utilize all experiences during the course of recovery to maximize change, personal growth, and overall outcome. In this framework relapse is viewed as an opportunity for more clearly understanding the use–abstinence cycle, associated chain of thoughts and behaviors, and system dynamics that play a role in maintenance and change. O'Farrell and Cowles (1989) state that up to 60% of couples seeking treatment for marital–family relationship difficulties have a problem with substance abuse.

PREPARATION OF INDIVIDUALS, COUPLES, AND FAMILIES FOR RECOVERY

1. Education on the use–abstinence cycle.
2. Identify possible family dynamics that can be helpful, threatening, or are points of resistance.

a. ambivalence

b. positive–negative roles of substances in family–social functioning

c. family substance use patterns

d. what experience has brought them to treatment

e. loyalty conflicts

f. shame regarding use

g. blaming

3. Promote the need for flexibility in relationship functioning.

4. Rebalance the system to view substance(s) as the problem.

5. Explore the degree of couple–family adaptation to the use–abstinence cycle so that the significance and predictability of the system's routine functioning can be used for anticipating the unfolding of the cycle. The information can also be used as a motivator for change.

a. family identity

b. rituals

c. problem solving

d. time structures

e. parenting

f. sexuality

g. issues of loss–grief

h. how emotions–feelings are managed

i. flexibility

j. power structure

k. life-cycle tasks

6. Clarify dual diagnosis issues. Two major points of treatment divergence will be clarified once recovery has been initiated and there is either (1) a decrease–elimination of psychiatric symptoms or (2) definition of the psychiatric symptoms that meet diagnostic criteria. If medication is required for psychiatric diagnosis(es), the following recommendations are important:

a. complete abstinence from alcohol and illicit substances

b. psychoactive medications used only as prescribed

c. medication only to be prescribed by a physician familiar with the individual's history and knowledgeable about substance abuse

7. Intimacy.

a. honesty

b. responsiveness

c. sharing

d. humility

e. forgiveness

f. risk

g. impact of use on sexual functioning (heightened experience–dysfunction)

8. Multigenerational assessment of substance use patterns.

a. helpful to clarify actual individual treatment needs

b. contributes to appropriate system interventions

9. Discuss treatment choices and engage in collaborative treatment planning.

10. Discuss the level of care best suited for achieving desired treatment goals.
    a. detox: inpatient or outpatient
    b. rehab: residential or outpatient
    c. outpatient: intensive outpatient, outpatient, self-help, aftercare, individual therapy

11. Level of treatment care discussed in association with conjoint–family system. There is benefit in developing a "system" consensus of support and motivation.

12. Develop treatment goals that include the partner, family, and appropriate extended social support system.
    a. enhancement of
        i. positive, appropriate, and effective system functioning
        ii. problem solving
        iii. conflict resolution
    b. development of new system behaviors to replace substance use behaviors–rituals
        i. improve system coping
        ii. change family rituals
    c. development of a healthy frame of reference from a new perspective of personal–system growth associated with the recovery process
        i. recovery consistent with stage of life issues
        ii. guidance to address general stages of life issues
        iii. how to effectively resolve stage of life issues
        iv. living a full life versus life centered around 12-step and treatment over time
        v. confronting complications relationship problems, financial problems, legal problems
        vi. relapse anticipated as a normal aspect of substance dependence recovery–understand relapse through unresolved systems dilemma
        vii. pace the momentum of recovery for thoroughness–the longer the problem has existed, the more entrenched and convoluted the associated sustaining patterns

Individualized treatment is the result of collaboration between the client and the therapist. It is based on the desired outcome. In other words, once the destination has been clarified, work is initiated on the best way for that individual to get there. The goals must be appropriate and fit the personality, situation, length of time of use, amount, etc. The less impaired the client, the greater the need for his or her involvement in treatment decisions. Psychotherapy is one component of a comprehensive, multidimensional treatment program.

According to Moos *et al.*, (1982), family, marital resources, positive work environment, and community support networks are the most significant social support systems affecting recovery. A successful recovery takes into consideration the entire life experience of the individual. In other words, the individualized treatment plan (ITP) must take into consideration the life context within which substance abuse takes place in order to provide a foundation for successful change when initiating the first step in treatment to interrupt the substance use behavior. The ITP provides the foundation and structure for success. It is a biopsychosocial perspective that is interpersonal and intrapersonal. Treatment goals and objectives are defined in a collaborative effort that is outcome-oriented. When reviewing the choices presented for formulating a treatment plan, the Axis V level of functioning defined for each assessed individual serves as a guide for intervention in the areas of psychological impairment, social skills, dangerousness, daily living skills, occupational skills, substance abuse, etc. In a thorough manner, all identified problems are outlined in the ITP, and the following issues are reviewed and considered for the purposes of necessary prioritization of interventions (crisis issues) and clarification of the course of treatment.

TREATMENT PRIORITIZATION

1. Seriousness of problems, need for detox and medical monitoring treatment.
2. Crisis intervention, harm to self, harm to others, issues of abuse (child, spouse, elder), severe mood and affective disorders, and psychosis.
3. Physical examination, tests for infectious disease, treating diseases, prevention, primary treatment.
4. Pharmacological intervention.
5. Abstinence, controlled drinking, obtaining and maintaining sobriety–substance free.
6. Setting and environmental atmosphere for recovery.
7. Prioritize goals.
8. Resolve or avoid legal problems.
9. Stabilize financial, employment, vocational, and educational issues.
10. Treatment time for given problems.
11. Motivation and positive treatment outlook. Program early treatment success by plugging in small manageable tasks to enhance self-esteem and self-efficacy.
12. Negotiation of treatment choices and preferences with the client's treatment choices.
13. Assess degree of support from significant other and family. These are important allies in treatment, offering encouragement and reinforcement.
14. Work environment and functions.
15. Situational preparedness.
16. Psychological well-being (depression, anxiety, unresolved grief, shame, guilt, abandonment, rejection, etc.).
17. Stress management.
18. Coping mechanisms (how to live free substance abused–dependence).
19. Problem solving.
20 Education regarding the nature and processes of addiction and recovery.
21. Education of associated family dynamics.
22. Self-care with corrective measures associated with general health and fitness.
23. Education associated with job, relationship, or financial issues and responsibilities.

The intrapersonal areas of evaluation from the preceding list include

1. Health
2. Psychological well-being
3. Coping mechanisms
4. Problem solving
5. Self-responsibility

The interpersonal areas of evaluation from the preceding list include

1. Relationships
   a. significant other
   b. family
   c. friends
   d. peers

2. Work
3. Situational preparedness
4. Community programs–self-help meetings

COURSE OF TREATMENT

An understanding of the course of treatment encourages motivation and hopefulness. The first step in the collaborative effort of treatment planning is the setting of goals. Goals can be viewed in terms of being short-term and long-term. Generally, short-term goals–problem resolution take 3–6 months. Long-term goals–problem resolution take up to 1 year with continued self-monitoring. One way to conceptualize this framework is by using a traditional hospital treatment plan outline. For example,

Treatment goal	Intervention	Estimated time	How change measured	Goal met (yes–no)

The second component, intervention, identifies the objectives utilized to reach the goal. The fourth component, measurement tool–self-monitoring, takes into consideration the different types of paper and pencil inventories, pre- and posttest derivatives, and the criteria that the client defines as markers of change and progress. When the goal is accomplished, it is noted on the treatment plan by date under the last component, goal met. When the goal has been met, efforts of self-monitoring demonstrated by evidence of documentation beside the date the goal was met may act as a reinforcer for the need and decision made to create effort(s), to maintain awareness, and to continue practice of the change.

AGENTS OF CHANGE

As previously stated, in making a personal assessment, it is important to identify all areas of life skills for the development of an ITP. A general review of agents of change for success would include the following.

1. Behavioral self-control (training where the client is taught skills to change and monitor behavior)
2. Contingency contracting (the rewarding and punishing of behavior)
3. Relaxation training
4. Shaping (how to break down tasks into small manageable steps)

5. Stress management
6. Social skills training
7. Relationship–conjoint therapy
8. Vocational counseling
9. Physical examination (endocrine functioning, diabetes, and other health issues that influence mood and energy level)
10. Cognitive restructuring (help to alter appraisal of self and environment)
11. Aversive conditioning (couples substance abuse with real or imagined unpleasant experience, Antabuse–Disulfuram, which is an antogonist to alcohol, methadone, which is a maintenance drug for heroin addicts considered more appropriate than illegal opiates)
12. Medication management (use of a psychotropic medication for a dual diagnosis issue or a medication that eases craving such as Naloxone for alcoholics)
13. Group therapy
14. 12-step meetings and other community choices (referral to self-help organizations and community programs–resources)
15. Didactic education on substances
16. Self-analysis of substance use
17. Self-monitoring
18. Self-reinforcement
19. Stimulus control methods
20. Active coping strategies
    a. cognitive strategies, such as self-statements and reappraisal of self–situations
    b. behavioral strategies, such as the use of modeling, instruction, behavioral rehearsal, homework assignments, learning alternative behaviors, development of appropriate alternative methods for responding to various situations
21. Systematic desensitization: Demonstrates usefulness for clients who have difficulty engaging in progressive muscle relaxation, extreme anxiety, and difficulty implementing new social skills in anxiety provoking situations. Once a hierarchy has been completed, the client should then be reintroduced to progressive muscle relaxation. Systematic desensitization will be accomplished over a number of sessions, and the time frame of course is individualized. Client self-report is the method used for determining progress. Desensitization is to be generalized to *in vivo*–real life situations.

The value of cognitive–behavioral therapy is to decrease, eliminate, and when possible prevent excessive emotional reactions and self-defeating behaviors. This is accomplished by confronting cognitive distortions, modifying maladaptive beliefs, and modifying ineffective behaviors. According to Beck *et al.* (1993), there are two significant types of beliefs associated with substance use:

1. Anticipatory beliefs: Beliefs that are activated on exposure to internal cues that have been linked to the choice of substance use (e.g., boredom or believing they need it to get through the day) or external cues or stimuli (e.g., being in the company of peers using substances or being invited to a party).

2. Permission giving: Choosing to use because "it has been earned" or minimization (e.g., "one drink won't be a problem—I can control it," "I've worked hard today, I deserve it").

Through genuine empathy, increased awareness, and understanding of the connection from maladaptive thoughts and behaviors to resulting consequences, therapists can facilitate desired change. This approach is helpful because it helps individuals to avoid substance stimulating environments, to develop effective ways of coping with the stimuli that cannot be avoided, and to recognize the difference. The therapeutic alliance, at least among outpatient alcohol-dependent individuals, is a factor that has an impact on treatment participation and outcome (Connor *et al.*, 1997).

AREAS OF PERSONAL VULNERABILITY FOR THOSE IN TREATMENT

Khantzian *et al.* (1990) propose five areas of vulnerability that emerge from common underlying characteristics:

1. Affect management: Unable to identify, label, or describe affective expressions. Lack of capacity to tolerate emotions.
2. Self-care: Poor lifestyle choices and ineffective prioritizing.
3. Judgment: Sensation seeking behavior, increased external stimuli, unable to utilize feelings of anxiety as a preemptive sign to avoid danger–risk.
4. Defensive functioning: Easily feeling overwhelmed, inability to tolerate affect, and issues associated with primitive defenses (projection, denial, and splitting).
5. Object relations: Building on defensive mechanisms is evidence of a narcissistic disturbance, which is manifested by grandiosity, arrogance, entitlement, unstable sense of self, and poor differentiation of self and objects.

OBSTACLES TO CHANGE

The preparation of someone to change is often the foundation of success. Change is stressful, which can provoke resistance, ambivalence, and/or fear. Although these responses can be a barrier to change, they can also represent an opportunity. Helping individuals to decide on a plan of action for change that offers adequate support and reinforcement allows them to begin to see that all of the changes associated with recovery is manageable. No matter how positive the change, it is stressful. Part of preparing individuals for change is acquainting them with the following points.

1. When individuals seek to avoid stress, it often creates more stress.
2. Set up realistic expectations and limitations regarding the speed of recovery. Individuals are sometimes disappointed that for all of their efforts, they do not feel better faster. Encourage consistent effort, allowing time for the body to heal and new skills and habits to be developed.

3. Life is hard, but when a person just does what he or she needs to do, it does not seem so difficult. Because recovery is hard and takes continuous effort, there is often resistance and the generation of excuses. Recognize what needs to be done for success and initiate new positive behaviors to substitute for the old self-defeating behaviors.

4. Habits are useful because the individual can function on autopilot and not think about it. Bad habits are resistant to change because they require little energy, whereas good ones are hard because it requires energy to initiate them and repeat them until they become habits. This means that, during the first stages of change, there may not be a feeling that the changes are paying off.

5. Individuals tend to cling to what is familiar. There is fear associated with change and the unknown.

6. The response of others plays a role in making and sustaining changes. When an individual changes, the people around must also change if the relationship is to continue. Sometimes people are very supportive and struggle with making changes, and other times they may be angry and resentful of feeling forced to change, which can result in emotional distress for the individual attempting to change.

7. A central task for individuals in recovery is learning to deal with emotions. Because they have been medicated and numbed, emotions have been blunted. This can result in the person feeling overwhelmed emotionally.

8. When the excuse for not being able to change is a lack of resources, encourage the individual to confront how he or she will deal with it, create resources, and continue with the plan for change.

9. It is not uncommon for someone who experiences a slip to move into a full-blown relapse because of his or her perspective that "I've blown it." Help the person learn to use mistakes, slips, and relapse as an opportunity to learn more about the self, choices, and what can be done differently in helping to achieve desired goals.

10. Goals are at times abandoned because they seem too big, too difficult, or too far away. Break goals down so that easier small steps toward a goal are achieved early to encourage the development of a self-reinforcing process.

OVERCOMING OBSTACLES TO CHANGE

1. The first step toward change is developing *awareness*.
2. Once there is awareness for changing specific behaviors, thoughts, and ineffective coping patterns, then it is time to *decide* what is a necessary or desired change.
3. Educate regarding the continuum of treatment *choices* and work with individuals in selecting the treatment interventions that best fit their needs.
4. There must be a *commitment* to change.

5. With commitment and realistic goal(s) in place, it is time to take *action*. When individuals talk about goals but do not take action, they become more frustrated. It negatively affects feelings of fear and self-efficacy.

6. To maintain motivation, build in *reinforcement*. Some changes are naturally self-reinforcing. In other instances, rewards linked to certain accomplishments will provide additional reasons for continued effort toward goals.

7. Decrease the attractiveness of use. Once individuals have clarified what they liked about, benefited from, or were seeking in substance use, help increase their awareness of the negative consequences associated with use.

8. *Personal feedback*, not lecturing, regarding harmful consequences: (1) health, (2) impairment, and (3) self-defeating aspects of substance abuse. The intervention of feedback begins following the intake interview. Information must be direct and objective.

9. *Self-monitoring*. Check in routinely to review progress, what is working, and what is not and make necessary changes or adjustments.

10. Once the individual has reached his or her goal(s), then help him or her use the skills that have been developed to set new goals.

Of all of the possibilities presented for overcoming the obstacles to change and motivating individuals toward change, a genuine, optimistic, and empathetic approach yields the most favorable results. Expectation of a positive outcome coupled with adequate support, reinforcement, and realistic expectations and limitations create an atmosphere encouraging appropriate and necessary changes. According to Kristenson (1983) and Leake and King (1977), an empathetic approach with the optimism of expecting a positive outcome yields the most favorable treatment results. Add to this Gerstein and Harwood's (1990) citation that the longer individuals stay in treatment, the better they do. The benefits of treatment begin to be enduring after about 6 months of participation and engagement.

INDIVIDUALIZED TREATMENT PLANNING

This author believes that the concept of individualized treatment planning (ITP) should be applied to all cases of substance abuse and mental health treatment if the goal is for the best possible outcome. Experience shows that insurance limitations, financial limitations, and geographical limitations are often the factors that impede treatment. However, there are also the personal issues of motivation and willingness to change, coupled with biological, psychological, and social factors, that play an equally important role in treatment outcome. As initially stated, these issues are integrated and very complex, which reinforces the importance of individualized treatment planning. Although the continuation of research and government-sponsored pilot treatment projects is imperative for clarifying and refining what works, they do not always effectively make the transition to the world of daily treatment practice because they generally fail to take into consideration cost, continuum of care, and treatment component availability. ITP requires collaboration with the individual in developing a treatment plan, and at times, because of the aforementioned limitations, requires the collaborative effort to creatively develop appropriate alternatives for getting treatment needs met. The ITP concept was developed as a result of the real challenges associated with realistic expectations and limitations.

FORMULATING THE TREATMENT PLAN

Research at the national level has resulted in three major recommendations for substance abuse treatment guidelines:

1. National Institute on Alcohol Abuse and Alcoholism (NIAAA) Project Match Research Group (1993)
   a. objective was to determine whether subgroups of alcoholism responded differentially to three treatments
      i. 12-step facilitation therapy
      ii. cognitive–behavioral coping skills therapy
      iii. motivational enhancement therapy
   b. although the concept is basic and makes sense, it was difficult to apply
      i. program access barriers
      ii. long waiting lists negatively impacting admission
      iii. geographical obstacles = limited participation
      iv. unstable funding

2. Center for Substance Abuse Treatment (CSAT; 1997) Comprehensive Care Model
   a. goal is to foster the application of treatment and recovery interventions known to be effective
   b. programming based on needs assessment and cultural sensitivity
   c. provide services through linkages in community agencies
   d. guidelines
      i. thorough assessment
      ii. same-day intake
      iii. documentation of findings and treatment
      iv. preventive and primary medical care
      v. testing for infectious diseases
      vi. weekly random drug testing
      vii. pharmacotherapeutic interventions
      viii. group counseling interventions
      ix. basic substance abuse counseling
      x. practical life skills counseling (vocational, educational, social skills, etc.)
      xi. general health education
      xii. peer support group (HIV–AIDS, sexual assault victims, spousal abuse, etc.)
      xiii. liaison services (legal aid, immigration, etc.)
      xiv. alternative housing
      xv. relapse prevention
      xvi. outcome evaluation (program improvement)

3. American Society of Addiction Medicine (ASAM; 1996) Patient Criteria Placement
   a. directed to refine a biopsychosocial model to specify treatment matching associated with clinical severity
   b. goal is the development of uniform patient placement and to determine appropriate level of care (early intervention, outpatient, intensive outpatient–patient hospitalization program, medically monitored intensive inpatient, medically managed inpatient)
   c. guidelines: stages of intervention and dimensional criteria
      Level 0.5 Early Intervention
      Level I   Outpatient Treatment

Level II   Intensive Outpatient and Partial Hospitalization
Level III   Medically Monitored Intensive Inpatient Treatment
Level IV   Medically Managed Intensive Inpatient Treatment
Dimensional criteria:
  i. acute intoxication, withdrawal potential, or both
  ii. coexistence of biomedical conditions–complications
  iii. emotional–behavioral conditions and complications
  iv. treatment acceptance or resistance
  v. relapse and continued use potential
  vi. recovery and living environment

As research continues, clarity on the issue of what composes the most effective treatment will be defined. Until then, therapists must continue to use what they and the individual seeking treatment are able to collaborate on as the goals of treatment.
Central issues will always be:

1. What the individual is willing to do.
2. How effectively a therapist can communicate and facilitate the acceptance of doing more when necessary.

RECORD KEEPING

There are numerous ways to structure a treatment plan for record keeping and review. The traditional format utilized by most hospital settings has found its way into outpatient settings. This particular format is designed for review, updating, and signing by a multidisciplinary team. Another example of a treatment plan outline is a checklist. This style allows for easy review and offers a clear presentation of treatment goals to the individual in treatment as well as the clinician. To develop a treatment checklist, think in terms of general criteria associated with clinical intervention and personal goals. Such a checklist might describe treatment areas of crisis intervention, management skills, self-care, and trauma issues in addition to direct substance abuse issues. Then, conceptualize an adequate time frame that coincides with the prioritization of the goals. Short-term treatment would be 3–7 days, moderate treatment would be 1–16 weeks, and long-term treatment would continue from 5 to 12 months or as long as specified. A condensed or abbreviated format would offer insight into the general course of treatment, whereas the checklist would offer a more specific outline for the course of treatment.

THE JOHNSON INDEPENDENT TREATMENT PLAN—SHORT FORM

Name _____ Date _____

Short-Term Treatment Goals	Estimated Time
__medical treatment	_____
__crisis issues	_____
__abstinence	_____
__monitor withdrawal	_____
__treatment of acute psychiatric symptomatology	_____
__provide a safe–supportive environment	_____
__stabilization	_____
__education	_____
__appropriate cognitive–behavioral interventions	_____

Moderate-Term Treatment Goals	
__assignment to treatment program	_____
__continued abstinence	_____
__relapse prevention	_____
__participation in self-help groups	_____
__appropriate management of affect–mood	_____
__challenge defense mechanisms	_____
__treatment of psychopathology	_____
__systems intervention (family–work)	_____
__improve interpersonal skills	_____

Long-Term Treatment Goals	
__recovery	_____
__individualized education	_____
__engage in successful–fulfilling relationships	_____
__education–job goal achievement	_____
__crisis-related issues	_____
__restructure personality	_____
__self-monitor	_____

THE JOHNSON INDIVIDUALIZED TREATMENT PLAN

Patient Name: _____   Date: _____

<u>Time Estimate</u>

__Crisis intervention
 Harm to self   _____
 Harm to others   _____
 Issues of abuse   _____
 Severe affective disorder–psychosis _____
 Gravely disabled   _____

__Detox–medical monitoring   _____

__Medication evaluation   _____

__Abstinence   _____

__Controlled drinking   _____

__Refusal skills   _____

__Review for other compulsive disorders
(eating disorders, gambling, sex, spending) _____

__Treatment format
 Inpatient–residential   _____
 Intensive outpatient   _____
 Partial hospitalization   _____
 Outpatient   _____
 Therapeutic group   _____
 12-step or other self-help program _____

__Increase ability to identify, label, and express emotions _____

__Increase ability to tolerate being alone _____

__Increase ability to manage mood and painful emotions _____

__Alleviate–eliminate vegetative symptoms of depression _____

__Increase ability to appropriately manage and express
frustration–anger _____

__Increase ability to express self assertively _____

__Improve problem solving skills _____

__Increase use of relaxation techniques _____

__Improve conflict resolution skills _____

__Identify and resolve issues of loss–grief _____

__Journal writing to vent, clarify, and problem solve _____

__Develop a physical exercise routine as part of lifestyle _____

__Develop appropriate daily structure–self-care plan _____

__Identify and modify lifestyle issues that contribute to stress _____

__Develop and utilize social support system _____

__Develop appropriate leisure activities _____

__Improve grooming and hygiene _____

__Develop and commit to long-term plans related to
job–education–relationships _____

__Develop skills to relax and decrease autonomic arousal _____

__Increase ability to manage escalating anxiety and
negative moods _____

__Increase ability to manage phobic response patterns _____

__Eliminate panic attacks _____

__Decrease self-defeating behaviors   _____

__Alleviate–eliminate intrusive thoughts   _____

__Decrease dissociation–time loss as a coping skill   _____

__Eliminate disturbing–recurrent dreams   _____

__Decrease–eliminate obsessive thoughts   _____

__Decrease–eliminate compulsive behaviors   _____

Some of the goals that have been identified are on a continuum that may be originated during the short-term-treatment phase and continue into the next stage of treatment or be an ongoing process. Therefore, designate from one term of treatment to the next if a specific task is continued or resolved. With an ever increasing demand for accountability, use the treatment goal information documented on either of the prior forms and integrate it with other necessary information to result in an easy treatment plan review. The basic format discussed is similar to outlines used by hospital-based programs, which generally include the interventions used, an estimation of time necessary for change to take place, how change will be measured, and if the treatment goal is met and resolved. This format makes it easy to maintain treatment focus and to discuss the treatment plan and associated progress or impediments to progress with the individual in treatment and other members of the treatment team. Following is an example of such a form.

BASIC TREATMENT PLAN FORMAT SAMPLE

Name _____   Date _____

Date Entered Treatment _____   DOB _____   SS£ _____

Review Date (weekly–monthly) _____

Brief History _____

_____

_____

DSM IV Diagnosis:

Axis I   _____

Axis II   _____

Axis III   _____

Axis IV   _____

Axis V   _____

Treatment Goals (short–moderate–long term)	Intervention	Estimated Time	How Change Measured	Goal met? (yes or no)
1				
2				
3				
4				
5				

UNDERSTANDING YOUR EXPERIENCE OF TREATMENT

Answer the following questions yes or no then please explain your answer.

1. Do you believe that treatment is helpful to you? _____

    _____

    _____

2. Are you having trouble making a commitment to recovery? _____

    _____

    _____

3. Is treatment what you expected? _____

    _____

    _____

4. Do you see treatment as an opportunity for positive changes? _____

    _____

    _____

5. At this point, what do you think about substance abuse? (concerns) _____

    _____

    _____

6. What will happen if you remain in recovery? _____

    _____

    _____

7. What are you going to do? Do you feel ready and willing to get help? Rate
   how committed you are to recovery, with level of commitment ranging from
   1 (no commitment) to 10 (totally committed): _____

    _____

    _____

TREATMENT RULES

1. Attendance at all meetings is mandatory. Any cancellation must be made in advance and with a good reason.
2. Everyone must be on time.
3. Abstinence is required.
4. Treatment compliance and completion are required.

TREATMENT CONTRACT

1. I agree to participate in treatment for _____ weeks, _____ times per week. If I choose to withdraw from treatment prior to completion, I will speak to my therapist about my decision before I terminate treatment.
2. I agree to attend all sessions.
3. I agree to always be on time.
4. I agree to always attend sessions clean and sober.
5. I accept responsibility for practicing the new skills I learn in treatment.
6. I agree to always complete my homework.
7. After talking with my therapist, I have chosen the following treatment goals:
   a. _____
   b. _____
   c. _____
   d. _____
   e. _____

I have reviewed the above information and agree to comply with it.

Client: _____   Date: _____

Therapist: _____   Date: _____

GUIDELINES FOR AN INTERVENTION

An intervention is defined as the precipitation of a crisis instead of waiting for one to unfold. It is a method for utilizing the problem that has already presented itself to clarify reality for the substance-dependent individual.

The goal of intervention is to present information about substance dependence to the substance-dependent individual in a caring and concerned manner as a means to motivate him or her to obtain professional help. It is anticipated that the substance-dependent individual does not acknowledge or lacks awareness of the degree of problem he or she experiences. An intervention creates the opportunity to present the reality of the situation to the substance-dependent individual in a manner that he or she can accept.

Information is presented as factually as possible without blaming or intense emotion, which can provoke conflicts and/or power struggles. Use the following outline of how to present facts.

1. All of the information offered during an intervention should be given with genuine care and concern.
2. Information should be relevant to substance-related behaviors or events.
3. Information that is shared has been witnessed by those sharing it or are they are sure of what has actually happened.
4. Information includes factual information of witnessed substance use and the associated consequences of use.
5. Information includes the consequences that others have suffered as a consequence of the substance use of the individual who is the focus of the intervention, not from the perspective of a victim or blaming but purely as a consequence.
6. Information offered is specific as to when, where, and with whom an incident happened. This is necessary for credibility.

It is helpful to write this information out for consistency and to avoid repetition.

CRITERIA FOR AN INTERVENTION

1. Two or more genuinely concerned individuals
2. Lists of factual and specific information.
3. For each incident described, clarify
   a. when
   b. substance used
   c. what happened
   d. who was there
   e. how what happened was associated with substance use
   f. how you felt
4. Be prepared with a minimum of five significant incidents associated with substance use.
5. Each person is to read directly from the list he or she has prepared.
6. Offer the information as an expression of concern, not blaming or judging.
7. It is recommended that an experienced professional be present.

8. There must be preparedness for specific and immediate alternatives and/or consequences.

9. All family members participating must present as a united front working for the benefit of the individual who is the focus of the intervention.

10. It is beneficial for all of those preparing to participate in an intervention to have met prior to reaffirm their motivation and clarify the procedure.

GUIDELINES FOR THOSE PARTICIPATING IN AN INTERVENTION

1. Everyone participating needs to have sufficiently addressed their own issues and behaviors so that there is no codependent or rescuing behavior.

2. The individual who is the focus of the intervention is asked to listen to all present prior to responding.

3. Even if the individual who is the focus of the intervention agrees to abstain,
   a. finish all prepared lists of concerns and issues.
   b. be prepared with alternatives for treatment.

4. Strive to understand the emotions expressed and do not react. For example, the more anger expressed, the greater the fear underlying it.

5. Education about disease concept and family process in the development and maintenance of substance abuse. It is also necessary to have commitment by all regarding their willingness to work on their own and shared problems. Family commitment to recovery is imperative.

6. Be prepared to confront excuses for avoiding immediate treatment. Provide directions and alternatives.

7. When those participating in the intervention meet prior to the intervention and lists are read, lists will be prioritized as to the sequence of reading.

8. Information about an intervention will not be shared with anyone not presenting in the intervention (even that it is going to take place to avoid the appearance of disrespect or sabotage).

9. Be respectful and genuine in your concern.

10. All information associated with the intervention is kept confidential.

Be sure that all individuals who participate in an intervention understand the principles of an intervention, what their role is, and the importance of consistency in their messages along with the avoidance of codependency.

11. Continue to expand on the positives associated with abstinence—many are simple pleasures:
    a. eat and sleep in a normal pattern
    b. able to deal with whatever issues are presented
    c. become someone that you can rely on
    d. become someone that others can rely on

12. Develop a positive association of ideas:
    a. associate substance use as a dead end and cause of shame and misery
    b. substances are the one thing that can destroy everything that you want that is important to you

13. Develop genuine gratitude that life is about choices.
14. Seek ways to be a positive role model and that abstinence is the best way to help others.
15. Develop and utilize resources that are supportive of recovery.
16. Seek the serenity to accept the things that cannot be changed, the courage to change what can be changed, and the wisdom to know the difference.

LEGAL ISSUES ASSOCIATED WITH SCREENING AND ASSESSING ADOLESCENT SUBSTANCE USE

Federal law and other regulations guarantee confidentiality for those receiving substance prevention and substance use treatment. This includes the protection of privacy on adolescents. Any program that specializes in providing assessment, referral, counseling, and/or treatment to adolescents with substance use disorders is required to comply with the laws and regulations of confidentiality.

Information may be shared under the following circumstances:

1. Appropriate consent has been given (by the adolescent or adolescent–parent)
2. Without the adolescent's consent when
   a. medical emergency
   b. child abuse reporting (consult to insure compliance with state law)
   c. program evaluations
   d. communication among staff for the benefit of the adolescent

The adolescent must always sign the consent form in order for a program to release information (even to a parent–guardian when applicable). The parents signature must be obtained in addition to the adolescent's signature only if the program is required by state law to obtain parental permission before providing treatment to the adolescent. The adolescent may revoke a consent at any time. Revocation need not be in writing.

ROLE OF AMERICANS WITH DISABILITIES ACT

The Americans with Disabilities Act (ADA) of 1990 referred to those protected by the ADA as a group of individuals who have historically been subjected to unequal treatment. The ADA was enacted to address and eliminate the major forms of discrimination:

1. Intentional exclusion
2. Over protection rules and policies
3. Segregation or regulation to lesser services–programs
4. Exclusionary standards
5. Architectural, transportation, and communication barriers

With regard to substance prevention and treatment programs, there is an acknowledgment that Americans with disabilities experience stressful demands, transectional periods, and some periods of depression, denial, grief, anger, social isolation, etc., according to the ADA, substance prevention and treatment programs serving individuals with disabilities are required to pay special attention to

1. the regular use of prescribed medication, both nonpsychoactive and psychoactive, which may serve to facilitate later legal or illicit substance use.
2. substance abuse that exists prior to disability acquisition, because it has significant potential to continue and get worse.

SUBSTANCE ABUSE SERVICES IN PRACTICE

As of January, 2003, *The Monitor on Psychology* journal identified how practitioners responding to a survey currently help their substance abusing clients:

- 31% utilize relapse prevention counseling
- 40% utilize cognitive-behavioral therapy
- 42% utilize motivational interviewing strategies

REFERENCES

Alcoholics Anonymous (1952). "Twelve Steps and Twelve Traditions." New York: AA World Services, Inc.

American Psychological Association (2003). Substance abuse services in practice. *The Monitor on Psychology*, January, p. 34.

American Society of Addiction Medicine (1996). "Patient Placement Criteria for the Treatment of Substance Related Disorders," 2nd ed. Chevy Chase, MD: American Society of Addiction Medicine.

Bean, M. (1981). Denial and the psychological complications of alcoholism. *In* "Dynamic Approaches to the Understanding and Treatment of Alcoholism" (M. Bean & N. Zinberg, Eds.), pp. 55–96. New York: Free Press.

Beck, A., Wright, F. O., Newman, C. F., & Liese, B. (1993). "Cognitive Therapy for Substance Abuse." New York: Guilford.

Bell, J. (1992). Treatment dependence: Preliminary description of yet another syndrome. *Br. J. Addiction* 87:1049–1054.

Berg, I. K. (1994). "Family Based Services: A Solution-Focused Approach." New York: W. W. Norton.

Berg, I. S., & Miller, S. D. (1992). "Working with the Problem Drinker: A Solution Focused Approach." New York: Norton.

Blatt, S. J., Rounsaville, B., Eyre, S. L., & Wilbur, C. (1984). The psychodynamics of opiate addiction. *J. Nervous Mental Dis.* 172:342–351.

Blumenthal, S. J. (1988). Suicide: A guide to risk factors, assessment and the treatment of suicide patients. *Med. Clin. North America* 72:937–971.

Brandsma, J. M., Maultsky, M. C., & Welsh, R. J. (1980). "The Outpatient Treatment of Alcoholism: A Review and Comparative Study." Baltimore, MD: University Park Press.

Brehm N. M., & Khantzian, E. J. (1992). The psychology of substance abuse: A psychodynamic perspective. *In* "Substance Abuse: A Comprehensive Textbook" (J. H. Lowinson, P. Ruiz, & R. B. Millman, Eds.), 2nd ed. Baltimore, MD: Williams & Wilkins.

Brownell, K. D. (1982). The addictive disorders. *In* "Annual Review of Behavior Therapy: Theory and Practice" (C. M. Franks, G. T. Wilson, P. C. Kendall, & K. D. Brownell, Eds.), Vol. 8. New York: Guilford Press.

Burkstein, O. G., Glancy, L. J., & Kaminer, Y. (1992). Patterns of affective comorbidity in a clinical population of dually diagnosed substance abusers. *J. Am. Acad. Child Adolescent Psychiatry* **31**:1041–1045.

Caetano, R., & Medina-Mora, M. E. (1990). Reasons and attitudes toward drinking and abstaining. *In* "Epidemiologic Trends in Drug Use: Community Epidemiology Work Group Proceedings, June, 1990," pp. 173–191. Rockville, MD: National Institute on Drug Abuse.

Carroll, J. (1993). Attitudes of professionals to drug abusers. *Br. J. Nursing* **2**:705-711.

Center for Substance Abuse Treatment (1997). Treatment improvement exchange: Opiod addiction special topic. On-line: http://www.samhsa.gov/csat/csat.htm.

Connor, G. J., DiClemente, C. C., Carroll, K. M., Longabaugh, R., & Donovan, D. M. (1997). The therapeutic alliance and its relationship to alcoholism treatment and outcome. *J. Consult. Clin. Psychol.* **65**(4):588–598 .

Cooney, N. L., Kadden, R. M., Litt, M. D., & Getter , H. (1991). Matching alcoholics to coping skills or interactional therapies: Two year follow-up results. *J. Consult. Clin. Psychol.* **59**:598–601.

Crissley, N. (1996). "Intersubjectivity: The Fabric of Social Becoming." Thousand Oaks, CA: Sage.

DeLeon, G. (1984). "The Therapeutic Community: Study of Effectiveness," NIDA Treatment Research Monograph. Rockville, MD: NIDA.

deShazer, S. D. (1989). Resistance revisited. *Contemp. Family Ther.* **11**(4):227–233.

Elder, I. R. (1990). "Conducting Group Therapy with Addicts: A Guidebook for Professionals." Blue Ridge Summit, PA: TAB books.

Ellis, A. (1994). Changing rational emotive therapy (RET) to rational emotive behavior therapy (REBT). *Behavior Therapist* **16**(10):257–258.

Ellis, A., & Dryden, W. (1987). "The Promotive of Rational Emotive Therapy." New York: Springer-Verlag.

Ellis, A., McInernery, J. F., Guiseppe, R., & Yeager, R. J. (1988). "Rational Emotive Therapy with Alcoholics and Substance Abusers." New York: Pergamon Press.

Evans, K., & Sullivan, J. M. (1990a). "Dual Diagnosis: Counseling the Mentally Ill Substance Abuser." New York: Guilford Press.

Evans, K., & Sullivan, J. M. (1990b). "Step Study Counseling with the Dual Disordered Client." New York: Guilford Press.

Finney, J. W., Moos, R. H., & Humphreys, K. (1999). A comparative evaluation of substance abuse treatment: Linking proximal outcomes of 12 step and cognitive behavioral treatment to substance abuse outcomes. *Alcoholism: Clin. Exp. Res.* **23**(3):537–544.

Frances, J., & Miller, S. I. (1991). "Clinical Textbook of Addictive Disorders." New York: Guilford press.

Gehart-Brooks, D., & Lyle, R. R. (Dec. 1998–Jan. 1999). What works in therapy: Client's perspectives. pp. 25, 33.

Gerstein, D. R., & Harwood, H. J. (1990). "Treating Drug Problems: A Study of the Evolution, Effectiveness, and Financing of Private and Public Drug Treatment Systems." Washington, DC: National Academy Press.

Gitlow, S. (1985). Considerations on the evaluation and treatment of substance dependency. *J. Substance Abuse Treatment* **2**:175–179.

Hester, R. K., & Miller, W. R., Eds. (1989). "Handbook of Alcoholism Treatment Approaches." New York: Pergamon Press.

Higgins, S. T., Delaney, D. D., Budney, A. J., Bickel, W. K., Hughes, J. R., Foerg, F., & Fenwick, J. W. (1991). A behavioral approach to achieving initial cocaine abstinence. *Am. J. Psychiatry* **148**:1218–1224.

Higgins, S. T., Bickel, W. K., Hughes, J. R., Foerg, F., & Badger, G. (1993). Achieving cocaine abstinence with a behavioral approach. *Am. J. Psychiatry* **150**:763–769.

Imhoff, J., Hirsch, R., & Terenzi, R. E. (1983). Countertransferential and attitudinal considerations in the treatment of drug abuse and addiction. *Int. J. Addictions* **18**:491–510.

Ja, D., & Aoki, B. (1993). Substance abuse treatment: Cultural barriers in the Asian American community. *J. Psychoactive Drugs* **22**(1):45–52.

Johnson, S. L. (1997). "Therapist's Guide to Clinical Intervention." San Diego: Academic Press.

Jones-Webb, R., Hsiao, C., & Hannan, P. (1995). Relationships between socioeconomic status and drinking problems among black and white men. *Alcoholism: Clin. Exp. Res.* **19**(3):623–627.

Khantzian, E. J., (1985). Psychotherapeutic intervention with substance abusers: The clinical context. *J. Substance Abuse Treatment* **2**:83–88.

Khantzian, E. J., Halliday, K. S., & McAuliffe, W. E. (1990). "Addiction and the Vulnerable Self: Modified Dynamic Group Therapy for Substance Abusers." New York: Guilford Press.

Kleber, H. D. (1994). Assessment and treatment of cocaine abusing methadone maintained patients. Treatment Improvement Protocol Series No. 10, NIH Pub. No. 94-3003. Rockville, MD: U.S. Department of Health and Human Services.

Kristenson, H. (1983). "Studies on Alcohol Related Disabilities in a Medical Intervention," 2nd ed. Malmo, Sweden: University of Lund.

Leake, G. S., & King, A. S. (1977). Effects of counselor expectations on alcohol recovery. *Alcohol Health Res. World* **1**(13):16–22.

Leshner, A. I. (1997). Addiction is a brain disease, and it matters. *Science* **278**:45–47.

Levin, J. D. (1987). "Treatment of Alcoholism and Other Addictions: A Self-Psychology Approach." New York: Jason Aronson.

Liberto, J. G., Oslin, D. W., Ruskin, P. E. (1992). Alcoholism in older persons: A review of the literature. *Hosp. Community Psychiatry* **43**:975–984.

Litt, M. D., Babor, T. F., DelBoca, F. K., Kadden, R. M., & Cooney, N. L. (1992). Types of alcoholism II. Application of an empirically derived typology of treatment matching. *Arch. Gen. Psychiatry* **49**:609–614.

Lowinson, J., Ruiz, P., Millman, R. B., & Langrod, J. G., Eds. (1992). "Substance Abuse: A Comprehensive Textbook," 2nd ed. Baltimore, MD: Williams and Wilkins.

Marlatt, A. G., (1998). "Harm Reduction: Pragmatic Strategies for Managing High Risk Behaviors." New York: Guilford Press.

Maxman, J. S., & Ward, N. G. (1995). "Essential Psychopathology and Its Treatment," New York: W. W. Norton & Company.

McClellan, A. T., Woody, G. E., Luborsky, L., O'Brien, C. P., & Druly, K. A. (1983). Increased effectiveness of substance abuse treatment: A prospective study of patient treatment "matching." *J. Nervous Mental Dis.* **171**:597–605.

McCourt, W., & Glantz, M., (1980). Cognitive behavior therapy in groups for alcoholics. *J. Studies Alcohol* **41**(3):338–346.

Miller, W. (1989). Matching individuals with interventions. *In* "Handbook of Alcoholism Treatment Approaches" (R. K. Hester & W. R. Miller, Eds.), pp. 261–272. New York: Pergamon Press.

Miller, W., & Rollnick, S. (1991). "Motivational Interviewing: Preparing People to Change Addictive Behavior." New York: Guilford Press.

Moos, R. H., Cronkite, R. C., & Finney, J. W. (1982). A conceptual framework for alcoholism treatment evolution. *In* "Encyclopedic Handbook of Alcoholism," (E. M. Pattison & E. Kaufman, Eds.), New York: Gardner.

Nace, E. P. (1987). "The Treatment of Alcoholism." New York: Bruner/Mazel.

National Institute on Drug Abuse (1990). "National Household Survey on Drug Abuse." Rockville, MD: NIDA.

O'Farrell, T. J., & Cowles, K. S. (1989). Marital and family therapy. *In* "Handbook of Alcoholism Treatment Approaches" (R. K. Hester & W. R. Miller, Eds.), pp. 183–205. New York: Pergamon Press.

Peck, M. S. (1978). "The Road Less Traveled." New York: Simon and Schuster.

Perry, S., Cooper, A. M., & Michaels, R. (1987). The psychodynamic formulation: Its purpose, structure and clinical application. *Am. J. Psychiatry* **144**:543–550.

Prochaska, J. O., DiClemente, C. C., & Norcross, J. C. (1992). In search of how people change: Applications to addictive behaviors. *Am. Psychologist* **47**:1102–1114.

Project Match Research Group (1993). Project MATCH: Rationale and methods for a multi-centered clinical trial matching alcoholism patients to treatment. *Alcoholism: Clin. Exp. Res.* **17**:1130–1145.

Ricour, P. (1992). "Oneself as Another." Chicago: University of Chicago Press.

Riley, D., & O'Hare, P. (2000). Harm reduction: Policy and practice. *Prevention Researcher* **7**(2):4–8.

Robinson, D. (1979). "Talking Out of Alcoholism: The Self-Help Process of Alcoholics Anonymous." London: Croom, Helm.

Schottenfeld, R., Carroll, K., & Rounsaville, B. (1993). Comorbid psychiatric disorders and cocaine abuse. *In* "Cocaine Treatment: Research and Clinical Perspectives," Research Monograph No. 135 (F. K. Tims & C. G. Leukenfeld, Eds.), pp. 31–47. Rockville, MD: National Institute on Drug Abuse.

Stark, M. J. (1992). Dropping out of substance abuse treatment: A clinically oriented review. *Clin. Psychol Rev.* **12**:93–116.

Steinglass, P., Bennett, L. A., Wolin, S. J., & Reiss, D. (1987). "The Alcoholic Family." New York: Basic Books.

Stewart, D. A. (1995). The dynamics of fellowship as illustrated in Alcoholics Anonymous. *Q. J. Studies Alcohol* **16**:251–262.

Substance Abuse and Mental Health Services Administration (1995). "National Household Survey on Drug Abuse: Population Estimates," DHHS Publication No. SMA 96-3095. Washington, DC: U.S. Government Printing Office.

Tatarsky, A., & Washton, A. (1992). Intensive outpatient treatment: A psychological perspective. *In* "The Chemically Dependent: Phases of Treatment and Recovery" (B. C. Wallace, Ed.), pp. 28–37. New York: Bruner/Mazel.

Treece, C. (1984). Assessment of ego functioning in studies of narcotic addiction. *In* "The Broad Scope of Ego Function Assessment" (L. Bellak & L. A. Goldsmith, Eds.), pp. 268–289. New York: Wiley.

Treece, C., & Khantzian, E. J. (1986). Psychodynamic factors in the development of drug dependence. *Psychiatr. Clin. North America* **9**:399–412.

Vannicelli, M. (1992). "Removing the Roadblocks: Group Psychotherapy with Substance Abusers and Family Members." New York: Guilford Press.

Wiens, A. N., & Manustik, C. E. (1983). Treatment outcome and patient characteristics in aversion therapy program for alcoholism. *Am. Psychologist* **38**:1089–1096.

Whircomb, R. B. (1999). "It's Time to Focus Drug War on Hard Core Users." Health Care Horizon, Manisses Communication Group, Inc., **4**(1):1–2.

Woody, G. E., McClellan, A. T., Luborsky, L., & O'Brien, C. P. (1986). Psychotherapy for substance abusers. *Psychiatr. Clin. North America* 9:547–562.

Wurmser, L. (1974). Psychoanalytic considerations of the etiology of compulsive drug use. *J. Am. Psychoanalytic Assoc.* 22:820–843.

Wurmser, L. (1985). Denial and split identity: Timely issues in the Psychoanalytic psychotherapy of compulsive drug users. *J. Substance Abuse Treatment* 2:80–96.

Zinberg, N. E. (1984). "Drug, Set and Setting." New Haven CT: Yale Univ.

Zweben, J. E. (1986). Recovery oriented psychotherapy. *J. Substance Abuse Treatment.* 3:255–262.

Zweben, J. E. (1989). Recovery oriented psychotherapy: Patient resistances and therapist dilemma. *J. Substance Abuse Treatment* 6(2):123–132.

Chapter 7

Continuum of Care

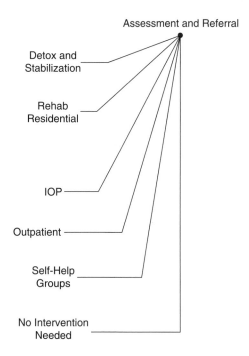

Recent studies suggest that, for every $1 invested in substance abuse treatment, $5–7 is saved in health care costs and $11 is saved in association with the criminal justice system and social services demands (Gerstein *et al.*, 1994).

KEY ASPECTS OF TREATMENT

The most effective and comprehensive treatment program is one that offers a continuum of care with a variety of treatment options that can be utilized to develop a treatment plan that best fits the individual's unique needs. According to Craig (1985), the most significant dropout rate occurs within the first 30 days. Therefore, attention to keeping individuals in treatment through this stressful early stage is potentially the key to successful treatment. The continuum of care should be designed to facilitate and support the client's optimal level of functioning. To accomplish this, all components in the continuum of treatment must be related conceptually into a unified framework, so that the focus of treatment, regardless of where the individual is along the continuum, is readily identifiable. Additionally, the logical sequence of treatment along the continuum enhances the client's understanding of his or her own treatment needs, which benefits his or her collaboration in developing the individualized treatment plan. Clients enter at a point on the continuum of care based upon their needs and related treatment focus. Global assessment functioning (GAF) is important for accurately identifying the level of care needed. The GAF is used to communicate functional impairment, and if not accurately diagnosed could result in a client being inappropriately placed in treatment. The appropriate client–treatment match offers a framework that supports the client's maximum level of functioning via the least restrictive and appropriate treatment intervention.

Key aspects of treatment are as follows:

1. Client safety.
2. To assure that individuals possess a knowledge and understanding of treatment issues, which encourage and benefit their participation in the treatment planning process.
3. Appropriate family involvement contributes to successful treatment and is supported by the program(s) and providers.
4. Treatment focus is developed with the least restrictive interventions along the continuum of care and implements a solution-focused therapy model.
   a. supports abstinence
   b. facilitates development of effective coping strategies
   c. independent adherence to the treatment plan
   d. stabilization of family systems
   e. utilization of community resources
   f. relapse prevention
   g. self-monitoring
5. Long-term recovery plan (discharge planning) that goes beyond programming.

SUBSTANCE ABUSE–DEPENDENCE CONTINUUM OF CARE SERVICES

As previously noted, the focus of treatment is to provide appropriate broad-based treatment options, promote the recovery process through the necessary acquisition of skills, and prevent relapse. The levels of care vary according to the degree of pathology and associated treatment intensity required; however, many of the components are similar or overlap. Additionally, not all of the services available must be utilized. The treatment plan is based upon the individual's needs and is selected collaboratively. Effective integrated substance abuse treatment requires expertise in all modalities and the ability to interchange the client between modalities as needed. Outpatient treatment is not merely inpatient treatment in a different setting. The treatment dynamics and treatment are very different and based upon need. Because of the potential health issues associated with substance abuse, a thorough medical examination is imperative.

OUTPATIENT TREATMENT PROGRAM

Depending on the needs of the individual and his or her family system, therapy sessions could be structured according to a time frame of bimonthly to biweekly, or as needed. Bien *et al.* (1993) suggest that there are substance abusers who clearly benefit from brief treatment, generally abusers of less severity. Galanter (1993) describes a treatment model called

Network Therapy, which can be utilized by individual therapists in a private practice setting. It is a model that focuses on decreasing substance abusing behaviors by using a cognitive-behavioral treatment orientation. Family system participation is a necessary component. This treatment format is important to refine because there are many geographical areas that do not offer substance treatment programs. However, a major concern is that insurance companies may inappropriately utilize this level of treatment and ignore the salience of matching the client to the appropriate treatment for optimal outcome. An individual who meets *DSM IV* criteria for severe substance abuse or substance dependence likely would not be a good candidate for this level of treatment. Components of treatment include the following:

1. Therapy
   a. individual
   b. conjoint
   c. family
   d. group (affect–mood management, skill development etc.)
2. Medication monitoring (if dual diagnosis)
3. 12-step meetings [or other self-help groups (Rational Recovery, Smart Recovery, SOS, etc.) and support for family such as Alanon, Codependents Anonymous (CoDA), Alateen, Adult Children of Alcoholics, etc.]
4. Problem solving current life stressors or adjustment issues
5. Support for dealing with overwhelming and difficult emotional reactions
6. Personal growth
7. Self-responsibility

Individuals in treatment and their family members should be made aware of all of the treatment choices. Additionally, they may utilize any of the treatment services provided by higher levels of care if necessary.

INTENSIVE OUTPATIENT TREATMENT PROGRAM

Generally structured to provide services 3–4 times per week for a period of 6–8 weeks. The program is offered during the evening hours so that clients can continue to participate in necessary daily activities of work and basic family responsibilities. This program structure offers the intensity of intervention with an effort to avoid unnecessary intrusiveness.

1. Deal with any crisis issues
2. Address issues related to addiction
3. Education covering disease concept, impact on personal and emotional growth, recovery, and relapse prevention
4. Long-term recovery plan
5. Education, identification, and intervention regarding dysfunctional family roles
6. 12-step program–meetings–step work
7. Smart Recovery, Rational Recovery, SOS
8. Individual therapy as indicated
9. Develop a social support system that encourages abstinence
10. Recovery maintenance and self-monitoring

11. Family–significant other participation in multifamily group and other groups for support such as Alanon, Naranon, etc.

12. Obtain a sponsor

13. Skills acquisition groups

14. Support groups for special populations (adults molested as children, PTSD, etc.)

PARTIAL HOSPITALIZATION SUBSTANCE DEPENDENCY PROGRAM

For individuals requiring more intensive intervention than that offered by intensive outpatient programming, partial hospitalization offers intervention 5 days per week during the core hours of the day. This level of intervention is designed for the individual who requires structure and an intensive environment to maintain abstinence, but does not require inpatient detox services. It is also used for the individual who will benefit from this level of structure for adjusting from an inpatient program or for the individual who is demonstrating symptoms of acute risk to decompensate and requires more support than is available at lower levels of care.

The programming used for partial hospitalization will have some components that may be available to those in an inpatient setting, if appropriate. For the individual requiring a higher level of structure and monitoring for a longer period of time, rehab–residential treatment is sought. The inpatient rehab offers an environment for the more acute case presentation and the client who has a history of failed attempt(s) in an outpatient setting. The program will generally span a 14- to 28-day time frame, which can be modified depending on the client's needs with a pending transfer to a residential program or partial hospitalization when appropriate.

1. Crisis issues

2. Individualized treatment–recovery plan

3. Explore, identify, clarify self-defeating behaviors that sabotage recovery

4. Identify healthy alternative behaviors

5. Identify leisure skills to promote abstinence and continued recovery

6. 12-step meetings–step work

7. Smart Recovery, Rational Recovery, SOS, etc.

8. Identify family enabling and codependent behaviors–patterns

9. Identify a social support system that promotes abstinence and recovery

10. Individual therapy as indicated

11. Family participation in Alanon, Naranon, CoDA, etc.

12. Recovery monitoring–maintenance

13. Case management

14. Some additional specialized groups include
    a. substance dependence process group
    b. substance dependence education group
    c. improved coping
    d. activity therapy
    e. relapse prevention
    f. individual recovery planning group
    g. family process group
    h. multifamily group (which includes family and significant other)

RESIDENTIAL TREATMENT PROGRAM

Residential treatment programs (RTPs), now generally referred to as treatment communities (TCs), are often recommended when an individual has had a long-term substance abuse problem and has experienced difficulty remaining in recovery. TCs can be described as fitting the treatment needs of someone who needs a supportive environment and significant support to achieve and maintain abstinence. The features of a TC are as follows:

1. Highly structured program
2. Generally an individual resides at the program site for 6–12 months
3. Therapy
4. Education
5. Social skills training and practice (often seriously impaired social functioning)
6. Redirect those with a history of criminal behavior
7. Develop an appropriate support system
8. Stabilized functioning
9. Vocational rehabilitation

Such a setting develops (or redevelops) a daily life structure, which prepares an individual to resume a functional and responsible clean and sober lifestyle. Time away may also serve to facilitate an appropriate social support system, which reinforces positive changes.

There are short-term variations of TCs whereby an individual participates in the following program:

1. 3–6 weeks of inpatient treatment
2. Extended outpatient treatment
3. 12-step orientation with significant structure

However, TCs are generally reserved for the most difficult cases or those that can afford the cost of residing in a therapeutic community. There are some well-known programs that offer such a service, but most people who enter substance abuse treatment will not be offered this choice. Most individuals will participate in an outpatient program, and some of them will require a brief hospital stay for detox.

INPATIENT DETOXIFICATION

Inpatient detox is utilized for individuals who present with a substance dependency disorder in which abstaining from the substance will result in withdrawal requiring medical detoxification and medical monitoring. The focus of treatment for inpatient detoxification includes

1. Medical detox from substances by an addictionist or other qualified physician
2. 24-h nursing care and monitoring for withdrawal symptoms
3. Introduction to a 12-step or other recovery program

The individual is encouraged to participate in all of the groups and milieu activities in the support services offered by the rehabilitation–partial hospitalization program as they are able due to decreasing intensity of withdrawal symptoms.

TREATMENT GROUPS

During participation in a substance abuse treatment program, there are several groups available to all clients and/or their families, regardless of the level of program intensity. These groups include the following.

Family–

Significant Other

Only Group

This group is offered one time per week for a 2-hr period (generally in the evening). Participants are expected to participate while the substance-dependent individual is in treatment. The group remains available to these individuals for 1 year after the individual has been discharged from his or her program. The focus of this group is

1. Identifying dysfunctional family and behavioral patterns
2. Self-responsibility
3. Participation in Alanon, Naranon, CoDA, etc.
4. Developing an appropriate social support system
5. Improved coping

There may be a variation of this group offered for children and adolescents of a substance abusing individual. The focus of this group would differ accordingly:

1. How have they been affected by the substance abuse?
2. What feelings do they have toward the substance abuser (anger, sadness, fear or concern for their parent)?
3. How do substances affect their relationship (with the parent)?
4. What have they learned?
5. Have they ever willingly, been tricked, or been coerced into a codependent–enabling role?
6. Processing issues of loss.

Multifamily–

Significant

Other Group

Family and significant other participation is generally mandatory. This group includes the substance-dependent individual. The group is facilitated by a professional trained in family systems and substance dependence dynamics and issues. Attendance takes place for the 6–8 weeks during the course of the core intensive outpatient program and for 6 consecutive weeks after the substance-dependent client is discharged. The structure of this group is also utilized when the substance abuser is an adolescent.

Aftercare–Relapse

Prevention Group

This group is available for a period of 1 year to all clients completing any level of treatment. The group meets one time per week for 2 hr and offers support for continued recovery. Some programs offer the flexibility that aftercare remains available in an open-ended manner to anyone who needs it.

ASAM-PPC-2 ASSESSMENT CRITERIA

The following section identifies diagnostic criteria described in the *DSM IV* as the foundation for determining level of care. Similar to this format of classification for referral for appropriate level of care is Assessment Criteria. The American Society of Addiction Medicine (1996) developed adult assessment criteria for substance abuse treatment. The criteria are a matrix of levels of care with associated dimensions that serve as identifiers of level of care–intervention, which demonstrates referral complementarity with the following section. The rendering of appropriate treatment recommendations requires a thorough understanding of all available treatment resources:

1. Comprehensive and current list of local and regional mental health treatment services
2. Comprehensive and current list of social service programs
   a. vocational rehab
   b. self-help programs
   c. churches–church-based programs
   d. legal aid
   e. financial aid

ASSESSMENT DIMENSIONS

1. Acute intoxication–withdrawal potential: alleviate or eliminate the severity of acute withdrawal syndrome. This may eliminate the need for intensive medical management.
2. Biomedical conditions and complications
   a. stabilization of medical problems, resulting in elimination of the need for medical monitoring
   b. resolve the biomedical problem to the degree allowing transition to a lower level of care
   c. a continuing care plan should include the following components
      i. a personal care physician (and/or necessary treating professional)
      ii. identification of medical–dental problem with associated treatment plan outline
      iii. development of a personal plan for health maintenance
      iv. development of a self-care plan
3. Emotional and behavioral conditions and complications
   a. alleviate severity of emotional–behavioral conditions
   b. ability to process the emotional experience
   c. ability to identify and discuss feelings associated with substance abuse (this includes an awareness of the connection between substance use and emotions such as guilt and shame)
   d. develop anger management skills
   e. develop impulse control techniques
   f. identify problems requiring the use of psychological services and how such services will be obtained and maintained
   g. develop cognitive–behavioral techniques for managing depression and anxiety
   h. learn or improve assertive communication skills
   i. learn or improve necessary interpersonal skills
4. Treatment acceptance and resistance
   a. acceptance of substance abuse problem(s) (awareness and acceptance of inability to control the use of substances)
   b. awareness of substance use and its consequences

c. recognition of the severity of the substance use disorder

d. acceptance of personal responsibility for recovery

e. acceptance of treatment goals

5. Relapse–continued use potential

   a. understand the relationship between triggers, craving, and relapse

   b. identify personal triggers

   c. integrate relapse prevention skills into general repertoire of behavior

      i. increased awareness

      ii. early identification

      iii. management of progressive relapse signs

      iv. early intervention and planning for relapse

   d. eliminate participation in high-risk activities–relationships–behavior–settings, etc.

   e. develop refusal skills

6. Recovery environment

   a. improve environmental supports sufficient to sustain recovery

   b. develop a lifestyle that promotes abstinence and recovery

   c. develop and use social supports that promote abstinence and recovery

   d. develop necessary interpersonal skills

   e. persue personal growth and development (i.e., education–vocation)

DIAGNOSTIC CRITERIA FOR DETERMINING LEVEL OF CARE

In order for an individual to be matched with the appropriate level of care, a thorough assessment must be made that identifies diagnostic criteria that are used to define the treatment foci for a particular level of care. Obviously, the first layer of diagnosis is associated with the criteria described in the *DSM IV* associated with the range of substance abuse disorders. The second level of criteria is related to programs within the continuum of care. The effectiveness of placement depends on the accurate collapsing of these two levels (Washton, 1995; APA, 1994, 1995; Galanter & Kleber, 1994; Lindstrom, 1992).

Intensive

Outpatient

Program

1. The individual satisfies criteria for substance dependence as defined by *DSM IV*.

2. There is a lack of life threatening signs and symptoms of withdrawal.

3. The individual requires a formal outpatient treatment program in order to effectively discontinue substance use and pursue recovery.

4. The individual is able to function in a community environment. However, there is some impairment in social, family, occupational, or medical functioning and GAF is > 50.

5. There is willingness to participate in the program and acceptance that absenteeism is not acceptable.

6. The individual demonstrates sufficient cognitive capacity to comprehend and respond to the content of the program.

7. The individual's living situation and support system are supportive of his or her efforts.

8. The individual does not satisfy criteria for a more intensive level of program intervention.

Partial
Hospitalization–
Rehabilitation

1. The individual satisfies *DSM IV* criteria for a substance dependence disorder.
2. The individual does not satisfy the severity of symptomatology for inpatient detoxification or a higher level of intervention for substance dependence rehabilitation.
3. The individual is unable to maintain abstinence without the support of the structured environment provided during the core hours of the day.
4. The individual is able to function in a community environment. There is significant impairment in social, family, occupational, or medical functioning. GAF is >40.
5. The individual demonstrates the cognitive capacity to comprehend and respond to the content of the program.
6. There have been previous treatment failures.
   a. willingly undergone outpatient treatment without success
   b. symptoms have been sustained or intensified
   c. relapse has occurred
7. The individual willingly participates in the partial hospitalization program (PHP) and accepts that program absence is unacceptable.
8. The individual requires the more intense PHP in order to minimize contact with a disruptive social environment.
9. The individual's living arrangement and family are supportive of recovery.
10. The individual does not satisfy criteria for a more intense level of care.

For consideration for admission to the inpatient rehabilitation program, add the following criteria:

1. The client is unable to live outside a controlled environment and maintain abstinence.
2. Functional impairment is to a degree that requires skilled observation and care.
3. Destructive influences in the home–social environments jeopardize abstinence.
4. Dual diagnosis issues that interfere with substance dependence recovery.

Detoxification

1. Medically monitored intensive inpatient
2. Medically managed intensive inpatient

The individual meets the criteria for *DSM IV* substance dependence and presents with a constellation of symptoms of withdrawal–toxicity representing compromised physical functioning and thus requiring medical support and 24-hr skilled observation, the need for medication stabilization, or monitoring of the individual's physiological or behavioral reactions to treatment. Under these conditions, fluids and medications are dispensed to prevent withdrawal complications that may threaten life or interfere with bodily functions. Criteria that are used to determine the severity of illness warranting detoxification services are as follows:

1. Severe anxiety
2. Depression and lassitude

3. Increased appetite
4. Headache
5. Muscle cramps
6. Anorexia–nausea–vomiting
7. Significantly disturbed sleep pattern
8. Diaphoresis
9. Significant increase or decrease in psychosomatic activity
10. Tremor
11. Clouding of consciousness with reduced capacity to shift, focus, or sustain attention
12. Pain, secondary to withdrawal
13. Suicidal ideation
14. Hallucinations–delusions
15. Incoherent speech

The following three symptoms are also considered, but placement is ultimately determined by the degree of medical necessity mediated by medical clearance from a primary care physician, specialist, or hospital staff:

1. Tachycardia
2. Hypertension
3. Orthostatic hypotension

Inpatient detoxification is contraindicated and hospitalization is required until medical clearance is obtained when the following symptoms are present:

1. Either the systolic or diastolic reading increases or decreases by 30 mm Hg from the baseline blood pressure.
2. Heart rate increases or decreases 30 beats from baseline rate.
3. The individual is at risk for acute disturbances associated with heart rhythm that are life threatening, such as complete heart block or premature beats associated with ventricular fibrillation.
4. Respiratory rate changes by 30% against baseline rate.
5. A history of withdrawal seizures or current excessive use of a substance indicating a propensity of recurring seizures.
6. Uncontrolled emesis or other life threatening medical states exist, such as acute pancreatitis, hepatorenal syndrome, acute alcohol hepatitis, or Wernicke's encephalopathy.
7. History of life threatening withdrawal episodes and current symptoms that present a strong clinical picture of severe withdrawal syndrome.
8. The individual experiences medical complications, such as acute pancreatitis, liver failure, or bacterial endocarditis, which can only be treated in an appropriate medical setting.

9. Altered level of consciousness, fluctuating from stupor to coma.

10. The individual experiences delirium associated with alcohol withdrawal.

11. Sympathetic nervous system activity, such as dilation, perspiration, or increase in dry mouth.

As the continuum of care is reviewed, it becomes evident that there are appropriate clinical reasons at every level to utilize individual therapy. Zweben (1986) states that individual therapy is often underutilized in substance abuse treatment and that it may be a key modality for keeping an individual in treatment. Naranjo and Bremner (1994) offer pharmacotherapy for treatment of substance use disorders.

SPECIFIC SUBSTANCE CLASS TREATMENT CONSIDERATIONS ASSOCIATED WITH CONTINUUM OF CARE

Helpful references in this area include Frances and Miller (1998) and Naranjo *et al.* (1994).

DEPRESSANTS

Alcohol

Treatment is initiated with an assessment for any medical emergency situations. Severe intoxication can threaten to compromise respiratory functioning. Severe withdrawal symptoms like delirium tremens or seizures are treated with medical intensive care. Even when no medical emergency is presented, an individual may still require careful medical and psychiatric treatment to avoid or manage symptoms of alcohol abuse or withdrawal. Early stages of alcohol withdrawal are effectively managed with a pharmacologic substitute for alcohol like librium. Other medical consequences of long-term alcohol abuse include organ system damage (such as cirrhosis of the liver) and nerve damage. Syndromes developed by chronic alcoholics associated with a prolonged inadequate diet resulting in a thiamine deficiency are Wernicke's encephalopathy and Korsakoff's syndrome. Wernicke's encephalopathy is an acute, life threatening condition with the following symptoms:

1. Clouding of consciousness

2. Opthalmoplegia (weakness of the muscles controlling movement of the eyes)

3. Ataxia (wide-based gait, falls easily, inability to walk or stand)

Korsakoff's syndrome remains as a chronic condition when Wernicke's encephalopathy is treated. It is also possible that it will occur after one or more episodes of delirium tremens. The most prominent symptom of this syndrome is recent memory impairment.

Treatment

Emergency situations must be treated first, such as severe intoxication and alcohol poisoning. There is concern of respiratory functioning being compromised. Other emergency concerns are delirium tremens and seizures. Even when individuals do not present in an acute symptomatic state, they may still require careful medical and psychiatric treatment to avoid dire consequences of withdrawal.

Detoxification is the first step of treatment for those who are likely to experience significant withdrawal symptoms. Although detox can be carefully monitored for some in an outpatient setting, it is generally carried out in a medical or psychiatric setting. Detox in an inpatient setting allows for more intensive monitoring of physical status and appropriate and timely intervention to prevent potentially lethal withdrawal reactions. Physiological withdrawal usually begins within 6–24 hr (may be as late as 36 hr) following the alcoholic's last intake of alcohol. Complications of alcohol withdrawal include (Frances & Miller, 1998; Kaplan & Sadock, 1990) the following.

1. Worsening of early symptoms
   a. rapid pulse
   b. sweating
   c. agitation
   d. tremor

2. Seizures
   a. most likely in the first 24–48 hr following the last drink
   b. usually nonfocal and generalized
   c. generally preceding agitation, delirium, and hallucinations

3. Alcoholic hallucinosis
   a. most likely 24–48 hr following last drink
   b. may be visual or auditory

4. Delirium tremens
   a. likely to occur 50–100 hr following last drink
   b. may last up to 14 days
   c. involves hallucinations, delusions, or both
   d. hypermetabolic state
   e. elevated body temperature
   f. dehydration
   g. blood chemistry imbalance

5. Mortality (as high as 15%)

Early treatment is the key to management and/or avoidance of allowing manifested symptoms to escalate. It is more difficult to treat after symptoms become more severe, as well as placing an individual at higher risk for severe complications.

Delirium tremens is treated effectively by a pharmacologic substitute for alcohol such as librium. This medication has a wide margin of safety and a long half-life (24–30 hr). Pharmacologic treatment of withdrawal acts to alleviate signs and symptoms of early withdrawal and prevents progression to more severe symptoms of delirium tremens and seizures.

Long-term treatments:

1. 12-step program or other self-help group
2. Psychodynamic therapy
3. Cognitive therapy
4. Behavior modification
5. Conjoint–family therapy
6. Appropriate group therapy
7. Disulfuram
8. Community programs and systems of support
9. Relapse prevention

Sedatives, Hypnotics, and Anxiolytics

All of these substances are central nervous system (CNS) depressants and referred to as downers. These CNS depressants are often used in combination with alcohol and opiates. Understandably, overdoses occur easily with these combinations. Symptoms of overdose with these substances are similar to those seen with drunkenness (Juergen, 1997; Frances & Miller, 1998).

Treatment

Intervening in an emergency such as overdose or withdrawal:

1. Overdose (hospitalization)
   a. induce vomiting
   b. lab testing on blood, urine, and gastric samples
   c. monitor–support respiratory and cardiac functions for at least 24 hr

2. Withdrawal
   a. CNS depressants pose danger if it occurs abruptly
   b. may experience seizures or cardiovascular collapse, possible death
   c. medically and pharmacologically treated

Withdrawal from benzodiazepenes can be protracted. Therefore, seizures can occur as late as two weeks after cessation of use. Medical monitoring is required.

Long-term treatments:

1. 12-step program or other self-help group
2. Psychodynamic therapy
3. Behavior therapy
4. Cognitive therapy
5. Conjoint–family therapy
6. Appropriate group therapy
7. Community resources and support
8. Relapse Prevention

Cannabinoids

Marijuana and hashish are mild euphorants that present some sedative effects. With heavy use they are also CNS depressants and offer some mild hallucinogenic properties. According to Washton (1995), anecdotal experiences have been reported of individuals combining a high dose of Zoloft (150–600 mg) with marijuana, resulting in enhanced creative abilities and improved productivity not experienced with either substance alone. A hypomanic episode may follow, requiring discontinued use of both substances with close follow-up.

Treatment

If psychotic symptoms are present, the individual needs a supportive environment and the use of benzodiazephines for calming. If psychosis persists, neuroleptics are indicated.

Long-term treatments:

1. 12-step program or other self-help group
2. Psychodynamic therapy
3. Behavior therapy
4. Cognitive therapy

5. Conjoint–family therapy

6. Appropriate group therapy

7. Community resources and support

8. Relapse prevention

Hallucinogens

Hallucinogens refer to a broad variety of substances that are grouped together based upon their ability to induce altered states of awareness similar to psychosis (Miller *et al.*, 1988; Daghestani & Schnoll, 1989; Frances & Miller, 1998).

Treatment

If severe panic is present, pharmacologic intervention is made. If seizures or severe muscle spasms are present, they will be treated pharmacologically. Unless psychosis is unusually severe and prolonged, antipsychotic medications may be avoided. Support, reassurance, and minimal environmental stimulation are important.

Long-term treatments:

1. 12-step program or other self-help group

2. Psychodynamic therapy

3. Behavior therapy

4. Cognitive therapy

5. Conjoint–family therapy

6. Appropriate group therapy

7. Community resources or support

8. Relapse prevention

Opiates

Opium has been around so long that it has served as an economic hub in some cultures. Although many opium-related compounds are used illegally, there are some that serve important medicinal purposes such as for pain (they are the strongest pain killers), slowing the gut, etc. All opiates are sedating and have a strong potential for the development of tolerance as well as physical and psychological dependence. As with other addicting substances, there are no socioeconomic boundaries that protect any given segment of the population from abusing these substances. Narcotic overdoses often take place because an individual is unaware of the strength and how his or her body will respond under various circumstances (Frances & Miller, 1998; Carroll, 1996; Garvin & Ellinwood, 1988).

Treatment

The first step in intervening medically with an acute overdose is to support vital functions with intravenous glucose. This is followed by an opioid agonist to block the effects of the substance. Withdrawal from opiates generally is not life threatening for a healthy individual. Opiate withdrawal has been likened to the experience of having the flu for a week, which is uncomfortable. Acutely addicted or recently detoxified individuals benefit from psychotherapy as a component of a multidimensional approach and as an adjunct to pharmacotherapy. Methadone substitution is effective treatment for withdrawal management during a course of inpatient treatment. However, clonidine has been found to be very effective for alleviating the signs and symptoms of withdrawal as well, and it is nonaddicting.

Long-term treatments:

1. Outpatient methadone maintenance

2. Long-acting opioid agonist (naltrexone)

3. 12-step program or other self-help group

4. Psychodynamic therapy

5. Behavior therapy

6. Cognitive therapy

7. Conjoint–family therapy

8. Appropriate group therapy

9. Community resources and support

10. Relapse prevention

STIMULANTS

Amphetamine and amphetamine-like substances are central nervous system stimulants referred to as uppers. Large doses can result in acute delirium and psychosis. Overdose is potentially lethal.

Treatment

Acute intoxication with severe symptoms requires intervention to decrease CNS irritability and control psychotic symptoms. Calming sedation with an antipsychotic medication may be used to ease agitation and diminish psychotic symptoms. Reassurance, support, and minimal environmental stimulation are also helpful.

Long-term treatments:

1. 12-step program or other self-help group

2. Psychodynamic therapy

3. Behavior therapy

4. Cognitive therapy

5. Conjoint–family therapy

6. Appropriate group therapy

7. Community resources and support

8. Relapse prevention

POLYSUBSTANCE ABUSE

Like other forms of substance abuse, the polysubstance abuser has substituted substances for human contact and relationships.

Lives revolve around

1. Process of obtaining substances

2. Daily structure associated with substances

3. Repetitive personal contacts within substance culture

4. Medicate "away" unpleasant emotions

Treatment

Short-term treatments

1. Detox

2. Stabilization

3. Substance abuse treatment

4. Initiate establishing a new support system
5. Self-help group
6. Vocational rehab
7. Day care center
8. Substance-free residential community
9. Psychodynamic therapy
10. Behavior therapy
11. Cognitive therapy
12. Conjoint–family therapy
13. Appropriate group therapy
14. Relapse prevention

COMMUNITY REINFORCEMENT

Another treatment choice is a behaviorally based treatment program that comprehensively reviews and matches interventions and community resources for the substance abuser and family members in need of support, education, and reinforcement of change (Hunt & Azrin, 1973; Mallams *et al.*, 1982). Some basic components of a community reinforcement program are the following:

1. Medication evaluation and monitoring for psychotropic medication
2. Encourage and reinforce program of change and growth
3. Marital–family therapy, encouraging participation of significant other
4. A job "club" (often offered by churches in a community)
    a. how to call upon a prospective employer
    b. filling out an application
    c. interviewing skills

5. Social skills training
6. Recommendations and problem solving associated with social, recreational, and leisure activities
7. Relapse prevention
    a. develop appropriate alternatives
    b. coping with urges to use
    c. refusal skills

8. Requires a higher degree of support; recognizes vulnerability

There are many individuals entering treatment who lack the necessary resources identified with a successful treatment outcome. The community reinforcement program format comprehensively provides for these needs by creating a new social support system for the substance abuser. Many substance abusers have alienated family and friends over time, have lost their jobs, and likely have experienced an erosion in their social skills. As a result they greatly benefit from, if not require, the degree of support offered by such a program.

CONTROLLED DRINKING: A TREATMENT ALTERNATIVE

Miller and Hester (1986) offer the following criteria for candidates for moderate or controlled drinking:

1. Early or low dependence problem drinking
2. Younger (under age 40)
3. Married, employed, and stable
4. Not presently committed to substances
5. Shorter time of use

TABLE 7.1   Diagram of Assessment and Treatment[a]

Screening and Evaluation
Substance Use
Behavior Patterns
Psychiatric Disorders–Syndromes
Health
Family Systems
Peer Relationships
Social Skills
Coping and Management Abilities
Work–Vocational Counseling–School
Leisure–Recreation

Treatment Options

Degree of support
and structure required
by presenting symptoms
and level of functioning
when entering treatment.

Lowest

No Intervention Needed

Self-Help Groups

Outpatient Therapy
pharmacotherapy
health interventions
marital–family treatment
relapse prevention
social skills training
mood management
anxiety management
stress management
community reinforcement
aftercare

Intensive Outpatient Therapy
drug aversion–maintenance treatment
self-control training
increased support

Rehab–Residential
controlled environment
increased structure

Stepwise progression
of recovery demonstrated
by the decreasing need of
structure and support.

Detox
Stabilization monitoring

Highest

[a]Adapted from Hester and Miller (1989).

TABLE 7.2   General Substance Abuse Treatment Diagram

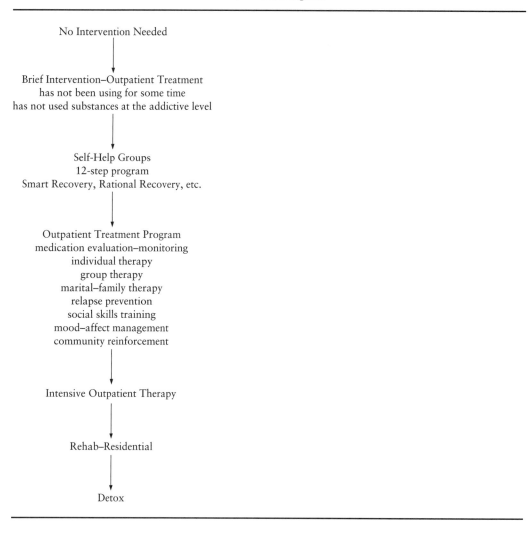

No Intervention Needed

Brief Intervention–Outpatient Treatment
has not been using for some time
has not used substances at the addictive level

Self-Help Groups
12-step program
Smart Recovery, Rational Recovery, etc.

Outpatient Treatment Program
medication evaluation–monitoring
individual therapy
group therapy
marital–family therapy
relapse prevention
social skills training
mood–affect management
community reinforcement

Intensive Outpatient Therapy

Rehab–Residential

Detox

6. Not prone to withdrawal symptoms

7. Physically healthy

8. Not subject to psychosocial problems associated with long-term drinking

A significant limitation may be the difficulty in attracting referrals of low-dependency problem drinkers to enter a treatment program in addition to learning controlled or moderate drinking (harm reduction). There is also controversy regarding controlled drinking as a viable treatment option. In contrast to treatment in the United States, the United Kingdom has for some time viewed controlled drinking as a treatment option for appropriate candidates. Research suggests that approximately 15–18% of problem drinkers are able to successfully drink in moderation following a standard treatment program (goal of abstinence) and that they continue to control their drinking as demonstrated by follow-up years later (Helzer *et al.*, 1985; Polich *et al.*, 1980). Nathan (1986) states that chronic alcoholics are the poorest candidates for moderate drinking.

According to the Institute of Medicine (1990), evidence suggests that possibly 80% of the alcoholics in the United States have never made contact with any self-help or professional treatment program. Miller *et al.* (1992) state that this is likely related to untreated individuals rejecting the disease concept model and the requirement for absolute abstinence offered by traditional treatment programs. Therefore, if total abstinence is not the desired goal for such individuals, they would lack motivation to invest in changes in their drinking behavior.

TABLE 7.3   Review of Inpatient versus Outpatient Differences

Inpatient	Outpatient
High level of patient support required (monitoring)	Support varies based upon need
Removal from vulnerable environment	Potential continued exposure to substance use environment
Immersion into therapeutic environment	Continued intermittent exposure to stressors and triggers
Focus on increased awareness, self-understanding, and disclosure	Focus on abstinence and relapse preventions
Break from daily problems	Immediate efforts to develop problem solving skills
Alleviation of craving and elimination of risk of relapse	Immediate efforts to develop skills needed to cope with craving and risk of relapse
Use of therapeutic confrontation to promote progress	Therapeutic support to promote change and decrease premature treatment termination
Consistent, dependable support made available	Intermittent support—must be sought after

TABLE 7.4   Substance Abuse Treatment

Assessment and referral

Initiation of treatment

A. Intervention
   Formal assessment utilizing motivational interviewing
   Listen to life experiences and perspectives
   Clarify why treatment now
   What are the beliefs about benefiting from substances
   Are there things that the individual feels he or she needs to change to improve life
   Is he or she ready for treatment and abstinence

B. Detox
   Inpatient or outpatient depending on the degree of medical supervision necessary

C. Referral options (refer to diagram)
   Inpatient
   Residential–rehab
   PHP
   Intensive outpatient
   Outpatient
   Each of the referral options offers a constellation of treatment components
      or choices, such as individual–group–family therapy, education, self-help meetings, etc.

D. Pharmacological treatment
   Alcohol
      Disulfuram (antabuse): it works by inhibiting the initial breakdown
         product of alcohol, which results in making the individual ill if he or she ingests
         alcohol while taking it
      Naltrexone: seems to help maintain sobriety as well as decreases the urge to use
      Antianxiety medication such as Ativan for calming physiological and psychological responses

(Continues)

TABLE 7.4 *(Continued)*

Opiates
    Methadone: is an addictive agonist. It is used as a replacement for the substance.
        Withdrawal requires tapering over 1–2 weeks. In a methadone program the individual
        is detoxed from the opiate over 21 days with the concomitant treatment with methadone.
        Unpleasant experience. Originally, it was believed that opiate addicts would never be
        clean (i.e., would never be able to stop methadone maintenance). However, after about 2 years
        they may attempt medically supervised cessation of the methadone
    Naltrexone: nonaddicting. It blocks opiate receptors, which could be a problem if
        emergency medical treatment is required
    Clonedine: for alleveating withdrawal symptoms
Stimulants–cocaine
    Most trials have been with antidepressant medications. Some evidence of decreased urge
        to use (for some individuals)
Dual Diagnosis
    Appropriate treatment for depression–anxiety and psychotic disorders

E. Four stages of recovery
    Precontemplation–using
    Contemplation–transition (work with resistance–ambivalence as much as possible)
    Active–early stages of recovery (self-help, dealing with issues of loss, growth, and adjustment)
    Maintenance–later stages of continued recovery (more typical psychotherapy issues)

F. Treatment selection (clarifying identified needs of personal intervention throughout the course of
    treatment)
    Individual therapy (personal growth for reinforcing substance abuse treatment
        interventions, continued skills development, support in adjustment, etc.)
    Conjoint therapy (may be useful throughout the course of treatment)
    Family therapy
        Role of family members in maintaining substance abuse
        Support in changing dysfunctional patterns
        Facilitate appropriate boundaries and developmental separation
        Assess for other cases of substance abuse in the family
    Group therapy
        Specific topic psychotherapy group
        Education–didactic format
        Specific self-help

G. Relapse prevention–continuing recovery
    Terminology
        Slip: one-time use following abstinence
        Lapse: use that does not go beyond several days
        Relapse: return to practice of addiction with reentry into drug subculture
    Educate individual regarding all steps that can lead to slip, lapse, and relapse. Predict what can
    happen under various circumstances (to plan prevention).

Miller (1983) cites that Canada, Australia, and Europe offer controlled drinking programs that attract individuals who are not interested in traditional abstinence-based treatment. Merely having the choice in treatment goals could result in encouraging some individuals to enter treatment who would not otherwise seek intervention. Although supporters of the disease concept theory often associated with traditional treatment oppose goals other than abstinence, findings indicate that continued but reduced consumption of alcohol is a successful treatment goal for some (Armor *et al.*, 1978; Polich *et al.*, 1981). The modification of such a fundamental treatment philosophy will, of course, impact the continuum of care's treatment options. At this time the debate continues. With continuing research and efforts to provide individualized treatment planning these, questions will be resolved in time.

TABLE 7.5 Substance Abuse–Dependence Continuum of Care[a]

Level of functioning with associated treatment format	General treatment goals	Focus of treatment	Possible treatment modalities
Outpatient	Cognitive restructuring–behavior modification work through necessary psychodynamic issues Improve self care, coping, problem solving, management of life stressors Develop–improve skills Relapse prevention Self-responsibility	Identify–resolve crisis issues Decrease symptomatology Diagnostic assessment initiated Stabilization of interpersonal relationships Medication intervention Reinforce independent utilization of internal–external resources Follow-up to ensure adequate crisis resolution Participation in 12-step or other self-help format Relapse prevention Self-efficacy Initiate vocational–educational plan	Case management (as needed) Individual therapy Conjoint therapy Family therapy Group therapy Educational group (skill building) 12-step–self-help meetings Random drug screen Medication consult–monitoring Appropriate referral to groups–classes aimed at skill building Urgent care or other higher level of care if warranted by crisis issues
Intensive outpatient	Treatment coordinance Abstinence Improve daily functioning and self-management, daily activity schedules, symptom management, decrease symptomatology, develop and utilize social support Relapse prevention Choices–alternatives	Identify–resolve crisis issues Diagnostic assessment initiated Monitor medication compliance Develop effective coping Facilitate adherence to treatment plan Utilize community resources Stabilize family system Relapse prevention Initiate step toward vocational–educational plan	Case management Evening programming (allows for work or school) Psychiatric home health Medication consultation–monitoring Multi family group Educational group (skill building) Family therapy Conjoint therapy Individual therapy 12-step or other self-help meetings Random drug screen After care program 24-hr crisis management
Partial hospitalization–rehabilitation	Treatment compliance Abstinence Behavior–affect stabilization Psychiatric rehabilitation Development–reinforcement of appropriate social support Improve coping–problem solving Improve judgement, insight, impulse control Relapse prevention–refusal skills	Identify–resolve crisis issues Provide safe environment Diagnostic assessment initiated Stabilize and decrease symptomatology Pharmacological monitoring Cognitive restructuring–behavior modification Supervised application–practice of coping skills Relapse prevention Clarify vocational–educational plan	Case management Monday–Friday daily programming Medication consultation–monitoring Support group Educational group (skill building) Vocational planning and support (i.e., appropriate referral) Drug screen (initial and random) 24-hr unit for acute crisis intervention
Inpatient–detox	Detox and medical stabilization Behavior–affect management Family prepared for discharged lower level of care	Provide safe environment Crisis intervention Diagnostic assessment initiated Medical management and monitoring Acute symptom alleviation–relief Mobilize support Reality testing Orientation to therapeutic process	Case management Detox with associated medical management of symptoms Medical monitoring Drug screen Introduction to substance abuse treatment programming

[a]Adult and adolescent options are collapsed. Engage or reinitiate lower level of care when individual is adequately stabilized. Treatment goals are cummulative from lower to higher level of functioning. Appropriate referrals assumed. Treatment goals determined cooperatively with patient.

REFERENCES

Alcoholics Anonymous (1996). "Alcoholics Anonymous: 1996 Membership Survey." New York: Alcoholics Anonymous World Services.

American Psychiatric Association (1994). "Diagnostic and Statistical Manual of Mental Disorders," 4th ed. Washington, DC: American Psychiatric Association.

American Psychiatric Association (1995). Practice guidelines for the treatment of patients with substance use disorders: Alcohol, cocaine, opioids. *Am. J. Psychiatry* **152** (Suppl.):5–59.

American Society of Addiction Medicine (1996). "Patient Placement Criteria for the Treatment of Substance Related Disorders," 2nd ed. Washington DC: American Society of Addiction Medicine.

Armor, D. L., Polich, J. M., & Stambul, H. B. (1978). "Alcoholism and Treatment." New York: Wiley.

Bezchlibnyk-Butler, K. Z. & Jeffries, J. J. (1998). "Clinical Handbook of Psychotropic drugs." Seattle: Hogrefe & Huber Publishers.

Bien, T. H., Miller, W. R., & Tonigan, J. S. (1993). Brief intervention for alcohol problems: A review. *Addictions* **88**:315–336.

Blume, S. B. (1985). Group psychotherapy in the treatment of alcoholism. *In* "Practical Approaches to Alcoholism Psychotherapy" (S. Zimberg, J. Wallace, & S. Blume, Eds.), 2nd ed., pp. 73–86. New York: Plenum Press.

Brown, S. (1985). "Treating the Alcoholic: A Developmental Model of Recovery." New York: Wiley.

Carroll, K. (1994). Relapse prevention as a psychosocial treatment: A review of controlled clinical trials. *Exp. Clin. Psychopharmacol.* 4(1):46–54.

Chaney, E. F. (1989). Social skills training. *In* "Handbook of Alcoholism Treatment Approaches" (R. K. Hester & W. R. Miller, Eds.), pp. 206–221. Boston: Allyn & Bacon.

Cooper, D. E. (1987). The role of group psychotherapy in the treatment of substance abusers. *Am. J. Psychother.* **41**(1):55–67.

Craig, R. (1985). Reducing the treatment dropout rate in drug abuse programs. *J. Substance Abuse Treatment* **2**:209–219.

Dackis C. A., & Gold, M. S. (1992). Psychiatric hospitals for treatment dual diagnosis. *In* "Substance Abuse: A Comprehensive Textbook" (J. H. Lowinson, P. Ruiz, & R. B. Millman, Eds.), 2nd ed., pp. 467–485. Baltimore, MD: William & Wilkins.

Daghestani, A. N., & Schnoll, S. H. (1989). Phenylcyclidine abuse and dependence. *In* "Treatments of psychiatric Disorders" (T. B. Karasu, Ed.), Washington, DC: American Psychiatric Press.

Daley, D., & Roth, L. (1992). "When Symptoms Return: A Guide to Relapse in Psychiatric Illness." Holmes Beach, FL: Learning Publications.

Davies, P. (1979). Motivation, responsibility, and sickness in the psychiatric treatment of alcoholism. *Br. J. Psychiatry* **134**:449–458.

DeLeon, G. (1984). "The Therapeutic community: Study of Effectiveness." Rockville, MD: National Institute on Drug Abuse Treatment Research Monograph.

Ellis, A., McInerney, J. F., DiGuiseppe, R., & Yeager, R. J. (1988). "Rational–Emotive Therapy with Alcoholics and Substance Abusers." New York: Pergamon Press.

Frances, R. J., & Miller, S. I., Eds. (1991). "Clinical Textbook of Addictive Disorder." pp. 146–170. New York: Guilford Press.

Frances, R. J., & Miller, S. I. (1998). "Clinical Textbook of Addictive Disorder," 2nd ed., New York: Guilford Press.

Galanter, M. (1993). Network therapy for addictions: A model for office practice. *Am. J. Psychiatry* **148**:1218–1224.

Galanter, M., & Kleber, H., Eds. (1994). "Textbook of Substance Abuse Treatment." Washington, DC: American Psychiatric Press.

Gawin, F. H., & Ellinwood, E. H., Jr. (1988). Cocaine and other stimulants: Actions, abuse and treatment. *New Engl. J. Med.*, **318**:1173–1182.

Geller, A. (1992). Rehabilitation programs and halfway houses. *In* "Substance Abuse: A Comprehensive Textbook" (J. H. Lowinson, P. Ruiz, & R. B. Millman, Eds.), 2nd ed., pp. 458–466. Baltimore, MD: Williams & Wilkins.

Gerstein D. R., Johnston, R. A., Harwood, H. J., Suter, N., & Malloy, K. (1994). "CAL DATA: Evaluating Recovery Services—The California Drug and Alcohol Treatment Assessment." Sacramento, CA: California Department of Alcohol and Drug Programs.

Gitlow, S. (1985). Considerations on the evaluation and treatment of substance dependency. *J. Substance Abuse Treatment* **2**:175–179.

Graham, K., & Timney, C. B. (1990). Case management in addictions treatment. *J. Substance Abuse Treatment*, **7**(3):181–188.

Heather, N., Miller, W. R., & Greely, J., Eds. (1991). "Self-Control and the Addictive Behaviors." New York: MacMillan.

Helzer, J. E., & Pryzbeck, T. R. (1988). The co-occurrance of alcoholism with other psychiatric disorders in the general population and its impact in treatment. *J. Studies Alcohol* **49**:219–224.

Helzer, J. E., Robbins, L. N., Taylor, J. R., Carey, K., Miller, R. H., Combs-Orne, T., & Farmer, A. (1985). The extent of long term moderate drinking among alcoholics discharged from medical and psychiatric treatment facilities. *New Engl. J. Med.* **312**:1678–1682.

Hesselbrock, M. N., Meyer, R. E., & Keener, J. J. (1985). Psychopathology in hospitalized alcoholics. *Arch. Gen. Psychiatry* **42**:1050–1055.

Hester, R. K., & Miller, W. R. (1989). "Handbook of Alcoholism Approaches." Boston: Allyn & Bacon.

Higgins, S. T., Budney, A. J., Bickel, W. K., Hughes, J. R., Foerg, F., & Badger, G. (1993). Achieving cocaine abstinence with a behavioral approach. *Am. J. Psychiatry* **150**:763–769.

Hirsch, R., & Imhof, J. E. (1975). A family therapy approach to the treatment of drug abuse and addiction. *J. Psychedelic Drugs* **7**:181–185.

Hunt, G. M., Azrin, N. H. (1973). A community reinforcement approach to alcoholism. *Behav. Res. Ther.* **11**:91–104.

Institute of Medicine (1990). "Broadening the Base of Treatment for Alcohol Problems." Washington, DC: National Academy Press.

Juergen, S. M. (1997). Benzodiazepines, other sedative, hypnotic and anxiolytic drugs and addiction. *In* "The Principles and Practice of Addictions in Psychiatry" (N. S. Miller, Ed.), pp. 177–187, Philadelphia: Saunders.

Kadden, R. M., Carroll, K., Donovan, D., Cooney, N., Monti, P., Abrams, D., Litt, M., & Hester, R. (1992). "Cognitive–Behavioral Coping Skills Therapy Manual: A Clinical Research Guide for Therapists Treating Individuals with Alcohol Abuse and Dependence." Rockville, MD: National Institute on Alcohol Abuse and Alcoholism.

Kadden, R. M., Litt, M. D., Cooney, N. L., & Busher, D. A. (1992). Relationship between role-play measures of coping skills and alcoholism treatment outcome. *Addictive Behav.* **17**:425–437.

Kaplan, H., Sadock, B. (1990). "Pocket Handbook of Clinical psychiatry." Baltimore, MD: Williams & Wilkins.

Kessler, R. C., Crum, R. M., Warren, L. A., Nelson, C. R., Schulenberg, J., & Anthony, J. C. (1997). Lifetime co-occurence of DSM-IIIR alcohol abuse and dependence with other psychiatric disorders in the National Comorbidity Survey. *Arch. Gen. Psychiatry* **54**:313–321.

Khantzian, E. J., Halliday, K. S., & McAulliffe, W. E. (1990). "Addiction and the Vulnerable Self: Modified Dynamic Group Therapy for Substance Abusers." New York: Guilford Press.

Kranzler, H. R., & Liebowitz, N. R. (1988). Anxiety and depression in substance abuse: Clinical Implications. *Med. Clin. North America* 72:867–885.

Liberman, R., DeRisi, W., & Mueser, K. (1989). "Social Skills Training for Psychiatric Patient." Elmsford, NY: Pergamon Press.

Lindstrom, L. (1992). "Managing Alcoholism: Matching Clients to Treatment." New York: Oxford University Press.

Lowinson, P., Ruiz, P., Millman, R. B., & Langrod, J. G. (1992). "Substance Abuse: A Comprehensive Textbook." Baltimore, MD: Williams and Wilkins.

Mallams, J. H., Godley, M. D., Hall, G. M., & Myers, R. A. (1982). A social systems approach to resocializing alcoholics in the community. *J. Studies Alcohol*, 43:115–123.

Marlatt, G. A., & Gordon, J. R., Eds. (1985). "Relapse Prevention: Maintenance Strategies in the Treatment of Addictive Behaviors." New York: Guilford Press.

McClellan, A., Woody, G., Luborsky, L., O'Brien, C., & Druley, K. (1983). Increased effectiveness of substance abuse treatment: A perspective study of patient–treatment matching. *J. Nervous Mental Dis.* 171:597–605.

Miller, W. R. (1983). Controlled drinking: A history and a critical review. *J. Studies Alcohol* 44:68–83.

Miller, W. R. (1989). Matching individuals with interventions. *In* "Handbook of Alcoholism Treatment Approaches" (R. K. Hester & W. R. Miller, Eds.), pp. 261–272. New York: Pergamon Press.

Miller, W. R., & Hester, R. K. (1986). Inpatient alcoholism treatment. *Am. Psychologist* 41(7):794–805.

Miller, W. R., & Rollnick, S. (1991). "Motivational Interviewing: Preparing People to Change Addictive Behavior." New York: Guilford Press.

Miller, N. S., Gold, M. S., & Millman, R. B. (1988). PCD: A dangerous drug. *Am. Family Physician* 38(3):215–218.

Miller, W. R., Lechman, A. L., Delaney, H. D., & Tinkcom, M. (1992). Long-term follow-up of behavioral self-control training. *J. Studies Alcohol* 53:249–261.

Miller, N. S., Belkin, B. M., & Gibbons, R. (1994). Clinical diagnosis of substance use disorders in private practice populations. *J. Substance Abuse Treatment* 2(4):387–392.

Nace, E.P. (1987). "The Treatment of Alcoholism." New York: Bruner/Mazel.

Naranjo C. A., & Bremner, K. E. (1994). Pharmacotherapy of substance use disorders, *Can. J. Clin. Pharmacol.* 1(2):55–71.

Naranjo, C. A., Odzemir, V., & Bremner K. E. (1994). Diagnosis and pharmacological treatment of alcoholic patients. *CNS Drugs* 1(5):330–340.

Nathan, P. E. (1986). Outcomes for treatment of alcoholism: Current data. *Ann. Behav. Med.* 8:40–46.

Osher, F. L., & Kofoed, L. (1989). Treatment of patients with psychiatric and psychoactive substance abuse disorders. *Hosp. Community Psychiatry* 40:1025–1030.

Polich, J. M., Armor, D. J., & Braiker, H. B. (1980). "The Course of Alcoholism: Four Years after Treatment." New York: Wiley.

Polich, J. M., Armor, D. J., & Braiker, H. B., Eds. (1981). "The Course of Alcoholism: Four Years after Treatment." New York: Wiley.

Rawson, R. A., Obert, J. L., McCann, M. J., Smith D. P., & Scheffey, E. (1989). "The Neurobehavioral Treatment Manual: A Therapist Manual for Outpatient Cocaine Addiction Treatment." Beverly Hills, CA: Matrix Center.

Rawson, R. A., Obert, J. L., McCann, M. J., Scheffey, E., & Ling, W. (1991). "The Matrix Treatment Model: A Therapist's Guide for the Outpatient Treatment of Alcohol-Related Problems." Beverly Hills, CA: Matrix Center.

Resnick, R. B., Washton, A. M., & Stone-Washton, N. (1981). Psychotherapy and naltrexone on opioid dependence. *In* "Problems of Drug Dependence, 1980," NIDA Research Monograph No. 34 (S. L. Harris Ed.), pp. 109–115). Rockville, MD: National Institute on Drug Abuse.

Rollnick, S., Heather, N., & Bell, A. (1992). Negotiating behaviour change in medical settings: The development of brief motivational interviewing. *J. Mental Health* 1:25–37.

Schuckit, M. A. (1989). Goals in treatment. *In* "Treatments of Psychiatric Disorders," Section 12, pp. 1072–1075. Washington, DC: American Psychiatric Association.

Smith, D. E., Buxton, M. E., Bilal, R., & Seymour, R. B. (1993). Cultural points of resistance to the 12-step recovery process. *J. Psychoactive Drugs* 25:97–108.

Vannicelli, M., Dillavou, D., & Caplan, C. (1988). Psychodynamically oriented group therapy with alcoholics: Making it work despite the prevailing bias. *Group* 13(2):95–100.

Volpicelli, J. R., Alterman, A. I., Hayashida, M., & O'Brien, C. P. (1992). Naltrexone in the treatment of opiate dependence. *Arch. Gen. Psychiatry* 49:876–880.

Washton, A., Ed. (1995). "Psychotherapy and Substance Abuse: A Practitioner's Handbook." New York: Guilford Press.

Whitcomb, R. B. (1999). It's time to focus drug war on hard core users. Health Care Horizon, Manisses Communication Group, Inc. 4(1):1–2.

Willis, C. S. (1992). "A Preliminary Look at Rational Recovery as an Alternative to Alcoholics Anonymous." Paper presented at AABT annual convention, Boston, MA.

Zweben, J. (1986). Recovery-oriented psychotherapy. *J. Substance Abuse Treatment* 3:255–262.

Zweben, J. E. (1987). Recovery-oriented psychotherapy: Facilitating the use of 12-step programs. *J. Psychoactive Drugs* 19:243–251.

Part IV

Chapter 8

Solution-Focused Therapy

```
M  D  A  B  S  F  E  S  D  C
O  T  L  D  U  A  D  V  A  H
T  R  E  A  T  M  E  N  T  A
I  M  E  Y  G  I  F  T  Q  N
V  A  R  C  R  L  E  E  I  G
A  I  D  S  O  Y  N  E  M  E
T  T  L  D  U  V  S  N  G  A
I  C  O  U  P  L  E  S  V  O
O  G  O  A  L  X  S  R  X  R
N  M  E  L  D  E  R  L  Y  N
```

The treatment plan should fit the specific needs of the individual. Traditionally, treatment has focused on the constellation of users at the end of the continuum where there is heavy use and dependence. Aside from primary prevention, more effective intervention should take place at much earlier stages of use, when problems and consequences have not been experienced or are just beginning to be experienced. Additionally, intervention at these stages would be much less intrusive and expensive. Thorough assessment not only identifies substance abuse and dependence, it also seeks to clarify such issues as perceived benefits, skill deficits, and self-medication associated with dual diagnosis. This approach is aimed at developing treatment planning that is focused on the specific needs of the individual. Individualized treatment is the result of collaboration between the individual and the therapist, which is based on a mutually understood desired outcome. The goals must be appropriate and fit the personality, life situation, and all variables associated with the problems of substance use. Although the types of interventions vary according to individual needs, the foundation of case conceptualization is initially based upon the level of care needed. According to Allan Leshner, director NIDA, "Addiction has diverse medical, behavioral and social consequences that affect one's ability to function in virtually every life domain. Thus, the target outcome for treatment cannot be just redirecting drug use; it must be restoring the individual to full functioning in the family, at work and in society. For these reasons, the best treatments combine as appropriate to the individual, medications, behavioral therapies and necessary psychosocial services." Regardless of the treatment setting, the therapist has an important role in helping the individual to become treatment ready by preparing him or her with information and criteria on the different modalities and treatment choices. The following is an overview of outpatient and inpatient treatment.

It must be recognized that, when an individual enters treatment, he or she is continuously confronted with daily life stressors and pressure. In all likelihood, this means easy access to a variety of substances. Support via program structure and testing for substance use is essential. The individualized treatment plan program length varies from 3 to 6 months with ongoing participation and is based upon

1. Responsible–reliable attendance at scheduled meetings
2. Clean drug screens
3. Developing an appropriate and supportive social network
4. Demonstrating adaptive (nonsubstance) coping–problem solving skills

Three phases of treatment are early abstinence, relapse prevention, and continuing care. Goals are as follows:

1. Improve motivation
2. Learn how to break addictive cycle
3. Controlled drinking (when appropriate)
4. Achieve abstinence from all substances
5. Learn adaptive coping skills–problem solving skills required to maintain long-term abstinence
6. Adequate support and guidance through difficult situations to prevent relapse

Therapists encourage recovery efforts by

1. Initiating contact using motivational interviewing
2. Reinforcing goals and associated objectives
3. Emphasizing strengths
4. Joining rather than confronting
5. Avoiding power struggles
6. Negotiating rather than dictating
7. Emphasizing individual responsibility

Detox is the initial intervention and is viewed as a prerequisite for the treatment of dependence on alcohol, opiates, and other sedatives. Hospitalization is usually unnecessary except in instances of severe alcohol, barbiturate, or benzodiazepine dependency when a withdrawal reaction may include delirium or potentially fatal seizures. Sometimes during the detox phase a prescribed substance is substituted that offers a similar effect in order to decrease the risk of medically problematic reactions and significant discomfort. Following detox, an individual either continues in treatment or resumes substance use. It is important to educate individuals that, if they resume substance use following detox, they will experience decreased tolerance and, therefore, require a lower dose to obtain the desired effect. With the decrease in tolerance there is an increased risk of overdose (*The Harvard Mental Health Letter*, August 1995; Gersten & Harwood, 1990).

When appropriate, naltrexone and disulfiram may be used to enhance relapse prevention for the alcoholic. The individuals with comorbid psychiatric disorders will require a specialized program component to deal wit dual diagnosis needs associated with medication, appropriate support, and effective interventions to meet their needs and to encourage treatment compliance.

Encourage 12-step or other self-help programs. Regarding AA, those who attended meetings consumed about 40% less alcohol than those who did not attend meeting, which may be attributed to the high frequency of abstinence among occasional and moderate participants of AA (Watson *et al*, 1997). If an individual refuses to participate in such meetings, do not use this as a reason for termination from the program. The alternative may be to develop other appropriate treatment choices that supply similar benefits, such as

1. Affiliation
2. Self-responsibility
3. Insight
4. Development of improved coping
5. Support for behavioral changes
6. Relapse prevention

POTENTIAL PROBLEMS

1. If an individual arrives at an appointment with clear signs of intoxication by alcohol or other substances, do not continue the meeting. An example of symptoms associated with alcohol intoxication may include the following: breath smelling of alcohol, lack of coordination, slurred speech, strange behavior, etc. Instead, make arrangements for him or her to be picked up by a family member, friend, or taxi and make an appointment as soon as possible or maintain the next appointment if there is a regular meeting time.

2. Unexcused absences: If the individual is not able to be consistent, he or she may need to be transferred to a group that focuses intensely on stabilization in order to facilitate overcoming early obstacles to abstinence and other necessary and associated changes.

3. Labeling the individual's behavior as unmotivated, a form of denial, or resistant can result in decreased motivation, poor collaboration, and distrust.

4. Reframing can increase motivation by identifying and seeking to understand in a respectful and caring manner an individual's ambivalence, fears, and reluctance to change.

5. Noncompliance can be challenged by joining the individual's resistance and using it as an opportunity to be creative and collaborative. Appropriate limit setting and constructive feedback are used as the boundaries of encouraging an individual's motivation to achieve the goal(s) on his or her terms and within limits.

STRATEGIES FOR IMPROVING MOTIVATION
(MILLER & ROLLNICK, 1991)

1. Express empathy: Therapists expressing accurate empathy results in the individual developing a sense of acceptance that frees him or her from defensiveness and improves his or her desire for change.
2. Developing discrepancy: The therapist clarifies the gap between where the individual is and where he or she wants to be. It is critical that the individual express concern him- or herself and that the therapist reflect this awareness.
3. Avoid arguments: Conflict over resistance can distract the therapist from the goal of motivating individuals toward change, while at the same time increasing the resistance of the individual.
4. Roll with resistance: When defensiveness or resistance is encountered, be creative in approaching the issue from a different perspective to which the individual may be open. Reflect questions back so that the individual may be placed in a better position to struggle to find a rational solution.
5. Support self-efficacy: The individual who is able to see him- or herself as successful in recovery is more likely to achieve the goal.

PREDICTIVE MEASURES OF OUTCOME

Project Match (1997) offered several predictive measures of outcome for drinking behavior:

1. Social support for drinking is associated with more drinking for those treated in inpatient and outpatient settings.
2. Higher alcohol involvement.
3. Being male.
4. Greater psychiatric severity.
5. Alcoholism typology familial alcoholism, greater alcohol dependence, impulsivity.

THERAPIST RESPONSES TO SLIPS

Slips are viewed as avoidable choices that reflect ambivalence. If a "slip" is experienced, use it as an opportunity to explore, clarify, and utilize all the information (feelings, thoughts, individuals involved, circumstances, etc.) that functions as part of the chain of behaviors–events that result in a slip.

If a slip occurs while the individual is intensely focusing on abstinence and stabilization, the goal is to achieve two consecutive weeks of abstinence and attend all agreed upon meetings. At that time the individual returns to the basic treatment program. If slips continue beyond this described situation, a review of the level of care is required. The individual may be at risk of being suspended from the program. Under these circumstances, it may be deemed that he or she requires the support of a residential treatment program. He or she may also opt for increased intensity of treatment in the outpatient setting, such as drug screens two times per week and individual therapy one time per week for 2–4 weeks. Two consecutive weeks of success will make the individual eligible to resume participation in his or her original programming.

DECREASING TREATMENT DROPOUT RATE

Because the dropout rate in treatment is so high, it is important to clarify what can be done to retain those seeking treatment. Consider the following recommendations in order to decrease the significant dropout rate of individuals who initially seek and begin to attend substance abuse treatment:

1. Be responsive. Facilitate admission to treatment as quickly as possible. The longer the wait, the greater the chance for ambivalence to swing the other way.
2. Prepare those entering treatment for what to expect. This decreases anxiety, increases the sense of a collaborative effort, and increases motivation by a discussion of treatment choices.
3. Ensure a smaller number of group participants.
4. Make sure that everyone participating receives the necessary and appropriate attention.
5. Increase treatment choices for better matching of treatment to the individual.
6. Focus on skill building to increase self-efficacy.
7. Respond to missed appointments with follow-up calls and a letter if necessary.
8. Use the least restrictive intervention(s).
9. Be respectful of the beliefs of others and sensitive to human diversity.
10. Address the treatment needs of significant others and family members. It is often these individuals who bring the substance abuser into treatment; therefore, help them to identify their own needs for treatment and support.

ROLE OF FAMILY TREATMENT

All significant others who play a central role in support of an individual's recovery are encouraged to participate in treatment (partner, family, close friend). Multifamily group generally meets weekly for 6 weeks to 3 months. Some programs may offer longer participation to those who need or desire to continue. Group provides education, support, and counselling, which are aimed at abstinence, increasing coping ability, and self-efficacy. This fits in with the individualized treatment planning model, which is focused on the importance of mobilizing the individual's own resources to bring about change by utilizing motivational and behavioral change principles.

INPATIENT TREATMENT

The inpatient setting provides an opportunity for development and practice of new skills, but in a supervised setting with increased support that lacks some of the stressors or negative feedback factors that may be inherent in the individual's environment. A major drawback is that an inpatient setting is artificial which places a limit on the skill rehearsal *in vivo* that is a significant aspect of treatment. The inpatient milieu may be recommended for some individuals as the treatment of choice for the initial stages of recovery because it offers an environment designed to maximize intensive skill training and structure, which encourages the practice of new skills based upon the functioning level of the individual. However, aside from detox, inpatient treatment often is not a choice due to cost and insurance limitations.

A review of the positive and negative attributes of inpatient treatment for substance abuse is useful for clarifying the decision to treat in an inpatient setting.
Benefits:

1. Supervision
2. Increased support
3. Breaking of well-established patterns of destructive or self-defeating behavior
4. Intense training of skills
5. Development of alternative behaviors
6. Development of coping skills–problem solving
7. Reinforcing active participation in treatment activities

Impediments:

1. Financial resources
2. Insurance limitations
3. Disruption of lifestyle
4. Therapist fear of losing clients to referral
5. Brevity of stay
   a. does not adequately address lack of social stability
   b. does not adequately connect with significant other–family and intervene

PATIENT–TREATMENT MATCHING

Kissin *et al.*, (1970) reported that the inpatient setting was presented as an advantage only to those demonstrating less social stability. This outcome was repeated by Welte *et al.* (1981), who found that the length of inpatient treatment made no difference for individuals with high social stability, whereas there was an improved outcome for longer stays when individuals presented with low social stability. Inpatient treatment offers safety from high-risk situations, it is a controlled environment, and it offers an opportunity to focus on acquiring skills to cope with situations that lead to relapse. Upon review, it appears that inpatient treatment is cost-effective when (Lindstrom, 1992):

1. There is poor social stability
2. Homelessness
3. Severe medical complications
4. Severe psychopathology (danger to self–other, unable to provide for own care)

Inpatient treatment should not be the treatment of choice when there have been only repeated treatment failures, which is often the case given the allocation of resources for substance abuse treatment and psychiatric treatment in general. The decision must be individualized based upon a clear demonstration of the need for effective treatment outcome.

DISCHARGE AND AFTERCARE

According to Graham and Timney (1990), aggressive case management with discharge planning initiated as early as possible has negatively impacted treatment and therefore outcome. Although a complete conceptualization of a case is important, a therapist (or treatment team) cannot become so involved in the endpoint "process" to the detriment of effective individualized treatment planning and treatment.

Aftercare is a decrease in program intensity and is a necessary phase of treatment in which there is continuity and reinforcement of skill development initiated during a more intensive treatment phase (inpatient or intensive outpatient). Factors taken into consideration for individualized aftercare include:

1. Length of addiction
2. Dual diagnosis (must address both diagnostic issues)
3. Propensity for switching addictions–compulsions (gambling, sex, self-destructive behaviors, eating disorders, etc.)
4. Adequacy of available social support–home environment
5. Prior treatment response(s)
6. Stress tolerance
7. Level of skill acquisition
8. Motivation

Treatment organization is the framework whereby the therapist's skills are used in a manner to facilitate a progressive course of treatment. This is often accomplished by reflection, lead-in, restatement, reframing, and questioning. An important aspect of treatment is the therapeutic relationship. The therapeutic relationship is based upon collaborative goal setting, trust, empathy, respect, and all other qualities that are considered in a non-substance-use treatment framework:

1. *Self-disclosure* of the therapist's own relevant experiences, feelings, and attitudes, which should only be used when the client can tolerate the information shared by the therapist and utilize it to result in
   a. increased self-esteem

b. decreased feelings of aloneness

c. increased understanding and acceptance of ups–downs

d. decreased feelings of being sick–defective.

2. *Confrontation* is a useful technique for educating, clarifying, and challenging discrepancies.

3. *Silence* is helpful when timing can facilitate introspection and therapeutic anxiety (dissonance) when an individual is resistant to approaching and working through difficult and painful issues.

TREATMENT INTERVENTIONS SUPPORTED BY RESEARCH

Miller and Hester (1986b) identified the following treatment interventions as being supported by research:

1. Aversion therapies
2. Behavioral self-control training
3. Community reinforcement
4. Marital and family therapy
5. Social skills training
6. Stress management

Additionally, individuals should be informed of the range of possible treatment interventions to increase their choices in the treatment planning process. Effective intervention is based upon collaborative efforts utilizing multiple treatment options, which allows treatment programming to be differentiated, targeted, and individualized. Therefore, individualized treatment planning (ITP) adds the following interventions to the above-listed methods:

7. Personal recovery goals
   a. educational–vocational counseling
   b. improved self-care–health behaviors

8. Relapse prevention skills (actually an ongoing part of good treatment from the onset)

9. Community resocialization
   a. development of appropriate recreational–leisure activities
   b. development of appropriate resources–support

10. Plan and rehearsal of abstinent–modified lifestyle, thinking, and behaviors

When developing an ITP, all of the aforementioned areas of intervention work in an interrelated manner to offer a social learning perspective for understanding substance use behavior, assisting clients to assess their substance use problem(s), identifying the antecedents associated with substance use, teaching relapse prevention skills, and facilitating self-reinforcement for abstinence. Developing skills and resources that enhance the control that clients have over their lives is necessary for attaining the goal of modification or abstinence. The cognitive–behavioral approach facilitates appropriate changes to avoid substance-associated stimuli, to effectively cope with substance associations that cannot be avoided, to improve judgment and recognize the difference between the two, and to encourage the development of skills that promote self-efficacy.

When dealing with the central issues of abstinence and relapse prevention it is necessary to develop a therapeutic conceptualization of change, individual struggles, adjustment, and integration. A thorough understanding of relapse results in the intervention of biological, psychological and sociological factors that influence the risk of relapse. Success in maintaining change and abstinence involves skill development, which enhances and promotes positive, self-responsible, and self-esteemed behavioral patterns. According to Brownell *et al.* (1986), it is when there is successful integration of these behaviors that the individual begins to experience the positive associations of abstinence. It is with this step that relapse prevention is firmly in place.

TREATMENT MODELS

COGNITIVE RESTRUCTURING

Treatment models are often a combination of interventions derived from cognitive restructuring, behavioral modification, and psychodynamic (insight-oriented) therapy. Cognitive restructuring encourages an individual to restate his or her beliefs in a more realistic and less distorted fashion, as well as helps him or her to take responsibility for his or her choices. It also acts to decrease negative self-evaluation–statements, negative self-fulfilling prophecies, anxiety, and fear. Another way of viewing cognitive restructuring is in terms of "rational thinking," which improves self-efficacy. Modification of ineffective beliefs should demonstrate early treatment changes in excessive emotional reactions, self-defeating behaviors, awareness of internal and external substance stimuli cues, and permission giving to use substances. Change requires motivation, awareness, and understanding of the connection between thoughts–beliefs, behaviors–choices, and consequences. Johnson (1997) outlines the impact that distorted thinking and negative self-talk have upon an individual. Utilization of a rational thinking framework is a necessary component. Some examples of rational thinking include the following:

1. Utilizing self-statements as reminders and reinforcers of his or her commitment to a clean and sober life.
2. Recognizing that what an individual thinks and feels is a choice related to how he or she views him- or herself and the world.
3. Benefitting from focusing on strengths and potential resources versus excess worrying, self-criticism, or taking the victim role.
4. Developing alternative ways to view the same situation and understanding the basis for previous viewpoints.
5. Identifying what an individual has control over versus being overwhelmed by the lack of control and taking responsibility where control–choices can be asserted.
6. Understanding possible secondary gain associated with negative thinking.
7. Identifying pleasing others or being part of the crowd versus the self-care behavior practiced with substance refusal.

Changes in negative patterns of thinking to rational thinking

1. Improve management of negative emotional states that influence the urge to use substances.
2. Improve coping skills by clarifying choices matched by ability and increased willingness to take appropriate risks (try something new without fearing failure or struggling for perfection).
3. Improve problem solving resulting from the freedom to think about an entire array of choices and associated consequences and feeling confident in making a choice and learning from it if it does not work out the way expected or intended.

Utilization of a journal–log is an excellent technique to identify what an individual is communicating to him- or herself under a specific set of circumstances. Have the individual include the following information in this type of journal writing:

1. The situation–circumstances
2. What happened prior
3. Was there an urge to use and if so how intense
4. What did he or she choose to do
5. What happened afterward
6. Assess the coping skills utilized—what was learned

Hester and Miller (1989) outline a five-component intervention for developing and improving effective coping skills.

1. Ask the individual to list the desired effects or benefits of using a substance:

buzz	disinhibition
courage	avoidance
mood change	sleep
forgetting	numbing
feeling carefree	stress management
relaxing	heightened experience

2. Make a list of the situations in which he or she likes to achieve the desired effect.
3. Discuss how he or she feels during these situations.
4. What would be appropriate alternatives to achieve the desired effects?
5. How will he or she best manage relapse prevention (after brainstorming all of the alternates available to him or her)?

BEHAVIOR MODIFICATION

Behavior modification offers learning new skills for improved intra- and interpersonal management. This is paramount to successful recovery. Social learning theory views substance use disorders as failing to adequately and effectively cope. Therefore, an individual must learn to decrease the risk of relapse by anticipating future stressors and avoiding people, places, and situations that he or she feels that he or she has not yet developed the skills to manage effectively. Examples of behavioral techniques utilized by clients include behavioral self-control training, which encompasses interventions that facilitate individuals in working toward desired behavioral changes. This includes the following:

1. Analysis of his or her own substance use patterns
   a. identify situations that are associated with substance use
   b. interventions such as the Inventory of Drinking Situations (IDS) to identify situations that place him or her at the highest risk of use
   c. once situations are identified, the individual can review, choose, and practice coping strategies for dealing with situations
   d. individuals can avoid situations that are too difficult to challenge
   e. individuals can work through a hierarchy of situations up to the most difficult
   f. individuals can prepare for anticipated situations, planning strategies to avoid or cope with the identified situations

2. Aversion therapy: A form of conditioning in which an aversive stimulus (shock, unpleasant smell, visualization) is paired with an undesired behavior. The least controversial form of aversion therapy is the use of visualization. The purpose is to decrease or eliminate the individual's desire or craving for a substance.

3. Consumption monitoring (actually a component of self-monitoring)
   a. can either start now and monitor day to day or recollect past
   b. identification of situations that are associated with substance use

4. Self-reinforcement: Individual rewards self for desirable behavior.

5. Stimulus control methods: Learning to respond differently in the presence of certain stimuli by evaluating and modifying behavior.

6. Stress management: The use of cognitive–behavioral techniques to enhance coping and relieve body tension (such as progressive muscle relaxation, visualization, self-hypnotism, exercise)

7. Assertive training: Honest and appropriate expression of thoughts and feelings. Premise is that assertiveness is incompatible with anxiety (e.g., use of assertiveness and refusal skills no longer allows antecedents of pressure to continue).

8. Learning alternative behaviors: Development of a repertoire of coping skills through instruction, behavioral rehearsal, and homework assignments.

9. Developing appropriate leisure activities

10. Contingency management: Does not deal directly with substance abuse, but instead establishes new contingencies that will increase behaviors that are incompatible with substance abuse.

11. Contingency contracting: Operant conditioning procedure that links a reward or punishment associated with the occurrence or absence of a specific response. An agreement regarding behavior change and the consequences (reward–punishment) associated with not honoring the contract.

12. Modeling
    a. can be videotape or audiotape, multiple models, and role-playing
    b. learning through observation and imitation of others to foster desired behaviors

c. types of skills developed include communication skills, eye contact, social skills, and refusal of subtances

13. Systematic desensitization
   a. time frame and progress are determined by client self-report
   b. useful for decreasing anxiety associated with social skills, dealing with authority figures, or any inhibiting fear or negative influence on an individual's ability or motivation in moderating or abstaining from the use of substances
   c. an excellent adjunct to comprehensive treatment

14. Flooding: Technique for extinguishing avoidant behavior by presenting a controlled stimulus (*in vivo* or imagined) while the individual is prevented from avoiding.

15. Implosion: Technique involving the extinction of a response by prolonged intense exposure to a stimuli that produces the response (may increase the anxiety experienced by some individuals).

16. Social skills training
   a. improve coping with high-risk situations
   b. develop or redevelop lost social skills resulting from years of substance abuse, and includes, but is not limited to
      i. body language
      ii. non verbal communication
      iii. initiating conversation
      iv. giving and receiving compliments
      v. identifying feelings and being able to describe them
      vi. listening skills
      vii. assertiveness
      viii. offering constructive criticism
      ix. able to articulate beliefs with confidence
      x. refusing requests
      xi. relationship development (boundaries, disclosure, trust, fear of rejection, etc.)
   c. develop and utilize social support
   d. refusal skills can be used for prevention and treatment
   e. to enhance success and reinforce the development of interpersonal skills (refusal skills are learned through modeling, role-playing, and performance feedback, with particular focus on generalizing refusal skill behaviors to real life experiences and environments; the first step is to identify the people and situations that are associated with risk of using.

17. Self-monitoring: A self-control technique in which an individual assesses factors associated with a target behavior and modification of the target behavior.

Types of behaviors targeted for development of refusal skills include the following:

1. Asking for help and utilizing resources
2. Giving instructions
3. Convincing others, demonstrating clarity and strength of choice
4. Able to identify feelings

5. Not frightened or overwhelmed by emotions of others, especially anger and rejection

6. Self-control

7. Assertive training is necessary because lack of assertiveness is a common dilemma for those who abuse substances. It is the difficulty they experience in appropriately expressing their personal rights and feelings. When responding assertively, the individual's affect must be appropriate to the situation:

   a. educate regarding behavioral patterns and associated outcome–consequences

   b. explore fears associated with assertive communication

   c. practice using all resources, i.e., modeling, coaching, behavioral rehearsal, role-playing, feedback, homework assignments

   d. may start with covert behavioral rehearsal, imagining themselves in a variety of situations assertively and effectively

   e. role reversal can be used to increase depth of understanding of how they have been affected by a lack of assertive communication

   f. increase awareness and acknowledgment of how the skill can serve them positively and encourage self-responsibility

   g. modeling to observe appropriate responses

   h. feedback to monitor progress and reinforce effort for skill acquisition

8. Asserting rights

9. Responding to teasing

10. Avoiding trouble, conflict, or fights with others

11. Coping with embarrassment

12. Coping with being left out

13. Responding to persuasion

14. Dealing with failure and disappointment

15. Dealing with accusation

16. Preparing for difficult conversation

17. Coping with peer group pressure

18. Decision making

19. Problem solving

PSYCHODYNAMIC THERAPY

Psychodynamic therapy is integral to the success and generalization of many, if not all, of the cognitive–behavioral skills listed, including self-care, emotional defense, management of emotions, and self-esteem. It is at this later stage of recovery that a psychodynamic approach may be of most value. For example, continuing the development of self-regulation mechanisms associated from impaired object relations. However, the exception to this is the insight-oriented work utilized to derive concrete practical strategies and related thinking and behavior necessary to maintain abstinence earlier in the recovery process.

1. Self-care is an internalized self-protective function that is established in early phases of development. Inadequate self-care in individuals who present with a history of substance abuse–dependence is demonstrated by their lack of or inability to appropriately worry about, anticipate, or consider the consequences of their behavior. As a result, the danger of substance abuse is disregarded (Khantzian, 1997).

2. Emotional defense: Problems associated with emotional defense are the foundation of substance abuse–dependence. These are circumstances where substances are used adaptively to insulate against overwhelming, painful, or confusing emotions. Specific substances are chosen because of their effect or "defense." According to Khantzian (1978), this is referred to as self-selection, whereby an individual discovers that short-term effects of substances are related to improved functions and a sense of well-being.

   a. depressants are used to diminish feelings of emptiness, isolation, and inadequacy
   b. stimulants are used to mask depression, hypomania (enhancement), low energy, powerlessness, and repression
   c. opiates are used to diminish rage, aggression, and self-hatred

3. Management of emotion: Over time, a substance abuser recognizes, understands, and controls conditions produced by taking substances. This way of combating the overwhelming emotions from which he or she suffers (but often that he or she does not understand) offers him or her the means of having perceived control. In line with Khantzian's view, substance abuse serves the need for a sense of well-being and security.

   a. identify emotions
   b. increased understanding of emotional experience
   c. improved connection between feeling and experience

4. Self-esteem: Low self-esteem can result in an individual relying on the external environment to fulfill needs and wants. If all of the biopsychosocial factors correlate, it can lead to addiction. This relationship to substances is a consequence of the failure to find basic solutions to the problems of coping with emotional distress and the seeking of satisfaction for wants and needs.

5. Troubled relationships: Low self-esteem and self-worth negatively impact the development of healthy relationships and intimacy. They are often associated with the individual's early life caretaker's lack of providing nurturing, caring, and a (emotionally–physically) safe environment. Thus, in the realm of substance use, the individual recreates this earlier relationship of dependency with a substance(s) as the central object to meet his or her needs.

Along with consideration for different therapeutic modalities of intervention, the issue of self-selection of substances and the consequences of detox and abstinence need to be understood for their therapeutic value. For example, in the case of alcohol treatment, psychodynamic therapy techniques, according to Levy (1987), require that the therapist be alert to the degree of physiological dependence that demands medical attention such as withdrawal. This highlights the importance of comprehensive assessment and treatment. Regardless of the treatment perspective, some basic treatment issues need being taken into account:

1. Propensity for the use of defense mechanisms of denial and projection (the individual addicted to alcohol will use defense mechanisms in a manner such that the consequences of the alcohol use become the reason for use).

2. Necessity of offering practical information, such as
   a. strategies for achieving abstinence and decreasing exposure to alcohol-related situations
   b. coping strategies for dealing with alcohol-related problems
   c. education related to the experience of craving and how to effectively cope without using

TABLE 8.1   Dynamic Cognitive Behavioral Model of Substance Abuse and Intervention Points[a]

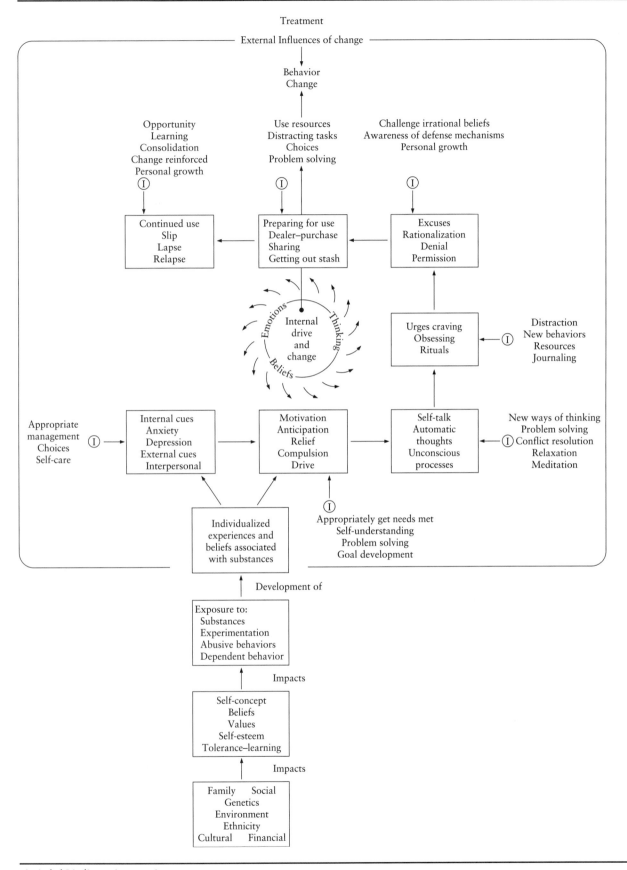

[a]A circled I indicates intervention.

d. the use of contingency contracting for committing to abstinence for a specific length of time for personal evaluation

e. social skills training that offers alternative behaviors for the development of a new perspective and associated skills

f. the benefit of role-playing to suggest and demonstrate non-substance-use choices for coping with problem situations

g. homework to facilitate generalizations of adaptive coping skills

h. teach stress management skills; learning effective stress management is imperative given that potential stressors impact every aspect of daily life (work, school, relationships, finances, health, etc.)

i. community reinforcement approach techniques (Hunt and Azrin, 1973; Azrin *et al.*, 1982) result in a decrease in drinking days while improving employment issues and other positive behavioral changes; this could be further enhanced by disulfiram treatment for those with a difficult history of relapse or long-term alcoholism (methadone or methadone maintenance for those with a heroin addiction)

MEDICAL TREATMENT FOR SUBSTANCE DEPENDENCE

The first step of treatment is acknowledgment that a problem exists. Resistance, medical problems, medical risks (associated with detox), and dual diagnosis complicate an already difficult and challenging clinical picture. As previously noted, substance abuse and dependence are the product of overlapping influences involving the substance effect, individual psychological functioning, and the social environment. Detox is the prerequisite for further treatment. Hospitalization usually is not necessary for detox except when a medical risk is identified, such as with severe alcoholism or benzodiazepine and barbiturate dependence where a withdrawal reaction may include delirium or potentially fatal seizures. Other circumstances that would meet criteria for a hospitalization for stabilization would be when an individual is a danger to self or others, when he or she is not able to provide for his or her basic needs and lacks an adequate and appropriate support system that can provide necessary care. Sometimes, during the detox phase, a long acting substance is substituted for a shorter acting one with a similar effect (e.g., diazepam for alcohol, methadone for heroin). Following detox, an individual either continues in treatment or resumes substance use. In the case of resumed substance use, an individual is likely to experience decreased tolerance (lower dose to experience desired effect) and an associated increased risk of overdose.

PHARMACOTHERAPY

Information regarding the pharmacological treatment of substance abuse was derived primarily from the following resources: Gerstein and Harwood (1990), *The Harvard Mental Health Letter* (August 1995, 1998), O'Brien (1997), and Frances and Miller (1998). In cases where substance abuse–dependence is the primary diagnosis, successful reduction in use or abstinence will generally result in alleviation of symptoms and improvement in other areas. When substance abuse–dependence is the secondary diagnosis, there may be indications for concomitant treatment of other psychiatric disorders. In the second case, the treating physician will take into consideration

1. Substance metabolism
2. Cross tolerance
3. Potential abuse of the prescribed substance

4. Special importance of counseling individuals regarding the prescribed substances (along with associated ethical and legal issues related to prescribing such medications)

Because much of the information from the sources listed earlier was overlapping, a composite outline of common treatments often listed in the literature was developed.

1. Alcohol detox
   a. benzodiazepines
   b. tricyclic antidepressants (used more when anxiety is present)
   c. these categories of substances present risks associated with sedation
   d. acomprosate (appears to act as a GABA receptor agonist)
   e. serotonergic agents
   f. naltrexone (useful for counteracting intoxication and decreasing craving)
   g. aversion therapy with disulfiram

2. Opiate withdrawal
   a. clonidine (α-agonist, antihypertensive)
   b. propranolol (beta-blocker to control tremor, tachycardia, and other withdrawal symptoms)
   c. naltrexone and naloxone (opiate agonist)
   d. methadone (detox and maintenance treatment)
   e. L-acetylmethadol (LAAM) (longer acting variant of methadone)
   f. buprenorphine (synthetic narcotic agonist–antagonist; has the neurochemical properties of both methadone and naltrexone)

3. Stimulants
   a. currently, there is no specific reliable antagonist for stimulant abuse
   b. naltrexone may slightly decrease the pleasure associated with use
   c. some prescription medications that demonstrate a reduction in cravings and relief of withdrawal are lithium, tricyclics, anticonvulsants, and dopamine agonists; methylphenidate results in a less intense response at the beginning and end states of use, however, it decreases the craving for cocaine only temporarily

INTEGRATION OF PSYCHOTHERAPY AND PHARMACOTHERAPY

According to Carroll (1997), the combination of psychotherapy and pharmacotherapy offers the following treatment benefits:

1. Improvement over a wide and variable range of symptoms. Because these two treatments work in individualized and complimentary ways, there is greater potential for symptom alleviation, which likely increases motivation.
2. Strategic combination of psychotherapy and pharmacotherapy offers numerous treatment choices to meet the needs of a diverse target population. Therefore, treatment is more likely to be effective.

3. Potential drawbacks or limitations associated with either treatment may be offset by the benefits of the other due to reciprocal reinforcement. In other words, cognitive–behavioral interventions may increase treatment compliance with medication. Likewise, symptom alleviation resulting from appropriate medication may increase treatment participation and facilitate increased motivation for change and personal growth.

EVIDENCE FOR EFFECTIVENESS OF COMBINED TREATMENT

For those with alcohol dependence, the pharmacological treatments of disulfiram and naltrexone may be offered under specific circumstances demonstrated by a difficult recovery history. According to Washton (1995), disulfiram removes the choice of drinking (negative physiological experience of side effects if mixed with alcohol), which decreases or eliminates the risk of relapse from impulsiveness. This eliminates breaks in treatment that interfere with the development of self-efficacy and increased motivation in treatment. Naltrexone (Revia) is an effective agent for helping recovering alcoholics establish a healthy, sober, solid recovery. They are less preoccupied with alcohol use and cravings and experience less loss of control and less pleasure drinking.

For individuals recovering from opiate addiction, little evidence supports general psychotherapy as a valuable singular treatment, but it may be valuable as an adjunct treatment. Relapse to opiates is extremely frequent. Withdrawal symptoms are similar to those experienced with the flu and are not life threatening. However, withdrawal may precipitate psychosis in those predisposed. Detox with methadone usually relieves symptoms. Woody *et al.* (1983) cited that cognitive–behavioral treatment in combination with pharmacotherapy facilitates mood management, skill development, goal setting, and personal growth, therefore supporting the value of psychotherapy as an adjunct to methadone maintenance.

1. Methadone maintenance
   a. retains those with an opioid addiction in treatment
   b. allows for the opportunity to evaluate and treat concurrent disorders (dual diagnosis, medical problems, family–relationship problems)

2. Naltrexone is an opioid antagonist that is nonaddicting. However, compliance and outcome have been poor in comparison to methadone.

In general, cocaine can be stopped abruptly without potential medical consequences. However, individuals may experience intense cravings and physical discomfort necessitating structured, medically supervised residential care to facilitate successful withdrawal. Additionally, if someone is psychologically impaired, emotionally ill (major depression, suicidal ideation, etc.), older, or frail (heart condition, etc.), his or her risk for complications increases if substances are stopped abruptly. This highlights another reason to reinforce the importance of a physical examination as part of the assessment process. Individuals with cocaine dependency have not, as yet, been able to seek symptom relief pharmacologically as have alcoholics (disulfiram and naltrexone) or heroin addicts (methadone and naltrexone withdrawal–maintenance). The continuing effort to find an effective pharmacologic treatment to use for cocaine has been set as a research priority by NIDA. Individuals with the most severe problems are more likely to demonstrate better outcomes with treatment in a long-term residential program 90 days or longer (Simpson *et al.*, 1999). Individuals with "increased treatment exposure were less likely a year later to use cocaine regularly, to use other drugs, to drink regularly, or to engage in criminal behavior"

(Hoffman *et al.*, 1996). Carroll *et al.* (1994) state that coping skills training in which individuals are taught ways to identify and cope with high-risk situations results in shorter and less severe relapses.

Higgins *et al.* (1991, 1993) adapted a behavioral treatment package:

1. Positive reinforcing voucher system (individuals can earn vouchers by giving urine samples that are opiate–substance free, which can be redeemed by a predetermined set of reinforcers with drug-free prosocial activities)
2. Counseling in behavioral techniques
3. Identifying antecedents and cues that ilicit craving
4. Reciprocal relationship counseling for both the individual and his or her significant other

This program led to substantial suppression of cocaine use, which was maintained over a 29-week period of time. Higgins *et al.* (1993) reviewed the treatment strategies with and without the voucher system and found that integration of the voucher system into treatment significantly improved treatment outcome. Facilitation of skill acquisition and adaptation requires that the therapist support, monitor, and offer positive reinforcement for the use of these new ways of thinking and behaving.

INDIVIDUAL THERAPY

Some patients choose individual therapy over other treatment modalities, and some require the support and facilitation of individual therapy to be able to remain active in the other forms of treatment beneficial to their recovery (Khantzian, 1986). Dodes and Khantzian (1991) state that the most frequently described function of substance use is the management of intolerable affect. In this case, individual psychotherapy may be useful for increasing understanding and facilitating working through areas of psychological vulnerability or dysfunctions that significantly contribute to the development and maintenance of addiction. For example, disturbances in

1. Self-regulation
2. Appropriate management of affect and mood
3. Development and maintenance of self-esteem
4. Self-care (intrarelationship)
5. Interrelationship functioning

Indications for individual psychotherapy depend on

1. ability to develop a positive therapeutic relationship
2. at least a moderate capacity to be introspective
3. experience and degree of emotional suffering–distress

These indications are similar to those for nonaddicted individuals.

IMPORTANCE AND USEFULNESS OF THE SUPPORT GROUP FORUM

McKenzie (1986) states that group therapy is an invaluable treatment method for overcoming low motivation. There are lower dropout rates than for individual treatment, and it appears to be especially effective with difficult to treat populations such as substance abusers. It is also more cost-effective. The additional support of individual treatment may be needed during the course of the group process for clients who present with dual diagnosis, character disorders, history of abuse, or extremely limited social skills and those needing or desiring insight-oriented work. Research by Toseland and Siporin (1986) and Budman, *et al.* (1988) has found that, given the choice of individual or group therapy, many chose individual treatment and expressed the belief that it was a more beneficial modality. Theses biases often result in a referral to group therapy as an adjunctive treatment. Given this treatment structure, it is important to acknowledge the positive reinforcement that takes place between these two treatment modalities.

Group therapy	Individual therapy
Peer pressure as a motivator	Validation–challenge of irrational beliefs
Reinforce behaviors–skills learned in individual	Development of new behaviors and skills therapy
Faster progress	Reinforcement
Learning from group members	Facilitate insight-oriented perspective
Confronting denial and negative patterns	Clarifying, supporting, and challenging
	positive change

The original self-help group, Alcoholics Anonymous (AA), was founded in 1935 and has become a worldwide organization. AA views abstinence from substances as the only choice. There is strong support in the affiliation of its members, along with the learning of survival skills. An important experience of AA membership is sponsorship. Members are encouraged to select a sponsor as quickly as possible into the recovery process. The sponsor is also in recovery with a history of abstinence. His or her goal in "sponsoring" someone is to encourage, support, and mentor the recovery of those he or she sponsors.

The group modality is a powerful tool for the substance abuser and his or her family members. Since its origination, many other 12-step and other self-help groups have evolved from the AA traditions and beyond. Some examples of these groups include

1. Narcotics Anonymous, Pills Anonymous, Pot Smokers Anonymous, etc.
2. Rational Recovery
3. Smart Recovery
4. Secular Organization for Sobriety (SOS)
5. Substance User's Recovery Group
6. Alanon–Alateen
7. Codependency Anonymous
8. Dysfunctional Families Anonymous
9. Emotions Anonymous

Treatment choices are expanding. Because of the difficulty some individuals have in embracing the AA 12-step program due to the requirement of acceptance of a higher power, recovery programs have developed that do not make reference to a higher power. Examples are Rational Recovery and Smart Recovery. However, all of the recovery programs offer the important components of fellowship and skill development needed for recovery. Other specialized groups that may be helpful as adjunctive treatment (some self-help and some in professional settings) include

1. Codependence
2. Shyness
3. Depression
4. Anxiety–stress management
5. Assertiveness training
6. Social skills training
7. Skills acquisition
8. Adult children of alcoholics
9. Adults molested as children
10. Domestic violence—offender
11. Domestic violence—victim
12. Understanding the impact on children (various parenting and family didactic groups)
13. Job seeking skills

BENEFITS OF SUPPORT GROUPS

Groups provide significant diverse interventions. Self-help groups provide focus and structure. Generally, self-help groups are not facilitated by a professional. There are numerous meetings, formats, rules, styles, and atmospheres to be considered when referring individuals to these community resources. They exist for the goal-oriented purpose of that group. It is helpful to prepare individuals for the differences that they may experience in such settings and identify the need to try numerous groups in order to find the one(s) that will be most useful and lead to regular attendance. The clinical and personal benefits associated with participation in therapeutic and self-help group programs are as follows:

1. Experience of affiliation and cohesion. Group offers a sense of belonging.
2. Identify and share with others facing similar problems.
3. Comfort, support, and acceptance balanced with identification and confrontation of addictive and maladaptive thinking and behavior.
4. Increased awareness and understanding of the individual's own attitudes toward substance abuse that interfere with abstinence. Decreased feelings of despair and shame.
5. Learn improved coping skills and appropriate behaviors.
6. Learn to effectively communicate thoughts, feelings, and needs.
7. Reinforcement of self-responsibility.
8. Development of adaptive and self-reinforcing lifestyle.
9. Support to remain abstinent.

10. An opportunity to observe and initiate the positive coping behaviors of others.

THERAPEUTIC GROUP

In a therapeutic group, there is also variance in how it will be experienced by an individual. Specific differences in comparison to self-help groups are as follows:

1. Psychological safety and support provided by the therapist
2. High level of structure
3. Specific issues are targeted
4. Goal-oriented
5. Smaller group size promotes earlier opportunities for reality testing of perceptions
6. Educational component
7. Group experience more closely approximates real life interactions
8. Viewing of the self *in lieu* of the responses made by others, resulting in an increase in self-understanding and facilitating clarification of individual goal setting
9. Allows for practice of social interactions, such as offering appropriate self-disclosure and soliciting feedback
10. Challenges self-focus by encouraging group behavior, empathy, and interest
11. Reinforces personal change
12. Facilitates and encourages the understanding and acceptance of individual differences
13. Feedback from group members improves perceptions
14. Over time, group participation helps to decrease defenses associated with increased honesty, motivation, and decreased cognitive distortions
15. Facilitates improved communication

The goal of the group is not "breaking through denial," but compliance, internalization, and empowerment. Compliance is achieved when the individual accepts the influence of the group (conforming) in the hope of achieving a positive reaction or outcome. Internalization is achieved when the individual accepts the influence of the group on his or her thinking and behavior and it is experienced as intrinsically rewarding. Empowerment is achieved when there is skill development, appropriate assertion and control over his or her life, encouragement of the empowerment of others, and a focus on self-responsibility. With such a clear direction focused on specific target problems, the emphasis is on behavior change and development of strategies for improved coping.

McCrady, *et al.* (1989) offer a group activity where group members are asked to brainstorm as many responses as possible to various questions. For example, "Why do you think some people develop substance abuse problems?" This technique can be useful in generating increased understanding and clarifying of coping mechanisms and antecedents of use. Second, it is also helpful for generating new ideas and new ways of looking at things, as well as emphasizing choices. Third, such group techniques offer encouragement that, throughout life, people continue to learn and have the opportunity to improve the quality of their lives by taking active responsibility for meeting their own needs.

BASIC AREAS OF EDUCATION

Basic areas of education include the following topics:

1. Understanding addiction
2. The ego-syntonic relationship to substance abuse
3. Social stigmatization issues
4. Categories of substances, their physiological and psychological effects, and long-term consequences
5. How to successfully survive weekends and holidays that have ritually included substances without using substances
6. How to create a healthy daily schedule with identified resources
7. Improved communication
   a. assertiveness
   b. understanding the role substances played to mask social distress
8. Understanding the reciprocal interaction between stress and addiction
   a. negative influences on self-care
   b. recreation
   c. social activity
   d. relationships
   e. conflicts
   f. avoidance
9. Relaxation training
10. Family roles of the addiction process
11. Refusal skills
12. Personal issues that play a role in recovery
    a. recidivism: prior treatment attempts, failures, and what happened
    b. insight: understanding of the addiction process
    c. motivation
13. Dealing with relapse
    a. craving
    b. thinking about substances–euphoric recall
    c. lying
    d. expecting too much
    e. acknowledging that recovery is a long-term process, not just achieving abstinence
    f. letting go
    g. meetings
    h. exercise
    i. good nutrition
    j. use of new resources

14. Relapse prevention
    a. acknowledge the lack of perfection and that mistakes will be made
    b. use mistakes as an opportunity to get back on track
    c. take and make the time to do it right
    d. utilize resources

15. Self-monitoring

As previously stated, the tasks of early recovery are focused on facilitating adequate, effective coping with distress without resorting to substance use. Most often cognitive–behavioral interventions provide the strategies necessary for the early stages of treatment where abstinence is achieved. Insight-oriented therapy may be useful in increasing awareness and self-understanding and developing the strategies necessary to maintain abstinence. It is insight-oriented therapy that leads to identifying circumstances and internal states that are likely to trigger substance use. Initial treatment efforts are expected to lead to the generation of an action plan that identifies appropriate and practical alternatives to substance use. Research by Brown (1985) demonstrated that an average time span of 20 months existed between initial contact and the acknowledgment and acceptance of AA membership. The role of the therapist is to facilitate the decision to elect for the difficult goals of commitment and transition to abstinence. Regardless of the presenting issues, individuals often enter treatment in crisis. The essence of the distress associated with crisis offers an opportunity for change.

STAGES OF SOLUTION-FOCUSED, OUTCOME-ORIENTED TREATMENT

To aid in the conceptualization of how the information presented may be utilized in one case, an outline initiated by a crisis and ensuing intake assessment could proceed in the following order.

1. Crisis (intake) inpatient if
    a. detox difficulties–complications
    b. psychosis
    c. suicidal ideation–plan–intent
    d. homicidal ideation–plan–intent to harm
    e. gravely disabled

2. Motivation (to alleviate distress)

3. Treatment contract (collaborative effort)
    a. specifying
        i. modalities (individual, conjoint, family, group)
        ii. frequency
        iii. time frame
        iv. commitment of significant other–family
        v. drug screening
    b. clarifying
        i. consequences of relapse (losses, higher level of care, etc.)
        ii. cessation of all substances (creates margin of safety against relapse with substance of choice or trading compulsions)

      iii. appropriate releases of information for case management and reinforcement of efforts–abstinence

      iv. self-care (appropriate nutrition, exercise, and structured activities)

4. Assess for the presence of differential diagnosis and complicated clinical issues that would add to the treatment contract
   a. personality disorder
   b. psychosis
   c. depression
   d. anxiety
   e. eating disorder
   f. history of sexual abuse–assault
   g. other
   h. not all issues can be reduced to recovery issues; therapy for some of these issues may not be instituted until a later date, possibly up to 1 year into recovery
   i. a period of abstinence is required for diagnostic clarification

5. Breaking the addiction cycle through education (educate client, significant other, and family members)
   a. disease concept–social learning theory
   b. resources and treatment choices
   c. benefits of abstinence
   d. review effects of intoxication and withdrawal
   e. identify losses and pending losses
   f. understanding of recovery process and required commitment
   g. role of denial (and other defenses)
   h. role of enabling
   i. relapse prevention and how to deal with relapse
   j. appropriate expectations and prediction of difficulties (i.e., high dropout rate in early recovery and how to avoid becoming a statistic)
   k. abstinence as the foundation of progress (i.e., psychological problems do not have to be solved to refrain from substance abuse)

The education process is easily accomplished in a group format. However, there is also a need to provide individual therapy so that concepts can be applied to the unique situations of an individual. This allows for necessary problem solving to insure adequate understanding and integration of new concepts. Be sure to distinguish between education versus therapy for each modality (individual, conjoint, family, group).

6. Journal for
   a. self-understanding
   b. increased awareness
   c. self-monitoring
   d. clarifying circumstances associated with use
      i. when occurs
      ii. who with
      iii. specifics of situation
      iv. what the individual was feeling
      v. what the individual did

      vi. what the individual wishes he or she had done differently

     vii. how the information helps him or her to move forward in recovery (focus on what works—successful outcome)

7. Support group (utilization of resources)
8. Self-help (12-step, Rational Recovery, Smart Recovery, etc.)
    a. survival skills
    b. support
    c. aids in transition of developing new identity
    d. resistance to this referral associated with
        i. unwillingness to admit substance dependency
        ii. fear of losing identity or individuality
        iii. discomfort of being new member feels like outsider
        iv. encourage the individual to take what he or she wants and leave the rest; he or she does not have to identify with everything

9. Develop a list of the negative consequences that substance abuse has had upon the individual's life. This is helpful to review when
    a. feeling ambivalent about recovery
    b. experiencing euphoric recall
    c. experiencing increased distress

10. Acknowledge and validate that the individual has given up something he or she liked and that he or she will continue to experience urges to use and may want to believe that he or she can use again.
    a. early recovery uses education to deal with these issues
    b. later stages of recovery are benefited by the earlier inquiry about his or her interest in substance(s), increased anxiety associated with emerging psychological or interpersonal problems. Social pressures, not feeling normal, etc.

11. Encourage strengthening behavioral supports for abstinence
    a. not uncommon to substitute one substance–compulsion for another
    b. use of another substance frequently precedes relapse to primary substance abuse

12. Negotiate a 6-month (short-term) period of abstinence from all substances versus insisting on total lifelong abstinence. Often when abstinence is achieved from all substances, individuals are more receptive to an abstinent lifestyle. Therefore, the advocated clinical perspective may be for lifelong abstinence, however, a short-term commitment offers a collaborative place to begin.

13. Relapse prevention (addressed throughout the recovery process)
    a. relapse is common; therefore, use the opportunity for reinforcing strength of overall recovery process and maintaining positive outcome
    b. increase understanding of varied causes (range from brain chemistry, early on, to factors that are clearly psychological)
    c. three significant associated areas
        i. negative mood states (boredom, depression, anxiety, fear, etc.)
        ii. interpersonal conflict
        iii. social pressure

14. Identification of specific vulnerabilities allows for prioritizing treatment issues. The specific problems are used to address how to avoid (these problems leading to) relapse.

15. Prepare for the experience of cravings and withdrawal symptoms, which can occur a month following the last episode of use. There is increased vulnerability associated with birthdays, anniversaries, holidays, and other celebrations.

16. Be on guard for progressive deterioration of physical, psychological, and behavioral functioning (increased vulnerability to relapse—high risk). Review list of warning signs:
    a. help individual increase awareness and track his or her feelings (journaling)
    b. develop skills to aid improved coping (contingency contracting, contingency management, stress management, skills development)
    c. learn to tolerate an experience versus the use of substances to cope
    d. help individual to accept disappointment that not everything is fixed with abstinence (and individual may experience and express significant disillusionment associated with abstinence not being the resolution to all of his or her problems)

17. Review and update treatment plan as needed to reinforce treatment gains, address evolving goals, and positively adjust to change and personal growth.

18. Facilitate the tenuous task of taking responsibility for past behavior without self-recrimination.

19. Psychological issues
    a. overwhelmed by emotions, personal growth
    b. early recovery: insight-oriented treatment focus
        i. help individuals to cope with pain without using substances
        ii. used to develop concrete, practical strategies and behaviors to abstain from substances
    c. later recovery focus
        i. explore and clarify to strengthen the understanding and need for support
        ii. increase behaviors associated with reinforcing abstinence
        iii. deal with personality-associated distortions
    d. increased relevance of insight-oriented therapy as an individual moves into solid foundation of recovery

Johnson (1997) offers an outline of group rules and a group contract, which clarifies for participants the expectations of the group. Such structure reinforces issues of respect and self-responsibility.

GROUP TOPICS

The following outlines identify some of the cardinal clinical issues presented under each topic. Group treatment is an excellent format for many of the underlying issues associated with substance abuse. Therefore, when a treatment plan is being developed, it is imperative to identify all of the treatment issues along with the variety of community resources available that can effectively treat the specific identified issues.

SUBSTANCE USE–ABUSE GROUP

This group is for the individual who has been assessed and needs review for greater understanding and reinforcement. The additional goals of this group are to offer validation, support, education, skill building, and problem solving. This group is not a substitute for self-help support groups, which offer affiliation, sponsorship, and increased availability for attendance as needed, at no cost. Alcoholics and other addicts are generally separated in some components of treatment because of

1. Different socialization-related issues (social bias of "drugs" versus alcohol)
2. Differences in lifestyle (alcohol is legal versus illicit substances)

Consider the following when selecting group members: gender, type of addiction, recidivism, and insight.

Group topics include the following:

1. Substance use history: Everyone identifies their first experience with substances, the mood altering effect, who else was involved, the circumstances, and how things have progressed to a history of current use. For concerned members of the group (who are not substance abusers), they may relate the history from the perspective of an observer who has been affected.

2. Patterns of substance use: Describe substance of choice, frequency, quantity, and circumstances associated with use.

3. Economics of substance use: Review the costs of substance use and how to utilize financial resources that were once used for substances.

4. Consequences of substance use: Review the history of substance use experiences and identify the negative consequences associated with use. Individuals should clarify in detail the relationship between use, negative behaviors, and consequences.

5. Emotional first step: How does the individual understand all of the factors that led to substance abuse–dependence.

6. Understanding family roles associated with substance abuse and dependency.

7. Outlining behavioral change and treatment choices: Important step for acknowledging, accepting, and reinforcing the collaborative treatment decisions made.

8. Substance use and the relationship to other activities: Impact of substance use upon education, vocation, leisure, etc.

9. Development of substance–free lifestyle: Environment, relationships, resources.

10. Personal inventory: A self-evaluation assessing the impact of substance abuse behavior and choices upon personal growth as well as reviewing how those in his or her life have been affected.

11. Self-care: Developing a lifestyle that includes rest, proper nutrition, appropriate support system, appropriate leisure activities, etc.

12. Surviving the weekend and holidays without substances.

13. Relapse prevention: Skill development.

14. Sharing: Concerns, how he or she is adjusting and coping with changes. A time for reinforcement of efforts and validation.

15. Problem solving: Although problem solving can take place at any time, this meeting is a formal opportunity to review what is working and what is not. How to strengthen individual programs and review personal growth.

CODEPENDENCY

Increases understanding of codependency, how it affects his or her life and relationships, and the ways in which it contributes to negative and unhealthy behaviors for him- or herself and others. A group that focuses on codependency can result in

1. Improved boundaries, setting limits, and maintained treatment gains
2. Improved self-efficacy and feelings of worthiness
3. Identified feelings
4. Appropriate expression of feelings
5. Honest and direct relationship functioning
6. Self-responsibility

Group topics can include the following:

1. What is codependency and how does it affect the individual
2. How does it work
3. Identify the codependency cycle in oneself
4. Identify efforts to control others
5. Ways to change codependency
6. Clarify what the individual has control over versus what he or she does not have control over
7. Self-responsibility
8. Individuality
9. Encouraging individuality and self-responsibility in others
10. Identifying feelings
11. Honest and effective communication of feelings
12. Dealing with difficult emotions
13. Clarifying boundaries
14. Setting limits
15. The importance of consistency with limits and boundaries
16. Congruence (thoughts, feelings, actions, and verbal communication match)
17. Improving self-esteem and feelings of worthiness
18. Identifying wants and needs
19. Appropriate expression of want and needs
20. Prioritizing
21. Self-care
22. Compassionate detachment
23. Identify hierarchy of difficult situations
24. Relapse prevention
25. Understanding codependency, the "family disease"

A group for codependents is important for the support and insight that can be achieved by working with others at varying levels of recovery. A significant amount of vicarious learning can take place and be reinforced by a group facilitator, with the result being an increased understanding of the individual's personal experience and appropriate substitute thoughts and behaviors. The healing effect achieved by working with other people who are struggling with the same or similar issues should not be underestimated. Group is also a useful method for encouraging those with low motivation.

SHYNESS

Some people are born with a shy disposition and others learn it from their life experiences, lack social skills, and/or struggle with negative thoughts and feelings. Shyness means unnecessary suffering from many people. Some find that they feel free from shyness when they use substances and need to find new ways of thinking, feeling, and coping.

1. Understanding shyness. Why is the individual shy? What triggers his or her shyness?
2. Identifying fears. How will the individual be able to do this substance-free?
3. Building self-esteem
4. Experiencing social interactions in a new way
5. Developing social skills
   a. education on assertive communication
   b. dealing with criticism
   c. conflict resolution
   d. negotiating
   e. giving and accepting compliments
   f. meeting new people
6. Systematic desensitization
   a. relaxation training
   b. visualization
   c. affirmations (positive self-statements versus put-downs)
7. New ways of thinking
   a. challenging irrational beliefs–fears
   b. developing positive and rational substitute statements to replace negative messages
8. Improving communication
   a. effectively expressing feelings, thoughts, and beliefs
   b. active listening
   c. "I" statements, taking responsibility for own emotions
   d. appropriate expression of emotions
9. Dealing with anger and other difficult emotions. What coping skills did the individual use?
10. Mood management
    a. depression
    b. anxiety
11. Freeing the individual of shyness. Role-play, beginning social interaction practice.
12. Is it working? Individual reports of *in vivo* practice and associated problem solving. More role-playing to increase repertoire of responses and improve comfort level.
13. Increasing social resources and contacts. Getting together with more people and in different environments.
14. Review what has been most helpful to every group member, what have they learned about their own experiences of shyness, and what specific tools they found helpful that they would share with someone else. What recommendations would they share for helping someone else?

ANGER MANAGEMENT

Anger is a normal healthy feeling. Everyone has felt it and will continue to experience it throughout their lives. Many learn to avoid problems, whereas others model those in their environment and use it to avoid, control, and intimidate others. For other individuals, it is a frustration because they feel it, but do not know how to appropriately express it. Individuals in recovery are looking for ways of expressing what they feel more clearly. Anger management may be an integral part of the recovery process.

1. Understanding anger in an individual's life.
   a. triggers
      i. the events that set off angry reponses
      ii. negative thinking that escalates and perpetuates anger
   b. learned behaviors
      i. anger as a defense
      ii. anger as control and distancing behavior
      iii. lack of developing appropriate skills for responding to various circumstances
   c. goal(s)

2. Understanding the chain of behaviors and emotions associated with the anger response and the important key to change: "calm down." It is necessary to slow down so that an individual learns to think instead of react.

3. Learn how to assess an individual's anger: When is it an appropriate response?
   a. problem solving
   b. decision making
   c. conflict resolution
   d. self-monitoring

4. What kind of thoughts contribute to the anger response?

5. Learning components of effective communication: "I" statements, active listening, reflection, and nonverbal communication.

6. What is assertive communication and how is it different from how the individual communicates?

7. Appropriate expression of anger.
   a. choices
   b. no blaming or shaming
   c. how to give feedback appropriately

8. Progressive muscle relaxation.
   a. systematic desensitization
   b. breathing techniques
   c. visualization
   d. affirmations (positive self-statements)
   e. step by step working through of a provocation

9. Using exercise to alleviate body tension (physical responses to anger)

10. Diffusing anger and how to respond to angry, aggressive responses from others.

11. Positive and negative consequences. Learning to connect the behavior with the consequences. The result is increased self-responsibility and positive outcomes, which improve self-efficacy.
12. Relapse prevention.

Rehearsal is used to practice scenarios associated with alternative responses to match desired outcomes and should be used throughout the group process.

ASSERTIVENESS TRAINING

Many individuals in recovery have lacked appropriate effective communicators in their lives and have replicated what they learned by modeling. They need the understanding, education, and practice to effectively convey to others what they think and feel. When individuals experience anticipatory anxiety, there is a disorganizing effect that heightens anxiety and decreases confidence. The result is avoidance of expressing their thoughts and feelings.

1. Define assertive communication and behavior.
2. Learn the difference between passive, assertive and aggressive.
3. Identify the range of one's own verbalization and behavioral trends.
4. Identify the rules, assumptions, or beliefs that influence feelings and associated responses in various situations
   a. what is he or she afraid will happen?
   b. what is the worst that could happen?
   c. would the outcome be intolerable? If not, what are his or her choices for managing it?
5. Assertive bill of rights.
6. Confront the fears associated with assertive behavior.
7. How to deal with criticism (versus rejection).
   a. how criticism can be beneficial
   b. dealing with honesty
   c. self-responsibility
8. Clarify the message he or she is trying to give.
9. When to take time out.
   a. responding in extremes (passive–aggressive)
   b. avoiding manipulative behavior
   c. mistake of setting up situations as win or lose
10. Give permission to be pleased.
    a. not required to respond immediately
    b. take the time to be clear about thoughts and feelings
    c. clarify consequences
11. Assertive listening.
    a. pay attention
    b. validate (everyone is entitled to their own feelings, thoughts, and beliefs)
    c. clarify one's own associated feelings and thoughts
12. Each individual is assigned the task of developing a list of situations where he or she experiences difficulty. Group members take turns role-playing in group to identify and reinforce positive responses, broaden their repertoire of behaviors and associated thoughts and feelings, and increase confidence.
13. Have group members predict the next time they expect to experience difficulties and problem solve it.
14. Self-monitoring (how will change be measured).
15. Relapse prevention.

SKILLS ACQUISITION

Johnson (1997) offers a brief outline of many of the skill building and self-care issues listed. A comprehensive understanding of the skill deficits of those in recovery is necessary for optimal outcome. Every deficit that is not identified and remediated contributes to risk factors. People who are most comfortable with themselves and the world are those who have a feeling of self-efficacy. Skill development is a prerequisite for this experience of self-confidence. Another way of viewing this issue is "having choices" and "feeling in control."

1. Prioritizing
2. Decision making
3. Problem solving
4. Coping with chronic problems
5. Conflict resolution–improved communication
6. Managing thoughts about using substances
7. Relaxation training
8. New ways of thinking
9. Goal development with associated self-responsibilty
10. Increasing leisure–recreational activities (supportive of recovery)
11. Negotiating
12. Managing stress
13. Management of depression and anxiety
14. Communication
15. Developing or increasing a social support network
16. Planning for a crisis
17. Self-responsibility
18. Refusal skills
19. Relapse prevention
20. Self-monitoring

Skill development is essential to a comprehensive recovery program. One of the significant contributors to and continuing reinforcers of substance abuse is the avoidance of thinking, feeling, and dealing with daily problems. The result is a snowball effect, which leaves an individual feeling overwhelmed with what he or she "has to cope with." Learning these skills provides a framework for his or her recovery to develop the ability to effectively cope with a variety of problems that occur in the daily lives of most people. It also offers the therapists a framework from which to evaluate the skills deficits of those in recovery (just as in traditional treatment of nonsubstance abusers) and appropriately structure treatment to facilitate development of these skills.

If more than one level of treatment is required, it is important that treatment team collaboration take place incorporating all of the professionals involved in the course of treatment so that appropriate and effective sequencing of treatment planning takes place and skills are continually practiced and reinforced. Throughout this text, there are numerous citations regarding the importance of skills acquisition being related to successful treatment outcome.

SOCIAL SKILLS TRAINING

Social skills training is appropriate for both the inpatient and outpatient population in substance abuse treatment. Parsons (1986) points out that one significant limitation of the use of cognitive techniques in skills training is for those who are cognitively impaired. This reinforces the issue of individualized treatment planning. Neuropsychological testing of alcoholics reveals a range of cognitive impairments of 50–85%. Skill development for these individuals can be facilitated in a reinforced manner in individual therapy and group. However, group is likely to demonstrate more rapid results. The focus of social skills training is a variation of the skills acquisition group.

1. Facilitate social development
   a. improved communication
   b. assertive communication
   c. receiving criticism
   d. conflict resolution
   e. problem solving
   f. anger management
   g. stress management
   h. mood and affect management

2. Strengthen adequate coping behaviors in various situations
   a. present situations and request each group member (or teams) to adaptively respond
   b. ask each member to offer a difficult situation specific to his or her life experience

3. All group members will be responsible for developing several situations (specifically assigned) and presenting them in group
   a. interpersonal
      i. situations that produce frustration and anger if not managed effectively
      ii. situations where coping is affected by negative emotional states
      iii. situations in which substances have been used to facilitate or enhance a positive emotional state
   b. intrapersonal
      i. situations in which the individual is in a negative physical state (appropriate remedies, relaxation, pain management)
      ii. testing personal control (clarify thought processes, generate appropriate alternatives for asserting personal control–choices)
      iii. situations that present or represent a temptation to use (unrealistic or resented demands from self or others, guilt, derailed activities)

4. Assign homework for each skill to be worked on in group for strengthening and reinforcement.

5. Develop realistic expectations and limitations.

ANXIETY AND STRESS MANAGEMENT

This is likely a group for everyone in recovery. Substance abusers often use substances to mask feelings of anxiety as well as a means of managing stress. Also, there are other substance use issues that complicate this situation. For example, if large amounts of alcohol are ingested for a long period of time, there can be a paradoxical response of it changing from an anxiolytic response to actually elevating anxiety.

1. Education about the thoughts, feelings, and physiological responses of anxiety and stress.

2. Understanding the complications of anxiety and stress associated with substance use.
   a. excess worrying and fears associated with life problems
   b. cognitive impairment
   c. detox–withdrawal symptoms
   d. hallucinosis
   e. paranoia
   f. psychosis

Detox may result in a significant diminishing or complete alleviation of intense anxiety, but the individual may then be confronted with a lack of skills and an overwhelming number of issues that have been avoided.

3. Learning to effectively manage anxiety and stress
   a. awareness of negative thinking (and its impact)
   b. decreasing reactiveness
   c. challenging irrational beliefs and cognitive distortions
   d. developing rational thinking
   e. learning relaxation techniques
   f. improved coping
   g. improved problem solving
   h. positive lifestyle changes
   i. alleviation–elimination of disabling and exhausting experiences that negatively impact health and sense of well-being (headaches, abdominal distress, etc.)

4. Continued management and relapse prevention
   a. predict the next anxiety–stress provoking circumstance and how it will be managed
   b. confront and resolve, when possible, associated external issues; often simple steps can make a significant difference regarding interpretation and management (family issues, legal problems, financial problems, education- or work-related issues)

5. Self-monitoring

ADULT CHILDREN OF ALCOHOLICS
(DYSFUNCTIONAL FAMILIES)

According to Johnson (1997), adult children of alcoholics appear to share common characteristics. These shared characteristics are likely the result of being raised in a home with certain dynamics that impact learning and coping. Participation in group can significantly contribute to challenging dysfunctional thinking and behavior associated with early life learning within the family. Specific issues of education and for group processing include the following:

1. Lack of trust
2. Loneliness
3. Denial of emotions
4. Feelings of guilt and shame
5. Need for control
6. Clarifying boundaries and self-responsibility
7. Perfectionism and compulsiveness
8. Avoiding assertiveness
9. Fear of anger
10. Fear of disappointing
11. Oversensitivity to criticism
12. Manipulative quality of behaviors
13. Understanding the positive and negative sides of these behaviors
14. Self-monitoring

DOMESTIC VIOLENCE (OFFENDER GROUP)

Domestic violence (DV) has serious consequences for everyone involved: the person who avoids intervention, the individual he abused, and the children who live in the shadows of violence in the family home. DV is never justified—it is a crime.

1. Assess lethality factor
    a. homicide–suicide risk
    b. cycle of violence frequency
    c. history of violence and assault in general–criminal history
    d. substance use
    e. isolation
    f. proximity to victim
    g. attitude toward role
    h. life stressors
    i. general psychological functioning

2. Anger management
3. Decrease social isolation to decrease dependency–focus on the relationship
4. Identify pattern of violence and associated red flags or warning signs
5. Increase self-understanding by weekly self-reporting of behaviors–thoughts–feelings
6. Problem solving how to withdraw and circumvent violence
    a. time out
    b. removing self from environment
    c. increased practice of utilizing support system (supportive of change)
    d. no use of substances (decreases inhibitions)

7. Goal setting (what does the individual want to accomplish)
8. Assertive communication
    a. honest appropriate expression of thoughts and feelings
    b. no intimidation

9. Accept the need to change
    a. acknowledge his or her history of abuse
    b. no blaming—take responsibility for own behavior
    c. identify socialization that has contributed to DV

10. Focus on self-responsibility
    a. identify how he or she sets him- or herself up for negative or positive outcome
    b. facilitate internalization of association between choices and outcome

11. Educate–confront the dangerousness of DV behavior (entire range of outcomes for his or her partner form emotional harm to death)
12. Empathy (learn to empathize with his or her partner)
13. Acknowledge the role of substance abuse in DV
14. Accept the legal consequences of DV (his or her behavior results in the consequences)
15. Stress management

Violence is sometimes passes from one generation to another in the homes where DV takes place. The basic concepts a child may learn from DV are

1. Being a man means dominating by force and using violence to deal with interpersonal conflicts.
2. Being a woman means being a victim.

TABLE 8.2   The Characteristics—Traits, Feelings, and Behaviors of Children of Alcoholics

The name of the game or the mode of survival	What is seen or visible traits, outside behavior	What is not seen or the inside story, feelings	What he or she represents to the family and why he or she plays along	As an adult without help, this is very possible	As an adult with help, this is also very possible
Family hero or super kid	"The little mother," "The little man of the family," always does what is right, overachiever, overresponsible, needs everyone's approval; not much fun.	Hurt, inadequate, confusion, guilt, fear, low self-esteem; progressive disease, so never can do enough.	Provides self-worth to the family, someone to be proud of.	Workaholic, never wrong, marry a dependent person, need to control and manipulate, compulsive, cannot say no, cannot fail.	Competent, organized, responsible, make good managers; become successful and healthy.
Scapegoat or problem kid	Hostility and defiance, withdrawn and sullen, gets negative attention, troublemaker.	Hurt and abandoned, anger and rejection, feels totally inadequate and no or low self-worth.	Take the heat: "see what he's done;" "leave me alone."	Alcoholic or addict, unplanned pregnancy, cops and prisons; legal trouble.	Recovery, has courage, good under pressure, can see reality, can help others, can take risks.
Lost child	Loner, daydreamer, solitary (alone rewards, i.e., food), withdrawn, drifts and floats through life, not missed for days, quiet, shy, ignored.	Unimportant, not allowed to have feelings, loneliness, hurt and abandoned, defeated and given up.	Relief at least one kid no one worries about.	Indecisive, little fun, stays the same, alone or promiscuous, dies early, cannot say no.	Independent, talented, creative, imaginative, assertive, and resourceful.
Mascot or family clown	Supercute, immature, anything for a laugh or attention; fragile and needful of protection, hyperactive, short attention span, learning disabilities, anxious.	Low self-esteem, terror, lonely, inadequate, and unimportant.	Comic relief, fun, and humor.	Compulsive clown, lampshade on head, etc.; cannot handle stress, marry us a "hero," always on verge of hysterics.	Charming host and person, good with company, quick wit, good sense of humor, independent, helpful.

DOMESTIC VIOLENCE (VICTIM GROUP)

The victim of domestic violence (DV) feels different or set apart from others. She may not feel that anyone will believe her or understand what her life is like. She may have been pushed, slapped, shoved, kicked, punched, choked, hit with an object, had things thrown at her, or been locked in small confining spaces. She may have been forced to have sex against her will or "raped." It is likely that she has been isolated from her family and everyone else. The parameters of her life are small and dictated. She is aware of what she is "allowed" to do.

1. The priority is always a safe environment
   a. educate regarding the right to safety
   b. increase protective skills for self and children

2. Assess lethality factor
   a. homicide–suicide risk
   b. cycle of violence frequency

3. History of violence in life
4. Decrease isolation
   a. develop a social support system
   b. participate in community-based activities

5. Increase self-care skills
6. Decrease helplessness
7. Decrease dependency on relationship
8. Increase understanding of family functioning and other factors that contribute to domestic violence
9. Increase self-efficacy by utilizing resources for taking care of self and setting limits
   a. legal services–rights
   b. medical treatment
   c. welfare

10. Improve communication (assertive, constructive, nonconfrontive expression of thoughts and feelings)
11. Identify whether she engages in behaviors that contribute to facilitating DV
12. Stress and mood management
13. No substance use
14. Goal development
    a. personal growth
    b. education
    c. vocation

Many communities have shelters to provide safety for women and children. There are also numerous books written by women who have survived the experience of DV, as well as those written by therapists. If a woman is unable to take action for herself, confront her with the impact of DV on her children and their right to a safe and stable home.

ADULTS MOLESTED AS CHILDREN

Sexual abuse issues are complex and challenging. They are interwoven from the individual to the societal level, which means overlays of sexism, family dysfunction, exploitation of power, sexual ignorance, issues associated with personality functioning, and coping. Sgroi and co-workers (Porter *et al.*, 1982) listed 10 treatment issues and related them to adolescents, but for those with a history of child sexual abuse, age is no boundary to these issues:

1. Experience of "damaged" goods
2. Guilt
3. Fear
4. Depression
5. Low self-esteem
6. Repressed anger and hostility
7. Inability to trust
8. Blurred boundaries, role confusion
9. Failure to complete developmental tasks
10. Self-mastery and control

Make a thorough assessment (substance abuse, eating disorders, etc.). Also, therapeutic work on child sexual abuse is so stressful that an individual with a diagnosis of strong compulsions like substance abuse and an eating disorder needs to be well-grounded in recovery and have ample resources prior to participation. There is increased risk of relapse with the experience of significant stress when adequate coping and resources are lacking.

Group Topics

1. Identifying a safe place and choices
2. Defining and developing a self-care plan
3. Identifying effective stress management techniques
4. "I'm in control" (requests for time out, compartmentalization, etc.)
5. Talking about the experience
6. Clarifying shame versus guilt
7. Clarifying boundaries
8. Confused feelings about family
9. Phenomenon of victim blaming (becoming self-blame)
10. Betrayal (used to gratify needs of adult, lack of parental protection, betrayal by the responses of his or her own body)
11. Identifying, understanding, and dealing with emotions
12. Coping mechanisms associated with sexual abuse (dissociation, etc.)
13. Separating the present from the past—assessing current choices
14. Trusting him- or herself (correcting distortions)
15. Effects on intimacy and sexual relationships
16. Avoiding the repetition of being victimized
17. Confronting the perpetrator
18. Reconceptualization of the experience to increase awareness, acceptance of what cannot be changed but has been survived, and a framework for resolution

Males may have homophobic concerns, issues of masculine identity, and socialization. Adolescents present with the developmental task of identity versus role confusion, egocentrism, self-consciousness, lack of responsibility, and acting out—possibly now sexualized. The adolescent victim–survivor has learned that sexual feelings can be exploited and controlling. He or she may use sexuality for pleasure, attention, affection, peer acceptance and financial independence. Adolescents are at higher risk for self-destructive behavior and suicide.

UNDERSTANDING THE IMPACT ON CHILDREN

Inadequate and ineffective parenting are often the hallmark of the substance abusing home. A parenting class with the flexibility for meeting didactic educational needs, increasing awareness, processing, and skill development is an important component for the family in recovery. It is imperative that a family in recovery be educated regarding what the potential impact of substance abuse in a family system has had upon a child along with guidelines for healthy family systems functioning. Some of the ways in which children are negatively affected include the following:

1. Family role development (hero, scapegoat, mascot, etc.)
2. Overdeveloped sense of responsibility
3. Negative impact on feelings of competence (resulting in such issues as perfectionism and feelings of insecurity)
4. Role reversal with parents
5. Lack of sufficient care or nurturing
6. Stress
7. Peer relationships (is it safe to bring a friend home)
8. Fetal alcohol syndrome
9. Limited resources; not comfortable, not safe, ashamed or embarrassed to bring friends home; avoidance of utilizing resources
10. Difficulty identifying feelings
11. Overall deficits in social development
12. Protecting family secrets
13. Developing age-appropriate realistic expectations and limitations
14. Behavior management skills
15. Shaping and reinforcing positive behaviors

Validating the rules learned by a child in a substance abusing family system:

1. Nobody talks about the problems in the family
2. There is no honest expression of emotion
3. It is not safe to address any issues
4. "Do as I say, not as I do"
5. Children do not learn to play, instead they become pseudo-parent

Review in Johnson (1997):

1. Parenting a Healthy Family
2. Guidelines for a Family Meeting
3. Developing Positive Self-Esteem for Children and Adolescents
4. Understanding and Dealing with Life Crises of Childhood
5. Talking to Children

Research has demonstrated the importance of positive relationships for emotional will-being and physical health. Therefore, it is not surprising that positive marital and family adjustment would be associated with a positive substance abuse treatment outcome. Although it is generally acknowledged that substance abuse leads to marital and family problems, there is also a reciprocal relationship whereby marital and family problems may play a role in the development and maintenance of substance abuse.

According to Stanton and Shadish (1997), conjoint and family therapy generally

1. Is more effective and less expensive than nonsystems treatment.
2. Is equally effective for adult and adolescent substance abusers.
3. Demonstrates higher rates of engagement and retention in treatment that nonsystems approaches.

Adopted from Prochaska and DiClemente (1986) is a three-stage framework for martial and family interventions in a substance abusing system.

1. Initial commitment to change
    a. acknowledge that a problem exists
    b. decide to seek intervention
    c. intervention
        i. how to encourage abstinence
        ii. how to encourage seeking professional treatment for specific needs
        iii. how to assist in treatment
        iv. use of appropriate reinforcement
        v. education and rehearsal confronting substance abusing partner
        vi. strengthen coping skills of nonusing partner
        vii. facilitate increased confidence for abstinence by substance abuser

2. Process of change
    a. abstinence (short-term trial of 6 months)
    b. stabilization
    c. once abstinence is achieved, partner can be encouraged to engage in increased positive interactions, i.e., mutually pleasing, caring behavior while focusing on nonsubstance issues
    d. decrease family interactional patterns that trigger or enable substance use
    e. dealing with slip, lapse, or relapse during the course of treatment
    f. planning shared leisure activities
    g. teach conflict resolution skills
    h. teach problem solving skills

3. Long-term maintenance of change
    a. focus on marriage
    b. relapse prevention
    c. prepare and facilitate readjustment of substance abuser to resume family role
    d. sex and intimacy

e. parent–child relationships
  i. communication
  ii. behavior management
  iii. limit setting
  iv. clear boundaries
  v. parent-centered versus child-centered family dynamics

Hester and Miller (1989) offer a check-off form for Monday–Sunday called the "marriage self-reminder," which lists positive relationship behaviors, such as

1. Compliments
2. Appreciation
3. Pleasant surprise
4. Affection
5. Pleasant conversation
6. Offer to help
7. Understanding–validation
8. Other

Couples counseling globally deals with the following issues: being specific with the breakdown of components within each issue that are intrapersonal, interpersonal within the couple's relationship, and family systems related.

1. Specific skills for dealing with substance use situations
2. Communication
3. Identifying and expressing feelings
4. Identifying and recognizing change in dysfunctional interaction patterns
5. Identifying and altering behavioral sequences associated with substance use
6. Dealing with parents and other transgenerational issues

Factors associated with a successful treatment outcome include the following:

1. At least a high school education
2. Full-time employment
3. Cohabitation or willingness to reconcile
4. Older–more mature
5. Enter treatment following a crisis (opportunity), especially if it threatens relationship
6. Spouse–partner and other family members are not substance abusers
7. Absence of first-degree crises (violence, danger to self or other, child abuse, etc.)
8. Evidence that substance abuser is motivated for treatment
  a. actively seeks treatment
  b. is interested in resources

c. accepts the need for change

d. accepts that abstinence is one component of recovery

FAMILY THERAPY

The focus of family therapy is on the relational and interactional characteristics of the family system. Family therapy is important as part of the recovery process:

1. To identify problems and facilitate change in interactions, behaviors, and beliefs within the family system that act to maintain substance abuse.

2. Family members often provide leverage for change. Generally, it is not the substance abuser who seeks therapy. The lack of confronting and working through family systems issues can be disastrous and lead to maladaptive generational patterns.

The reciprocal interaction between the substance abuser and his or her social environment, particularly the family, can have a significant influence on abstinence, recovery, and resolution.

A family systems background is helpful in understanding the dynamics of patterns, rituals, reciprocal interaction, and motivation. When working with a system, a central challenge is that all members have a different degree of readiness initially, and clinical efforts strive to bring some level foundation that results in facilitation of movement for the entire system. Just as substance abuse behavior interferes with or interrupts functional homeostasis in the family system, abstinence likewise will affect family homeostasis. Therefore, what role substance abuse plays in the family must be considered and integrated into assessment, treatment, and recovery plans for rational goals setting and maximum results.

One of the ways to conceptualize the family in recovery is to understand its journey of change through the course of the recovery process. Three central factors are the following:

1. Achieving abstinence destabilizes the system by interrupting ongoing patterns and roles. Abstinence itself can create distress in which the system finds it easier to reestablish homeostasis by returning to use patterns. Therefore, interpret the family's level of distress in working toward change. Another possibility is that abstinence facilitates the family to work toward accepting treatment and initiating disengagement from behavioral patterns that have maintained the unhealthy and dysfunctional system.

2. *Adjusting to abstinence* signifies working toward redefining and restabilizing the system using new understanding and initiating healthy interactional patterns. Factors associated with adjustment include

   a. acceptance and self-responsibility

   b. improved communication

   c. identification of resources

   d. treatment internalization and facing the reality of change

   e. skills acquisition

   f. reorganization or "putting it all together," which leads to healing and repairing relationships

   g. consolidation or increased comfort with decreased chaos, new lifestyle behaviors, improved intimacy, and a sense of efficacy

3. *Maintenance,* whereby positive changes are maintained by continued stabilization of the new lifestyle functioning; self-monitoring–self-responsibility by each family member.

FAMILY PATTERNS OF SUBSTANCE DEPENDENCY

According to Stanton *et al.* (1982), there are family patterns of substance dependency. Some characteristics that describe or distinguish substance abusing families include the following:

1. A high rate of multigenerational substance abuse–dependency.
2. Primitive, indirect expression of conflict.
3. Overt alliances and triangulations in the family system.
4. Substance culture peer group where an individual finds solace from family systems stressors, difficulties, and expectations. This additionally, offers the illusion of independence.
5. Symbiotic parenting behavior (e.g., enabling mother of addict).
6. Themes of premature, unexpected deaths in addict's family.
7. Pseudo-individuation.
8. Acculturation problems.
9. Amplified parent–child problems.
10. Poor communication.

STAGES OF FAMILY INTERVENTION

1. Identification of the problem. The therapist often bonds with the most motivated family member, but must be respectful and empathic to all family members. It is beneficial to use a standardized questionnaire to assess the degree of substance abuse. The use of an objective questionnaire can be especially beneficial for confronting denial.
2. Collaborative prioritizing of treatment goals. The primary goal is abstinence (sometimes moderation). All other goals are related indirectly or directly. This helps to clarify family treatment issues and their association to the primary treatment goal.
3. Development of a treatment alliance toward the collaborative effort of change. This alliance with nonusing family members functions as a motivator.
   a. joining (therapist affiliates and is respectful to each family member)
   b. encouragement
   c. benevolent influence
   d. therapist must maintain neutral, nonblaming stance toward the entire family. Reframe or "sandwich" the difficult issues to confront the family system with a positive intent to problem solve and avoid alienation. This lessens resistance and promotes compliance. The "sandwich" technique frames a difficult issue between two positive statements or reinforcers and is a method that decreases defensiveness.

e. identify the problem as a "family problem." Everyone in the family system plays a role in recovery. This related to strengthening the family in healthy ways: facilitating development of appropriate boundaries, developing improved problem solving and conflict resolution, and increased self-responsibility.

4. Negotiation of a treatment contract
   a. abstinence (or modification) is a prerequisite for further treatment. However, another view is to focus on other substantial changes of corrective thinking and behaving in the family system, which increases pressure on the substance abusing member and can lead to abstinence. Some individuals are not initially convinced that abstinence is necessary, and it may need to be proved during the course of treatment as loss mounts with the improvement of a healthier family system that moves forward without them. Contract with them for at least 30 days of abstinence; 60–90 days are preferable. Establishing an abstinence contract allows the therapist, identified patient, and family members the opportunity to experience the impact of abstinence. Contracting for abstinence and other specific treatment issues helps to reinforce the need for structure in the family system.
   b. list goals
   c. clarify objectives and time line for accomplishment–mastery
   d. self-monitoring to improve self-responsibility and increase self-efficacy

5. Stabilization I : Refers to the strategies that aid abstinence and are needed to improve functioning. Initial treatment efforts are aimed at
   a. appropriately intervening in crisis–health issues
   b. decreasing emotionality
   c. decreasing reactiveness
   d. clarifying the importance of each family member working from a position of self-responsibility
   e. destabilizing self-defeating or self-destructive patterns of behavior and personal interactions
   f. considering the importance of other community resources and integrating them into treatment for additional support and reinforcement (12-step, Rational Recovery, Smart Recovery, SOS, church, etc.)
   g. self-help groups for significant other and family members
   h. education regarding the course of behavior change
      i. regression is a normal sequence in recovery
      ii. it is the nature of addictive craving that "motivates" using behaviors
      iii. directly discuss addictive craving with the individual and family
      iv. encourage family members to try to imagine what it is like to experience drive from a strong craving; how would they respond (possibly quite similar)?
      v. educate family on how substance use has invaded family routines and rituals and what can be done to restructure the daily functioning of the family so as to not reinforce substance using behaviors and dynamics
      vi. family members also need to learn to tolerate stress
   i. encouraging detachment from substance abusing culture and associated behaviors (24-hr crisis support through 12-step sponsor, meetings, and hot lines)
   j. emphasizing personal responsibility and choices, being sure to facilitate connection of choices to consequences to improve effective problem solving
   k. predicting and preparing family members for the difficulties and "ups and downs" of recovery; pain, physical discomfort, feeling emotionally overwhelmed, suicidality, etc., along with the choices and resources for managing while the individual is learning how to effectively cope with life. Possible escalation in pathology that places him or her at risk to be "hooked" back into old patterns (with a general

increase in substance abuse, which provides increased health risks if he or she has been abstaining, i.e., decreased tolerance and overdose).

    l. therapist must be creative and flexible, being prepared to intervene with a variety of strategies to keep the family in treatment during this stage

6. Choices and adjustment
   a. the substance abusing individual is now in treatment, where family changes and goals are in direct conflict with continuing substance use and related behaviors. As a result, the substance abuser will have to choose between the substance object or his or her family and associated changes. With increasing separation from the desired substance and substance culture, there may be a heightening of feeling abandoned. This may lead him or her to turn to the therapist for support, seek reassurance, and decrease feelings of being overwhelmed as he or she initiates the path of recovery.
   b. it is imperative, regardless of the substance abusing individual's choice, that the rest of the family remain in treatment and work toward the process of change so that all share in the success of treatment.

7. Stabilization II: With abstinence comes a new set of problems. Family members may experience distress associated with changes in the substance abusing family member and begin to sabotage treatment. This is a point of significant risk of relapse. The expectation of joy and relief by family members may not be experienced. Instead, there may be feelings of depression, loss, emptiness, and anger. There is now a greater challenge presented to them as they must change their interactional family system patterns. This must be framed as an opportunity for correcting the family system's homeostasis to being parent-centered, improving communication, clarifying boundaries and limits, and establishing healthy, developmentally appropriate family activities. At this point, system reorganization has not yet shifted from the focus of substance abuse and resolving associated issues.

8. System reorganization: This stage signifies that the substance abuser has stabilized and family members are all prepared to work together toward recovery. Therefore, family therapy begins to focus on general systems issues, such as
   a. improved communication
   b. stress management
   c. problem solving
   d. conflict resolution
   e. improved marital relationship
   f. improved parent–child relationship(s)
   g. identifying and dealing with family of origin issues
   h. codependency
   i. complimentary role–team work
   j. resolving issues of power and control
   k. new changing role identified (changing old expectations and behaviors)
   l. problem solving how to facilitate family members to break their old behaviors so that increased self-responsibility and reinforcement for the efforts of the substance abuser can take place
   m. problem solving how to facilitate desired level of couple's intimacy
   n. during this stage of treatment, skill acquisition plays an important role in changing old patterns of behavior and increases self-efficacy

The family has likely learned to avoid affective-laden issues for fear of "pushing" someone into the use of substances. Legitimately, the individual in recovery may become overwhelmed by anxiety and depression in the early stage of recovery if too much pain is uncovered because he or she lacks effective coping skills. Therefore, both the recovering individual and his or her family are often threatened by the emergence of affective material early in the process. Education, support, and skill development are needed for successful navigation through such distressing periods of learning and adjustment.

If the substance abuser in the family system is an adolescent, a shift in treatment focus would be on appropriate developmental issues:

a. school
b. peer relationships and teen culture
c. increased self-responsibility
d. facilitation of connection between behaviors and consequences
e. clarification between rights and privileges
f. goal development
g. vocational counseling–getting a job
h. living arrangement and associated responsibilities
i. appropriate separation and individuation

As the family system demonstrates continued growth and progress in recovery, longer intervals between sessions are scheduled. This eventually leads to "checkup" appointments, which occur over intervals of months. This format is designed to serve as a reinforcer and maintains increased awareness of task orientation and consistency in behavior change in anticipation of the checkup session. It is made clear to the family that, if an appointment is needed prior to a checkup session, they should simply call and schedule an appointment as needed.

9. Treatment consolidation and termination: It is best if termination of treatment is mutually agreed upon. In preparation of discharge from treatment, the therapist helps the family to consolidate its treatment experience by
   a. reviewing the goals and objectives met
   b. reviewing the development to new skills and their demonstrated benefit
   c. reviewing resources
   d. predicting difficulties that may be experienced and ways in which they can be dealt with
   e. discussing and reinforcing the importance of new family rules, boundaries, respect, and responsibility
   f. reinforcing new international patterns
   g. being on guard for changes in compulsions (some are socially acceptable and some are not, i.e., workaholic, gambling, etc.)

Termination of treatment is not "a last session;" it is a process of reviewing, consolidating, and preparing. The process identifies what has changed and what has demonstrated benefit and predicts some of the issues confronting the family following termination. It facilitates the family system to take the education and newly acquired skills and as successfully as possible make the transition to independent practicing of the new ways to functioning.

10. Termination: The family reflects an experience that major problems are better understood and that adequate changes have taken place. The family members also feel satisfied with their accomplishments, accompanied by feelings of increased self-efficacy. They understand that this is not a point of being "cured." Instead, it is a level of stabilization and skill acquisition that has prepared them to continue to move forward in a physically, psychologically, and emotionally healthy manner. They are prepared and encouraged to continue their efforts outside the frame and support of therapy. Therapy is not meant to be a way life. For those needing ongoing support and affiliation, attendance of an AA or other appropriate self-help group is recommended.

If premature termination takes place, it is recommended that the therapist make the effort to clarify the reason and, if necessary, make appropriate referrals or offer additional services and resources.

RELAPSE

The most frustrating issue for many therapists working in the field of substance abuse intervention is relapse. Outcome studies suggest 40–80% rates of relapse among substance-dependent individuals. According to Catalano *et al.* (1988), psychiatric impairment is highly associated with substance use relapse. Daley (1988) and Marlatt and Gordon (1985) state that the greatest rate of relapse, two-thirds, occurs during the first 90 days of abstinence. Generally, it is not a single casual factor, but rather multiple factors that cause the actual lapse or relapse to substance abuse.

1. Affect and mood: Negative mood states are associated with relapse (anger, anxiety, boredom, depression, emptiness, guilt, and loneliness). Sometimes these symptoms are the result of comorbidity with psychiatric disorders.
2. Behavior: Lack of social and personal coping skills.
3. Cognitive: Deficits in cognitive functioning, attitudes, beliefs, and expectations.
4. External (environment–relationships): Life changes, interpersonal conflicts, deficits in social skills (listening, self-disclosure, expression of feelings, negotiating conflict), living arrangement, indirect social pressure, substance availability, and negative social network.
5. Physiological: Chronic pain, chronic illness, physical craving, acute–protracted withdrawal.
6. Psychiatric–psychological factors: Personality disorder–features, psychiatric illness, psychological problems, addiction–compulsions, problems with impulse control, or history of abuse (physical, sexual, emotional, verbal).
7. Spirituality: Lack of meaning–purpose in life, emptiness, lack of connection with others, excess feelings of guilt or shame.

Gorski (1988) identified relapse vulnerabilities, stating that relapse is a state of mind that precedes actual substance use. Individuals often conceal slips, lapses, and relapses to avoid disappointing their therapists, as well as to avoid being confronted. Gorski offered two basic lines of experience for self-monitoring, or taking an inventory, of those potential shifts (warning signs). A quick inventory of these internal and behavioral warning signs would be as follows:

Internal warning signs:

1. Difficulty thinking clearly
2. Difficulty in managing feelings and emotions
3. Difficulty with memory
4. Difficulty with stress management
5. Daydreaming and magical thinking
6. Feeling hopeless and helpless
7. Feeling irritable–on-edge

Behavioral warning signs:

1. Irregular sleep and change in eating patterns
2. Loss of or inconsistency in daily structure (lack of routine)
3. Inconsistent 12-step attendance
4. Inconsistency in treatment (not working on his or her program)
5. Episodes of anger, frustration, resentment
6. Lying
7. Manipulation

RELAPSE PREVENTION TECHNIQUES

The foundation of recovery and relapse prevention is initiating and maintaining change. Marlatt and Gordon (1985) assert that the relapse process begins with a lifestyle imbalance, which manifests itself as overwhelming stress in an individual's life. Teaching of self-control strategies is intended to increase an individual's ability to deal with stress and cope with high-risk situations. The role of treatment is to increase self-efficacy and self-confidence through the management or mastery of hierarchy of high-risk situations. Homework assignments are given between sessions to facilitate practice in the natural environment (with progressive risk as he or she works through the hierarchy) and promote maintenance via improved self-efficacy. Keep in mind that the substance abuser likely found substance use to be particularly rewarding. Therefore, it is important to develop appropriate replacements of indulgence that are not harmful or self-defeating. These gratifying substitutes must have a reinforcement potential matching or greater than that of substance use.

Bandura (1977, 1978, 1986) and Annis (1986) assert that the procedures or strategies that initiate change may not be the keys for producing maintenance and generalization of change. Therefore, relapse prevention must introduce strategies that facilitate change over time. Bandura's theory of efficacy views relapse prevention as actually beginning with assessment, identifying high-risk situations followed by determining an individual's cognitive appraisal of each situation (using past experiences). According to Brown *et al.* (1990, 1995), among abstaining alcoholics, personal threat and chronic life stress may lead to relapse. The most vulnerable to stress are those lacking in adequate coping skills, self-efficacy, and social support. Stress-related relapse is greatest among those with less self-confidence in their ability to resist using substances and those who rely on others who use substances for support. Stress may exert its greatest influence on the initial lapse or relapse following a period of abstinence.

The goals of relapse prevention are (O'Farrell, 1993)

1. To maintain treatment gains.
2. To deal with unresolved issues that emerge during the first year of recovery.
   a. difficulties experienced by the individual in recovery as he or she attempts to assume a more dominant or assertive role in the family
   b. issues associated with substance abuse by other family members
   c. issues associated with intimacy

3. To develop and rehearse cognitive–behavioral strategies for effectively dealing with relapse.
   a. discuss relapse
   b. identification of high-risk situations
   c. identification of early warning signs
   d. plans for prevention of relapse
   e. plan for minimizing the intensity and duration of any occurrence of relapse
   f. alternatives of management should he or she be confronted by a high-risk situation
   g. how to deal with any substance use that might occur

The components of relapse prevention are

1. Adequate motivation for entering treatment and making changes
2. Incentive(s) to change (recognize the benefits of abstinence); positive correlates include
   a. belief that substance use has hindered meeting personal goals
   b. belief that substance use has impaired relationship functioning
   c. accept the value of learning relapse prevention
   d. if, for example, moderate drinking is the goal and the individual is a good candidate for successful moderation, collaboratively develop effective guidelines and monitor success
   e. clearly defined areas of risk versus generalized risk across situations

3. Assessment of high-risk situations
   a. use of inventories such as the Inventory of Drinking Situations (IDS 100), which offers eight categories of drinking situations and renders a risk profile. The information is then integrated into treatment planning. There are numerous inventories available, or the same questions can be integrated into an assessment format utilized by the therapist.
   b. self-monitoring

4. Outline with the individual a hierarchy of high-risk situations, microanalysis:
   a. when
   b. where
   c. who present
   d. what happened before, during, and after use
   e. how did the individual appraise that event (thoughts and feelings before, during, and after use)

f. what is his or her current level of self-efficacy to cope successfully in a similar situation

g. due to the high degree of the individual's involvement in all aspects of decision making, there is a natural transition for maintaining change as he or she learns to act as his or her own therapist, i.e., thinking methodically through all the issues confronting him or her and demonstrating appropriate and effective problem solving

5. Identifying strengths and resources
   a. personal strengths–assets
   b. support
      i. family–significant other
      ii. friends
      iii. clergy
      iv. self-help groups
      v. community agencies
      vi. employer

6. Developing effective coping responses
   a. behavioral
      i. alternative activities
      ii. history of successful management of high-risk situations
      iii. utilization of appropriate resources
      iv. self-care–health choices
   b. cognitive
      i. reasoning ability
      ii. developing helpful–reinforcing thoughts
      iii. problem solving and conflict resolution
      iv. appreciated benefits associated with abstinence
   c. affective
      i. appropriate management of affective experiences
      ii. ability to confront negative emotions constructively–productively
      iii. comforted by spiritual beliefs
      iv. able to accept what cannot be changed (let it go or deal with it)
      v. appropriate emotional outlets to ease distress

7. Stress management (achieving positive daily structure and balance)
   a. deal with one thing at a time
   b. exercise to relieve body tension and clear mind
   c. challenge and change perfectionism
   d. use resources appropriately
   e. learn to be alone (enjoy own company)
   f. develop leisure activities that do not involve substances
   g. strive for moderation in life versus being rigid or extreme
   h. adequate rest and nutrition

8. Homework assignments (designed to coincide with working through progressively difficult hierarchy of high-risk situations)
   a. generally be prepared to develop three or more assignments per session to promote increased awareness, skill development, and reinforcement of recovery
   b. early in treatment have a tentative plan(s) of action for each difficult situation

c. development of realistic expectations and limitations in association with anticipation of problem situations

d. initital assignments must offer maximal reinforcement; therefore, design assignments that are programmed for success to result in increased self-efficacy

e. later stages of homework must focus on promoting a strong maintenance program with demonstrated increase in self-efficacy
   i. challenging tasks
   ii. moderate effort required to cope effectively, signifying that abstinence is not experienced as aversive
   iii. little external support required (but validated and reinforced if needed)
   iv. task success associated with overall improvement
   v. increased personal control (internal locus of control)
   vi. individual associates success with personal growth, confidence, and skill development

9. Self-monitor with log–journal
   a. continued identification of triggering antecedents
   b. initiation of individual's planning–coping
   c. continued problem solving associated with increasing self-responsibility
   d. reinforcement of efforts
   e. this is one of the first tools used in training individuals to identify high-risk situations. It serves both as an assessment procedure and as an ongoing observational and learning technique, where it reinforces what works and identifies what does not and needs to be changed.
   f. planning for difficult situations–crises and rehearsal of alternative responses
   g. practicing new behaviors
   h. as the end of treatment is approached, the task of developing homework assignments should be transitioned to the individual in treatment
   i. increases awareness and reinforces change

10. Consolidates treatment gains by having the individual give an objective review of his or her behavior and overall responses to different risk situations
    a. clarify with him or her points of competency to reinforce confidence
    b. monitor outcome of improved self-efficacy across all areas. If there is a demonstrated lack of confidence in coping with any of the identified areas or situations, discharge should be considered as being premature

Specific Relapse Prevention Techniques

In order to prevent relapse, an individual must be able to identify the causes of relapse, typical warning signs, ways to cope with thoughts of using, cues that trigger craving to use, social pressure to use, social interactions–network, lifestyle issues, and how to deal with setbacks and relapse.

1. Educate about relapse warning signs
   a. avoid high-risk people, places, and situations
   b. educate about how to deal with high-risk people, places, and situations

2. Explore beliefs about recovery and relapse in order to confront cognitive distortions

3. Detachment
   a. to overcome urges and craving
   b. identify–observe bodily responses and sensitivity to environmental influences

c. allows a degree of separation (labeling and detachment) because as an observer he or she is able to talk him- or herself through the conditional response (urge–craving): "the feeling is temporary and it will pass," while understanding that responding to it strengthens the conditioned response

4. Prepare to effectively deal with psychiatric–psychological factors that increase risk

5. Identify necessary lifestyle changes because of association and risk of relapse

6. Facilitate development of realistic expectations and limitations

7. Deal with defense mechanisms
   a. rationalization and denial are precursors to high-risk situations
   b. goal is to avoid engaging in faulty thinking and recognize the warning signs of his or her own decision making, which could lead to the process of relapse

8. Role-play: Behavioral rehearsal to prepare individuals to deal with pressures

9. Develop interpersonal skills
   a. initiating conversation
   b. giving and receiving compliments
   c. giving and receiving criticism associated with substance abuse
   d. refusing substances
   e. developing close, positive relationships
   f. improving support system
   g. using resources appropriately (practice)

10. Develop assertive communication skills so that emotions can be appropriately communicated

11. Journaling
    a. self-reflective writing for the purpose of identifying, clarifying, exploring, and problem solving personal and recovery issues
    b. review potential setbacks or relapse experiences or identify previously ignored–unidentified warning signs as well as possible coping strategies for a pertinent range of potentially difficult situations. If there is a history of relapse, identify clear, predictable patterns associated with relapse.
    c. daily inventory of
       i. high-risk situations
       ii. relapse warning signs
       iii. dealing with any current problems

12. Develop refusal skills (adapted from Goldstein et al., 1990)
    a. asking for help
    b. giving instructions
    c. convincing others
    d. knowing his or her feelings
    e. expressing his or her feelings
    f. dealing with someone else's anger
    g. dealing with fear and other difficult emotions
    h. using self-control
    i. standing up for his or her rights
    j. responding to teasing
    k. avoiding problems–trouble with others

TABLE 8.3   Relapse Prevention Decision Tree[a]

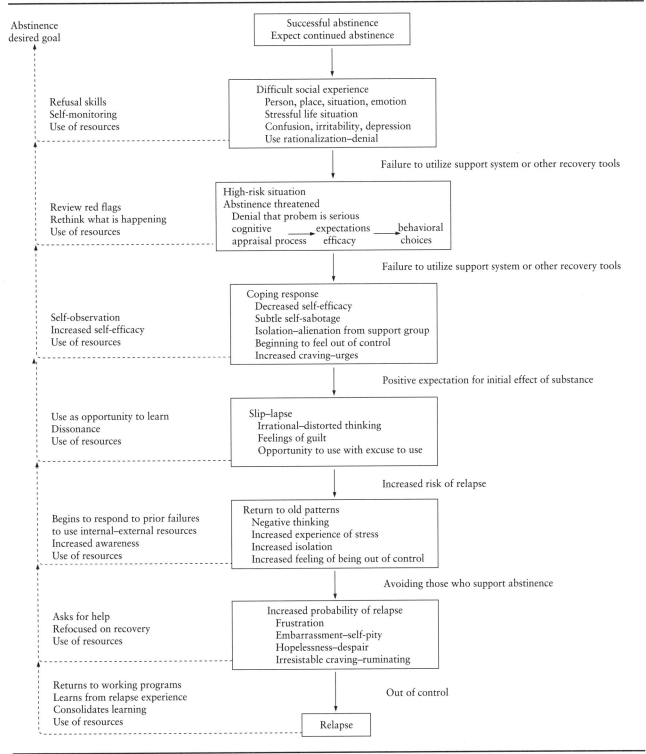

[a]Self-talk has a significant influence on recovery it every juncture. Examples of useful positive self-statements include (1) recalling good things about oneself and life; (2) challenging irrational beliefs about unrealistic expectations; (3) decatastrophizing (deal with "what is" not "what if"); (4) relabeling distres as a signal to use coping skills; (5) hopefulness and optimism (optimism and pessimism often become self-fulfilling prophecies); (6) stay on task and do the best one can. (if there is something where choices can be asserted, do something; Let go of things where one does not have control).

l. avoiding fights and provocation

m. dealing with embarrassment

n. dealing with being left out

o. responding to failure and disappointment

p. dealing with an accusation

q. preparing for difficult conversation

r. dealing with group–peer pressure

s. decision making

t. prioritizing

u. goal setting

Curry and Marlatt (1987) recommend that individuals use every opportunity to examine and learn from their experiences, and they suggest keeping the following points in mind:

a. stop, look, and listen (to what is happening)

b. keep calm

c. renew the commitment to behavior change

d. review the situation leading up to the slip or lapse (or the potential of it)

e. make an immediate plan for recovery

f. ask for help

13. Problem solving cards
   a. 3×5 in. index cards with various information for reminding, imaginal rehearsal, specific coping strategies, and affirmations
   b. carry a small card in his or her wallet that has tips on what to do should a slip occur (obviously a time when he or she is having difficulty thinking clearly on his or her own; having it written down decreases stress and facilitates him or her to go through the "right" motions) and outlines coping skills, helpful thoughts to utilize, and numbers to call

14. Develop lifestyle changes, activities, and social events that are enjoyable and supportive of goals (do not present threat–pressure which may lead to relapse)

15. If the individual is dually diagnosed, prepare him or her to work closely with the prescribing physician to take medication as prescribed, i.e., to stop taking neuroleptics, antidepressants, or mood stabilizers would present an increased risk of relapse as well as an exacerbation of psychiatric symptoms

16. Development of a recovery support network
   a. family and social support
   b. 12-step or other self-help group
   c. therapy (individual, conjoint, family, special topic group)

DEALING WITH A SLIP, LAPSE, OR RELAPSE

Should any of these occur, deal with it immediately to facilitate reimmersion into recovery and maxime what the individual can learn with the least amount of damaging delay in time.

1. Call someone immediately for support and to reinforce the positive choices for self-care.

2. Understand why it happened.

3. Identify the accompanying fellings (guilt–shame) associated with "failing."
4. Learn from it.
5. Understand that a slip or lapse does not have to result in a total relapse.

A slip is one time, a lapse is use that does not go beyond several days, and relapse is a return to the practice of dependence.

AVERSION THERAPY FOR ALCOHOL DEPENDENCE

The purpose of aversion therapy is to decrease or eliminate an individual's desire for a substance. Probably the most well-known use of aversion therapy has been the Schick Program. Aversion therapy is generally considered when an individual has experienced difficulty with remaining abstinent; however, it could also be an initial treatment modality. Examples of this form of treatment include the following:

1. Imagery or covert desensitization: Pairs imagined unpleasant scenes with imagery of drinking to produce nausea. This treatment may be augmented with an aversive odor. Positive factors of use as a treatment
   a. involves minimal risk to individuals
   b. no special equipment required
   c. can be administered in an outpatient setting by an appropriately trained paraprofessional
   d. preparing the individual for treatment:
      i. prepare him or her to experience nausea or fear (anxiety), which may continue briefly following treatment
      ii. breath alcohol test (BAT) is used prior to session to assure that the individual is not using alcohol, which could diminish the effectiveness of treatment
      iii. setting: quiet room, comfortable chair–position, distractions eliminated
   e. imagery
      i. individual imagines drinking in a familiar setting, then imagines association of aversive consequences (nausea, vomiting, feared natural consequences, or excess consumption)
      ii. steps of treatment: simple pairing—escape—avoidance
      iii. goal is to develop an avoidance response in addition to the aversive response. Once the pairing scene becomes an established conditioned response, as evidenced by nausea or discomfort, the escape scene is initiated. Alternate pairing of the imagined aversive consequences and the escape scene acts to strengthen the conditioned response. The avoidance scene is introduced to reinforce avoidant behavior.
      iv. administration of treatment if there is a desire to pair a noxious odor. Valeric acid is commonly used as the noxious odor. Generally, use a glass jar with a tight fitting lid that is easy for the therapist to use. The jar is opened close to the individual's nose at appropriate timing for stimulus pairing. To determine the physiological response to imagery scenes, inexpensive biofeedback devices that measure skin conductance level–response, heart rate, and/or breathing rate can be utilized.
   f. contraindications
      i. history of gastrointestinal disorders
      ii. history of heart disease

iii. current experience of major depression with suicidal ideation

iv. psychosis

2. Electrical conditioning: Pairs a painful shock to the hand or arm as the individual reaches for or tastes the beverage. The stimulus may be self-administered. However, requires trained medical supervision.

3. Disulfiram
   a. may be beneficial for older individuals who have a history of relapse but are motivated and have at least moderate social stability
   b. may be effective in preventing relapse when utilized in a treatment with social context
   c. poor compliance is an obstacle to effectiveness
   d. side effects and potential danger of disulfiram–alcohol reactions contraindicate use with individuals who present with a wide array of medical and psychiatric conditions and with pregnant women

4. Emesis: The oldest and most commonly used approach of aversion therapy. Substances are used to produce nausea. The substance is administered so that severe nausea occurs following tasting, sipping, or swallowing alcoholic beverages. The substances used are emitine hydrochloride, lithium, and apomorphine. Requires trained medical supervision.

5. Apnea: This treatment produces a brief (60-sec) but terrifying paralysis of breathing. Alcohol is placed on the individual's lips during the paralysis episode.

MODERATION OF USE

There is an ongoing debate about this treatment alternative and harm reduction. For more information, review the concept of harm reduction in Chapter 6. According to Heather and Robertson (1983), data indicate that a treatment goal of moderation regarding alcohol appears to result in rates of success comparable to a treatment goal of abstinence. The goal of moderation is likely to be achieved by individuals with less severe problems and a lower degree of dependency; abstinence is a more stable outcome among severe alcohol abusers. The success rate of more severe alcohol dependent individuals to learn to consume alcohol moderately is very low. Harm reduction acknowledges that, whereas the ideal outcome may be abstinence, moderation of use is an alternative that reduces harm. Hester and Miller (1989) propose the following considerations for the goal of moderation in alcohol use:

1. Individuals who refuse to consider abstinence and do not present with a prior effort to achieve moderation (not committed to abstinence)

2. Young

3. Married, employed, stable

4. Shorter duration of a drinking problem

5. Less severe problems–dependency

6. No health issues associated with drinking

7. More individuals might enter treatment if abstinence was not the only goal. However, they may be willing to abstain for a brief period such as 6 months. During the period of abstinence, some individuals may acknowledge their need for abstinence and continue in treatment accordingly.

BEHAVIORAL SELF-CONTROL TRAINING (HESTER & MILLER, 1989)

1. Self-directed format with minimal therapist consultation
2. Goal setting
3. Self-monitoring
4. Specific changes in drinking behavior
5. Rewards for goal attainment
6. Analysis of drinking situations
   a. following several weeks of self-monitoring
   b. patterns, antecedents, factors associated with overdrinking
7. Learning alternative coping skills
8. Homework tasks assigned between sessions
9. Individual maintains primary responsibility for decision making throughout the course of treatment
10. Therapist-directed groups (8–10 participants, 90-min sessions, one time per week for 8 weeks)

SETTING LIMITS OR GUIDELINES FOR MODERATE DRINKING

1. Set a limit for number of drinks
2. Avoid hard liquor or drink mixed drinks (avoid straight drinks)
3. Wait until 5 PM (never drink in the morning)
4. A glass of wine or beer is acceptable with dinner
5. Take at least 20–30 min to finish a drink
6. Learn how to say no when offered a drink
7. If out at a party or socializing, drink an occasional glass of water or soda to help space out drinks
8. Eat something when having a drink

The central goal for all of the mental health professionals working in the field of substance abuse treatment is to continue to improve treatment while maintaining a concern for the cost of treatment and an awareness of the impact of the manner in which services are delivered, facilitating the use of multidisciplinary treatment teams, and ever exploring what works best in the constellation of multidimensional treatment applications. It is both an opportunity and a challenge for the mental health community to be scientific and creative and to apply common sense in the effort to advance the treatment of substance abuse and dependence disorders. One such issue has been case management being increasingly instituted in substance abuse programs in order to facilitate a positive impact on treatment outcome. According to Rapp *et al.* (1998), "confidence in case management may be warranted as long as treatment professionals realize that case management's value in improving outcome may be the result of its role in retaining clients in treatment." Therefore, there is a need to highlight the importance of what may be effective and why.

RECOMMENDATIONS FOR IMPROVING SUBSTANCE ABUSE TREATMENT

1. Increase treatment options by decreasing the dominance of disease concept, allowing improved matching of treatment to individual.
2. Individualize treatment planning.
3. Utilize the least intrusive interventions.
4. Increase the utilization of broad-based cost-effective services.
5. Gather more information on people who are able to successfully abstain or modify.
6. Increase research on comparative treatment outcome studies.
7. Consider substance abuse in the context of an individual's level of functioning across all areas.
8. Increase the development of practical interpersonal and intrapersonal skills.
9. Accept modification as a goal in the context of consequences and outcome.
10. Better understand and treat the phenomenon of multiple compulsions and the trading of compulsions during the course of treatment.

REFERENCES

Annis, H. M. (1986). A relapse prevention model for treatment of alcoholics. *In* "Treating Addictive Behaviors: Process of Change" (W. R. Miller & N. Heather, Eds.), pp. 407–433. New York: Plenum Press.

Annis, H. M. (1990). Relapse to substance abuse: Empirical findings within a cognitive–social learning approach. *J. Psychoactive Drugs* **22**:177–124.

Annis, H. M., & Davies, C. S. (1989). Relapse prevention. *In* "Handbook of Alcoholism Treatment Approaches." (R. K. Hester & W. R. Miller, Eds.). New York: Pergamon Press.

APA Monitor on Psychology, June 2001, Vol. 32, No.6.

Azrin, N. H., Sisson, R. W., Myers, R., & Godley, M. (1982). Alcoholism treatment by disulfiram and community reinforcement therapy. *J. Behav. Ther. Exp. Psychiatry* **13**:105–112.

Baker, T. B., & Cannon, D. S. (1979). Taste aversion therapy with alcoholism: Techniques and evidence of a conditioned response. *Behav. Res. Ther.* **117**:299–242.

Bandura, A. (1977). Self-efficacy: Toward a unifying theory of behavior change. *Psychol. Rev.* **84**:191–215.

Bandura, A. (1978). Reflection's on self-efficacy. *Adv. Behav. Res. Theory* **1**:237–269.

Bandura, A. (1986). "Social Foundation of Thought and Action: A Social Cognitive Theory." Englewood Cliffs, NJ: Prentice Hall.

Bean, M., & Zinberg, N., Eds. "Dynamic Approaches to the Understanding and Treatment of Alcoholism." New York: Free Press.

Boland, F. J., Mellor, C. S., & Revusky, S. (1978). Chemical aversion treatment of alcoholism: Lithium as an aversive agent. *Behav. Res. Ther.* **16**: 401–409.

Brown, S. A. (1985). "Treating the Alcoholic: A Developmental Model of Recovery." New York: Wiley.

Brown, S. A., Vik, P. W., McQuaid, J. R., Patterson, T. L, Irwin, M. R., & Grant, I. (1990). Severity of psychosocial stress and outcome of alcoholism treatment. *J. Abnormal Psychol.* **99**(4):344–348.

Brown, S. A., Vik, P. W., Patterson, T. L., Grant, I., & Schuckit, M. A. (1995). Stress, vulnerability, and adult alcohol relapse. *J. Studies Alcohol* **56**(5):538–545.

Budman, S. N., & Gurman, A. S. (1988). "Theory and Practice of Brief Therapy." New York: Guilford Press.

Budman, S. H. (1981). Significant treatment factors in short term group psychotherapy. Group **5**: 25–31.

Cannon, D. S., Baker, T. B., & Wehl, C. K. (1981). Emetic and electric shock alcohol aversion therapy: Six and twelve month follow-up. *J. Consult. Clin. Pychol.* **49**:360–368.

Carroll, K. M. (1997). Integrating psychotherapy and pharmacotherapy to improve drug abuse outcomes. *Addictive Behav.* **22**(2):233–245.

Carroll, K. M., Rounsaville, B. J., & Gordon, L. T. (1994). Psychotherapy and pharmacotherapy for ambulatory cocaine abusers. *Arch. Gen. Psychiatry* **51**:177–187.

Catalano, R., Howard, M., Hawkins, J., & Wells, E. (1988). Relapse in the addictions: Rates, determinants, and promising prevention strategies. *In* "1988 Surgeon General's Report on Health Consequences of Smoking," pp. 157–181. Washington, DC: U.S. Government Printing Office.

Chaney, E. (1988). Social skills training. *In* "Handbook of Alcoholism Treatment Approaches" (R. K. Hester & W. R. Miller, Eds.), pp. 206–221. New York: Pergamon Press.

Chaney, E. (1989). Social skills training. *In* "Handbook of Alcoholism Treatment Approaches" (R. K. Hester & W. R. Miller, Eds.), pp. 206–221. Boston: Allyn & Bacon.

Chaney, E., O'Leary, M. R., & Marlatt, G. A. (1978). Skill training with alcoholics. *J. Consult. Clin. Psychol.* **46**:1092–1104.

Chiaruzzi, E. (1991). "Preventing Relapse in the Addictions: A Biopsychosocial Approach." New York: Pergamon Press.

Craig, R. (1985). Reducing the treatment dropout rate in drug abuse program. *J. Substance Abuse Treatment* **2**:209–219.

Curran, J. P., & Monti, P. M. (1982). "Social Skills Training." New York: Guilford.

Curry, S. G., & Marlatt, G. A. (1987). Building self-confidence, self-efficacy, and self-control. *In* "Treatment and Prevention of Alcohol Problems: A Resource Manual" (W. M. Cox, Ed.), pp. 117–136. New York: Academic Press.

Daley, D. (1988). "Relapse Prevention: Treatment Alternatives and Counseling Aids." Bradenton, FL: Human Services Institute.

deShazer, S. D. (1985). "Keys to Solution in Brief Therapy." New York: W. W. Norton.

deShazer, S. D. (1989). Resistance revisited. *Contemp. Family Ther.* **11**(4):227–223.

deShazer, S. D., Berg, I. K., Lipchick, E., Nunnally, E., Molnar, A., Gingerich, W. C., & Weiner-Davis, M. (1986). Brief therapy: Focused solution development. *Family Process* **25**:207–221.

Dodes, L. M., (1990). Addiction, helplessness, and narcissistic rage. *Psychoanalytic Q.* **59**:398–419.

Dodes, L. M., & Khantzian E. J. (1991). Psychotherapy and chemical dependence. *In* "Clinical Manual of Chemical Dependency" (D. Ciraulo & R. Shader, Eds.), pp. 345–358. Washington, DC: American Psychiatric Press.

Elkins, R. L. (1980). Covert sensitization and alcoholism: Contributions of successful conditioning to subsequent abstinence maintenance. *Addictive Behav.* **5**:67–89.

Ellis, A. (1994). Changing rational–emotive therapy (RET) to rational–emotive behavior therapy (REBT). *Behav. Therapist* **6**(10):257–258.

Ellis, A., Mclnerney, J. F., DiGiuseppe, R., & Yeager R. J. (1988). "Rational Emotive Therapy with Alcoholics and Substance Abusers." New York: Pergamon Press.

Eriksen, L., Bjornstad, S., & Gotestam, K. G. (1986). Social skills training in groups for alcoholics: One year treatment outcome for groups and individuals. *Addictive Behav.* **11**:309–329.

Farrell, T. J., & Cowles, K. S. (1989). Marital and family therapy. *In* "Handbook of Alcohol Treatment Approaches" (R. K. Hester & W. R. Miller, Eds.). New York: Pergamon Press.

Ferrell, W. L., & Galassi, J. P. (1981). Assertion training and human relationship training in the treatment of chronic alcoholism. *Int. J. Addictions* **16**:959–968.

Fleiger, D. L., & Zingle, H. W. (1973). Convert sensitization treatment with alcoholics. *Can. Counsellor* 7:267–277.

Foy, D. W., Nunn, B. L., & Rychtarik, R. G. (1984). Abstinence and controlled drinking goals in behavioral treatment for chronic alcoholics: Effects of training controlled drinking skills. *J. Consult. Clin. Psychol.* **52**:213–230.

Galanter, M., Egelko, S., & Edwards, H. (1993). Rational Recovery: Alternative to AA for addictions. *Am. J. Drug Alcohol Abuse.*

Gerstein, D. R., & Harwood, H. J., Eds. (1990). "Treating Drug Problems," Vols. I and II. Washington, DC: National Academy Press.

Gitlow, S. (1985). Considerations on the evaluation and treatment of substance dependency. *J. Substance Abuse Treatment* 2:175–179.

Goldenberg, I., & Goldenberg, H. (1985). "Family Therapy: An Overview." Pacific Grove, CA: Brooks/Cole.

Goldstein, A. P., Reagles, K. W., & Amann, L. L. (1990). "Refusal Skills: Preventing Drug Use in Adolescents." Champaign, IL: Research Press.

Gorski, T. (1988). "The Staying Sober Workbook. Exercise Manual." Independence, MO: Independence Press.

Gorski, T. (1991). "Understanding the Twelve Steps." New York: Prentice Hall.

Graham, K., & Timney, C. B. (1990). Case management in addiction treatment. *J. Substance Abuse Treatment* 7(3):181–188.

Haley, J. (1990). "Problem Solving Therapy." San Francisco: Jossey-Bass.

Hawkins, J. D., Catalano, R. F., & Wells, E. A. (1986). Measuring effects of a skills training intervention for drug abusers. *J. Consult. Clin. Psychol.* **54**:661–664.

Heather, N., & Robertson, I. (1983). "Controlled Drinking." London: Methuen.

Heather, N., Rolnick, S., & Winton, M. (1983). A comparison of objective and subjective measures of alcohol dependence as predictors of relapse following treatment. *Br. J. Clin. Psychol.* **22**: 11–17.

Heather, N., Miller, W. R., & Greeley, J., Eds. (1991). "Self-Control and the Addictive Behaviors." New York: MacMillan.

Hedberg, A. G., & Campbell, L. M. (1974). A comparison of four behavioral treatment approaches to alcoholism. *J. Behav. Ther. Exp. Psychiatry* 5:251–256.

Hedberg, A. G., & Dunn, R. B. (1974). "Predicting and Evaluating the Response of Alcoholics in Treatment." Paper presented at the Western Psychological Association Convention, San Francisco, California.

Hester, R. K., & Miller, W. R. (1989). "Handbook of Alcoholism Treatment Approaches." New York: Pergamon Press.

Higgins, S. T., Delaney, D. D., Budney, A. J., Bickel, W. K., Hughes, J. R., Foerg, F., & Fenwick, J. W. (1991). A behavioral approach to achieving initial cocaine abstinence. *Am. J. Psychiatry* **148**:1218–1224.

Higgins, S. T., Budney, A. J., Bickel, W. K., Hughes, J. R., Foerg, F., & Badger, G. (1993). Achieving cocaine abstinence with a behavioral approach. *Am. J. Psychiatry* 150:763–769.

Hirsch, R., & Imhof, J. E. (1975). A family therapy approach to the treatment of drug abuse and addiction. *J. Psychedelic Drugs* 7:181–185.

Hoffman, J. A., Caudill, B. D., Koman, J. J., Luckey, J. W., Flynn, P. M., & Mayo, D. W. (1996). Psychosocial treatment for cocaine abuse. 12-month treatment outcomes. *J. Substance Abuse Treatment* 13(1):3–11.

Holder, H. D., Longabaugh, R., Miller, W. R., & Rubonis, A. V. (1991). The cost effectiveness of treatment for alcoholism: A first approximation. *J. Studies Alcohol,* 52:517–540.

Hunt, G. M., & Azrin, N. H. (1973). A community reinforcement approach to alcoholism. *Behav. Res. Ther.* 11:91–104.

Institute of Medicine Report (1990). "Broadening the Base of Treatment for Alcohol Problems." Washington, DC: National Academy Press.

Johnson, S. L. (1997). "Therapist's Guide to Clinical Intervention." San Diego: Academic Press.

Kang, S.-Y., Kleinman, P. H., Woody, G. E., Millman, R. B., Todd, T. C., Kemp, J., & Lipton, D. S. (1991). Outcome for cocaine abusers after once-a-week psychosocial therapy. *Am. J. Psychiatry* 148:630–635.

Kaufman, E. (1985). "Substance Abuse and Family Therapy." Orlando, FL: Grune & Stratten.

Khantzian, E. J. (1978). The ego, the self, and opiate addiction: Theoretical and treatment considerations. *Int. Rev. Psychoanalysis* 5:189–198.

Khantzian, E. J. (1985). Psychotherapeutic intervention with substance abusers: The clinical context. *J. Substance Abuse Treatment* 2:83–88.

Khantzian, E. J. (1986). A contemporary psychodynamic approach to drug abuse treatment. *Am. J. Drug Alcohol Abuse* 12:213–222.

Khantzian, E. J. (1997). The self-medication hypothesis of substance use disorders: A reconsideration and recent applications. *Harvard Rev. Psychiatry* 4:231–244.

Khantzian, E. J., Halliday, K. S., & McAuliffe, W. E. (1990). "Addiction and the Vulnerable Self: Modified Dynamic Group Therapy for Substance Abusers." New York: Guilford Press.

Kissin, B., Platz, A., & Su, W. H. (1970). Social and psychological factors in the treatment of chronic alcoholism. *J. Psychiatr. Res.* 8:13–27.

Levy, M. (1987). A change in orientation: Therapeutic strategies for treatment of alcoholism. *Psychotherapy* 24:786–793.

Lindstrom, L. (1992). "Managing Alcoholism: Matching Clients to Treatments." New York: Oxford University Press.

Litman, G. K., Stapleton, J., Oppenheim, A. N., Peleg, M., & Jackson, P. (1983). The relationship between coping behaviors, their effectiveness, and alcoholism relapse and Survival. *Br. J. Addiction* 79(3):283–291.

Low, A. A. (1978). "Mental Health through Will-Training: A System of Self-Help in Psychotherapy as Practiced by Recovery, Inc." Winnetka, IL: Willett.

Maistro, S. A., McKay, J. R., & O'Farrell, T. J. (1998). Twelve month abstinence from alcohol and long-term drinking and marital outcomes in men with severe drinking problems. *J. Studies Alcohol* 59:591–598.

Marlatt, G. A. (1985). Situational determinants of relapse and skills-training interventions. *In* "Relapse Prevention: Maintenance Strategies in the Treatment of Addictive Behaviors." (G. A. Marlatt & J. R. Gordon, Eds.), pp. 71–127. New York: Guilford Press.

Marlatt, G. A., & Gordon, J. R., Eds. (1985). "Relapse Prevention: Maintenance Strategies in the Treatment of Addictive Behaviors." New York: Guilford Press.

McGrady, B. S., & Irvine, S. (1989). Self help groups. *In* "Handbook of Alcoholism Approaches" (R. K. Hesly & W. R. Miller, Eds.), pp. 153–168. NY: Pergammon Press.

McGrady, B. S. (1972). Conjoint behavioral treatment of an alcoholic and his spouse. *In* "Clinical Case Studies in the Behavioral Treatment of Alcoholism" (W. M. Hay & P. E. Nathan, Eds.), pp. 127–156. New York: Plenum Press.

McKenzie, K. R. (1986). Commentary: when to recommend group treatment. *Int. J. Group Psychother.* **36**(2):207–210.

Miller, W. R. (1992). The effectiveness of treatment for substance abuse: Reasons for optimism. *J. Substance Abuse Treatment* **9**:93–102.

Miller, W. R., & Dougher, M. J. (1984). Covert sensitization: Alternative treatment procedures for alcoholics. *Alcoholism: Clin. Exp. Res.* **8**:108.

Miller, W. R., & Hester, R. K. (1986a). Matching problem drinkers with optimal treatment methods. *In* "Treating Addictive Behaviors: Process of Change" (W. R. Miller & N. Heather, Eds.), pp. 175–204. New York: Plenum Press.

Miller, W. R., & Hester, R. K. (1986b). The effectiveness of alcohol treatment. What research reveals. *In* "Treating the Addictive Behaviors: Processes of Change" (W. R. Miller & N. Heather, Eds.), pp. 121–174. New York: Plenum Press.

Miller, W. R., & Munoz, R. (1982). "How to Control Your Drinking Rev. ed. Albuquerque, NM: University of New Mexico Press.

Miller, W. R., & Rollnick, S. (1991). "Motivational Interviewing: Preparing People to Change Addictive Behavior." New York: Guilford Press.

Minuchin, S. (1979). Constructing a therapeutic reality. *In* "Family Therapy of Drug and Alcohol Abuse" (E. Kaufman & P. Kaufman, Eds.), pp. 5–18. New York: Gardner Press.

Mirin, S., Ed. (1984). "Substance Abuse and Psychotherapy." Washington, DC: Psychiatric Press.

Monti, P. M., Rohsenow, D. J., Michalec, R. A., & Abrams, D. B. (1997). Brief coping skills treatment for cocaine abuse: substance use outcomes at three months. *Addiction* **92**(12):1717–1728.

O'Brien, C. P. (1997). A range of research-based pharmacotherapies for addiction. *Science* **278**:68–69.

O'Brien, C. P., & McLellan, A. T. (1996). Myths about the treatment of addiction. *Lancet* **347**:237–240.

Oei, T. P. S., & Jackson, P. R. (1982). Social skills and cognitive behavioral approaches to the treatment of problem drinking. *J. Studies Alcohol* **43**:532–547.

O'Farrell, T. J. (1993). "Treating Alcohol Problems: Marital and Family Intervention." New York: Guilford Press.

O'Farrel, T. J., & Birchler, G. R. (1987). Marital relationships of alcoholics, conflicted and nonconflicted couples. *J. Marital Family Ther.* **13**:259–276.

O'Farrell, T. J., & Cutter, H. S. G. (1984). Behavioral marital therapy groups for male alcoholics and their wives. *J. Substance Abuse Treatment* **1**:191–204.

Olitzky, K. M., & Copans, S. A. (1991). "Twelve Jewish Steps to Recovery." Woodstock, VT: Jewish Lights.

Parsons, O. A. (1986). Alcoholic's neuropsychological impairment: Current findings and conclusions. *Ann. Behav. Med.* **8**:13–19.

Prochaska, J. O., Crimi, P., Lapanski, D., Martel, L., & Reid, P. (1982). Self-change processes, self-efficacy, and self-concept in relapse and maintenance of cessation of smoking. *Psychol. Rep.* **51**:983–990.

Prochascka, J. O., DiClemente, C. C., & Norcross, J. C.(1992). In search of how people change: Applications to addictive behaviors. *Am. Psychologist* **47**(9):1102–1114.

Prochaska, J. O., & DiClemente, C. C. (1983). Toward a comprehensive model of change. *In* "Operating Addictive Behavior: Process of Charge" (W. R. Miller & N. Heather Eds.), pp. 3–27. NY: Plenum Press.

Project Match Research Group (1993). Project Match: Rationale and methods for a multi-centre clinical trial matching alcoholism patients to treatment. *Alcoholism: Clin. Exp. Res.* **17**:1130–1145.

Rapp, R. C., Siegel, H. A., Li, L. I., & Saha, P. (1998). Predicting post primary treatment services and drug use outcomes: A multivariate analysis. *Am. J. Alcohol Abuse* **24**(2):603–615.

Rawson, R. A., Obert, J. L., McCann, M. J., Smith, D. P., & Scheffey, E. (1989). "The Neurobehavioral Treatment Manual: A Therapist's Manual for Outpatient Cocaine Addiction Treatment." Beverly Hils, CA: Matrix Center.

Rist, F., & Watzl, H. (1983). Self-assertion and relapse risk and assertiveness in relation to treatment outcome of female alcoholics. *Addictive Behav.* **8**:121–127.

Rollnick, S., Kinnersley, P., & Stott, N. (1993). Methods of helping patients with behavior change. *Br. Med. J.* **307**:188–190.

Rounsaville, B. J., & Kleber, H. D. (1985). Psychotherapy/counseling for opiate addicts: Strategies for use in different treatment settings. *Int. J. Addictions* **20**:869–896.

Schottenfeld, R., Carroll, K., & Rounsaville, B. (1993). Comorbid psychiatric disorders and cocaine abuse. *In* "Cocaine Treatment: Research and Clinical Perspectives," Research Monograph No. 135 (F. K. Tims & C. G. Leukenfeld, Eds.), pp. 31–47. Rockville, MD: National Institute on Drug Abuse.

Simpson, D. D., Joe, G. W., Fletcher, B. W., Hubbard, R. L., & Anglin, M. D. (1999). A national evaluation of treatment outcomes for cocaine dependence. *Arch. Gen. Psychiatry* **56**:507–514.

Smith, D. E., Buxton, M. E., & Seymour, R. B. (1993). Cultural points of resistance to the 12-step recovery process. *J. Psychoactive Drugs* **25**:97–108.

Stanton, M. D., & Shadish, W. (1997). Outcome, attrition and family-couples treatment for drug abuse: A meta-analysis and review of the controlled, comparative studies. *Psychological Bulletin* **122**(2):170–191.

Stanton, M. D., Todd, T. C., & Associates (1982). "The Family Therapy of Drug Abuse and Addiction." New York: Guilford Press.

Steinglass, P., Bennet, L. A., Wolin, S. J., & Reiss, D. (1987). "The Alcoholic Family." New York: Basic Books.

Stockwell, T., & Town, C. (1989). Anxiety and stress management. *In* "Handbook of Alcoholism Treatment Approaches" (R. K. Hester & W. R. Miller, Eds.), pp. 222–230. Bosten: Allyn & Bacon.

Tatarsky, A., & Washton, A. (1992). Intensive outpatient treatment: A psychological perspective. *In* "The Chemically Dependent: Phases of Treatment and Recovery" (B. C. Wallace, Ed.), pp. 28–37. New York: Bruner/Mazel.

The Harvard Mental Health Letter. August 1995, **12**(2):1–4.

The Harvard Mental Health Letter. September 1995, **12**(3):1–3.

The Harvard Mental Health Letter. July 1998, **15**(1):1–3.

Walant, K. B. (1995). "Creating the Capacity for Attachment: Treating Addictions and the Alienated Self." Northvale, NJ: Jason Aronson.

Washton, A. M. (1989). "Cocaine Abuse: Treatment, Recovery, and Relapse Prevention." New York: Norton.

Washton, A. M. (1995). "Psychotherapy and Substance Abuse: A Practitioner's Handbook." New York: Guilford Press.

Watson, G. C., Hancock, M., Gearhart, L. P., Mendez, C. M., Malvorh, P., & Raden, M. (1997). A comparative outcome study of frequent, moderate, and nonattenders of Alcoholics Anonymous. *J. Clin. Psychol.* **53**(3):209–214.

Wegscheider, S. (1981). "Another Chance: Hope and Health for the Alcoholic Family." Palo Alto, CA: Science and Behavior Books.

Welte, J. W., Hynes, G., Sokolow, L., & Lyons, J. P. (1981). Effect of length of stay in inpatient alcoholism treatment on outcome. **42**:483–491.

Wieder, H., & Kaplan, E. (1969). Drug use in adolescents. *Psychoanalytic Study Child* **24**:399–431.

Woody, G. E., Luborsky, L., McClellan, A. T., & O'Brien, C. P. (1983). Psychotherapy for opiate addicts: Does it help? *Arch. Gen. Psychiatry* **40**:639–645.

Woody, G. E., Luborsky, L., McClellan, A. T., & O'Brien, C. P. (1989). "Individual Therapy for Substance Abuse Disorders," pp. 1417–1430. Washington, DC: American Psychiatric Association Press.

Wurmser, L. (1974). Psychoanalytic considerations of the etiology of compulsive drug use. *J. Am. Psychoanalytic Assoc.* **22**:820–843.

Zackon, F., McAuliffe, W., & Ch'ien, J. (1985). "Recovery Training and Self-Help." Rockville, MD: NIDA Treatment Research Monograph Series.

Zimbardo, P. G., & Radl, S. L. (1979). "The Shyness Workbook." New York: A & W Visual Library.

Zweben, J. E. (1986). Recovery oriented psychotherapy. *J. Substance Abuse Treatment* **3**(4):255–262.

Zweben, J. E. (1987). Recovery oriented psychotherapy: Facilitating the use of 12-step programs. *J. Psychoactive Drugs* **19**(3):243–251.

Zweben, J. E. (1989). Recovery oriented psychotherapy. Patient resistances and therapists dilemmas. *J. Substance Abuse Treatment* **6**(2):124–132.

Zweben, J. E. (1993). Recovery oriented psychotherapy. A model for addiction treatment. *Psychotherapy* **30**(2):259–268.

Zweben, A., & Barrett, D. (1993). Brief couples treatment for alcohol problems. *In* "Treating Alcohol Problems: Marital and Family Interventions" (T. J. O'Farrell, Ed.), pp. 353–380. New York: Guilford Press.

Zweben, A., Pearlman, S., & Li, S. (1983). Reducing attrition from conjoint therapy with alcoholic couples. *Drug Alcohol Dependence* **11**:321–331.

Chapter 9

Special Populations and Dual Diagnosis

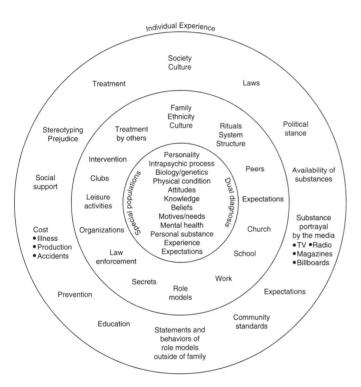

The issue of mental illness is a labyrinth of possibilities. There is not a simple way to explain most diagnoses of mental illness. Many factors contribute in a causal manner to the development of becoming mentally ill. In some cases, when someone has engaged in the abuse of substances, mental problems can develop. In other cases, it is the distress associated with an inability to cope, mental illness, or health problems that lead people to abuse substances as a means of self-medication. Obviously, it is often difficult to separate and identify which issue is primary. The biopsychosocial model directs causation of mental illness to three areas:

1. Biological: Some forms of mental illness run in families, demonstrating an apparent genetic predisposition. Other problems may play a role, such as health problems, medical problems, or substance abuse.

2. Psychological: Personality, coping style used for stress management, thinking processes, relationship functioning and choices, motivation, realistic expectations and limitations, and internal versus external locus of control.
3. Social and cultural: People are affected and influenced by their home environment and associated social interactions of family, neighborhood, school peers, cultural beliefs, rituals, and expectations. In other words, the compendium of life experiences.

As a result of the biopsychosocial factors, a possible relationship exists between addictive behavior and coexisting psychopathology:

1. Substance using behavior and symptoms of psychopathology may become meaningfully related over the course of time.
2. Psychopathology may be a risk factor for addictive behaviors.
3. Symptoms of psychopathology may develop during the course of chronic intoxications or during any episode of use that perpetuates disturbances or psychosis.
4. Certain psychiatric disorders emerge as a consequence of substance use and remain while the individual is in remission.
5. Psychopathology may influence the course of substance dependence in terms of time frame of course, response to treatment, constellation of symptoms, and outcome.

There is an increased incidence of psychiatric problems with those identified as substance-dependent. Substance abuse may be both the cause and the result of emotional illness and social dysfunction. Substances not only interact with many psychiatric disorders but also imitate similar symptomatology, making it difficult to ascertain an accurate diagnostic picture. This issue is made even more difficult when symptom presentation has been severe or chronic. Thorough evaluation is essential to the development of appropriate individualized treatment planning and successful treatment outcome. Collateral contact with family, friends when appropriate, current–referring outpatient therapist, prior therapist, physician, etc. may be useful in clarifying the clinical picture. If the individual has been treated pharmacologically, a medication-free period (when appropriate) will offer some diagnostic clarity as well. Some of the psychiatric diagnoses that may diminish following a period of abstinence from all substances are depressive disorders, anxiety disorders, and drug-induced psychosis. Therefore, the diagnosis of psychiatric disorders should only be given tentatively until a clear clinical picture can be established. However, just as with all initial evaluations, crisis issues are assessed to determine the level of risk that requires immediate intervention such as danger to self–other, gravely disabled, or abusive situations. Obviously, those individuals presenting with acute symptomatology of active psychosis, severe depression, and acute anxiety that is unmanageable and impedes effective coping set a priority for stabilization, with careful consideration regarding appropriate substance abuse treatment.

According to Wallen and Weiner (1989), a minority of substance-dependent individuals actually fulfill the criteria of dual diagnosis. These authors estimate that 5–10% of the individuals diagnosed with substance dependence suffer from significant psychiatric disorders, such as mood disorders, anxiety disorders, and psychotic disorders. They also state that a larger percentage, 25–35%, likely have an underlying personality disorder. Regier *et al.* (1990) present a much different finding of the comorbidity of mental illness and substance abuse at about 81%. In the middle, Helzer and Pryzbeck (1988) state in their review that more than half of the substance abusers had at least one comorbid diagnosis of mental illness. For example, in males alcoholism precedes depression in 78% of the cases, with the reverse being true for female alcoholics where depression preceded alcoholism in 66% of the cases.

Cocaine abusers demonstrated comorbidity in approximately 76% of cases. Additionally, antisocial personality disorder is the most prevalent personality disorder among male alcoholics whereas Grande *et al.* (1984) state that for women it is borderline personality disorder. Helzer and Pryzbeck state that schizophrenia is four times more prevalent in alcoholics than nonalcoholics. Osher and Kofoed (1989) state that individuals with dual diagnosis represent about half of those presenting in acute psychiatric settings. Ross *et al.* (1988) found that, of the substance abusers in their study, 26% met the criteria for generalized anxiety disorder and 30% for a phobic disorder. When they reviewed the criteria for depression, it was revealed that 23% of the alcoholics had major depression and 13% had dysthymia. These varying statistics demonstrate that the complex relationship between psychopathology and substance abuse makes it difficult to achieve diagnostic clarity.

Acute and chronic psychotic disorders may be precipitated by use of amphetamines, cocaine, marijuana, hallucinogens, and severe withdrawal experiences from alcohol, barbiturates, benzodiazepines, and opiates. Zweben (1992) points out that this unique population of dual diagnosis individuals has benefitted from an evolving treatment conceptualization that offers the integration of a variety of theories and interventions that better fit the *individual* needs. This is an extremely important issue because those who are dually diagnosed are a heterogeneous group who differ according to

1. Psychiatric disorder
2. Level of functioning
3. Family history and associated dynamics
4. Social support
5. Capacity for change
6. Capacity for independent living

Reviewing these issues reinforces that no single treatment modality or methodology can adequately serve the needs of such a diverse population. Services need to be tailored to the presenting issues of the individual. For example, someone with a psychotic disorder needs treatment services to match his or her treatment needs, not generic treatment programming (Sciacca, 1991). In other words, level of functioning, ability to deal with various stimuli, and development of realistic expectations and limitations are vital considerations when developing a treatment plan. According to Evans and Sullivan (1990), it could take a month of abstinence to determine a drug-free clinical picture. In a situation where psychiatric symptoms develop secondarily to substance abuse and toxicity, dual diagnosis is ruled out. Contrary to this diagnostic outcome, if psychiatric symptoms continue beyond the detox period and initial recovery, this indicates dual diagnosis (Zweben, 1992). Adding to the issue of diagnostic clarification, Zweben (1992) suggests a longitudinal approach to assessment throughout the first year of sobriety to observe the emergence of the "true or real" personality. This can be particularly difficult because of the percentage of premature terminations associated with substance abuse treatment. Pettinati *et al.* (1999) identified three predictors of adverse outcome in substance abuse treatment:

1. Axis II psychopathology
2. Psychiatric comorbidity (Axis I)
3. Illegal substance use

Lehman *et al.* (1989) offer four dual diagnosis hypotheses in an effort to categorize the complicated clinical picture presented by dual diagnosis individuals:

1. Primary mental illness with subsequent substance abuse
2. Primary substance abuse with subsequent mental illness

3. Dual primary diagnoses
4. Situations whereby a common factor causes both diagnoses

The appropriate treatment for dual diagnosis individuals can be difficult to determine due to the range in symptom presentation. For example, an individual presenting with features of impaired emotional and psychological functioning may be disqualified from various substance abuse treatment programs (rehab facility, therapeutic milieu, halfway house, etc.). The opposing situation is where the individual's substance abuse complicates acceptance by peers in a therapeutic community, staff is not appropriately prepared to deal with his or her specific issues, or other biases. Successful inpatient treatment requires an integrated program that can intervene in a spectrum of diagnostic symptoms: psychiatric, substance abuse, and dual diagnosis. Comprehensive outpatient treatment requires case management, a necessary continuum of interventions, and adequate support to meet individual needs. If an outpatient therapist is functioning as a case manager, he or she must be prepared to enlist necessary resources and make appropriate referrals. Treatment considerations include the following:

1. Medical evaluation
2. Necessary medical care
3. Outpatient detox
4. Psychiatric–medication evaluation
5. Facilitation of the steps of early recovery with a codeveloped treatment plan
6. Psychotherapy services
   a. individual therapy
   b. various groups (therapeutic, support, didactic)
   c. conjoint therapy
   d. family therapy
7. Referrals for family members
   a. self-help
   b. community programs
   c. therapy as indicated
8. Skills development
9. Relapse prevention

KEY ISSUES FOR TREATING DUAL DIAGNOSIS INDIVIDUALS

1. Entry into treatment: Period of engagement, ambivalence, and potentiating motivation where individuals accept the reality and consequences of the substance use disorder. Also, many individuals do not enter treatment voluntarily, which may play a role in denial and minimization. They may choose to believe that, if the psychiatric disorder is effectively treated, they will be able to continue using substances.
2. Treatment retention: Tims *et al.* (1991) state that there is significant evidence that the length of time in treatment is associated with positive outcome.

Individuals with personality disorders represent a population that has a high rate of premature termination.

3. Treatment compliance: Three areas associated with compliance are
   a. noncompliance with negotiated treatment goals and objectives
   b. inadequate use of social supports
   c. failure to complete–follow through on individualized treatment tasks

4. The need for social support that encourages abstinence and decreases distress.

5. Relapse prevention: Individuals with dual diagnosis are at risk for high rates of relapse.

Additional individual issues that should be considered when treatment is initiated:

1. Difficulty tolerating the rules and structure of a substance abuse program
2. Difficulty tolerating the demand for participation
3. Increased need for orientation, sensitivity, support, and creativity
4. Importance of focusing on strengths, abilities, and successes
5. Use trouble areas–weaknesses for their predictive value of preparing for making different–positive choices
6. Difficulty managing with increased environmental stimulation (as for those who experience a thought disorder)
7. How time alone is used, i.e., as disengagement or as a stress reliever, which is a positive self-care issue
8. Decrease focus on misbehavior, instead redirect
9. Explore and educate about the role of substance abuse in exacerbating or intensifying psychiatric symptoms
10. Reality testing with relevant coping skills

Regarding treatment, Ouimette *et al.* (1999) state that dual diagnosis individuals benefit as much as those with only a substance abuse disorder from

1. A formal (programmed treatment plan) and an informal continuum of care (improved consistency in continuum of care is associated with improved outcome with abstinence and psychosocial changes).
2. Increased 12-step attendance (associated with alleviation of psychological symptoms and level of distress).
3. Increased mental health visits.

SHORT-TERM TREATMENT PLAN

1. Medical treatment
2. Monitoring of withdrawal
3. Address issues of safety
4. Cognitive–behavioral interventions

5. Education
6. Prepare individuals
    a. to attend self-help groups
    b. to identify road blocks and red flags
    c. regarding tendencies associated with their presenting psychopathology with appropriate support and skills for initial success, which will be reinforced
    d. to predict potential negative experiences and role-play how to manage them
    e. to avoid the focus on what they "don't have in common with others"

LONG-TERM TREATMENT PLAN

1. Maintain gains achieved in early recovery
2. Work toward goals
    a. continued abstinence
    b. improve interpersonal skills
3. Challenge defense mechanisms
4. Relapse prevention
5. Appropriate treatment of psychopathology
6. Participation in self-help group

Generally, group treatment is the central modality of intervention during the initial phase of recovery. However, individual therapy may serve an additional function for individuals who struggle through group therapy and demonstrate a need for more support with personal conflicts. Due to the unique role of individual therapy, it should be scheduled at regular intervals throughout the course of treatment. This is particularly true for dual diagnosis individuals in most cases. Dual diagnosis individuals are expected to make progress over a longer period of time and at a slower pace. For them, abstinence is only one significant step in the recovery process, and treatment retention is often a challenge.

Once an individual reaches stabilization with abstinence and psychiatric functioning, the next step is to broaden and strengthen his or her abstinence and to continue symptom alleviation and abstinence. This is accomplished in aftercare. Aftercare is open-ended in duration, generally lasting at least a year. In this phase of treatment, weekly group participation decreases from two to four times per week to one time per week. This may be accompanied by individual therapy with a focus on recovery issues and continuing self-help group participation. A successful transition in treatment modality requires consideration of the prior treatment experience whereby skills are expanded and integrated:

1. Review progress
2. Clarify relative strengths–weaknesses and which resources will continue to play a role in maintaining treatment gains
3. Social rehabilitation
    a. disengagement from destructive relationships
    b. couples–family work
    c. fellowship in AA or other support group
4. Outline remaining treatment goals and objectives

As per Khantzian *et al.* (1990), individual therapy is the treatment of choice in the later stages of recovery because character structure is exposed and treatment shifts inward. This can be a very difficult time, without self-medication, when an individual feels emotionally overwhelmed with extremes in mood–anxiety and object relationship disturbances become more pronounced. A therapist can help the individual to experience increased awareness through

1. Self-understanding
2. Development of realistic expectations and limitations
3. Development of appropriate means of meeting needs
4. Working through distressing issues
5. Learning how to self-nurture
6. Accepting the necessary work as a personal investment
7. Resolution, making peace, and letting go of what cannot be changed and making decisions and taking action where changes can be made

DUAL DIAGNOSIS

Among those in substance abuse treatment programs, there is a prevalence of dually diagnosed individuals whose degree of psychopathology differs. Three general areas of dual diagnosis stand out as the most clinically prominent: mood disorders, anxiety disorders, and personality disorders. When considering these three diagnostic areas, think in terms of the full spectrum of diagnoses that fall under these categories. Generally, mood disorders and anxiety disorders can be conceptualized as those with nonchronic psychiatric symptoms and those with chronic psychiatric symptoms.

NONCHRONIC VERSUS CHRONIC SYMPTOMS

Following abstinence, the range of symptomatology may intensify, remain stable, or be alleviated.

Intensified Symptoms

Be alert to the coexistence of obsessive–compulsive disorder, posttraumatic stress disorder (PTSD) and associated dissociation, and attention deficit disorder. Particularly at risk are the individuals presenting PTSD symptoms with dissociation. Without self-medication to mask the severity of the symptoms, they may experience an emergence of traumatic memories and become frightened and overwhelmed, with a possible escalation to suicidality or psychoticism. As a result, their behavior may be unpredictable and disruptive to the therapeutic environment. For those demonstrating an exacerbation of symptoms, the program norms and expectations may need to be adjusted. Therefore, these cases may be managed by emphasizing individual counseling services.

Treatment is complicated by cautious avoidance of medications (such as benzodiazepines) because of their addictive qualities. Therefore, individuals in recovery requiring medication should be evaluated by a physician who specializes in addiction medicine and who will prescribe necessary appropriate and effective medication in an adequate dosage level and regimen. This will allow the management of symptoms that would otherwise interfere in treatment and cause a protracted recovery.

Additional treatment benefits include the potential for increased self-management and focus on the development and utilization of appropriate resources. An individual must be educated thoroughly regarding the importance of medication compliance and the negative consequences of mixing prescribed medications and other substances.

Stable or

Persistent

Symptoms

Determine early in treatment whether symptoms of depression or anxiety existed prior to substance abuse or during earlier trials of abstinence. In either case, pharmacological intervention may be beneficial for a brief period of time. Those with persistent psychiatric symptoms generally respond well to medication following abstinence. Educate individuals regarding the importance of not using other substances with prescribed medications.

Other treatment tools that may be of particular benefit to this population include psychotherapy, biofeedback, and exercise. Reassess at 2–4 weeks. If depression or anxiety symptoms remain untreated, the individual is at increased risk of relapse and/or premature termination from treatment.

Alleviated or

Eliminated

Symptoms

Symptoms decrease or cease following abstinence. If difficulty with withdrawal is experienced, psychotropic medication may be beneficial for a brief period of time for alleviation of symptoms and psychological distress. Clarify that psychiatric symptoms developed as a result of substance abuse.

In addition to basic substance abuse treatment, a dual diagnosis program will offer

1. Dual diagnosis group (educating that recovery may take longer).
2. Education regarding variances in the course of treatment (such as how to identify problems before they escalate or treatment sabotage occurs).
3. Education on medication management and compliance through the course of treatment.

MOOD DISORDERS

Helzer and Pryzbeck (1988) cite that major depression and dysthymia are 1.5–2 times greater in the substance abusing population. Hasselbrock *et al.* (1985) state that mania also has a higher rate of prevalence in this population; female alcoholics about 10 times more than the general population and males about 3 times more. Martin and Jasinki (1969) identified that, with successful abstinence, there are often symptoms such as somatic complaints, dysphoria, anxiety, craving, poor concentration, poor coping, sleep disturbance, and decreased activity. It is important to predict this as a component of recovery that abates over time. When individuals are prepared to identify symptoms and associated coping strategies, their risk of relapse decreases.

Treatment of individuals for substance abuse who have a comorbid mood disorder will be offered additional treatment associated with

1. Medically supervised detox (if needed)
2. Thorough medical examination with lab tests
3. Pharmacological treatment
4. Education on how mood symptoms are exacerbated by specific substances
5. The importance of treatment compliance (medication)
6. Mood management
7. Identifying and problem solving their interpreted positive benefits of substance use
8. Positive daily structure
9. Self-care
10. Development and utilization of a support system

ANXIETY DISORDERS

Regier *et al.* (1990) concurred in general with Boyd and Burke (1988), who found that individuals diagnosed with anxiety disorders had approximately 13–14% comorbidity with alcohol dependence. A study by Kushner *et al.* (1990) found that acute anxiety and panic attacks correlated to compulsive consumption of alcohol. PTSD commonly occurs with other psychiatric disorders, including substance abuse, and, therefore, these individuals should always be screened for substance abuse (Brady, 1997). Abstinence from sedative–depressant substances (opiates–alcohol) may result in a worsening of symptoms, which over time will abate. However, until distress is alleviated, treat appropriately medically, validate, support, and encourage. Initially, the use of substances may alleviate anxiety symptoms, but over time anxiety symptoms may become a conditioned stimulus for substance craving that reinforces the continued use of substances (Linnoila, 1989).

Treatment considerations:

1. Medically supervised detox
2. Thorough physical examination with lab testing
3. Appropriate pharmacological treatment
4. Supportive counseling
5. Peer support
6. Cognitive–behavioral treatment
    a. challenge irrational thinking
    b. importance of aerobic exercise
    c. progressive muscle relaxation–meditation
    d. biofeedback or hypnosis
    e. skill development
    f. affect management
7. Educate and validate regarding the experience of withdrawal–crisis associated with anxiety symptoms

PERSONALITY DISORDERS

Often substance use is symptomatic of the dynamics of an underlying personality disorder. According to O'Malley *et al.* (1990), many individuals with dual diagnosis meet the criteria for narcissistic or borderline personality disorder. Helzer and Pryzbeck (1988) state that antisocial personality disorder is most prevalent among male alcoholics, and Grande *et al.* (1984) cite borderline personality disorder as being most prevalent among female alcoholics. Unfortunately, people with these pervasive personality dynamics have a tendency to act out behaviorally, which may precipitate premature termination from a treatment program. This lack of tolerance for a structured environment should be addressed in conjunction with treatment philosophy and overall treatment goals. It is this author's position that successful treatment must consider the entire psychiatric picture.

There must be careful consideration of the diagnosis of a personality disorder with the substance abuse population. They are already dealing with a socially negative label. The effect of labeling can be counterproductive, stigmatizing, and create a sense of hopelessness to change "one's character." The diagnosis of a personality disorder should be given cautiously and only if there is a lack of clarification in determining which diagnosis preceded the other. According to Khantzian and Treece (1985), 65% of a diverse sample of narcotic addicts met the diagnostic criteria for a personality disorder. Some researchers believe that personality disorders are frequently overdiagnosed as a result of associated events surrounding an individual who is abusing substances, such as legal problems and interpersonal violence, which lead to treatment. Gertsley *et al.* (1990) propose that overdiagnosis takes place because of the failure to require antisocial behaviors to be in occurrence independently of substance abuse. In other words, a diagnosis of antisocial personality disorder is based upon substance-use-related behaviors versus pervasive underlying personality dynamics. Grande *et al.* (1984) suggest that a diagnosis of antisocial personality disorder only be applied when dysfunctional behavior patterns precede substance-use-related behaviors, signifying an independent diagnosis. Another perspective is offered by, Zinberg (1975), who states that chronic use of a substance(s) may cause changes in personality correlated to pharmacological actions of the substances, denial, and societal rejection of substance users. One possibility may be the amplification of personality disorder features associated with substance use.

In congruence with the individualized treatment plan is the concept that treatment must be commensurate with the degree of psychopathology associated with self-defeating and self-destructive behavior patterns. Often, when a brief hospitalization is indicated and abstinence is achieved, there is recognizable alleviation of dysfunctional personality symptoms. If dysfunctional behavior persists throughout the course of treatment and aftercare, and if there is an underlying personality disorder, diagnostic clarity will emerge.

Treatment of personality disorders is difficult, and positive results are often elusive in traditional, individual outpatient therapy. However, the structured programming of substance abuse treatment may be useful. It is group-oriented, which offers peer support, appropriate confrontation of denial and dysfunctional self-defeating behaviors, and the learning of social skills along with new cognitive–behavioral response patterns. It is important that therapists maintain acute awareness of subtle sabotaging behaviors, which can lead to relapse, and during the course of treatment facilitate the individual's awareness of such patterns of thinking and behavior to enhance the efficacy of self-responsibility and self-monitoring. One central treatment approach is to identify dysfunctional behavioral patterns and cognitive style that interfere with effective and appropriate functioning and to avoid stigmatizing labeling.

An additional diagnostic issue is the individual who presents with a triple diagnosis. A triple diagnosis includes substance abuse, an Axis I–Axis II diagnosis, and a medical diagnosis. Literature addressing this issue comes from Batki (1990) and Smith (1989). Batki suggests that individuals who present with a triple diagnosis may show improved outcomes through case management with interdisciplinary communication and coordinated treatment. Smith states that frequent communication among involved professionals led to increased treatment consistency, decreased anxiety, and increased treatment compliance.

Treatment can be difficult with this population as demonstrated by noncompliance and premature termination. Johnson (1997) offers a brief cognitive–behavioral review of treatment for personality-disordered individuals. Strategies that can be utilized as an effort to support and reinforce appropriate and consistent treatment include the following:

1. The use of a cotherapist to dilute challenges and confrontations.
2. Reframe the fact that it will be more detrimental to the individual to continue substance use than to abstain by indentifying the negative consequences associated with use.
3. It may be less threatening or feel less controlling when there is collaboration that considers realistic expectations, i.e., the use of a time-limited abstinence contract versus possible unrealistic expectations of committing to lifelong change.
4. Identify and focus on specific coping skills, speaking in terms of treatment success.
5. Clear rules and consequences.
6. Modeling empathic behavior. This population often lacks the ability to empathize and express feeling misunderstood.
7. Use of privileges–rewards to reinforce development of appropriate behaviors.
8. Structured exercises–homework.

9. Keep in mind an awareness of special issues associated with motivation and behaviors that may undermine treatment.

10. Group therapy is an effective tool for diffusing transference issues, which subtly undermine treatment.

11. Identify the value attached to substance use and what beliefs are held that substance use benefitted him or her, so that appropriate coping mechanisms can be substituted.

12. Identify dysfunctional–self-sabotaging behavior.

13. Help the individual to understand his or her role in maintaining dysfunctional behaviors.

14. Address the anxiety experienced in association with change.

15. Identify behaviors that may have been initiated as adaptive, but over time have become dysfunctional.

As successes and difficulties are experienced throughout the course of treatment, this information can be utilized for problem solving and decision making regarding future behavior and motivation for change.

To conceptualize substance abuse treatment in the same frame with personality disorders, review the pervasive elements of each personality disorder within a given cluster:

Cluster A (Odd or Eccentric)

1. Paranoid personality disorder
   a. suspicious of being exploited by others
   b. never lets guard down–preoccupied with doubt
   c. avoids bonding–developing relationship
   d. holds a grudge

2. Schizoid personality disorder
   a. relationships are not necessary; they are neither desired nor enjoyed
   b. emotionally cold and detached–flat affect
   c. takes little pleasure in activities–generally chooses solitary activities
   d. lacks close relationships

3. Schizotypal
   a. ideas of reference–odd beliefs and behaviors
   b. suspicious or paranoid
   c. inappropriate affect
   d. excessive social anxiety–lacks close relationships

Cluster B (Dramatic, Emotional or Erratic)

1. Antisocial personality disorder
   a. lacks social conformity, consistently irresponsible
   b. disregards safety for self and others
   c. impulsivity–aggression of violence
   d. lacks remorse

2. Borderline personality disorder
   a. identity confusion
   b. issues of abandonment
   c. extreme and inappropriate emotional expression–self-destructive behaviors
   d. difficulty tolerating emotional pain–impulsivity

3. Histrionic personality disorder
   a. strives to be the focus of attention
   b. interpersonal interactions often sexually seductive or provocative
   c. dramatic and impulsive
   d. focused on own needs–shallow and superficial

4. Narcissistic personality disorder
   a. self-focus–overdeveloped sense of importance
   b. insecure–entitled–lacks empathy
   c. needs admiration of others
   d. envious of others and is interpersonally exploitive

Cluster C (Anxious or Fearful)

1. Avoidant personality disorder
   a. important to be liked but views self as socially inept
   b. fears abandonment and may choose isolation to avoid risk of being hurt
   c. avoids taking risks
   d. exaggerated fear and response to criticism

2. Dependent personality disorder
   a. difficulty initiating projects or making decisions
   b. support and approval of others is viewed as necessary
   c. fears that assertiveness will result in loss of approval or abandonment
   d. insecure and often preoccupied with fears

3. Obsessive–compulsive personality disorder
   a. preoccupation with details
   b. rigid and perfectionistic
   c. excessive devotion to productivity and reluctance to delegate tasks
   d. reluctant to make changes–stubborn

The literature indicates that a prevalence of individuals dually diagnosed with a substance abuse disorder and a personality disorder are likely to have personality styles found in cluster B. The constellation of symptoms with these personality disorders tend to be self-focus, little regard for the impact of his or her behavior upon others, and inappropriate modulation of emotion. These issues present obvious challenges in any treatment setting and highlight the importance of individualized treatment planning that goes beyond the goal of abstinence. Therapists need to assist individuals to identify and learn to manage these risk factors (impulsivity, behavioral acting out, and negative mood states).

A study by Thomas *et al.* (1999) looked at 104 subjects with diagnoses of a substance abuse disorder and one or more personality disorders. A follow-up at 1 year to monitor treatment outcome and relapse revealed the following information:

1. No consistent relationship between substance of choice and personality disorder. However, a high proportion of those diagnosed with antisocial personality disorder indicated a preference for cocaine, other stimulants, or polysubstance use.

2. Likelihood of relapse increased significantly with a diagnosis of personality disorder.
   a. 6% of the individuals with one or more personality disorders maintained abstinence at the end of 1 year

b. 44% of individuals not diagnosed with a personality disorder remained abstinent

3. Preference for cocaine was a significant predictor of relapse.

Marlowe *et al.* (1997) investigated the premise of an expected adverse impact of comorbid personality disorder with a substance abuse disorder on treatment outcome. Axis II diagnoses were generated using the SCID-II. The following results were found:

1. There were no significant differences between individuals with or without an Axis II diagnosis on the outcome measure.
2. Axis II diagnoses minimally correlated with substance use severity, depression, and anxiety at intake.
3. Borderline personality disorder symptoms were associated with negative treatment outcome.
4. Dependent personality disorder symptoms were associated with positive treatment outcome.
5. Antisocial, paranoid, and compulsive personality symptoms were negatively associated with some outcome measures.
6. Substantial rates of clinical depression and anxiety were found at intake.
7. Although affective lability, impulsivity, antisocial behavior, and paranoia are common features of character pathology, they may also be symptomatic of acute physiological changes or even adaptive coping attempts to dangerous and chaotic environments.

PSYCHOTIC DISORDERS

This is a very difficult population to work with because these individuals have so few positive reinforcers in their lives. Encouraging them to abstain does not hold the same promise of positive outcomes as it does for others. Substance abuse exacerbates negative outcomes for those with severe mental illness, including high relapse rates, rehospitalization, medication noncompliance, isolation, suicide risk, increased financial distress, increased family distress and alienation, and legal problems. According to the Epidemiologic Catchment Area study, the rate of lifetime substance abuse for those with schizophrenia is very high versus only 17% for the general population. The scope of integrated treatment is necessary to treat both the mental illness and the substance abuse diagnoses in a single setting. For many there is chronicity of illness and few social supports or other resources. Treatment offers education, minimal stressful stimuli (avoid processing emotions and loss in depth), affiliation, support, and reinforcement. It is imperative to have collateral contacts–therapy with family, board and care, etc., which will serve as the central key to helping these individuals. Often family members are also in strong need of support, validation, and skill development [*The Brown University Digest of Addiction Theory and Application (DATA)*, 1998]. A review of 13 NIMH demonstration projects integrating treatment for young adults with severe mental illness and substance abuse problems yielded the following information (Mercer-McFadden & Drake, 1995):

1. All of the programs were successful in engaging individuals in outpatient dual diagnosis services at a rate of 75–85%.
2. The participation in the dual diagnosis services generally resulted in decreased utilization of inpatient treatment and institutional services.
3. Minimal or no reduction in substance abuse over the course of 1 year.

4. Substance abuse treatment was complicated by
   a. measurement difficulties
   b. short-term follow-up
   c. these individuals were not motivated to participate in the abstinence-oriented treatment offered

Bartels *et al.* (1995), in their study of dual diagnosis individuals, found that approximately 25% of the individuals with alcohol use disorders and 35% with other substance use disorders achieved abstinence over 7 years. They also found that a slightly higher percentage achieved remission for a 6-month period of abstinence. Although these individuals were not in a truly integrated treatment program, there was an outpatient case manager who provided 12-step counseling and actively linked individuals with traditional substance abuse treatment and self-help programs. *DATA* states that, in 9 out of 10 cases of dual diagnosis, the mental health disorder (such as schizophrenia) develops 5–6 years before the substance abuse disorder. This period of time is a window of opportunity for substance abuse prevention, particularly for increasing awareness of adolescents exhibiting warning signs.

Because individuals with severe mental illness and substance abuse disorders tend to be associated with higher treatment and societal costs, it is imperative to consider the benefits of longer term treatment with associated overall decreased costs versus short-term intervention with unrealistic expectations for this population. In other words, their needs exceed those of the average dual diagnosis individuals. This necessitates specialized services:

1. Support and treatment that consider cognitive deficits and reality testing
2. Care for deteriorated physical condition
3. Social skills training and reinforcement
4. Community resources offering positive daily structure
5. Case management with close medication monitoring and reinforcement for medication compliance

Treatment is likely to be slow and protracted, often as a consequence of limited interpersonal resources and social skills. The coordination of care and reinforcement of efforts toward treatment goals are essential for effective treatment. These individuals may benefit from the structure of a specialized intensive outpatient program. Specialized daily programming would offer the repetition necessary for developing and reinforcing adequate social skills by providing positive structure. It is essential that such treatment be coordinated with other demands for attendance or goals asserted by social service agencies in which they are enrolled (current treatment is generally from multiple programs). This requires effective case management. Additionally, unlike most substance abuse treatment programs, which promote a fixed time, a treatment program for those with psychotic disorders should be open-ended and coordinated with social service agency programming.

Treatment issues:

1. Use of substances that exacerbate or cause psychotic symptoms
2. Prescription medication noncompliance
3. Self-medication
4. Inability to tolerate the structure or stimuli in traditional treatment settings
5. High risk of relapse
6. High risk of harm to self

7. Inability to care for basic needs
8. Anticholinergic medications may be abused in an effort to obtain a "sense of feeling"

Treatment interventions:

1. Deal with crisis issues
2. Offer an environment that is comfortable and feels safe
3. Treatment must be comprehensive in the context of facilitating life changes
4. Have a goal of shared decision making to encourage a knowledge of
   a. greater treatment choices
   b. increased self-responsibility
   c. improved self-management
   d. potential for greater satisfaction
   e. improved quality of life
5. Involves long-term commitment
6. Assertive outreach
7. Reinforcement and support of case management
8. Need for more community-oriented and less treatment-program-based services to encourage and facilitate progress and generalization
9. Facilitate development of trust (be honest)
10. Encourage medication compliance
11. Educate regarding the significant negative influence of substances
12. Reality testing
13. Positive daily structure with physical activity and rewarding or self-reinforcing activities–experiences
14. Intervention must match the level of functioning with realistic expectations and limitations

ADOLESCENTS

Adolescence is a particularly challenging stage of life for many individuals. Many of the symptoms and underlying issues associated with substance abuse are the same as those identified and presented by adults:

1. Environmental antecedents, dynamics, and reinforcers
2. Genetic predisposition–multigenerational history of substance abuse
3. Defense mechanisms of denial, projection, and rationalization
4. Shame–damage to the self associated with continued behavior, which is contrary to values and is generally self-destructive
5. Craving or the desire to continue using substances with an increased negative association to all areas of life and choices of activities

6. Dysfunctional family issues
    a. other family members who abuse substances
    b. poor communication
    c. ineffective management of mood–affect
    d. ineffective problem solving, conflict resolution, collaboration, etc.

Other symptoms presented by the substance abusing teenager are associated with the developmental features of adolescence:

1. Rebellion against parents and other authority figures
2. Poor coping skills
3. Fewer responsibilities or overwhelmed by responsibilities
4. Hormonal changes
5. Adolescent confusion
6. Need/desire to try things on his or her own regardless of rules and limits
7. Peer pressure
8. Seeking adult status

According to *DATA* (October 1998), the setting and social situation strongly influenced how much adolescents drink. The most common setting for adolescent drinking was at the home of a peer. Most adolescents reported drinking in groups of 8–10 people, with those reporting the heaviest drinking in groups of 11 or more. The changing social context for 9–12th graders also had an influence. These findings were consistent with the social context of adult drinkers and adult heavy drinkers:

1. Larger groups
2. Later part of the day
3. Other heavy drinkers present

In 1989, Christiansen *et al.* used years of research to develop a theory to account for the influence of children's early life experience with alcohol on later drinking behavior. They defined the primary sources of learning about alcohol:

1. Parental modeling
2. Peer modeling
3. Media dissemination of cultural values

In utilizing the outcome information of studies documenting the presence of alcohol-related beliefs and values as being established as early as age 6, Christiansen *et al.* make a case for an earlier role of modeling influences. The theory of alcohol-related expectancy is an effort to connect prior experience with the proximal decision to drink. On a more sophisticated level, it strives to integrate psychological with pharmacological effects. This means that an individual receives information about alcohol

1. Through drinking (direct experience).
2. Through subjective experience of alcohol effects.

3. Through the observation of others (indirect experience with associated expectancy).

What is clear from the research is that well-developed expectancies exist before children–adolescents have had substantial drinking experience. Significant roles in this acculturation process are played by parental modeling, mass media, and peer group influences. Therefore, once an individual has acquired alcohol-associated expectancies, he or she may actually produce desired effects when alcohol is consumed. The result is the reinforcement of drinking through a mechanism akin to self-fulfilling prophecy. It is generally prudent to anticipate that expectancies may be elevated in high-risk adolescents. This is due to high-risk adolescents being more likely to hold strong expectancies of social, cognitive, and motor functioning facilitation associated with alcohol use.

OVERVIEW OF ADOLESCENT SUBSTANCE ABUSE

According to O'Malley *et al.* (1995), retrospective data given by eighth graders suggest that the use of three substances was initiated by more than 50% of those using substances in the sixth grade or earlier: alcohol, tobacco, and inhalants. They also report that, in general, males use substances of all kinds more than females. The one exception is by younger adolescents, which is viewed as resulting from the earlier maturation rate of younger females and their tendency to associate with older males.

1. Substance use among adolescents increased by 33% between 1994 and 1995 (Institute of Medicine, 1995).
2. Since 1992, 12- to 17-year-olds' use of marijuana increased by 14%, and their use of hallucinogens increased by 183% (Institute of Medicine, 1995).
3. Adolescent use of cocaine increased by 166% between 1994 and 1995 (Folsom & Jenkins, 1997).
4. Abuse of substances is associated with behavioral problems associated with home, school, peer relationships, and mood management.
5. Rapid progression from substance abuse to substance dependence (Washton (1995) cites 6–18 months for adolescents versus 2–7 years for adults).
6. Tend to be polysubstance abusers.
7. System of denial is particularly strong (by both adolescents and the adults in their lives).
8. Significant enabling from family system, peers, etc.
9. Developmental delays are directly associated with substance use
   a. academics
   b. social skills development
   c. impulse control
   d. decreased tolerance for gratification delay
10. Decreased motivation–productivity. They have not yet experienced years of negative consequences associated with substance use: "it won't happen to me."
11. As substance abuse increases, functional impairment increases.

Bachman *et al.* (1991) offered the following breakdown of substance use by racial–ethnic group in the 12th grade:

1. Caucasians: highest rate of substance abuse
2. Native Americans: rate at the top with that of Caucasians
3. Hispanics: highest for cocaine, heroin, and steroids (this group was highest for all substances in the 8th grade)
4. African Americans: reported lowest rate of substance abuse
5. Asian Americans: reported low use

According to the National Association of Judges, the leading cause of death for people 16–24 years of age is homicide, followed by automobile accident. Respectively, 83% of the homicides and 53% of the auto accidents involve the use of substances. Although adolescents compose approximately 17% of the population, they are involved in 48% of the fatal auto accidents. Substance abuse demonstrates no demographic boundaries. Listed below are some characteristics of family dynamics that are noted in substance-dependent adolescents:

1. Rigidity
2. Diffused boundaries
3. Triangulations
4. Enmeshment
5. Secrecy
6. Enabling

Cultural or lifestyle issues that predispose adolescents to vulnerability are associated with the changes, pressures, and choices they face during the course of development:

1. Physiological changes: Significant changes associated with puberty, such as physical changes and sexual urges.
2. Cognitive development: A shift from concrete to abstract thinking, resulting in new ideas and changes in perceptions.
3. Peer relationships: Increased identification with peers as the central reference group instead of family. The practice of new behaviors within a different social system. Increased separation from family. Substance abuse may play a role here as a rite of passage phenomenon. For example, adolescents do not tolerate differences very well, and drinking can give the illusion of belonging by providing entry into a new group of peers. Substances are hard to resist for this age group because they are tied to seeking an identity within a group and reducing the anxiety associated with exploration and experimentation (such as sexuality).
4. Family relationships: Parents are engaged in the process of conflict and resolution as adolescents move toward autonomy. Values and morality are reevaluated as adolescents form their own individual and peer group perceptions.
5. Identity: Identity is individualized as the adolescent moves away from their peer group.

Goodwin (1985) suggests that children of alcoholics may have increased tolerance for alcohol, be deficient in serotonin, or experience an increased level of serotonin in the presence of alcohol. All of these factors would act to increase their vulnerability to alcoholism. This could account for the addictive cycle, whereby initially an individual drinks to feel good and at a later point in time, following a brief abstinence, will have to resume drinking to avoid feeling bad. Psychiatric comorbidity also demonstrates an association. Adolescents with a substance use disorder show a rate of conduct disorder ranging from 50 to 80%. Additionally, ADHD is commonly identified in substance abusing adolescents, and there appears to be a relationship between ADHD and conduct disorder (Levin & Kleber, 1995). In addition to the association of substance abuse disorders and ADHD, there is also comorbidity of depression with risk of suicidal behavior (preceding and consequential to use). Therefore, the case is presented for self-medication on the one hand "to feel better," whereas on the other hand use increases dysphoria, disinhibition, impaired judgment, and increased impulsivity (Schuckit, 1986). It is also pointed out that aggressive behavior is present in many adolescents who use substances, and their choice of substances (alcohol, amphetamines, phenylcyclidine) may increase subsequent aggressive behavior. Other adolescent clinical populations associated with substance abuse disorders are

1. Suicidality (Kaminer, 1996)
2. Anxiety disorders (Clark *et al.*, 1995)
3. Social phobia (Kushner *et al.*, 1990)
4. PTSD (Clark *et al.*, 1987)
5. Bulimia (Bulik, 1987)
6. Schizophrenia (Kutcher *et al.*, 1992)
7. Personality disorders, especially from cluster B (Grilo *et al.*, 1995)
8. Language deficits–learning disabilities (Moss *et al.*, 1994)

The adolescent experience of substance use is that substances help the adolescent to cope, mediate stresses rather quickly, provide him or her with a kind of status, and provide a feeling of belonging to a group. As adolescents struggle with their own development and life stresses, their tenuous sense of self slips and substances offer them relief. Therefore, counter to the beliefs of many, adolescents are not preoccupied with getting high, but rather are seeking the relief of distress associated with substance use. Under these circumstances, the use of substances can become the primary relationship in their teen life and continue into adulthood if appropriate intervention, personal growth, and adequate skill development do not take place. Adolescents, like others who self-medicate, would identify one of the following reasons for using substances:

1. To numb painful feelings or diminish distressing thoughts.
2. Belief that they function better under the influence of a substance.
3. They feel good when they use.

Within the family system, the adolescent's substance abuse evolves into an integral part of family balance or homeostasis. The family tries to bring the adolescent's out-of-sync behavior into line in order to regain homeostasis. Through this process, the family system unknowingly begins to take responsibility for the adolescent behavior. The outcome is a shielding of the adolescent from the consequences of his or her behavior. The most unfortunate result of this enabling is that the adolescent not only remains entangled in his or her substance abuse but also ends up moving deeper into his or her substance using peer group and drug culture in an effort to separate. Family members generally acknowledge the experience of their efforts to help as being rejected, leaving them feeling fearful and angry. A central task to intervening with the family is to help family members identify their feelings and facilitate resolving them so that they can be adequately prepared to participate in both the appropriate support and limit setting with the adolescent and clarify their own points of separation, thereby achieving a healthier family homeostasis. They must confront and resolve their preoccupation with and compulsive need to make the adolescent the focus of their lives. The parents also need to confront the impact on their marital relationship. For this to happen, the symbiotic codependency–dependency must end. Conceptualization of a family system working through the stages of grief bears some analogy to the work toward resolution required for the family of a substance abusing or dependent adolescent.

Some characteristics of adolescence that contribute to difficulties with treatment include the following:

1. Lack of self-responsibility, blaming others
2. Lack of anxiety and guilt
3. Denial
4. Depression (masked behaviorally)
5. Anger (associated with experiences and used as a defense)
6. Manipulation
7. Self-destructive or self-defeating behavior
8. Disturbed interpersonal relationships
9. Refusal to communicate and/or participate

The therapist needs to maintain awareness for countertransference with this population. Adolescents can be persistent in their reluctance to comply, which can be frustrating. Therefore, be clear regarding the principles of intervention employed to alter behavior. There are four possible consequences that alter behavior:

1. Increase desirable behavior by positively reinforcing it.
2. Increase desirable behavior by removing a feared object or negative reinforcer.
3. Decrease undesirable behavior by removing positive reinforcement.
4. Decrease undesirable behavior by administering punishment.

Treatment for adolescents tends to be longer and more intense. The Personal Experience Inventory (PEI; Winters & Henley, 1989) is designed for adolescents to assess patterns of substance use and substance-use-associated behaviors. The PEI has two norms: (1) a comparison to normal adolescents and (2) a comparison to adolescents normally seen in substance abuse treatment. Random drug screens are an expected component of treatment.

The interaction of the therapist during the interview of the family and the adolescent is key to obtaining information and initiating the development of a collaborative therapeutic alliance. Accomplishing this requires the following:

1. Be direct and ask specific questions.
2. Separate the person from the behavior.
3. Awareness of adolescent fears
   a. the therapist is going to take away a desired object
   b. the therapist is going to try to change the adolescent

4. Offer nonjudgmental acceptance.
5. Be persistent in order to obtain answers to questions.
6. Sidestep denial, minimization, and excuses.
7. Do not engage in discussing excuses, i.e., blaming and justifying.
8. Avoid conflict and power struggles.
9. Be very clear about confidentiality.
10. Demonstrate genuine empathy and support by consistently reinforcing efforts and acknowledging the adolescent's struggle with change and developing new skills.
11. Offer feedback in a genuine and concerned manner in association with the education of harmful consequences and conflicted value system.
12. Express how the adolescent could benefit from treatment by confronting and resolving the problems associated with substance abuse.
13. Reinforce the adolescent for asking appropriate questions, indicating concern for him- or herself and others.
14. Validate the adolescent's developmental (separation–individuation) and personal goals.
15. Summarize the information gathered during the interview, framing the adolescent's problems and struggles as an effort to achieve identified goals with a closure of numerous appropriate choices available for reaching those goals.

The clinical interview is performed in two parts:

1. Conjoint interview of adolescent and parents
   a. discuss confidentiality issues
   b. history of presenting problem
   c. history of prior treatment
   d. history of substance use (personal and family history) and consequences
   e. history of psychiatric problems–self-destructive behavior or prior suicidal gestures
   f. any history of friends with suicidal gestures or successful commission of suicide
       i. does the adolescent feel loved?
       ii. what has the adolescent been like to live with for the past 6 months?
   g. childhood–developmental problems
   h. academic functioning
       i. grades
       ii. attendance
       iii. extracurricular activities
       iv. behavior states while at school
       v. self-evaluation of school performance
   i. legal problems
   j. assess family system functioning, including extended family (genetic predisposition and environmental factors)
   k. prenatal exposure to alcohol or other substances (may be a predictive factor)
   l. diagnosis of ADD and/or learning disabilities
   m. clarify that a medical exam included an evaluation of vision and hearing

n. discuss behaviors associated with escalated risk of being danger to self
  i. increased secretiveness
  ii. increased isolation
  iii. sneaking out of home
  iv. deterioration in conduct
  v. shift in peer group
  vi. shift in functioning level

2. Individual interview with adolescent
  a. substance use profile, inquire regarding the entire spectrum of substances
  b. age when used first substance, substance of choice, substance most used
  c. how has it progressed since use was initiated–pattern of use (amount, frequency)
  d. what meaning is attached to use
  e. periods of abstinence
  f. ever experience a need to decrease use, if so why and what happened
  g. shift in peer group—why and what searching for
    i. do peers use?
    ii. does the adolescent have friends who have stopped using–are they still friends?
    iii. is the adolescent involved in a significant relationship?
    iv. self-evaluation of peers
    v. has the adolescent had–does her or she have a job?
    vi. if no job, how does the adolescent obtain spending money?
    vii. where does the adolescent see him- or herself in 5 years?
    viii. what would the adolescent like to change?
    ix. how does the adolescent feel about treatment?
  h. ever behave in a way that is inconsistent with personal values (illegal behavoir, violence, sexual acting out)
  i. Mental Status Exam (MSE) with special attention to
    i. unexplained mood swings
    ii. current affective state
    iii. processes
  j. treatment—why now?
  k. motivation for treatment

Additional information can be gathered with psychological testing, a urine drug screen, structured questionnaires, and observation during the interview as well as during the course of clinical intervention. For a review of some of the formal assessment tools specifically designed for yielding information about substance abusing adolescents, refer to Chapter 5.

FAMILY EDUCATION AND INTERVENTION

1. Educate the family regarding the dynamics of adolescent substance abuse–dependency and its impact on developmental delays and educational delays.

2. With minimization of the problem by adolescents, request they abstain.
  a. those who can stop will as consequences become significant and intrusive
  b. those who cannot stop will continue even with the intrusive circumstances of treatment and negative consequences

3. Developmental behaviors along continuum within normal limits versus unacceptable behaviors. Clearly specify rights versus privileges, limits, and consequences. When the adolescent is given the opportunity to learn that choices exist, how he or she reacts to daily life, and the positive and negative experiences associated with his or her choices, he or she can then begin to make the connection between his or her behavior (choices) and the associated consequences. As a result, the adolescent often begins to make more positive choices.

4. Abstinence is required.

5. Resistance and anger are common, but with consistency from treatment and family it often does not persist long term.

6. Group therapy with other adolescents in varying stages of recovery.

7. Learning about recovery lifestyle.

8. Ongoing monitoring with random drug screens.

9. Continue to assess (maintain an attitude of healthy skepticism).

It is not uncommon for adolescents to test a therapist, distorting the outcome as being an indication of outsmarting the therapist or getting away with something. This should be addressed up front as a potential issue that is accurately described as self-sabotaging, with the continuation of negative behavioral patterns. Indications of increasing problems on a continuum toward being out of control and demonstrated lack of care and concern or connection between behavior and consequences include the following:

1. Running away

2. Legal problems (especially possession, sale, distribution of substances)

3. Inability to function effectively at school or job

PREGNANCY AND SUBSTANCE USE

The pregnant adolescent in substance abuse treatment requires intensive support, education, and resources. These adolescents are often referred by case managers and those in outreach programs. Alcohol (38%) and marijuana (24%) use was higher among female adolescents than among adult females. Polysubstance use and cocaine use was the about the same in both groups (Farrow *et al.*, 1998). Difficulties exist associated with early identification of pregnancy and a commitment to substance abuse treatment. Additional problems:

1. The number in treatment is small despite intensive recruitment efforts.

2. Many adolescents present with a history of sexual and physical abuse in addition to the chaos of street life, resulting in a view of adults as being exploitive and manipulative.

3. Substance using pregnant teens are at the same risk for labor and delivery complications as their adult counterparts, as well as the increased risk of problems for their infants.

INTERVENTION

1. Crisis issues

2. Random drug screens (normal part of treatment that is positively reinforcing)

3. Focus on developmental issues and health
   a. health–biogenetic issues
   b. education
   c. social skills
   d. influence of peer group choice
   e. appropriate leisure activities
   f. family dynamics
   g. spirituality
   h. psychological functioning
   i. defenses (against real or imagined threats to self)
   j. vocation–goals
   k. legal issues
   l. relapse prevention

4. Appropriate limit setting with rules and consequences (development of realistic expectations and limitations; they are not adults)

5. Development of effective management skills
   a. problem solving
   b. conflict resolution
   c. assertive communication

6. Behavioral contract

7. Collateral contact with school for support in dealing with education-related issues

8. Referrals

Next is a brief diagram of the role of self-awareness and the influence upon change,

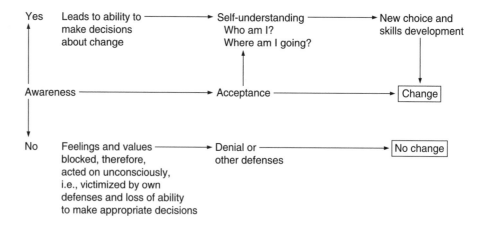

Treatment dynamics will be maximally positive with the following:

1. Confidentiality–avoid collusion and codependence.

2. Respect–avoid labeling and avoid power struggles.

3. Genuine empathy.

4. Reflection of individual's awareness of where he or she is and where he or she wants to be, and amplify it with increasing dissonance by clarifying values–beliefs versus behavior (be careful).

5. Accept resistance; "put the ball in his or her court." Allow the adolescent to struggle with answering his or her own questions.

6. Acknowledge and support appropriate and effective navigation through developmental tasks and weave these issues into treatment, thereby increasing self-esteem, personal growth, and goal development.

7. Appropriate referrals where there can be affiliation and fellowship with other adolescents in recovery.

INTERVENTION WITH PARENTS

1. Adolescent substance abuse must be confronted along with parental–familial substance abuse.

2. Encouragement.
   a. deemphasize guilt
   b. focus on self-responsibility
   c. facilitate age-appropriate separation, mutual respect, and allowing the adolescent to experience the consequences of his or her behavior

3. Reframe the difficulties experienced with the adolescent and with their marriage as presenting an opportunity for increased understanding and improving relationships.

4. Ventilation and clarification of feelings.
   a. disappointment
   b. frustration
   c. failure

5. Validate normalcy of feelings.

6. Focus on couple's relationship (improved understanding, communication, cooperativity, and intimacy).

7. Development of improved communication and other couple's skills.

8. Permission giving technique, which is used for serious feelings as well as the absurd. It is used for relieving tension. Therefore, it must be kept light or humorous.

9. Homework assignments for increased understanding and skill development.

10. Participation in multifamily group and parenting group.

The common sense approach is to acknowledge the importance of

1. Sitting down together as a family at dinner.
   a. communication
   b. demonstrating interest–commitment to family structure
   c. helps to maintain clear family roles

2. Being active in religion.
   a. clarifies values
   b. is something done as a family

3. Doing homework with children.
   a. sit with them
   b. go over their work with them
   c. reinforces interest in children
   d. reinforces time management

4. Going to children's sporting events or other extracurricular activities (demonstrates support, interest, and involvement in children's lives).

5. Being consistent with a clear message regarding "no drugs accepted in this home" and reinforcing it with own choices.

6. Being a parent, not a friend.

Guidelines for Establishing Privileges and Responsibilities

1. Family cooperation and communication (know how to reach one another by phone).
2. Either be awake when adolescents come home from an evening out or have them awaken parents when they come in.
3. Assure adolescents that they can phone parents to pick them up whenever needed.
4. It is imperative to know their friends and meet the parents of their friends.
5. Discipline must be appropriate, consistent, and given out of love and concern.
6. If problems persist, parents need to utilize all of their resources, i.e., treatment program, therapy, school counselor.

Curfew

Reasonable hours are necessary for respect, responsibility, safety, and a sense of security. Suggested curfew hours are as follows:

1. School nights: home evenings except for school or community events (expected to be home 30 min following event)
2. Weekends
   a. 9th grade: 11:00–11:30 pm
   b. 10th grade: 11:30–12:00 am
   c. 11th grade: 12:00–12:30 am
   d. 12th grade: 12:30–1:00 am
3. Vacations or school breaks: Parents to discuss if they feel any modifications are necessary and agree on time limits.

Social Life

Parents are legally responsible for minor children and their actions. As previously identified, it is important to meet their children's friends and the parents of their friends.

1. Be alert to the signs and symptoms of substance abuse.
2. Be aware that driving under the influence is a criminal offense.

Another situation about which parents are often confused is how to respond to the issue of permission to attend or give a party. Some suggestion are as follows:

1. Parents of the adolescent requesting to attend a party
   a. verify the occasion
   b. verify adult supervision
   c. be sure that there will not be any substances
   d. be appropriately concerned if the preceding criteria were not met

2. Parents of adolescent giving party
   a. encourage a reasonable–manageable number of guests
   b. make it clear that substances are not allowed, and anyone disrespectful of that request will be asked to leave
   c. anyone who leaves is not allowed to return
   d. make selves visible

If parents are going out of town, make sure to alert neighbors to keep a watchful eye on their home.

Adolescents benefit from participation in a support group. They may have a substance abuse problem or may have just experimented with substances. Whatever the circumstances, affiliation and support that reinforce positive choices and their efforts are important, and group is one means to facilitate continued recovery and/or personal growth with increased self-awareness and associated increases in self-responsibility.

Group goals:

1. Provide an opportunity for affiliation with peers who choose to be clean and sober.
2. Add to their social support network.
3. Encouragement to identify and develop goals.
4. Facilitate development of self-esteem and confidence.
5. Identify and change enabling behavior.
6. Provide feedback, appropriate confrontation, and associated problem solving.
7. Demonstrate genuine care and concern.
8. Provide an opportunity to discuss and problem solve difficult issues.
9. Develop consequences for continuing harmful behavior.
10. Increase awareness for defenses and how they are used.
11. Facilitate increased awareness for their feelings.
12. Encourage increased self-responsibility.

GERIATRICS

There is a negative stereotype and stigma in our culture about growing old. The elderly are often discounted and ignored. This is likely to be especially true for those from minority cultural and ethnic groups. Therefore, it is important to be sensitive but astute in approaching the elderly about substance abuse and treatment. Substance abuse in the elderly may be difficult to detect. Many symptoms of physical deterioration may not be identified as the possible consequences of substance abuse. As a result, lower tolerance in the elderly means a lower observed quantity consumed, which can be a contributor to misidentification of use for abuse. Additionally, there is a great potential for polysubstance abuse and dependence. Simply put, the effort to adjust to current life stressors could be facilitated in many ways. One of these ways is to abuse substances, which is a primary reason that assessment of substance abuse is warranted in the geriatric population.

According to Liberto et al. (1992), a clear relationship has yet to be defined between ethnic origin or geographic residence and alcoholism among the elderly. The following statistics and information on geriatric alcoholism are cited in the literature:

1. 4–20% of the geriatric population in the United States and the United Kingdom exhibit problem drinking (Atkinson et al., 1992; Bridgewater et al., 1987).

2. Alcoholism is the third most frequent disorder in the geriatric population (Myers et al., 1984).

3. 10–15% of all elderly individuals seeking medical treatment are found to have an alcohol-related problem (Blixin, 1988).

4. High rates of lifetime alcohol abuse have been found in the elderly, deinstitutionalized, and homeless (Caton et al., 1994).

5. Alcohol-related hospitalizations (over age 65 and based upon Medicare claims data) have been estimated to be 54.7% for men and 14.8% for women (Adams et al., 1993).

6. A clinical picture of geriatric alcohol abuse, depression, and significant medical illness probably comprises the group at highest risk for suicide in the general population (Conwell & Brent, 1995; Moscicki, 1995).

7. Estimates of alcohol use associated with suicide in the elderly population range from 25 to 50% (Blumenthal, 1998).

8. Elderly alcohol-related dementia is estimated to be between 25 and 60%. Cognitive impairment is one of the most significant consequences of alcoholism (Bienenfeld, 1990).

Adams et al. (1992) stated that elderly individuals seen in the emergency room demonstrated a 24% lifetime and 14% current prevalence of alcoholism. Schuckit (1979) found benzodiazepines to be a commonly abused substance among the elderly. There is often a concomitant abuse of these two substances, which could be a lethal combination. Simon et al. (1968) found that, of the 23% of elderly alcoholic hospital admissions, 7% became alcoholic after the age of 60 and 16% were alcoholic before age 60 and presented with a long history of abuse. Therefore, this indicates that two-thirds had been alcoholic for a long period of time and one-third had developed alcoholism later in life.

The National Council on Patient Information and Education (NCPIE) released a study that focused on the elderly and prescription medications, citing the following:

1. People over 65 fill twice as many prescriptions as younger people.
2. People over 60 account for 40% of all adverse drug reactions.
3. One out of six of all hospital admissions for patients over the age of 70 result from adverse drug reactions.
4. Approximately 25% of older people's hospital admissions are the result of improperly taking a prescribed medication.
5. People over 65 comprise 12% of the total population, yet they consume 25% of all prescription medications.

ASSESSMENT

Problems associated with identifying and treating substance abuse in the elderly:

1. They may lack the obvious signs of withdrawal.
2. Level–amount of substance use.
3. Feelings of shame leading to increased efforts to hide.
4. Greater denial.
5. Less severe health consequences in some cases.
6. Confusion with manifestations of health issues, signs of aging, and depression.
7. Few psychosocial consequences associated with substance abuse that are easily identifiable:
   a. social (probably have already experienced a decrease in support system, etc.)
   b. legal (few legal issues associated)
   c. financial (are not likely to be using substances at a level that results in a significant fiscal impact)
   d. occupational (retired)
   e. interpersonal (live alone)

Therefore, utilization of the assessment criteria established for younger adults may not identify a substance abuse problem in the elderly. Instead of focusing on frequency and amount in this population, review symptoms and experiences that are often viewed as being within normal limits for older adults. Although many of these symptoms may be attributed to non-alcohol-related diseases, disorders, or situations, it could also present a missed opportunity of appropriate screening for substance abuse if not considered as potential risk factors to be explored. Just as age 50 is a hallmark developmental age for a thorough medical review, as someone is entering his or her sixth decade of life a thorough screening of substance use (alcohol, over the counter and prescription medications) should be a standard. For example, assessment may include the following.

Physical Level

1. Older adults tend to take more medications (over the counter and prescribed)
2. Increased possibility for substance interactions (medications and alcohol, medication and medication)

3. Increased risk of substance interactions due to chronic disease states
4. Slowed metabolism and excretion (result is a slowed response to resolving unfavorable reactions)

Screening of
General Physical
Symptoms

1. Cognitive impairment
    a. memory or concentration disturbances
    b. disorientation or confusion

2. Sleep disturbance
    a. changes in sleep pattern
    b. daytime fatigue–drowsiness
    c. appearing sedated
    d. oversleeping

3. Not keeping appointments or maintaining or regular activities
4. Seizures
5. Fainting–loss of consciousness
6. Malnutrition-changes in eating
    a. muscle wasting
    b. obvious weight loss

7. Abnormal liver function
8. Altered mood
    a. persistent irritability
    b. depression
    c. anxiety

9. Unexplained complaints
    a. chronic pain
    b. somatic complaints (dry mouth, nausea–vomiting, gastrointestinal distress)

10. Urinary tract complications
    a. incontinence
    b. urinary retention
    c. difficulty urinating

11. Poor hygiene and grooming
    a. obvious self-neglect
    b. difficulty with associated daily living skills

12. Unusual restlessness and/or agitation
13. Increased visual or auditory problems
14. Slurred speech
15. Observed physical instability–change
    a. tremor
    b. motor coordination changes
    c. shuffling or unstable gait

16. Frequent falls or accidents
17. Unexplained bruising
18. Increased use of medication
19. Compliance with medical recommendations, medication regimes, etc.

Psychosocial Level   The later years of life often are not what people expected, and they may not be adequately prepared for the associated losses and general changes. Assessment of the elderly should explore the following factors regarding the influence so that they can be integrated into the individualized treatment plan:

1. Financial distress
2. Fewer choices
3. Housing problems
4. Emotional role associated with physical decompensation–changes in physical functioning
5. Losses (death of spouse, family members, or friends, difficult adjustments associated with declining health and physical functioning, independent living, etc.)
6. Loneliness–social isolation
7. Loss of social support
8. Apathy
9. Avoidance of meeting with primary care physician
10. Transitions–adjustments
11. Depression
12. Diminished ego and other changes associated with retirement
13. Empty nest
14. Menopause
15. Caretaker role for ailing relatives and/or grandchildren
16. Level of interactive activity
17. Helplessness and diminished hope for the future

Assessment needs to be multidisciplinary and comprehensive. A thorough assessment takes into consideration how the aforementioned factors–problems interrelate:

1. Medical examination
   a. recent or past medical problems
   b. trauma–injuries suffered throughout the life span
   c. exposure to toxins
   d. sight
   e. hearing
   f. energy level
   g. list of past and current medications (prescribed and over the counter)
   h. substance use–abuse

2. Mental status examination [refer to Johnson (1997)]
3. Social–cultural review
   a. level of education
   b. employment history
   c. financial status
   d. current living arrangement
   e. social supports

f. religious affiliation

g. social activities

h. list of past and current pleasurable activities

i. ethnicity–cultural background

j. primary language spoken

4. Ability to maintain daily activities
   a. grooming
   b. eating
   c. toileting
   d. mobility
   e. household chores
   f. shopping
   g. health maintenance

Two well-known alcohol screening instruments that have been well-validated for their use with geriatric population are the CAGE Questionnaire (Ewing, 1984) and The Michigan Alcohol Screening Test-Geriatric Version (MAST-G) (Blow *et al.*, 1992a). The CAGE is widely used because it is a brief, four-question assessment tool that can be self-administered, even by those with a low reading level. Graham (1986) asserts that a helpful method for identifying elderly alcoholics is to combine

1. CAGE

2. MAST

3. X corpuscular volume (MVC; abnormalities seen in lab results)

4. X corpuscular hemoglobin (MCH; abnormalities seen in lab results)

The CAGE Questionnaire scoring for the responses to the four items is 0 for "no" and 1 for "yes," with a higher score being indicative of alcohol problems. A total score of 2 or greater is considered clinically significant. However, a single positive response should encourage further exploration of an alcohol problem. The CAGE questions are as follows (Ewing, 1984):

1. Have you ever felt that you should <u>C</u>ut down on your drinking?

2. Have people <u>A</u>nnoyed you by criticizing your drinking?

3. Have you ever felt bad or <u>G</u>uilty about your drinking?

4. Have you ever had a drink first thing in the morning to steady your nerves or to get rid of a hangover (<u>E</u>ye opener)?

The MAST-G is an instrument that was specifically developed for the geriatric population and demonstrates a high degree of specificity and sensitivity in assessing the elderly. Scoring of five or more responses as "yes" is indicative of an alcohol problem.

Because this can be a population that is difficult to engage, consider the following points in addressing substance abuse issues following an assessment:

1. Offer information regarding the negative impact that alcohol (or other substances) may be having upon the individual's health.

2. Clarify that the condition is treatable and that there are treatment options. Be prepared to speak to people regarding the range of choices from abstinence to varying degrees of modification. Ultimately, the individual may make the "better" choice for his or her health if he or she feels in control.

3. Continue interviewing in a motivational style, exploring the individual's willingness for change and follow-up.

4. Be familiar with community resources before a recommendation for treatment is given and collaborative decision making takes place. A tentative treatment plan that cannot be executed successfully may be the demise of an opportunity for improving health and quality of life.

At this developmental stage, there are two groups of identified substance abusers:

1. Those who begin abusing substances as a reaction to issues confronted in later life (retirement, financial distress, widowhood, diminished physical functioning, etc.)

2. Those who have been abusing substances over a much longer course of time, but due to medical advances are living longer.

When applying the *DSM IV* diagnostic criteria for general substance dependence, special considerations should be made for the geriatric population. According to the *DSM IV*, dependence is defined as a "maladaptive pattern of substance use, leading to clinically significant impairment or distress, as manifested by three (or more) of the following occurring at any time in the same 12-month period" (American Psychiatric Association, 1994, p.181). Each criterion will be followed by the special consideration of when the criterion is applied to an older adult, with a focus on alcohol:

1. Tolerance: May have problems with even a low intake due to increased sensitivity to alcohol and higher blood alcohol levels.

2. Withdrawal: It is not uncommon for late onset alcoholics to not develop physiological dependence.

3. Taking larger amounts over a longer period of time than was intended.
   a. increased cognitive impairment may interfere with self-monitoring
   b. drinking may exacerbate cognitive impairment

4. Unsuccessful efforts to cut down or control use: Issues do not differ across life span.

5. Spending excessive time to obtain and use alcohol and to recover from effects: Possible negative effects with relatively low use.

6. Giving up activities due to use: The elderly may engage in fewer activities anyway, which makes detection of negative consequences more difficult.

7. Continuing use despite physical or psychological problems caused by use: Even after a medical evaluation and advisement, they may not understand or connect the problem to alcohol use.

Before reviewing treatment considerations, it may be helpful to have an overview of psychoactive prescription drug abuse as it exists along the continuum from appropriate prescribed use to dependence, along with effects of aging on response to drug effect and substance–alcohol interactions.

CONTINUUM OF USE TO ABUSE OF PRESCRIBED PSYCHOACTIVE MEDICATIONS

Physicians play a role in prescription misuse by

1. Not clearly explaining how to take the medication appropriately and why
2. Not thoroughly explaining side effects
   a. which side effects to be concerned about
   b. which side effects to expect and not be concerned about
3. Prescribing a higher dose than necessary
4. Prescribing without clarifying all of the medications a person is taking
5. Not following up on a regular basis

Patient's role (adopted from the American Psychiatric Association, 1994):

1. Appropriate prescribed use
2. Misuse
   a. does not take as prescribed
      i. higher dose–lower dose
      ii. inconsistent skipping dose, loading dose
   b. use for contraindicated purposes
   c. undesirable effects resulting from use with other medications
   d. hoarding drugs
   e. use with alcohol, over the counter medications, or other substances
3. Abuse (by patient)
   a. use resulting in decline in functioning
      i. work
      ii. home–family–significant relationships
      iii. school
      iv. legal problems
   b. impaired judgment [use that increases risk of harm (self or others) because of being under the influence]
   c. continued use despite adverse social or interpersonal consequences
4. Dependence (by patient)
   a. use resulting in
      i. tolerance
      ii. withdrawal symptoms
      iii. negative change in normal activities
      iv. unsuccessful attempts to cut down or control–modify use when desired to do so
   b. use of substance in increasingly larger amounts
   c. use of substance for longer periods of time than intended, including time to acquire substance and to recover from its effects

d. continued use despite knowledge that it caused (or aggravated)
 i. social interpersonal problems
 ii. legal problems
 iii. physical problem(s)
 iv. psychological problem(s)

EFFECTS OF AGING ON RESPONSE TO SUBSTANCE EFFECTS

As an individual ages, metabolism and excretion of substances change, requiring appropriate attenuation of medication dosage. Following is a list of some commonly prescribed medications and the associated effects of aging [adopted from Cusack and Vestal (1986)].

No change in response to medication effects:

Analgesics	Aspirin
Anticoagulants	Heparin
Bronchodilators	Albuterol
	Ipratropium
Cardiovascular medications	Adenosine
	Phenylephrine
	Timolol
Psychotropics	Diphenhydramine

Increased response to medication effects:

Analgesics	Morphine
	Pentazocine
Anticoagulants	Warfarin
Cardiovascular medications	Diltiazem
	Enaleprin
	Verapamil
Psychotropics	Diazepam
	Midazolam
	Temazepam
	Triazolam
Others	Levodopa

Decreased response to medication effects:

Cardiovascular medications	Isoproterenol
	Prazocin
Diurectics	Furosemide
Psychotropics	Haloperidol
Others	Tolbutamide

The American Society of Addiction Medicine (1996) offers an outline of six dimensions to consider as the criteria for placing older adults in the appropriate treatment setting in the continuum of care. The range of treatment settings in the continuum are from medically managed inpatient to various outpatient services. As previously stated, for the geriatric population the process of prioritizing treatment services if often significantly influenced by factors other than the severity of a substance use problem. This is the reason behind weaving in age-related issues.

TREATMENT CONSIDERATIONS

Older substance abusing individuals tend to receive less intensive care than their younger counterparts, and less than 25% received any outpatient substance abuse treatment, which is the opposite of what is needed given the general degree of isolation (Moos *et al.*, 1993). Prior to referral for treatment, individuals should receive a thorough physical and psychiatric examination for diagnostic clarity and appropriate treatment planning.

TABLE 9.1 ASAM PPC-2 Assessment Dimensions[a]

1. **Acute intoxication and/or withdrawal potential**
   –risk associated with current level of intoxication
      severe withdrawal symptoms or seizures, based upon
         prior withdrawal history
         amount
         frequency
         recentness of discontinuation/reduction of substance(s) used
         current signs of withdrawal
         adequate social support available if medically safe

2. **Biomedical conditions and complications**
   –aside from withdrawal, are there current medical illnesses that complicate treatment?
   –are there chronic conditions that affect treatment?

3. **Emotional/behavioral conditions and complications**
   –are there current emotional, psychological or behavioral problems that complicate treatment?
   –are there chronic conditions that affect treatment?
   –are these problems a part of addiction or autonomous?
   –do these problems require specific mental health intervention?

4. **Treatment acceptance resistance**
   –acceptance or resistance to treatment (do they feel coerced?)
   –are they prepared for change?
   –do they accept and acknowledge their addiction?
   –are they compliant only to avoid consequences or genuinely motivated?

5. **Relapse/continued use potential**
   –is there immediate danger of continued severe distress and substance use?
   –is there recognition, understanding or skills to cope with addiction problems and relapse prevention?
   –is there awareness of relapse triggers, coping with cravings, and impulse control skills?

6. **Recovery environment**
   –any individuals, living situation, school or work situations that present a threat to entering treatment
      and being successful
   –do they have supportive family/friends?
   –adequate financial resources
   –vocational/educational resources that increase likelihood of treatment success
   –legal, vocational, social services, or criminal justice mandates that encourage and enhance their
      motivation for treatment

[a]Adapted from American Society of Addiction Medicine, 1996.

According to Atkinson *et al.* (1993), older alcoholic men are more likely to remain in treatment provided:

1. They are matched with peers in a group paced to their needs for socialization, reminiscence, and, of course, social support.
2. Family is included in treatment (crucial).
3. Third parties are involved (which includes spouse, court, probation).
4. Later onset of problem drinking has a weak positive effect on treatment compliance.

Reflection upon traditional substance abuse treatment and maximal benefit to the elderly reveals that some adjustments are required:

1. Appropriate setting: An environment identified by seniors may readily decrease a barrier. For example, senior center, VA hospital, or any community gathering place.

Meeting places need to be
a. easily accessible
b. safe
c. convenient

2. Focus confrontation on problems experienced rather than substance problem
   a. depression
   b. isolation
   c. medical problems

3. Treatment of coexisting depression

4. Identify and deal with financial impediments (basic needs being met adequately, access to treatment)

5. Housing stability

6. Transportation
   a. this factor may present as a hardship for some seniors, especially night meetings
   b. be prepared to be resourceful
      i. family
      ii. public transportation
      iii. special senior transportation program services

7. Cognitive issues
   a. distinguish between chronic physiological–psychologically based impairment versus acute impairment; clarify source by
      i. comprehensive medical history
      ii. physical examination
      iii. substance abuse history
   b. medication monitoring–management: under specific circumstances, inpatient treatment may be necessary for detox to deal not only with medical concerns associated with detox but also with the secondary and overwhelming cognitive problems, withdrawal, or interaction of prescribed medications or other substances
   c. cognitive impairment and/or confusion associated with acute fear and anxiety

8. Medication management–case management
   a. physiological changes in the elderly adult affects tolerance via metabolism rate and excretion
   b. interaction between substances–prescribed medications can lead to toxic reactions or confusion
   c. this population is particularly susceptible to the effects of multiple medication use (they are often prescribed numerous medications by different physicians, which emphasizes the importance of case management)

9. Activity therapy directed toward the goal of developing meaningful life activities with continued reason to live

10. Peer support
    a. meetings should be peer- and age-appropriate
    b. meeting content relative to stage of life issues
    c. designation of age-appropriate social services
       i. community social resources
       ii. senior center and activities
       iii. meals delivered when available

11. Utilization of social services

12. Follow through to assure referral services are in place
13. Follow up with the individual to remind him or her of appointment times
14. Home visits should be considered under certain circumstances
15. Treatment needs to be comprehensive, addressing the biopsychosocial experience of the individual (an individualized treatment plan)
16. Specific attention for follow-up regarding the issue of social isolation and keeping these individuals in appropriate and pleasurable social activities in order to develop an adequate support system
17. Relapse prevention strategies; risk of relapse may be predicted by (Moos *et al.*, 1994a)
    a. lack of match between individual and treatment
    b. inadequate or insufficient aftercare
    c. unmarried–widowed, comorbid psychiatric disorders, lack of socioeconomic resources

Treatment goals are integrated into general treatment recommendations, which focus on all of the issues associated with substance use, risk, and relapse. Respectful behavior as outlined in motivational interviewing should be adhered to. Additionally, case management plays an important role in monitoring as well as encouraging changes recommended in the individualized treatment plan.

1. Eliminate or decrease (harm reduction) substance abuse
   a. education on effects of substances
   b. relapse prevention
   c. stress management
   d. group therapy
   e. medication management

2. Management of slips, lapses, or relapse during the course of treatment
   a. removal from regular treatment program
   b. refer for detox or medical supervision
   c. understand what happened, why, and desire for change with consolidation of experience

3. Improved relationship functioning
   a. marital–significant relationship (conjoint therapy, group therapy)
   b. family (group therapy)
   c. social skills development (individual therapy, group therapy)
   d. psychodynamic relationship issues (individual therapy, group therapy)

4. Increase health behaviors: This area of treatment is the ultimate reflection of self-responsibility. Self-care that promotes health is a fundamental characteristic of an individual taking the responsibility to utilize the information, resources, and support offered by comprehensive, case-managed treatment. Modalities include primary care medicine and group therapy for education and self-management skills training. Areas of focus:
   a. nutrition
   b. exercise
   c. sleep

d. stress management–relaxation training

e. utilization of social support

f. reduce–eliminate substance abuse

5. Stabilization: Resolve and treat medical and psychiatric comorbidities

a. medical care

b. depression–anxiety management

c. pain management

Because the establishment of a basic level of functioning is particularly important in assessing the needs of the geriatric population, three instruments are given. Although numerous screening instruments exist, these have been chosen to offer the reader a more comprehensive picture of the assessment of the geriatric population. The information extracted from screening instruments being added to a more general assessment is extremely useful in multidisciplinary consulting, which ultimately results in more effectively meeting the treatment needs of an individual. With a review of mental status, activities of daily living, mood, and health behaviors, a clearer picture emerges of where to start in the intervention process.

Assessing
Activities
of Daily
Living (ADL)

While assessing the level of functioning it is very easy to review basic daily living skills with the following questions. Before proceeding:

1. Clarify the medications that the individual takes.

2. What side effects (if any) do they experience from the medication. Clarify which side effects coincide with which medication.

3. Do they take their medications on their own or are they assisted (if so, by whom).

4. Do they have any difficulty remembering the dosage they need to take.

5. Do they take their medication in the proper time frames or do they occasionally miss taking their medication.

6. What medications are they currently taking (i.e. prior to the interview which may affect their presentation).

Once these issues have been clarified review the following information with the individual:

1. Do you dress yourself
   –independently
   –minimal help
   –unable to do it, someone must help

2. Are you able to get out of bed and a chair
   –independently
   –minimal help
   –unable to do it, someone must help

3. Do you bathe yourself, how often and by sponge, shower, or tub. (This is an opportunity to thoroughly review hygiene)
   –independently
   –minimal help
   –unable to do it, someone must help

4. Are you able to use the toilet on your own, clean properly and put your clothes back together
    –independently
    –minimal help/supportive devies over toilet, etc.
    –unable to do, someone must help

5. Do you do your own laundry
    –independently
    –minimal help
    –unable to do it, someone must help

6. Do you drive
    –yes (to what extent/where/how often/any difficulties/do medications or medical condition prohibit but they have been driving anyway)
    –no
    –what arrangements are made to get you to appoints, stores, visiting other places

7. Do you have any difficulty walking
    –yes
    –no

8. Do you shop for your own groceries
    –independently
    –minimal help
    –unable to do it, someone must help

9. Do you do your own cooking
    –independently
    –minimal help
    –unable to do it, someone must help

10. How many meals do you eat

11. What do you eat. (use questions 10 & 11 to assess nutrition)

12. Do you do your own housework
    –independently
    –minimal help
    –unable to do it, someone must help

13. Do you do your own handyman repairs (clarify which tasks they do and which ones they get help with any why. They may be able but choose to not do some things)
    –independently
    –minimal help
    –unable to do it, someone must help

14. Do you manage your own money
    –independently
    –minimal help
    –unable to do it, someone must help

15. Are there some things that you feel you are currently needing help with that you have been doing on your own with increasing difficulty.

Brief Geriatric Depression Review

Answer each one of the following questions with a yes or no. If information is shared that is beneficial to problem solving and case management document it while as you go through these questions. Also once the review is completed clarify (how often, for the last week, month, longer etc. to clarify experience) all questions answered in a manner which indicates the possibility of depression

1. Are you happy with your life?
2. Do you often feel bored?
3. Do you have activities that you look forward to every week?
4. Do you no longer find pleasure in activities that used to be pleasurable?
5. Do you sometimes experience a loss of appetite?
6. Have you ever felt sad or blue and couldn't get over it?
7. Do you get upset, frustrated or bothered by things that normally wouldn't bother you?
8. Do you have difficulty staying focused on what you are doing?
9. Have you ever felt depressed?
10. Do you feel hopeful about the future?
11. Do you ever feel fearful or overwhelmed?
12. Would you rather stay at home by yourself than go out and do things or be with people?
13. Do you experience any problems with your memory?
14. Do you experience serious health problems or chronic pain?
15. Are you glad to be alive?
16. Do you feel happy and in a good mood?
17. Do you feel worthless?
18. Do you feel that other people are better off than you are?
19. Do you feel that everything you do takes an effort?
20. Do you ever have crying spells?
21. Do you get sick a lot?
22. Do you feel helpless to make any changes?

Health Screening

1. What medical problems are you being treated for?

_____

_____

_____

2. Please list the medications that you take, the dosage, and what time of the day they are taken:

_____   _____

_____   _____

_____   _____

3. Do you exercise regularly?

    –what do you do? _____

    –how often do you do it? _____

    –are you able to do it for 20 minutes without stopping? ____ yes ____ no

4. Do you smoke?

    If yes, …

    –what?

    –how much per day or week?

    If no, …

    –have you never smoked? ____ yes ____ no

    –if you quit, when? _____

5. Do you drink alcohol?

    If yes, …

    –what? _____

    –how much? _____

    –how often? _____

    –what circumstances? _____

6. Have you been dieting to lose weight?

    If yes, …

    –describe your diet _____

    –approximately how many calories/day? _____

    –how long have you been dieting? _____

    –how much weight have you lost? _____

    –what is the amount of weight you plan to lose? _____

7. Have you been getting restful sleep? _____

    –how many hours of sleep/night? _____

    –are you able to sleep well without sleep medication? ____ yes ____ no

SUBSTANCE-ALCOHOL INTERACTIONS

If a person takes medication and drinks alcoholic beverages, they need to be educated about the potential interactions so that health consequences can be avoided. There are two considerations of this topic when applied to a geriatric population. First of all is the effects of changed physiology in the aging person taking medication (generally lower dosages). Second is the overlay of the interaction of medications and alcohol on an aging person with a changed physiology.

Substance	Potential adverse affects with alcohol
Acetomenophen	liver toxicity in chronic alcoholics
Anticoagulants (oral)	decreased effect of the anticoagulant
*Heparin	increased bleeding
Antidepressants (tricyclic)	CNS depression evidenced by psychomotor performance
Aspirin	gastritis, gastrointestinal bleeding
Non-steroidal anti-inflammatories	gastritis, gastrointestinal bleeding
Barbiturates	additive CNS depressant
Benzodiazepines	additive CNS depressant
Beta-adrenergic blockers	masked signs of delirium, tremors
Bromocriptine	gastrointestinal side effects
Caffeine	decreased reaction time
Cephalosporins	disulfiram-like reaction (with some of these meds)
Chloramphenicol	disulfiram-like reaction (with some of these meds)
Chloral Hydrate	extends hypnotic effect, cardiovascular effects
Cimetidine	CNS depressant effect
Cycloserine	increased alcohol effects, *convulsions
Digoxin	decreased effect of digitalis
Guanadrel	increased sedation, orthostatic hypotension
Glutethimide	additive CNS depressant
Sulfonylurea	increased drug effect (acute ingestion) decreased drug effect (chronic ingestion)
Tolbutamide chlorpropamide	disulfiram-like reaction
Isoniazid	liver toxicity
Ketoconazole griseofulvin	disulfiram-like reaction
Lithium	liver toxicity
Meprobamate	CNS depression
Methotrexate	liver damage (chronic ingestion)
Metronidazole	disulfiram-like reaction
Nitroglycerin	hypotension
Phenformin	lactic acidosis
Phenothiazines	additive CNS depressant
Phenytoin	increased toxicity (acute ingestion) decreased anticonvulsant effect (chronic ingestion)
Quinacrine	disulfiram-like reaction
Tetracyclines	decreased effects

*Disulfiram-like reaction=abdominal cramps, flushing, vomiting, hypotension, confusion, blurred vision, psychosis.
Adapted from Korrapati & Vestal 1995.

AIDS–HIV

OVERVIEW

In the fourth decade of the "AIDS epidemic," few people can say they do not know of someone who has experienced an HIV–AIDS crisis in their life or the life of someone they love or care about. It is no longer a disease affecting someone else; it has come to every neighborhood. The HIV-infected individual shares with the substance-dependent individual issues of moral judgment, stigmatization, and blame by society. Therefore, be aware of one's own biases as a therapist so that clear and genuine compassion and competence can be extended to those so desperately in need of acceptance, understanding, support, and problem solving.

Take the time to educate oneself regarding transmission of this disease, issues associated with different developmental stages, and prevention information. There are many sociocultural issues that need to be considered when assessing how to intervene and educate the individuals who present for treatment, some of which include the following:

1. Educational level
2. Language barrier
3. Ability to understand
4. Motivation to appropriately use the information and treatment offered
5. Sexual functioning–behaviors
6. Attitudes
7. Belief system

Guidelines to Minimize Cultural Clashes (University of Hawaii AIDS Education Project)

1. Plan to spend more time with clients holding values different from one's own. The relationship is more complex, and it may take longer to establish trust.
2. Anticipate that past frustrations with insensitive or inappropriate providers may have made the client angry, suspicious, and resentful.
3. Acknowledge past frustrations.
4. Acknowledge the difference between one's own experience and that of the client.
5. Individualize (the clear message of all treatment planning)—a client is more than an "addict," an Asian, or a person with HIV–AIDS. Get to know the whole person.
6. Encourage disagreement and negotiation to ensure a workable plan.
7. Anticipate multiple needs: medical, legal, social and psychological.
8. Be prepared to advocate for the client who may not have the resources, knowledge, or experience to negotiate the HIV–AIDS and substance abuse services systems.
9. Assist the client in getting other resources.
10. Involve friends and family. This can help ensure that the client receives other needed services.
11. Pay attention to communication: nonverbal, expressive style, and word usage and meaning.
12. Make use of providers from other cultures.
13. Learn the strengths of a culture. In Hispanic culture, for example, the value of "respeto," demonstrating appropriate social respect, can be used to support an intervention plan.
14. Expect differences in beliefs about
    a. help-seeking behaviors
    b. caretaking–caregiving
    c. cause of disease–illness

d. sexuality–homosexuality

e. death and dying

f. making eye contact and touching

15. Broadly define family.

The Learn Model (Berlin & Fowkes, 1983)

L: Listen with empathy and understanding. Ask the client, "What do you feel may be causing the problem? How does this affect you?"

E: Elicit cultural information, explain one's perception of the problem, have a strategy, and convey it to the client.

A: Acknowledge and discuss differences and similarities. Find areas of agreement and point out areas of potential conflicts so they can be discussed, understood, and resolved.

R: Recommend action, treatment, and intervention. Incorporate cultural-knowledge to enhance acceptability of the plan.

N: Negotiate agreements, and differences. Develop a partnership with the client and the family.

Prevention of HIV Transmission

1. Do not share needles (if not abstaining from substance abuse)

2. Engage in safer sex practices

a. use of condoms

b. masturbation

c. mutual masturbation

3. HIV testing if history of sexual activity or other high-risk behaviors deems it warranted

4. Co-meeting of individual and potential sex partner with primary care physician or county health worker for education and testing so that both share the same information

5. Identify personal importance of substance abuse

6. Education regarding importance of substance abstinence

Interrelationship of Substance Abuse and HIV

1. Excuse, rationalize, or justify high-risk behavior (decreased inhibition)

2. Use of some substances to heighten sexual experience (such as use of cocaine)

3. Trading sex for substances

4. Poor judgment (increased high risk behaviors)

5. Decreased inhibition

ASSESSMENT OF THE SUBSTANCE ABUSING HIV–AIDS-INFECTED INDIVIDUAL

1. Cultural-ethnic sensitivity

2. Crisis issues

a. danger to self

b. danger to others

c. gravely disabled

     d. child abuse–neglect

     e. domestic violence

     f. assaultive

3. Individual's emotional response to diagnosis

     a. individual therapy

     b. group therapy

     c. family therapy

        i. disclosure

        ii. support for all of those involved

        iii. system coping

        iv. concerns about what will happen

     d. conjoint therapy

        i. disclosure

        ii. support for both

        iii. coping (individually and as a couple)

        iv. concerns about what will happen

        v. intimacy issues

        vi. sexual dysfunction

4. High risk behaviors

     a. sexually permiscuous

     b. unprotected sex

     c. substance abuse

     d. "tempting fate"

5. Medical history

     a. HIV date of diagnosis

     b. stage of disease according to CDC classification–criteria

     c. other medical illness

     d. current medications

     e. medical crisis counseling

        i. HIV status

        ii. fears associated with decompensating health, potential dependency, financial worries, lack of control, pain management (current–future), death and dying

     f. reproductive issues

     g. need for psychoeducational counseling

6. Developmental–social history

     a. developmental milestones

     b. childhood trauma–illness

     c. level of education–history of academic performance

     d. employment history

     e. sexual orientation

     f. relationship history

     g. current support system

     h. use of community support system

7. Substance use history

8. Psychiatric history: History of psychiatric illness

     a. age problems first became evident

     b. past diagnoses and medication treatment

    c. outpatient–inpatient treatment history

    d. current diagnosis and medication

9. Current psychiatric presentation

    a. mental status

    b. symptom presentation

10. Family

    a. family constellation

    b. family relationships

    c. family psychiatric history

    d. family substance abuse history

    e. family expectations and participation in individual's life

11. Social support

    a. if socially isolated, identify or develop appropriate social support

    b. if isolating by choice, confront the issues and problem solve them

12. Losses

    a. loss of health–sense of well-being

    b. loss of loved one to AIDS

    c. loss of independence and control–loss of employment and financial stability

    d. associated with changes in identity and self-esteem

13. Death and dying

    a. what tasks are important for the individual to accomplish

    b. spirituality and meaning–beliefs associated with death

    c. coming to terms with dying

    d. utilization of support system (partner, family, friends, community resources)

    e. medical issues–choices

    f. guardianship

    g. placement in skilled nursing facility

    h. hospice

14. Stress management

    a. self-care

    b. exercise

    c. relaxation training

    d. visualization

    e. meditation

    f. yoga

15. Treatment compliance

    a. assess

        i. mental status (is individual able to consistently comply)

        ii. substance abuse (need for specific treatment, education, problem solving, development of appropriate management skills, impact on treatment compliance)

    b. therapeutic alliance

    c. self-defeating or self-destructive behaviors

TABLE 9.2 Psychosocial Assessment of HIV-Infected Individuals[a]

	Individual	Family system	Healthcare system	Sociocultural context
Physical	Food, clothing Shelter, halfway house Treatment program Safety Ability to carryout ADL's	Physical home environment Financial resources Availability of family members to provide support	Availability and accessibility of Treatment Medications Medical equipment Home health	Availability and accessibility of Social services Financial resources Community resources
Affective	Feelings about HIV disease Having a fatal illness Current status Healthcare providers Medical treatment Caregivers	Feelings about HIV disease HIV+ family member Medical treatment Sexuality issues Alternative lifestyle issues Addiction	Healthcare providers feelings about HIV disease Psychiatric illness Addiction Poverty Sexuality–lifestyle issues Addiction	Social stigma associated with HIV disease Physical disfigurement Psychiatric illness Sexuality–lifestyle issues Addiction
Cognitive	Level of cognitive functioning Knowledge of HIV Health beliefs Expectations related to illness Expectations related to treatment Expectations related to caregivers Spiritual beliefs Coping style–stress management	Knowledge of HIV disease Attitude toward HIV+ family member Expectations of HIV+ family member Family coping style	Healthcare providers attitudes toward The individual HIV disease Psychiatric illness Sexuality–lifestyle issues Addiction	Cultural attitudes toward HIV disease Treatment Psychiatric illness Sexuality–lifestyle issues Addiction
Behavioral	Health promoting behaviors Self-destructive behaviors Activity level Treatment compliance Degree of social interaction Substance use history Safe sex practices Parenting ability History of abuse	Degree of involvement in care of individual Crisis issues Danger to self Danger to others Child abuse–neglect Domestic violence	Communication between the healthcare provider and the individual Healthcare providers behavioral responses to the individual's health behavior	Ethical issues Legal issues Employment Insurance Community and social network response to individual's health behaviors

[a]Adapted from Belar and Deardorff (1995).

TABLE 9.3 HIV/AIDS related neurocognitive decompensation is a gradual process. At San Francisco General Hospital they developed the "Neuropsychiatric AIDS Rating Scale (NARS). The NARS Indicates the degree of Impairment that may be seen a different stages in the course of dementia. A neuropsychological examination encompasses the cognitive functions of orientation, memory and problem solving, motor functioning, and the behavioral functions which includes ADL"

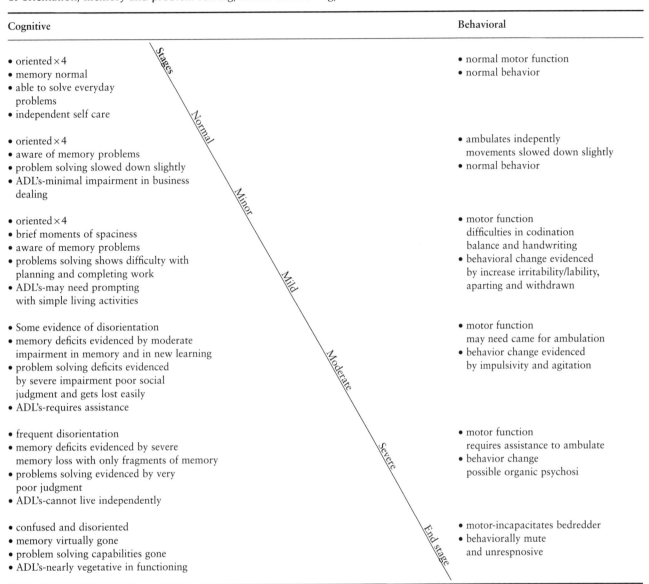

Cognitive	Behavioral
• oriented×4 • memory normal • able to solve everyday problems • independent self care	• normal motor function • normal behavior
• oriented×4 • aware of memory problems • problem solving slowed down slightly • ADL's-minimal impairment in business dealing	• ambulates indepently movements slowed down slightly • normal behavior
• oriented×4 • brief moments of spaciness • aware of memory problems • problems solving shows difficulty with planning and completing work • ADL's-may need prompting with simple living activities	• motor function difficulties in codination balance and handwriting • behavioral change evidenced by increase irritability/lability, aparting and withdrawn
• Some evidence of disorientation • memory deficits evidenced by moderate impairment in memory and in new learning • problem solving deficits evidenced by severe impairment poor social judgment and gets lost easily • ADL's-requires assistance	• motor function may need came for ambulation • behavior change evidenced by impulsivity and agitation
• frequent disorientation • memory deficits evidenced by severe memory loss with only fragments of memory • problems solving evidenced by very poor judgment • ADL's-cannot live independently	• motor function requires assistance to ambulate • behavior change possible organic psychosi
• confused and disoriented • memory virtually gone • problem solving capabilities gone • ADL's-nearly vegetative in functioning	• motor-incapacitates bedredder • behaviorally mute and unrespnosive

Stages: Normal, Minor, Mild, Moderate, Severe, End stage

Adapted from Price and Perry (1994).

TREATMENT

Treatment begins with a thorough assessment that takes place in a caring, respectful, and responsible manner. The goal is to understand the biopsychosocial experience of the individual so that appropriate and effective intervention can take place. Therefore, be prepared to take the information learned from assessing the individual and intervene in the following areas with a clearly defined multidisciplinary treatment team (be sure to have releases to communicate with all pertinent collateral contacts):

1. Individual knowledge, attitude, emotional response to HIV
2. Reality-based–motivated to fight for life and actively living life, not just focused on disease state

3. Current medical status
   a. HIV symptomatology
   b. other medical conditions

4. Medications
   a. prescribed, over the counter, herbal remedies, street substances
   b. dosage and treatment goal of each medication
   c. compliance (if not compliant, why?)

5. Additional medical treatment: What role (if any) does it play in the treatment of HIV, what choices are associated with treatment modality, and what has been the general response to every treatment?
   a. acupuncture
   b. chiropractic
   c. physical therapy
   d. occupational therapy
   e. neurology
   f. ophthalmology
   g. endocrinology
   h. dietitian
   i. nurse practitioner
   j. home health
   k. herbalist
   l. religious–spiritual support
   m. other self-treatment

6. Neurological–psychoneurological condition
   a. baseline functioning
   b. neurotoxic impact of medication(s)
   c. symptoms of CNS involvement (cognitive deficits, memory loss, etc.)

7. History of traumatic abuse experience (sexual, emotional, verbal, physical), which is experienced with some degree of repetition by HIV infection

8. Feelings of unworthiness, defect, shame, or guilt associated with HIV–substance use

9. Experience of inappropriate or ineffective treatment

10. Effectiveness of support system: Anyone in support system diagnosed with HIV, if so how does this affect the individual?

For the focus of therapy to be on appropriate treatment goals, require that the following be continuously monitored to insure that an individual is receiving the appropriate level of care and support.

1. Neuropsychological–health issues
2. Hallucinations or other perceptual disturbances
3. Difficulties in communication
4. Cognitive impairment
5. Delirium–dementia

If an individual reports headaches, fever, seizures, or any medical symptoms that lack prior history, refer him or her to the primary care physician and let the individual know that the therapist will also follow up with his or her physician.

HARM REDUCTION: UNDERSTANDING THE RISKS

Reducing Sexual Behavior Risks

1. Identifying high-risk behavior
   a. sexual (safe sex)
   b. substance abuse related (decrease–abstain)

2. Identifying risks associated with current sexual behavior
   a. teaching basic safe sex behaviors
   b. role-playing
      i. limit setting–boundaries
      ii. how to talk to a partner
      iii. how to assert the use of safe behaviors (condom use, etc.)

3. Steps taken for choosing a sexual partner
   a. identify qualities desired in a partner
   b. meeting people through friends
   c. relationship development
   d. self-responsibility in using safe sex behaviors

4. Building an appropriate social support system
5. Developing, practicing, and self-monitoring social skills

Factors Indicating HIV–AIDS Risk

1. Participating in unprotected sex (vaginal, anal, oral)
2. Exchanging sex for money or substances
3. Unprotected sex with multiple partners
4. Unprotected sex with intravenous drug user
5. Unprotected sex with partner that is HIV–AIDS-infected
6. When the individual has sex:
   a. are condoms used?
   b. are drugs used before or after?

7. When the individual uses substances:
   a. does he or she use or share syringes?
   b. does he or she clean own works?
   c. does he or she use more than one substance at a time?

CONTINUUM OF CARE WITH ASSOCIATED TREATMENT

1. Detox
   a. medical supervision
   b. possible complicated schedule of HIV treatment medications
   c. HIV–AIDS-related medical illness

2. Inpatient–residential treatment
   a. treatment issues include
      i. consciousness raising
      ii. contemplation of behavior and personal changes around risky behavior
      iii. developing plans for action

  iv. discuss problems associated with relapse

  v. interaction of competing problems from sex and drug domains

 b. group therapy

  i. sets the stage for actual change

  ii. optimal for consciousness raising

  iii. influences move toward a more consistent level of safe behaviors (harm reduction, what are the individual's concerns about HIV–AIDS, increasing cognitive dissonance)

  iv. role modeling

  v. support for recovery

  vi. initiate self-evaluation feeling about consistent bleaching, are there times the individual is willing to take risks (when, why), thoughts–[feelings about protected sex, how does the individual's addiction affect those close to him or her]

  vii. consolidation of gains in individual therapy work

 c. individual therapy

  i. used to clarify group experience

  ii. expressing need to make own decisions

  iii. feeling HIV–AIDS diagnosis and problems have not hit him or her

  iv. predicting outcomes associated with "unchanged" behaviors

  v. validate "no one knows all the answers"

  vi. support for harm reduction

  vii. explore what the individual is willing to consider changing (with associated problem solving of possible actions–choices)

  viii. resolving barriers

  ix. self-reevaluation

3. Outpatient treatment (continuation of individual–group therapy)

 a. consolidates the gains of detox–inpatient treatment

 b. reinforce treatment–discharge plan from inpatient or residential treatment

 c. identify increased risk of relapse

 d. reinforce development–utilization of increased social support

 e. increased vulnerability as those close to the individual struggle with his or her changing (others may feel threatened, abandoned, angry, etc.)

 f. increase awareness of sabotage by self–others

 g. reinforce relapse prevention [problem solve high-risk situations (sex–substances)]

4. Counseling the terminally ill: This stage of treatment should be supportive and nonconfrontational. Issues need to be addressed at the individual's pace. General issues include the following:

 a. denial associated with HIV–AIDS diagnosis

  i. normal response

  ii. help in accepting illness and need for home health or hospice care

 b. planning for death

  i. discussion of death and dying, e.g., "if you become too ill to care for yourself, what would you do? Who would you want to help? Where would you go? Where would you choose to die (home, hospital, etc.)? What arrangements at death do you want?"

  ii. many individuals fear dying alone, in pain, or losing control over bodily functions

  iii. listen to fears and help with problem solving

  iv. does the individual know what to expect (understanding the process of dying and planning the details can give a sense of control)

c. pain management
   i. complicated issue for those in recovery
   ii. appropriateness of pain management (when it might escalate death process)
   iii. encourage discussions of pain management with his or her physician
d. unfinished business
   i. making a will
   ii. living will
   iii. health care proxy
   iv. granting power of attorney
   v. appointment of guardian for children
   vi. family issues needing to be addressed
   vii. assisting the individual in preparing children for the loss of a parent (leaving a legacy of memories)

HIV–AIDS AND PAIN MANAGEMENT

The management of acute and chronic pain for an individual confronting substance abuse issues and HIV–AIDS is challenging. These individuals often have pain problems similar to those with cancer. Goals, concerns and points of clarification include the following:

1. Potential drug seeking behavior
2. Appropriate use of narcotic analgesics when other efforts have failed (medication for pain management should not be withheld because of a history of substance abuse)
3. Goal is to maximize comfort and minimize side effects
4. Treatment plan using narcotics for pain management must be clear

The World Health Organization (WHO) outlines the following pain management protocol:

1. Local measures (rest, heat, ice, analgesic rubs)
2. Tylenol (acetaminophen), nonsteroidal anti-inflammatory drugs (NSAIDs); naprosyn, ibuprophen (do not use tylenol if liver disease is present)
3. Use of weak opioid (codeine, oxycodone, hydrocodone, etc.)
4. Add adjuvant to weak opioid to potentiate effect
5. Use of strong opioid (morphine, duragesic patches, hydromorphine, methadone)

Other points to consider regarding pain management:

1. Make sure the source of pain is being treated.
2. Professional treating the pain should have training and expertise in this special area of treatment.
3. When appropriate, include input from family.
4. Use least invasive route of administration of pain medication.
5. Continually reevaluate.
6. Require collaboration across all disciplines.
7. Develop a pain management plan that prevents pain.

8. Do not interfere with HIV–AIDS treatment.
9. Clarify treatment interactions.
10. Be aware that individuals actively abusing substances often manifest psychological disorders.

ASSESSMENT OF NEEDS IN ADDITION TO SUBSTANCE ABUSE TREATMENT

Because of the double social bias associated with having a diagnosis of HIV–AIDS and a diagnosis of substance abuse, these individuals often have numerous basic needs being neglected or inadequate support to access available resources. Therefore, in addition to the substance abuse assessment, explore the following areas:

1. Does the individual have a primary care physician?
   a. when last seen
   b. how often seen
   c. what seen for
   d. satisfaction with physician and medical care
2. Are there medical–health concerns that the individual has that he or she has not discussed with his or her physician?
3. Does the individual take medication (prescribed by which physician)?
   a. name of medication
   b. dosage
   c. how long taken
   d. what medication is for
   e. when taken
   f. any medication side effects experienced
4. Does the individual have stable housing?
5. Does the individual have financial concerns?
6. Does the individual have needs for child care?
7. Does the individual have transportation problems?
8. Does the individual need mental health services?
9. Is the individual's support system adequate?
10. Does the individual need dental care?
11. Is daily nutrition adequate?
12. Is there a need for legal services?

ADULTS MOLESTED AS CHILDREN

It is not unusual for an individual with a history of sexual abuse who presents for treatment to lack awareness of the impact of sexual abuse on his or her current behavior, making it a primary issue. Rankin (1989, p. 90) views relapse as a "return to the former coping style in a context of recovery." As abstinence is initiated and an individual withdraws from addictive behavior, he or she may become emotionally overwhelmed and struggle with relapse. Farther along the continuum of abstinence, underlying emotional issues begin to emerge, revealing a deeper degree of pain and impairment. Along this continuum of abstinence with revealing layers of emotional impact, the path is fraught with risk of relapse—fearing to let go of addictive behaviors that for years have masked and numbed pain and memories. Should relapse be experienced, reframe it as an opportunity to strengthen the process of abstinence through the resolution of precipitating factors in the development of addictive behavior.

Gil-Rivas *et al.* (1997) found that the results of sexual abuse in association with substance abuse treatment outcome demonstrated the following:

1. Sexual abuse among women was associated with higher levels of depression, anxiety, suicidal ideation, suicide attempts, and post traumatic stress disorder (PSTD).
2. Physical abuse among women was associated with fewer psychological disturbances than the experience of sexual abuse.
3. Sexual abuse among men demonstrated a central association only with anxiety.
4. Physical abuse among men was associated with depression, anxiety, suicidal ideation, and posttraumatic stress disorder.
5. There was no significant association found between sexual and physical abuse and lower levels of treatment participation or substance use at follow-up.

Regarding women with PTSD and substance abuse treatment (Najavits *et al.*, 1998):

1. Evidence of a decrease in trauma-related symptoms at 3 months. By post treatment there were improvements in suicide risk, suicidal ideation, social adjustment, problem solving, depression, thoughts of substance use, and didactic knowledge associated with treatment.
2. Honesty is essential to improvement.
3. There was a strong degree of retention by women who felt helped by treatment.
4. Those who completed treatment in this study were more symptomatically severe than dropouts on all measures. They also demonstrated more engagement in the treatment process and, therefore, greater alliance with treatment.
5. Individuals gave the highest rating to the treatment philosophy, "abstinence from all substances."
6. A strong focus on coping skills was found helpful by participants.

This study suggests that, when an individual is in early recovery from PTSD or substance abuse, cognitive–behavioral strategies may be the preferred treatment.

Therapeutic focus must be consistent, empathic, and neutral and must have very clear boundaries. This population is vulnerable to decompensation. The individuals need a lot of support, patience from those who work with them clinically, and reinforcement for their efforts. There are times when they do not trust themselves, let alone their environments. In fact, it may take considerable time for them to develop trust for their counselors and therapists and to feel safe in the treatment environment. It is not uncommon for those presenting with a history of sexual abuse and PTSD to have been repeatedly victimized and present themselves in a physical and emotional manner that easily identifies them to others who would exploit and abuse them, but they have little or no awareness of this presentation that is predisposing them to continued abuse. Probably the most challenging clinical presentation involves both psychic numbing and a reexperiencing of the trauma. Psychic numbing may take place in the form of (1) memory loss, (2) compartmentalization of affect, or (3) dissociation. Additionally, it may appear that they respond in one extreme or the other when they have become out of control with the abuse of substances, and it takes a while working with them to determine what the triggers may be. Add self-destructive, acting out behavior to such a profile and one begins to easily see how complicated the treatment picture can become.

Issues that impact clinical intervention:

1. Unpredictable boundaries
2. Triangulating
3. Bargaining
4. Enmeshment
5. Difficulty trusting
6. Significant lack of self-awareness
7. Insecurity
8. Transference
9. Projection
10. Testing–power struggles
11. Masked communication
12. Secrets–misrepresentation
13. Sexualizing of relationships
14. Feelings of anger, fear, vulnerability, guilt, shame, damage, and fear of abandonment
15. Self-control through extremes in work, perfectionism, eating, sexuality, etc.
16. Multiaddictions
    a. substances
    b. food
    c. gambling
    d. sex
17. Dissociation

DISSOCIATIVE EXPERIENCES SCALE

The Dissociative Experiences Scale II (Carlson & Putnam, 1993) is a brief, self-report instrument that measures in a quantified manner the frequency of dissociative experiences. It is useful as a screening instrument and in determining the influence of dissociation on various psychiatric disorders. A high score on the DES II is not intended to be construed as an indicator of a dissociative disorder diagnosis. This instrument was developed for use with adults (individuals 18 years of age and older).

WOMEN AND MINORITIES

The reference to the special populations of women and minorities is the issue of sensitivity to human diversity:

1. Gender
2. Race

3. Ethnicity
4. Culture
5. Immigrant experience
6. Language
7. Acculturation
8. Belief systems
9. Values
10. Education
11. Socioeconomic status
12. Employment experience
13. Stereotyping
14. Issues of loss
15. Feeling lack of power–helplessness
16. Defenses (shame, overwhelming guilt defended against by grandiosity)
17. Compulsive, self-destructive behavior
18. Poor self-regulation (impulse, interpersonal behavior, self-esteem, self-efficacy)
19. Abuse issues
20. Rejection
21. Negative expectations

When assessing women or those from diverse racial and ethnic populations, it is important for the therapist to consider and be prepared to deal with the following:

1. When problem solving and facilitating the development of healthier and more effective ways of coping, the individual's cultural strategies and his or her reference group must be taken into consideration.
2. Expand the information base to include information about racial–ethnic identity, acculturation, migration history, language, traditional versus nontraditional family structure, social support system, future goals, socioeconomic issues, values–beliefs associated with the use of substances, problem identification, and perceived problem solving alternatives.
3. Do not make assumptions. Identify the psychosociocultural issues in a sensitive and competent manner that facilitates the development of a therapeutic relationship and positively impacts the individual's self esteem.

INTERVENTION CONSIDERATIONS

1. Be aware of how the individual's unique psychosociocultural background and experience impact the utilization of treatment and treatment compliance. Whenever possible, integrate treatment options that are culturally congruent with the individual's belief system.
2. Awareness of the impact of how lifelong social problems contribute to a vulnerability to physical and mental health problems. This requires caring, comprehensive treatment.

3. Acknowledge the potential information and support to be gained in expanding information gathering and treatment to include family members, extended family members, and other salient participants.

4. Listen. Personal accounts of life experiences may offer pertinent information regarding "what is important" to the individual. Identify these factors and incorporate them into treatment.

5. Always be respectful acknowledging the mutual learning experience that is taking place.

Relapse Prevention

1. Identify relapse symptom(s) substituted by engagement of other compulsive behaviors
2. Prepare for specific high-risk situations with alternative behaviors versus conditioned response
3. Learn to perceive triggers
4. Remediate underlying psychopathology
5. Develop appropriate and adequate resources (may be difficult for dealing with losses associated with prevalent cultural issues)
6. Self-regulation and self-monitoring

Treatment

1. Resolve past trauma–losses
2. Cognitive restructuring
3. Ego strengthening
4. Improved self-regulation
5. Appropriate alternative behaviors
6. Shape–reinforce more adaptive behaviors
7. Empower
8. Identify and resolve individual issues

WOMEN

As with most research, for studies examining substance abuse the subjects have traditionally been white males and the information gleaned form those studies was extrapolated to other populations. The classic studies served to shape the professional understanding of the nature and course of substance use and abuse. Most programs developed from this research have merely been adapted for women and minority populations. Although there has been improvement, bias in addiction research continues (Brett *et al.*, 1995). However, there is a growing body of literature adding to the overall knowledge of the clinically relevant features of addictive disorders to be considered for women and minority populations (Center on Addiction and Substance Abuse 1996; NIDA, 1990). Clinical studies suggest that the needs of women alcoholics–addicts are better met in single sex treatment programs. In these settings, women are more likely to discuss problems that may have contributed to their substance abuse, such as sexual abuse–assault and physical abuse. Women for Sobriety may be a support group option in some communities. According to the National Institute of Alcohol Abuse and Alcoholism (NIAAA, 2001).

1. Number of Americans with a drinking problem: 13.8 million
2. Number of women with a drinking problem: 4.5 million

3. Number of children who live in households with at least one alcoholic parent: 6.6 million

DATA (September 1998) cites a report issued by the National Center on Addiction and Substance Abuse that $30 billion per year in healthcare costs associated with substance abuse remain hidden from primary care physicians for women over the age of 59. Warner *et al.* (1995) demonstrated gender difference in the rate of substance abuse–dependence with information from the National Comorbidity Study using the U.S. population of 15- to 54-year-olds. An overall prevalence in men masked some subgroup gender differences. Women in the 45–54 age range reported a higher lifetime prevalence of substance dependence than men in the study (not including alcohol and nicotine). During the same age range, women and men show a similar prevalence of substance use for the past 12 months. In the 15–24 age range, substance dependence was 4.5% for males and 2.1% for females. Researchers such as Amarao and Hardy-Foster (1995) illuminate the influence of significant other males upon the substance use pattern of females, where the males are likely to:

1. Introduce their partners to substances.
2. Supply substances to their female partners.

Other demographics offered in the research on women identify several other areas where increased acuity in assessment and treatment are needed:

1. Those involved in the criminal justice system (Teplin et al., 1996)
2. Those convicted of homicide (Eronen, 1995)
3. Those identifying themselves as lesbian (McKirnan & Peterson, 1989)
4. Education regarding
   a. fetal alcohol syndrome (FAS) (Institute of Medicine, 1995)
   b. negative impact on sexual dysfunction, which is contrary to the myths about women and the use of substances (Malatesta, 1982)
   c. negative impact on ovulation and fertility (Gavaler, 1985)
   d. onset of health consequences is often more rapid with heavy alcohol use than for men (Miller & Doot, 1994)
   e. genetic and environmental use factors (Sigvardsson *et al.*, 1996)

Lack of effective assessment of women of childbearing age likely leads to preventable birth defects. Additionally, later stage dependency treatment is more costly and less successful due to physiological, psychological, and social consequences. Factors that impact the seeking of treatment include:

1. Lack of awareness of the seriousness of their substance abuse
2. Secretive use of substances
3. Stigma of diagnosis and treatment
4. Lack of child care
5. Cost of treatment
6. Support for women seeking treatment
7. Socialization issues (needs of others come first)

8. Cultural barriers
9. Unhealthy relationships
10. Sexuality issues
11. Transportation
12. Fear of losses associated with diagnosis and treatment (such as loss of child custody)

Many women who use substances do not seek treatment because they are afraid that they will not be able to take care of their children or will lose custody of their children. They fear retaliation from the men in their lives to use it against them in some way, and they fear social sanctions.

The norms, attitudes, and stereotypes associated with substance use differ for men and women. There is a protective element associated with the expectation that women will drink less and not as often (Kubricka *et al.*, 1995). Coincident with this is a decreased tolerance for intoxicated behavior by a woman, which may not vary from that of a man. The social perspective of the substance abusing woman is one of moral degradation and sexual promiscuity. An unfortunate relationship is that the involvement of substances increases the probability of these women being the victims of violent crimes and society adhering to a victim blaming stance that they are responsible for their own victimization (Blume, 1991). As of January 1997, the Center for Disease Control (CDC) had documented approximately 85,500 cases of AIDS among adolescent and adult women in the United States. Among these cases,

1. Approximately 62% were related to the female's own use of injecting substances or having sex with an intravenous substance user.
2. Approximately 37% were related to heterosexual contact, and about half of these women acquired HIV–AIDS by having sex with a intravenous substance abuser.

According to Blume (1997) and Lewis *et al.* (1996), women with substance dependence differ from men in the following ways:

1. More likely to have a reported prior psychiatric problem and treatment (with alcohol)
2. Higher incidence of dual diagnosis (with alcohol and cocaine)
3. Higher incidence of comorbid prescription medication dependence (with alcohol)
4. More likely to have a history of physical or sexual abuse (with alcohol, cocaine, and other substances)
5. Onset of problematic substance use associated with a specific stressful event (with alcohol and cocaine)
6. Significant other is likely a substance abuser (with alcohol, cocaine, and other substances)
7. Substance use is started later in life (with alcohol)
8. Disease progression is more likely (with alcohol and cocaine)
9. Generally women drink less and use other substances less than men

10. More likely to attempt suicide (with alcohol)

11. Increased rate of mortality (with alcohol)

Uziel-Miller *et al.* (1998) attempted to assess the treatment needs of substance abusing African-American females. The outcome review included multiple choice questions and open-ended questions on substance abuse, employment, education, child care, relapse, and perceived degree of overall improvement. At the time of discharge, 88% of the women had remained substance-free, and 49% had jobs or were enrolled in school or job training. The results demonstrate the efficacy of an integrated gender- and culture-based treatment approach to substance abuse treatment for women and their families.

A study whose sample comprised primarily ethnic minorities from disadvantaged backgrounds who supported themselves with public assistance offered the following information (Hein & Scheir, 1996):

1. A high rate of detox completed with low dropout in a women only program.

2. On short-term follow-up, 60% were considered to have a positive outcome.

3. Nearly all women in the study reported themselves as "extremely likely" to follow through on the referral for detox, but 40% did not follow through.

4. Those with multiple prior detox attempts were more likely to pursue further help.

5. Nearly two-thirds experienced a childhood history of physical or sexual abuse.

6. No significant relationship between a history of violence and short-term outcome.

7. Identifying and discussing early history of abuse did not interfere with treatment.

8. The more experience a substance-dependent woman had with substance abuse treatment, the more likely she was to pursue ongoing treatment and assistance.

The physical differences between male and female abusers of alcohol need to be addressed as part of the education offered in treatment. Women are generally smaller in size and have more body fat and less body water than males, which all contribute to higher blood alcohol levels. Additionally, females may be more likely to avoid snacking while drinking due to the social pressures to be weight conscious, therefore, drinking on an empty stomach. This pattern can lead to malnutrition and quicker adsorption of alcohol into the blood stream. The effects of hormonal changes during menstruation can cause a higher blood alcohol levels, and the premenstrual phase of decreased estrogen and progesterone can decrease tolerance and increase depression and general tension.

According to *The Harvard Mental Health Letter* (December 1998), 13% of men qualify for a current diagnosis of alcohol abuse–dependence versus 4% of women. The rate of alcoholism is highest among females in their 20s, showing a steady decline with age. The risk factors for females at various ages of adulthood are as follows:

1. Age 20–30
   a. age is a risk factor
   b. never married
   c. not employed full-time
   d. may not have fully assumed an adult social role

2. Age 30–40
   a. divorced
   b. unemployed
   c. lacks a strong sense of self and goal direction
   d. no children living at home

3. Age 50–60
   a. married
   b. not working outside of the home
   c. no children at home (empty nest syndrome)
   d. unfulfilled personally and professionally

Female alcoholics tend to drink less beer, but more wine and hard liquor. They also tend to not eat while drinking, thereby drinking on an empty stomach. Women progress to the middle and late stages of alcoholism more rapidly than males because of their physiology. With males there appears to be more of a heritable type of alcoholism with antisocial personality disorder, which is predominantly male. Females demonstrate less heritability and more environmentally medicated predominance. However, as previously stated, biology certainly does play a role for women, especially in the context of trying to keep up with the alcohol consumption of their male counterparts.

Physiological factors include the following:

1. Increased sensitivity, even after adjusting for body weight; at a given dose, female blood level of alcohol is higher and they are more intoxicated. This is due to
   a. higher proportion of body fat
   b. lower proportion of water (alcohol is less diluted)
   c. fewer enzymatic secretions to break down alcohol in the stomach before it reaches the bloodstream
   d. hormonal changes lessen tolerance
   e. poor nutrition with increased vitamin deficiency

2. Metabolism of alcohol
   a. females develop symptoms of alcohol dependence progressively
   b. more rapid development of physical complications (increased blood pressure, peptic ulcers, weakening of heart and skeletal muscles)

3. More depression in females

Women alcoholics often remain undetected because they tend to not get in the kind of trouble that men often do, which reveals their alcoholism. Additionally, if a woman is an alcoholic and a primary caretaker of children, it may result in increased suffering by the children in that family system. Women and substance abuse are a combination that can result in the legacy of fetal alcohol syndrome (FAS). Approximately 10–20% of all women who drink moderately during their pregnancy will give birth to FAS babies. This is compared to alcoholic women, who demonstrate a rate of about 45% of their babies being diagnosed as having FAS. FAS children experience retarded physical development and a range of intellectual functioning that is below normal. Babies of alcoholic mothers are victimized twice: (1) being raised by an alcoholic mother and (2) FAS (Institute of Medicine, 1995).

Children of crack-dependent mothers (*The Harvard Mental Health Letter*, December 1998) show the same intellectual development as others living under similar circumstances. Newborns may show signs of withdrawal, demonstrated by being excessively cranky, stiffening to the touch, crying at the sound of voices, experiencing disturbed sleep, and unreliable regulation of body temperature and blood pressure. Cocaine can harm the fetus in several ways:

1. Constricts blood vessels in the umbilical cord and placenta, which reduces the flow of oxygen and nutrients (note that nicotine is also a vasoconstrictor).
2. Interferes with the action of the neurotransmitters serotonin and dopamine, which is associated with the growth of nerve cells, their branching, and connection.

The amount of cocaine needed to sustain damage in the fetus is not known. It does not appear that anything similar to a distinct pattern of deformities or disabilities is seen as in the case of FAS. However, the following reports of physical effects and pregnancy have been made:

1. Cardiac abnormalities
2. Poor control of newborn heart rate
3. Malformation of the urinary tract
4. Spontaneous abortion
5. Premature birth
6. Abrupted placenta
7. Small brain hemorrhages

As the children grow older, they may exhibit symptoms of ADD as well as other symptoms, such as

1. Impulsivity
2. Distractibility
3. Hyperactivity
4. Low frustration tolerance
5. Easily startled
6. Difficult to arouse or too easily excited once aroused
7. Impaired habituation (inability to ignore or accommodate repeated stimuli and recover interest upon introduction of a new stimulus)

According to the National Institute on Drug Abuse (1994):

1. An estimated 46,000 mothers inhaled or injected cocaine at least one time during pregnancy
2. 35,000 smoked crack during pregnancy
3. 757,000 drank alcohol
4. 320,000 smoked tobacco

Given the areas of difference demonstrated by women and men who are substance-dependent and their different sociological experiences, the following considerations for prevention and treatment of women appear logical:

1. Early education on the physiological differences and consequences of substance abuse and dependence.
2. Early education regarding the genetic and environmental risk factors, particularly aimed at high-risk groups such as
    a. adolescents and adult daughters of those who are substance-dependent
    b. victims of aggression
    c. those at vulnerable points of transition (divorce, widowed, job reentry, role of caretaker for elderly parent)
3. Learning effective stress management skills.
4. Increased awareness of positive female role models and what they can learn.
5. Increased awareness of the impact of social stigma and sexism.
6. Adequate access to health care.
7. Increased awareness of the role of dual diagnosis and its consequences along with treatment choices.
8. Comprehensive medical exam with awareness of physical complications and comorbid disorders.
9. Assessment of prescription medication abuse and dependence.
10. Evaluation and treatment of significant other and their children.
11. Provide child care and other interventions–support for women in treatment (parenting education and other social support for improving their lives and, therefore, the lives of their children).
12. Increased awareness of the intervention for minority women, lesbians, and those who have encountered legal problems.

Treatment

1. Provide for safe environment of women and children
2. It may be necessary to provide food and clothing
3. Parenting education
4. Child care
5. Medical care–dental care
6. Conjoint therapy–family therapy
7. Vocational training–literacy training–educational opportunities
8. Transportation
9. Social services
10. Social support
11. Assertiveness training
12. Social skills training–living skills
13. Psychological assessment and associated mental health services
14. Family planning
15. Legal assistance

Obviously the need is for integrated treatment. After completing treatment, women need continuing services to assist them in sustaining their recovery and in rejoining the community. Factors that may play an important role in facilitating the maintenance of recovery include the following:

1. Complete follow-up, making sure that she is linked with necessary services and adequate aftercare.
2. Overcome cultural and social barriers that contribute to the difficulty in accessing services and to feelings of helplessness.
3. Facilitate establishment of boundaries, clarification, self-esteem, self-sufficiency, and other factors that contribute to healthy relationships.
4. Therapist attitudes that encourage women to develop goals and make choices about their future.
5. Participation in self-help groups in order to facilitate recovery, responsibility, personal growth, values clarification, and increasing their choices.

MINORITIES

In general, members of any race must not be assumed to be all alike. There must be respect for human diversity and a genuine effort to understand the values, modes of communication, standards of behavior, and specific conditions of their life experiences. Therefore, it is of particular importance that the information presented in this section not be utilized to profile different segments of the population. Instead, this information is intended to increase awareness of all possible issues of diversity to be considered as influencing an individual's experience, presentation, and treatment needs. There are no clear-cut divisions. Even within an ethnic group there are variations in origin, religious–spiritual orientation, political ideology, socioeconomic status, education, occupation, housing, marital status and associated beliefs, age, gender, multigenerational home life, etc. Clearly, experiences within an ethnic group can be vastly different. Additionally, there is not sufficient data on ethnic differences regarding biological vulnerability for substance abuse to allow a between groups review (Berrettini & Persico, 1996; Chan *et al.*, 1994). Therefore, whereas racial–ethnic differences are significant, the clinical picture of human diversity cannot be limited. Sensitivity to the diversity of the human condition is a necessary requirement in respectfully and effectively treating everyone entering treatment. The individualized treatment plan (ITP) is the most respectful and beneficial method of collaborating on a plan of change and associated action for the individual to commit to because it is distinctly his or her program.

Special Considerations for Providing Culturally Sensitive and Competent Treatment

1. Advocacy for special services
2. Unbiased assessment instruments
3. Convenient program location
4. Staff with backgrounds similar to these of program participants
5. Staff training in multicultural issues
6. Sensitivity to differences in spirituality
7. Ongoing assessment of the utilization of special services
8. Community liason

According to NIDA (fax update 3/4/99), there were approximately 1.9 million admissions to publicly funded substance abuse treatment programs in 1995. Associated statistics included the following information:

1. Approximately
    a. 54% were admitted to alcohol treatment programs
    b. 46% were for illicit substance abuse treatment
    c. 38% were treated for cocaine dependence
    d. 25% were treated for heroin dependence
    e. 12% were treated for marijuana dependence

2. Approximately 70% who entered treatment were male, with females filling the remaining 30%

3. Ethnic–racial breakdown was as follows
    a. 56% Caucasian
    b. 26% African American
    c. 7.7% Hispanic
    d. 2.2% Native American
    e. 0.6% Asian–Pacific Islander

Native Americans

Native Americans represent a very heterogeneous grouping of cultures. However diverse, Native Americans do share beliefs in unity, the sacredness of nature, and a focus on the community versus the individual. They are the most researched minority population, and the research focus has been most specifically on alcoholism (Burns, 1995). Although the mortality rate for Native Americans has been 3–4 times the national average, statistics indicate a decrease in mortality since 1969. It is believed that this decrease is directly related to the doubling of alcohol treatment programs by Indian Health Services during the 1980s. The negative consequences of alcoholism are much greater for Native Americans: 36 times more cirrhosis of the liver, 7 times more FAS, and 75% of deaths are alcohol-related. Why is alcohol dependency such a big issue for this population (for some but not all)?

1. "To drink" and "to get drunk" are the same in their native language.
2. It is rude to refuse to accept a drink.
3. To be drunk does not necessarily have a negative connotation.
4. There is no evidence for lower tolerance, different rates of metabolism, or a mystery enzyme.

As previously stated, the Native-American population is highly diverse, making it virtually impossible to make ethnic generalizations or general recommendations regarding treatment. Not only do tribes vary from one another, but any one individual may differ significantly from other members of his or her own tribe. Therefore, it is imperative to avoid stereotyping. Intracultural differences can sometimes be greater than intercultural differences. Traditional Native-American healers do not segment physical problems from mental or emotional problems because there is no such thing as a problem isolated in one area (Thomason, 1991). Preparation of a Native American for therapy would include an understanding of the following and must take into consideration the fact that many Native Americans are pulled between traditional tribal culture and mainstream American culture (Edwards & Edwards, 1989; Attneave, 1982, 1985; Lewis & Ho, 1989; Everett *et al.*, 1983):

1. The necessity of giving a positive orientation to treatment with a hopeful outcome at the first session.
2. The expectation that a therapist will not pry deeply with intimate questions of the individual's personal life. Instead, spend time in social conversation to build rapport.
3. The use of self-disclosure may prompt self-disclosure on behalf of the individual.
4. It may be expected that the therapist would solve the individual's problems. This population has been controlled and patronized for a long time. Therefore, educate members in advance about the mutual responsibilities of treatment.
5. Seek to explore, in a respectful manner, the tribe's family structure, age, gender roles, and characteristics of nonverbal and paralinquistic behavior.
6. Gather information on the natural support system, developmental stress points, and coping strategies.

Characteristics of the therapist and his or her personal approach should include the following:

1. The therapist must be genuine and sincere.
2. He or she must have a basic understanding of the history and status of Native Americans.
3. Exploration of the individual's concerns is best undertaken informally.
4. Be prepared to include the individual's family, visiting his or her home, and possibly involve a traditional healer from the tribe.

To aid in the understanding of the diversity of this population, the following information may be helpful. LaFramboise *et al.* (1990) offers a schema of acculturation or "Indianness" [first developed by Spindler (1958) and then modified by Ryan and Ryan (1982)]:

1. *Traditional* individuals generally speak and think in their native language and know little English. They observe "old time" traditions and values.
2. *Transitional* individuals generally speak both English and the native language in home. They question basic traditionalism and religion, yet do not fully accept dominant culture and values.
3. *Marginal* individuals may be defensively Indian, but are unable either to live the cultural heritage of their tribal group or to identify with the dominant society. This group tends to have the most difficulty in coping with social problems due to their ethnicity.
4 *Assimilated* individuals, for the most part, have been accepted by the dominant society. They generally have embraced dominant culture and values.
5. *Bicultural* individuals are those who are, for the most part, accepted by the dominant society. However, they also know and accept their tribal

traditions and culture. They can thus move in either direction, from the traditional society to the dominant society, with ease.

Substance abuse must be assessed and treated with reference to the unique context that surrounds the individual. Some guidelines for setting up a "task-centered group" approach for Native Americans with a culturally marginal status include the following:

1. Belief that abstinence is a goal. It is likely that the use of alcohol has been viewed as a means for short-term coping.
2. Homogeneity of tribal and non-Indian culture. Inner conflict of two distinct, often contradictory cultural references used for personal identity. Therefore, there is the challenge of being a good member of the tribe and a good contributor to the mainstream world. It is this struggle of conflicting values that is often at the foundation of substance abuse.
3. Organize the group around specific tasks for managing abstinence and emphasizing adaptive coping for situations in which different values impose conflicting expectations behaviorally.
4. With increased confidence and trust in the therapist, group members are more likely to discuss their problems with substances.
5. Acknowledge and define problems in a way that is congruent with the life circumstances and perceptions of the group members.

Whereas the aforementioned information on the degree of acculturation and its clinical implications were specific to Native Americans, there is credence in its generalized application to all of those who have a traditional and a dominant cultural experience with which to contend.

African Americans

African Americans experience 2 times the cirrhosis of the liver than any other group, and it is more common among males than females. This population tends to be more receptive to treatment than Native Americans, but more outreach is needed. When African Americans are compared with their Caucasian counterparts regarding substance abuse disorders and associated problems, the following has been found (Herd, 1990, 1994; Rosenheck & Seibyl, 1998; Hanson, 1985; Kandel & Davies, 1991):

1. Heavy alcohol use peaks in the middle years versus Caucasian men, whose alcohol use peaks in the 20s.
2. Racial composition of a program, rather than therapist–client matching, is most salient.
3. African-American men demonstrate lower rates in frequency of heavy drinking, but more symptoms of physical dependence and health problems. This could be attributed to limited financial resources and associated access to health care.
4. African-American males at a lower socioeconomic status have more social consequences than their Caucasian counterparts.
5. African-American males at higher socioeconomic status reported fewer social consequences than their Caucasian counterparts. It appears that socioeconomic

status has more of an impact on African-American males than Caucasian males, i.e., higher income translated to lower rates of drinking for African-American males. However, income appears to have little influence upon the alcohol consumption of Caucasian males.

6. African-American males are overrepresented in categories of heroin and cocaine abuse.

7. Early sexual intercourse (age 13 for males, age 14 for females) is associated with elevated lifetime cocaine use across African Americans, Hispanics, and Caucasians.

Nobles and Goddard (1989) identify three central processes that contribute to the degree of substance abuse among African Americans:

1. Disenfranchisement, racism, and environmental stressors.

2. Availability of substances in their communities-neighborhoods.

3. Use of advertising media to heavily target them.

Treatment Considerations

Although it is important for anyone in substance abuse treatment to acknowledge and accept what he or she has in common with others who are also in treatment, individuality from a perspective of cultural diversity is tantamount to successful treatment. Such culturally and ethnically relevant issues include the following:

1. Positive cultural–ethnic identity

2. Facilitate and encourage self-determination

3. Enhance self-esteem

4. Identify, respect, and encourage living in accordance to personal and traditional values

5. Show empathy and respect for cultural experiences

6. Acknowledge and accept that an individual may desire and benefit from ethnic-cultural matching with therapist

Hispanic Americans

Hispanic and Asian Americans are the least researched of the minority populations. Hispanic Americans offer significant cultural and ethnic diversity: Mexican Americans, Cuban Americans, Puerto Ricans, and Hispanic Americans with roots from various other locales in Central and South America. When surveyed (National Household Survey on Drug Abuse 18+, 1995), Hispanic Americans demonstrate the lowest rate in the "ever used any illegal drug" category. However, they appear to have 2 times the rate of alcoholism.

A significant relationship between acculturation and alcohol use exists (Black & Markides, 1993). It appears that the probability of alcohol use and frequency of consumption are positively correlated with acculturation. Acculturation is described as the degree that language, traditions, and values are adopted into the family system. Caetano and Medina-Mora (1990) presented the following drinking patterns, comparing Mexicans living in Mexico to Mexican Americans:

1. Increased permissive attitudes about drinking are associated with acculturation.

2. The increased consumption associated with acculturation was true for both males and females.

3. Mexican Americans report fewer alcohol-related problems than their counterparts living in Mexico.

A delineating factor between Mexican Americans, Puerto Ricans, and Cuban Americans is the relationship that each location has with the United States. Ruiz *et al.* (1981) define these three relationships as follows:

1. The United States has an ambivalent relationship with Puerto Rico, which results in cultural identity confusion.
2. Mexican Americans and Puerto Ricans are viewed as a burden on the U.S. economy and resources.
3. There are varying levels of struggle with the language barrier.
4. A politically motivated relationship with Cuba offers a more protective experience to Cuban immigrants, unlike the more alienating experience for immigrants from Mexico and Puerto Rico.

Treatment Considerations

1. Support for decreased language barriers such as English as a Second Language (ESL) classes, which are offered in locations and at times to more readily accommodate individuals.
2. Respect and sensitivity to the Hispanic-American family structure and the associated factors of intimacy, sexuality, family, and parenting. Additionally, there may be issues of fear and distrust related to security of staying in the United States (Szapocanzik & Fein, 1995).
3. Be aware that traditional family roles are extended multigenerationally, where the elderly are highly regarded and respected for their experience and wisdom.
4. Understand the role–function of every family member, including extended family members. They are useful when family support is integrated into treatment.
5. When working with Hispanic-American teens (12–17), recognize the influencing role associated with parents' attitudes and use of substances. Parents need to be educated regarding this influence (Gfoerer & DeLa Rosa, 1993).

Asian Americans

The Asian-American population includes Chinese, Japanese, Korean, Filipino, Vietnamese, Thai, Cambodian etc. Obviously, a combination of many cultures, languages, religions, and political belief systems is represented. All of these factors, particularly religion, play a role in substance use and the acceptance of substance abuse. Unfortunately, there is even less information on Asian Americans, in that they often have not even been represented with other ethnic minority populations in data collected on alcoholism. The continuum of highest to lowest rate of heavy alcohol consumption is as follows: Korean Americans, Japanese Americans, and Chinese Americans (Kitano & Chi, 1989).

Although there is a continuing pursuit for understanding of the biological differences associated with ethnicity and specific biological mechanisms, much remains to be learned. Those of Asian-American heritage experience a phenomenon referred to as "flushings" which is the result of a limited ability to break down acetaldehyde to acetic acid. The resulting symptoms are headache and nausea. The estimated percent of Asian Americans who experience flushing is 47–85% (U.S. Department of Health and Human Services, 1993).

Treatment Considerations

1. Decrease language barriers, utilizing ESL classes at times and locations to easily accommodate the needs of individuals.

2. In general, members of the Asian–American community do not accept substance dependence as an illness to be treated (Ja & Aoki, 1993). Substance abuse problems are often ignored and denied. The family is likely to make efforts to keep the "problem" concealed from the community in order to avoid embarrassment. For the family members, there is a sense of failure if they are required to seek help from the outside.

3. Be respectful of and sensitive to family systems issues.

4. There must be appropriate acknowledged recognition of the dominance of family and community over the needs of the individual.

COURT-MANDATED TREATMENT

When individuals are forced into treatment by an employer, the court, or a family member, the results can be as follows:

1. Defensiveness–dishonesty
2. Lack of motivation
3. Complicated emotional picture (anger, resentment, embarrassment, distrust, etc.)
4. Confidentiality issues
5. Resistance to collaborative treatment planning

Encourage a collaborative effort even under strained circumstances.

Miller and Rollnick (1991) offer a process of motivational interviewing with a client-centered approach to assess an individual with a substance abuse or addiction problem. It is a perspective that emphasizes the following:

1. The acceptance of the applied labels such as addict or alcoholic is not a prerequisite for change.
2. Treatment is viewed as a personal choice.
3. The individual is responsible for change.
4. Resistance is viewed as a relationship of influence by the therapist's attitude or behavior toward the individual.
5. Encourage collaborative treatment planning.
6. View ambivalence versus denial as a central treatment issue.

Many individuals mandated to treatment fulfill the criteria for a personality disorder. They may be distrustful and guarded, lack motivation, and lack an appropriate peer–support group reinforcing positive changes such as abstinence and self-care. Several strategies that may be helpful in engaging them in treatment include the following:

1. Empathize with the individual's circumstances (coercion).
2. Accept where he or she is coming from without challenging his or her motivation for coming to treatment.
3. Validate the individual's response to mandated treatment.
4. Praise him or her for facing the reality of the situation and encourage him or her to focus on gaining benefit.
5. Encourage the individual to not focus on the coercive agent that brought him or her to treatment.
6. Be open and honest regarding confidentiality and reporting.
7. Recognize the treatment goal of getting an accurate picture of the individual's life experience.
8. Use treatment as an opportunity to complete a life inventory and utilize support for personal growth, goal setting, and redirection.

If there have been any prior episodes of treatment, assessment of the following issues may offer some direction and effective problem solving associated with the development of the treatment plan:

1. Who was the individual in treatment with and when?
2. What were the events that led to treatment?
3. Reason–goal for entering treatment (his or her own reasons and/or the reasons of others).
4. What type of treatment did he or she receive?
5. Treatment completed.
6. Premature termination (if so, why).
7. What was helpful?
8. What was not helpful?
9. Past–present experience of 12-step program participation.
10. Explore the meaning of the chosen substance to the individual.
11. Length of time abstinence has ever been maintained (was it helpful).
12. What factors contributed to relapse?

Institute of Medicine (1990) suggests that substance abuse treatment programs that are sufficiently comprehensive and well-integrated into the criminal justice system do result in a significant decrease in recidivism. These findings are contrary to the belief that coerced treatment does not work. In the treatment of substance abuse disorders, it may be the review of this population with appropriate comprehensive treatment that clarifies retention as being the variable most highly related to a positive treatment outcome. It appears that, regardless of whether treatment is voluntary or involuntary, those who remain in treatment demonstrate similarity in outcome.

Substance abuse treatment programs in prison are often viewed as mandated from the standpoint of monitoring and limited choice availability. According to NIDA (3/4/99), the "Delaware Model" is such a program. It is an ongoing study of comprehensive treatment of substance-dependent inmates. The program statistics demonstrate a 57% decrease in the probability of a rearrest. The program includes

1. A therapeutic community setting.
2. A work release therapeutic community.
3. Community-based aftercare.

REFERENCES

Adams, W. L., Magruder-Habib, K., Trued, S., & Broome, H. L. (1992). Alcohol abuse in elderly emergency room patients. *J. Am. Geriatr. Soc.* **40**:1236–1240.

Adams, W. L., Zhong, Y., Barboriat, J. J., & Rimm, A. A. (1993). Alcohol related hospitalizations of elderly people: Prevalence and geographic variations in the United States. *J. Am. Med. Assoc.*

Adler, R. A. (1992). Clinically important effect of alcohol on endocrine function. *J. Clin. Endocrinol. Metab.* **74**:957–960.

American Psychiatric Association (1994). "Diagnostic and Statistical Manual of Mental Disorders," 4th ed. Washington, DC: American Psychiatric Association.

American Society of Addiction Medicine (1996). "Patient Placement Criteria for the Treatment of Substance Related Disorders," 2nd ed. Washington, DC: American Society of Addiction Medicine.

APA Monitor on Psychology, June 2001, Vol. 32, No. 6, p. 11.

Aponte, J. F., Rivers, R. Y., & Wohl, J. (1995). "Psychological Interventions and Cultural Diversity." Boston: Allyn & Bacon.

Arentzen, W. P. (1978). Impact of alcohol misuse in family life. *Alcoholism* 2(4):345–351.

Atkinson, R. M., Ganzini, L., & Bernstein, M. J. (1992). Alcohol and substance use disorders in the elderly. *In* "Handbook of Mental Health and Aging." (J. Birren, R. Sloane, & G. Cohen, Eds.), pp. 515–555. San Diego: Academic Press.

Atkinson, R. M., Tolson, R. L., & Turner, J. A. (1993). Factors affecting outpatient treatment compliance of older male problem drinkers. *J. Studies Alcohol* **54**:102–106.

Attneave, C. L. (1982). American Indian and Alaska Native families: Emmigrants in their own homeland. *In* "Ethnicity and Family Therapy" (M. McGoldrick, J. Pearce, & J. Giordano, Eds.), pp. 55–83. New York: Guilford.

Attneave, C. L. (1985). Practical counseling with American Indian and Alaska Native clients. *In* "Handbook of Cross Cultural Counseling and Therapy" (P. Pederson, Ed.), pp. 135–140. Westport, CT: Greenwood Press.

Bachman, J. G., Wallace, J. M., O'Malley, P. M., Johnston, L. D., Kurth, C. L., & Neighbors, H. W. (1991). Racial/ethnic differences in smoking, drinking, and illicit drug use among American high school seniors 1976–1989. *Am. J. Pub. Health* **81**:372–377.

Bartels, S. J., Drake, R. E., & Wallach, M. A. (1995). Long term course of substance use disorders among patients with severe mental illness. *Psychiatr. Services* **46**:248–251.

Bass, E., & Davis, L. (1988). "The Courage to Heal." New York: Harper & Row.

Batki, S. L. (1990). Drug abuse, psychiatric disorders and AIDS: Dual and triple diagrams. *Western J. of Med.* **152**:547–552.

Beck, A., Freeman, A., & Associates (1990). "Cognitive Therapy of Personality Disorders." New York: Guilford Press.

Beck, A., Wright, F., Newman, C., & Liese, B. (1993). "Cognitive Therapy of Substance Abuse." New York: Guilford Press.

Belar, C. D., & Deardorff, W. W., Eds. (1995). "Clinical Health Psychology in Medical Settings. A Practitioner's Guidebook." Washington, DC: American Psychological Association.

Beletsis, S., & Brown, S. (1981). A developmental framework for understanding the children of alcoholics. Focus on women. *J. Health Addictions* **2**(Winter):1–32.

Berlin, E. A., & Fowkes, N. C., Jr. (1983). A teaching framework for cross cultural health care. *Western J. Med.* **139**(6):934–938.

Bernstein, E. M., & Putnam, F. W. (1986). Development, reliability, and validity of a dissociation scale. *J. Nervous Mental Dis.* **174**:727–735.

Berrettini, W. H., & Persico, A. M. (1996). Dopamine D2 receptor gene polymorphisms and vulnerability to substance abuse in African Americans. *J. Biol. Psychiatry* **40**:144–147.

Bienenfeld, D. (1990). Substance abuse in the elderly. *In* "Vervoerdt's clinical geropsychiatry," 3rd edition (Bienenfeld, Ed.), Bartimone: Williams and Wilkins.

Birrin, J. E., Sloan, R. B., & Cohen, G. D., Eds. (1992). "Handbook of Mental Health and Aging," 2nd ed. San Diego, CA: Academic Press.

Black, S., & Markides, K. S. (1993). Acculturation and alcohol consumption in Puerto Rican and Mexican American women in the United States. *Am. J. Pub. Health* **83**(6):890–893.

Blazer, D. G. (1993). "Depression in Late Life," 2nd ed. St. Louis, MO: Mosby.

Blixin, C. E. (1988). Aging and Mental Health Care. *J. Gerontol. Nursing* **14**:11–15.

Blow, F. C., Brower, K. J., Schulenberg, J. E., Demo-Daranber, L. M., Young, M. S., & Beresford, T. P. (1992d). The Michigan Alcohol Screening Test: A new elderly specific screening instrument. *Alcoholism: Clin. Exp. Res.* **16**:372–377.

Blow, F. C., Loveland Cook, C. A., Booth, B. M., Falcon, S. P., & Friedman, M. J. (1992b). Age related psychiatric comorbidities and level of functioning in alcoholic veterans seeking outpatient treatment. *Hosp. Community Psychiatry* **43**:990–995.

Blumenthal, S. J. (1988). Suicide: A guide to risk factors and treatment of suicidal patients. *Med. Clin. North America* **72**:937–971.

Bode, J. C., & Bode, C. (1992). Alcohol, malnutrition, and gastrointestinal tract. *In* "Nutrition and Alcohol" (R. R. Watson & B. Watzy, Eds.), pp. 402–428. Boca Raton, FL: CRC Press.

Bollerud, K. (1990). A model for the treatment of trauma-related syndromes among chemically dependent inpatient women. *J. Substance Abuse Treatment* **7**:83–87.

Brady, K. T. (1997). Posttraumatic stress disorder and comorbidity: Recognizing the many faces of PTSD. *J. Clin. Psychiatry* **58**(Suppl. 7):12–15.

Brehm, N. M., & Khantzian, E. J. (1992). A psychodynamic perspective. *In* "Substance Abuse: A Comprehensive Textbook" (J. H. Lowinson, P. Ruiz, & R. B. Millman, Eds.), pp. 106–117. Baltimore, MD: Williams and Wilkins.

Breitbart, W. (1993). Suicide risk and pain in cancer and AIDS patients. *In* "Current and Emerging Issues in Cancer Pain: Research and Practice" (C. R. Chapman & K. M. Foley, Eds.), pp. 49–65. New York: Raven Press.

Bridgewater, R., Leigh, S., James, O. F. W., & Potter, J. F. (1987). Alcohol consumption and dependence in elderly patients in an urban setting.

Brown, S. (1985). "Treating the Alcoholic: A Developmental Model of Recovery." New York: Wiley.

Browne, A., & Finkelhor, D. (1986). Impact of sexual abuse: A review of the literature. *Psychol. Bull.* **99**:66–77.

Brunner-Orne, M. (1956). The utilization of group psychotherapy in enforced treatment programs for alcoholics and addicts. *Int. J. Group Psychother.* **6**:272–279.

Buchsbaum, D. L., Buchanan, R. G., & Lawton, M. J. (1991). Alcohol consumption patterns in a primary care population. *Alcohol Alcoholism* 26:215–220.

Bulik, C. M. (1987). Drug and alcohol abuse by bulimic women and their families. *Am. J. Psychiatry* 144:1604–1606.

Burkenstein, O. G., Glancy, L. J., & Kaminer, Y. (1992). Patterns of affective comorbidity in a clinical population of dually diagnosed substance abusers. *J. Am. Acad. Child Adolescent Psychiatry* 31:1041–1045.

Caetano, R. & Medina-Mora, M. E. (1990). Reasons and attitudes toward drinking and abstaining: A comparison of Mexicans and Mexican-Americans. *In* "Epidemiological trends in drug use: Community epidemiology work group proceedings." June 1990, pp. 173–191. Rockville, MD: National Institute on Drug Abuse.

Carlson, E. B., & Putnam, F. W. (1993). An update on the Dissociative Experiences Scale. *Dissociation* 6(1):16–27.

Carter, R. T. (1995). "The Influence of Race and Racial Identity in Psychotherapy." New York: Wiley.

Caton, C. M., Shrout, P. E., Eagle, P. E., Opler, L. D., & Felix, A. (1994). Correlates of codisorders in homeless and never homeless indigent schizophrenic men. *Psychol. Med.* 24:681–688.

Center for Substance Abuse Treatment (1995). Detoxification from alcohol and other drugs. "Treatment Improvement Protocol Series," No. 19, DHHS Pub. No. (SMA) 95-3046. Washington, DC: U.S. Government Printing Office.

Chaney, E. F., O'Leary, M. R., & Marlatt, G. A. (1978). Skill training with alcoholics. *J. Consult. Clin. Psychol.* 46:1092–1104.

Chavkin, W. (1990). Drug addiction and pregnancy. Policy crossroads. *Am. J. Pub. Health* 80(4):483–487.

Chesney, M. A., & Flkman, S. (1994). Psychological impact on HIV disease and implications for intervention. *Psychiatr. Clin. North America* 17:163–182.

Christiansen, B., Roehling, P., Smith, G., & Goldman, M. (1989). Using alcohol expectancies to predict adolescent drinking behavior after one year. *J. Consult. Clin. Psychol.* 57(1):93–99.

Clark, D. B., Burkstein, O. G., Smith, M. G., Kacynski, N. A., Mezzich, A. C., & Donovan, J. E. (1995). Identifying anxiety disorders in adolescents hospitalized for alcohol abuse and dependency. *Psychiatr. Service* 46:618–620.

Clark, H. W. (1987). On professional therapists and alcoholics anonymous. *J. of Psych. Drugs* 19:233–242.

Clinebell, H. J. (1963). Philosophical–religious factors in the etiology and treatment of alcoholism. *Q. J. Studies Alcohol* 24:473–488.

Conwell, Y., & Brent, D. (1995). Suicide and aging: I. *Int. Psychogeriatr.* 7:149–164.

Cougton, S. S. (1986). Facing the clinical challenge of women alcoholics: Physical, emotional, and sexual abuse. *Focus Family* 3:10–11, 9(37):42–44.

Curtis, P. A. (1990). The consequences of acculturation to service delivery and research with Hispanic families. *Child Adolescent Social Work* 7(2):147–159.

Cusack, B. J., & Vestal, R. E. (1986). Clinical pharmacology: Special considerations in the elderly. *In* "Practice of Geriatric Medicine" (E. Calkins, P. J. Dovin, & A. B. Ford, Eds.), pp. 115–136. Philadelphia: W. B. Saunders.

Daniolos, P. T., & Holmes, V. F. (1995). HIV public policy and psychiatry: An examination of ethical issues and professional guidelines.

Davies, P. (1979). Motivation, responsibility, and sickness in the psychiatric treatment of alcoholism. *Br. J. Psychiatry* 134:449–458.

DeVita, V. T., Jr., Hellman, S., & Rosenberg, S. A., Eds. (1997). "AIDs: Etiology, Diagnosis, Treatment, and Prevention." Philadelphia: Lippincott-Raven.

Dickey, B., & Azeni, H. (1996). Persons with dual diagnosis of substance abuse and major mental illness: Their cost of psychiatric care. *Am. J. Pub. Health* **86**(7):973–977.

Dilly, J. W., Pies, S., & Helquist, M., Eds. "Face to Face: A Guide to AIDS Counseling." Berkeley, CA: Celestial Arts.

Dobson, K. S., Ed. (1988). "Handbook of Cognitive Behavioral Therapies." New York: Guilford Press.

Dunlop, J. (1990). Peer groups support seniors fighting alcohol and drugs. *Aging* **361**:28–32.

Dupree, L. W., Broskowski, H., & Schonfeld, L. (1984). The gerontology alcohol project: A behavior treatment program for the elderly. *Gerontologist* **24**:510–516.

Dworkin, S. H., & Pincu, L. (1993). Counseling in the era of AIDS. *J. Counseling Dev.* **71**:275–281.

Edwards, E. D., & Edwards, M. E. (1989). American Indians: Working with individuals and groups. *In* "Counseling American Minorities" (D. R. Atkinson, G. Morten, & D. W. Sue, Eds.), pp. 72–84. Dubuque, IA: William C. Brown Publisher.

Erikson, E. (1980). "Identity and the Life Cycle." New York: Norton.

Eronen, M. (1995). Mental disorders and homicidal behavior in female subjects. *Am. J. of Psychiatry* **152**(8):1216–1218.

Evans, K., & Sullivan, J. M. (1990). "Dual Diagnosis: Counseling the Mentally Ill Substance Abuser." New York: Guilford Press.

Everett, F., Procter, N., & Cartmell, B. (1983). Providing psychological services to American Indian children and families. *Profess. Psychol.* **14**:588–603.

Ewing, J. A. (1984). Detecting alcoholism: The *CAGE* questionnaire. *J. Am. Med. Assoc.* **252**(14):1905–1907.

Fanon, F. (1968). "Black Skin, White Masks." New York: Grove Press.

Fawzer, F. I., Namer, S., & Wolcott, D. L. (1989). Structured group intervention model for AIDS patients. *Psychiatr. Med.* **7**:35–45.

Finkelhor, D. C., & Browne, A. (1986). The traumatic impact of child abuse: A conceptualization. *Am. J. Orthopsychiatry* **55**:530–541.

Finley, D. G. (1978). Alcoholism and systems theory: Building a better mousetrap. *Psychiatry* **41**(3):272–278.

Fleming, M. F., & Barry, K. L. (1991). A three sample test of a masked alcohol screening questionnaire. *Alcohol Alcoholism* **26**(1):81–91.

Folsom, R. E., & Judkins, D. R. (1997). "Model based estimates from the 1991–1993 national household surveys on drug abuse: Methodology report." Rockville, MD: Dept. of Health and Human Services, Substance Abuse and Mental Health Services Administration.

Friedman, H., Kline, T., & Specter, S., Eds. (1991). Immunosuppression by marijuana and its components. *In* "Psychoimmunology" (R. Adler, D. L. Felten, & N. Cohen, Eds.), 2nd ed., pp. 931–953. New York: Academic Press.

Gavaler, J. S. (1985). Effects of alcohol on endocrine function in postmenopausal women. *A Review J. of Studies on Alcohol* **46**:495–516.

Gawin, F. H., & Kleber, H. D. (1986). Abstinence symptomology and psychiatric diagnosis in cocaine abusers. *Arch. Gen. Psychiatry* **43**:533–545.

Gertsley, L. J., Alterman, A. I., McClellan, A. T., & Woody, G. E. (1990). Antisocial personality disorders in patients with substance abuse disorders: A problematic diagnosis. *Am. J. Psychiatry* **147**:173–178.

Gfroerer, J., & De la Rosa, M. (1993). Protective and risk factors associated with drug use among Hispanic youth. *J. of Addictive Disease* **12**(2):87–107.

Gil, E. (1988). "Treatment of Adult Survivors of Childhood Sexual Abuse." Walnut Creek, CA: Launch Press.

Gil-Rivas, V., Fiorentine, R., Anglin, M. D., & Taylor, E. (1997). Sexual and physical abuse: do they compromise drug treatment outcomes? *J. Substance Abuse Treatment* **14**(4):351–355.

Gloria, A. M., & Peregoy, J. J. (1996). Counseling Latino alcohol and other drug abusers: Cultural issues for consideration. *J. Substance Abuse Treatment* **8**:1–8.

Gomberg, E. S. (1976). Alcoholism in women. *In* "The Biology of Alcoholism, Social Pathology" (B. Kissin & H. Begleiter, Eds.), vol. 4. New York: Plenum Press.

Goodwin, D. W. (1985). Alcoholism and genetics: The sins of the fathers. *Arch. Gen. Psychiatry* **42**:171–174.

Graham, K. (1986). Identifying and measuring alcohol abuse among the elderly: Serious problems with existing instrumentation. *J. Studies Alcohol* **47**:322–326.

Grande, T. P., Wolfe, A. W., Shubert, D. S. P., Patterson, M. B., & Brocco, K. (1984). Associations among alcoholism, drug abuse, and antisocial personality: A review of the literature. *Psychol. Rep.* **55**:455–474.

Grilco, C. M., Becker, D. F., Walker, M. L., Levy, K. N., Edell, W. S., & McGlashan, T. H. (1995). Psychiatric comorbidity in adolescent inpatients with substance use disorders. *J. of the Am. Acad. of Child and Adolescent Psychiatry* **34**:1085–1091.

Haley, W. E. (1996). The medical context of psychotherapy with the elderly. *In* "A Guide to Psychotherapy and Aging: Effective Clinical Interventions in a Life Stage Context" (H. S. Zarit & B. G. Knight, Eds.), pp. 221–239. Washington, DC: American Psychological Association.

Hanson, B. (1985). Drug treatment effectiveness: The case of racial and ethnic minorities in America. Some research questions and proposals. *Int. J. Addictions* **20**(1):99–137.

Hasselbrock, M. N., Myer, R. E., & Kenner, A. S. (1988). Psychopathology in Hospitalized Alcoholics. *Archives of Gen. Psych.* **42**:1050–1055.

Heilman, R. O. (1975). "Early Recognition of Alcoholism and Other Drug Dependence." Center City, MN: Hazelden.

Hein, D., & Scheir, J. (1996). Trauma and short term outcome for women in detoxification. *J. Substance Abuse Treatment* **13**(3):227–231.

Hellman, J. (1981). Alcohol abuse and the borderline patient. *Psychiatry* **44**:307–317.

Helzer, J. E., & Burnam, A. (1991). Epidemiology of alcohol addiction: United States. *In* "Comprehensive Handbook of Drug and Alcohol Addiction" (N. S. Miller, Ed.), pp. 9–38. New York: Decker.

Helzer, J. E., & Pryzbeck, T. R. (1988). The co-occurrence of alcoholism with other psychiatric disorders in the general population and its impact on treatment. *J. Studies Alcohol* **49**:219–224.

Herd, D. (1990). Subgroup differences in drinking patterns among black and white men: Results from a national survey. *J. Studies Alcohol* **55**:61–71.

Herd, D. (1994). Predicting drinking problems among black and white men: Results from a national survey. *J. of Studies on Alcohol* **55**:61–71.

Hester, R. K., & Miller, W. R. (1989). "Handbook of Alcoholism Treatment Approaches: Effective Alternatives." New York: Pergamon Press.

Hollon, S. D., Evans, M. D., & DeRubeis, R. J. (1990). Cognitive mediation of relapse prevention following treatment for depression. Implications for differential risk. *In* "Contemporary Approaches to Depression" (R. E. Ingram, Ed.), pp. 117–136. New York: Plenum Press.

Huberty, D. J. (1975). Treating the adolescent drug abuser: A family affair. *Contemp. Drug Problems* 4(2):179–194.

Huberty, C. E., & Huberty D. J. (1976). Treating the parents of adolescent drug abusers: The necessity for marriage counseling. *Contemp. Drug Problems* 5(4):573–592.

Imhoff, J., Hirsch, R., & Terenzi, R. (1985). AIDS and the substance abuse treatment clinician (editorial). *J. Substance Abuse Treatment* 2:137.

Institute of Medicine (IOM) (1990). Broadening the base of treatment for alcohol problems. Washington, DC: National Academy Press.

Institute of Medicine (IOM) (1995). "Fetal Alcohol Syndrome: Research Base for Diagnostic Criteria, Epidemiology, Prevention and Treatment." Washington, DC: National Academy Press.

Ja, D., & Aoki, B. (1993). Substance abuse treatment: Cultural barriers in the Asian American community. *J. of Psychoactive Drugs* 25(1):61–71.

Jaffe, J. H., & Ciraula, D. A. (1986). Alcoholism and depression. *In* "Psychopathology and Addictive Disorders" (R. E. Meyer, Ed.), pp. 293–320. New York: Guilford Press.

Jelinek, J. M., & Williams, T.(1987). Post-traumatic stress disorder and substance abuse: Treatment problems, strategies, and recommendation. *In* "Post-traumatic Stress Disorders: A Handbook for Clinicians" (T. Williams, Ed.). Cincinnati: Disabled American Veterans.

Johnson, S. L. (1997). "Therapist's Guide to Clinical Intervention." San Diego: Academic Press.

Johnson, J. G., Williams, J. G. W., Raskin, J. G., Goetz, R. R., & Remien, R. H. (1995). Axis I psychiatric symptoms associated with HIV infection and personality disorder. *Am. J. Psychiatry* 152:551–554.

Kaminer, Y. (1996). Adolescent substance abuse and suicidal behavior. *In* "Adolescent Substance Abuse and Dual Disorders. Child Adolescent Psychiatry Clinics in North America" (S. L. Jaffe, Ed.), pp. 59–72. Philadelphia: Saunders.

Kandel, D. B., & Davies, M. (1991). Cocaine use in a national sample of U.S. youth (NISY):Epidemiology, predictors, and ethnic patterns. *In* "The Epidemiology of Cocaine Use and Abuse" (C. Schade & S. Shober, Eds.), NIDA Research Monograph No. 110, pp. 151–188. Washington, DC: U.S. Government Printing Office.

Katz, S., Ford, A. B., Moskowitz, R.W., Jackson, B. A., & Jaffe, M. W. (1963). Studies of illness in the aged. The Index of ADL: A standardized measure of biological and psychosocial function. *J. Am. Med. Assoc.* 185:914–919.

Khantzian, E. J. (1985a). Psychotherapeutic intervention with substance abusers: The clinical context. *J. Substance Abuse Treatment* 2:83–88.

Khantzian, E. J. (1985b). The self-medication hypothesis of addictive disorders: Focus on heroin and cocaine dependence. *Am. J. Psychiatry* 142:1259–1264.

Khantzian, E. J. (1997). The self-medication hypothesis of substance use disorders: A reconsideration and recent applications. *Harvard Rev. Psychiatry* 4:231–244.

Khantzian, E. J., & Treece, C. (1985). DSM-III psychiatric diagnosis of narcotic addicts. *Arch. Gen. Psychiatry* 42:1067–1070.

Khantzian, E. J., Halliday, K. S., & McAuliffe, W. E. (1990). "Addiction and the Vulnerable Self: Modified Dynamic Group Therapy for Substance Abusers." New York: Guilford Press.

Kitano, H. H. L., & Chi, I. (1989). Asian Americans and alcohol: The Chinese, Japanese, Koreans, and Filipinos in Los Angeles. *In* "Alcohol Use among U.S. Ethnic Minorities"(D. Spiegler, D. Tate, S. Aitkins, & C. Christian, Eds.), NIAAA Research Monograph No. 18, DHHS Publication No. ADM 89-1435, pp. 373–382. Washington, DC: U.S. Government Printing Office.

Kofoed, L., Kania, J., Walsh, T., & Atkinson, R. M. (1986). Outpatient treatment of patients with substance abuse and coexisting psychiatric disorders. *Am. J. Psychiatry* 143:867–872.

Kofoed, L., Tolson, R. L., Atkinson, R. M., Toth, R. F., & Turner, J. A. (1987). Treatment compliance of older alcoholics: An elder specific approach is superior to "mainstreaming." *J. Studies Alcohol* **48**:47–51.

Korrapati, M. R., & Vestal, R. E. (1995). Alcohol and medications in the elderly: Complex interactions. *In* "Alcohol and Aging" (T. P. Beresford & E. Gomberg, Eds.), pp. 42–69. New York: Oxford University Press.

Kovner, R., Lazar, J. W., Lesser, M., Perecman, E., Kaplan, M. H., Hainline, B., & Napolitano, B. (1992). Use of the dementia rating scale as a test for neuropsychological dysfunction in HIV-positive IV drug abusers. *J. Substance Abuse Treatment* **9**:133–137.

Kranzler, H. R., & Liebowitz, N. R. (1988). Anxiety and depression in substance abuse. Clinical implications. *Med. Clin. North America* **72**:867–885.

Krystal, H. (1982). Character disorders: Characterological specificity and the alcoholic. *In* "Encyclopedia Handbook of Alcoholism" (E. M. Pattison & E. Kaufman, Eds.), pp. 607–618. New York: Gardner Press.

Kubler-Ross, E. (1969). "On Death and Dying." New York: MacMillan.

Kurtines, W. M., Ball, L. R., & Wood, G. H. (1978). Personality characteristics of long term recovered alcoholics:A comparative analysis. *J. Consult. Clin. Psychol.* **46**(5):971–977.

Kushner, M. G., Sher, K. J., & Bertman, B. D. (1990). The relation between alcohol problems and anxiety disorders. *Am. J. Psychiatry* **147**:685–695.

Kushner, M. G., Kachur, E., & Marton (1992). Substance use among adolescents with chronic mental illness:A pilot study of descriptive and differentiating features. *Can. J. Psychiatry* **37**:428–431.

Kutcher, S., Kachur, E., & Marton, P. (1992). Substance use among adolescents with chronic mental illness: A pilot study of descriptive and differentiating features. *Can. J. of Psychiatry* **37**:428–431.

LaFromboise, T. D., Trimble, J. E., & Mohatt, G. V. (1990). Counseling intervention and American Indian tradition. An integrative approach. *Counseling Psychologist* **18**(4):628–654.

Land, H., Ed. (1992). "AIDS: A Complete Guide to Psychosocial Intervention." Milwaukee, WI: Family Service America.

Lawton, M. P., Moss, M., Fulcomer, M., & Kleban, M. H. (1982). A research and service oriented multilevel assessment instrument. *J. Gerontol.* **37**:91–99.

Lehman, A. F., Myers, C. P., & Corty, E. C. (1989). Assessment and classification of patients with psychiatric and substance abuse syndromes. *Hosp. Community Psychiatry* **40**:1019–1030.

Leigh, B. C., & Stall, R. (1993). Substance use and risky sexual behavior for exposure to HIV. *Am. Psychologist* **48**:1035–1045.

Levin, F. R., & Kleber, H. D. (1995). Attention deficit/hyperactivity disorder and substance abuse: Relationships and implications for treatment. *Harvard Rev. Psychiatry* **2**:246–258.

Leverich, G. S., Post, R. M., & Ross, A. S. (1990). Factors associated with relapse during maintenance treatment for affective disorders. *Int. Clin. Psychopharmacol.* **5**:135–156.

Lewinsohn, P. M., Rohde, P., & Seeley, J. R. (1993). Adolescent psychopathology:III. The clinical consequences of comorbidity. *J. Am. Acad. Child Adolescent Psychiatry* **34**:510–519.

Lewinsohn, P. M., Rohde, P., & Seeley, J. R. (1996). Alcohol consumption in high school adolescents:Frequency of use and dimensional structure of associated problems. *Addiction* **91**: 375–390.

Lewis, R., & Ho, M. (1989). Social work with Native Americans. *In* "Counseling American Minority" (D. Atkinson, G. Morten, & D. Sue, Eds.), pp. 51–58. Dubuque, IA: William C. Brown Publisher.

Liberto, J. G., Oslin, D. W., & Ruskin, P. E. (1992). Alcoholism in older persons: A review of the literature. *Hosp. and Comm. Psychiatry* **43**:975–984.

Linnoila, M. (1989). Anxiety and alcoholism. *J. Clin. Psychiatry* **50**(11):26–29.

Mahler, M. (1968). "On Human Symbiosis and the Vacissitudes of Individuation." New York: International University Press.

Malatesta, V. J., Pollack, R. H., Crotty, T. D., & Peacock, L. J. (1982). Acute alcohol intoxication and female orgasmic response. *Journal of Sex Research* **18**:1–17.

Marlatt, G. A., & Gordon, J. R. (1985). "Relapse Prevention: Maintenance Strategies in the Treatment of Addictive Behaviors." New York:Guilford Press.

Marlowe, D. B., Kirby, K. C., Festinger, D. S., Husband, S. D., & Platt, J. J. (1997). Impact of comorbid personality disorders and personality disorder symptoms on outcome of behavioral treatment for cocaine dependence. *J. Nervous Mental Dis.* **185**(8):483–490.

McGoldrick, M., Pearce, J. K., & Giordano, J., Eds. (1996). "Ethnicity and Family Therapy," 2nd ed. New York: Guilford.

McKirnan, D. J., & Peterson, P. L. (1989). Alcohol and drug abuse among homosexual men and women: Epidemiology and population characteristics. *Addictive Behaviors* **14**:545–553.

Mercer-McFadden, C., & Drake, R. E. (1995). "A Review of 13 NIMH Demonstration Projects for Young Adults with Severe Mental Illness and Substance Abuse Problems." Rockville, MD: Community Support Program, Center for Mental Health Services, U.S. Department of Health and Human Services.

Miller, N. S., & Doot, M. C. (Eds.), (1994). Principals of addiction medicine: Section XVI. "Women, Children and Addiction." Chevy Chase, MD: American Society of Addiction Medium.

Miller, W. R., & Rollnick, S. (1991). "Motivational Interviewing: Preparing People to Change Addictive Behavior." New York: Guilford Press.

Mirin, S. M., & Weiss, R. D. (1991). Substance abuse and mental illness. *In* "Clinical Textbook of Addictive Disorders" (R. J. Frances & S. I. Miller, Eds.), pp. 271–298. New York: Guilford Press.

Moos, R. H., Mertens, J. R., & Brennan, P. L. (1993). Patterns of diagnosis and treatment among late middle aged and older substance abuse patients. *J. Studies Alcohol* **54**:479–487.

Moos, R. H., Brennan, P. L., & Mertens, J. R. (1994a). Diagnostic subgroup and predictors of one-year readmission among late middle aged and older substance use patients. *J. Studies Alcohol* **55**:173–183.

Moos, R. H., Mertens, J. R., & Brennan, P. L. (1994b). Rates and predictors of four year readmission among late middle aged and older substance abuse patients. *J. Studies Alcohol* **55**:561–570.

Morrison, M. A., Knauf, K. J., & Hayes, H. R. (1989). A comprehensive treatment model. *Alcoholism Addiction*, 12–17.

Moscicki, E. K. (1995). Epidemiology of suicide. *Intl. Psychogeriatrics* **7**:137–148.

Moss, H. B., Kirisci, L., Gordon, H. W., & Tarter, K. E. (1994). A neuropsychological profile of adolescent alcoholism. *Alcoholism: Clinical and Experimental Research* **18**:159–163.

Moss, H. B., & Tartar, R. E. (1993). Substance abuse, aggression, and violence: Where are the connections? *Am. J. Addiction* **2**:149–160.

Myers, J. K., Weissman, M. M., Tischler, G. L., Holzer, C. E., Leaf, P. J., Orvaschel, H., Anthony, J. C., Boyd, J. H., Burke, J. D., Kamer, M., & Stoltzman, R. (1984). Six month prevalence of psychiatric disorders in three-communities. *Archives of General Psychiatry* **41**:959–967.

Nace, E. P., Davis, C. W., & Gaspair, J. P. (1991). Axis II comorbidity in substance abusers. *Am. J. Psychiatry* **148**:118–120.

Najavits, L. M., Weiss, R. D., Shaw, S. R., & Muenz, L. R. (1998). "Safety-seeking:" Outcome of a new cognitive–behavioral psychotherapy for women with posttraumatic stress disorder and substance dependence. *J. Traumatic Stress* **11**(3):437–456.

National Council on Patient Information and Education (NCPIE), 666 11th St., Suite 810, Washington, DC 2001.

National Institute of Alcohol Abuse and Alcoholism (1974). "An Assessment of the Needs of and Resources for the Children of Alcoholic Parents," PB 241, 119. Rockville, MD: National Institute of Alcohol Abuse and Alcoholism.

National Institute on Drug Abuse (1990). "National Household Survey on Drug Abuse." Rockville, MD.

National Institute on Drug Abuse (1994). "National Household Survey on Drug Abuse." Rockville, MD.

NIDA Infofox, National Institute of Health. http://www.drugabuse.gov, ph: 1-888 644 6432, fax: 301 8977 400.

Nielsen, L. A. (1984). Sexual abuse and chemical dependency: Assessing the risk for women alcoholics and adult children. *Focus Family Chem. Dependency* 7(6):10–11.

Nobles, W. W., & Goddard, L. (1989). Drugs in the African American community: A clear and present danger. *In* "The State of Black America" (J. Dewart, Ed.). New York: The National Urban League.

North, R. L., & Rothenberg, K. H. (1993). Partner notification and the threat of domestic violence against women with HIV infection. *New Engl. J. Med.* 329:1194–1196.

O'Malley, S. S., Kosten, T. R., & Penner, J. A., Jr. (1990). Dual diagnosis: Substance abuse and personality disorders. *New Directions Mental Health Services* 47:125–137.

O'Malley, P. M., Johnston, L. D., & Bachman, J. G. (1995). Adolescent substance use: Epidemiology and implications for problem solving. *In* "Substance Use. Pediatric Clinical North America" (P. D. Rogers, & M. J. Werner, Eds.), pp. 241–260. Philadelphia : Saunders.

Osher, F. I., & Kofoed, L. (1989). Treatment of patients with psychiatric disorders and psychoactive substance abuse disorders. *Hosp. Community Psychiatry* 40:1025–1030.

Ouimette, P. C., Gima, K., Moos, R. H., & Finney, J. W. (1999). A comparative evaluation of substance abuse treatment IV. The effect of comorbid psychiatric diagnosis on amount of treatment, continuing care, and 1 year outcomes. 23(3):552–557.

Paul, J. P. (1991). Clean, sober and safe. "18th Street Services Group Client Workbook." San Francisco, CA.

Perry, S., & Jacobsen, P. (1986). Neuropsychiatric manifestation of AIDS-spectrum disorders. *Hosp. Community Psychiatry* 37:135–142.

Pettinati, H. M., Pierce, J. D., Belden, P. P., & Myers, K. (1999). The relationship of Axis II personality disorders to other known predictors of addiction outcome. *Am. J. Addiction* 8:136–147.

Piercy, F., & Frankel, B. (1989). The evolution of an integrative family therapy for substance-abusing adolescents. Toward the mutual enhancement of research and practice. *J. Family Psychol.* 2:149–171.

Price, R. W., & Perry, S. W., III (1994). "HIV, AIDS and the Brain." New York: Raven Press.

Prochanka, J. O., DiClemente, C. C., & Norcross, J. C. (1997). In search of how people change: Applications to addictive behaviors. *A. Psychologist* 47:1102–1114.

Radloff, L. S. (1977). The CES-D Scale: A self-report depression scale for research in the general population. *Applied Psychol. Measurement* 1(3):385–401.

Raskin, V. D. (1992). Maternal bereavement in the perinatal substance abuser. *J. Substance Abuse Treatment* 9:149–152.

Regier, D. A., Farmer, M. E., Rae, D. S., Locke, B. Z., Keith, S. J., Judd, L. L., & Goodwin, F. R. (1990). Comorbidity of mental disorders with alcohol and other drug abuse. *J. Am. Med. Assoc.* 264:2511–2518.

Rohde, P., Lewinsohn, P. M., & Seeley, J. R. (1996). Psychiatric comorbidity with problematic alcohol use in high school students. *J. Am. Acad. Child Adolescent Psychiatry* 35:101–109.

Rosenheck, R., & Seibyl, C. L. (1998). Participation and outcome in a residential treatment and work therapy program for addiction disorders. The effects of race. *Am. J. Psychiatry* **155**:1029–1034.

Ross, H. E., Glaser, F. B., & Germanson, T. (1988). The prevalence of psychiatric disorders in patients with alcohol and other drug problems. *Arch. Gen. Psychiatry* **45**:1023–1031.

Roth, M. (1989). Anxiety disorders and the use and abuse of drugs. *J. Clin. Psychiatry* **50**(Suppl. 11): 30–42.

Ruiz, P., Langrod, J., & Alksche, L. (1981). Rehabilitation of the Puerto Rican addict: A cultural perspective. *Intl. J. of Addictions* **16**(5):841–847.

Ruiz, R. A., & Padillo, A. M. (1977). Counseling Latinos. *Personnel Guidance J.*, **55**.

Russel, M., Martier, S. S., Sokol, R. J., Jacobson, S., Jacobson, J., & Bottoms, S. (1991). Screening for pregnancy risk-drinking: TWEAKING the tests (abstract). Alcoholism: *Clin. Exp. Res.* **15**(2):368.

Schliefer, S. J., DeLaney, B. R., Tross, S., & Keller, S. E. (1991). AIDS and addictions. *In* "Clinical Textbook of Addictive Disorders" (R. J. Frances & S. I. Miller, Eds.), pp. 299–319. New York: Guilford Press.

Schlossberger, E., & Hecker, L. (1996). HIV and family therapist's duty to warn: A legal and ethical analysis. *J. Marital Family Ther.* **22**:27–40.

Schonfeld, L., & Dupree, L. W. (1991). Antecedents of drinking for early and late onset elderly alcohol abusers. *J. Studies Alcohol* **52**:587–592.

Schottenfeld, R., Carroll, K., & Rounsaville, B. (1993). Comorbid psychiatric disorders and cocaine abuse. *In* "Cocaine Treatment:Research and Clinical Perspectives." (F. K. Tims & C. G. Leukefeld, Eds.), Research Monograph No. 135, pp. 31–47. Rockville, MD: National Institute on Drug Abuse.

Schuckit, M. (1979). Geriatric alcoholism and drug abuse. *Gerontologist* **17**:168–174.

Sciacca, K. (1991). An integrated treatment approach for severely mentally ill individuals with substance disorders. *In* "Dual Diagnosis of Major Mental Illness with Substance Disorder" (K. Minkoff & R. E. Drake, Eds.), pp. 69–84. San Francisco: Jossey-Bass.

Sheikh, J. I., & Yesavage, J. A. (1986). Geriatric Depression Scale (GDS): Recent evidence and development of a shorter version. *Clin. Gerontol.* **5**(1&2):165–173.

Sigvardsson, S., Bokman, M., & Cloninger, C. R. (1996). Replication of the Stockholm adoption study of alcoholism: Confirmatory cross-fastering analysis. *Archives of Gen. Psych.* **53**(8):681–687.

Simon, A., Epstein, L. J., & Reynolds, L. (1968). Alcoholism in the geriatric mentally ill. *Geriatrics* **23**:125–131.

Smith, D. (1989). The role of substance abuse professions in the AIDS epidemic. *Adv. Alcohol Substance Abuse* **7**:175–195.

Smith, D., Buxton, M. E., Bilal, R., & Seymour, R. B. (1993). Cultural points of resistance to the 12-step recovery process. *J. Psychoactive Drugs* **25**:97–108.

Stall (1986). Change and stability in quantity and frequency of alcohol use among aging males: A 19 year follow-up study. *Br. J. Addiction* **81**:537–544.

Stratton, K., Howe, C., Battaglia, F., & Institute of Medicine (1995). "Fetal Alcohol Syndrome: Diagnosis, Epidemiology, Prevention, and Treatment." Washington, DC: National Academy Press.

Sue, D. (1981). "Counseling the Culturally Different." New York: Wiley.

Sue, S. (1988). Psychotherapeutic services for ethnic minorities. *Am. Psychologist* **43**:301–308.

Sue, S., & McKinney, H. (1975). Asian Americans in the community mental health system. *Am. J. Orthopsychiatry* **45**:111–118.

Szapocanik, J., & Fein, S. (1995). "Issues in Preventing Alcohol and Other Drug Abuse among Hispanic/Latino Families," CSAP Cultural Competencies Series 2, DHHS Publication No. SMA 95-3034. Washington, DC: U.S. Government Printing Office.

Takaki, R. (1990). "Iron Cages: Race and Culture in 19th Century America." New York: Oxford University Press.

The Brown University Digest of Addiction Theory and Application (DATA), September 1998, **17**(9).

The Harvard Mental Health Letter, December 1998, **15**(6):1–4.

Thomas, V. H., Melchert, T. P., & Banken, J. A. (1999). Substance dependence and personality disorders: Comorbidity and treatment outcome in an inpatient treatment population. *J. Studies Alcohol* **60**:271–277.

Thomason, T. C. (1991). Counseling Native Americans: An introduction for non-Native American counselors. *J. Counseling Dev.* **69**:321–328.

Tucker, C. (1990). Acute pain and substance abuse in surgical patients. *J. Neurosci. Nursing* **22**:339–349.

Uziel-Miller, N. D., Lyons, J. S., Kissel, C., & Love, S. (1998). Treatment needs and initial outcomes of a residential recovery program for African American women and their children. *Am. J. Addiction* **7**:43–50.

Walker, L. E. (1979). "The Battered Woman." New York: Harper and Ross.

Walker, L. E. (1983). The battered woman syndrome study. *In* "The Dark Side of Families: Current Family Violence Research" (D. Finkelhor, R. S. Gelees, G. Hottaling, & M. Straus, Eds.). Beverly Hills, CA: Sage Production.

Wallace, B. C. (1992). Treatment models for special groups: Criminal, pregnant, uninsured, adolescent, HIV positive, methadone-maintained, and homeless populations. *In* "The Chemically Dependent: Phases of Treatment and Recovery" (B. C. Wallace, Ed.), pp. 310–336. New York: Bruner/Mazel.

Wallace, B. C. (1993). Cross-cultural counseling with the chemically dependent: Preparing for service delivery within our culture of violence. *J. Psychoactive Drugs* **24**(3):9–20.

Wallen, M. C., & Weiner, H. D. (1989). Impediments to the effective treatment of the dually diagnosed patient. *J. Psychoactive Drugs* **21**(2):161–168.

Washton, A. W. (1989). Preventing relapse to cocaine. *J. Clin. Psychiatry* **49**:34–38.

Weider, H., & Kaplan, H. (1969). Drug use in adolescents: Psychodynamic theory and pharmacogenic effect. *Psychoanal. Study Child* **24**:399–431.

Weisman, M. M., & Myers J. K. (1980). Clinical depression in alcoholism. *Am. J. Psychiatry* **137**:372–373.

Williams, T., Ed. (1987). "Posttraumatic Stress Disorder: A Handbook for Clinicians." Cinncinati, OH: Disabled American Veterans.

Winiarski, M. G. (1991). "AIDS-Related Psychotherapy." Elmsford, New York: Pergamon Press.

Young, E. B. (1990). The role of incest issues in relapse. *J. Psychoactive Drugs* **22**:249–258.

Zimberg, S. (1990). Management of alcoholism in the elderly. *Addictions Nursing Network* **2**:4–6.

Zinberg, N. (1984). "Drug, Set, and Setting." New Haven, CT: Yale University Press.

Zweben, J. E. (1992). Issues in the treatment of the dual-diagnosed patient. *In* "The Chemically Dependent: Phases of Treatment and Recovery" (B. C. Wallace, Ed.), pp. 298–309. New York: Brunner/Mazel.

Part V

Chapter 10

Skill Building Resources

Hope

Opportunity

Motivational

Ego strengthening

Working through

Ownership of change

Relapse prevention

Knowledge

To ensure the best use of these resources for each individual's personal growth with associated changes in thinking and behaving, remember the following:

1. There are variations of some homework assignments, which provide more than one approach for achieving an identified task.
2. Homework exercises can be modified to fit the specific details of an individual and his or her circumstances.

RISK FACTORS FOR SUBSTANCE ABUSE

As part of a continuing effort to help parents prevent drug and alcohol problems with their children, the following risk factors below need to be explored:

1. Family history of alcoholism
2. Family management problems
3. Early antisocial behavior
4. Parental drug use and positive attitude toward use
5. Academic failure
6. Little commitment to school
7. Alienation, rebelliousness, and lack of bonding to society
8. Antisocial behavior at early adolescence
9. Friends who use drugs
10. Favorable attitude toward drug use
11. Early first use of drugs
12. Experience of abuse (emotional, physical, sexual)
13. Closed family system
14. Experience of social anxiety
15. Lack of goals

CONSEQUENCES OF SUBSTANCE ABUSE

Following is a list of *some* of the consequences of substance abuse.

1. Loss of control when using
   a. getting into trouble
   b. fighting and arguing
   c. poor judgment
   d. embarrassing behavior
   e. blackouts

2. Physical functioning
   a. feeling ill (hangover–crash)
   b. dependence on substances
   c. increased deterioration (often ignored by person using substances)
   d. health risks (heart, brain, nervous system, digestive system, liver, immune system, and reproductive); potential problems vary per substance

3. Social roles
   a. problems with work or school
   b. legal problems
   c. deterioration in social skills
   d. risk taking behavior
   e. difficulty coping

4. Relationships
   a. interpersonal difficulties
      i. partner
      ii. family
      iii. friends
   b. intrapersonal difficulties
      i. disappointed in self
      ii. low self-esteem–lack of self-worth
      iii. feelings of guilt

5. Mood
   a. mood swings
   b. feeling overwhelmed and avoiding
   c. numb
   d. decreased motivation, "don't care"

SIX CARDINAL SIGNS INDICATING
SUBSTANCE DEPENDENCE

The diagnosis can be made if two or more of these signs are present. Under each, write down what you recognize in yourself.

1. Denial: Minimizes, defensive, blaming.

2. Preoccupation: Time, money, and energy are spent to get substances; boasting, reminiscing, and anticipating; do "just about anything" to get substance.

3. Loss of control: Urgency of first drink; larger amounts over longer time; "blackouts;" attempts to limit use fail; using alone; hiding the "evidence" of use; regrets afterward; using to escape worries.

4. Continued use despite negative consequences: Complaints–trouble with family, friends, employer; neglected responsibilities; health problems; legal problems.

5. Change in tolerance: More needed to get same effects; lower tolerance in late stage of alcoholism.

6. Withdrawal symptoms: Withdrawal and intoxication interfere with everyday responsibilities; abrupt symptoms after discontinuation of substance use.

SYMPTOMS OF ALCOHOLISM

The diagnosis of alcoholism is made primarily from obtaining a history of a drinking pattern that is predominantly not social drinking. Elicitation of a history of any consequences that result from this nonsocial drinking pattern reflects the seriousness or the degree of the alcoholism.

The following list represents a nonsocial, or pathological, use of alcohol.

1. Preoccupation with alcohol or the next opportunity to drink.
2. Gulping drinks. The alcoholic usually drinks a double or downs the first couple of drinks rapidly.
3. Increased tolerance for alcohol. The alcoholic can usually drink much more than others and still function relatively well.
4. Drinking alone. This includes drinking in bars, but alone.
5. Use of alcohol as a medicine for relief of tension or anxiety or as an aid to sleep.
6. Blackout. Drinking sufficiently such that the next morning brings amnesia for some of the events of the previous evening.
7. Secluded bottle. Have a bottle hidden in the home or somewhere in case a drink is needed.
8. Nonpremeditated drinking. Drinking much more than planned or drinking differently from what was planned.
9. Morning tremors. Fine tremor of fingers from overindulgence.
10. Morning drink. To help one over a hangover.

If 4 or more of the 10 criteria are fulfilled, this constitutes a problematic nonsocial drinking pattern and a positive diagnosis of alcoholism.

DO I HAVE A DRINKING PROBLEM?

Most alcoholics today are unrecognized as such by themselves or by others. They are unaware that their drinking pattern is different, and they subconsciously defend themselves quite effectively from this knowledge. Therefore, considerable skill is needed in choosing the right questions to ask the suspected alcoholic in order to secure an accurate history. The following questions for each of the 10 criteria listed are suggested.

1. Preoccupation
   a. Do you ever look forward to the end of a day's work so that you can have a couple of drinks and relax?
   b. Do you sometimes look forward to the end of the week so that you can have some fun drinking?
   c. Does the thought of drinking sometimes enter your mind when you should be thinking of something else?
   d. Do you sometimes feel the need to have a drink at a particular time of the day?

2. Gulping Drinks
   a. Do you usually order a double or like to have your first two or three drinks quickly?
   b. Do you sometimes have a couple of drinks before going to a party or out to dinner?

3. Increased Tolerance
   a. Do you find that you can often drink more than others and not show it too much?
   b. Has anyone ever commented on your ability to hold your liquor?
   c. Have you ever wondered about your increased capacity to drink and perhaps felt somewhat proud of it?

4. Use of Alcohol as a Medicine
   a. Do you ever drink to calm your nerves or reduce tension?
   b. Do you find it difficult to enjoy a party or dance if there is nothing to drink?
   c. Do you ever use alcohol as a nightcap to help you get to sleep at night?
   d. Do you ever use alcohol to relieve physical discomfort?

5. Drinking Alone
   a. Do you ever stop in a bar and have a couple of drinks by yourself?
   b. Do you sometimes drink at home alone or when no one else is drinking?

6. Blackout
   a. In the morning after an evening of drinks, have you ever had the experience of not being able to remember everything that happened on the night before?
   b. Have you ever had difficulty recalling how you got home after a night's drinking?

7. Secluded Bottle
   a. Do you sometimes hide a bottle in the house in the event you may need a drink some time?
   b. Do you ever keep a bottle in the trunk of your car just in case you may need a drink?

8. Nonpremeditated Drinking
   a. Do you ever stop in to have two or three drinks and have several more than you planned?
   b. Do you ever find yourself stopping in for a drink when you had planned to go straight home or someplace else?

c. Are you sometimes one of the last ones to leave a bar or a drinking party when you had planned to go home earlier in the evening?

d. Do you sometimes drink more than you think you should?

e. Is your drinking sometimes different from what you would like it to be?

9. Morning Tremors

a. Have you ever had the shakes or tremors of the hands after a night of drinking?

10. Morning Drink

a. Have you ever taken a drink in the morning to help you over a hangover?

If a therapist is not sure of the diagnosis of alcoholism after a review of the drinking history, then an exploration of the possible complications or consequences of drinking is necessary. As a result of drinking, a problem in any **ONE** of the following areas is all that is necessary to establish a diagnosis of alcoholism.

1. Marital

a. Does your partner think you drink too much?

b. Does your partner object to your drinking?

c. Has your partner ever threatened to leave you because of your drinking?

2. Economic

a. Do you ever drink although sometimes you cannot afford to?

3. Industrial

a. Have you ever missed work because of a hangover?

b. Have you ever lost a job because of drinking?

c. Has drinking ever caused you to be less efficient at work?

d. Have you ever been threatened with loss of job because of drinking?

4. Physical

a. Has a doctor ever told you to cut down or stop drinking for any reason at all?

b. Have you ever been hospitalized because of drinking or from a complication due to your drinking?

5. Social

a. Do you have a very definite preference to associate with people who drink rather than those who do not?

b. Do you sometimes do things while drinking and are ashamed later?

c. Has drinking become so important or time consuming that previous hobbies or interests are neglected?

PROBLEM DRINKER

The following situations indicate that a person has a problem with alcohol. Here is the affirmation to get help for yourself, whether you are the person with a drinking problem or the significant other of someone with a drinking problem.

1. Anyone who by his or her own personal definition or by the definition of his or her immediate family (friends) has been intoxicated four times a year is a problem drinker.

2. Anyone who goes to work intoxicated is a problem drinker.

3. Anyone who must drink in order to get to and perform at work is a problem drinker.

4. Anyone who was intoxicated and drives a car is a problem drinker.

5. Anyone who sustains bodily injury requiring medical attention as a consequence of an intoxicated state is a problem drinker.

6. Anyone who experiences a lot of conflict as a consequence of an intoxicated state is a problem drinker.

7. Anyone who under the influence of alcohol does something he or she contends he or she would never do without alcohol is a problem drinker.

8. Anyone who has become dependent on alcohol as a way of life and is uncomfortable in situations where no alcohol is available is a problem drinker.

9. Anyone who frequently, progressively loses the capacity to drink according to his or her intentions is a problem drinker.

10. Anyone whose work performance or attendance is impaired by his or her own use of alcohol is a problem drinker.

SUBSTANCE USE OR ABUSE: DIAGNOSING DEPENDENCY

Dependence on substances is a widespread problem, though often people do not recognize it. Substance dependence is an inability to control the use of a substance. In other words, not being able to quit or not being able to limit the amount used.

Symptoms of substance dependency:

1. Not been able to cut down or quit

2. Lapses of memory or "blackouts"

3. Using substances alone

4. Hiding the evidence of substance use

5. Using substances in an effort to forget about problems

6. Regretting things done while under the influence

7. Not being able to enjoy activities without substance use

8. Using more than others at social gatherings

9. Neglecting responsibilities in order to use substances

10. People expressing concern about substance use

11. Willing to do almost anything to get a substance

12. Financial or legal problems as a result of substance use

13. The loss of an important relationship

What needs to be done:

1. Acknowledge the problem

2. Get help—and abstain

3. Learn how to deal with problems and recover

SELF-DIAGNOSIS: DO YOU HAVE A PROBLEM WITH SUBSTANCE USE?

Sometimes substance abuse and dependence are difficult for an individual to recognize because he or she evaluates his or her life and sees that he or she has a job and family and has not had financial or legal problems. The individual does not think that his or her life has become unmanageable. However, when many of these people use substances, there are problems. Therefore, when self-diagnosing, focus on the influence of substance use upon behavior, relationships, finances, etc.

	Yes	No
1. Have you ever lost or forgot what you did with your Social Security or SSI check because of alcohol or drug use?	_____	_____
2. Do you ever use alcohol or drugs to cope with your disability?	_____	_____
3. Do you ever use alcohol or illicit drugs to cope with physical pain?	_____	_____
4. Do you ever use prescribed medication for either physical or psychological pain?	_____	_____
5. Is alcohol or drug use affecting your disability?	_____	_____
6. Do you seek admission to hospitals because alcohol or drug use has caused complications with your disability?	_____	_____
7. Do you use alcohol or drugs to build your self-confidence?	_____	_____
8. Do you look for your physician to treat your disability as opposed to treating your problem with alcohol or drug use?	_____	_____
9. Have you ever had a complete loss of memory because of your alcohol or drug use?	_____	_____
10. Have you ever fallen out of your wheelchair or, if blind, fallen or walked into a barrier because of alcohol or drug use?	_____	_____
11. Do you drink or use drugs alone?	_____	_____
12. Do you drink or use drugs to escape the realities of your disability?	_____	_____
13. If you are deaf, do you use alcohol or drugs to deal with the frustration of your deafness?	_____	_____
14. Has anyone ever suggested to you that you have a drinking or drug use problem?	_____	_____
15. Have you ever received (by mistake) any medication through the mail or clinic and not returned it?	_____	_____

16. Have you ever lost your balance and/or fallen due to being under the influence of drugs or alcohol?   _____   _____

17. Have you ever missed an appointment because you were covering up a hangover?   _____   _____

18. Do you like to associate with people who abuse drugs, medication, and/or alcohol?   _____   _____

19. If your disability is a result of a traumatic injury, did drugs or alcohol have anything to do with it?   _____   _____

20. Is drug, medication, and/or alcohol use a very important part of you or your family's lifestyle?   _____   _____

RELATIONSHIP ADDICTION

When considering this possibility that you may experience addictive issues in the realm of relationships, the key is to understand who you are and why you make the decisions that you do in relationships. To help you explore these issues, keep a journal about how the following statements apply to you. Self-awareness is the first step toward change.

1. You grew up in a home where emotional needs were not met.
2. Growing up, you lacked the feeling of security.
3. You have low self-esteem and feel unworthy of being happy.
4. You learned as a child how to "predict" what you needed to do to please people.
5. You are attracted to partners that are emotionally unavailable, which is similar to your experience as a child with your parents.
6. You have a tendency to seek out needy partners and become their caregiver, trying to fill your own need for nurturing that you did not receive as a child.
7. You generally take responsibility for more than half of the problems in the relationship.
8. Out of your fear of rejection and abandonment, you will do almost anything to keep from losing a relationship.
9. You have a strong need for control in a relationship.
10. You dream of how it could be instead of dealing with the reality of how it is.
11. While it hurts to not get your needs met in a relationship, you stay because it is familiar to you.
12. When you don't get the love you want, you give more, try harder, and are willing to wait in the hopes of being loved and cared for.
13. You are drawn to people who have problems and become enmeshed in their chaos, while avoiding taking responsibility for yourself. (You avoid dealing with yourself by remaining focused on the problems of others.)
14. You are not attracted to people who are attentive, caring, and interested in you.
15. You find nice people boring.
16. You have a history of depression.
17. You look for a relationship to make you happy instead of working on the inside and making yourself happy by being the best you can be.
18. You are overly helpful and do everything as a way to control your relationships.
19. You choose partners who are emotionally unavailable and think you can change them.
20. You may be predisposed to substance abuse and addiction, such as addiction to food, etc.

COMPULSIVE GAMBLING

If you are questioning whether or not you have a gambling problem, or others are telling you that you have a problem and are in denial, the following information may help you clarify what is the reality and what you need to do.

1. Has gambling ever led to arguments and fights with those close to you?
2. Has gambling affected the way that people think about you?
3. Has gambling influenced people's trust in you?
4. Have you ever experienced feelings of guilt or embarrassment following gambling?
5. Have you ever missed work because of gambling?
7. Have you ever gambled away money that was needed for rent, food, or other bills?
8. Have you neglected the needs of your family?
9. After losing at gambling do you feel that you would be lucky if you could get right back to it?
10. After winning do you feel compelled to continue to win more?
11. Have you ever gambled until you didn't have any money left?
12. Have you ever borrowed money or sold possessions to gamble?
13. Have you ever set aside money for gambling and been resistant to using it for more or family needs?
14. When something good happens, do you want to celebrate by gambling?
15. Do you think that your gambling is self-destructive?
16. Have you ever stayed and gambled longer than you had expected to?
17. When you get upset and frustrated, do you want to gamble?
18. Do you ever gamble to avoid worry, stress or trouble?
19. Have you ever considered or done something illegal to get money for gambling?
20. Do you sometimes think about gambling so much that you can't sleep?
21. Has gambling ever negatively affected your being effective in your life?
22. Do you feel like you can't stop gambling?

Adapted from The Twelve Step Program of Gamblers Anonymous

SEXUAL ADDICTION

If you question whether or not you have a sex addiction problem, or someone has ever tried to bring such a problem to your attention, you may use the following information to clarify if you do indeed have such a problem.

1. Do you obsess about sex, thinking about it all of the time?
2. Have you ever considered getting professional help for sexual thoughts or behaviors?
3. Do you feel controlled by sex?
4. Do you think you would be better off if you weren't controlled by sex?
5. Have you ever tried to modify or stop the sexual behaviors that are causing you a problem (or could cause you a problem)?
6. Does your sexual thinking and behavior cause problems between you and your partner?
7. When you experience stress and anxiety, do you use sex as an escape?
8. If sexual overtures are made to you, are you able to resist?
9. During sex, do you have other images, memories or fantasies?
10. Have you ever felt depressed or guilty after sex?
11. Do you feel that your sexual needs, thoughts and behaviors are self-destructive or self-defeating?
12. Do you have serial relationships or serial lovers?
13. Do you ever think that the right relationship would resolve your sexual obsession?
14. Have you ever been careless in pursuing sex?
15. Has pursuing sex ever interfered with your work?
16. Do you want to escape a sexual partner when sex is over?
17. Has your pursuit of sex ever potentially harmed your family or put them at risk?
18. Do you feel a need to masturbate or have sex with others even though you are very compatible with your partner?
19. Do you shop for sex in neighborhoods that you would not otherwise visit?
20. Have your sexual thoughts and behaviors affected your self-esteem?
21. Has your obsession with sex interfered with your effectiveness in taking care of responsibilities?
22. Do you feel like you can't stop your sexually obsessive thoughts and behaviors?

Adapted from Sexaholics Anonymous

SUBSTANCE DEPENDENCY: A FAMILY ILLNESS

These questions are to be answered by family members. Please answer these questions with as much honesty as possible. Circle the questions to which you answer yes.

1. Do you lose sleep because of a substance user?
2. Do most of your thoughts revolve around the problem user or the problems that arise because of him or her?
3. Do you make exact promises about the substances that are not kept?
4. Do you make threats or decisions about the substances and then not follow through on them?
5. Has your attitude changed toward the substance user (alternating between love and hate)?
6. Do you mark, hide, dilute, and/or empty bottles or bags of substances?
7. Do you think that everything would be okay if only the substance user would stop or control his or her use?
8. Do you feel alone, fearful, anxious, angry, or frustrated most of the time?
9. Do you find your mood fluctuating as a result of the substance problem in your life?
10. Do you feel responsible and guilty about the substance problem?
11. Do you try to conceal, deny, and protect the substance user?
12. Have you withdrawn from outside activities and friends because of embarrassment and shame associated with the substance use?
13. Have you taken over many responsibilities that would normally be the substance abuser's?
14. Do you feel like you have no choice but to take more control over many or all of the family responsibilities?
15. Do you feel the need to justify your actions and attitudes and at the same time feel that you are superior to the substance user?
16. If there are children in the home, do they often take sides with the substance user or the other parent?
17. Are the children showing signs of emotional stress, such as withdrawing, having trouble with authority figures, or acting out?
18. Have you experienced physical symptoms associated with stress, such as stomach problems, headaches, shakiness, etc.?
19. Do you feel helpless that nothing you say or do will change the substance user?
20. Do you fear or believe that the substance user cannot get better?

Share your answers to these questions with your therapist. You may find it helpful to write about every question to which you answered yes. Writing will offer you more information on the extent to which your life has been affected by substance use. Once you have this information, you can begin to develop your own recovery program. Self-responsibility is the key to healing.

UNDERSTANDING THE DYNAMICS OF THE CHEMICALLY DEPENDENT FAMILY

Circle or underline the descriptors that clarify individual and family functioning.

	Dependent	Chief enabler	Hero	Scapegoat	Lost child	Mascot
Motivating inner feeling	Shame Guilt Pain Fear Hurt	Anger Hurt Pain Fear Guilt	Inadequacy Hurt Lonliness Guilt Confusion Anger	Lonliness Fear Rejection Hurt Anger Betrayal	Lonliness Hurt Inadequacy Anger Invisible Unimportant	Fear Insecurity Confusion Lonliness

Wall of defenses	Perfectionism
	Righteousness
	Grandiosity
	Charming
	Aggression
	Rigidity
	Anger
		Hyperresponsible
		Powerlessness
		Self-pity
		Self-blaming
		Seriousness
		Fragile
		Manipulative
		Indirect
			Hyperresponsible
			Earns approval
			Special
			Successful
			Independent life
			  from family
				Withdrawn
				Acting out
				Sullen
				Defiant
				Substance use
				Increased
				  value of peers
					Withdrawn
					Distance
					Aloof
					Quiet
					Hyperindependent
					Rejection
						Clowning
						Attracts
						  attention
						Hyperactivity
						Fragile
						Humorous

Identifying symptoms, visible qualities, characteristics	Substance use	Powerlessness
		Caretaker
		Rescuer
			Successful
			Overachiever
			Friends
			Grades
			Athletic
			Does all the
			  right thing
				Negative attention
				Hostility
				Anger
				Avoid competition
				  with hero
					Loner
					Solitariness
					Shyness
					"Easy child"
						Immature
						Needs
						  protection

Perceived benefit	Relief of pain	Important
		Self-righteousness
		-
			Positive attention	Negative attention	Escape	Amused–
						  playful
						  attention

Perceived benefit for family	None	Responsibility	Self-worth	Focus away from dependent	Relief	Fun

Possible consequence	Addiction	Martyr
		Illness
			Compulsive
			  drive
				Addiction
				Self-destructive
					Social isolation	Emotional
						  illness

No intervention	Losses
	Possible death
		Controlling
		Mental illness
		Repeat pattern
			Never wrong
			Workaholic
			Responsible for
			  everything
			Marries
			  dependent
				Troublemaker at
				  school–work–
				  prison
				Unplanned
				  pregnancy
				Self-defeating
				  behavior
					Possible
					  promiscuity
					Stays alone
					Remains invisible
					At risk for poor
					  health
						Cannot manage
						  stress
						Compulsive
						  clown marries
						  hero for care
						Ulcers

With intervention	Quality of life
	Happiness
	Personal
	  growth with
	  self-acceptance
	Serenity
		Letting go
		Peacefulness
		Increased self-
		  responsibility
			Accepts failure
			Responsible for
			  self not the
			  world
			Good executive
				Accepts
				  responsibility
				Good counselor
				Able to take
				  appropriate risks
				Reality-based
				  thinking
					Independent
					Talented
					Creative
					Imaginative
						Self-care
						No longer clown
						Fun to be with
						Good sense of
						  humor

RECOVERY NEEDS OF FAMILY MEMBERS

Chemically dependent needs:

1. Get out of own head, i.e., stop intellectualizing.
2. Develop awareness of how others feel.
3. Become flexible.
4. Work through problems.
5. Express anger without blaming.

Strengths: heightened awareness, gutsy, sensitivity to pain, empathy.
Chief enabler needs:

1. Let go of responsibility.
2. Get in touch with feelings.
3. Refocus on self (wants and needs).
4. Become aware of self-responsibility and let others do the same.
5. Deal with anger without blaming or falling apart.

Strengths: nurturing, giving, loving.
Family hero needs:

1. Learn to ask for and take what he or she needs.
2. Learn to accept failure.
3. Let down, relax, and be.
4. Focus on self—stop "fixing" the family.

Strengths: hard worker, know how to get what they want
Family scapegoat needs:

1. Get through anger to the hurt.
2. Learn to negotiate instead of rebel.

Strengths: can see reality, has good insight, sensitive, courageous.
Lost child needs:

1. Reach out.
2. Deal with loneliness.
3. Face pain.
4. Make new close relationships.

Strengths: patient, creative, independent.
Family mascot needs:

1. Take responsibility.
2. Risk being serious.
3. Assertiveness.

Strengths: humor, knows how to enjoy.

IDENTIFYING PATTERNS OF CODEPENDENCY

1. My good feelings about who I am come from being liked by you.

2. My good feelings about who I am come from approval from you.

3. Your struggle affects my serenity. My attention is focussed on solving your problems and relieving your pain.

4. My attention is focused on pleasing you.

5. My attention is focused on protecting you.

6. My attention is getting you to do what I want you to do (manipulation).

7. My self-esteem is increased by solving your problems.

8. My self-esteem is increased by relieving your pain.

9. My own desires and interests are put aside. My time is spent sharing your desires and interests.

10. How you dress and your personal appearance are dictated by my desires because you are a reflection of me.

11. My behavior is dictated by my desires because you are a reflection of me.

12. I am not aware of how I feel; instead, I am aware of how you feel.

13. I am not aware of what I want—I ask what you want, though most often I assume what you want.

14. My dreams of the future are linked to you.

15. My fear of rejection or abandonment determines what I say and do.

16. My fear of your anger determines what I say and do.

17. I use giving and taking care of you as a way of feeling safe and secure in our relationship.

18. The more I become involved with you, the less I am involved with my friends and other people.

19. I put my values aside in order to connect with you.

20. I value your opinions and way of doing things more than my own.

The Quality of My Life Is Related to the Quality of Your Life.

DOES SOMEONE YOU KNOW HAVE A PROBLEM WITH SUBSTANCES?

This questionnaire will clarify your observations of someone important in your life. Be truthful and fair in your responses to the following questions. Circle the questions to which you answer yes.

1. Has he or she ever lost time from work due to his or her use of substances?

2. Is his or her substance use making home life stressful?

3. Does he or she use substances because of stress in social settings?

4. Is substance use affecting his or her reputation?

5. Has he or she gotten into financial difficulties as a result of substance use?

6. Has he or she ever expressed feeling remorse after using substances?

7. Does he or she use substances with low class people or in low class environments?

8. Does substance use make his or her careless of family responsibilities?

9. Has his or her motivation decreased in the last year?

10. Does he or she need to use substances at specific times?

11. Does he or she use substances in the morning?

12. Does his or her substance use cause sleep problems?

13. Has his or her effectiveness and efficiency decreased as a result of substance use?

14. Is substance use putting his or her job at risk?

15. Does he or she use substances alone?

16. Has he or she ever had a complete loss of memory associated with substance use?

17. Has he or she ever been treated by a physician for substance-related problems, such as stomach problems, sleep disturbance, anxiety, etc.?

18. Does he or she use substances for a feeling of increased self-esteem?

19. Has he or she ever been hospitalized as a result of substance use?

20. Has there been a change in friends over the last year?

STAGES OF RECOVERY

Procheska *et al.* (1992) offers a model comprising six stages of change. These models suggest that all *self-changing* individuals will pass through these stages of recovery.

Stage 1. **Precontemplation:** You either do not realize you have a problem or you are having such a difficult time coping and functioning that you are not even able to think about trying to change.

Stage 2. **Contemplation:** You are not sure whether you want to change, but you are beginning to think about it.

Stage 3. **Preparation:** You begin to prepare for changes by seeking information (reading, questions, other) in recovery, inquiring about possible programs of interest.

Stage 4. **Action:** You begin to make some attempts to change. This is a time of relapse and greater understanding for what changes are required to achieve abstinence.

Stage 5. **Maintenance:** Relapse prevention is the central focus and realization that taking action is not enough; it takes a lot of work–effort to maintain change.

Stage 6. **Termination:** Change has become–is becoming a normal aspect of your function, without requiring the prior focus on abstinence and the energy to maintain the change.

RECOVERY IS A CHOICE

You can meet and talk with a lot of people about the choice of abstinence and recovery. Many of them may recommend abstinence and recovery because they care about you, they have already seen the results of your substance abuse, or they know what can happen. Everyone has an opinion, but your opinion is the only one that counts. It may be helpful for you to spend a few minutes writing down what you believe would be good reasons to abstain from substances. As you work through recovery, you will identify information that is helpful and reinforcing to your recovery. Put this information on index cards. Then, any time you need reinforcement and encouragement to remain abstinent and in recovery, you can read through your key cards and get back on track.

Reasons for Recovery

1. _____

2. _____

3. _____

4. _____

5. _____

6. _____

7. _____

8. _____

9. _____

10. _____

Are there reasons preventing you from entering recovery? If yes, please list them.

1. _____

2. _____

3. _____

4. _____

5. _____

YOUR CHOICE

Recovery bound	Relapse bound
__ Honest, realistic about self and problems	__ Minimizing, maximizing, distorting
__ Socializes with others	__ Isolated, avoids others
__ Listens, accepts input from others	__ Not listening, knows it all
__ Asks for help, accepts help from others	__ Will not ask for help
__ Positive attitudes	__ Negative attitudes
__ Focusing on personal recovery	__ Too many concerns outside recovery
__ Trusting, sharing with others	__ Suspicious, distrustful
__ Harmonious relationships	__ Conflicts with others
__ Turns will over to higher power	__ Depends on personal willpower
__ Stable lifestyle	__ Unstable lifestyle
__ Takes full responsibility for own behavior	__ Blaming, resentful, feels "victimized"
__ Appears, warm, friendly, caring about others	__ Appears hostile
__ Attends plenty of 12-step group meetings	__ Not attending 12-step or other group
__ Has close working relationship with sponsor	__ Has no sponsor
__ Reasonable expectations of self and others	__ Pities self, focuses on what is missing
__ Shares thoughts and feelings openly	__ Acts immature
__ Considerate, displays humility	__ Not working on the 12 steps of recovery
__ Has an attitude of gratitude for blessings of life	__ Does not accept the need for abstinence
__ Acts mature	__ Rejects reality of associated health and personal risks
__ Actively working with 12 steps of recovery or other self-help program	__ Hides, unwilling to discuss recovery
__ Fully accepts need for abstinence	__ Hides–denies disease to others
__ Understands–accepts disease concept of addiction	__ Appears angry, agitated
__ Open and sharing about recovery process	__ Looks for "magic solutions" to problems
__ Openly shares about personal disease experience	__ Acts depressed, withdrawn
__ Appears peaceful, comfortable with self	__ Unwilling to be helpful, supportive
__ Takes personal responsibility for solutions	__ No evidence of spiritual growth
__ Acts cheerful, outgoing	__ Returns to old relationships associated with substance use
__ Actively helpful and supportive of others	__ Returns to old substance using environments
__ Discusses spiritual aspects of recovery	__ Beginning to think "just using once will not be a problem"
	__ Lack of self-care
	__ Quits practicing newly learned skills

WHY IS SUBSTANCE ABSTINENCE IMPORTANT?

Although it is difficult for many people to commit to abstinence, it is necessary if you have a substance dependency. Recovery requires abstinence, which means choosing not to use any substances. If you question the need for abstinence, thoroughly review the consequences of substance use. Also, you have probably gone for periods of time not using. When you returned to using, was it a different experience of purely social–recreational use or did you get back into a pattern of abuse? If you could have limited use to being social or recreational, you would have. Dependency is a permanent issue that goes into remission with abstinence. Give a history of your prior experiences of abstinence and what happened:

_____

_____

_____

_____

_____

_____

_____

_____

_____

_____

_____

_____

_____

_____

_____

_____

_____

_____

_____

_____

HOW HAS SUBSTANCE ABUSE AFFECTED YOUR LIFE?

For each area identified, write five ways that substance abuse has negatively affected intimacy, honesty, stress, coping, expectations, problem solving, conflict resolution, losses, disappointments, etc.

1. How you see yourself:

   _____

   _____

   _____

2. Relationship with life partner:

   _____

   _____

   _____

3. Family relationships (children, parents, etc.):

   _____

   _____

   _____

4. Friendships:

   _____

   _____

   _____

5. Social life:

   _____

   _____

   _____

6. Work–social:

   _____

   _____

   _____

   _____

HOW TO CUT DOWN ON YOUR DRINKING

Are you drinking too much?

1. Do you drink alone when you feel angry or sad?
2. Does your drinking or hangovers ever make you late for work?
3. Does your drinking ever worry your significant other or family?
4. Do you ever drink after you have decided to not drink?
5. Do you ever forget what you have done while you were drinking?
6. Do you ever feel bad physically after drinking?

If you are drinking too much and have decided to cut down:

1. Write down your reasons for wanting to cut down your drinking.
   a. what have been your negative experiences associated with drinking?
   b. what would be anticipated benefits of cutting down?

2. Set a drinking goal.
   a. choose a limit for how much you will drink
   b. if you are cutting down, keep below these limits
      wome: no more than one drink per day
       men: no more than two drinks per day

If you have medical problems that are negatively affected by drinking, these limits may be too high for you. Therefore, consult your physician to find out what limit is right for you.
   Tips:

1. Keep little or no alcohol at home (decreases temptation).
2. Drink slowly. Take an hour break between drinks.
3. Do not drink on an empty stomach. Eat while you are having a drink.
4. You do not have to drink when others do; learn to day "no."
5. Stay busy. Write out what you can do for fun besides drinking.
6. Because cutting down on drinking can be difficult, get support.
7. Increase your awareness of people, places, times, or situations that tempt you to drink.
8. Stay focused on your goal!

AN OVERVIEW OF WHERE I AM AND WHERE I AM GOING

1. Self-diagnosis (what is the problem?)

_____

_____

_____

_____

_____

_____

2. Identify sources of support:

_____   _____

_____   _____

_____   _____

_____   _____

_____   _____

3. Examine and discuss your lifestyle:

_____

_____

_____

_____

_____

4. What is your commitment to recovery and change?

_____

_____

_____

_____

_____

_____

5. What is your plan of action (your recovery program)?

_____

_____

_____

_____

_____

_____

RECOVERY INVENTORY

Recovery is hard work that requires a lot of motivation and commitment. To get the most out of treatment:

1. Consistently use the resources available to you.
2. Be prepared to change old habits.
3. Practice new behaviors (to replace old habits).

Use this list to monitor what you need to change. Check off what you have already done:

___Physical examination

___Attend self-help meetings

___Sponsor

___Avoid substance using environments

___Avoid substance users

___Throw away substance paraphernalia

___Stop using substance

___Identify substance using behaviors

___Identify triggers

___Relapse prevention

___Honest discussion of thoughts, behaviors, feelings

___Individual therapy

___Daily schedule

___Educational meetings

___Good nutrition

___Daily exercise

___Journaling

___Rational self-talk

___Thought stopping (for craving or others)

1. What have been the easiest tasks on the list to accomplish?

_____

_____

_____

2. What seem to be the hardest tasks on the list for you?

_____

_____

_____

3. What have you not accomplished and why?

_____

_____

_____

MY RECOVERY PLAN

For any goal to be successful, an individual must take the time to identify what needs to be done to insure meeting his or her goals.

1. What changes do you want to accomplish with recovery? _____

_____

_____

_____

2. What has happened to encourage you to choose recovery? _____

_____

_____

_____

3. What do you need to do in order to reach your goals? _____

_____

_____

_____

4. What resources (people, community resources, etc.) will be helpful to you in reaching your goals? _____

_____

_____

_____

5. What things could interfere with you reaching your goal(s)? _____

_____

_____

_____

6. How will you know if your recovery plan is working? _____

_____

_____

_____

REVIEWING YOUR RECOVERY PROGRAM

During the course of your first year of recovery, review and update your recovery program regularly to assure the best use of resources, practices of change, and personal growth. Compare the changes in your recovery program with an understanding of why a change has been made and how it will benefit your recovery. This requires a thorough review of thoughts, feelings, behaviors, situations, and what you have learned about your own recovery and the potential for relapse.

1. What have you learned from self-monitoring?
2. What has been more difficult than what you expected?
3. What new information will add to a successful recovery plan?
4. What do you think when you review the strategies developed to manage the warning signs of relapse?
5. What new coping skills have you learned?
6. Have you identified new warning signs that could jeopardize your recovery?
7. What is the most useful information you have learned about yourself recently?
8. Review and update the progress toward your goals.
9. Review and update the list of social resources.
10. What has been the most difficult aspect of your recovery so far, and how have you managed it?

Now take your prior recovery plan and update it with the information form this review:

_____

_____

_____

_____

_____

_____

_____

_____

_____

_____

_____

_____

PREPARATION FOR ATTENDING A 12-STEP MEETING

Talk to your therapist about the specific 12-step meeting to which you have been referred (AA, NA, etc.) regarding the differences in meeting format and the goals associated with attending meetings. It would be necessary to attend numerous meetings in order to identify which meet your needs. Also, be prepared to focus on what you have in common with other people attending the meetings. To find out more about 12-step programs, you can go to the drug and alcohol council in your community, go to a bookstore, or contact:

AA World Services, Inc.
Box 459 Grand Central Station
New York, NY 10163

WHAT IS A 12-STEP PROGRAM?

Alcoholics Anonymous is a self-help program that offers fellowship for men and women who once had a drinking problem. Self-help means nonprofessional, nondenominational, multiracial, and self-supporting. Membership is open to anyone in need of support and wanting to stop the substance abuse–dependence problem.

WHAT DOES A 12-STEP PROGRAM DO?

1. 12-step members share their experiences with anyone seeking help with a substance abuse–dependence problem. Members with a history of abstinence offer "sponsorship," which is one-to-one support.

2. 12-step programs offer a way to develop good, satisfactory life choices without the use of substances.

3. There are different types of 12-step meetings:
   a. open-speaker meeting: open to everyone (substance abusers and nonsubstance abusers). This is the best way to learn about 12-step groups. Members share their life experiences with substance abuse, how long they have been coming to a 12-step program, and how it has changed their lives.
   b. open discussion meeting: one member offers a brief summary of his or her substance experience, which leads to discussion on many substance-related problems.
   c. closed meeting: conducted like an open meeting but is *only* for those with a substance problem.
   d. step meeting (generally closed): focuses on one of the 12 steps.

Twelve-step meetings share a message and the method of recovery, offering fellowship, survival skills, and support.

THE 12 TRADITIONS OF ALCOHOLICS ANONYMOUS

1. Our common welfare should come first: personal recovery depends upon AA unity.

2. For our group purpose, there is but one ultimate authority—a loving God as He may express Himself in our group conscience. Our leaders are but trusted servants: they do not govern.

3. The only requirement for AA membership is a desire to stop drinking.

4. Each group should be autonomous except in matters affecting other groups of AA as a whole.

5. Each group has but one primary purpose: to carry its message to the alcoholic who still suffers.

6. An AA group ought never endorse, finance, or lend the AA name to any related facility or outside enterprise, lest problems of money, property, and prestige divert us from our primary purpose.

7. Every AA group ought to be fully self-supporting, declining outside contributions.

8. Alcoholics Anonymous should remain forever nonprofessional, but our service centers may employ special workers.

9. AA, as such, ought never be organized, but we may create service boards or committees directly responsible to those they serve.

10. Alcoholics Anonymous has no opinion on outside issues; hence, the AA name ought never be drawn into public controversy.

11. Our public relations policy is based on attraction rather than promotion: we need always maintain personal anonymity at the level of press, radio, and films.

12. Anonymity is the spiritual foundation of all our traditions, ever reminding us to place principles above personalities.

TWELVE STEPS OUTLINE

The 12 steps of AA offer a program of hope, with a structure to help you address and work through problems in order to live a more healthy lifestyle. The 12 steps from Alcoholics Anonymous cover the following points:

1. Admit that you are powerless over alcohol—that your life had become unmanageable.

2. Believe that a power greater than yourself can restore you to sanity.

3. Make a decision to turn over your life and will to the care of God.

4. Make a thorough, fearless, moral inventory of yourself.

5. Admit openly and honestly what you have done wrong.

6. Be ready to have God heal all the areas of your life.

7. Humbly ask God to help you change your weaknesses to strengths.

8. Make a list of all persons who have been affected by your behavior and be willing to make amends to all of them.

9. Make amends to those affected by your behavior, except when to do so would cause them more harm.

10. Continue to take a personal inventory, and when you are wrong promptly admit it. Each day take an inventory of yourself and your activity.

11. Seek through prayer and meditation to improve your conscious contact with God as we understand him, praying only for knowledge of His will for us and the power to carry it out. Keep growing in your relationship with God by daily prayer and Bible reading. Ask God for guidance.

12. Express gratitude to God for the changing of your life experience by working the 12 steps.

Working a 12-step program offers affiliation, support, and survival skills.

TEN STEPS (MODIFICATION OF 12 STEPS)

To be successful in recovery means more than abstinence. It requires awareness, self-understanding, personal growth with associated changes, self-responsibility, and taking responsibility for the ways in which your substance abuse has affected others.

1. Due to substance use, I and my life are out of control.

2. I will seek whatever supports are necessary to become responsible and respectful to myself and to others.

3. I will learn to accept things that I cannot change and take responsibility to change the things I can, so that I can set appropriate goals and be the best that I can be.

4. I will not be afraid to do an inventory of my values and my morality.

5. I am ready to be honest about my mistakes and take responsibility for what I have done.

6. I am willing to learn from all of my previous mistakes and experiences and live according to my values in a responsible and respectful manner.

7. I will make amends to the people who have been negatively affected by my substance use.

8. I will continue to focus on my goals by taking a regular inventory and being responsible.

9. I will take the information from the prior eight steps to develop a respectful and responsible life plan of action and put it to work.

10. Through my thoughts, feelings, and behavior, I declare my daily commitment to recovery.

TWELVE STEPS

Do you experience difficulties in your life associated with the abuse of substances? If yes, explain: _____

_____

_____

_____

_____

1. How do you know your life is unmanageable? _____

_____

_____

_____

_____

2. What is the difference between spirituality and religion? _____

_____

_____

How are spirituality–religion and self-responsibility related, and how do they play a role in recovery? _____

_____

_____

_____

_____

3. Make the decision to enter recovery. Turn over your old ways of doing things and learn new ways of coping, problem solving, managing overwhelming emotions, and taking responsibility for yourself. You will do this by: _____

_____

_____

_____

_____

_____

4. Make a searching and fearless inventory of yourself. On a separate piece of paper, identify your positive and negative points.

5. Admit to yourself, to others, and to your higher power (if you believe) the exact nature of your wrongs.

6. What is(are) your character, values, and beliefs? How have you not lived according to your own values, beliefs, and character? Write it out.

7. What is an amend? _____

    _____

    _____

8. Make a list of all of the persons you have harmed and become willing to make amends to them all. This may be something that you need to do more than once throughout the course of your recovery as your understanding of you and what you have lived becomes more clear.

9. Make direct amends to people whenever possible, except when to do so would injure them or others.

    What are the benefits for you to make amends to others? _____

    _____

    _____

    _____

    _____

    How would you make an amend? _____

    _____

    _____

    _____

10. Why is it important to continue to take a personal inventory and when wrong to promptly admit it? _____

    _____

    _____

    _____

11. Strive through meditation, prayer, or other techniques to understand yourself and take responsibility for all the choices you make.

12. In experiencing the awakening that has led you to the choice of recovery, how do you practice the principles of your values and beliefs to live daily life in a self-responsible manner? _____

    _____

    _____

_____

_____

_____

_____

Try to remain focused on who you are, where you are going, and how you will get there.

TWELVE STEPS TO RECOVERY

STEP 1

Answer the following questions about your use of substance(s) (drugs–alcohol) to help you clarify whether you are in control of substance use or whether it is controlling you.

	Yes	No
1. Do you ever spend money on substances more than you expect to?	____	____
2. Do you ever use more substances than you expect to?	____	____
3. Have you ever set a limit on how much of a substance you would use, but then end up using too much?	____	____
4. Do you ever spend money on substances that was needed for rent, bills, or other things?	____	____
5. Do you ever binge on substances?	____	____
6. Do you ever make repeated stops at the bank ATM more than one time in a day to get money for substances or to "party"?	____	____
7. Have you ever purchased substances to share with other people, but either used some or all it before it could be given to them?	____	____
8. Do you ever borrow money to use substances?	____	____
9. Have you ever dealt substances?	____	____
10. Have you ever tried to deal substances but used it all yourself?	____	____
11. Have you ever traded sex for substances?	____	____
12. Do you–have you ever missed appointments because of use?	____	____
13. Do you ever make promises that you do not keep or miss family events because of substance use?	____	____
14. Do you use substances more during the holidays?	____	____
15. Have you ever gotten sick by using too much of a substance?	____	____
16. Do you believe you are addicted to drugs–alcohol?	____	____

Take the time to review how you answered these questions. Use the information to help you make choices that fit with life goals of change.

STEP 2

If you could have abstained without support and definite efforts toward clear changes in thoughts, feelings, and behavior you would have

1. Developed a recovery program:

_____

_____

_____

_____

_____

_____

_____

2. Developed recovery goals:

_____

_____

_____

_____

_____

_____

_____

3. Developed a recovery support system:

_____

_____

_____

_____

_____

_____

_____

STEP 3

Acknowledge and accept the problem of substance abuse in your life. Make the decision to develop a recovery program to which you are committed. Work toward self-understanding, mood management, developing coping skills, and goals for change and personal growth. To get started, develop a brief outline of information that will clarify some of these issues.

1. Self-understanding:
   a. Describe yourself—who are you?

   _____
   _____
   _____

   b. How do you want to be known?

   _____
   _____
   _____

   c. How are you known (based upon how your behavior is seen by others)?

   _____
   _____
   _____

2. Is there a history of anxiety or depression (etc.), or are you currently experiencing any emotional difficulties? Please explain:
   a. _____
   b. _____
   c. _____
   d. _____
   e. _____

3. Identify difficulties coping:
   a. _____
   b. _____
   c. _____
   d. _____
   e. _____

4. What do you want to change about how you do things or think about things?
   a. _____
   b. _____
   c. _____
   d. _____
   e. _____

5. What are your current goals (recovery, education, job, relationship with self or others)?
   a. _____
   b. _____
   c. _____
   d. _____
   e. _____

STEP 4

Realize the importance of and make a searching and fearless inventory of your morals and values for your recovery. Often people do not take the time to clarify their morals and values. Generally, when people do not live according to their morals and values, the results are poor emotional function, relationship problems, and poor judgment. Identify your morals and values and then review how your life is not guided by them.

Morals

Ethics, honesty, honor, integrity, character, "right and wrong."

1._____

2._____

3._____

4._____

5._____

6._____

7._____

8._____

9._____

10._____

Values

What do you esteem, value, and prioritize in your life, love, and relationships?

1._____

2._____

3._____

4._____

5._____

6._____

7._____

8._____

9._____

10._____

STEP 5

It is time to take an honest look at the choices you made as substances became a bigger part of your life. Look back before the time of substance use influenced your life. What were your goals and your dreams? How did you think things would turn out? How did the use of substances change the direction you thought your life would take?

_____

_____

_____

_____

_____

_____

_____

_____

_____

_____

_____

_____

_____

_____

_____

_____

_____

_____

_____

_____

_____

_____

STEP 6

Prepare to let go of feelings of guilt and shame and begin to take responsibility for your behaviors. List the choices or behaviors for which you experience the feelings of guilt or shame. Then write the action you plan to take to confront it, take responsibility for it, and then make peace with yourself.

1. _____

   Action: _____

2. _____

   Action: _____

3. _____

   Action: _____

4. _____

   Action: _____

5. _____

   Action: _____

6. _____

   Action: _____

7. _____

   Action: _____

8. _____

   Action: _____

9. _____

   Action: _____

10. _____

   Action: _____

STEP 7

1. How will your strengths help you in recovery and with achieving other goals?

_____

_____

_____

_____

_____

_____

_____

2. How could your weaknesses negatively affect recovery and achieving other goals (write specifically)? What do you plan to do to ensure that does not happen?

_____

_____

_____

_____

_____

_____

_____

_____

_____

_____

_____

3. Strengths are your assets—the things about you that are helpful to you. Weaknesses are the things that make it hard for you to create problems.

Strengths	Weaknesses
a. _____	a. _____
b. _____	b. _____
c. _____	c. _____
d. _____	d. _____
e. _____	e. _____

STEP 8

Make a thorough inventory of everyone who has been affected by your past behaviors and prepare yourself to make amends. Who has been affected by your past behavior and in what way?

1. _____

_____

2. _____

_____

3. _____

_____

4. _____

_____

5. _____

_____

6. _____

_____

7. _____

_____

8. _____

_____

9. _____

_____

10. _____

_____

STEP 9

Be prepared and willing to make amends to everyone who has been affected by your behavior, unless it is upsetting for them. Write out how you plan to make amends to everyone (listed in step 8). Who has been affected by your past behaviors? Also, identify any reason that is preventing you from taking the action to make amends.

1. _____

_____

_____

2. _____

_____

_____

3. _____

_____

_____

4. _____

_____

_____

5. _____

_____

_____

6. _____

_____

_____

7. _____

_____

_____

8. _____

_____

_____

9. _____

_____

_____

10. _____

_____

_____

STEP 10

Though it was difficult, it feels good to make amends. Therefore, continue to take responsibility for your behaviors whenever you do something wrong. Write about the experience(s) of making amends, what you learned from it, and how it will help you to do things differently in your daily commitment to recovery.

_____

_____

_____

_____

_____

_____

_____

_____

_____

_____

_____

_____

_____

_____

_____

_____

_____

_____

_____

_____

_____

STEP 11

Through meditation (and prayer if chosen) seek peace and self-understanding.

Grant me the serenity to accept the things I cannot change,

The courage to change the things I can,

And the wisdom to know the difference.

Purchase a meditation tape or make your own. Meditate regularly for peace and the development of comfort being with yourself.

Write out how you plan to accomplish Step 11

_____

_____

_____

_____

_____

_____

_____

_____

_____

_____

_____

STEP 12

How you will continue to practice all that you have learned from your step work to improve your life and continue your personal growth:

_____

_____

_____

_____

_____

_____

_____

_____

_____

_____

_____

_____

_____

_____

_____

_____

_____

_____

_____

_____

_____

_____

_____

TAKING INVENTORY

Taking inventory means looking at your assets and liabilities. Another way of thinking about it is in terms of what it is about you that works for you and against you in achieving goals and the impact on relationships.

How has substance abuse affected:

1. How you feel about yourself?

    _____

    _____

    _____

2. How family and friends have reacted?

    _____

    _____

    _____

3. Your job–school?

    _____

    _____

    _____

4. How have your social life and significant relationships been affected?

    a. spouse _____

    _____

    _____

    b. children _____

    _____

    _____

    c. parents _____

    _____

    _____

    d. siblings _____

    _____

    _____

5. How other areas of your life been affected (i.e., health)?

    _____

    _____

    _____

AN OUTLINE FOR MAKING AMENDS

1. Make a factual statement of what has happened. Be honest with yourself.

   _____

   _____

   _____

   _____

   _____

2. Acknowledge how the person was negatively affected by your behavior (discomfort, emotional pain, financial distress, feelings of loss–sadness, etc.).

   _____

   _____

   _____

   _____

   _____

3. Write out a brief, direct apology and/or commitment to further necessary amends (paying money back, etc.).

   _____

   _____

   _____

   _____

   _____

4. Write out a final statement about your future expectations (continued abstinence, improved character, life on track, etc.).

   _____

   _____

   _____

   _____

   _____

Once you have made your amends to a person, let go and move on. He or she may or may not respond or accept your amends. That is his or her choice. Your goal is to heal and learn by taking responsibility. Prepare yourself for a wide range of responses:

1. If a person insists you have done no harm, accept his or her kindness and in return offer your own kindness and goodwill.
2. If a person begins to vent his or her anger or pain, listen and validate the truth of what he or she says. Stay calm and avoid being defensive or argumentative. Stay focused on your goal of making amends, validated by acknowledging that you can understand how he or she feels.

THE FIVE S's OF RECOVERY

1. Surrender
2. Sobriety
3. Sanity
4. Sincerity
5. Serenity

How are the five S's accomplished?

1. Honesty
2. Open mindedness
3. Willingness
4. Changing old ideas
5. Changing old behavior
6. Self-responsibility

What are the principles behind the accomplishment?

1. Self-honesty (1)
2. Hope (2)
3. Faith (3)
4. Courage (4–6)
5. Humility (7)
6. Responsibility (8–10)
7. Patience (11)
8. Charity or love (12)

These are taken from the 12 steps [numbered to the right of each principle is the associated step(s)]. Write about each word–concept on this page and discuss how it will play a part in your recovery by giving examples.

UNDERSTANDING CRAVING

Craving substances is a common experience especially early in recovery. It may be a brief experience lasting for weeks or months, or it may last for a very long time (years). The experience of craving does not mean that something is wrong. However, it is uncomfortable and you need to be prepared to deal with it. Some important information about craving substances:

1. Craving is time-limited (few minutes to a few hours).
2. It usually peaks after a few minutes and then urges decrease.
3. Craving tends to decrease over time.
4. Craving can be triggered by
   a. environmental factors that remind you of using
   b. psychological factors such as the positive consequences of use (felt good, helped you cope, etc.). A very strong psychological factor is euphoric recall, which is an experience that feels like a reliving of what it felt like to be under the influence when a substance has not been used. The images during euphoric recall can be detailed.
5. Craving becomes less intense as you learn to cope with the common triggers.
   a. contacts with association of use (people, places, situations)
   b. emotional reactors (overwhelmed, fatigue, fear, stress, frustration)
   c. exposure to substances–seeing other people use

Write about craving experiences you have had:

_____

_____

_____

_____

_____

_____

_____

_____

_____

_____

_____

_____

_____

COPING WITH CRAVING

It can be difficult to identify the triggers of craving. Keeping a self-monitoring journal can help you to recognize what these triggers are so that you can problem solve how to do things differently to decrease stress and encourage recovery. The best way to cope with craving is to avoid the triggers, but there are other choices for coping with craving as well:

1. Avoid contact with triggers.
   a. get rid of all substances in the home
   b. do not go to environments where there are substances
   c. decrease or eliminate time spent with friends or acquaintances who use
2. Make a list of triggers and prioritize them from the easiest to the most difficult with which to deal.
3. Develop a plan for dealing with craving. Go back to your list of triggers and think through what choices you could use to cope with each potential experience.
4. Get involved in new activities (hobby, exercise, art, reading, etc.).
5. Talk about your craving urges (to identify the source of craving) and get relief. It will help you to be honest with yourself.
6. Ride the wave of craving: use visualization to "see" yourself overcoming urges to use.
7. Challenge undermining or unnatural thinking.
   a. counter a focus on what the positive experiences of use were with the negative experiences
   b. remind yourself of the negative consequences of continued use
   c. identify messages or self-talk statements that precede craving so that you can develop substitute statement to replace them: "it is normal to crave, but it will pass" and "it feels bad, but I can survive it"

What do you think will help you to cope effectively with craving?

1. _____

2. _____

3. _____

4. _____

5. _____

ASSESSING HIGH-RISK SITUATIONS

1. In what kind of situations do you use substances?

   _____

   _____

   _____

2. What are your triggers for use?

   _____

   _____

   _____

3. What are your experiences of relapse (in detail)?

   _____

   _____

   _____

4. What were your thoughts and feelings when that happened (relapse description from no.3)?

   _____

   _____

   _____

5. What do you identify as the positive consequences of substance use?

   _____

   _____

   _____

6. What do you identify as the negative consequences of substance use?

   _____

   _____

   _____

7. Why did you choose to keep using substances instead of doing something different?

   _____

   _____

SELF-MONITORING JOURNAL

Day and time	Behavior	Thoughts and feelings	Coping behaviors			
			Triggers (of used substances)	Positive outcome	Negative outcome	What you have learned

DAILY LOG

PART I

If you have never kept a log or journal before, initially you may want to make the effort to keep an in-depth self-report of what you are experiencing as you prepare for your recovery. A log will offer you the opportunity to vent your thoughts and feelings, to clarify the underlying issues, and to initiate problem solving. You may also want to keep a basic log of your days to clarify how you actually use your time and what your feelings and throughout the course of the day. This log will either reinforce the efforts you are currently making or identify what you need to do to increase self-responsibility and feeling more in control of your choices and your life.

	Activity	How you felt
Day Date Time		
Day Date Time		
Day Date Time		
Day Date Time		
Day Date Time		
Day Date Time		
Day Date Time		

PART II

Once you have practiced keeping a log and feel that you have a clear idea of what you need to do, you may choose to keep a brief weekly record listing choices that supported recovery as well as choices that did not. This can be helpful for your work in a recovery program with a sponsor and/or therapist. Label helpful choices H and nonhelpful choices N.

M	
T	
W	
Th	
F	
S	
S	

When you have established a lifestyle pattern supporting recovery, you can begin to plan out activities in advance that have demonstrated being supportive of your recovery. Write out a monthly plan.

EXPERIENCE LOG

Record each occurrence or habit for 3–4 weeks. Use these sentence stems to describe what the task was, where to took place, with whom, how you felt, and what the consequences were.

Keeping an experience log will help you to develop regular self-monitoring of "what I am doing" and "why I am doing it."

Date: _____   Time: _____

I was with _____ at _____

This is what happened: _____

_____

_____

_____

Just before then I had been _____

_____

I said to myself _____

_____

And I felt _____

_____

Afterward I said to myself _____

_____

I felt _____

_____

And I did _____

_____

_____

The negative consequences I experienced were (natural) _____

_____

_____

_____

The positive consequences were _____

_____

_____

_____

DAILY RECOVERY SCHEDULE

Recovery is dynamic. That means that it is ever changing—sometimes up and sometimes down. This requires awareness and efforts to identify and cope with thoughts, feelings, and behaviors that can lead to relapse. Chances are you have been engaging in these old habits for a long time, making them deeply rooted habits. To change habits means to change thoughts, feelings, and behaviors. Once you have identified what you need to change, use the following outline to reinforce your efforts:

1. Practice new effective ways of coping.
2. Have adequate support for maintaining change.
3. Self-monitor to maintain awareness.
4. Use journaling to help identify what you are doing that is helpful and those things you do that are not helpful or supportive of your recovery.

When trying to change life patterns, it can be helpful to write out a daily plan. This scheduling of daily goals will keep you focused on recovery and help practice the new skills needed to replace the old ones.

Day	Plan–changes (new behaviors–thoughts, use of resources, meetings, positive or negative effects on recovery)	Rate the day (good or bad and why difficult and why, how you responded)
M		
T		
W		
Th		
F		
S		
S		

JOURNAL WRITING AS PART OF YOUR RECOVERY

PART I

Journal writing can be useful for increasing awareness, developing goals, and monitoring progress. A journal is a history of your life experience. Keeping a journal will help you to clarify appropriate goals and what you need to do to achieve your goals.

Steps to Journal Writing

1. Write down your goals. Remember that, as you learn more about yourself and start to make changes associated with recovery, some of your goals may change or new ones may be added. Therefore, it is a good idea to review your goals from time to time. Goals should be specific and realistic. Write
   a. daily goals (you may write them out daily or have them previously written to help establish new patterns)
   b. weekly–monthly goals
   c. long-term goals (year or more to accomplish)

2. Self-monitoring.
   a. keep track of where you are now and the progress you make
   b. this step also helps to identify trouble areas where you need to do additional problem solving or seek support

3. List your fears, negative messages you say to yourself, and patterns that you are experiencing difficulty changing. Keeping a journal will help you to identify these patterns if you lack awareness of the patterns that keep you stuck or cause you problems.

4. Each day write down a minimum of three successes and forgive yourself for something you have done (act responsibly and respectfully).

5. Be willing to do things differently. If you do not, nothing will change.

Learn to enjoy journal writing. It is a very useful skill and, like a best friend, is available to you 24 hr per day and 7 days per week. Get started journalizing immediately. [Adapted from Johnson, S. (1997). "Therapist's Guide to Clinical Intervention." San Diego: Academic Press.]
Keeping a journal can be useful to:

1. Clarify the triggers, emotions, behaviors, and people that play a role in substance use. Keep a record of exactly what happens before, during, and after an episode of craving or use.
2. Problem solve how to effectively change behaviors in order to successfully abstain.
3. Self-monitor what works and what does not.

There are numerous ways to keep track of and create a daily record. For example,

1. What was the social setting?
2. Who were you with?
3. What were you doing?

4. When?
5. What was the situation?
6. How did you feel?
7. What did you do?
8. What have you learned?

Prepare a sample and go over it with your sponsor or therapist, and then write your entries in a notebook.

_____

_____

_____

_____

_____

_____

_____

_____

_____

_____

_____

_____

_____

_____

_____

_____

_____

_____

_____

EVENING AND WEEKEND SCHEDULE AND JOURNAL

Sometimes people do quite well during the day when their lives are structured by the demands of work or other activities. However, the evening time or weekends are sometimes more difficult to manage. Here are several steps that you can take to decrease stress and risk of relapse during these times:

1. Write out a plan that is supportive of recovery efforts.
2. Keep a journal to self-monitor what you are following through on, what is helpful, what requires problem solving, etc.

EVENING JOURNAL

Evening recovery behaviors (e.g., 12-step meetings–self-help group, meeting with sponsor, gym, stress management techniques, etc.):

1. _____
2. _____
3. _____
4. _____
5. _____
6. _____
7. _____
8. _____
9. _____
10. _____

JOURNAL

Date and time	Activity or behavior	What is beneficial and how did you feel?

CONSEQUENCES

When people hear the word "consequence," the association is that it is something negative. However, consequences are merely the outcome of your choices, thoughts, and behaviors. It is the positive consequences that reinforce, perpetuate, and result in repetition of certain choices. Sometimes when people use a substance, they believe it is helping them. Consequences are complex, and they are biological, social, and psychological.

Sometimes consequences include:

1. To feel more comfortable in social situations.
2. To think less about distressing issues or feel less distressed.
3. To get numb and not feel.
4. To avoid low self-esteem.
5. Hangover, exacerbation of medical problems, etc.

For example, socially you may experience approval or disapproval. Psychological consequences:

1. Low self-esteem or inflated self-esteem
2. Issues of self-worth
3. Mood changes
4. Impact on personal growth and effective coping

Physical consequences:

1. Sleep disturbance
2. Poor nutrition
3. Lack of exercise
4. Part of substance use

When keeping a journal to clarify the outcome of your choices, try to include as much information as possible so that you can understand the complexity of your involvement in each experience.

CONSEQUENCE JOURNAL
1. Date
2. Time
3. Who with
4. Where
5. What happened
6. What you had been doing previously

7. What you felt before
8. What you felt after
9. How you dealt with those feelings
10. Negative consequences
11. Positive consequences
12. What you learned
13. How it will improve your recovery

RELAPSE PREVENTION

PART I

How an individual chooses to think about specific situations will play a role in the decisions he or she makes. The following tasks will help you to clarify information that will help you to stay focused on your recovery.

1. Identify your goals:

_____

_____

_____

_____

2. Identify negative emotions that influence your urge to use substances:

_____

_____

_____

_____

3. Identify peer relationships that influence your urge to use substances:

_____

_____

_____

_____

4. Start a journal to increase your awareness and include
   a. date
   b. situation
   c. who is involved
   d. what happens (do you give in to influence–impulses or use recovery resources)
   e. what happens afterward
   f. what did you learn–which coping skills helped or would help

5. Problem solving: Identify appropriate alternative responses to specific substance-related situations (Social pressure, patterns of thinking, relationship problems, craving, slip, etc.).

6. Remind yourself of the benefits of not using:
   a. list 5–10 benefits associated with not using substances
   b. list 5–10 negative consequences associated with using substances
   c. list 5–10 high-risk situations that are difficult to manage

PART II

Five things I can do to avoid relapse:

Substance dependent   Codependent

1. _____   1. _____

2. _____   2. _____

3. _____   3. _____

4. _____   4. _____

5. _____   5. _____

Slippery situations and how I will avoid or deal with them:

1. _____

   _____

   _____

2. _____

   _____

   _____

3. _____

   _____

   _____

4. _____

   _____

   _____

5. _____

   _____

   _____

The most helpful things my family can do for me if I relapse:

1. _____

_____

2. _____

_____

3. _____

_____

4. _____

_____

5. _____

_____

PART III

Behavior change is associated with successful abstinence from substances. Recovery **SUCCESS** is accomplished by first making the decision to quit using substances and then changing patterns of thought and behavior to reinforce and maintain your goal. The following statements are a helpful reminder of some of the basic changes that are necessary to assure that you reach your goal.

Study your emotional and behavioral responses to experiences that trigger use. It may be your own thoughts and feelings (inside–internal) or associated with others (interpersonal–external).

Use your recovery resources (make a list of resources).

Change problem behaviors and behavioral patterns.

Change "Stinking thinking," also described as irrational thinking and distortions (e.g., having one drink will not matter). Work hard at becoming increasingly aware of how you think and how that thinking influences your choices and quality of life.

Explore areas of desired growth and monitoring of progress on goals (in other words, where are you going and how are you going to get there). From time to time, review and refine your goals.

Start practicing self-care behaviors as part of your daily structure:
   a. good nutrition
   b. exercise
   c. adequate sleep
   d. meditation–progressive muscle relaxation
   e. use of recovery reinforcing resources

Start to develop healthy recovery reinforcing leisure activities
   a. participate in activities that you enjoy
   b. spend time with people you enjoy who support your recovery
   c. always consider the potential for personal growth

PART IV

Rehearsal

In order to increase successful abstinence and recovery, it can be helpful to think through the way you think and behave in various situations. This "thinking through" or mental rehearsing is a way to use the information you have learned and apply it in mental images for practice. When you do this, it acts to prepare you for making choices that are in the "helpful to your recovery" category of choices.

1. Identify potentially difficult situations:
   a. _____
   b. _____
   c. _____

2. What could you say to yourself that would not be helpful?
   a. _____
   b. _____
   c. _____

3. What could you say to yourself that would be helpful?
   a. _____
   b. _____
   c. _____

4. What mental images could you use to reinforce your recovery goals?
   a. _____
   b. _____
   c. _____

5. How do you see yourself dealing with substance using peers?
   a. _____
   b. _____
   c. _____

6. What behaviors are you changing that make your recovery stronger? Create a mental image of you carrying out these behavioral changes.
   a. _____
   b. _____
   c. _____
   d. _____
   e. _____

MAINTAINING PROGRESS

Because recovery is new to you, it is important to gain a thorough understanding of yourself, your choices, and the associated consequences of those choices. Seek to understand how and why some sources of support are helpful to your recovery and some are not. Keep the following points in mind to help you maintain recovery progress.

1. Always practice good self-care behaviors
   a. adequate sleep
   b. good nutrition
   c. regular exercise
   d. positive leisure activities
   e. relationships that support your recovery

2. Positive reinforcement
   a. positive, rational, and realistic thoughts and feelings "keep your cup half full"
   b. relaxation coupled with positive affirmations
   c. review successful efforts

3. Positive feedback: Focus on what is right and what works. This can be done by appraising daily experiences:
   a. what was helpful–pleasing
   b. what you learned from approaching things differently
   c. accept what you cannot control or change
   d. do something about things you can change
   e. positive use of feedback from meetings, sponsor, or others in your support group

4. Develop realistic expectations and limitations
   a. acknowledge what you do not know and need to learn
   b. take responsibility to learn and make appropriate changes
   c. accept that personal growth continues throughout your life

5. Acknowledge and accept that there are a lot of resources available to support recovery, but that you are responsible for you.

Keeping a journal to maintain a log of experiences, how you respond, and what you learn from each experience is a very helpful skill for building a strong recovery.

INTERRUPTING POTENTIAL RELAPSE

An important aspect of recovery is changing patterns of behavior, feelings, and thinking as well as avoiding or problem solving situations that lead to substance use. Once you have identified such patterns and situations, there are a number of ways to prepare yourself to respond differently. Use the list you generated of thoughts, feelings, behaviors, and situations that place you at risk for relapse for rehearsal of responding differently for a helpful homework assignment.

For this work you can do the following:

1. Write it out to increase your understanding of the stepwise events that increase your risk of relapse.
2. Visualization can be used to mentally practice successful recovery behaviors.
3. Role-play responses supportive of recovery.
4. Learn from modeling the successful behavior of others.
5. Present situations to sponsor, therapist, or others supportive of your recovery.

Utilizing as many of these techniques as you can for practicing change will increase the potential for the change you desire by increasing your awareness and being prepared. Begin practicing now by writing out new choices for managing these thoughts, feelings, and behaviors.

_____

_____

_____

_____

_____

_____

_____

_____

_____

_____

_____

_____

_____

_____

_____

CHOICES—LEARNING MORE ABOUT YOURSELF

Life is about choices. Success requires evaluating each choice and its associated consequences. Recovery is a particularly important time to carefully consider the choices ahead of you and how those choices support your recovery or make you vulnerable to relapse. Each choice you make could be an important step toward self-responsibility, which creates the opportunity for increased awareness, increased self-understanding, and identifying helpful alternatives. All of this improves the possibility of a positive future outcome under similar circumstances. Therefore, learn from every choice you make. Take the time to review previous experiences to make sure you learned everything possible to benefit you in recovery.

1. Write down five problem situations:
   a. _____
   b. _____
   c. _____
   d. _____
   e. _____

2. What feelings did you experience prior to choosing to use substances?
   a. _____
   b. _____
   c. _____
   d. _____
   e. _____

3. What were you thinking?
   a. _____
   b. _____
   c. _____
   d. _____
   e. _____

4. What were your choices?
   a. _____
   b. _____
   c. _____
   d. _____
   e. _____

5. What did you do?

   _____

   _____

   _____

6. How do you feel about what happened? Can you use that to benefit your recovery?

_____

_____

_____

7. What would you do differently now?

_____

_____

_____

PRACTICING CHANGE

Development of a new repertoire of assertive behaviors and improved communication requires practicing the changes you desire. Make a list of social situations to which you would like to respond differently. Then write out how you normally deal with each situation and how you would like to deal with it. The following are some of the techniques you can use for practicing change:

1. Role-playing: If you are anticipating a specific situation, ask someone to play the part opposite you. Role-play every possibility to see which one works best for you. Practice with your therapist, sponsor, a group member, or someone else you trust.
2. Self-talk: Affirmations, rational substitute statements, and rational thinking.
3. Empty chair: Imagine that the individual you are anticipating dealing with is sitting in a chair and play out the interaction.
4. Talk to yourself in a mirror.

On the following lines, develop some situations for practicing change. Practice will allow you to feel more comfortable about trying the change in an actual situation. Be patient with and encouraging to yourself. Practice makes perfect.

1. _____

   Old response: _____

   _____

   New response: _____

   _____

2. _____

   Old response: _____

   _____

   New response: _____

   _____

3. _____

   Old response: _____

   _____

   New response: _____

   _____

INCREASING SELF-UNDERSTANDING

Complete each of the following sentences with five endings. It is important to complete them as quickly as possible. Then go back over the endings to each sentence to determine which ones are a good fit for you. Use this information to increase self-awareness, self-understanding, and in guiding yourself in recovery-related decisions.

1. I am now becoming aware that _____

_____

_____

_____

2. The kind of thinking that increases a risk of relapse is _____

_____

_____

_____

3. The kind of feeling that increases a risk of relapse is _____

_____

_____

_____

4. I can see a pattern of substance use associated with _____

_____

_____

_____

5. The excuses have I used to relapse are _____

_____

_____

_____

6. The next time I begin to experience the signs of relapse, I can avoid relapse by

_____

_____

_____

Think about where you are, who you are with, and what is happening when you experience a warning sign of relapse.

LINGERING WITHDRAWAL

If you have been abusing your body with substances for a long time, it could take a long time (6 months to 2 years) to recover to a level of consistent positive changes. As with all changes, there is a tendency to fall back into old patterns when there is increased stress, not getting enough rest, or not feeling well. Experience of any of these symptoms is an opportunity to interfere with and fill any gaps in your recovery program. If you do not acknowledge the problem and take action, your risk of relapse is increased. Do you experience any of these difficulties? If yes, explain:

___difficulty with concentration or attention

___thoughts that repeatedly come into your mind

___difficulty dealing with problems that you generally manage fine

___difficulty dealing with stress

___poor memory

___sleep disturbance

___difficulty with balance or coordination

___difficulty managing emotions

___difficulty making decisions and setting priorities

___craving

Talk about it and deal with it.

WHAT TO DO WHEN CONFRONTED WITH THE URGE TO USE

Having made the choice for recovery, being clean and sober is of central importance because without it you may lose your family, job, sanity, or even life. If you believe that everything in life depends on your being clean and sober, you are more likely to be successful. If you make other things a priority, your chances for success will be compromised. Here are some things to help you clarify your goal and how to make it happen.

1. Continue to acknowledge and accept that your choice is between a happy, satisfying life or using substances.
2. Learn to be grateful for what you have.
3. Expect that you will experience recurring craving.
4. Develop and rehearse a daily plan of thoughts and behaviors that will guide you through even difficult moments in a day.
5. Never allow yourself to think "it isn't fair that I can't drink or use drugs like other people."
6. Never allow yourself to think of using substances as a substitute for coping with stressors.
7. Continue to identify all of the pleasures in life that are not associated with substance use.
8. Seek ways to help other people—mostly by staying clean and sober yourself.
9. Use your resources—meetings, friends, sponsor, therapist, etc.
10. Do something about the things you can and let go of the things you cannot.

Recovery is an opportunity for personal responsibility, self-awareness, and growth. Abstinence is just the first step of recovery. Although it is an extremely important step, it is just the beginning of a journey of life change.

Write about how the preceding information (ways of thinking and behaving) has influenced your life: _____

_____

_____

_____

_____

_____

_____

_____

_____

_____

POINTS TO CONSIDER WHEN CONFRONTED WITH THE URGE TO USE SUBSTANCES

The individual who yearns to enjoy life as he or she once knew it, but cannot experience it because of continuing addictive behavior, is a very unhappy individual. He or she may have difficulty even forming a mental image of life without substances on some days because the obsessions and urge to use substances seem to control his or her life. Without achieving the goal of abstinence, the self-defeating cycle will continue. If you are able to reprioritize what is important, placing abstinence at the top of the list, all of the other important "priorities" will be possible; marriage, family, job, home life, etc. If you choose a different lineup of priorities and goals, it is possible that you are guaranteeing what you believe you desire most will never happen.

1. Continue to reinforce the fact that your choice is between continuing a life of addiction and doing without a drink, snort, pill, or fix.

2. Work on developing a true sense of gratitude. Be grateful that you have found the out what was wrong and have the opportunity to achieve the life you desire.

3. It is a realistic expectation that for a period of time you will repeatedly experience
   a. conscious, nagging craving to get high
   b. a sudden, compelling impulse to get high
   c. that the craving experienced is not for the substance, but for the soothing, warm euphoria that the substance gave you

4. Use the times when you are not craving as an opportunity to strengthen your recovery.

5. Develop and rehearse a daily plan of thinking and behaving that will guide you through each day of your life regardless of whether you experience the urge to use substances.

6. Do not allow yourself to feel self-pity that you can no longer get high.

7. Do not allow yourself to talk or think about the real or imagined pleasures associated with substance use.

8. Avoid thinking about substance use as a choice for dealing with your problems.

9. Reinforce the positive thoughts and feelings of abstinence, how good it feels to be
   a. free of shame and self-condemnation
   b. free of the fear of the consequences of using substances
   c. free of hangovers or residual side effects of substances
   d. free of the negative perception that others you care about have about you
   e. free of fear!

PLANNING HOW TO COPE WITH A LAPSE

When someone experiences a slip or lapse, he or she often feels shame or guilt for using. Deal with it immediately. If you put off dealing with it, your risk of relapse significantly increases. Use the experience as an opportunity to better understand yourself and what you need to do differently to encourage success in your recovery. Do not allow it to escalate.

Review your refusal skill flash cards. A slip or lapse must be recognized as a crisis in your recovery. If you experience a slip or lapse, do the following immediately.

1. Get rid of the substance.
2. Remove yourself from the people, places, situations, or environment where it occurred
3. Call to talk to someone in your recovery support group immediately.
4. Go to a meeting.
5. Write about it in your journal and then process it with your therapist (or sponsor).
6. Recognize that a slip or lapse does not have to result in a total relapse. Use the experience to strengthen your recovery.

Write about an experience that you have had.

1. What was the situation? _____

_____

_____

2. What did you do? _____

_____

_____

3. What were you thinking (before, during, after)? _____

_____

_____

4. What did you feel (before, during, after)? _____

_____

_____

5. What did you learn? What will help you in the future? _____

_____

_____

DEALING WITH A SLIP, LAPSE, OR RELAPSE

If you have recently experienced a slip, lapse, or relapse, take the time to understand what happened and learn from it. This will help you to build upon the success of abstinence:

1. What happened and when?
2. Understand what happened that brought you to that point and that choice.
3. What were the feelings associated with "failing"?
4. What could you have done differently?
5. Where and when would specific interventions have been most helpful?
6. Understand that a slip or lapse does not have to result in a total relapse.
7. What will be different the next time under similar circumstances?

Think through your experience, replaying a mental picture of what took place. Now write about it using previous statements and questions.

_____

_____

_____

_____

_____

_____

_____

_____

_____

_____

_____

_____

_____

_____

_____

_____

ANTICIPATING HOW TO COPE WITH AN EMERGENCY

Sometimes a person in recovery relaxes, and the result is a decrease in awareness and an increased risk of recovery crisis. Therefore, it is important to have thought out a plan so that you can get back on track immediately. Use your resources. Immediately journal about the crisis and talk with your sponsor or other supportive people who will encourage and reinforce effective coping and problem solving.

If you find yourself in a high-risk situation, do the following:

1. Remove yourself from the situation.
2. Put off using the substance for 15–30 min (craving generally lasts for a brief period of time—wait it out).
3. Challenge stinking thinking (minimizing, rationalizing, justifying).
4. Think about something else or go and do something else that is supportive of recovery.
5. Review your recovery program.
6. Call someone that is supportive of your recovery.

Emergency contact   Phone number

1. _____   _____

2. _____   _____

3. _____   _____

4. _____   _____

5. _____   _____

To help you get through a crisis:

1. _____

2. _____

3. _____

4. _____

5. _____

GETTING UNSTUCK

Understanding
Nurture yourself
Self-acceptance
Truthfulness
Utilization of resources
Choices
Keep doing what works in your step by step efforts toward gaining control
over your life

Chances are you have had negative feelings about yourself and how you have responded to experiences for a long time. This may seem like a difficult if not impossible pattern to break, but with commitment and the use of resources it can change.

1. Learn to accept yourself, both the strengths and the weaknesses.
2. Learn new skills for how to decrease self-defeating, unhealthy thoughts, behaviors, and emotions. Substitute rational and believable thinking, feelings and behaviors.
3. Learn to tolerate normal negative emotions like feelings of sadness and loss. These feelings change, but not immediately because they are connected to experiences that are often unresolvable, where other choices for closure must be pursued.

BEAST

Rational Recovery and Smart Recovery have created the following mnemonic:

Boozing opportunity, when you think of drinking
Enemy recognition, when you hear the inner voice
Accuse the thought of drinking as being the real enemy
Self-control and self-worth are yours now if you choose them
Treasure your sobriety—a lot is at stake

How can you use this to help you in your recovery?

_____

_____

_____

_____

_____

_____

_____

_____

_____

_____

_____

_____

_____

_____

_____

Remember, relapse does not just happen. There are many feelings, thoughts, and behaviors in place before use of a substance occurs.

HELP ME

Head: Negative, irrational thinking. Fantasies, euphoric recall. Get help or move to the next step.

Emotion: Negative or difficult emotions triggered by negative thinking or lack of effective coping. Negative emotions can be a source of permission to use. Get help or move on to the next step.

Lapse: Opportunity to use is present. Placing self in harm's way, making it more difficult to refuse. Use resources, go to a meeting, call your sponsor, call your therapist, talk to people in your support system who will be honest and supportive of your abstinence. Journal to clarify choices and consequences. Get help or move on to next step.

Plan: Negative dysfunctional thinking paves the way for relapse. Old patterns are at greater risk to return. Identify the thoughts and feelings associated with the slip or lapse. If you do not take appropriate action, you are allowing a plan for relapse to unfold. Instead, use this as an opportunity to strengthen your recovery. Get help or move on to the next step.

Move: Move back into a drug culture lifestyle. Relapse. Get help. Understand what has happened and why. Also, identify your supports and choices. If you do not do this, the consequences are likely to increase. Get help or move on.

Enclosed: Cut off from resources who reinforce your recovery. Consequences of returning to use result in conflict and losses. You have been there before. Reinitiate recovery. Go to a meeting, call your sponsor, call your therapist—GET HELP.

Did you realize as you read through this information that you have the opportunity and choice at every step to get help and reestablish your recovery? Life is about choices.

REFUSAL SKILLS

If someone has been abusing substances for some time, chances are that he or she has a very narrow social circle, comprised mostly of other people who also abuse substances. If these relationships are continued, the risk of relapse is increased by

1. Spoken and unspoken pressures to use.
2. Increased craving issues with people, places, situations, emotional states, and activities that had a prior association with the use of substances.
3. Continued thinking about the positive consequences associated with using substances (dull emotions, social lubricant, relaxation, etc.).
4. Continued increased availability of substances.
5. Fear of change—the unknown, which feels like hard work or is overwhelming.

WHAT TO DO

Some of the choices associated with recovery are difficult and feel like losses. However, successful recovery requires changes so that healthy new ways of thinking and behaving can take place. Next is a list of those things that will help you be successful with your choice for abstinence. Make flash cards of your "what to do" refusal skills list so that you always have them to refer to, especially when you are confused and distressed.

1. Avoid people, places, and situations associated with substance use.
2. Refuse the requests to use (turn them down). Hesitation in saying no is a sign of risk. Following hesitation in saying no is rationalization: "One time isn't a problem."
3. Use your flash cards for problem solving the high-risk people, places, emotional states, and situations.
4. Predict the next situation(s) that has a risk of social pressure and using—what are your choices?
5. During the first 90 days of recovery, there is a high risk of relapse. Who do you anticipate that you will see who is supportive of abstinence and recovery and who will encourage or tempt you to use?
6. Visualize and rehearse in your mind your refusal skills.
7. Put off the decision to use for 15–30 min (craving generally does not last too long).
8. Challenge stinking thinking.
9. Remind yourself of your success up until now.
10. Call or visit your support system members or activities.

Surviving the crisis strengthens the recovery.

SUBSTANCE USE AGGRAVATES STRESS

Many individuals turn to substances to help relieve tension and stress. They fail to recognize that substances actually make stress worse. Common responses to stress are

1. Fatigue
2. Depression
3. Easily frustrated
4. Feeling sad and helpless
5. Illness

These reactions can take place whether the stressor is negative or positive. Individuals are also more likely to become ill or find that it takes longer to get well when they experience a lot of stress. Stress can also have a negative influence on maintaining concentration and attention.

Substance dependence is viewed as progressive and plays its own role in stress, because

1. As time passes, the consequences seem to get worse.
2. A person's health and emotional well-being are affected.
3. As effective coping decreases, stress increases.
4. Substance abuse interferes with proper body functioning. When health problems arise they increase stress. Direct influences of harmful physical effects can be
   a. immune system (run-down and poor nutrition)
   b. circulatory system
   c. nervous system

5. The emotional stressors associated with choices made when a person is substance-dependent can include
   a. job loss or demotion
   b. sabottaging a relationship
   c. ruining a marriage
   d. family dysfunction
   e. lowering self-esteem
   f. causing an accident (harm to self, others, financial distress)

It is clear that substances do not get rid of stress. Instead, they can create stress or make it worse in the long run. If you have problems with substances, get help so that you can

1. Take responsibility and resolve issues.
2. Learn new ways of coping.

SELF-CARE PLAN

Self-care is an important aspect of recovery. A good plan considers all of your needs. Develop a personalized self-care plan for optimal emotional health and a positive sense of well-being. This does require a commitment to health and follow through. It is recommended that you have a medical exam for clearance to participate in desired physical activity. Components of a self-care plan include new ways of thinking, mood management, and learning new behaviors. [Adapted from Johnson, S. L. (1997). "Therapist's Guide to Clinical Intervention." San Diego: Academic Press.]

1. Utilization of relaxation techniques to decrease body tension and to manage stress and regular exercise.
2. Review the social supports available to you. If necessary, work at developing an adequate and appropriate support system. Utilization of your social supports can offer relief, distraction, and pleasure. Make a list of your supports.
3. Initiate a journal. Instead of keeping thoughts and feelings inside where they can build up and cause confusion and emotional–physical distress, get them down on paper. A journal is useful for venting thoughts and feelings, clarifying issues, and problem solving. It can also be helpful in determining patterns, relationships, health, and emotional functioning. Keeping a journal will help you monitor progress toward life goals.
4. Get adequate sleep and rest.
5. Smile and have laughter in your life. Be spontaneous at times and playful.
6. Feed your body, mind, and spirit. Eat meals regularly and nutritionally. Practice good hygiene and grooming. Participate in life for personal, spiritual, and professional growth.
7. Approach each day with purpose. Be productive by outlining daily structure. No task is too small to feel good about. Each step can be important to reach goals that you develop.
8. Avoid being self-critical. Be as kind to and understanding of yourself as you would be to another person. Use positive self-talk to reassure yourself, cope effectively, and allow yourself to see that there are always choices.
9. Be sure to build into your schedule time for relationships and pleasurable activities.
10. Take responsibility for your own life. Life is about choices. Understand yourself, your behaviors, your thoughts–beliefs, and your motivations. Be honest with yourself and consistent in your recovery program.

RELAXING WITHOUT SUBSTANCES

Everyone needs to relax and get adequate rest. There are also times when people have difficulty sleeping. Take some time to think about different choices you have to get enough sleep and relaxation without substances.

REST

1. Read a book
2. Meditate–progressive muscle relaxation–yoga
3. Take the time to appreciate the beauty of the outdoors
   a. walk in the forest
   b. watch the clouds
   c. watch birds
   d. star gazing
4. Take an art class and develop a skill
5. Get a massage
6. Listen to classical music or the sounds of nature

SLEEP

1. Get adequate exercise
2. Develop a ritual for unwinding to help prepare your body for sleep
   a. hot bath–shower
   b. herbal tea
   c. relaxing sounds (sound of surf)
   d. meditation–progressive muscle relaxation
   e. no stimulating conversation

Write down your plans for improving rest and sleep:
Rest

1. _____

2. _____

3. _____

4. _____

5. _____

Sleep

1. _____

2. _____

3. _____

4. _____

5. _____

Some people choose to end their day by taking a few moments to reflect upon the good things in their life and their gratitude. We all have things for which to be grateful. You may want to spend a few minutes each evening writing down three to five things for which you feel grateful. To do this, you can use a specific "gratitude journal" or put the entry in a general journal you are using as part of your recovery.

EXCITEMENT WITHOUT SUBSTANCES

Using substances is dangerous. It is this danger seeking that is appealing to many people. This is a difficult issue, because at the beginning of substance use there may be reinforcing experiences when you feel you had fun or a rush of excitement. However, you may be flirting with losses and even death. There are a lot of ways to have a good time and find excitement that are appropriate and safe. Challenge yourself to find some appropriate ways to meet your need for excitement.

Make a list of activities that offer "safe" excitement when you are by yourself and with others. Some examples are sports, sky diving, volunteer firefighting, drama class or plays, rock climbing, or roller coasters.

1. _____

_____

2. _____

_____

3. _____

_____

4. _____

_____

5. _____

_____

6. _____

_____

7. _____

_____

8. _____

_____

9. _____

_____

10. _____

_____

DEEP BREATHING: A RELAXATION SKILL

When you are under stress, your breathing becomes shallow and rapid and your muscles tense. A simple way to decrease stress and relax your body is to breathe deeply and slowly.

HOW IT WORKS

1. Shallow breathing from the chest takes in less oxygen.
2. Blood has to move more quickly to get enough oxygen to the brain, and this can result in high blood pressure.
3. Deep breathing can reverse these effects.
4. Breathe through your nose.
5. Count to 5, filling your lower abdomen with air (diaphragm).
6. Breathe deeply for about 2 min.

Deep breathing used with pleasant mental images like sitting on a beach can increase your relaxation.

RESULTS OF DEEP BREATHING

1. Decreases body tension
2. Relieves body aches
3. Improves sleep
4. Releases endorphins (natural painkillers)
5. Helps blood pressure return to normal (if stressed)

What mental image(s) could you use with deep breathing?

_____

_____

_____

_____

_____

_____

_____

_____

_____

_____

_____

RELAXATION

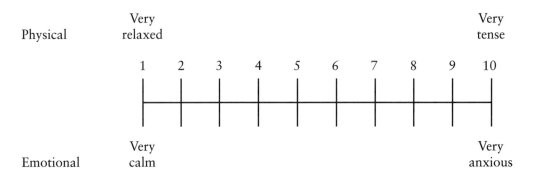

Day and date	Time of day	Length of time	Physical		Mental–emotional		Comments
			Before	After	Before	After	

SELF-CONTROL

Self-control is an important social skill. If you have given yourself permission to be reactive for a long time, it will be a challenge to practice self-control. However, the positive consequences, especially the way you feel about yourself, will reinforce your efforts. Consider the following steps for achieving self-control:

1. Stop to think
2. Pay attention to how you feel inside and what you need to do to be in the best frame of mind to make a good choice
3. Decide whether you are losing self-control
4. Think about your choices
5. Relax and calm yourself
6. Make a choice
7. Do not react to another person's response
8. Review in your mind whether you made the best choice for you
9. Learn from every experience of practicing self-control
10. Be honest with yourself and feel good about your efforts

Write three experiences where you have not demonstrated self-control and then identify what you would do differently:

1. _____

_____

_____

_____

2. _____

_____

_____

_____

3. _____

_____

_____

_____

MODIFIED DRINKING

My Drinking Goals:

1. I will stop drinking alcohol or
2. I will not drink more than _____ drinks per day.
3. I will not drink more than _____ drinks per week.
4. I will start on this day: _____.

Keep a journal of your drinking to help you reach your goal. A journal will show you exactly how much you drink and when.

DRINKING JOURNAL

Day	No. of drinks	Type of drinks	Place consumed	With whom	Feelings– thoughts
Monday					
Tuesday					
Wednesday					
Thursday					
Friday					
Saturday					
Sunday					

WHAT IS RESPONSIBILITY?

Please answer the following questions for increased self-understanding.

1. What does responsibility mean to you?

_____

_____

_____

2. Who is responsible for your behavior and why?

_____

_____

_____

3. Who is responsible for your problems and why?

_____

_____

_____

4. Who is responsible for resolving your problems and how?

_____

_____

_____

5. What are the consequences if you do not take responsibility for yourself?

_____

_____

_____

6. Why is it important for you to be responsible for you?

_____

_____

_____

7. What happens if you try to take responsibility for someone else?

_____

_____

_____

8. What are you responsible for and how will you demonstrate this responsibility?

_____

_____

_____

_____

COPING WITH DISAPPOINTMENT

Everyone has hopes and dreams for the future. Sometimes things do not work out the way we planned. Sometimes things do not turn out because the right decisions and actions were not taken, and other times things just did not work out. Whatever the case, you have a choice to get so frustrated and disappointed that you want to give up or to use the disappointment to better understand what has happened and work at having a different outcome in the future.

THE MEANING AND VALUE OF DISAPPOINTMENT

When you have been planning and hoping for something that does not happen, it is normal to feel disappointed. Generally, you accept the loss and move on. Be careful not to use this as an excuse to relapse. Instead, use it as an opportunity to learn and change. Expectations need to be realistic. Take an honest look at how things really are. There are different kinds of disappointment:

1. Simple disappointment (with an entire range of how you experience it)
   a. small and easy to forget
   b. happens to everybody
   c. deep and painful
   d. could be the result of poor decision making
   e. could be the result of bad luck (bad things happen to good people all the time)
   f. could have been an unrealistic expectation

2. Chronic disappointments: Tend to be a lifestyle pattern associated with not learning from experience or having unrealistic expectations.

3. Life stages
   a. expectations–plans that certain accomplishments will be made at a specific time of life (security, job position, accomplishments)
   b. children growing up
   c. changes in health or physical functioning

HOW TO DECREASE DISAPPOINTMENT

1. Develop realistic expectations and limitations.
2. Be flexible. There are a lot of things that you cannot control.
3. Recognize disappointments, talk about them, and learn from them.
4. Work hard at making your plans a reality.
5. Accept when you cannot influence a situation.

SURVIVING THE HOLIDAY BLUES

Because you cannot control the arrival of the holidays, develop some skills that can lift your spirits and see you through without becoming depressed and self-defeating.

1. Start new traditions: If you have negative or painful memories attached to the holidays, you may dread them and feel unable to celebrate like other people do. If this is the case, then start a new tradition that gives you something to which you can look forward. It may not seem like much at first, but after doing it for several years it will bring new meaning to this time of year.

2. Participate when you can: Even if you do not have much enthusiasm, participate at a level that is comfortable to you. Do not isolate—that will make things worse.

3. Volunteer: Help out at a social service program. This can be a good way out of the holiday blues:
   a. feeling like you have made a contribution to others who have less
   b. helping others can distract you from an overfocus on negatives
   c. recognizing that you can almost always look around and find others in a much more difficult circumstance

4. Talk things out: A lot of people experience holiday blues. If it begins to lead to depression, get professional help.

5. Self-care
   a. nurture yourself
   b. listen to peaceful music or read a book
   c. write to people you care about
   d. plan activities that you will enjoy

Only you can change things for you. Because you know why the holidays lead to feeling bad, take the "Self-responsibility" to deal with it and change what you can. You cannot change the past; however, you can take steps to change your current experience. Do it for yourself. Time passes too quickly, and if you do not take any steps to begin to make a difference, you will soon find yourself confronted with the holidays once again.

STINKING THINKING

In the 12-step tradition, there is a line of thinking patterns that is identified as interfering with staying on task and causing a high risk of relapse. It is referred to as "stinking thinking." Following are some examples. If you find yourself preoccupied in any of these thinking patterns so that you are not able to concentrate on other things, start talking about it immediately so that you can get back on task with your recovery. Recovery requires rational thinking. These thoughts can be present even if you are abstinent.

1. Obsessive thoughts about using: "I'm not using, but I can't seem to stop thinking about it."
2. Craving: Continuing to experience strong cravings to use.
3. Euphoric recall: Focusing on "good experiences" associated with substance use or reexperiencing feelings associated with substance use.
4. Compulsion to use substances: Evidenced by a strong image to use substances.
5. Imaginal thinking or fantasizing about how problems can be solved by using substances.
6. Negaholic thinking: Focus on all of the fears, hard times, and bad feelings associated with abstinence. Minimizing negative associations with relapse.

All of these issues, if not addressed and confronted, increase the risk of relapse.

Because you have been taking the time to increase your awareness and self-understanding, you can predict some situations that may present themselves, which increase the risk of relapse. What things do you say when you are giving permission to use?

Write five situations that may result in you wanting to use substances again. Be thorough in your description of each situation of indulging feelings, thoughts, and self-defeating behaviors that could contribute to the experience of relapse.

_____

_____

_____

_____

_____

_____

_____

_____

_____

_____

_____

_____

_____

_____

Now, go back to each situation you described and write effective responses to

a. self-defeating behavior
b. unimaginable or negative feelings
c. negative thinking

_____

_____

_____

_____

_____

_____

_____

_____

_____

_____

_____

_____

_____

_____

_____

_____

UNDERSTANDING THE ROLE OF THINKING AND RELAPSE

Because people talk to themselves constantly, the content of these messages or repetitive tapes can influence or predispose a person to relapse. Work to be aware of the messages that replay in your mind so that you can develop more helpful and rational thoughts to replace the negative thoughts. AA refers to this type of thinking as "stinking thinking."

Stinky thinking → leads to → drinking thinking → leads to → drinking without thinking.

This path of negative thinking is generalized early to the use of any substance. Sometimes it is a case of excuses being made that takes a person down the path to relapse. Other times it is avoiding taking responsibility or just plain errors in thinking. Some examples of thinking that can lead to relapse (or just feeling bad in general) include the following:

1. Escapism
   a. "I can't deal with it"
   b. "I can't stand feeling this way"
   c. "I want to get away from my problems"

2. Relaxation
   a. "I just wanted to unwind"
   b. "I need to feel better now"

3. Overwhelmed
   a. "This is too much for me"
   b. "It's too hard"

4. Socialization
   a. "I don't know what to say or do when I'm with others"
   b. "I feel anxious in social settings"

5. Lack of control
   a. "Recovery is too hard"
   b. "I don't want to have to do all this"

6. Who cares?
   a. "What is the benefit of this?"
   b. "Does any of this even really matter?"

7. Magical thinking
   a. "I've done so many things wrong"
   b. "Everything is awful because of what I've done"

8. Jumping to conclusions:
   a. "No one talked to me at the meeting"
   b. "I don't belong"

9. Minimizing
   a. "I'll only have one drink, it's no big deal"
   b. "So I used, nothing bad happened"

10. Magnifying
    a. "This is the worst thing that could happen"
    b. "I've blown it now, why stop? Everything I worked on is down the tubes"

COPING WITH NEGATIVE THINKING

Nonnegative thinking begins with honest and rational statements of reality. For those in recovery, there is acknowledgment that they will at some point think about using substances. Acknowledgment creates honest awareness that clarifies the need to appropriately counter these thoughts and have a recovery plan to deal with triggers. There are basic steps to changing your thinking. Changing thinking requires consistent awareness and new behaviors to match the changes in thinking. The steps to changing your thinking are as follows:

1. Awareness

2. Develop realistic statements for replacing or substituting the negative thinking

3. Practice the change consistently

To effectively deal with thoughts of using substances requires the following.

1. Affirmation of commitment to recovery.

2. Consistent substitution of thoughts about using substances.

3. Abstinence.

4. Avoidance of using defense mechanisms as an excuse to use substances.

5. Maintenance of a high level of awareness, being on guard for the risks of relapse and preparedness to deal with it.

6. Use of resources and talking through thoughts as a means of problem solving and validation.

7. Write out a list of the expected positive consequences of substance use.

8. Use visualization to recreate images of the negative consequences associated with substance use.

9. Write out a list of the negative consequences of substance use.

10. Write out the issues or situations that make it difficult to maintain abstinence.

11. Write out a plan for dealing with these issues and situations to encourage and support abstinence.

MANAGING THOUGHTS ABOUT USING SUBSTANCES

One of the major ways to cope with thoughts about using substances is to quit thinking about how you felt it was a benefit to you. Choose to remind yourself of the benefits of not using (make an index card with this list and carry it with you). Focus on the unpleasant side effects and other consequences of use. Doing the following will be helpful.

Benefits of not using substances:

_____

_____

_____

_____

1. Challenge unhelpful thinking.
2. Think of things that are not associated with substance use.
3. Remind yourself of your successes so far and what works.
4. Practice using positive pictures of success in your mind.
   a. successfully refusing
   b. successfully getting past craving

5. Practice using negative pictures associated with how your substance use has harmed or caused pain or disappointment to others.
6. Change your environment (leave a place, be with different people, etc.) when needed.
7. Delay a decision: Give yourself 15 min to make a decision. Call someone supportive of your recovery while waiting to talk about it.

Unpleasant effects and other consequences of using substances:

_____

_____

_____

_____

LIST OF SYMPTOMS LEADING TO RELAPSE

1. *Exhaustion:* Allowing yourself to become overly tired. Not following through on self-care behaviors of adequate rest, good nutrition, and regular exercise. Good physical health is a component of emotional health. How you feel will be reflected in your thinking and judgment.

2. *Dishonesty:* It begins with a pattern of small, unnecessary lies to those with whom you interact in your family, socially, and at work. This is soon followed by lying to yourself or rationalizing and making excuses for avoiding working on your program.

3. *Impatience:* Things are not happening fast enough for you. Or, others are not doing what you want them to do or think they should do.

4. *Argumentative:* Arguing small, insignificant points, which indicates a need to always be right. This is seen as sometimes developing an excuse to drink.

5. *Depression:* Overwhelming and unaccountable despair may occur in cycles. If it does, talk about it and deal with it. You are responsible for taking care of yourself.

6. *Frustration:* With people and because things may not be going your way. Remind yourself intermittently that things are not going to be the way you want them.

7. *Self-pity:* Feeling like a victim, refusing to acknowledge that you have choices and are responsible for your own life and the quality of it.

8. *Cockiness:* "Got it made." Compulsive behavior is no longer a problem. Start putting self in situations where there are temptations to prove to others that you do not have a problem.

9. *Complacency:* Not working on your program with the commitment that you started with. Having a little fear is a good thing. More relapses occur when things are going well than when not.

10. *Expecting too much from others:* "I've changed, why hasn't everyone else changed too?" All that you control is yourself. It would be great if other people changed their self-destructive behaviors, but that is their problem. You have your own problems to monitor and deal with. You cannot expect others to change their lifestyles just because you have.

11. *Letting up on discipline:* Daily inventory, positive affirmations, 12-step meetings, therapy, meditation, prayer, therapy. This can come from complacency and boredom. Because you cannot afford to be bored with your program, take responsibility to talk about it and problem solve it. The cost of relapse is too great. Sometimes you must accept that you have to do some things that are routine for a clean and sober life.

12. *Use of mood-altering chemicals:* You may feel the need or desire to get away from things by drinking, popping a few pills, etc., and your physician may participate in thinking that you will be responsible and not abuse the medication. This is about the most subtle way to enter relapse. Take responsibility for your life and the choices you make.

Printed with permission from Johnson, S. L. (1997). "Therapist's Guide to Clinical Intervention." San Diego: Academic Press.

SYMPTOMS OF RELAPSE

1. Return to denial
   a. Not being truthful
   b. "I may not be an alcoholic–addicted"
   c. About work, sports, relationships
   d. Not being truthful to people around you

   e. _____

   f. _____

2. Avoidance .... the defensive behavior
   a. "It's not possible for me to do it again"
   b. "I'll never do it again"
   c. "I don't need to go to meetings"
   d. "I'm OK, and I don't need meetings"
   e. "I'm not like them"
   f. "They are probably doing it"
   g. "I have a handle on it"

   h. _____

   i. _____

3. Crisis building note; is it really a crisis (patterns)?
   a. "Unable to plan things"
   b. "Family is not doing right"
   c. "This is very important and must be taken care of now!"
   d. Roommate, co-workers, fellow members problems
   e. Him–her problems
   f. "Look at what you made me do"

   g. _____

   h. _____

4. Immobilization (no action can be taken)
   a. Magical thinking: "If I could just win the lotto"
   b. Immature thinking: "I wish that I could just be happy," "if this would happen I could stay sober and have a happy life"

   c. _____

   d. _____

5. Confusion and overreactions
   a. Crisis
   b. Unexpected events
   c. Moody
   d. "I sure would like to use"

e. _____

f. _____

6. Depression
   a. A change in regular eating or sleeping patterns
   b. Deep depression at times
   c. Thinks of suicide
   d. Stays in room more than 12 hr each day
   e. Avoids friends or roommates
   f. Loses daily structure (work, school, chores)
   g. Loses need for recovery structure

   h. _____

   i. _____

7. Behavioral loss of control (the dry drunk syndrome)
   a. Behaviors are like before cleaning up
   b. Avoiding meetings
   c. The feelings of powerlessness
   d. Finding fault
   e. Not forgiving
   f. Not joining in with the "program"
   g. Isolation, not sharing what is inside

   h. _____

8. Recognition of loss of control
   a. Feelings of guilt
   b. Feelings of hopelessness
   c. Feelings of powerlessness
   d. Sadness–shame

   e. _____

   f. _____

9. Option reductions (less and less options)
   a. Unreasonable resentment
   b. Blaming others for his or her state: "If they would have done what
      I told them to do, this would not have happened"
   c. Generalized resentment: "They are all like that"
   d. Loneliness

   e. _____

   f. _____

10. Acute relapse (doing it)
    a. Feeling like a complete failure
    b. An emotional collapse

c. Not belonging to either or any group
d. Thoughts of suicide
e. Suicidal

f. _____

g. _____

EARLY WARNING SIGNS

If you find yourself experiencing any of the following symptoms, get help immediately.

1. Violations of value system
2. Increased use
3. Preoccupation with use
4. Increased planning for use
5. Spending time with friends who use
6. Blackouts–losing time
7. Mood changes with use
8. Sexual acting out
9. Behavioral and personality changes

Talk with someone to better understand yourself.

1. What has been happening?
2. Why has it been happening?
3. What are your choices for changing it?

REVIEWING PERSONAL RISKS OF RELAPSE

You have already identified some thoughts, feelings, and behaviors that are associated with increasing the risk of relapse. Write appropriate and rational alternatives to each relapse-prone thought, feeling, and behavior.

Thoughts:

1. _____

_____

_____

_____

2. _____

_____

_____

_____

3. _____

_____

_____

_____

Feelings:

1. _____

_____

_____

_____

2. _____

_____

_____

_____

3. _____

_____

_____

_____

Behaviors:

1. _____

_____

_____

2. _____

_____

_____

2. _____

_____

_____

FEELING LIKE YOUR LIFE IS OUT OF CONTROL

When you feels like your life is out of control, your negative thinking increases, you feel overwhelmed and desperate, your self-esteem plummets, and there does not seem to be anything that you can do to get back in control. It is like having a lot of conversations in your head with yourself and you cannot turn it off. It is such a frightening feeling that suicide may appear like the only way to get away from it all. Most people experience this feeling a little bit when they have a lot of different things going on at one time and the demand is greater than what they can give to take care of everything.

It may not be what would be expected, but when a person is feeling like this, he or she tends to engage in behaviors that contribute to feeling and being more and more out of control. It can be like a vicious cycle. The thing to do is to get help from someone who is trusted and can be objective. There are choices, but to effectively make good choices, a person will have to slow things down, evaluate and define what the problems are, and then prioritize the identified issues so that they can be systematically resolved one by one. A person can only do one thing at a time. When this process is followed, it becomes possible to take one step at a time toward any goal that has been set. It helps to deal with "what is" instead of "what if." [Printed with permission from Johnson, S. L. (1997). "Therapist's Guide to Clinical Intervention." San Diego: Academic Press.]

If you are feeling like your life is out of control, describe it. _____

_____

_____

What are all of the things that you are feeling pressure from? _____

_____

_____

What resources can you use to help you slow things down to get a handle on your situation?

_____

_____

_____

Remember :

1. Take one day at a time.
2. You can only do one thing at a time.
3. Give yourself credit for your efforts and accomplishments, because every step you take contributes to regaining control over your life.

DEALING WITH FEELING EMOTIONALLY OVERWHELMED

When someone has used substances for a long time, there tends to be emotional blunting or masking of what he or she would normally feel in many different situations. He or she may also experience feeling emotionally overwhelmed if he or she has used substances to "cope" with his or her emotions and stress, which results in a lack of developing effective coping. This in turn increases feelings of stress and the "need" to use substances to cover up the feelings of inadequacy.

When someone chooses recovery, the result, aside from abstinence, is twofold:

1. *Feeling emotionally overwhelmed* is at times so intense that a person may find him- or herself totally focused on how to escape or avoid the distress. Therefore, take the time to break down what feels overwhelming into manageable steps:
   a. identify the emotion [accurately describe what emotions(s) you are experiencing]
   b. think about what you need to do
      i. write about it in your journal (problem solve or let go)
      ii. where does the distress come from?
      iii. how would you normally respond?
      iv. how do you want to respond?
      v. how can you share the information so that another person can hear what you are saying and understand your experience?

2. *Inability to effectively cope* is the result of stunted personal growth and lack of adequate social skills. Learn to cope effectively:
   a. read or join a support group to get the information you need
   b. observe others who demonstrate effective coping
   c. consider your choices in responding to a variety of situations
   d. clarify the consequences associated with each choice
   e. practice doing things differently, and remember that you are in the process of learning and will make mistakes

If you take responsibility for what you say and what you do, you will make progress in recognizing what you have control over and can do something about and what you have no control over and must let go.

The Serenity Prayer
   God grant me the serenity to accept the things I cannot change,
   The courage to change the things I can, and
   The wisdom to know the difference.

PREVENTION

ADULTS

1. Examine your own use of substances as objectively as possible. Be aware of utilizing the defense mechanisms of
   a. denial
   b. rationalizing use
   c. projecting (blaming)
   d. minimizing use
   e. changing the topic
   f. repressing the facts that are painful

2. Recognize and follow "unsafe" drinking periods (HALT):
   a. H=being hungry
   b. A=being angry
   c. L=being lonely
   d. T=being tired

3. Recognize media messages contradicting these rules

4. Recognize that social customs regulating use of substances are changing

5. Realize that our drinks are "larger and stiffer" these days (2–3 oz versus 1 oz)

6. Be aware of underestimating the amount consumed per setting, occasions

7. Be aware of underestimating your frequency of using substances (self-delusion)

8. Recognize behaviors used that could classify you as a "pusher" (soliciting and encouraging attendance at after-work get-togethers, TGIF, walking around refilling drinks at events, encouraging someone to have "just one more," etc.)

9. Take an inventory of activities that you enjoy doing, going to, participating in. How many include substance use? What alternatives do you have to getting "high?"

10. If substance use is a part of your life, FOLLOW THESE RULES:
    a. measure drinks
    b. count drinks
    c. drink when relaxed
    d. drink slowly
    e. confine–reduce occasions to drink
    f. do not cluster drink (week's allowance in a day)
    g. move around while drinking
    h. stop when effects begin to show
    i. eat while drinking
    j. do NOT drink if you do not enjoy it!
    k. RESPECT ALCOHOL–DRUGS!!!

DEVELOPING AND UTILIZING SOCIAL SUPPORT

When someone lacks emotional support, he or she tends to withdraw from pleasureable activities and socially isolate. One important way to regain emotional health, encourage recovery, and develop new ways of thinking and behaving is to develop and utilize appropriate social supports.

We all need several good friends to talk to, spend time with, and be supported by with their care and understanding. For someone to be part of your support system requires that you care for them and/or trust them. A partner or family member is a likely candidate for your support system. You may develop relationships with people through activities or interests that you share. These relationships could become strong enough to become part of your support system. Other resources could be clubs or other social group affiliations that you feel a part of and have regular contact. Whoever the person or group is, it is necessary that there be mutual care, positive regard, and trust. It is reasonable to expect that some of the people or activities in your life would be related to recovery. Such support offers affiliation, the learning of survival skills, increased self-understanding and an environment and people who support recovery.

CHARACTERISTICS OF A SUPPORTIVE RELATIONSHIP

1. Objectivity and open-mindedness. They let you describe who you are and how you feel. They validate you.
2. They support and affirm your individuality and recognize your strengths. They validate and encourage your goals.
3. They empathize with you. They understand your life circumstances and how you are affected by your life experiences.
4. They accept you as you are without being judgmental. You ask one another for help and support. However, they are also honest with you.
5. You can laugh with them and be playful. You will both enjoy it.

They are at your side, supporting you to do whatever is important to you. And most importantly, they accept and support your goal of recovery.

List the people that make up your recovery support system:

1. _____

2. _____

3. _____

4. _____

5. _____

List the activities that are part of your recovery support system:

1. _____

2. _____

3. _____

4. _____

5. _____

HOW TO BUILD A RECOVERY SUPPORT SYSTEM

The people comprising your recovery support system could include a life partner, family, friends, and those who may be supportive within a variety of environments (self-help groups, church, or other community organizations). Being a part of a recovery support system is a commitment and a responsibility. Be sure that you communicate in what ways you would like to be able to seek support from them so that they understand your current and future needs. There may be some people you would like to be a part of your support system but who, for a variety of reasons, are not able to. Respect their honesty and pursue other resources.

Characteristics of people in a social network supportive of recovery are as follows:

1. Do not have a substance abuse problem
2. Knowledgeable about substance abuse or willing to learn about it
3. Accepting and supportive of your decision and need for being in recovery
4. Supportive of your goals of recovery and personal growth
5. Available to be supportive

List 10 characteristics of people who would not be a good choice for your recovery support system. You know your special needs at this time and will benefit from surrounding yourself with supportive people, environments, and activities. You also need to identify the negatives that are not supportive of recovery.

1. _____
2. _____
3. _____
4. _____
5. _____
6. _____
7. _____
8. _____
9. _____
10. _____

List 10 places or activities that increase your risk of relapse.

1. _____
2. _____
3. _____

4. _____

5. _____

6. _____

7. _____

8. _____

9. _____

10. _____

MAINTAINING A SUPPORT SYSTEM

Maintaining a positive support system is an important part of recovery. Answer the following questions to increase your awareness and understanding of this topic.

1. List things that will help you maintain recovery.

_____

_____

_____

_____

_____

2. What do you do to maintain emotional well-being and stable moods?

_____

_____

_____

_____

_____

3. List self-care behaviors.

_____

_____

_____

_____

_____

4. In recognizing and accepting that others can help, but that you are responsible for making yourself okay, define what you must do for yourself versus what is reasonable support form others.

_____

_____

_____

_____

_____

5. Developing appropriate social skills can be done by working with a sponsor or therapist, reading and practicing the techniques you read about, participating in activities in the community or special groups, taking a class at an adult education program if available, or observing other people who demonstrate successful behaviors. Explore your community and identify what resources would be helpful and what is available to you.

_____

_____

_____

_____

6. Doing volunteer work and being supportive of others can be a helpful technique that encourages you to be a contributing member of your community and decrease the focus on the negatives in your life. When you participate as a volunteer in your community, take the time to make an inventory of all the things for which you have to be grateful. Where could you volunteer that is of interest to you? Who supports you and how can you be supportive back?

_____

_____

_____

_____

7. Make it a point to stay in touch with friends and acquaintances who are supportive of your recovery. When was the last time you invited someone to do something or made an effort to get together? If it did not work out, was it because of the timing, the activity, or someone who really is not capable of being a social support to you? What are you going to do to increase your success in being active and growing through the use of your social support system?

_____

_____

_____

_____

8. How will you know if you are making progress in developing a social support system? How does that social support system work to encourage your recovery?

_____

_____

_____

_____

As you worked through these questions, you may have noticed that the way to build and keep a support system is by working on being the best you can be. From time to time, just as you reevaluate your recovery plan, review your social support system and make changes as needed. Developing and maintaining a support system that encourages and reinforces your efforts toward recovery are very important and are your responsibility. [Adapted from Johnson, S. L. (1997). "Therapist's Guide to Clinical Intervention." San Diego: Academic Press.]

FACTORS THAT INTERFERE WITH DEVELOPING A SOCIAL SUPPORT SYSTEM

If you do not have anyone to list as your support system or only one or two people, do not feel bad about yourself and give up. What you have done is to accomplish the first step in understanding what you need to do: change your situation. The good news is that there is a lot you can do to change your situation.

What stands in your way of developing your support system (check the items that apply to you)?

1. You are afraid of change
2. You have a hard time reaching out
3. You have a hard time making and keeping friends
4. You have low self–esteem, fear of being rejected
5. You tend to be very needy and draining to others
6. You become overly dependent and wear people out
7. You lack the social skills necessary to develop relationships
8. You have inappropriate behaviors that embarrass others
9. You are unreliable

What is it you need and want from your recovery support system (check the items that apply to you)?

1. Someone to talk to
2. Understanding
3. Someone to stand up for you
4. Companionship
5. Caring
6. Sharing
7. Someone to watch or monitor you
8. Someone who will listen to you
9. Someone to do things with
10. Someone who writes to you or phones you
11. Someone who encourages your recovery
12. Someone who encourages your personal growth

Are there other things you would want or expect from a friend?

_____

_____

_____

People that help you get started in making the changes necessary to develop a strong support system include your therapist, minister, and various support groups. There are also many helpful books that have been written that you can find in the psychology or self-help sections of a bookstore. The main thing is to make a commitment to yourself, develop a support system, and not give up. [Adapted from Johnson, S. L. (1997). "Therapist's Guide to Clinical Intervention." San Diego: Academic Press.]

THE ROLE OF RELATIONSHIPS AND SUBSTANCE USE

Because you may be asking people who come from a variety of backgrounds and experiences as well as those who have played a prior role in your life to become a part of your recovery support system, it may be helpful to clarify how their relationships with you may have unknowingly or knowingly played a role in your substance use. For them to take the time to explore some of the same recovery issues you have explored would be very helpful and a sign of their commitment to support your recovery. Anyone with whom you have had a relationship has undoubtedly been affected by your substance use. Likewise, there have been some things that they did that may have played a role in your substance use behaviors.

You may want to ask those who you are requesting to be a part of your support system to take the time to complete the following brief inventory.

QUESTIONNAIRE FOR POTENTIAL SOCIAL SUPPORT MEMBER

Name: _____ Relationship to Person in Recovery: _____

1. If you have unresolved issues or feelings of anger with this person, then address it honestly and appropriately. If it is a difficult issue that you are concerned about addressing on your own, ask him or her to attend a therapy session or have a counselor–sponsor mediate.
2. How has this person's behavior affected you?
3. Identify any behaviors or statements that may contribute to a relapse.
4. What signs of relapse have you seen in this person that concerns you when you are with him or her?
5. Do these signs of relapse affect you in any way?
   a. how do you react when this happens?
   b. how does your response affect him or her?
6. Can you think of any alternative responses for either of you that may be helpful in supporting recovery efforts?
7. What role are you willing to play in this person's recovery support system?
8. Can you predict any situations that would be too stressful for you as a support system member?
9. In what manner could you be supportive if this person returned to prior substance abuse patterns?
10. What would you do differently if this person did experience relapse (than you might have responded in the past)?

DEFENSE MECHANISM DEFINITIONS

These definitions have been provided to help you understand what defense mechanisms you may be using to avoid dealing with issues. As you read through them, circle the ones that you use. Writing and talking about how you use defense mechanisms will increase your awareness to avoid excuses and confront the problems. [Modified from Johnson, S. L. (1997). "Therapist's Guide to Clinical Intervention." San Diego: Academic Press.]

1. Denial: Protecting oneself from unpleasant aspects of life by refusing to perceive, acknowledge, or face them.

2. Rationalization: Trying to prove one's actions "made sense" or were justified; making excuses.

3. Intellectualization: Hiding one's feelings about something painful behind thoughts; keeping opposing attitudes apart by using logic-tight comparisons.

4. Displacement: Misdirecting pent-up feelings toward something or someone that is less threatening than that which actually triggered the response.

5. Projection: Blaming, assuming that someone has a particular quality or qualities that one finds distasteful.

6. Reaction formation: Adopting actions and beliefs to an exaggerated degree that are directly opposite those previously accepted.

7. Undoing: Trying to superficially repair or make up for an action without dealing with the complex effects of that deed; "magical thinking."

8. Withdrawal: Becoming emotionally uninvolved by pulling back and being passive.

9. Introjection: Adopting someone else's values and standards without exploring whether they actually fit oneself; "shoulds" or "ought to's."

10. Fantasy: Trying to handle problems or frustrations through daydreaming or imaginary solutions.

11. Repression: Unconsciously blocking out painful thoughts.

12. Identification: Trying to feel more important by associating oneself with someone or something that is highly valued.

13. Acting out: Repeatedly performing actions to keep from being uptight without weighing the possible results of those actions.

14. Compensation: Hiding a weakness by stressing too strongly the desirable strength. Overindulging in one area to make up for frustration in another.

15. Regression: under stress, readopting actions performed at a less mature stage of development.

DEFENSE MECHANISMS

You may have been offered much evidence about having a substance use problem and chose to ignore or deny it. You may have refused to take an honest look at you: your thoughts, feelings, behaviors, coping style, reference group, efforts toward goals. What you need to do may seem so hard and overwhelming that you do not want to face it and take responsibility. Be honest with yourself, search for answers about you and necessary resources and supports.

Defense mechanisms are ways of coping that are sometimes used by people when they want to avoid or distance themselves from a problem. Part of recovery is the development of self-responsibility, which requires being honest with yourself and others. In order to do this, you must be willing to be honest about your thoughts, feelings, behaviors, and coping style. [Modified from Johnson, S. L. (1997). "Therapist's Guide to Clinical Intervention." San Diego: Academic Press.]

1. Defense mechanism: _____

_____

_____

_____

_____

2. Defense mechanism: _____

_____

_____

_____

_____

3. Defense mechanism: _____

_____

_____

_____

_____

4. Defense mechanism: _____

_____

_____

_____

_____

5. Defense mechanism: _____

_____

_____

_____

_____

DEALING WITH FEAR

Fear can feel overwhelming and seem to stand in the way of making necessary changes. Answer the following questions to clarify your fear, how it affects you, and what you can do to resolve it and move forward in your goal of recovery.

1. What are you afraid of? _____

_____

_____

_____

2. Identify the cause(s) of your fear: _____

_____

_____

_____

3. Is your fear rational? _____

_____

_____

_____

4. What is the worst thing that could happen associated with your fear? _____

_____

_____

_____

5. What is the best thing that could happen if you resolve your fear? _____

_____

_____

_____

6. Are you concerned that more will be expected of you if you overcome your fear?

_____

_____

_____

_____

7. What have you done in the past to get over your fear? _____

_____

_____

_____

8. What do you think would decrease your fear?_____

_____

_____

_____

9. What are your current choices in helping you to overcome your fear? _____

_____

_____

_____

10. What are you going to do? _____

_____

_____

_____

BREAKING THROUGH THE NEGATIVE THOUGHTS CYCLE

When you decide to stop using substances, you will likely experience certain thoughts that lead to craving. When this happens, there are thoughts that rationalize the use of substances, justifying that it is okay: only one drink, one hit, etc. It is a way of giving permission. When you have decided to stop using substances and you have these thoughts, it creates internal conflict. "Continued recovery or relapse." Although this seems like an automatic process that comes out of nowhere, it is not.

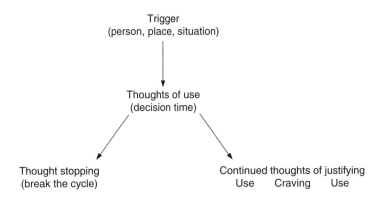

Trigger
(person, place, situation)

Thoughts of use
(decision time)

Thought stopping
(break the cycle)

Continued thoughts of justifying
Use   Craving   Use

Because this process has been going on for a long time, it seems automatic; therefore, it takes a lot of effort to make yourself aware of and choose to stop the thoughts. However, if you do not make the effort to break this cycle, you must acknowledge that you are making the choice that sets you on a course to relapse. The best way to prevent it is to stop the thoughts immediately before they build up to the point of craving.

THOUGHT STOPPING

A technique that is useful for breaking one of the cycles that triggers use is thought stopping. This is not an automatic cycle. You have a choice.

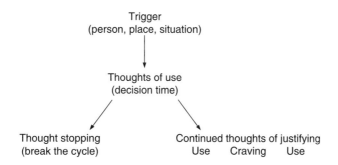

Thought stopping is accomplished by interfering (stopping) thoughts of using by distracting yourself with something else. Here are some choices you can make.

1. *Snap:* A loose rubber band on your wrist. Every time you become aware of a substance using thought, snap the rubber band, say "no" to that thought, and choose to think about something else.
2. *Call someone:* Supportive of your recovery. Talk out your feelings to improve your awareness and to reinforce the positive changes of recovery.
3. *Visualization:* Create a picture in your mind of a peaceful, serene place. See yourself successfully abstaining from substances.
4. *Meditation:* You can learn meditation by taking a meditation or yoga class, getting a tape, or developing your own meditation from the outline of a book.
5. *Progressive muscle relaxation:* Use a tape you have purchased or ask your therapist to make–lend you a tape. If you use it daily, pretty soon you will be asked to do it without a tape.

FIFTEEN RULES FOR EMOTIONAL HEALTH

1. Remain committed to recovery and personal growth.

2. Take care of yourself. Take time to relax, exercise, eat well, spend time with people you enjoy, and participate in activities you find pleasurable. When you are the best you can be for you, then you will be the best you can be in all other relationships.

3. Choose to find the positives in life experiences instead of focusing on the negatives. Most clouds have a silver lining of opportunity for personal understanding and growth. When you accept that things are difficult and just do what needs to be done, it no longer seems so hard.

4. Let go of the past. If you cannot change it, and you have no control over it, then let it go. Do not waste your energy on things that you cannot change. Forgive yourself and others.

5. Be respectful and responsible. Do not worry about other people and their choices. Do what you know is right for you. When you take care of business it feels good. Do not get caught up in planning what other people should do.

6. Acknowledge and take credit for your accomplishments and successes. Avoid false modesty.

7. Take the time to develop close relationships in which you can be honest about your thoughts and feelings.

8. Talk positively to yourself. You may not be aware of it, but you talk to yourself all day long. If you are saying negative and fearful things, that is what you will feel.

9. Remove yourself from potentially risky or damaging situations. Walk away from a difficult or confusing situation and give yourself time to think about your choices for dealing with it.

10. Accept that life is about choices and that there is always change of some sort to deal with. Making positive adjustments means being clear about your values, but flexible to grow with new knowledge.

11. Have a plan for the future. Develop long-range goals for yourself, but work on them one day at a time.

12. Recognize that you will reexperience difficult situations until you learn to improve your judgment. Make appropriate changes.

13. When you find yourself in a repetitive negative experience, ask yourself
    a. what am I doing?
    b. why am I doing it?
    c. what do I need to do?

14. Clarify your values and live by them. They are your life rules. When people do not live according to their values, it makes them sick in some way.

15. Accept that making mistakes and learning from them is an ongoing life experience. Strive to get the most out of every learning experience.

Adapted from Johnson, S. L. (1997). "Therapist's Guide to Clinical Intervention." San Diego: Academic Press.

DEALING WITH DIFFICULT PEOPLE

Everyone will be confronted with having to deal with a difficult person. It can lead to feeling fearful or avoiding activities and interests. The best approach is to

1. Identify the pattern.
2. Define the behavior.
3. Clarify your choices.
4. Decide how to best deal with them.
5. Recognize any contribution you have to a difficult situation. You only have control over what you do.

Try the following techniques with people who make your life difficult or frustrating.

1. Bullies: Avoid fighting, but make your point clear.
2. Silent types: Ask them open-ended questions that require more than a yes–no response.
3. Negaholics: Enlist them to be part of a solution.
4. Complainers: Ask them directly, "What is it that you want?"
5. Know-it-alls: Gather the facts before talking with them.
6. Procrastinators: Find out the reason behind the delay. Ask for their help.

Write about two situations dealing with difficult people that you have encountered where things have not gone well. What would you do differently?

1. _____

_____

_____

_____

_____

_____

2. _____

_____

_____

_____

_____

_____

SURVIVING THE LOSS OF A RELATIONSHIP

When a relationship ends as a result of a breakup or divorce, it is a very stressful and emotional experience. There is no doubt that it is a crisis. However, it is also a time of opportunity:

1. Focus on self-care and personal growth
2. Learn from the experience
3. Develop new relationships

Emotional stress can be experienced as follows:

1. Separations are painful
2. Feeling like a failure
3. Loss of security, friendship, intimacy, nurturing
4. Resentment and anger
5. Feelings of guilt, worry, loneliness
6. Issues associated with child support and custody
7. Depression and anxiety

Physical stress can be experienced as follows:

1. Headaches
2. Abdominal distress (stomach hurts)
3. Sleep disturbance
4. Appetite disturbance

Self-care and healing:

1. Acknowledge and accept your feelings
2. Reach out for support, attend a support group, get a book on the subject, journal
3. Take risks, try new things, create opportunities
4. Eat right and get enough sleep
5. Do not self-medicate

THE ART OF NEGOTIATION

When more than one person has something to offer about a decision being made, negotiation may be necessary. Negotiation is an important skill for resolving conflict, promoting a "brainstorm" of choices, offering a careful review of the input–outcome as negotiators try to persuade one another, and creating a collaborative atmosphere. The components of negotiation are the following:

1. Identify the problem–area of conflict.
2. Offer your ideas about how to deal with the problem.
3. Discuss all the choices for resolution.
4. Listen to each other with open minds.
5. Be respectful of one another's opinions.
6. Think through the information presented by the other person.
7. Struggle to understand why he or she feels the way he or she does.
8. Avoid blaming and conflict-oriented behavior, such as finger pointing or name calling.
9. Try to work toward a mutually satisfying compromise.
10. Reinforce a collaborative effort to bring the issue to a resolution (thank the other person for his or her positive efforts).

How to negotiate differences:

1. Communicate in a positive manner
   a. do not be angry or accusing
   b. be direct
   c. express yourself honestly and in a manner in which you can be heard

2. Be cooperative
   a. work together
   b. listen, do not be defensive
   c. acknowledge the contribution of everyone
   d. suggest "win–win" solutions
   e. assume both of you have a desire for peaceful resolution

3. Be understanding
   a. negotiate wisely
   b. put yourself in the other person's shoes
   c. avoid criticizing

SELF-CONFIDENCE

A part of recovery is learning more about yourself and what you are capable of doing. List positive statements about yourself to each of the following questions.

1. What can I do now that seemed difficult or impossible before?

    a. _____

    b. _____

    c. _____

    d. _____

    e. _____

2. What can I accomplish if I make a commitment and put my mind to work on it?

    a. _____

    b. _____

    c. _____

    d. _____

    e. _____

3. What personality traits am I working at acquiring?

    a. _____

    b. _____

    c. _____

    d. _____

    e. _____

4. What are the long-term goals I am working on that will add to my feelings of being successful?

    a. _____

    b. _____

    c. _____

    d. _____

    e. _____

You can see that building self-confidence is an active process that requires

1. Taking action
2. Choosing to think in a positive and productive way
3. Observing others who are successful (how they do it)
4. Developing and using resources
5. Developing goals and breaking them down into manageable steps

COPING WITH CONFRONTATIONS

Confrontations may take place for numerous reasons. Generally, when one person confronts another, it is because he or she is displeased with something and needs to vent or wants to resolve it. Whatever the case, it is an attempt to educate someone about a specific situation. Use the following suggestions to diffuse and resolve confrontational situations.

1. Remain calm.
2. Show appropriate concern.
3. Use good social skills and avoid blaming.
4. Speak reassuringly.
5. Do not raise your voice unnecessarily; discuss things in a business-like or problem solving manner.
6. Monitor the tone of your voice. Pay attention to how you may sound to someone else.
7. Be positive in your attitude and presentation.
8. Do not use provocative, angry language.
9. Do not use threatening behavior such as pointing in someone's face or shaking your fist.
10. Be respectful. Do not invade the other person's personal space.
11. Try to gain control over the situation by appropriately validating and speaking calmly.
12. Attempt to diffuse the situation by redirecting the focal point of anger to the issue instead of the person.

Write about three situations when you were confronted that you would like to have had a better ending. Use the preceding recommendations to determine how you could have responded differently.

1. _____

_____

_____

2. _____

_____

_____

3. _____

_____

_____

DEALING WITH EMBARRASSMENT OR
BEING SELF-CONSCIOUS

Sometimes people avoid or withdraw from a situation because they experience some type of embarrassment. Instead of limiting your resources, learn to deal with a feeling that everyone experiences at some point. Some ways of dealing with embarrassment include the following:

1. Decide why you are feeling embarrassed.
2. Clarify what happened that made you feel embarrassed.
3. Decide what can be done to decrease feelings of embarrassment.
4. If possible, correct the problem.
5. If not correctable, make a comment about it.
6. Use humor, laugh it off.
7. Ignore the embarrassment. Do not make it a big deal.
8. If someone has a habit of saying or doing things that embarrass you, confront the issue.
9. Challenge irrational thoughts you have that may contribute to feeling embarrassed.
10. Assure yourself that you are all right and that the embarrassment is not long lasting or important.

Write about an experience or issue that has been embarrassing for you. How has it created limitations? How are you going to take charge of the situation and not let it limit you?

_____

_____

_____

_____

_____

_____

_____

_____

_____

_____

_____

_____

COPING WITH EMBARRASSMENT

Everyone will experience feelings of embarrassment at some time. Therefore, learning to effectively deal with it in a positive manner is an important social skill. Following are some ways of learning to deal with the difficult feelings of embarrassment.

1. Clarify why you feel embarrassed.
2. Talk to someone or write about what has happened that resulted in you feeling embarrassed.
3. Clarify what can be done to make you feel less embarrassed.
4. If possible, correct any problems that contribute to feelings of embarrassment.
5. Use laughter. Learn to laugh at yourself and make light of situations when appropriate.
6. Assure yourself with positive self-talk that you will survive this and it will pass.
7. Confirm your self-worth.
8. Talk yourself through it and be rational.

Describe three situations where you have or would experience embarrassment. How would you choose to deal with each situation?

1. _____

_____

_____

_____

_____

_____

_____

_____

_____

2. _____

_____

_____

_____

_____

_____

_____

_____

3. _____

_____

_____

_____

_____

_____

_____

_____

EMOTIONAL FIRST STEPS FOR DUAL DIAGNOSIS

1. Self–understanding
2. How you have managed your symptoms
3. Improving coping with new thinking and behaviors

It is assumed that you have already given a thorough review of your substance use history, identified your recovery goals (including how to manage high-risk situations, sources of recovery support, supportive daily structure such as meetings and journaling, and ways of increasing self-responsibility), and are participating in a treatment program.

An important component of successful recovery is developing the ability to find appropriate and necessary help. Treatment staff, therapist, sponsor, and clergy are some of the sources who can offer helpful information. You can also read or talk to others who have been successful in recovery. Ask for help if you feel stuck or need more support.

Many people who have dual diagnosis will benefit from medication. Medication can make you feel better, and it may help you to think more clearly as well. Taking prescription medication as prescribed, by a physician who understands addiction, is different than using other substances or abusing prescriptions to get high. It is important that you develop a good awareness of your symptoms and share them with your doctor. If you are unclear about your symptoms, keep a journal of your symptoms and accept feedback from those who care and are objective. When you talk to your doctor, ask questions. The more you learn about your illness, the better prepared you will be for learning to effectively manage your symptoms.

Some of the illnesses often associated with substance abuse include the following. If you have a diagnosis that is not on the list, your counselor or therapist can provide you with a list of symptoms to better understand your life experience.

__Anxiety Disorders
    __Generalized Anxiety
    __Obsessive Compulsive Disorder
    __Panic Anxiety
    __Phobic Disorders
    __Posttraumatic Stress Disorder

__Mood Disorders
    __Bipolar Disorder
    __Depression
    __Mania

__Personality Disorder
__Thought Disorder

Following are symptom lists associated with the general diagnoses already given. This is just the beginning of finding out about your illness. Beside each symptom that applies to you, do the following:

1. Mark with an "s" if the symptom is experienced under the influence of substance use.
2. Mark with an "x" if the symptom is experienced when clean and sober.
3. Mark with a "b" if the symptom is experienced under both of those conditions.

Marking the conditions that you experience and your symptoms will help you understand which symptoms are associated with your use of substances and which are associated with your illness. There may be some overlap of symptoms. Also, if you have a symptom that is not listed, add it.

ANXIETY DISORDER SYMPTOMS

__trembling, twitching, shaking
__restlessness
__feeling keyed up, on edge
__shortness of breath
__sleep disturbance
__palpitations, fast heart rate
__nausea or abdominal distress
__chest pain
__fear of going crazy
__avoiding people–places–things
__recurrent–distressing recollections
__sense of reexperiencing trauma
__efforts to avoid distressing thoughts
__inability to recall aspects of trauma
__feelings of detachment
__irritability–outbursts of anger
__hypervigilance
__do not expect to have a career, marriage, children, or long life
__fear is excessive–unreasonable
__repetitive intentional behaviors

__muscle tension
__fatigue
__frequent urination
__dizziness or faintness
__stress
__sweating, cold flashes, hot flashes
__numbness or tingling
__fear of dying
__fear of doing something uncontrolled
__you–your environment do not seem real
__recurrent distressing dreams
__intense emotional distress
__efforts to avoid activities–situations that bring up recollections of the trauma
__restricted range of feelings (e.g., cannot feel love)
__difficulty with concentration
__exaggerated startle response
__recurrent thoughts–images
__checking rituals or routines to decrease anxiety

Additional

Symptoms

_____   _____

_____   _____

_____   _____

Comments:

_____

_____

_____

_____

_____

MOOD DISORDER SYMPTOMS

__depressed mood

__appetite disturbance

__fatigue

__poor concentration

__feeling helpless–hopeless

__thoughts, plans of suicide

__abnormally elevated mood

__inflated self-esteem–grandiosity

__distractibility

__flight of ideas–racing thoughts

__psychomotor agitation

__mood disturbance impairs functioning

__hallucinations

   __see things that are not there

   __hear thing that others do not hear

__delusions

   __distortions in thinking
    (such as ideas of reference)

__irritable mood

__sleep disturbance

__low self-esteem

__difficulty making decisions

__feelings of despair

__prior suicide attempts

__abnormal irritability

__decreased need for sleep

__more talkative–pressure to speak

__increased goal–directed activity

__excessive pleasurable activity
  (sex, gambling, shopping, etc.)

PERSONALITY DISORDER SYMPTOMS

Paranoid

_____

__expects to be harmed by others

__holds grudes for slight
  insults

__questions without justification fidelity of
  partner

__reads hidden demeaning or threatening
  meaning from benign remarks or behaviors

__distrusts others without justification

__reluctant to confide in others
  for fear
  information will be used against him
  or her

Antisocial

_____

__truant–runaway

__cruel to animals

__destroyed the property of others

__stolen from others (including forgery)

__unable to sustain consistent work

__irritable–aggressive

__impulsive–does not plan ahead

__reckless safety behaviors

__often initiates physical fights

__physically abusive to others

__deliberately sets fires

__often lies

__does not respect laws or rules

__fails to honor financial obligations

__use of alias or conning

__is not a responsible parent

Borderline	__unstable–intense relationships	__black–white thinking
	__self-damaging impulsiveness (sex, spending, shoplifting, binge eating)	__self-mutilation–suicidal
		__chronic feelings of emptiness
	__frantic efforts to avoid real or percieved abandonment	
	__identity disturbance (self-image, sexual orientation, goals, career choice, values)	

Histrionic	__constantly seeking reassurance	__inappropriately sexually seductive
	__overconcerned with physical appearance	__exaggerated expression of emotions
	__uncomfortable if not center of attention	__self-centered

Narcissistic	__reacts negatively to criticism	__takes advantage of others
	__believes his or her problems are unique	__grandiose sense of self-importance
	__preoccupied with fantasies of success	__sense of entitlement
	__requires constant attention–admiration	__lack of empathy
	__preoccupied with feelings of empathy	

Avoidant	__easily hurt by criticism–disapproval	__no close friends or confidants
	__avoids social–occupational activities	__fear of being embarrassed
	__exaggerates potential difficulties or dangers	
	__unwilling to get involved without guarantee of positive experience or of being liked	

Dependent	__unable to make everyday decisions confidently	__allows others to make important decisions
	__agrees with others when believes they are wrong	__has difficulty doing things on own
	__feels uncomfortable when alone	__preoccupied with fear of being abandoned
	__easily hurt by disapproval	

Obsessive–Compulsive	__perfectionism interferes with task completion	__preoccupation with details
	__insistence that things be done his or her way	__excessive devotion to work
	__inflexible on ethics, values, morals	__restricted expression of affection
	__unable to discard worthless objects	__lack of generosity

Passive–Aggressive	__procrastinates	__irritable, argumentative
	__works deliberately slowly	__protests without justification
	__avoids obligations ("forgot")	__unreasonable criticism of authority
	__obstructs the efforts of others by not doing his or her share of a job–project	
	__resents useful suggestions on increasing productiveness	

THOUGHT DISORDER SYMPTOMS

__impaired level of functioning

__odd–magical beliefs

__impaired personal hygiene

__social isolation–withdrawal

__thinking that does not make sense

__talking about things that are not related

__hearing, seeing, smelling, or feeling
things that are not there

__blunted–inappropriate affect

__unusual perceptual experiences

__peculiar behavior

__lack of interest and energy

__believing he or she is someone else

__difficulty at home, work, school

ACCEPTING YOUR ILLNESS

Accepting your illness, just as in admitting to substance abuse, is the first step to begin to recognize how your life is affected. As you increase your understanding of what does not work well and what you have difficulty coping with, you then can begin to make necessary changes for improving the quality of your life. Sometimes the symptoms are so distressing that it feels like they are unmanageable. However, with the proper treatment, treatment compliance, and self-responsibility, most symptoms are improved and the level of distress decreases.

When did you first notice symptoms of your illness?

_____

_____

_____

_____

_____

How was your life being affected?

_____

_____

_____

_____

_____

How did you finally get diagnosed (what happened that led to diagnosis)?

_____

_____

_____

_____

_____

Did symptoms happen when you were sober or under the influence of substance(s)?

_____

_____

_____

What was your treatment and how did it work?

_____

_____

Has treatment improved your functioning (are you doing better, why or why not)?

_____

_____

_____

_____

_____

Recognizing how you used substances in an effort to control symptoms is important. How did substance use make you feel? _____

_____

_____

How did substance use make things worse? _____

_____

_____

In the space provided, list all of the ways that you have tried to control your distressing symptoms:

_____

_____

_____

_____

_____

In an effort to cope and sometimes to survive, people change their behavior. This is a normal response to difficult or crisis situations. Describe situations or crises where you changed your behavior:

_____

_____

_____

_____

_____

_____

_____

_____

_____

What do you think would have–might have happened if you had not changed your behavior, remained in denial about the problem, and realized that your effort to cope was no longer helping the situation?

_____

_____

_____

_____

_____

Give yourself credit for adjusting and trying to help your situation. Do not feel guilty or bad about yourself. That can become an excuse to stay stuck and not find more positive ways to cope. Use your experience as an opportunity to learn about yourself, what helps, and what does not. Acceptance and self-responsibility are the keys to change and recovery for both emotional illness and substance abuse.

Write about the thoughts and feelings you had when you first realized you had an emotional illness:

_____

_____

_____

_____

_____

_____

_____

How did denial affect what happened to you and your life?

_____

_____

_____

_____

_____

Assuming that you have been in treatment and recovery, what are your current thoughts and feelings about your emotional illness?

_____

_____

_____

_____

_____

List five ways that you think accepting your emotional illness helps you:

1. _____.

2. _____.

3. _____.

4. _____.

5. _____.

What are the warning signs of your emotional illness (list a minimum of five)?

1. _____.

2. _____.

3. _____.

4. _____.

5. _____.

6. _____.

7. _____.

8. _____.

9. _____.

10. _____.

Have you ever had a relapse of your emotional illness? If so, please write about what happened to increase your understanding of how to prevent it from happening again:

_____

_____

_____

Some of the information you have written down has probably involved the impact of your illness on your family and family relationships. Use the information that you have learned about your emotional illness to educate your family members on how they can be most helpful in your treatment and recovery.

1. Have you talked with family members about your emotional illness? Write about what you think is important for them to understand in an effort to be thorough and helpful to them as well:

_____

_____

_____

_____

_____

2. Does your family understand the possibility of relapse? Please explain.

_____

_____

_____

_____

3. What do you want your family members to do if they see symptoms of a relapse?

_____

_____

_____

_____

4. If you refuse to listen to family members when they see signs of relapse, what should they do?

_____

_____

_____

_____

If you commit yourself to recovery, you will improve your chance of recovery and experiencing an improved quality of life. In the beginning of treatment and recovery, there may be times when you feel worse. If this happens, you may find yourself thinking about using substances. You may have felt better using substances sometimes; however, there were a lot of consequences and you did not always feel better—like the hangover, paranoia, conflicts with family, missing work, etc. Remind yourself that, whereas it is true that you may be having a rough time, you are learning to be with genuine emotions and how to effectively cope with difficult emotions. The use of substances numbs your emotional experiences, so when you are clean and sober emotions may feel overwhelming. Be patient in your recovery from substances and emotional illness. Stay positive, use your resources, and things will get better.

Take the time to write about thoughts and behaviors that make things more stressful or get in the way of recovery from your emotional illness:

Thoughts:

1. _____

2. _____

3. _____

4. _____

5. _____

Behaviors:

1. _____

2. _____

3. _____

4. _____

5. _____

Write your affirmation for recovery:

_____

_____

_____

_____

_____

THE TWELVE STEPS AND DUAL DIAGNOSIS

The building blocks of recovery work for those with an addiction and a psychiatric illness. Recovery is an active process, and the following exercises will offer a plan for personal growth and self-understanding. Recovery takes time, patience, and practice. Take your recovery one day at a time.

THE FIRST STEP

Writing a thorough and honest history of your life experience will help you to

1. Understand how substance abuse and emotional illness have affected your life
2. Develop insight and awareness for what has happened to you over time
3. More clearly see the problems that substance abuse and emotional illness have caused

Use the following questions to develop a history for substance abuse and a history of your emotional illness.

Addiction

1. Family history of drug abuse?
2. What were your drugs of choice (that you continue to want to use)?
3. What was the pattern of use?
   a. how much?
   b. how often?
   c. under what circumstances?
   d. with whom did you use?
   e. where did you use?

4. How recently have you used drugs (what did you use and how much)?
5. Have you attempted to hide your drug abuse from others?
   a. who?
   b. how?

6. Have you ever tried to stop using or switch to a different drug?
   a. what happened when you stopped using or cut down on use?
   b. how did this change your life?
   c. if you started using after stopping, what happened to cause you to start using again?

7. Have you ever gotten into trouble for using drugs?
   a. how did you deal with it?
   b. did you lie and/or blame others?
   c. did drug abuse cause other problems?
      i. relationship problems (family, friends)
      ii. work–school
      iii. financial matters
      iv. health–safety
      v. legal issues

8. How has drug use affected your emotional illness?

9. Why did you enter treatment and begin recovery?

10. Why is recovery important to you?

Psychiatric Illness

1. Family history of emotional illness?

2. How old were you when you first experienced symptoms of your emotional illness?

3. What symptoms did you experience (ask your therapist for a symptoms list if you have difficulty identifying the symptoms you have experienced)?

4. Is there a pattern to the symptoms that you experience?
   a. do they come and go?
   b. do they ever go away totally?
   c. do they get worse under certain circumstances?

5. Give a history of the medications you have taken:
   a. how do they make you feel?
   b. how do they help you deal with your symptoms?
   c. are you compliant in taking your medication as prescribed (if not why)?

6. Have you attempted to stop taking medication?
   a. what happened?
   b. what did you learn?

7. Have you ever pretended that you were okay when you were not?
   a. what did you do?
   b. was there anyone in particular you were trying to hide your illness from?

8. Have you tried to control your symptoms on your own?
   a. what did you do?
   b. what did you learn?

9. What is your history of treatment from mental health providers, and what has been helpful?
   a. individual–couples–family–group therapy
   b. hospitalization–day treatment–residential care–case management
   c. medication–electroconvulsive treatment
   d. vocational training
   e. other

10. Has emotional illness created problems?
    a. in relationships
    b. work–school
    c. health–safety
    d. legal issues

By addressing the issues of addiction and emotional illness, you have written down a lot of information that will help you with the next part of the dual diagnosis first step: understanding the mutual influence of addiction and emotional illness that has created a negative feedback loop in your life, which has prevented your growth, healing, and recovery.

Interaction

Influence of Dual

Diagnosis

1. Which diagnosis started first?
2. How does drug use affect symptoms?
   a. worse
   b. improved
   c. what happened

Effect of dual diagnosis on self-esteem and self-image: how do you feel about the following?

1. Being addicted
2. Being diagnosed with emotional illness
3. Taking psychiatric medication
4. Treatment

It is important to remind yourself that your dual diagnosis disorders are not your fault. However, using the resources for recovery is your responsibility.

It may take you several tries to complete your first step so that you feel satisfied that it is honest and thorough. It is an opportunity for you to know yourself better, to clarify how you have been affected, and to clarify what you need to do. It is this action, the "doing," that will improve your self-esteem and self-image.

As you work through the 12 steps, you will begin to recognize the value of the process. The 12 steps provide a framework for self-understanding and change. It is up to you to use the outline provided in a thorough, committed, and conscientious manner that encourages your recovery from addiction and emotional illness.

THE SECOND STEP

The second step offers hope. Whether you choose to focus your belief on a higher power that is spiritual in nature or other tools that will be your source of help in recovery, it is a very important step in your recovery. The second step is about improving your quality of life: it is learning how to cope and making your life more manageable.

The second step is the application of information from your first step:

1. Organize your life
2. Make healthier lifestyle choices
3. Stop self-defeating–self-destructive behaviors
4. Practice new ways of thinking
5. Develop an appropriate support system
6. Develop new behaviors

For each of the following areas, write out a plan to accomplish your goal(s).

1. Changing thoughts
   a. what thinking do you need to stop?
   b. what thinking needs to start?

2. Changing behaviors
   a. what behaviors do you need to stop?
   b. what behaviors do you need to start?

3. What attitude is going to benefit your recovery?
4. What are your resources?
5. What places you at risk in your recovery?
6. Do you have any negative experiences related to religion?
   a. religious–church experiences
   b. psychiatric symptoms with religious ideas

7. What can you learn from these experiences that might benefit your recovery?
8. Have you been resistant to making more positive life choices?
   a. not convenient
   b. simply do not want to make changes
   c. do not want to take the time required for recovery (want a quick fix)

9. Are you seeking greater stability and balance in your life?
   a. how would this be accomplished?
   b. what resources would be helpful?
   c. how do you demonstrate responsibility for your recovery?

10. How do you describe having a satisfying and fulfilling life?
    a. spiritually
    b. physically
    c. emotionally
    d. relationships
    e. personal growth
    f. professional or educational growth

THE THIRD STEP

The third step has to do with developing trust. It means accepting help and learning a better way of living one day at a time. Dual recovery is challenging and requires that you actively work on the changes you identify as important to your recovery and use the resources that are supportive to your recovery efforts.

The third step is your recovery plan: it is your commitment to maintain positive daily activities. Some people use daily affirmations, prayer, or meditation to reaffirm their commitment to recovery every day.

Consider the following if you are struggling with the third step:

1. What are you afraid of in recovering from your dual diagnosis?
2. Are you overwhelmed when you think about rebuilding your life?
   a. what have your losses been?
   b. what abilities do you want to develop?
   c. what opportunities do you want to pursue?

Write out your general recovery plan:

_____

_____

_____

_____

_____

_____

_____

_____

_____

_____

_____

_____

_____

THE FOURTH STEP

The fourth step is about exploring your life in depth to make a searching and fearless personal inventory of yourself. When you work on the fourth step, it reinforces your recovery, improves the quality of your life, and prevents relapse. This self-exploration is an opportunity to

1. Identify the losses and pain of the past.
2. Heal the past pains.
3. Arrest the progression of drug addiction and emotional illness (for dual diagnosis).

Because dual diagnosis affects every area of your life, the fourth step encourages the following:

1. Improved self-knowledge in all of the identified areas (make a list for each of the following)
   a. spiritually
   b. physically
   c. emotionally
   d. values–beliefs
   e. behaviors
   f. relationships
   g. personal growth
   h. professional–educational growth

2. Identification of your strengths and weaknesses
   a. assets (benefit and support recovery)
      i. social supports (people)
      ii. things that decrease symptoms
      iii. things that improve functioning
   b. liabilities (contribute to potential risk of relapse–roadblocks to recovery)
      i. fear
      ii. pain
      iii. self-defeating–self-destructive thoughts or behaviors

The challenge is to be aware of problems, be prepared to cope more effectively and to make better choices.

When you have completed a thorough inventory, it is time to apply that information to your daily recovery needs, short-term recovery goals, and long-term recovery goals. Make a list for each of the following (address addiction and emotional illness):

1. Daily recovery needs
   a. what you do that helps you
   b. what you do that is not helpful
   c. basic needs
      i. do not use substances
      ii. management of psychiatric symptoms
      iii. adequate rest

iv. proper nutrition

v. healthy relationships

vi. recovery-reinforcing leisure activities and fun

vii. adequate coping with stress

2. Development of short-term goals (to be completed in 6 months to a year)

3. Development of long-term goals (beyond a 1-year time frame).

Keep a list of your liabilities an assets in a convenient place and check your progress on a regular basis.

THE FIFTH STEP

The fifth step takes you beyond the self-reflection and insight derived from completing the first four steps. Once the information is identified in the prior four steps you increase your commitment to recovery by sharing the information with at least one other person. This means that, as you are allowing yourself to know exactly who you are, you also let another person get to know who you really are. The shame of addiction and psychiatric illness begins to be replaced by self-forgiveness and acceptance. Likewise, there is the seeking of acceptance from another. Apply this to addiction and emotional illness.

Working on the fifth step can be anxiety provoking. Ask yourself, "What fears do I have in sharing my personal inventory with another?"

What would be some benefits of sharing your personal inventory, and what characteristics should the person with whom you share your inventory have?

Because you have had some time to review you personal inventory, what have you learned about yourself?

What personal strengths or assets can help you with self-forgiveness and self-acceptance?

Do you identify any patterns of thinking or behavior that interfere with effective coping and overall recovery?

As you prepare to share your personal inventory with another person, also be prepared to nurture yourself with peaceful music, relaxation exercises, deep breathing, or spending time with people you enjoy who support your recovery.

THE SIXTH STEP

Once you have identified your liabilities, problem solving your recovery plan is strengthened and there is awareness of the desire to make important changes. This process of change is challenging because the patterns or habits of thoughts and behaviors that have been a part of addiction and psychiatric illness while distressing are also comforting because they are familiar. They have become the protective defenses that have seemed to help you to cope. However, you have already acknowledged that your life had become unmanageable. As a result, three very important things take place when you complete the sixth step:

1. There is a willingness to change.
2. There is belief and hope that change is possible.
3. A *commitment to change* is made.

The sixth step is signified by the commitment to change. Write an affirmation describing your willingness to change. Some changes will be easy and some will be difficult. The difficult changes become a priority because these are the thoughts and behaviors that place you at highest risk for relapse. Therefore, identify those thoughts and behaviors that could stand in the way of your commitment to change. Make a list of these thoughts and behaviors.

1. Thoughts that interfere with being prepared to change and to be successful with change (think in terms of both the addiction and emotional illness):

   _____

   _____

   _____

   _____

   _____

   _____

2. Behaviors that interfere with being prepared to change and to be successful with change (think in terms of both the addiction and emotional illness):

   _____

   _____

   _____

   _____

   _____

   _____

   _____

THE SEVENTH STEP

This is another challenge. The sixth step was the commitment, and the seventh step is the action of change behind the commitment. The seventh step is a reminder of the courage it takes to embrace abstinence and the associated changes in thoughts and behaviors necessary to continue in the recovery process. You are ready to let go of the "old ways" and learn a new way of being. How do you *choose* to move forward in your recovery of addiction and emotional illness? It is important that you continue to review your previous step work so that you can apply the information to your process of change. Much of this information becomes your instrument for change. Although it is you that must make the changes, you continue to benefit from the support, encouragement, and reinforcement for change from your recovery support system. Be patient, and continue to review your commitment to change and the worthiness of your recovery goals. Write about the changes you need to make and the benefits you will have by continuing to work on the changes that you need to make.

1. The changes that you need to make (in recovery from addiction and emotional illness):

_____

_____

_____

_____

_____

_____

2. The benefits of making these changes (in recovery from addiction and emotional illness):

_____

_____

_____

_____

_____

_____

_____

THE EIGHTH STEP

The task of the eighth step is to make a list of all the persons that you have harmed and be willing to make amends to all of them. During periods of drug use and difficult episodes of emotional illness, there have been behaviors that have harmed others. It was back in the fourth step that this was first explored as liabilities or weaknesses. Because you felt badly about yourself for your own thoughts and behaviors, you also came to believe that others felt negatively about you as well. It is this repetitious replay of your "unforgiven" past that increases your risk of relapse. These thoughts are self-defeating and self-destructive. You have clarified your values and beliefs. The result is that, in doing so, you have also clarified how your behaviors affected other people.

1. Write how you feel about your past behaviors and their influence on your recovery.

_____

_____

_____

_____

_____

2. Because some of your behaviors were related to addiction and others were related to emotional illness, write about the people you have harmed and how.

_____

_____

_____

_____

_____

_____

_____

_____

_____

_____

_____

_____

_____

THE NINTH STEP

The ninth step offers an opportunity to be released from the past by making amends to those you have harmed by your words or behavior. It is a process of alleviating a weight that you have been carrying so that you can heal and so that others can heal as well. It is the taking of responsibility for yourself. Self-responsibility is the key to a successful enduring recovery from addiction and emotional illness. It is acknowledging what abilities for change rest solely with you. The ninth step is about asking for forgiveness, forgiving yourself, and forgiving others. Be patient with yourself; this can be a difficult process.

It is recommended that whenever possible amends should be made in person, but is also okay to contact the individuals by phone, e-mail, or in writing if you are not able to meet. The only exception for seeking someone out to make amends is if doing so would cause him or her harm. It demonstrates your desire for a healthier relationship with yourself and with others. Making amends means being honest, respectful, and responsible. It means being true to yourself. This is a significant step in working toward being the best you can be. Be prepared that not everyone to whom you offer your amends will be pleased to hear from you or accept your apology. Contacting people may in some instances be planned and in others be an informal meeting that was unplanned.

1. Make a list of the people to whom you need to make amends and why.

2. Review the people on your list; who will be easiest to contact and make amends?

3. Who will be difficult to make amends to and why? Is there anyone you have difficulty forgiving?

4. As you prepare to ask the forgiveness of others, write a letter of forgiveness to yourself. Is there anything for which you have difficulty forgiving yourself? If so, how does this affect your recovery?

5. How do you choose to meet with this person (formally contact him or her and request meeting, or is it someone that you bump into from time to time and will make amends next time you see each other)?

6. Think about what you need to say when you are making amends.

7. Write out what you will say when you make amends.

8. What do you think it will feel like when you make amends?

9. Do you have any anxiety or fears about making amends?

10. What are positive ways to deal with your anxiety as you make amends?

11. How will making amends benefit and strengthen your personal recovery?

THE TENTH STEP

Your recovery from addiction and emotional illness is a daily struggle. It is one thing to achieve abstinence and emotional stability, but it is another to maintain them. The maintenance of dual diagnosis recovery means staying very aware of what you are doing and why you are doing it. It is a stage of recovery where you have become better at recognizing the warning signs of relapse and take the appropriate actions to stay on the course of recovery. Remember that when you were doing the fourth step, it was recommended that you keep a list of your assets and liabilities. Hopefully you have been reviewing it intermittently. Right now you are going to use it to thoroughly review where you have been, what you have accomplished, and where you are going. The tenth step is the self-monitoring of your recovery progress.

1. Are you working on your dual diagnosis program and following your treatment plan?

2. What liabilities or areas of potential difficulty do you need to continue to watch for?

3. How are you dealing with symptoms of emotional illness?

4. How are you managing challenging situations that arise?

5. Are you taking good care of yourself (rest, nutrition, personal growth, use of resources supportive of your recovery, etc.)?

6. How do you benefit from continuing to take a personal inventory?

7. What personal assets do you need to continue to build on to strengthen your recovery?

8. Write out your current daily schedule of activities. For each activity, review how your assets or liabilities played a role.

9. Have you neglected doing the right thing or procrastinated and put off personal responsibilities in your recovery plan? The tenth step is an active process of monitoring progress, staying on task with your responsibilities, and quickly taking responsibility for what you have done.

10. What is the importance of humility (look it up in the dictionary if you are not sure of what it means) in your recovery from addiction and emotional illness? Humility is important to the development of seeing yourself honestly and taking responsibility. Write about the important role of humility in your recovery.

THE ELEVENTH STEP

For some people, the eleventh step is working on improving their conscious relationship with their higher power through prayer and meditation. If you struggle with the issue of a higher power, do not use that as an excuse to not be thorough in your recovery. Another way of defining the eleventh step is that it encourages you to stay focused on your goals and is reflected in your daily decision making. Regardless of your view of a higher power, it is helpful to set aside some quiet time each day to reflect on your beliefs, coping skills, and behaviors. A part of this quiet time may be participation in activities requiring discipline, music, dance, martial arts, exercise, or inspirational books or tapes—whatever you find to be a helpful reinforcer for staying on task. Regarding reflections on daily decision making, think about all of the decisions with which you are confronted every day:

1. Getting out of bed and getting started
2. Work–school
3. Self-care
4. How you spend money
5. Responsibility and respect in relationships
6. Recovery-supportive leisure activities
7. Treatment choices
8. Living arrangements
9. Choices in thinking

1. Write about what you have accomplished in your recovery from addiction and emotional illness and what has helped you to accomplish it:

_____

_____

_____

_____

_____

_____

2. What do you identify as the risks of relapse, and what are you prepared to do about them?

_____

_____

_____

_____

_____

_____

THE TWELFTH STEP

The twelfth step is an awakening to who you have become through hard work, self-responsibility, and humility. Again, review all of the major areas of your life and clarify your current level of functioning. When you compare this to earlier writing as you worked through the steps to recovery, it will highlight areas of change and continuing struggles.

1. After making a review of your recovery efforts, write down examples of positive change in the different areas of your life.
   a. emotional:
   b. spiritual:
   c. physical
   d. social:
   e. significant relationships:
   f. leisure activities:
   g. financial:
   h. life goals (updated):

2. What has helped you to become more open, honest, and willing to make the changes necessary for a successful recovery?

3. How would you explain your journey of recovery from addiction and emotional illness in a way that might encourage others in their journey of recovery?

4. What has been most important and helpful to you in your recovery?

5. What are limits or rules you currently live by that were not in place at the beginning of your recovery journey?

6. When confronted with a difficult or challenging situation, what are the tools you have developed that you use to deal with it?

7. How does using these tools strengthen your recovery and prevent relapse?

8. Acknowledge the improved quality of your life that has been found in recovery.

IDENTIFYING DEPRESSION

Depression affects a person physically, emotionally, and in how he or she thinks. Following are some of the symptoms of depression. Review the symptoms to determine whether you have been experiencing depression and did not know it.

1. Physical effects
    a. appetite is increased or decreased
    b. there may be weight loss or gain
    c. sleep disturbance (too much or too little)
    d. agitation (inability to sit still, pacing, hand-wringing, outbursts)
    e. slowing down (slowed speech, thoughts, movements)
    f. fatigue (decreased energy)
    g. lack of sexual desire
    h. body aches

2. Emotional effects
    a. sad
    b. lonely
    c. fearful
    d. tearful
    e. overwhelmed
    f. no motivation
    g. self-critical
    h. easily frustrated
    i. stress
    j. feeling hopeless
    k. feeling helpless
    l. despair
    m. withdrawn
    n. apathetic

3. Thinking effects
    a. irrational thinking
    b. sense of worthlessness
    c. self-hate
    d. guilt
    e. suicidal thoughts
    f. difficulty concentrating
    g. memory problems
    h. difficulty staying focused–attention
    i. excess worrying
    j. homicidal thoughts

Depression and anxiety are often experienced at the same time. If you recognize that you are depressed, talk with your physician or call a mental health professional. There are a lot of things that you can do that would help you to feel better. It may also be helpful to you to go to a book store and look through the self-help books on depression. Educate yourself about the different reasons that people can have depression and the different types of treatment available.

MANAGING DEPRESSION

Most people will experience depression sometime during their lives. The difference between major depression and other forms of depression is that the symptoms are more severe, last longer, and make daily functioning much more difficult. If you think that you are suffering from depression, talk to your physician to find out about the different forms of treatment available to you.

Goals for managing depression:

1. Understand the source of your depression.
   a. biological–genetic
   b. environmental–situational
   c. thinking patterns–personality style

2. Take responsibility for improving the quality of your life.

3. Challenge irrational thinking that contributes to your feeling depressed.

4. Develop a positive daily structure that includes positive things to which to look forward.

5. Exercise. It improves mood, increases energy, improves sleep, and gives you an overall sense of well-being.

6. Develop relaxation skills.

7. Identify and change self-defeating behaviors.

8. Keep a journal. It is a great tool for venting, clarifying, and problem solving what you have control over and what you choices are.

9. Develop assertive communication and clarify boundaries.

10. Develop a self-care program.
    a. working a recovery program
    b. adequate sleep
    c. good nutrition
    d. laughter
    e. positive leisure activities
    f. goal development

UNDERSTANDING GRIEF

Grief is experienced as intense emotional suffering caused by a loss. When grief is not resolved, it can lead to anxiety and depression. Loss associated with grief is not always related to a death of a loved one. With loss, there are feelings of hurt, sadness, fear, and loneliness.

Elizabeth Kubler-Ross has identified five stages of grief:

1. Denial: Not allowing oneself to accept the truth. A protective or defensive position to buffer the pain.
2. Anger: May be reasonable and may take the form of blaming, regrets, or anger turned inward.
3. Bargaining: As people calm down, they attempt to strike a bargain, sometimes in an attempt to turn back the hands of time or to take it away. "What if," an attempt to regain control.
4. Depression: When bargaining does not work, people become depressed (sad, guilty, helpless, self-destructive thoughts–behavior). Emotional, empty, immobilizing.
5. Acceptance: Not necessarily a pleasant stage, but people begin to find peace, learn to cope, accept the loss, and adjust. Belief that it is possible to recover and heal.

As you think about this information, you will recognize that grief is sometimes a part of recovery. It may feel like having to give up something that you feel benefited you in some way.

Write about the grief you have experienced in making the choice for recovery and what has helped you to begin your journey of healing. Identify losses that you have experienced and how they have affected your life.

_____

_____

_____

_____

_____

_____

_____

_____

_____

_____

_____

DAILY ACTIVITY SCHEDULE

Date: _____

Mood(s): _____

Time	Planned activity and expectations	Actual activity	How it felt
7–8 AM			
8–9 AM			
9–10 AM			
10–11 AM			
11–12 noon			
12–1 PM			
1–2 PM			
2–3 PM			
3–4 PM			
4–5 PM			
5–6 PM			
6–7 PM			
7–8 PM			
8–9 PM			
9–10 PM			

Keep a daily activity schedule until your depression is manageable and you feel that you do not need the support of this strategy to remain stable. [Printed with permission from Johnson, S. L. (1997). "Therapist's Guide to Clinical Intervention." San Diego: Academic Press.]

IDENTIFYING ANXIETY

Anxiety affects a person physically, emotionally, and psychologically (thinking). Following are listed some of the effects of anxiety. Take the time to review the lists and determine whether you experience some of the symptoms of anxiety.

1. Physical effects
   a. body tension
   b. headaches
   c. nausea–diarrhea
   d. sleep disturbance
   e. dizziness
   f. fatigue
   g. restlessness
   h. feel shaky–trembling
   i. change in appetite
   j. palpitations

2. Emotional effects
   a. anxious
   b. fearful
   c. overwhelmed
   d. easily frustrated
   e. stressed
   f. on edge
   g. easily irritated
   h. nervous

3. Thinking effects
   a. irrational thinking
   b. obsessive thoughts
   c. excess worrying
   d. difficulty with concentration
   e. catastrophizing
   f. intrusive thoughts
   g. problems with memory
   h. difficulty staying focused

Other symptoms that you believe may be associated with anxiety:

_____

_____

_____

Anxiety and depression are often experienced at the same time. Identification of the symptoms of anxiety is the first step toward recognizing the problem, being able to find out about the different treatments available to help you, and determining what you can do to help yourself.

MANAGING ANXIETY

Anxiety is a normal emotional experience. However, some people suffer from extreme feelings of anxiety that interfere with their daily activities. This anxiety is more intense, lasts longer, and may be associated with a specific person, place, situation, and/or pattern of thoughts.

MANAGEMENT SKILLS

1. Understand your personal reaction to anxiety provoking people, places, situations, and ways of thinking.
   a. learn new skills
   b. problem solve
   c. role and risks of medication

2. Be willing to do things differently.
   a. make a commitment to change
   b. be consistent in following through with new ways of responding

3. Develop rational self-talk.
   a. develop realistic expectations and limitations
   b. nonnegative thinking

4. Use journal writing.
   a. venting thoughts and feelings
   b. clarifying patterns of thinking, feeling, and behaving
   c. problem solving

5. Exercise.
   a. decreases body tension
   b. improves sleep
   c. results in a feeling of well-being

6. Develop relaxation skills.
   a. progressive muscle relaxation
   b. meditation

7. Identify and change self-defeating behaviors and personality traits.
8. Develop a positive daily structure and utilize your support system.
9. Develop assertive communication.
10. Nurture yourself with positive self-care behaviors.
    a. good nutrition
    b. positive leisure activities
    c. laughter

ANXIETY RELAPSE

Managing anxiety is very important. In the past it may have been an excuse to use substances, or when symptoms are experienced strongly it may create vulnerability to relapse. Therefore, if you find yourself falling back into old behaviors and old ways of thinking you are likely recycling an old pattern.

1. Assess your reactions
2. Evaluate your feelings and behaviors
3. Intervene: DO SOMETHING TO BREAK THE CYCLE
    a. manage stress
        i. relaxation
        ii. meditation
        iii. exercise
        iv. utilization of support system
    b. challenge negative–irrational thinking
        i. positive self-talk
        ii. remind yourself that anxiety will not last forever
        iii. use positive affirmations
        iv. journaling
    c. resolve internal–external conflicts

Break the anxiety relapse cycle with:

1. Increased awareness
2. Use of management skills
    a. critical problem solving
        i. identify the problem
        ii. generate all possible solutions and associated consequences
        iii. select the best option and follow through
        iv. evaluate the outcome
    b. assertiveness
        i. stand up for yourself
        ii. express yourself honestly and appropriately
        iii. exercise your right without diminishing the rights of others
    c. conflict resolution: combine problem solving, good listening skills, assertiveness, and mutual respect
    d. time management
        i. clarify tasks to be completed and a plan of action
        ii. clarify priorities
        iii. divide the plan of action into manageable goals
        iv. allow reasonable time to complete tasks
    e. self-care
        i. positive health behaviors (sleep, nutrition, exercise)
        ii. development and utilization of a support system
        iii. relaxation and other strategies for decreasing tension
        iv. self-monitoring for staying on task

IDENTIFYING FEELINGS

Level of Intensity	Happy	Sad	Angry	Scared	Confused	Strong	Weak
Strong	Excited Elated Over joyed	Hopeless Sorrowful Depressed	Furious Seething Enraged	Fearful Panicky Afraid	Bewildered Trapped Troubled	Potent Super Powerful	Overwhelmed Impotent Small
Mild	Cheerful Up Good	Upset Distressed Down	Annoyed Frustrated Agitated	Threatened Insecure Uneasy	Disorganized Mixed up Foggy	Energetic Confident Capable	Incapable Helpless Insecure
Weak	Glad Content Satisfied	Sorry Lost Bad	Uptight Dismayed Put out	Timid Unsure Nervous	Bothered Uncomfortable Undecided	Sure Secure Durable	Shaky Unsure Soft

UNDERSTANDING YOUR FEELINGS

Name: _____

Date: _____

Date	Event (what happened)	Expected feeling(s)	How I felt	What I did (behavior)	How it worked (result)-

SELF-HONESTY

What are the rewards for accomplishing the principles of self-honesty?

1. Hope

2. Faith

3. Courage

4. Humility

5. Responsibility

6. Patience

7. Charity or love

Remember:

1. Hope will replace desperation.

2. Faith will replace despair.

3. Courage will replace fear.

4. Peace of mind will replace confusion.

5. Self-respect will replace self-loathing.

6. Self-confidence will replace helplessness.

7. Respect for others will replace anger, pity, or frustration.

8. A clear conscience will replace feelings of guilt.

9. Genuine friendship will replace loneliness.

10. A task- and goal-directed life will replace a lack of purpose and confusion.

11. The love, acceptance, and understanding of those we love will replace the fear, concerns, and doubts.

12. The freedom of a happy life for which I gladly take responsibility.

COMMUNICATION

Good communication has two basic components, and each of these has several parts.

1. Be able to appropriately and effectively express your thoughts and feelings:
   a. starting a conversation
      i. greet a person in a positive manner
      ii. establish eye contact
      iii. explore areas of interest to the other person
      iv. determine whether the other person is listening to you
      v. keep the conversation interesting
      vi. allow the other person to express him- or herself
   b. asking for support–help
      i. first be clear about the problem
      ii. find the right person to trust (the first person you approach may not be the last); he or she is not responsible for you, but may have ideas about how you can help yourself and be supportive of you
      iii. use the person's suggestions in a positive manner if possible
   c. persuasiveness
      i. allow yourself to be influenced by what is right for you
      ii. be clear about what you want others to understand from your point of view
      iii. share your ideas and ask about the ideas of others'
      iv. explore why your idea is a good one to be able to support it
      v. ask for feedback

2. Be a good listener
   a. interested
      i. attentive
      ii. open posture
      iii. eye contact
   b. reflect
      i. repeat what you believe has been said to clarify shared understanding
      ii. do not make emotional assumptions
   c. accept the right of individual beliefs and feelings

Communication offers the opportunity to both share and learn.

COMMUNICATING DIFFICULT FEELINGS

HOW TO DEAL WITH UNCOMFORTABLE FEELINGS

1. Talk to someone or journal
   a. speak specifically about the facts
   b. clarify the issue and try to remove the emotion
   c. problem solve and review the various choices for dealing with the situation

2. Take action
   a. follow through on your course of action
   b. be prepared to handle the range of possible responses
   c. clarify your issue, which may be different from another person's issue; be prepared to negotiate
   d. if necessary, seek support for dealing with thoughts and feelings that you are experiencing difficulty resolving
   e. write an uncensored letter that you do not intend to send that allows you to vent the emotions and clarify the important points of a situation
   f. clarify what you want as an outcome

3. Physical activity: Discharge your tension with exercise. It will also help clear your mind.

Whatever the problem, when you neglect to deal with your emotions, things seem to get worse. Three common errors in response to dealing with difficult feelings are the following.

1. Fight: If you know how to argue or negotiate things through to resolution, it can be helpful. However, most people lack the skills beyond "fighting," which can cause more problems. Learn the skill of negotiation.
2. Flight: Walking out on others and avoiding your own emotions can have a negative impact on a relationship as well as your own physical and emotional well-being over time.
3. Withdrawal: When you do not deal with things, they pile up and become overwhelming. This creates an increase in stress, which can lead to headaches, fatigue, depression, anxiety, etc.

Overall, if you improve your communication skills and learn how to manage difficult feelings, you will feel better and relationships are likely to have less distress. [Adapted from Johnson, S. L. (1997). "Therapist's Guide to Clinical Intervention." San Diego: Academic Press.]

CONSTRUCTIVELY EXPRESSING ANGRY FEELINGS

Here are some examples of how to express feelings of anger:

1. Take responsibility for your own angry feelings. Acknowledge and accept that you are angry when you are. Do not blame your anger on others. No one but you can make you angry.

2. Express your feelings of anger at the time you become angry. Do not allow angry feelings to build up hostility until you explode. This helps keep anger in control so that it is not destructive to you or others.

3. Express your feelings honestly and assertively, so that no one is hurt in the process. This means communicating your feelings in a way that does not put the other person on the defensive and that gives the other person a chance to understand the problem along with the opportunity to change his or her behavior.

4. When anger is intense and you feel like exploding, it may be helpful to use nondestructive ways of decreasing tension:
   a. physical exercise (walking, running)
   b. write a letter you do not intend to deliver

5. Learn to express your feelings as they are developing. Using "I" statements is especially helpful. They are useful for avoiding blaming or putting down others.

6. Combining "I" statements with a request is often a helpful way to prevent hostility from building up. For example, "I get angry when you are late for dinner. I would appreciate you being on time from now on."

DEALING WITH CRITICISM AND GIVING FEEDBACK

Two important skills from which everyone benefits are being able to deal with the criticism of others and giving feedback.

DEALING WITH CRITICISM

1. Allow your defensiveness to be put aside so that you can hear what is being said.
2. Do not personalize it. It is an opinion.
3. Is the information helpful? If so, find a way to use it and benefit from it.
4. If the information is shared in a negative way, respond assertively.
5. Validate. If what is being said is accurate regarding something you have said or done, and it created a problem for someone else, own it. Take responsibility for your actions. Taking responsibility and validating diffuses conflict and heals hurt feelings.
6. If you responded in a defensive manner, make the effort to understand why and how you can remedy the situation.

TEN STEPS FOR GIVING FEEDBACK

1. Describe what you see instead of being judgmental.
2. Be specific. Do not speak in generalities (i.e., always, never).
3. Feedback should be helpful and provide information.
4. Consider the timing, but do not use it as an excuse to put it off.
5. Make sure that what you say is not misinterpreted.
6. Do not overwhelm others with information.
7. Use "I" statements.
8. Share your feedback in such a way that others can hear what you have to say.
9. Do not insist yourself in how the other person chooses to use your feedback.
10. Demonstrate personal honesty and openness to the response to your feedback.

UNDERSTANDING ANGER

It is important to understand the difficulties that you have had with anger so that you can learn to express your anger assertively. Check off any of the following statements that describe your anger:

_____taught or socialized to believe–feel that anger is wrong

_____anger is always associated with anxiety

_____fear of your anger

_____fear of other's anger

_____pretend that you are not angry when you are

_____try not to think about anger (maybe it will go away)

_____fear of disapproval

_____fear of the power of your anger

_____others deny your right to be angry

_____avoid all feelings

_____deny all feelings (no longer aware of feeling angry, sad, or happy)

_____disguise anger

Write about any of the statements that you checked off:

_____

_____

_____

_____

_____

_____

_____

_____

_____

_____

_____

_____

_____

MANAGING ANGER

The purpose of leaning more about anger is to

1. Identify when anger becomes a problem.
2. Learn how to appropriately express anger.

Understanding anger:

1. Anger is a normal emotion.

   _____

   _____

2. What do you do when you are angry?

   _____

   _____

3. What are the consequences when anger is kept inside or experienced inappropriately?

   _____

   _____

Identify five situations in which anger has been a problem and a corrective action of "what needs to be done differently" so that you can achieve the outcome you want.

1. Problem situation: _____

   Corrective action: _____

   _____

   _____

   _____

2. Problem situation: _____

   Corrective action: _____

   _____

   _____

   _____

3. Problem situation: _____

   Corrective action: _____

   _____

   _____

   _____

4. Problem situation: _____

   Corrective action: _____

   _____

   _____

   _____

5. Problem situation: _____

   Corrective action: _____

   _____

   _____

   _____

WAYS OF DEALING WITH ANGER

1. Learn to recognize when you are feeling anger (raise awareness).
2. Express anger appropriately when it occurs: "I am feeling angry."
   Use an "I" statement in a courteous, respectful, and assertive manner.

Write five things that make you angry:

1. _____

2. _____

3. _____

4. _____

5. _____

What can you do to deal with your anger?

1. Express it
2. Talk about it
3. Write about it
4. Exercise to discharge muscle tension
5. Think about how you want to deal with it

Most of all, take responsibility for how you feel and deal with your emotions appropriately. No longer give yourself permission to behave badly or withdraw.

Write about your observations of someone whom you feel expresses anger appropriately and effectively. What can you learn from him or her?

_____

_____

_____

_____

_____

_____

_____

_____

_____

_____

THE STEPS FOR LETTING GO OF ANGER

1. Awareness of your feelings and behaviors.[1]
2. Take responsibility for your emotions and responses.
3. Attitude will greatly influence your success or failure. If you have a negative attitude, do not expect good things to happen.
4. Self-talk. What you say to yourself will determine how you think and feel. It is a choice.
5. Do not take responsibility for other people and things that you do not have control over.
6. Develop resources and a support system that encourage the positive changes in you and in your life.
7. Self-care behaviors. People who take care of themselves feel better about who they are, have more energy, and are more likely to be happy.
8. Develop positive self-esteem.
9. Develop positive alternative responses to counter the older anger responses.
10. Practice rehearsing the new responses. Keep a journal to track and reinforce change. A journal will also clarify issues that require further problem solving or dysfunctional patterns that are keeping you from the progress and change that you desire.

[1]Adapted with permission from Johnson, S. L. (1997). "Therapists Guide to Clinical Intervention." San Diego: Academic Press.

GOAL SETTING

When people are engaged in change, especially a significant life change such as abstinence, goal development offers direction and a way to monitor progress. Following find some examples of possible goals.

1. *Emotional*: Feelings of self-worth, happiness, satisfaction, accomplishment.
2. *Positive attitude*: Affirmations, improve relationships, increase support system.
3. *Intellectual*: Increase and improve your knowledge, take classes, increase reading, take music or art classes, attend community events.
4. *Personal*
   a. work toward a change or promotion
   b. develop skills–personal growth
   c. develop relationships
5. *Physical*: Exercise (walk, weight training), relaxation, nutrition.
6. *Spiritual*: How to add to spiritual growth (read, study, prayer–meditation).

Brainstorm possibilities, then begin to single out those that are realistic and contribute to accomplishing your goals. There is no such thing as too much detail or steps that are too small.

Make a list of goals you are considering and write out the steps needed to accomplish your them.

1. _____

_____

_____

2. _____

_____

_____

3. _____

_____

_____

4. _____

_____

_____

5. _____

_____

GOAL DEVELOPMENT

Before a person can reach goals, he or she must set goals. Often, a person has a lot of different things on his or her mind that he or she would like to see happen. However, the individual has not taken the time to sit down and thoroughly think through all that is required to see those things happen. Strategizing for success is an easy process that does not take much time, and when you are completed you will have a much clearer idea of what you want and how you are going to go about making it happen. Recovery is like any other goal. Take time to outline the specific changes required, how the changes can be achieved, and how the changes can be made a part of your daily structure.

STEPS FOR DEVELOPING GOALS

1. Keep it simple. Define the goal as clearly as possible. If you are not sure of exactly what you want, consult with others who are supportive of your goals.

2. Break it into small steps. Once you have clearly defined the goal, break it down into small steps that you take to reach your goal. Small steps are helpful because they are manageable, require the least amount of stress, and allow you to see the progress you are making toward your goal.

3. Choose a starting point. Once you have broken your goal down into steps, the next thing is to choose a starting point. When will you begin working on your goal? This is a question that clarifies how much of a priority it is to you. Life is about choices, and each person is responsible for the quality of his or her own life.

4. Redefine the goal. Sometimes it becomes necessary to redefine a goal that you have set. In redefining the goal, you go through the same steps as you did in setting the original goal. Redefinition of goals is often related to personal growth. As you learn more about yourself, feel secure in the changes you are making, and experience increased self-esteem, you may find yourself expanding your goals. This is a normal process, because through personal growth our lives are always changing, which means we have new opportunities.

5. Act on your plan. By the time you actually initiate a formal starting point for your goal, you will already have completed several steps toward it. You will have thought it through and actually planned it out. Accomplishing steps toward your goal will reinforce positive self-esteem and follow through on other important changes in your life. Development of goals and efforts to accomplish them result in feelings of security and "I can do this!"

Write five basic goals associated with initiating recovery:

1. _____

2. _____

3. _____

4. _____

5. _____

SETTING PRIORITIES

Once you have set major goals and have decided on your plan of action, you need to determine how important it is for you to reach your goal. This is what is meant by "setting priorities." Sometimes people get frustrated with themselves because they start things they never finish. It is important to explore the reason behind the lack of accomplishment. It could be that motivation is low, avoidance is at work, or it is simply not a priority for you. Begin to take the time to understand how you got to where you are now and what have you learned. Learning to set priorities is an important step in learning how to manage your life more effectively.

STEPS FOR SETTING PRIORITIES

1. Develop a strategy. Another way to say it is to develop your recovery program. This relates back to the steps of clearly defining your goals. Once the goals are decided, you then break them down into steps that will ensure that you are able to reach them. When a goal is broken down into manageable steps, it does not seem so overwhelming.

2. Know what is important. To be satisfied with the outcome of your goal, it is important to be aware of all the issues related to it. In some ways your goal may open the door for other opportunities, or it may present some limitations. Understand where you are going and how things may change over time, which may alter priorities. Spend time with people and engage in activities that support and reinforce your recovery. Make these people and activities a part of your daily life.

3. Investigate alternatives. Use your resources, take the time to educate yourself, and ask as many questions as possible. Life is about choices, so be clear about the positive and negative consequences associated with each choice. Ask yourself what is necessary for you to reach your goal.

4. Reach your goal. By having a clearly defined goal and a plan that is broken into manageable steps, you will be able to reach your goal. You will have put your priorities into place and will be on your way to accomplishing your goal.

Write down five priorities and develop a plan (on a separate piece of paper) for reaching the goal you have identified as a priority.

1. _____

2. _____

3. _____

4. _____

5. _____

PROBLEM SOLVING

Effective problem solving requires changing the way you behave and the way you think about people, places, and situations that creates roadblocks to recovery. Sometimes it is the behavior that needs to be changed, sometimes it is the way you think about things, and sometimes it is both the behavior and the thinking that need to be changed.

Consider how you would change your behavior, thinking, or both in the following situations.

1. Situations in which substance use has occurred in the past.
2. Coping with certain people associated with substance use.
3. Difficult situations associated with abstinence (cravings, slips, social pressures, changes in relationships).
4. Difficulty in developing recreational leisure activities supportive of abstinence and recovery.
5. Difficulty encountered in reaching personal goals.

Make a list of problem solving difficulties that you are currently experiencing and the choices you can make that will help resolve them. With each potential choice, consider the associated positive and negative consequences.

1. _____

   Choices: _____

   _____

2. _____

   Choices: _____

   _____

3. _____

   Choices: _____

   _____

4. _____

   Choices: _____

   _____

5. _____

   Choices: _____

   _____

   _____

DECISION MAKING

Life is about choices. Decision making is a skill that can help you to make choices that are necessary and right for you. It is an active process that requires you to take responsibility for yourself, your life, and your own happiness. People who are good at making decisions have the self-confidence that comes from knowing how to make good choices in their lives. Because you are making changes and learning new ways to think about things and new behaviors, think through all of your decisions. Making a conscious effort to think through your decisions no matter how small will (1) increase awareness, (2) help to connect the consequences with the choices, (3) reinforce your efforts, and (4) decrease the use of defenses like minimizing, rationalizing, and justifying.

STEPS FOR DECISION MAKING

1. Isolate the problem. Sometimes things are not what they seem. Be careful to not just look at the surface issues and make a decision based on them. Instead, try to understand the underlying issues that may actually be the source of the problem. Review all of the factors associated with your substance use: people, places, emotional states, and situations. The more options you have, the better your chance of making the best choice.

2. Decide to take action. Once you have isolated the problem, the next step is deciding whether you need to take action now. Sometimes the best action is to do nothing. However, there is a difference between making a choice to do nothing and procrastination or avoidance of dealing with an uncomfortable situation. Ask yourself "what am I doing" and "why am I doing it?"

3. Gather resources. Ideally it is best to gather as much information as possible about the situation. Journal about the issue for clarification and talk about it at a meeting with your sponsor, therapist, and/or other members of your recovery support system. Gathering information could be a way to delay taking any action based on the premise that you do not have all of the information that you know is out there.

4. Make a plan. In other words, "make a decision." Once you have clarified what the problem is and what your choices are, decide on a course of action. Now it is time to decide how you will carry out your decision.

5. Visualize your plan of action. Do a test run on your plan by visualizing the potential outcome of your decision. Use all the information you have and your gut feeling or intuition. If it does not feel right, do not ignore it: try to understand the source of your discomfort with the decision. Again, talk about it.

6. Take action. You have successfully completed all the steps required for good decision making. Now it is time to take action and put your decision to work. At this point, you should feel confident about the work you have done on making this decision, and you will be able to maintain that feeling of self-confidence as you take action. The more you practice this process in your recovery, the more aware and less impulsive you become.

TIME MANAGEMENT

Sometimes when a person's life has been centered around the use of substances, he or she either does not learn or becomes distant from how to effectively use his or her time to take care of responsibilities and priorities. Therefore, when a person enters recovery, he or she feels overwhelmed and recovery seems like it is too hard. Remind yourself of the benefits of recovery, utilize your social supports for reinforcement, and practice a new way of doing things and thinking about things.

FOUR CENTRAL STEPS TO EFFECTIVE TIME MANAGEMENT

1. Establish priorities. This will allow you to base your decision on what is important instead of wasting your time.
2. Create time by realistic scheduling. People tend to misjudge how much time tasks will really take to accomplish. Therefore, give yourself adequate time accomplish a given task and eliminate low-priority tasks.
3. Develop the skill of decision making.
4. Delegate tasks to others as appropriate. You do not have to know everything yourself. However, you are responsible for what you choose. If you are confused, ask for help and support. But remember, you have to make the walk.

HOW TO START YOUR TIME MANAGEMENT PROGRAM

1. Make an initial assessment of how you spend your time. This takes approximately 1 week of observation. Keeping a journal specifically to log how you spend your time will clarify your time management or lack thereof. This will be easy to manage if you break up the day into three parts:
   a. from waking through lunch
   b. from the end of lunch through dinner
   c. from the end of dinner until you go to sleep

2. You may find that defining and prioritizing some goals can be done in a day, whereas others continue to be updated as you learn more about yourself, your potential, and all of your choices.
3. To adequately develop a habit of effective time management will take between 3 and 6 months.

Once you begin your time management program, continue to complete a weekly review to monitor your consistency and progress. Maintain an awareness of what you are doing and why. You will find that effective time management will significantly reduce stress.

HOW TO BUDGET

Be in control of your spending. Be realistic and budget your money efficiently. If you are out of money by payday or always feel in debt, consider learning some strategies that will decrease your financial distress.

Getting started:

1. Purchase a notebook
2. Keep track of daily expenses
3. Keep track of how you spend cash and use credit cards versus checks
4. Review expenditures at the end of the month

You will probably be very surprised at how much money is spent on miscellaneous and unnecessary items. When you see the pattern of your spending, it will be easier for you to choose how to spend your money.

1. Be reasonable
   a. start out with a budget you can live with
   b. be realistic about responsibilities and leisure expenses

2. List priorities
   a. have a concrete financial goal
   b. make a list of things you need
   c. make a list of things you want
   d. set your priorities and save each month toward major purchases

3. Be flexible
   a. if your budget is too tight or not tight enough, problem solve how to make it more realistic
   b. expect that it may take a few months to get it all worked out
   c. feel good about your efforts and goals

Debt has become more of a problem because of the availability of credit cards. As a result, people spend money they do not have on items they do not need and end up feeling overwhelmed by debt. If you are overwhelmed by debt, make an appointment with a credit counselor to work out a plan. The longer you put off dealing with a problem, the longer you will feel stressed and overwhelmed about it.

YOUR PERSONAL BUDGET

Month _____	Planned Budget	Actual Expenses	Under or Over
INCOME			
Your salary (income)			
Spouse's salary (income)			
Other income			
Alimony, child support			
Tax refund			
Reimbursements			
Interest			
Dividends			
TOTAL INCOME			
EXPENSES			
Mortgage (or rent)			
Taxes			
Tuition–books			
Child care			
Utilities			
Telephone			
Insurance (life, homeowner's, renter's, auto, medical, disability)			
Household maintenance and supplies			
Food (including meals out)			
Car maintenance			
Other transportation			
Clothing			
Laundry, dry cleaning, and personal care			
Medical and dental (excluding insurance)			
Credit card payments			
Entertainment–vacations			
Charitable contributions			
Personal allowances			
Miscellaneous			
TOTAL EXPENSE			

APPLYING FOR A JOB

The first impressions a prospective employer has of you are:

1. Your appearance
2. Your presentation
3. The information on your application and resume

Therefore, when you are preparing to apply for a job, pay attention to how you dress, groom, and care for your personal hygiene. When you get a job application, practice filling out a copy so that when you fill out the one to be turned in it will be neat, thorough, and have good grammar and spelling.

Before you pursue a job, find out information about what is required so that you can answer the following questions for yourself:

1. What specific position are you seeking?
2. Do you qualify for the job?
3. Will the job hold your attention?
4. Will the job pay you what you need to make a living?
5. Do you think you can get the job (confidence level)?
6. Write out an application or resume that outlines and focuses on your interests and qualifications for a specific job, such as
   a. specific information (dates, addresses, names of prior employers)
   b. personal qualities (reliability, works well with people, learns quickly, self-starter, motivated, positive attitude, team player, etc.)
7. Ask someone you respect, who knows you well, to review your resume information and to offer any recommendations he or she may have.
8. Read a book on interviewing or practice interviewing with a knowledgeable peer.

There are numerous resources that offer examples of resumes. Use these resources to determine which format would be best for the job for which you are applying.

HOW TO GIVE A GOOD JOB INTERVIEW

It is important to be prepared for the job interview:

1. Dress appropriately
2. Use good social skills and manners
3. Know the qualifications for the job
4. Choose words to describe your positive characteristics that would be an asset to the position
5. Have several questions to ask the potential employer
   a. is there advancement potential?
   b. are training and/or further education offered?
   c. how long has the average employee worked there?
   d. what is the benefit package?

Demonstrate how prepared you are for the interview by:

1. Being on time.
2. Bringing your resume and being prepared to offer references.
3. Being prepared to fill out an application (better if you had been able to pick one up prior to the interview and have it filled out when you go in and introduce yourself). For a formal interview, the employer would have requested the application to even consider you for an interview.
4. Being courteous and patient.
5. Making eye contact with the interviewer.
6. Listening carefully. Answer the questions you are asked—do not ramble.
7. Speaking in a familiar manner about the tasks to be performed on the job for which you are applying.
8. Answering questions carefully and thoughtfully.
9. Expressing your interest in this job by offering your strong points and relevant experience.
10. Expressing why you are particularly interested in this job.
11. Being genuinely enthusiastic.
12. Thanking the interviewer for the interview and ask when he or she expects to let you know the outcome of his or her decision.

SETTING CAREER GOALS

Many people fail to make a connection between what they do now and their future success. If you have a future goal, it would be helpful to clarify what you need to do now in order to take steps in the direction of your planned goal. Take the time to consider the following and then write about the possibilities. You can change or update your goals any time you choose.

1. Clarify the difference between short- and long-term goals.
2. Match your interests and abilities to your future goals.
3. Clarify what success and failure are to you.
4. What education and/or experiences are necessary to fulfill the success you desire?
5. What are some short-term goals that build toward longer term goals?
6. Get as much information as possible so that you become increasingly clear about the path to take in order to achieve your long-term goals.

POTENTIAL CAREER GOALS AND HOW TO REACH THEM

Steps:

1. _____

_____

_____

2. _____

_____

_____

3. _____

_____

_____

4. _____

_____

_____

5. _____

_____

_____

WORK ETHICS

Being able to work well with other people is a valuable asset. Develop skills for judging and dealing fairly with others. Treat everyone as you would want to be treated. Be motivated to perform well the tasks you are given. Be respectful.

The following work ethics will make you a good employee and reinforce positive feelings about you and how you work on your own and with others.

1. Set an example of what you expect from others.
2. Treat everyone equally and according to their qualifications.
3. Emphasize the future instead of the past.
4. Do not blame. Deal with causes, not with symptoms.
5. Learn from mistakes.
6. Do not pass the buck—deal with it.
7. Consider both easy and difficult results to achieve.
8. Make sure that everyone involved benefits.
9. Maximize your potential and encourage the potential of those around you.
10. Praise achievements and reinforce efforts.
11. Promote positive professional relations.
12. Help create an atmosphere of trust and confidence.
13. Do not show favoritism or gossip.
14. Be supportive of the group effort to achieve the best outcome.
15. The bottom line is "be the best you can be."

SURVEY OF PERSONAL STRENGTHS

Everyone possesses strengths and weaknesses. Often people rely on their strengths to compensate for their weaker points. Take the time to identify and understand your strengths and weaknesses.

Check the words that describe you:

__take charge

__determined

__assertive

__firm

__self-starter

__competitive

__enjoy a challenge

__spontaneous

__bold

__decision maker

__leader

__self-reliant

__goal-directed

__adventurer

__controlled

__reserved

__predictable

__detail-oriented

__analytical

__inquisitive

__patient

__problem solver

__supportive

__subtle

__shy

__practical

__orderly–organizational skills

__persistent

__scheduled–good with routines

__take risks

__motivated

__energetic

__verbal

__like variety

__creative

__group-oriented

__optimistic

__loyal

__nondemanding

__even-keeled

__avoid conflict

__dislike change

__adaptive

__empathic

__thoughtful

__good listener

__nurturing

__direct

__good social skills

__resourceful

others:

_____

_____

_____

_____

_____

_____

WRITING A THANK YOU LETTER

Writing a letter to express your appreciation of someone's time to interview you is a courtesy as well as a way to stand out and market yourself in a competitive job market.

Why write?

1. It demonstrates courteous and professional behavior.
2. Keeps your name out in front of the employer.
3. May appeal to and stand out to the employer.
4. It is an opportunity to reinforce your strengths—positive points.
5. Offers a second chance to include something you may have forgotten during the interview.
6. Confirms your understanding of the issues discussed.
7. Reinforces that you are looking forward to the next step in the hiring process.
8. It is an opportunity to restate your interest in the job.

When to write?

1. Write the follow-up letter within the next day (24 hrs).
2. Follow the letter with a phone call 10–14 days if you have not heard from the employer.

How to write it (sample):

Date

Name of the Interviewer
Title–Position
Company Address

Dear _____,

Thank you for taking the time to meet with me/interview me.

1. Reflect how it was helpful–what you learned during the interview.
2. Offer clarification on an issue brought up during the interview.
3. Confirm your interest in the job.
4. Close with thank you or an impressionable statement.

SAMPLE LETTER

January 5, 2000

Robert Smith
Manager
A-1 Business Services
555 Success Way
Utopia, CA 34567

Dear Mr. Smith,

   Thank you for taking the time to meet with me yesterday regarding the employment opportunities with A-1 Business Services. I am impressed with the state of the art technology used by your company. I am confident that my management skills and business training would make an asset to your company. I hope to have the opportunity to discuss the position with you in more detail very soon. Thank you again for your time.

Regards,

Mary Jones

COPING SKILLS FOR CAREGIVERS

When you are in the role of taking care of someone who is chronically ill, it is not uncommon that your own needs get put on the back burner. Your focus is on the care of the person in need. However, if you do not take adequate care of yourself and get your own needs met, you will likely be a candidate for burnout, substance abuse, and possibly become run-down and ill. To prevent burnout, depression, resentment, illness, or other negative experiences and emotions you will need to take care of yourself. Taking care of yourself is actually the best way to insure that you will have the energy to care for someone important to you.

Common problems:

1. Concern about medical care, advice, and costs.
2. There may be multiple health issues and a lack of hope for recovery.
3. Strain upon other relationships.
4. Less time and energy for yourself and for other relationships.
5. The stresses of additional responsibilities.

All of this can leave you exhausted, nervous, depressed, and easily frustrated. Often, caregivers do not want to think about their own situations. They hope it will improve, and when it does not they can begin to feel trapped or hopeless. Caregivers are also at risk for silently abusing substances to numb their stress and to feel better. Do not hold your thoughts and feelings in—talk about it with someone you trust or seek professional help.

What to do:

1. Attend a caregiver support group. Find support by talking with others in a similar situation.
2. Take time for yourself. Exercise regularly, eat well, spend time with people, and participate in activities that you enjoy.
3. Ask for help from others.
4. Let the person you are caring for, and others, know what you need to do to take care of yourself, maintain your energy, and have a meaningful life.

GUIDELINES FOR FAMILY MEMBERS–SIGNIFICANT OTHERS OF THE ALCOHOLIC–CHEMICALLY DEPENDENT INDIVIDUAL

1. Do not view alcoholism–chemical dependency as a family or social disgrace. Recovery can and does happen.

2. Do not nag, lecture, or preach. Chances are that the individual has already told him- or herself everything that you might say. People tune out what they do not want to hear. Being nagged or lectured may lead to lying and may put the individual in a position of making promises he or she cannot keep.

3. Be careful that you do not come off sounding and acting like a martyr. Be aware, because you can give this impression without saying a word. Look at your own attitudes and behavior.

4. Do not try to control the individual's behavior with "if you loved me." Because the individual using substances is compulsive in his or her behavior, such pleas only cause more distress. He or she has to decide to stop because it is his or her choice.

5. Be careful to guard against feelings of jealousy or being left out because of the method of recovery that the individual chooses. Love, home, and family are not enough to support abstinence from substance abuse. Gaining self-respect is often more important in the early stages of recovery than other personal relationship responsibilities.

6. Support responsible behavior in the chemically dependent individual. Do not do for him or her what he or she can do for him- or herself or do what he or she must do for him- or herself. No one can do this for the individual: he or she must do it for him- or herself. Instead of removing the problem, allow him or her to see it, solve it, and deal with the consequences of it.

7. Begin to accept, understand, and live one day at a time.

8. Begin to learn about the use of substances, what role it plays in an individual's life, and what role you have played in the life of a substance abuser. Be willing to assume responsibility for your own life and totally give up any attempt to control the behavior of or change the substance abuser—even for his or her own good.

9. Participating in your own support group, like a 12-step meeting such as Alanon, can help you in your own recovery from the dysfunctional behaviors in this relationship and possibly similar behaviors in other relationships as well.

10. Recognize and accept that whatever you have been doing does not work. Understand what your own behavior is about. Acknowledge that your life has become as unmanageable as that of the substance abuser, so that you can learn to be free to make better choices instead of reacting to what is the responsibility of someone else. Know where you end and he or she begins.

Printed with permission from Johnson, S. L. (1997). "Therapist's Guide to Clinical Intervention." San Diego: Academic Press.

DETACHING WITH LOVE VERSUS CONTROLLING

One of the hardest, but most important goals for people close to an individual in recovery to learn is to detach from the behaviors–substance abuse process and continue to love the person.

What does detachment mean? It can sound frightening, given that everyone's lives (especially family members) have revolved around the chemically dependent person—always trying to anticipate what will happen next, covering up for him or her, etc. Detaching with love is an attitude that is associated with behaviors that are not controlling.

What does controlling mean? Controlling behavior is the need to have people, places, and things be "my way:" expecting the world to be what you want it to be for you, living your life with "should" and "ought to be," not expressing your feelings honestly but with self-centeredness and manipulation of the environment around you, and feeling okay if things are the way you want them to be regardless of the needs to desires of others. It is a behavior that comes from fear—fear of the unknown, fear of "falling apart" if people and situations are not the way you want them to be. It is a symptom of a family or systems dysfunction. It is a reaction to the substance abuse that evolves out of feeling increasing responsibility for the substance abusing person.

As the illness within the substance abusing individual progresses, so do the projections: "If it were not for you, I would not drink to drink–use other substances." Statements like this contribute to a deterioration of self-worth, with the result being that you believe that you are the key to changing this awful mess by controlling your world and the people in it. You become exhausted, frustrated, and resentful. Resentment comes from people not doing what you want them to do—and resentment kills love.

You must accept that

1. Chemical dependency is an illness.
2. You did not cause it.
3. You cannot control it.
4. You cannot cure it.

Detachment from the illness and the substance abusing individual's behaviors allows him or her to take responsibility for him- or herself and allows you to be free to feel love for the individual. When you begin taking care of yourself and doing and being responsible for yourself, you have the key to peace, serenity, sanity, and really feeling good about who you are. [Printed with permission from Johnson, S. L. (1997). "Therapist's Guide to Clinical Intervention." San Diego: Academic Press.]

THE ENABLER—THE COMPANION TO THE DYSFUNCTIONAL–SUBSTANCE ABUSING PERSON

Substance abuse and substance dependency can have devastating consequences for the individual using the substances, as well as for those closely associated with him or her. Of most concern is the individual who may reside with the substance abusing individual or who spends a significant amount of time with him or her. Typically, this person begins to react to the symptoms of the individual, which results in the "concerned person" unsuspectingly conspiring with the dysfunctional behavior–illness and actually enabling it to progress and get worse. This "enabling behavior surrounds and feeds the dependency.

How does the dysfunctional behavior–illness affect the dependent individual? For the substance-dependent individual, he or she completely loses his or her ability to predict accurately when he or she will start and stop substance use. Because of this, he or she becomes engaged repeatedly and unexpectedly in such behaviors as

1. Breaking commitments that he or she intended to keep.
2. Spending more money than he or she planned.
3. Driving under the influence (DUI) violations.
4. Making inappropriate statements to friends, family, and co-workers.
5. Engaging in arguing, fighting, and other antisocial behaviors.
6. Using more of the substance(s) than he or she had planned.

These types of behaviors violate the individual's internal value system, resulting in feelings of guilt, remorse, and self-loathing. However, these feelings get blocked by rationalizations and projections. The rationalization that "last night wasn't that bad." The projection causes the individual to believe that "anyone would be doing what I am doing if he or she had to put up with what I do." The effects of such use of defenses is to progressively lead the individual to be out of touch with reality. This distortion becomes so solid that the individual using substances or engaging in other dysfunctional behaviors is the last to recognize that his or her behavior represents any type of personal problem.

What is an enabler? It is the person who reacts to the preceding symptoms of illness–dysfunctional behavior in such a way as to shield and protect the individual from experiencing the consequences of his or her problem. Thus, he or she loses the opportunity to gain insight regarding the severity of his or her behavior. Without this insight, the individual remains a victim of the defenses and is incapable of recognizing the need to seek appropriate and necessary help. Tragically, the enabler's well-intentioned behavior plays an increasingly destructive role in the progression of the illness–dysfunctional behaviors.

The enabler continues his or her behavior because he or she sees all that he or she has done as a sincere effort to help. Although the enabler sees the negative behavior as isolated attempts to cope with difficult situations or something that just got a little out of hand, his or her behavior serves to reinforce the issues of rationalization, denial, and projection related to the substance abuse–dysfunctional behaviors.

The enabler may be in denial him- or herself about the significance or severity of the problem. His or her thinking may be that the problem does not really exist or that it will disappear as soon as the real problem disappears. This makes the enabler highly vulnerable to developing beliefs and attitudes that victimize the individual engaging in substance abusing–dysfunctional behavior. The rationalizations of both persons are now supporting each other's misunderstanding of the true nature of the problem. The result is that they are both engaged in a successful self-deception, which allows the disease to remain hidden and to progress to a more serious stage.

The substance abuse–dysfunctional behaviors continue to have an increasingly adverse effect on both individuals. To understand the progression of the type of thinking that the individual engaged in substance abuse–dysfunctional behavior has, it is important to under-stand what a successful defense system projection is.

1. The individual takes the unconscious and growing negative feelings about the self and puts them onto other people and situations. This relieves some of stress that he or she feels inside and allows him or her to continue to live in an increasingly painful situation. The individual does not have any insight, and as a result he or she continues to experience more pain, which leads to further projections or putting it off on others—what a vicious circle.

2. As the individual with the substance abuse–dysfunctional behavior problem continues to verbalize his or her projections on the other person, there is no realization from either party that this is being said out of hatred. Both believe that the individual hates the enabler and for good reason (because of the view that he or she is the source of the problem). The consequence is that they now both focus on the enabler's behavior, and this allows the problem behavior to continue to go unseen as the central issue.

It is easy to see how this defense can have a significant emotional effect on the enabler. This becomes a pivotal point in the process of enabling. As the pain from the projections becomes more painful and uncomfortable, the enabler reacts by feeling hurt, injured, and guilty. The result is avoidance behavior. Less and less is expected of the individual with the substance abuse–dysfunctional behaviors because of the distress that it causes. These avoidant reactions only allows the progression of the problem. The individual with substance abuse–dysfunctional behaviors remains out of touch with reality and does not receive honest feedback on the behaviors causing the difficulties at home, work, school, etc. What develops is a "no talk" rule. By the enabler not directly expressing the issues, the individual with substance abuse–dysfunctional behaviors becomes more removed from any insight into his or her behavior and its harmful consequences.

The enabler is not always able to avoid the individual with substance abuse–dysfunctional behaviors. Where relationships are very close, the increasing projections create in the enabler a growing feeling of guilt and blame. He or she begins to feel responsible for the individual's self-defeating and self-destructive behavior. These feelings of self-doubt, inadequacy, and guilt continue to increase with the progression of the severity of the problem.

Unfortunately, the tendency is for the enabler's controlling behavior to escalate. The only way for him or her to feel positive is to "try to make sure that the behavior does not get out of control." "If there are things that I did to cause this, then I can make it go away." Most of the enabler's efforts are manipulative. He or she does things indirectly in an effort to get the behavior he or she wants. These manipulations are destined to fail. Nothing is being confronted and dealt with. As the enabler's feelings of low self-worth increase, it triggers even more desperate attempts of control. The cycle continues and escalates as both parties become increasingly alienated and dysfunctional.

The way to break the cycle is through knowledge and understanding:

1. Learn about the dynamics of chemical dependency and other dysfunctional behaviors.
2. Learn about the dynamics of being an enabler and the importance of self-care.
3. Become aware of the personal identification with the compulsive behavior of enabling.

[This section printed with permission from Johnson, S. L. (1997). "Therapist's Guide to Clinical Intervention." San Diego: Academic Press.]

HEALING FOR THE SUBSTANCE ABUSING FAMILY: FROM ENABLING TO RECOVERY

When one person in a family has a problem with substances, the entire family is affected. Well-meaning efforts to protect the substance abuser make the problem worse over time. Understanding how family members enable the substance abuser to continue using and how to correct their own behavior is the first step toward family recovery. Families who confront their difficulties can achieve recovery and create a harmonious home life.

Examples of enabling are the following:

1. Covering up for the substance abuser's behavior.
2. Denial of the problem.
3. Calling in sick for someone who is hungover, etc., and not able to work.
4. An older child taking over parental responsibilities.
5. Denying adolescent substance abusing behavior as "typical teenage stuff."

Family members in a substance abusing household often feel isolated and ashamed. They feel unable to confront the problems affecting them. They may also have feelings of guilt, wondering if they are some way at fault for the substance abuser's behavior. The emotional damage of substance abuse can be horrible for everyone affected. However, by confronting the problem, getting help, and dealing with the family issues, the path to recovery can be established.

The first step of recovery is acknowledging the problem. The next step is to seek the appropriate level of support and intervention for the entire family. Family treatment includes the following:

1. Acknowledging the problem and its effect on the family system.
2. Recognizing and accepting each person's feelings and needs.
3. Learning good skills.
   a. communication
   b. problem solving
   c. resource development
4. Reassuring the children in the family that they are not at fault for the problems.
5. Each family member appropriately fulfilling his or her family role
   a. adults as adults
   b. children as children

FAMILY LESSONS AND RULES LEARNED IN SUBSTANCE DEPENDENCY AND DYSFUNCTIONAL HOMES

In a substance abusing home, "life lessons" and "rules" are learned that influence the lives of family members and the quality of their relationships. It is common that these beliefs and rules are passed from one generation to the next. Some of problems include the following.

1. General tendencies:
   a. being too loyal to the rules that have been learned
   b. a closed family system that isolates and prevents learning from others
   c. the child's only choice is to accept the reality of the family
   d. the child experiences fear and attempts to overcontrol
   e. living with a substance abuser means living alone
   f. the family tradition of perfection turns children into parents
   g. hypervigilance is developed instead of trust

2. Children leave their family with:
   a. controlling behaviors (bossy, caretaking, rebellious)
   b. difficulty trusting
   c. lack of awareness or ignoring personal needs
   d. poor boundaries
   e. difficulty saying "no" and hearing "no"
   f. denial of feelings
   g. addicted to potential (could be, would be, should be)
   h. difficulty receiving from others

3. Children need to learn:
   a. self-acceptance
   b. trust of themselves and others
   c. set appropriate boundaries
   d. overcome feelings of shame
   e. develop effective coping skills
   f. accept parents as they are versus overidealization
   g. take responsibility for getting needs met

STAGES OF FAMILY ADJUSTMENT TO
SUBSTANCE DEPENDENCE

1. Attempts to deny the problem: Occasional episodes of inappropriate substance use are explained away by family members and/or significant other. The use of substances may be rationalized as taking place due to excess worry, nervousness, tiredness, or having a bad day. Such circumstances allow it to be believable as something other than abuse. Therefore, the assumption is that it is an isolated incident and not a problem.

2. Attempts to eliminate the problem: A partner begins to recognize that the substance use is not normal and tries to pressure the dependent person to be more careful, cut down, or quit. At the same time, the significant other tries to hide the problem from the outside world and make it look as if everything is okay. Children in the family start having problems in response to the family stress.

3. Disorganization and chaos: The equilibrium or status quo of the family is broken down. The significant other can no longer pretend that everything is all right and spends most of his or her time going from crisis to crisis. There may be financial problems. The significant other may question his or her own "rational" thinking, feeling totally stressed out and trapped.

4. Attempts to reorganize in spite of the problem: The significant other begins to take on the larger share of responsibility for the family system. This may mean getting a job, working more hours, taking over the finances, being in charge of children's activities and schedules, etc. The substance-dependent person often loses respect and loses his or her place as a parent with family leadership. Another scenario would be the angry, reactionary person that the family reorganizes to avoid.

5. Efforts to escape the problem: There may be attempts to separate or divorce. Often the marriage is over but they continue to live together. The children do not experience the freedom and consistency to be children. The children may act out, trying to force a different outcome and bring the parents together. Behavior patterns are reinforced.

6. Family reorganization: A family environment centered around substance abuse results in a strong tendency to repeat familiar behavioral patterns and reactions. Most people are not aware of how they have been affected or how they respond. "It seems normal." It is now clear that the entire family needs support and intervention for recovery. Regardless of whether there has been a separation or divorce or the family remains intact, all family members must learn new roles and new ways of responding. If the family is intact, there must be a realignment of roles.

TEN STEPS TO FEELING BETTER IF YOU ARE AN ADOLESCENT LIVING WITH SOMEONE WHO USES SUBSTANCES

1. *Talk about your feelings* with a close friend, relative, teacher, minister, or therapist. Sharing your feelings is not being mean or disrespectful to family. Talking to someone about your feelings can help you feel less alone, and that person might be able to give you needed support.

2. *Get involved in doing things you enjoy.* Activities can help you feel better about yourself and give you something to look forward to, an opportunity to meet new people, and an opportunity to focus less on problems at home.

3. *Observe others that have good relationships.* Learn what you can about what they do that helps them to have a successful relationship.

4. *Remember that your thoughts and feelings are normal.* It is okay to hate substance abuse and still love the person at the same time. All people have self-doubt and mixed up feelings at times. It is part of growing up.

5. *Recognize that with every crisis there is opportunity for change.* The more you learn about yourself and why you do what you do, the more positive choices you will have. This means a greater chance of success.

6. *Educate yourself about substances and their effects.* You are living the consequences of substance abuse.

7. *Realize that your parent's behavior is his or her business.*

8. Recognize that the only thing you have control over is you. Do not try to change other people.

9. *Try to let go of angry and sad feelings.* You have a right to your feelings, but do not let them get you down.

10. *Remember how to have fun.* Sometimes people from substance abusing families worry so much that they forget how to just be themselves and to be carefree.

The more that you talk about these problems, learn how you are affected, and learn what you can do to be the best you can be improves your chances of not growing up and doing the same thing. Attending Alateen or an other support group would be supportive of dealing with current circumstances and learning how to do things differently.

FIRST STEP FOR FAMILY MEMBERS AND SIGNIFICANT OTHER

This exercise offers the opportunity for understanding how your responses and behavior play a role in maintaining the patterns of behavior of others, efforts to control their use of substances, or efforts to control the behavior of others. If you do any of the following, identify it, write about what you do, how it affects your life, and how you will go about changing it. Regarding the preoccupation with someone else's behavior and use of substances, do you:

1. Worry
2. Lose sleep
3. Lecture or nag
4. Moralize–preach
5. Reason with him or her to not use
6. Bargain or barter ("If you don't use … you can have … ," "I'll do … if you stop using … ")
7. Search for stashes
8. Have emotional displays
9. Avoid conflict
10. Cover up–make excuses for someone
11. Engage in destructive behavior (self–others)

Review the following questions and statements

1. As your involvement becomes more clear (in how you are trying to control the behavior of someone else), take responsibility for making changes.

_____

_____

_____

2. Do you accept that you cannot control someone else's behavior? If yes, what are you going to do about it?

_____

_____

_____

3. Do you recognize that your efforts to control result in anger, resentment, and an excuse to not deal with your own issues?

_____

_____

_____

4. Do you want to be responsible for the behavior and consequences of others? What are you going to do?

_____

_____

_____

5. Start your own new beginning or recovery of being free from the efforts to control the behavior of others by developing your own goals.

_____

_____

_____

FUNCTIONAL VS. DYSFUNCTIONAL FAMILIES

Characteristics of the Healthy Functional Family	Dysfunction Caused by an Alcoholic Parent
Safety and security	Parent is not emotionally available Lack of safety and security Lack of protectiveness for children Exposure to loss of parental control Emotional , physical, sexual abuse
Open, assertive communication	No talk of the obvious Keeping peace means keeping secrets Pretense of normalcy Feelings are kept silent Children are used as confidants
Self-care/self-responsibility	Needs of the alcoholic come first Learn that the needs of others come first It is not okay to ask for what you need Thinking of yourself is "selfish" Learn to question one's values and worth
Individual identity	You are not an individual You are what your family needs you to be Family roles are rigid When there is stress everyone automatically takes on their role
Continuity	Lack of security Chaos and conflict Arbitrary and without reason Uncertainty and fear Breakdown of family
Respect and privacy	Individual differences not respected Secrecy confused with privacy Closed family system Parents intrusive Lack of boundaries
Appropriate focus of attention	Not determined by child's needs Needs of the alcoholic is the focus
Quality of family life	Restricted range of emotions Comfort with conflict and chaos develops Emotional problems are never resolved

Adapted from T. L. Cerrnak and J. P. Tarcher (1988) A Time to Heal.

PARENTING STYLE AND ADOLESCENT SUBSTANCE USE

For centuries, mothers have been identified as the parent most responsible for how children develop and form their subsequent behavioral patterns. As children become problem-oriented adolescents, mothers are generally blamed. However, if their children develop into respectable and admirable adolescents, both parents usually share in the pride and glory of their children's accomplishments. How unfair. How incorrect.

Recent psychological research indicates that the father plays a much more significant role in the development of children's behavior patterns than has been thought previously. Both parents directly affect the development of the lifestyle of their children. It is not so much the identity of the mother or father in the home, but rather the parenting style utilized in the home in the rearing of children.

A total of 443 young people, ages 9–17, were interviewed along with their respective parents. Of particular interest was the amount of drugs used by the youths and the parenting style of the parents of these youths. To best understand the relationship between parenting style and drug usage among adolescents, the youths in this research study were subdivided into four groups: (1) abstainers, (2) infrequent drug users, (3) weekly drug users, and (4) daily drug users. Each of the four groups was balanced so that there was an equivalent number of youths of the same age, sex, ethnic background, and perceived social class. In conducting this research, the four groups were then compared on a number of interpersonal and attitudinal dimensions so that parental relationships and parenting styles could be correlated with subsequent drug usage among the 443 young people comprising this research study.

The results of this research study indicate that abstainers and infrequent drug users came from homes where the following were present: (1) a feeling of closeness to a parent (father or mother) prevailed; (2) emphasis in the home was placed on getting along with the parents; (3) there was a desire on the part of the youth to be like the parent (father or mother); (4) there was a perceived attitude of trust for the youth by the mother; (5) there was encouragement and praise from a parent (father or mother); and (6) there was the ability to talk about personal problems with the father. In addition, there were three dynamics that prevailed in the relationship between parent and youth. These were parental strictness or firmness, parental limit-setting, and parental involvement in the decisions made by their children and adolescents. Interestingly, it is important to note that substance use by adolescents was not at all related to whether the parents set rules regarding the prohibition of drug usage. Yet, parents frequently invoked such a rule, thinking that it would deter their children from using drugs. On the other hand, rules about homework and television were significantly related to no or little substance usage. Parents of nonusers were generally considered to be less permissive and had more conduct rules in the home. They were not particularly punitive in their management approach either.

The preceding research results strongly indicate that adolescent drug usage is a family matter. Drug usage is also a behavior pattern that can be prevented by the way families live together and treat each other. [Printed with permission from Allan G. Hedberg, Ph.D.]

HEALTHY PARENTING, HEALTHY FAMILY

Remember, healthy parenting starts first with healthy parents who have a good partnership. This means that the parents work well together. Here are two basic guidelines for healthy parenting:

1. Be a leader
   a. make appropriate family rules that reflect values, are rational, promote safety, and help the family to function well
      i. be specific (what is wanted and what is not)
      ii. make sure rules are understood
   b. stick together
      i. couples need to make rules they both believe in and support
      ii. negotiate your differences (you need to support one another)
      iii. no splitting (good parent–bad parent scenario)
   c. stay in charge and demonstrate what you want your child to learn
      i. show your child ways to do what needs to be done
      ii. talk less and act more
      iii. make rewards and consequences practical and reinforcing of the desired outcome
      iv. be consistent
      v. follow through

2. Be a role model
   a. Plan time to be with children
      i. children learn by role modeling
      ii. demonstrate your love by actions
      iii. establish routines and rituals
      iv. have some one on one time with each child
   b. involve children in family life: children learn values and skills by doing things with you

THE HEALTHY FAMILY IS A PARENT-CENTERED FAMILY

People often misinterpret the statement, "the children must always come first." In doing so, they are always putting off their partner because they need to do this or that for a child. Take some time to rethink what a child needs. The parental relationship must be the center of family life. If the parents do not have a healthy relationship, many of a child's needs are not met. Children have the right to

1. Security
2. Stability
3. Be children
   a. not to be put in the middle of parent issues
   b. not to choose one parent over the other
   c. not to be used as confidant

These rights are protected when there is a healthy parental partnership and two people are working together to fulfill the needs of family life and raising children. Several things automatically fall into line when there is a healthy parental relationship and there are good boundaries between parents and children:

1. There are effective family rules
2. Values are clear and modeled by parents
3. The role of parents is clear and respected
4. Parents are active in their children's lives
5. All family members are involved
6. Good communication is learned and practiced

To achieve this, the following may be helpful:

1. Couple's therapy to clarify how to achieve your goals as a couple
2. Reading books on marriage and family
3. Taking community-based classes (adult education, church, etc.) for couples, such as
   a. communication–relationship enhancement
   b. parenting
   c. skill development

Adapted from Johnson, S. L. (1997). "Therapist's Guide to Clinical Intervention." San Diego: Academic Press.

PARENTS HELPING CHILDREN

Before you take the step to help your children, make sure you can do it effectively. That means you must first take a look at how you live, your values, and how you deal with things. It is common sense that if you are experiencing your own difficulties coping, then you will not be able to offer your child the help you know he or she needs. Get support and educate yourself as needed.

Prevention is the best method for helping children learn to make the right choices about substance use and other life issues. The following information will give a general overview of the parenting role when it comes to the issue of substance use and abuse. Make your children resistant to substance abuse by

1. Love and emotional availability
2. Guidance and role modeling
3. Offering strong personal values
4. Offering a good moral foundation
5. Building self-confidence and self-esteem
6. Helping them learn how to resist peer pressure
7. Offering good family communication
8. Educating yourself and them about substances and their effects
9. Revisiting a discussion on substances from time to time
10. Being supportive and reinforcing of positive, healthy choices

People who feel good about themselves tend to make better choices than their peer counterparts. They learn at an early age that doing the right thing feels good to them.

SUMMARY OF SUBSTANCES

Drug name	Physical dependence	Psychological dependence	Effects	Withdrawal
Alcohol	High	High	Euphoria Drowsiness Slurred speech Impairment in Judgment, Coordination, and Inhibition	Vomiting Headache Delirium Tremors Convulsion Possible death
Cocaine	Possible	High	Hyperalert Excitation Euphoria Paranoia	Apathy Irritability Depression Disorientation
Amphetamines	Possible	High	Same as above Rapid pulse Insomnia Poor appetite	Same as above
Barbiturates	High to moderate	High to moderate	Slurred speech Seems "Drunk" Disorientation	Anxiety Insomnia Delirium Tremors Convulsion Possible death
Narcotics	High	High	Euphoria Drowsy Slow respiration Small pupils Nausea	Watery eyes Runny nose Low appetite Irritability Tremors Panic Cramps Chills Sweats
LSD	None	Unknown	Hallucinations Illusions Change in perceptions	Possible flashbacks
Marijuana	Unknown	Moderate	Euphoria Relaxed inhibitions High appetite Disoriented behavior Apathy	Insomnia Hyperactive

I THINK MY CHILD MAY BE USING SUBSTANCES

If you find paraphenalia for substance use, that is a strong indicator that your child is using substances. You should be involved enough in your child's life to be aware of changes that suggest his or her involvement in substance use. Such changes would include the following:

1. Abrupt changes in mood
2. Negative changes in academic performance
3. Suddenly uncooperative at home
4. Change in peer relationships
5. Relationship problems at home and at school
6. Ignoring rules
7. Resistant to discipline efforts at home and at school
8. Demonstrations of anger and an unusually quick temper
9. Borrowing money, things missing at home
10. Suddenly becomes very sensitive about "his or her things"

What have you seen that is causing you concern for your teenager?

_____

_____

_____

_____

_____

_____

_____

_____

_____

_____

If these things are happening, do not wait for it to get worse. Get help immediately. Talk to a school counselor or family physician to get a referral for an evaluation and recommendation for treatment.

A PARENT'S CHECKLIST ABOUT ADOLESCENT SUBSTANCE USE

For any question that follows to which you would answer yes, circle the number.

1. Is your adolescent lying consistently, especially about the use of money and activities (who he or she is with, what he or she is doing)?
2. Does your adolescent demonstrate lapses of memory?
3. Has your adolescent been isolating him- or herself from family and old friends?
4. Is your adolescent acquiring new friends that you do not know and changing his or her appearance?
5. Has your adolescent's physical condition deteriorated by looking ill–pale, weight loss, etc.?
6. Is your adolescent's behavior causing constant conflicts?
7. Has your adolescent been demonstrating a lot of secretive behavior?
8. Is your adolescent showing a change in sleep pattern, such as sleeping during the day or staying up at night?
9. Are items of value disappearing from your home?
10. Has your adolescent become susceptible to frequent accidents?
11. Do you frequently experience hang-ups on your phone when you answer or callers who refuse to give their names?
12. Is your adolescent being defiant against authority (family, school, community)?
13. Has alcohol or prescription medications been missing at home?
14. Is there a noticeable decline in respectful and responsible behavior?
15. Did your adolescent talk about his or her goals before, but now states he or she does not care, does not worry about it, or does not expect to live to be very old?

ADOLESCENT SUBSTANCE ABUSE QUIZ

1. Does it make you feel more grown-up or more relaxed to use substances?

   _____

   _____

2. Do you find yourself using substances alone more often?

   _____

   _____

3. Do you use substances even when you do not want to?

   _____

   _____

4. Do you feel like you have to use substances when you go to a party?

   _____

   _____

5. Do you have to become numb to deal with your problems?

   _____

   _____

6. Have you done things under the influence of substances that you would not do
   otherwise? _____

   _____

7. Have you changed friends to ones who like to party and use substances?

   _____

   _____

8. Do you use substances before you go to school?

   _____

   _____

9. Are your grades going down?

   _____

   _____

10. Are you acting differently and not as responsibly as you used to?

_____

_____

11. Do you sometimes not remember what happened when you have used substances? _____

_____

12. Do you lie about your substance use?

_____

_____

13. Have you tried to cut down on your substance use or stop, but could not? _____

_____

14. Have you ever gotten in trouble because of substance use?

_____

_____

15. Has using substances changed or hurt important relationships?

_____

_____

16. Has the use of substances interfered with your values (right and wrong)?

_____

_____

17. Do you think you have a substance abuse problem?

_____

_____

18. Do you spend time that is supposed to be for work or school using substances?

_____

_____

19. Does it bother you if someone recommends that you cut down or stop using substances? _____

_____

20. Has your substance use caused any financial problems for your family (fines, attorney fees, damaged property, medical bills, etc.)?

_____

_____

Go back and read over your responses. Are you being honest with yourself? If you have answered "yes" to just three of these questions, it is recommended that you seek help.

ACTIONS TO TAKE IF YOUR CHILD IS USING SUBSTANCES

If you are concerned that your child is using substances, then you need to intervene. Speak to your child, making your position on substance use very clear (hopefully this is not the first time that he or she has heard it). Be very clear that you intend to enforce your opposition to the abuse of substances. Do this example first:

1. Seek understanding
2. Be consistent and true to your own beliefs
3. Be supportive
4. Examine your own behaviors (you may be negatively influencing your child)

Avoid the following:

1. Accusations
2. Sarcasm
3. Shame or humiliation (you are worthless)
4. Seeking of sympathy–manipulation (you are hurting me)
5. Self-blame (it is my fault)

How to stop substance use:

1. Get help immediately
2. Reinforce with your behavior your love and commitment to helping your child learn to make better choices
3. Provide rational consequences for behavior
4. Reinforce appropriate behaviors
5. Always make sure that boundaries are clear between parents and children
6. Make sure that there is adequate accountability

NO RESCUING: If you make protective, enabling choices in dealing with your child, it will make things worse by allowing him or her to get deeper in trouble with substances and take longer to have effective recovery. Do not do it!!!!

DEALING WITH PEER PRESSURE

PART I

Learning to cope with feeling left out by your old group as you make changes or by the new group that you are getting to know is important to a successful recovery. If you have chosen abstinence, being left out by the group–person with whom you used to do drugs may feel lonely, but it is something that needs to be confronted and problem solved. Sometimes making changes seems difficult because you may feel like you do not fit anywhere. This in between period of growth and change is definitely a challenge and can leave you vulnerable to falling back to the risk of influence by your old peer group. Learn to deal with peer pressure and adjust to change by doing the following:

1. Explore your attitudes (think, feel, act) and beliefs.
    a. being around friends–significant other getting high (how does it affect you?)
    b. does it affect your recovery?

2. Are others putting pressure on you, or are you struggling with the difficulties associated with change and feelings of loss?

3. Do you feel like an outsider at recovery meetings whereas others seem to be a part of the group?
    a. do you participate and try to get to know people at meetings?
    b. are there things you could do to help out at meetings?
    c. are you working at developing resources?
    d. do you leave right after the meeting instead of introducing yourself and talking with people?

4. Clarify your situation (being left out, adjusting, etc.).

5. Clarify and affirm what you need to do to achieve a successful recovery.

6. What activities could you seek out that fit in with your recovery goals?

7. What activities could make you vulnerable to relapse?

8. Decide how to deal with these issues.
    a. seek to be included in activities supportive of your recovery
    b. talk about your thoughts and feelings
    c. journal to vent, clarify, and problem solve choices and associated consequences
    d. choose the best solution and take action

Write about three situations in which you struggle with feeling left out. How would you have dealt with it in the past? How will you deal with it now?

1. _____

_____

_____

2. _____

_____

_____

3. _____

_____

_____

DEALING WITH PEER PRESSURE

PART II

Peer pressure is described as feeling influenced or pushed to do something that you know is wrong for you to do. Although it feels difficult to resist such influence or pressure, it is rewarding and reinforces your recovery. Each person has to find his or her own way. That means that each person must take the responsibility of making decisions for him- or herself—not being a follower. When learning to deal with peer pressure, consider the following:

1. Listen to what others say or encourage you to do.
2. Decide what you think about it yourself (your own thoughts, feelings, and values).
3. Separate your ideas from theirs. You know what is right for you.
4. Compare what they say or do with your own thoughts. Is it supportive of your recovery?
5. Decide what is best for you:
   a. what is supportive of your goals
   b. what places your recovery at risk
6. Make a decision and take action.

Write about three situations in which you are struggling with negative influence or pressure to do something that you know is wrong. What are your choices for dealing with it? What are you going to do?

1. _____
   _____
   _____
   _____
   _____
   _____
   _____
   _____

2. _____
   _____
   _____
   _____

3. _____

DEALING WITH PEER PRESSURE

PART III

A factor that is very helpful in your efforts to deal with negative peer pressure is to clarify your values. Your values are responsible for giving you that tight feeling in your stomach that reminds you that you are doing something wrong. When people do not live according to their values, they are not being honest or responsible to themselves, which results in unhappiness and underachievement. Clarify your values by the following steps.

1. What are your values or rules that guide you in knowing what is right or wrong for you to do?
2. Decide what you want to do and how it agrees or disagrees with your values.
3. What is the reason for your decision?
4. Learn to say "no" to choices that do not agree with your values.

Here are some examples of values. If you have difficulty understanding what values are, then look them up in a dictionary.

1. Honesty
2. Leadership
3. Self-responsibility
4. Respect
5. Being the best you can be
6. Commitment
7. Integrity
8. Character
9. Doing the right thing
10. Lack of envy–jealousy
11. Good work ethic
12. Being true to yourself and others

Write out your values:

1. _____
2. _____
3. _____
4. _____
5. _____

Discuss how you have and have not lived by your values:

_____

_____

_____

_____

_____

_____

_____

_____

_____

_____

_____

_____

_____

_____

PART IV: MAKING YOUR OWN DECISIONS

To resist giving in to negative influence and peer pressure requires the use of independent thinking. Consider the following when you are being–feeling pressured by someone to do something that you know is wrong.

1. Clarify what you want to do and why.
2. What are the consequences associated with your decision?
3. Decide how you will inform others of your decision.
4. Prepare yourself to deal with the response from others for your independent thinking.
5. Tell why you have made the decision you have chosen (good practice for assertive communication).
6. Saying "no" to negative influence and pressure demonstrates your ability to distinguish between what is right and wrong for you.
7. If necessary, use social supports for validating and reinforcing your decision.
8. Reaffirm yourself with positive self-talk.

Write about a peer pressure experience you have dealt with or are currently dealing with. What have you learned about yourself and what is right for you to do?

_____

_____

_____

_____

_____

_____

_____

_____

_____

_____

_____

_____

_____

_____

_____

_____

Remember, when you do not live in accordance with your values, you will suffer with negative consequences.

FAMILY RULES AND EXPECTATIONS

As parents develop rules, they should consider the following:

1. Have as few rules as possible.
2. Expectations and consequences should be very clear.
3. Natural consequences and rational consequences.
4. Whenever possible, take a positive approach and create learning experiences.
5. Be clear about what is negotiable and what is not.

Parents often confront situations when they are tired and stressed. As a result, they may find it difficult to avoid conflict with their teen. Maintaining awareness of what you are doing and why you are doing it is necessary at all times. Just as you are trying to teach your teen to not use excuses for poor choices or negative behaviors, remember that you are the role model and must avoid those pitfalls yourself. Therefore, as you maintain your awareness, always consider the following:

1. What is the positive approach to take?
2. Is there a pattern to what we are going through?
3. What can we both learn from this?
4. Are the rules appropriate for this age (i.e., have you updated child rules)?
5. Are there some situations where natural consequences will be the best teacher?
6. Is the behavior in question potentially harmful?
7. Are our values and morals being reflected?
8. Are you managing your emotions or do you get pulled into conflicts easily?
9. Do you struggle with being a friend versus being a parent?
10. Is there a possible negotiation?

Always be respectful and responsible in your relationship with your children. Parents often demand it but are not sure how to demonstrate it themselves. Taking a parenting class at every stage of development can help to prepare you for the changing challenges. It is also validating because most families struggle with the same issues.

TIPS FOR PARENTS

1. Know your children's friends.
2. Be clear about the values that you are teaching your children and the behaviors that go along with good family values.
3. Know what your children do in their free time.
4. Demonstrate interest in your children and encourage their personal growth and development of self-esteem.
5. How are your children influenced by the friends that they have chosen?
6. Keep your children busy and know how they spend their money.
7. Give your children responsibility.
8. Develop good communication with your children.
9. Spend time with your children.
10. Have a "no tolerance" family philosophy about substance use and abuse.
11. Be knowledgeable about substances.
12. Do not let your children dress in gang colors or gang clothing.
13. Set an appropriate curfew.
    a. supervise them
    b. know where they are going and with whom
14. Have a "no tolerance" family philosophy about gangs.
15. Be knowledgeable about gangs.
16. Participate in your children's education.
17. Join a neighborhood watch and participate in any other neighborhood activities that support the safety of children.
18. Set a good example for your children by teaching self-discipline and respectful, responsible behavior.
19. Do not be afraid to appropriately discipline your children.
20. If you keep firearms or other weapons in your home, keep them locked in a safe.

KEEPING CHILDREN DRUG-FREE

Factors that increase children's risk for substance abuse:

1. Child factors
   a. serious behavioral problems
   b. attention deficit hyperactivity disorder
   c. violent acting out
   d. alienation
   e. rebelliousness
   f. low self-esteem
   g. academic difficulties
   h. losses

2. Family factors
   a. poor communication
   b. too much or too little discipline
   c. parent's use of substances
   d. child abuse or neglect
   e. ineffective parenting or parent splitting
   f. stresses of a blended family

3. Environment factors
   a. peer difficulties or rejection
   b. exposure to criminal behavior in the home or neighborhood
   c. poverty
   d. excessive lifestyle
   e. school problems–difficulty mainstreaming or fitting in

Protecting children from substance abuse:

1. Child factors
   a. positive attitude
   b. positive adaption and coping to changes
   c. belief in one's own ability
   d. goals and active in interests

2. Family factors
   a. good family values
   b. warm, close family relationships
   c. consistent discipline
   d. parental supervision of daily activity
   e. positive role modeling

3. Environment factors
   a. close, positive peer relationships
   b. extended family interest and support

c. community resources and activities

d. family and community attitudes that do not tolerate substance use–abuse

Parents are encouraged to

1. Talk with their children about the dangers of substance abuse.
2. Use community programs when necessary to intervene in family crises.
3. Participate in programs or classes that improve parenting and family management skills.
4. Attend and participate in community programs and discussions: speak up, ask questions, express concerns, and share ideas.

HOW SUBSTANCE ABUSE HARMS AN UNBORN CHILD OR NURSING CHILD

Although fetal substance exposure is associated with a variety of effects, there are a number of similar consequences resulting from maternal use of different substances.

1. When a mother uses substances, her unborn or nursing child is also affected. The substances in the bloodstream cross the placenta into the bloodstream of the fetus and into the mother's milk for the breast-feeding baby.

2. Substance use during the fourth through the eighth weeks of pregnancy is more likely to cause spontaneous abortion or noticeable physical abnormalities in the newborn than use of substances later in pregnancy.

3. After the eighth week of pregnancy, maternal substance use is associated with
   a. retardation in growth
   b. premature birth
   c. neurological damage

4. Substance use close to the time of delivery may cause premature labor and can be associated with numerous dangers for the unborn child, such as
   a. increased rates of respiratory problems
   b. sudden infant death syndrome
   c. developmental delays

5. Women who smoke, drink, and/or use other substances experience increased risk of
   a. spontaneous abortion
   b. miscarriage
   c. stillbirth

6. Infants who were exposed to maternal substance abuse prior to their birth are at risk to experience the following difficulties:
   a. low birth weight (small head size and body length for gestational age)
   b. central nervous system damage
   c. mild to severe withdrawal effects
   d. congenital physical malformations
      i. cleft palate
      ii. abnormal facial features
      iii. heart murmurs–abnormalities in other organ systems

7. Although not all babies show the effects of maternal substance use, their risk for problems, defects, and death is increased. The only way to insure the avoidance of substance-related risks of harm is to abstain from substance use.

8. Chronic substance abuse by a female can result in infertility and changes in sexual functioning.

9. Newborns with substance-related impairments are often difficult to manage. This can interfere with mother–infant bonding and requires the input and support of family and social services.

10. In many cases, substance-associated deficits only become apparent as a child matures.

If you are pregnant or considering getting pregnant and use substances, stop using substances immediately, get professional substance abuse treatment immediately if necessary, and talk with your physician about your situation and concerns.

FETAL ALCOHOL SYNDROME (FAS)

What is it? Birth defects or other abnormalities that may occur in some children whose mothers drank alcohol during pregnancy. Alcohol poses possible risks to your unborn child. So do not take a chance. A new life is too important.

Effects of alcohol on children:

1. Low birth weight–small size
2. Difficulty with balance and coordination
3. Mental retardation
4. Facial abnormalities
5. Central nervous system problems and damage

Alcohol is dangerous throughout pregnancy. When it reaches the fetus, it may interfere with normal development.

1. First trimester (1st–3rd months of pregnancy):This is a crucial time in fetal development.
   a. cells are dividing rapidly
   b. alcohol may damage cells that are dividing and also damage the new cells growing from them
   c. the brain is especially vulnerable to damage because it is being formed at this time

2. Second trimester (4th–6th months of pregnancy):The fetus is growing a lot.
   a. the fetus grows the most during this stage
   b. alcohol use results in a poor nutritional state for both mother and baby, so that the proteins and vitamins needed for growth and strength are not there

3. Third trimester (7th–9th months of pregnancy): The last stages of organ development and brain development occur.
   a. brain cells are maturing and connections between them are being made
   b. alcohol use can interrupt these connections
   c. alcohol use during this stage can result in dulled mental activity (retardation)

If you are a pregnant woman or a couple planning a pregnancy, take the safest course of action:

DO NOT DRINK ALCOHOL OR USE ANY OTHER SUBSTANCES

IDENTIFYING CHILDREN OF SUBSTANCE ABUSING PARENTS

General indications of parental substance abuse:

1. Morning tardiness (especially on Mondays)
2. Poor attendance
3. Consistent concern about getting home quickly when school is over or activities end
4. Appearance of neglect
   a. body odor
   b. poor grooming
5. Dressed inappropriately for weather
6. Regressed or immature behavior (thumb sucking–wetting–age-inappropriate behaviors)
7. Avoids arguments or conflicts
8. Frequent illness and visits to school nurse
9. Isolated or withdrawn from peers
10. Difficulty concentrating
11. Hyperactivity
12. Sudden emotional outbursts
13. Poor anger management
14. Exaggerated concern about pleasing authority figures
15. Perfectionism and psuedo-maturity
16. Fear associated with situations involving contact with parents

How to assess:

1. Ask simple, direct, and straightforward questions.
2. Try to understand what it is like to walk in another person's shoes.
3. Try to grasp the degree of helplessness and despair. Share the feelings that this evokes.
4. Reinforce courage and good judgment to not run away or become self-destructive, but to seek appropriate help. These are very difficult choices.

Common feelings of preadolescent children of substance abusers:

1. Confusion
2. Unimportant to parents who do not spend time with them
3. Upset about parental conflicts, possible spousal abuse

4. Feeling older than their peers as a result of role reversal with parents
5. Loneliness and isolation
6. Fear
7. Concern that they are the reason for their parent's substance abuse
8. Angry
9. Disappointed by broken promises
10. Protective of parents or embarrassed. Often will not even bring friends into their home.

Mentoring for children who have substance abusing parents can be a very useful tool for demonstrating the numerous positive life choices that can result in breaking the chain of generational substance abuse.

SELF-ESTEEM AND MENTORING

Self-esteem is the term used to describe how a person feels about him- or herself.

1. High–positive self-esteem: feel good about yourself.
2. Low–negative self-esteem: do not like yourself very much.

Self-esteem begins to develop early in infancy and is shaped by the feedback and visual reflection that children receive from their parents or other important people in their lives. Children learn to believe in themselves and their abilities from the encouragement and reinforcement of their efforts. Some assert that self-esteem is the single most important factor in children's experiences of personal growth. It is easy to see how self-esteem affects everything children do.

1. Children with high–positive self-esteem
   a. are motivated to learn
   b. get along better with others
   c. are physically healthier
   d. cope more effectively with difficulties

2. Children with high–positive self-esteem are more willing
   a. to be curious, questioning, adventurous, and enthusiastic
   b. to see themselves as being able
   c. to take appropriate risks
   d. to be openly creative

3. High–positive self-esteem facilitates
   a. self-confidence
   b. self-responsibility
   c. motivation and self-direction
   d. self-reliance

How does a mentor help to facilitate the development of high–positive self-esteem?

1. Be a good listener.
2. Acknowledge and validate thoughts and feelings.
3. Allow the experience of successes that reinforce ability.
4. Model your own healthy self-esteem.
5. Treat children with mutual respect.
6. Recognize and acknowledge the value in personal differences and cultural diversity.
7. Teach by example that failure can be turned into success by learning and trying again.

8. Demonstrate stability in relationships. For example, some behaviors are not acceptable, but emotional commitment does not change.

9. Encourage new experiences.

10. Identify and encourage strengths.

These goal is to help children see themselves as capable, valuable, and potentially successful individuals. Life is about choices. It is important to clarify who you are and where you are going.

CHARACTERISTICS OFTEN FOUND IN MEMBERS OF SUBSTANCE-DEPENDENT FAMILIES

Aside from the substance-dependent individual, other identifiable roles in the family include the following:

1. Chief enabler
2. Hero
3. Scapegoat
4. Mascot
5. Adjuster

Each family role is defined by specific characteristics. Following are the listed roles and the features that identify them. Although all substance abusing families are different and all children react differently, there are similarities in coping strategies used by the children of substance abusing parents.

1. Substance-dependent person
   a. behaviors: blaming, charm, self-righteousness, perfectionism, grandiosity, rigidity, self-pity, anger, hostility
   b. feelings: anger, fear, guilt, remorse, self-hate, shame
   c. provides the family with a focus and an excuse

2. Chief enabler (generally the partner)
   a. behaviors: overresponsible, serious, manipulative, self-blame, self-pity, martyring, control seeking
   b. feelings: anger, fear, guilt, helplessness, inadequacy, self-doubt
   c. provides the family with respectability

3. Hero
   a. behaviors: serious, leadership, control seeking, approval seeking, focus on tangible tasks (example: workaholic)
   b. feelings: anger, fear, confusion, inadequacy, guilt, loneliness
   c. provides the family with self-worth
   d. how to help:
      i. decrease the need to be perfect, encourage him or her to take appropriate risks
      ii. decrease the need to be responsible for everything (aside from him- or herself)
      iii. learn to accept failure
      iv. learn to value the self instead of accomplishments
      v. learn to value the enjoyment of cooperation and sharing with others
      vi. encourage social cooperation
      vii. learn self-efficacy and decrease–eliminate approval seeking

4. Scapegoat
   a. behaviors: strong identification with peers, confrontative, rebellious, defiant, early substance use, low self-esteem

b. feelings: anger, fear, inadequacy, rejection, resentment, loneliness

c. provides the family with distraction and is a target for blame

d. how to help:

    i. disengage from power struggle

    ii. allow the experience of consequences without lecturing–shaming

    iii. avoid expressing shock and disgust over behaviors

    iv. be calm

    v. provide opportunities for him or her

    vi. take positive action and build a positive, respectful relationship with him or her

5. Mascot

    a. behaviors: sensitive, warm, good listener, hyperactive, avoids conflict, clowns around, approval seeking

    b. feelings: anger, guilt, fear, inadequacy, insecurity, loneliness

    c. provides the family with distraction and emotional relief

    d. how to help:

        i. teach the appropriate use of a sense of humor, but do not reinforce "clowning"

        ii. learn self-care

        iii. teach him or her to identify and appropriately express feelings

        iv. learn to manage his or her compulsive need for attention

        v. develop appropriate ways to get attention

        vi. be consistent and firm using natural and logical consequences

6. Adjuster

    a. behaviors: compliant, responsible, spontaneous, aloof–detached, imaginative, materialistic, eating disorder

    b. feelings: anger, fear, inadequacy, isolation, loneliness, powerlessness, feels unworthy

    c. provides the family with flexibility

    d. how to help:

        i. encourage use of creativity and imagination

        ii. avoid pampering

        iii. do not criticize

        iv. provide successful experiences

        v. encourage

        vi. develop self-goals and associated necessary skills

When the coping strategies used by these identifiable roles are reviewed, one thing they all have in common is the attempt at and adaptation of certain survival skills. Some of these skills are functional and some are dysfunctional.

HOW TO HELP CHILDREN THROUGH A CRISIS

1. First understand your own reaction and deal with it. Remember the focus is on what your child needs from you to deal with a crisis.
2. Attempt to understand your child's experience of the situation–event.
   a. how is he or she coping?
   b. how does he or she feel?
   c. what does he or she think?
3. Validate your child's feelings.
4. Understand that with loss everyone, in his or her own way, deals with and must work through issues like denial, anger, depression, bargaining, and acceptance. What do you need to do to help your child accomplish this?
5. Acknowledge and accept your child's efforts to deal with the crisis. Listen and validate. Do not deny his or her experience.
6. Meet your child where he or she is in dealing with whatever the crisis is and communicate at his or her level. Be direct and simple.
7. Do not push your child to talk about the crisis. However, be available and interested if he or she wants to talk to you.
8. Try to understand what it is like from your child's perspective.
9. Promote objectivity by helping your child to see all sides of the situation.
10. Facilitate problem solving and taking appropriate action. Whenever possible, prepare your child for a difficult situation to encourage better coping and closure. Make a list of issues you think you may need to help your child work through.
    a._____
    b. _____
    c. _____
    d. _____
    e. _____

You do not have to have all of the answers. If you feel your child needs help and you are not sure what to do, then talk to someone or use other resources such as books. Also, in many communities there are programs to help children deal with losses. [Adapted from Johnson, S. L. (1997). "Therapist's Guide to Clinical Intervention." San Diego: Academic Press.]

A PARENTS' PLEDGE[1]

As parents of _____,
we sincerely and openly pledge to live our lives and take decisive action to keep our home free of drugs. Alcohol consumption will likewise be absent from out lifestyle or limited to minimal levels and occasions. To fulfill this pledge, we commit:

1. To communicate with our child–children. That means not only transmitting but receiving. Truly listening. We pledge to respect their ideas and opinions even when they differ from ours. If we disagree, we will explain why and calmly try to guide them to the best of our abilities.
2. To respond to our child–children's problems, rather than reacting to them.
3. To educate ourselves about drugs and their dangers so that we can, in turn, effectively impress upon our children why substances are bad for them.
4. To instruct our child–children in realistic terms how to turn down offers of substances.
5. To monitor our child–children's moods, habits, attitudes, and friendships, which will better enable us to recognize potential substance abuse and prevent it.
6. To help build our child–children's self-esteem, providing and promoting alternative to chemicals, helping them feel grown up in ways other than with drugs, and teaching them how to confront problems instead of seeking escape through substances.
7. To confront any youthful drug or alcohol crises quickly and calmly so that we can make informed, rational decisions that are in our child–children's best interest.
8. To get counseling for ourselves if we have difficulty handling child–children's substance use, so that we may be better able to help them recover and be drug-free.
9. To remember what it was like to be a child, never forgetting where we came from.

_____
Signature of Father

_____   _____
Signature of Mother   Date

Read and acknowledged by child–children _____

_____

[1]Printed with permission from Allan Hedberg, Ph.D.

THE HOUSE WITH THE PINK ELEPHANT

In a substance abusing home, children learn "life lessons" and "rules" that influence their lives and the quality of their relationships. It is common that these beliefs and needs are passed on from one generation to another. Some of the problems include the following:

1. Being too loyal to what parents taught
2. A closed family system, where isolation negates learning from others and promotes dysfunctional thinking and behaving
3. The child experiences "fear" and tries to overcontrol
4. Living with an alcoholic means learning to live alone
5. The family tradition of perfection makes children into parents
6. Trust is underdeveloped; hypervigilance is developed instead
7. Ability to negotiate usually is not developed
8. Lack of honesty (with self and others)

Children leave their family of origin with the following:

1. Controlling behaviors (being bossy, care taking, sick, rebellious)
2. Difficulty with trust (too much or not at all)
3. Either not knowing or ignoring personal needs
4. Denying feelings
5. Being addicted to potential
   a. would be
   b. should be
   c. could be
6. An inability to receive from others
7. Feeling overwhelmed
8. Feeling defective (shame, i.e. something is wrong with me)

These children need to learn

1. True sense of self-worth (accept themselves)
2. Sense of trust (of self and of others that are worthy of their trust)
3. How to set boundaries and then establish primary relationships
4. How to overcome shame
5. To develop healthy coping skills
6. To say goodbye to the parents they wished they had and say hello to the real people their parents are. To live in the here and now by taking responsibility for what they know and making appropriate changes.

PARENTS, TEENAGERS, AND HONEST COMMUNICATION

Being a teenager is a difficult time of life—for everyone involved. Teens are working toward independence and a separate identity from their family, but they do not always make the best choices doing it. Parents need to learn to let go while at the same time setting appropriate guidelines that help to encourage positive growth. This requires

1. Mutual trust
2. Respect for personal privacy
3. Open communication

Teenagers want to talk about their thoughts, feelings, and body changes. They may have concerns such as

1. Are their body changes normal? Reassure them and avoid joking; this is a sensitive issue.
2. Substance use
   a. be a good role model
   b. talk about substance use, values, rules, and responsibility
   c. educate yourself about substances
   d. sign up for Students Against Drunk Driving (SADD, P.O. Box 800, Marlboro, MA 01752)
3. Social status: It is so easy to get caught up in teen social structure. Instead, encourage your teens to participate in different activities. The social status issue will not be so significant if they are involved in activities with other people their own age.
4. Relationship issues
   a. romance (breakups are emotional and devastating)
   b. friendships (conflicts, loss, being left out, etc.)
   c. listen, empathize, and encourage your teens to express and work through feelings
5. Sexuality: Teens have many questions about intimacy, sex, and sexual identity. Parents can be a useful and trusted source of information. Additional issues about which teens need to be educated are birth control, pregnancy, and sexually transmitted diseases.
6. Legal problems and consequences that may interfere with choices such as driving

Make yourself available:

1. Fun family activities
2. Chores together

3. Shared interests
4. Do not be intrusive, but make sure that there is plenty of opportunity for natural conversation.
   a. be a good listener
   b. reinforce efforts and positives

SKILLS FOR POSITIVE PARENTING

No matter their age, children test the limits, which can result in stress and conflict. Learn how to resolve such conflicts in an emotionally healthy and productive way. This not only helps to keep peace in the home but also helps your child to learn good role modeling as they grow up and become independent. Beyond the toddler years, children go through three stages, and with each stage life is experienced differently. The more awareness you have of each stage your child goes through, the more you will be able to offer him or her the appropriate and necessary guidance.

1. Young children
   a. parents are primary role models
   b. use a firm, but loving tone
   c. set clear limits
   d. make sure that their world feels safe and secure
   e. encourage appropriate exploration
   f. give them a lot of attention

2. School-age children
   a. actively involved in a wider social group
   b. influenced by other adults and peers
   c. experiences can be both exciting and scary
   d. be loving, supportive, and believe in them
   e. consistency in messages is important
   f. offer more learning about the relationship between choices and consequences

3. Teenagers
   a. they may feel grown up, but they are not
   b. tend to be secretive and strive toward independence
   c. influence by peers is strong
   d. they need to feel that their parents listen to them and respect them
   e. help them to understand that life is about choices
   f. offer them reinforcement in connecting consequences to their choices

Work with your children:

1. Spend time with them
2. Speak with them
3. Reinforce and praise their efforts
4. Encourage goal development and achievement
5. Focus on specific behavior changes versus personality

UNDERSTANDING THE EXPERIENCE OF THE SIGNIFICANT OTHER

This assignment is designed to help you clarify your role in the recovery process. This means taking the time to think about your participation in change and personal growth.

1. How have you been affected by your partner's use of substances?

_____

_____

_____

2. Are you more concerned now than before?

_____

_____

_____

3. What do you think will happen if substance use does not stop?

_____

_____

_____

4. How do you think you can be encouraging of your partner's recovery?

_____

_____

_____

5. What has discouraged you from trying to help in the past?

_____

_____

_____

6. What are the things you like most about your partner when he or she is not using substances?

_____

_____

_____

7. Why the decision for treatment now?

_____

_____

_____

8. Do you feel that this is also an important time for you to have support and to learn some new ways of thinking, understanding and behaving that will be helpful to you and supportive of your partner's recovery?

_____

_____

_____

_____

TWELVE THINGS YOU CAN DO IF YOUR LOVED ONE IS A SUBSTANCE ABUSER

1. Do not regard this as a family disgrace. Recovery is possible, but it is the substance abuser's choice.

2. Do not nag, preach, or lecture to the substance abuser. Chances are he or she is already aware of everything you can say to him or her. You may only increase his or her shutting you out or lying or may force him or her to make promises he or she cannot possibly keep.

3. Guard against self-righteous and martyr-like attitudes. It is possible to create this impression without uttering a word. A substance abuser's sensitivity is such that he or she judges other people's attitudes toward him or her more by small things that are said or done than by outspoken statements.

4. Do not use the "If you loved me" appeal. Because the substance abuser's problem is compulsive, this approach only increases his or her guilt.

5. Avoid any threat unless you think it through carefully and intend to carry it out. However, there may be times when a particular action is necessary to protect children. Idle threats only make the substance abuser believe that you do not mean what you say.

6. Do not hide substances. Usually this only pushes the substance abuser into a state of desperation. In the end he or she will simply find a way to replace it.

7. Do not allow the substance abuser to persuade you to use with him or her. When you condone substance use, he or she puts off doing something to get help.

8. Do not be jealous of the substance abuser's recovery program. There is often the belief that a love of family and willpower are enough to simply make the choice to change. It is difficult to see your loved one turn to someone or something else for support in his or her recovery. Get your own support to understand what has happened in your life and identify what changes you need to make.

9. Do not expect immediate 100% recovery. Substance abuse and dependence is generally a personally complex issue. As with any recovery, you should expect ups and downs.

10. Do not try to protect the substance abuser in recovery from challenging situations. That could help to push him or her into a relapse. He or she must learn on his or her own to say "no." If you warn other people against his or her exposure to substances, it will stir up feelings of resentment and inadequacy. These issues are all a part of the substance abuser's recovery.

11. Do not do for the substance abuser what he or she cannot do for him- or herself. Allow him or her to face each problem, solve it, or suffer the consequences.

12. Do offer love, support, and understanding in the substance abuser's recovery.

EIGHT STEPS FOR FEELING BETTER IF YOU LIVE WITH SOMEONE WHO ABUSES SUBSTANCES

1. Talk about your thoughts and feelings with someone that you trust (friend, relative, minister, therapist). Sharing your feelings is not a betrayal or being mean. It is necessary to talk about these things so that you can get it out and understand the boundaries of what is your responsibility versus the responsibility of someone else. Talking about your feelings can help you to feel less alone and to get the support that you need.

2. Get involved in doing things that you enjoy. Participate in activities that can help you feel better about yourself. Being active also helps you to meet new people and focus less on problems that belong to someone else that you do not have any control over.

3. Remember that your thoughts and feelings are normal. It is okay to hate the disease of substance dependence and continue to love the person—both at the same time. Under these circumstances, it is not uncommon to experience self-doubt and confused feelings. However, it is your responsibility to understand you, what is contributing to how you feel, and what your choices are for dealing with it.

4. Educate yourself about substance abuse and its effects.

5. Acknowledge and accept that another person's behavior is his or her own business. Try to not feel embarrassed yourself for something that he or she does.

6. Work at finding a way to let go of angry or sad feelings. Everyone has a right to his or her feelings, but do not let your feelings get you down.

7. Remember the importance of having fun. Sometimes you can get so caught up in worrying that you can forget how to just be yourself and be carefree. Spend time doing things and being with people that bring laughter and enjoyment to your life.

8. Do not copy the painful mistakes of others. Instead learn from them. Attend Alanon or other group meetings that promote self-understanding and growth.

If an adolescent looks at this list, he or she would need to consider the following:

1. You are not an adult and should not be taking the role of an adult.
2. You cannot use this experience as an excuse to behave badly.
3. Get involved in fun things at school or near where you live (music, sports, drama).
4. Go to Alateen meetings or other support groups.

BREAKING THE CODEPENDENCY CYCLE

If you have a history of codependency, it is time that you learn to begin to do things differently. It is easier to talk about necessary changes than it is to actually make the changes associated with codependent behavior. As with most difficult changes, it is the small, manageable changes that lead to new behavior when the overall change itself seems too big and overwhelming.

This is your assignment: EVERY DAY you will do at least one thing for yourself (minimum 15 min). It may be helpful to identify how you feel about making such changes so that you can talk it out and problem solve how you feel about this challenge. Do you feel

1. depressed?
2. anxious?
3. guilty?
4. fearful?
5. overwhelmed?
6. confused?
7. excited?
8. ready?

1. Write about your feelings (what do you feel and why).

_____

_____

_____

_____

2. What are somethings you can do for yourself?

_____

_____

_____

_____

3. In 3 months what changes have you made?

_____

_____

_____

_____

4. In 6 months what changes have you made?

_____

_____

_____

_____

If you feel that you do not have time for taking care of yourself, fill out the following schedule.

Time	Typical Activity	Time	Typical Activity
7:00 AM		7:00 PM	
7:30 AM		7:30 PM	
8:00 AM		8:00 PM	
8:30 AM		8:30 PM	
9:00 AM		9:00 PM	
9:30 AM		9:30 PM	
0:00 AM		10:00 PM	
0:30 AM		10:30 PM	
1:00 AM		11:00 PM	
1:30 AM		11:30 PM	
Noon		Midnight	
2:30 PM		12:30 AM	
1:00 PM		1:00 AM	
1:30 PM		1:30 AM	
2:00 PM		2:00 AM	
2:30 PM		2:30 AM	
3:00 PM		3:00 AM	
3:30 PM		3:30 AM	
4:00 PM		4:00 AM	
4:30 PM		4:30 AM	
5:00 PM		5:00 AM	
5:30 PM		5:30 AM	
6:00 PM		6:00 AM	
6:30 PM		6:30 AM	

SIGNS OF AN UNHEALTHY RELATIONSHIP

To have a healthy relationship requires that first you be healthy. This means being the best you can be with honesty, awareness, cooperativity, and appropriate management of feelings and moods. You have to be okay as an individual to be a partner in a healthy relationship. If you depend on others to make you feel okay, you likely are not at the point of being the healthy person that you need to be. Consider the following red flags of an unhealthy relationship.

1. Putting the needs of your partner ahead of your own (protecting, covering up, etc.).
2. Putting your partner's goals ahead of the importance of your own goals.
3. Focusing on helping your partner to change.
4. Focusing on the appearance of your partner's appearance.
5. Recognizing "all" of the problems that your partner has and feeling the need to remake him or her.
6. Always able to quickly point out what is wrong with your partner.
7. Caring for you partner because of what he or she can give you: financial security, intimacy, protection.
8. Bouncing back and forth between extremes of love and hate or a general lack of understanding of what it is like for your partner and not particularly interested in what it is like for him or her.
9. Feeling the need to rescue your partner.
10. Having the expectation that your partner will take good care of you in areas or ways that are really an issue of self-responsibility (exploitation).

These are just a few of the indicators that demonstrate relationship functioning to be unhealthy. So much of the potential for success is related to each person spending the time to take a long, hard, honest look at him- or herself, taking responsibility for being strong as an individual, and offering the best to the person with whom he or she shares his or her life. Ask yourself the following questions:

1. Who am I?
2. Where am I going?
3. How do I get there?
4. How do I offer the best and the healthiest me, which would benefit my relationship?

TEN WAYS TO IMPROVE YOUR MARRIAGE

1. Work together in achieving substance abstinence.
   a. what are your own responsibilities?
   b. do not work your partner's program

2. Increase the positive rewards in your marriage: Enjoy one another, have fun, play, laugh.

3. Develop good communication skills.
   a. think before you speak
   b. say things in a way that can be heard (e.g., if you react emotionally, that will be the focus instead of what you are saying)

4. Reinforce your partner's efforts: Efforts are made because a partner cares.

5. Deal with existing problems.
   a. identify a problem
   b. brainstorm choices for dealing with it (individually and shared)
   c. select the method of dealing with it that appears to result in the most positive outcome
   d. assess the effectiveness of your choice; if it did not work, try again

6. Do not expect your partner to read your mind.
   a. be open, honest, and direct
   b. ask for what you want and need

7. Express your thoughts and feelings in a positive and assertive manner.
   a. do not criticize the person
   b. confront the issue–problem

8. Practice being calm instead of angry and reactive.

9. If there are problem behaviors, make a specific request for change and reinforce all efforts.

10. Do not let problems or negative feelings build up.
    a. deal with things as they happen
    b. explore the possibility of repetitious problems (use self-responsibility and collaborative problem solving to deal with it)

WORKING TOGETHER

This couple's exercise is to be completed by both to increase awareness for goals of improvement or change, reinforce strengths of partnership, and define phased responsibilities. Therefore, for each of the following topics, think in terms of

1. What needs to be accomplished or what is desired.
2. What "I" contribute to the success of each area.
3. What "I" would like from my "partner" in each area.

Topics:

1. Communication
2. Problem solving–conflict resolution
3. Intimacy (affection and sex)
4. Child rearing
5. Money management
6. Independence–personal growth
7. Social–leisure activities
8. Jobs
9. Household responsibilities
10. Honor and support

RELATIONSHIP SELF-MONITORING

Behavior	M	T	W	Th	F	S	S
Affection							
Appreciation							
Compliments							
Conversation							
Listening							
Offers support–help							
Surprise–romance							
Understanding							

BEING A HEALTHY COUPLE

1. Review your commitment to one another and what it means
   a. respect mutually demonstrated
   b. responsibility (for yourself and your partnership)
   c. honor one another
   d. validate one another

2. Develop your skills as a couple
   a. communication
      i. appropriate and accurate expression of thoughts and feelings
      ii. good listening skills
      iii. be clear
   b. conflict resolution
      i. be respectful to one another's perspectives
      ii. work toward what is best for the relationship
      iii. honesty
      iv. self-responsibility
   c. problem solving
      i. work as a team
      ii. listen to one another
      iii. collaborate–cooperate
   d. mutually caring and nurturing behaviors
      i. thoughtful
      ii. helpful
      iii. loving

3. Recognize your differences that are the result of how you were each raised
   a. how do you deal with strong emotions (anger, loss, disappointment, etc.)?
   b. what are problem areas that you need to work out?
   c. what are the strengths?
   d. how do your differences compliment each other?

4. Learn to negotiate
   a. the importance of both of you getting your needs met
   b. how do you continue to grow as a couple?
   c. the use of assertive communication
   d. reinforce the efforts of one another
   e. each must feel like he or she gets out what he or she puts in (fairness)

5. Consider goals, interests, and friendship
   a. as an individual (the effects upon partnership)
   b. as a couple

SELF-ACCEPTANCE

If you have chosen to remain in a difficult situation with a substance abusing partner, it does not mean that you cannot reclaim your "self" or your identity. You could leave if you chose to, but for whatever reason your decision is to stay in the relationship. That does not mean that you cannot develop your own goals and appropriately get some of your needs met. However, it does require that you be honest with yourself. You must be true to yourself to truly accept yourself.

1. Write out what self-acceptance means:

_____

_____

_____

_____

2. What are some goals that would reflect you and what is important to you being the best you can be?

_____

_____

_____

_____

3. Make a list of five ways that you can change your attitude so that it reinforces self-acceptance:

_____

_____

_____

_____

_____

4. Make a list of five behavioral changes that reinforce self-acceptance:

_____

_____

_____

_____

_____

STOP THE RESCUING

Let the crisis happen!!! You and others have stood in the way of the natural course of events—*the natural consequences*. For every choice a person makes there is a consequence. This is true unless it is a substance abuser surrounded by codependent protectors. Unfortunately, although these protectors feel they are saving the substance abuser from pain, what they are really doing is

1. Prolonging and supporting the substance abusing behavior and thinking
2. Avoiding taking responsibility for themselves

As you explore this issue, take a serious look at your rescuing role and the roles of other rescuers in the life of the substance abuser you are protecting from the natural consequences of his or her behavior.

1. Identify all of the rescuers and explain what you understand about their behaviors (i.e., the need to rescue, the need to control, avoidance of guilt, avoidance of self-care, avoidance of self-responsibility).

_____

_____

_____

_____

_____

_____

_____

_____

_____

_____

2. After completing this exercise, what changes are you prepared to make and what help do you need in order to successfully accomplish these changes?

_____

_____

_____

_____

ADULT CHILDREN OF ALCOHOLICS

Adult children of alcoholics (ACAs) share numerous characteristics as a result of having been raised in an alcoholic household. This list could be generalized to those who grew up in a home where there was any substance dependence issue. Read the following list of characteristics and honestly identify any issues you recognize in yourself. Then respond to each one in writing, addressing how your life has been affected as well as your goals for change.

1. Isolated and afraid of people and authority figures.
2. Constantly seeking approval to the point of losing your identity.
3. Frightened by angry people and personal criticism.
4. A tendency to become a substance abuser, marry one, or both.
5. Find some other compulsive behavior such as being a workaholic to fulfill abandonment needs.
6. Overdeveloped sense of responsibility, put the needs of others first.
7. Feel guilty if you stand up for yourself.
8. Addicted to excitement or chaos and crisis.
9. Confuse love and pity (tend to love people you can rescue).
10. Have stuffed the feelings of a traumatic childhood.
11. Lost the ability to express feelings because it hurts so much (even good feelings are difficult to experience and express).
12. Harsh self-judgment and low self-esteem.
13. Dependent personality who is terrified of abandonment and will do almost anything to hang on to a relationship to avoid feelings of reexperienced abandonment.
14. React versus respond to stressful situations.

The goal is to learn to challenge and change irrational beliefs, develop healthy and functional behaviors with appropriate boundaries, and live your own life in a meaningful manner.

CHILDREN OF ALCOHOLICS

Millions of American children have alcoholic–substance abusing parents. These children are at greater risk than their peers who do not have to deal with substance abuse issues in their homes. Alcoholism runs in families, and children of alcoholics are four times more likely than other children to become alcoholics. Children from substance abusing homes have a variety of problems aside from their increased risk to abuse substances.

1. Guilt: The child may see him- or herself as the main cause of the parent's substance use.
2. Anxiety: The child may worry constantly about the situation at home. He or she may fear that something will happen to his or her parent or fear a fight–violence between parents.
3. Embarrassment: Living with the family secret and shame. The child does not invite friends over and is afraid to ask for help.
4. Inability to have close relationships: Disappointment and broken promises lead to distrust of others.
5. Confusion: The substance abusing parent can suddenly change from being loving to being angry without any association to the child's behavior. It is likely that home life lacks routines of nurturing and care for children, often leaving them to fend for themselves.
6. Anger: The child feels angry at the parent for substance abuse and anger at the nonsubstance abusing parent for his or her lack of support and protection.
7. Depression: The child feels lonely and helpless to change the situation.

Although a child may believe that he or she is maintaining the "family secret," relatives, teachers, other adults, or friends may sense that something is wrong. The following may signal a substance abuse problem in the home of a child:

1. Grades going down, failure in school, truancy
2. Lack of friends, withdrawn from peers
3. Delinquent behaviors (stealing, violence, etc.)
4. Frequent physical complaints
5. Own abuse of substances
6. Low frustration tolerance–acting out

Some children of substance abusing parents may act like responsible "parents" within the family and among friends. They cope with the substance abuse of their parents by becoming very controlled and overachieving. At the same time, they may be emotionally isolated from others. Their emotional problems may not become evident until they are older and their efforts to control become more stress-laden. This role reversal robs them of their childhoods. As early as possible, seek professional help, Alateen, Alatot, or other supports.

THE CONSEQUENCES OF CODEPENDENCY

Although the focus of codependency is often on the effects of the enabler upon a substance abuser, the price the codependent individual pays warrants increased self-awareness and appropriate change. Following is a list of some of the consequences and characteristics of being codependent.

1. Not able to identify what is normal.
2. Difficulty in following through on tasks.
3. Difficulty feeling free (or knowing how) to have fun.
4. Judges self harshly and has low self-esteem.
5. Difficulty developing and maintaining meaningful relationships.
6. Difficulty letting down guard to share true intimacy.
7. Overreact to change and feelings of fear or anxiety.
8. Constantly seeking approval and deriving identity from the feedback of others.
9. Feeling of being different from others.
10. Confusion and feelings of inadequacy.
11. Extremes of being overresponsible or irresponsible.
12. Difficulty making decisions. Lacks a sense of personal power.
13. Denial or lack of awareness for feelings of guilt, insecurity, inadequacy, shame, and other experiences of emotional pain.
14. Tendency to respond impulsively and find it difficult to see alternatives.
15. Social isolation.
16. Fear of anger and criticism.
17. Fear of being abandoned.
18. Confusion between love and pity–sympathy.
19. Dependency upon others associated with fear of abandonment.
20. Tendency to find people who need help.
21. Needs to control and a tendency to be rigid.
22. Lies when it would be just as easy to tell the truth.
23. Difficulty trusting.
24. Engages in compulsive behaviors to avoid thinking and feeling.
25. Over time develops feelings of resentment for always having to take care of everything.

If you see numerous points on this list with which you identify, think of it as an opportunity to better understand yourself. With increased self-knowledge comes the potential for change and the hope for an improved quality of life.

FEELINGS

Addicted person	Codependent person
Shame	Shame
Guilt	Guilt
Fear	Fear
Anger	Anger
Inadequacy	Inadequacy
Loneliness–isolation	Loneliness–isolation
Unworthy	Unworthy
Failure	Immobilized
Impotent	Lack of intimacy

When you look at these lists, two things are evident:

1. Addiction affects those close to the addicted person. Therefore, the feelings are a shared experience.
2. Because of poor boundaries, it is hard to tell where one ends and the other begins.

Clearly, individuality, self-responsibility, and shared goals contribute to a healthy partnership.

Write out what you identified about yourself on the above list, and how you understand the effect on your life.

_____

_____

_____

_____

_____

_____

_____

_____

_____

BEHAVIORS OF THE CODEPENDENT

1. Denial
2. Rigid, set in his or her ways
3. Perfection, my way
4. Demand for agreement, no discussion
5. Controlling
6. Closed off
7. Sarcastic
8. Inferiority, passive
9. Martyr, self-righteous
10. Self-pity
11. Manipulate by guilt
12. Superperson (he or she does it all)
13. Hyperactive
14. Protective
15. Overresponsible

Write out what you identified about yourself in the above list, and how it affects you in relationships.

_____

_____

_____

_____

_____

_____

_____

_____

_____

_____

HOW TO DEAL WITH CODEPENDENCY

1. Educate yourself.
   a. read books
   b. Codependents Anonymous (support group)
   c. individual–group therapy

2. Increase self-awareness.
   a. what am I doing?
   b. why am I doing it?

3. Take responsibility for yourself.
   a. emotions
   b. goals
   c. desires, needs, wants, happiness

4. Learn to deal with reality and unpleasant feelings.

5. Quit covering up and taking responsibility for others.

6. Learn assertive communication.

7. Understand the reason(s) behind the choices you make being an enabler.

8. Clarify boundaries.
   a. specifically where you end and someone else begins
   b. what is truly your responsibility versus the responsibility of others

9. If you have children, learn what it means by providing a healthy, stable environment for children.

10. Resolve feelings of anger, hurt, abandonment, and resentment that have built up over the years and prevent you from having the life that you need and want.

Recovery from codependence comes from resolving those toxic feelings left over from childhood, which continued to be reinforced by the coping mechanisms that you used in adult relationships. Work at identifying your codependent behaviors, how those behaviors affect others, and how they affect you. Work at developing the skills you need to live a life with mature and satisfying relationships.

COUPLES HOMEWORK

In an effort to improve your marital relationship, here are some recommendations for practice. Plan to do your homework for the next month, but start immediately to learn how to be a better partner and be prepared to discuss how things have gone at your next therapy session. Every day:

1. Say three kind or loving things to your partner
2. Do three helpful or pleasing things to or for your partner
3. Listen to what your partner says to you
   a. reflect–repeat back to him or her what you hear him or her saying; this gives your partner the opportunity to correct or elaborate for improved understanding
   b. talk with him or her about it
   c. be interested
   d. do all of these things to assure your partner that you are listening
4. Plan couple's activities
5. Plan a time to talk about couple's issues without interruption
6. Catch your partner being good and reinforce his or her efforts
7. Begin to discuss short-term goals and how each of you contribute
8. Laugh together
9. Critical thinking—what do you think would be helpful?

This may seem like a lot to do; however, once you have been practicing it for a while, you will begin to recognize what little effort it takes. You will also begin to recognize several other things:

1. It takes as much effort, if not less, to be respectful, attentive, and caring as it does to be distant or angry.
2. The positive difference you will feel as a couple.
3. How much better your quality of life is.

Get practicing!!!

COUPLES LEARNING TO SOLVE PROBLEMS

There is no way to avoid all conflicts between two people. However, good communication strengthens a couple's relationship by giving them the foundation for effective listening in conjunction with the appropriate expression of thoughts and feelings.

Problems that most couples experience are related to their differences in style, beliefs, goals, and finances. Therefore, when a problem arises:

1. Talk about it
   a. ideas
   b. concerns
   c. fears
   d. frustrations
   e. desired outcome

2. Agree on some basic rules
   a. mutually supportive
   b. mutually respectful
   c. validating (everyone is entitled to his or her own thoughts and feelings)

3. Define the problem: If you do not agree on what the problem is, avoid a conflict by clarifying what needs to be the focus of your problem solving.

4. Generate alternatives to solve the problem
   a. brainstorm all the possibilities
   b. discuss the consequences associated with each possibility
   c. have realistic expectations and limitations

5. Choose a path for resolution and take action

Be prepared for the possibility that things might not work out as you planned. This means that there may be the need for a backup plan. A backup plan is merely one of the alternatives that is generated during your problem solving. Avoid blaming each other. You are a team. Be respectful and kind.

RELATIONSHIP CHALLENGES

Substance use affects your relationships. Now that you have chosen to change, some of the people closest to you may be skeptical and doubtful about your abstinence and growth.

What You Do	What You Do Not
Stay focused on your recovery	Try to please others
Focus on the benefits of abstinence	Try to convince others of change
Acknowledge skepticism and doubt	Pretend everything is okay
Prepare a plan for dealing with difficult personal situations where your goals are in doubt	Procrastinate until the time feels right
State your intention to change	Make your intention given work by being ambivalent
Ask for cooperation and support	Give into goading and temptation
Assertively take responsibility for your own behavior	Take responsibility for the thoughts, feelings, or behaviors of others
Be patient, calm, logical, and respectful of your rights and the rights of others	Ignore your respect and responsibility in relationships
	Fall into old patterns

Make a list of the ways that you demonstrate *behaviorally* your chosen path of recovery and other positive changes that will have a positive effect on relationships.

1. _____

2. _____

3. _____

4. _____

5. _____

IMPROVING RELATIONSHIPS BY USING CLEAR COMMUNICATION

Developing a relationship is a continuous process. Some relationships, like a life partner, family, or best friend, will be with you through many experiences during the course of your life. Through all the changes and stress, clear communication may be what maintains these relationships.

Be aware that people pay significantly more attention to how you say something and your body language while you are saying it than what you say. Therefore, when you have something to say:

1. Speak honestly and directly
2. Avoid emotional escalation
3. Acknowledge the possibility of being misunderstood
4. Avoid responding defensively
5. Try to clarify if necessary (the goal is to be understood)
6. Use humor when appropriate (it can lighten a difficult topic)
7. Be sensitive
8. Be patient and do not interrupt
9. Be specific
10. Be fair

Because people spend more time talking than sharing in any other way, it is a very important component of a satisfying relationship. Consider the following points:

1. Listen without giving advice
2. Use "I" instead of "you"
3. Repeat back what is said to validate listening and clarify mutual understanding
4. Be friendly
5. Match your expression to your message

How does the other person know that you are listening to him or her?

1. Look at him or her while he or she is speaking
2. Concentrate on what he or she is saying
3. If asked a question, respond
4. Ask questions if you do not understand
5. Repeat back to him or her what you think he or she has communicated to you

Practice your communication skills. Because the goal is to be understood, take responsibility for saying things in a way that the other person can "hear" what you are saying to him or her.

COMMUNICATION GUIDELINES

1. Be a good listener: do not make a statement, interrupt, or answer until the other person is finished. Make sure that you understand what the other person is saying.

2. Think first. Think before you speak. Do not be hasty in offering your opinion.

3. Speak in such a way that the other person can understand you.

4. Speak the truth, but in a kind way.

5. Be clear about your facts before you speak.

6. Be smart. Will what you have to say help you or hurt you?

7. Timing is important. Is this the best time to say whatever it is you have to say?

8. Do you have the right attitude?

9. Is your motivation positive or do you have a hidden agenda?

10. Do not use what you have to say *or* what you withhold from saying as a punishment.

11. Always try to think in terms of what is the best way of saying something.

12. Avoid power struggles. Be respectful of differences in opinion.

13. Being willing to acknowledge what role you may play in difficulties when you are talking through issues.

14. Avoid using emotions to hurt others or speaking in extremes such as "always" and "never."

15. Take responsibility for your own emotions, words, actions, and reactions. Do not blame others for what you feel, say, and do.

16. Do not recycle old arguments. Resolve the issue or let it go. Choose your battles carefully.

17. Do not dredge up the past. Deal with here and now issues. Use the past to learn from and increase understanding about feelings and differing points of view.

18. Deal with one problem at a time. Be clear on what the identified issue is and resolve it. If another problem exists, then work on resolving it but do not confuse things by talking about several issues at one time.

19. Focus on positives instead of negatives. Focus on what works, not what does not.

20. Pay close attention to how others experience you. Remember that the words you choose are only part of communication. Other parts of communication include how your body looks when you say it (body language), tone of voice, and facial expression.

21. Part of good listening is the effort to understand what is being said to you so that you can respond appropriately.

22. Take responsibility for responding instead of reacting. This means that if you start getting upset, take a time out and think about how to respond.

23. Admit when you are wrong and make amends. Also, accept the apologies of others.

24. Avoid repetitious nagging.

25. If someone is speaking negatively to you, avoid responding in a similar manner. Instead, validate him or her. Acknowledge his or her thoughts and feelings.

26. Learn to empathize. This means to try to understand what it is like to be in the other person's shoes. Treat others as you wish to be treated.

27. Be respectful of the opinions of others. Maybe the difference in view is an opportunity to learn.

28. As you learn to be respectful of the views held by others, you will find yourself feeling less judgmental.

29. Become more observant of the behavior of others as you try to understand the motives and reasons for their choices. You can care for another even when you do not approve of his or her behavior.

30. Learn to find peace in yourself. Accept others as they are, and take responsibility for the positive role you can play in creating a positive and respectful environment for the sharing of information.

A SENIOR'S GUIDE FOR USING MEDICATIONS WISELY

DO

1. Make sure you tell your doctor
   a. all the medications you are taking
   b. about any medication allergies–sensitivities you have

2. Make sure you understand the instructions before you begin taking a new medication
   a. when
   b. what with
   c. how long to continue
   d. what to do if a problem occurs

3. Make sure you take medications as you are supposed to.
4. Contact your doctor if there is a medication-related problem or concern.
5. Store medications as directed.
6. Maintain a record of
   a. all medications
   b. regimen of how medications are taken
   c. vaccines
   d. medication allergies–sensitivities

DO NOT

1. Take more or less of a medication than what is prescribed.
2. Stop taking a medication without talking with your doctor.
3. Mix medication with alcohol or other medications without speaking to your doctor.
4. Take a medication prescribed for someone else.
5. Transfer medications from one container to another.
6. Keep old–expired medications.

NAIL IN THE FENCE

There was once a boy who had a bad temper.
His father gave him a bag of nails and told him that every time he
lost his temper, he must hammer a nail into the back of the fence.

The first day the boy has driven 37 nails into the fence.
Over the next few weeks, as he learned to control his anger,
the number of nails he used began to dwindle down.
He discovered that it was easier to hold his temper than to drive
the nails into the fence. Finally the day came when the
boy did not lose his temper at all. He told his father about it, and
the father suggested that the boy now pull out one nail for each
day that he was able to hold his temper.

The days passed and the young boy was finally able to tell his father
that all the nails were gone. The father took his son by the hand
and led him to the fence. He said, "You have done well my son,
but look at the holes in the fence. The fence will never be the same.
When you say things in anger, they leave a scar just like this one.
You can put a knife in a man and draw it out. It will not matter how
many times you say you are sorry, the wound is still there."

A verbal wound is as bad as a physical one. Family and friends are
rare jewels, indeed. They make you smile and encourage you to succeed.
They lend an ear, they share words of praise, and they always want to
open their hearts to you.

Author Unknown

INFORMATION SHEETS

ALCOHOL

Drug	Dependence (physical–psychological)	How used	Duration (hours)
Ethyl alcohol	Possible–possible	Oral	1–4

What is alcohol?	Liquid distilled product of fermented fruits, grains, and vegetables Used as solvent, antiseptic, and sedative Moderate potential for abuse
Possible effects	Intoxication Sensory alteration Anxiety reduction
Symptoms of overdose	Staggering Odor of alcohol on breath Loss of coordination Slurred speech, dilated pupils Fetal alcohol syndrome (in babies) Nerve and liver damage Nausea, vomiting Shallow respiration Cold–clammy skin Coma
Withdrawal syndrome	Sweating Tremors Altered perception Psychosis, fear, auditory hallucinations Agitation Anxiety Chills Insomnia
Indications of possible misuse	Confusion, disorientation, loss of motor nerve control Convulsions, shock, shallow respiration Involuntary defecation, drowsiness Respiratory depression and possible death

CENTRAL NERVOUS SYSTEM (CNS) DEPRESSANTS

Drug	Dependence (physical–psychological)	How used	Duration (hours)
Barbiturates	High–moderate	Oral	1–16
Methaqualone	High–high	Oral	4–8
Tranquilizers	Low–low	Oral	4–8
Chloral hydrate	Moderate–moderate	Oral	5–8
Glutethimide	High–moderate	Oral	4–8

What are depressants?	Drugs used medicinally to relieve anxiety, irritability, tension High potential for abuse, development of tolerance Produce a state of intoxication similar to that of alcohol Combined with alcohol, increase effects and multiply risks
Possible effects	Sensory alteration, anxiety reduction, intoxication Small amounts cause calmness, relaxed muscles Larger amounts cause slurred speech, impaired judgment, loss of motor coordination Very large doses may cause respiratory depression, coma, death Newborn babies of abusers may show dependence, withdrawal symptoms, behavioral problems, birth defects
Symptoms of overdose	Shallow respiration, clammy skin, dilated pupils Weak and rapid pulse, coma, death Low margin of safety
Withdrawal syndrome	Anxiety, insomnia, muscle tremors, loss of appetite, nausea, weakness Abrupt cessation or reduced high dose may cause convulsions, irritability, delirium, death
Indications of possible misuse	Behavior similar to alcohol intoxication (without odor of alcohol on breath) Staggering, stumbling, lack of coordination, slurred speech Falling asleep while at work, difficulty concentrating, retrograde amnesia Dilated pupils

CANNABIS

Drug	Dependence (physical–psychological)	How used	Duration (hours)
Marijuana (pot, grass)	Unknown–moderate	Smoked, oral	2–4
Hashish	Unknown–moderate	Smoked, oral	2–4

What is cannabis?	Hemp plant, from which marijuana and hashish are produced Hashish consists of resinous secretions of the cannabis plant Marijuana is a tobacco-like substance
Possible effects	Euphoria followed by relaxation Loss of appetite Apathy, impaired memory, concentration, knowledge retention Loss of coordination More vivid sense of taste, sight, smell, hearing Stronger doses cause fluctuating emotions, fragmentary thoughts, disoriented behavior, psychosis May cause irritation to lungs or respiratory system May cause cancer
Symptoms of overdose	Fatigue, lack of coordination, paranoia, possible psychosis
Withdrawal syndrome	Insomnia, hyperactivity, sometimes decreased appetite
Indications of possible misuse	Animated behavior, loud talking, followed by sleepiness Dilated pupils, bloodshot eyes Distortions in perception, hallucinations Distortions in depth and time perception, loss of coordination

NARCOTICS

Drug	Dependence (physical–psychological)	How used	Duration (hours)
Opium	High–high	Oral, smoked	3–6
Heroin	High–high	Smoked, injected, sniffed	3–6
Morphine	High–high	Oral, smoked, injected	3–6
Codeine	Moderate–moderate	Oral, injected	3–6
Meperidine	High–high	Oral, injected	3–6
Methadone	High–high	Oral, injected	12–24

What are Narcotics?	Drugs used medicinally to relieve pain High potential for abuse Cause relaxation with an immediate "rush" Initial unpleasant effects—restlessness, nausea
Possible effects	Euphoria, depression Drowsiness, respiratory depression Constricted (pinpoint) pupils
Symptoms of overdose	Slow, shallow breathing, clammy skin Convulsions, coma, possible death
Withdrawal Syndrome	Watery eyes, runny nose, yawning, cramps Loss of appetite, irritability, nausea Tremors, panic, chills, sweating (feels like a bad case of the flu)
Indications of possible misuse	Scars (tracks) caused by injections Constricted (pinpoint) pupils Loss of appetite Sniffles, watery eyes, cough, nausea Lethargy, drowsiness, nodding (Paraphernalia, syringes, bent spoons, needles, etc.)

HALLUCINOGENS

Drug	Dependence (physical–psychological)	How used	Duration (hours)
LSD Acid Green–red dragon	None–unknown	Oral	8–12
Psilocybin	None–unknown	Oral, injected, smoked, sniffed	Variable
Mescaline, peyote	None–unknown	Oral, injected	8–12
PCP Angel dust Loveboat	Unknown–high	Smoked, oral, injected	Up to days

What are hallucinogens?	Drugs that produce behavioral changes that are often multiple and dramatic No known medical use, but some block sensation to pain, and use may result in self-inflicted injuries "Designer drugs," made to imitate certain illegal drugs, are often many times stronger than the drugs they imitate
Possible effects	Rapidly changing feelings, immediately and long after use Chronic use may cause persistent problems, depression, violent behavior, anxiety, distorted perception of time Large doses may cause convulsions, coma, heart–lung failure, ruptured blood vessels in the brain May cause hallucinations, illusions, dizziness, confusion, suspicion, anxiety, loss of control Delayed effects—"flashbacks" may occur long after use Designer drugs—one use may cause irreversible brain damage
Symptoms of Overdose	Longer, more intense "trip" episodes, psychosis, coma, death
Withdrawal syndrome	No known withdrawal syndrome
Indications of possible misuse	Extreme changes in behavior and mood, person may sit or recline in a trancelike state or may appear fearful Chills, irregular breathing, sweating, trembling hands Changes in sense of light, hearing, touch, smell, and time Increase in blood pressure, heart rate, and blood sugar

CENTRAL NERVOUS SYSTEM (CNS) STIMULANTS

Drug	Dependence (physical–psychological)	How used	Duration (hours)
Amphetamines	Possible–high	Oral, injected	2–4
Methamphetamine	Possible–high	Oral, injected	2–4
Cocaine	Possible–high	Sniffed, smoked, injected	1–2
Crack	High–high	Smoked, oral	4–14
Other Stimulants	Possible–high	Oral, injected	2–4

What are stimulants?	Drugs used to increase alertness, relieve fatigue, feel stronger and more decisive Used for euphoric effects or to counteract the "down" feeling of tranquilizers or alcohol
Possible effects	Increased heart and respiratory rates, elevated blood pressure, dilated pupils and decreased appetite High doses may cause rapid or irregular heartbeat, loss of coordination, collapse May cause perspiration, blurred vision, dizziness, a feeling of restlessness, anxiety, delusions
Symptoms of overdose	Agitation, increase in body temperature, hallucinations, convulsions, possible death Disorientation, apathy, headaches, hypertension
Withdrawal syndrome	Apathy, long periods of sleep, irritability, depression, disorientation, nausea, diarrhea, psychosis, social withdrawal
Indications of possible misuse	Excessive activity, talkativeness, irritability, argumentativeness, or nervousness Increased blood pressure or pulse rate, dilated pupils Long periods without sleeping or eating Euphoria

STEROIDS

Drug	Dependence (physical–psychological)	How used	Duration (hours)
Dianabol	Possible–possible	Oral	Days to weeks
Nandrolone	Possible–possible	Oral	Days to weeks

What are steroids?	Synthetic compounds available legally and illegally
	Drugs that are closely related to the male sex hormone, testosterone
	Moderate potential for abuse, particularly among young males
Possible effects	Increase body weight
	Increase muscle strength
	Enhance athletic performance
	Increase physical endurance
	Changes in mood
	Rageful
	Broken out skin
Symptoms of overdose	Quick weight and muscle gains
	Extremely aggressive behavior or "roid rage"
	Severe skin rashes
	Impotence, withered testicles
	In females, development of irreversible masculine traits
Withdrawal syndrome	Significant weight loss
	Depression
	Behavioral changes
	Trembling
Indications of possible misuse	Increased combativeness and aggressiveness
	Jaundice
	Purple or red spots on body, unexplained darkness of skin
	Persistent unpleasant breath odor
	Swelling of feet or lower legs

NATIONAL HELPLINES

Adult Children of Alcoholics (ACA/ACoA)	310-534-1815
Alanon/Alateen Family Groups	800-344-2666
AIDS Hotline	800-551-2728
Alcoholics Anonymous	866-701-1206
Alcoholics Anonymous World Service Office	212-870-3400
American Association of Retired Persons Health Advocacy	202-434-AARP
Anxiety Disorders Association of America	301-231-9350
Battered Women's Hotline	800-640-0333
Child Abuse Hotline	800-422-4453
Clearing House on Abuse and Neglect of the Elderly	302-831-8546
Council on Alcoholism and Drug Dependence	212-269-7797
Eating Disorders Treatment	800-841-1515
Families Anonymous	800-736-9805
Narcotics Anonymous	818-780-9725
National Adolescent Suicide Hotline	800-621-4000
National Alliance for the Mentally Ill (NAMI)	800-950-NAMI
National Black Alcoholism Council (NBAC)	202-296-2696
National Council on Alcoholism and Drug Dependence (NCADD)	800-622-2255
National Health Information Center	800-336-4797
National Institute on Aging Information Center	800-222-2225
National Mental Health Association	800-969-NMHA
National Rural Institute on Alcohol and Drug Abuse (NCADI)	800-729-6686
National STD Hotline	800-342-2437
Rational Recovery Systems	800-303-2873
Recovering Couples Anonymous	510-336-3300
Runaway Hotline	800-231-6946
Secular Organizations for Sobriety (SOS)	323-666-4295
The National Alliance for Hispanic Health	202-387-5000

Develop a summary page of resources and support. Collect important community resource phone numbers and put them on your list. Place this list where you can easily get to it when needed. The back of your journal is one place to keep such information.
Resource List

1. _____   6. _____

2. _____   7. _____

3. _____   8. _____

4. _____   9. _____

5. _____   10. _____

Phone numbers change from time to time. Therefore, check numbers ahead of time and update numbers as needed.

INDEX

A

Absorption 14–15
Activities of daily living (ADL) 327–328
Addictive middle stage 57–58
Addictive severity index (ASI) 84
Adolescent drinking index (ADI) 85
Adolescent drug abuse diagnosis (ADAD) 85
Adolescents
    communication with parents 625–626
    curfew 314
    living with substance abuser 586
    est. privileges-responsibilities 314
    group goals 315
    intervention with parents 313–314
    legal issues 185
    parenting style 590
    peer pressure 601–608
    pregnancy 311–312
    role of self-awareness 312
    social life 314–315
    substance abuse quiz 597–599
    treatment dynamics 312–313
Adolescent parent communication form 85
Adult children of alcoholics 256, 641
Adults molested as children 261–262, 342–344
    clinical issues 344
    dissociation experience scale 344
    PTSD 343
Aftercare relapse prevention group 196
Age 17
Agents of change 170–171
Agonist 13
AIDS-HIV 331–342
    assessment 333–335
    harm reduction 339
    LEARN model 333
    neurocognitive decompensation (NARS) 337

    pain management 341–342
    psychosocial 336
    sociocultural issues 332
    treatment 337–338, 342
Alcohol 19
Alcoholics anonymous
    12 steps 154, 408, 409, 410–412, 413–425
    12 traditions 155, 407
    preparing for a meeting 406
Alcohol detox
    medical treatment 235
Alcohol use inventory (AUI) 84
Americans with Disabilities Act 185–186
amphetamines 28
Anger
    dealing with 561
    expressing 556
    letting go 562
    managing 559–560
    understanding 558
ASAM assessment criteria 196–197
    criteria placement 175–176
    dimensions 197
Asian American 358–359
Assessment
    adult psychosocial 100–103
    adolescent screening assessment 132–133
    alcohol involvement scale 127
    assessment questions 78
    brief psychosocial assessment 123–126
    chemical dependency assessment 111–113
    chemical dependency psychological
        assessment 114–116
    components of history 79–81
    conceptual assessment 87–88
    diagnostic criteria codependency 133–134
    dimensions 197

Assessment *(continued)*
  early phase 118–119
  employment setting 134–141
  factors indicating need for adolescent
      assessment 132–133
  family substance use history 122
  follow-up assessment 87
  functional importance of use 86
  individualized treatment plan 77–78
  inventories 83–85
  Johnson brief initial assessment 104–107
  Johnson psychological questionnaire 89–99
  late phase 121
  middle phase 120
  motivational interviewing 76
  mnemonic screening devices 86
  multivariate treatment planning 79
  objective assessment 81–82
  outline for diagnostic summary 129–130
  personal evaluation 128
  psychosocial brief form 123–124
  psychological/neurological assessment 82–83
  prevention
    class topics 142–143
    health behaviors 145–146
    health-education model 146
    goals 145
    models 143–145
    program 145–146
  substance use history 117
    early phase 118–119
    middle phase 120
    late phase 121
  substance use psychological questionnaire
    89–99
  substance use survey 108
  withdrawal symptoms checklist 131
Assessment and treatment diagram 207
Assessment of chemical health inventory
    (ACHI) 85
Anger Management 250–251
Antagonist 13
Anxiety and stress management 255
Anxiety disorder 296
  identifying 548
  managing 549
  relapse 550
Assertiveness training 252
Assessing high risk situations 432
Aversion therapy 279–280

B

Barbiturates 20–21
Behavioral self-control training 281
Benzodiazepines 21
Biological mechanism 42–43
Biopsychosocial perspective 154, 289–290

Brief drinker profile (BDP) 84
Budget
  how 569
  personal plan 570

C

Caffeine 31
CAGE 86, 320
Cannabinoids 22, 23
Caregivers
  coping skills
Center for substance abuse treatment
    (CSAT) 175
Characteristics of substances 11, 12, 13
Chemical dependency adolescent assessment
    project (CDAAP) 85
Children of alcoholics 642
Chloral hydrate 21
Chronic, late stage 58
Classification of substances 19–32
Clinical interview, adolescent 309–310
Club drugs 32
Cocaine 29–30
  crack 30–31
  freebase 30
Codeine 25
Codependent professional 166
Codependency 65–66, 247–248
  behaviors 645
  braking the cycle 632–633
  consequences 643
  how to deal with 646
  identifying patterns 393
Cognitive appraisal questionnaire (CAQ) 84
Common drugs of abuse 36–37
Communication 554
  difficult feelings 555
  expressing anger 556
  guidelines 651–652
  parents and teens 625–626
  pink elephant 624
Comparison
  recovery-mental health models 155–156
Compromising health behaviors 145
Compulsive gambling 387
Conditioning of substances 13, 14
Constructively confronting
  employee 135–136
  outline 136–137
Continuum of prevention model 143
Coping skills 228
Consequences 441–442
Course of treatment 170
Court mandated 359–361
  Delaware model 360–361
  results 359
  treatment 360

Continuum of care 191
   AIDS-HIV 339–341
   inpatient vs outpatient 209
   chart 211
Community reinforcement 206
Controlled drinking 207
Coping with confrontations 514
Coping with disappointment 475
Dealing with embarrassment 515, 516–517
Coping with negative thinking 480
Crack, cocaine 30–31
Craving
   coping 431
   understanding 430
Cross tolerance 234

D

Daily activity schedule 547
Dealing with criticism 557
Dealing with difficult people 509
Dealing with fear 504–505
Decision making 567
Defense mechanisms 501, 502–503
Defensive strategies of employees 138
Delaware model 360–361
Demerol 15
Depression
   identifying 544
   managing 545
   review 329
Depressants 19–22
Developmental stages of dependency
     and recovery
   adolescent 69, 304, 308
   adult 68
Dextroamphetamines 29
Discharge and aftercare 225
Distribution 13
Domestic violence (offender group)
     257–258
Domestic violence (victim group) 260
Drug dosage 12
Drug equivalence 12
Drug interactions 13
Drug use screening inventory-revised
     (DUSI-R) 85
Dry drunk 62–64
DSM IV criteria
   abuse 6
   dependence 7
   geriatric 321
   specifiers 7
Dual Diagnosis 8, 161, 289–290
   adolescent 307
   anxiety disorder 296
   increased self-awareness 295
   long term treatment 294

models of treatment 162
mood disorders 296
nonchronic vs chronic symptoms 295–296
personality disorder 296–301
psychotic disorder 301–303
short term treatment 293–294

E

Early onset variables 50–51
Education 241–242
Eights steps for feeling better if living with a
     substance abuser 631
Emotional first step for dual diagnosis
     518–528
Emotional health rules 508
Employee behavioral patterns 141
Employer and supervisor training 134–135
Enabler 581–582
   detaching 580
   healing 583
Excitement without substances 468
Excretion 13
Expectations 18
Experience of object loss 59–60
Ecstasy 28, 32

F

Family patterns 267
   characteristics 620–621
   identify substance abusing parents
     616–617
Family response to dependence 64
   actions to take 600
   functional vs dysfunctional 589
   guidelines 579
   stages of adjustment 585
Family-significant other group 196
Family therapy 266
   education and intervention 310–311
   first step 587–588
   helping children through crisis 622
   keeping children drug free 611–612
   parenting 591
   parent centered 592
   parents helping children 593
   parent's pledge 623
   positive parenting 627
   rules and expectations 609
   stages of intervention 267
   tips for parenting 610
Fetal alcohol syndrome (FAS) 311–312,
     350–351, 613–614, 615
Feelings 644
Form 90 84
FRAMES 162
Freebase, cocaine 30
Frequency of use 12

G

Geriatric 316–331
  Activities of daily living 327–328
  aging and substance effects 323
  assessment dimensions 324
  assessment problems 317
  depression review 329
  guide for using medication 653
  health screening 329–330
  men 324
  prescribed medication 322–323
  psychosocial 319–320
  statistics 316
  substance-alcohol interactions 331
  treatment considerations 323, 324–326
  treatment goals 326–327
GHB 32
Goal
  development 564
  setting 563
Group 238, 239, 240
  benefits 239–240
  examples 238
  therapeutic 240–241
  topics 245–263

H

Hallucinogens 26–28, 204
Harm reduction
  clinical rationale 161
    integration with traditional treatment 160–161
    principles 160
Health screening 329–330
Heroin 24–25
Hispanic American 357–358
Hydrocodone 25

I

Increased self-awareness 295
Increasing self-understanding 453
Increasing treatment engagement 158
Identifying feelings 551
  understanding 552
Individual therapy 237, 238
Individualized treatment planning 174
  formulation 175–176
  short form 177
Inhalant 22
Inpatient treatment 224
Intensive outpatient 193–194, 198
Inpatient detox 195, 199
Inpatient treatment 224
Integrated treatment 162
Intervention
  criteria 183–184
  guidelines 183
  participation guidelines 184–185

Intrapersonal evaluation 169–170
Intervention
  criteria 183–184
  guidelines 184–185
Inventory of drinking situations (IDS) 84

J

Job
  applying 571
  career goals 573
  interview 572
  personal strengths 575
  sample letter 577
  thank you letter 577
  work ethics 574
Journal writing 228, 243, 433, 434–436, 438–440

K

Ketamine 28, 32

L

Lapse 278
Late onset variable 51
LSD 26–27
LEARN model 333
Level of care
  criteria 198–201
  alcohol 201–202
  cannabinoids 203–204
  hallucinogens 204
  opiates 204–205
  poly substance 205–206
  sedative, hypnotics, anxiolytics 203
  stimulants 205
Level of functioning associated with use 156
Lipid solubility 28

M

Magnetic resonance spectroscopy 43
Maintaining progress 448
Making amends 427
Managing thought about using 481
Marital and family therapy 264–266
  being a healthy couple 638
  challenges 649
  clear communication 561
  communication guidelines 651
  couple's homework 647
  learning to solve problems 648
  ten ways to improve 636
  working together 637
Medical treatment 234
Merperidine 15
Metabolism 13, 234
Methadone 16, 236
Methamphetamine 29–30

Methaqualone 21
methymedroxymethamphetamine
 (MDMA) 28
Michigan alcohol screening test (MAST) 84
 geriatric (MAST-G) 320–321
Minorities 353–359
 African American 356–357
 Asian American 358–359
 Hispanic American 357–358
 Native American 354–356
Moderation of use 280–281
 setting limits 282
Modified drinking 472
Mood 18
 dealing with feeling overwhelmed 489
Morphine 25
Motivational interviewing 76–77, 162, 359
Multifamily group 196

N
Narcotic 23
National helplines 662
Native American 354–356
Negative thinking
 braking the cycle 506
 thought stopping 507
Negotiation 511
Neuropsychiatric AIDS rating scale 337
Neurotransmitters 26
Neurotransmission, altered 26
Nonbarbiturates 21
No talk rule 584

O
Obstacles of change 172–173
 overcoming 173–174
Opiate withdrawal medical treatment 235
Opioids 23–26
Opium 24
Outcome measures 222
 treatment effectiveness 236–237
Outpatient treatment 192–193
Oxycodone 25

P
Pain management, AIDS 341–342
Parallel treatment 162
Partial hospitalization program 194, 199
Patient treatment matching 224–225
Patterns of use 55–56
Peer pressure 601–608
Personal experience inventory (PEI) 85
Peyote (mescaline) 27
Pharmacotherapy 234
 integrated with therapy 235–236
Phases of addiction and recovery 67
Phenylcyclidine (PCP) 28

Physiological functioning
 pharmacodynamics 16, 17
 pharmacokinetics 14, 15
 user factors 17, 18
Positive health behaviors 145
Positron emission tornography 43
Potency 12
Psilocybin 27
Psychosocial, geriatric 319–320
Practicing change 452
Pre-addictive stage 56
Prescribed medication, geriatric 322–323
Prevention 142–146
Prevention-intervention management and
 evaluation system (PMES) 85
Problem drinker 380–381, 382
Problem oriented screening instrument for
 teenagers (POSIT) 85
Problem solving 566
Professional codependent 166
Professional helper 166
Progressive stages of relapse 70
Project match 175
Psychological factors of user 18
Public health model 143–145

Q
Quaalude 21

R
Rational emotive behavior therapy (REBT) 164
Rational emotive therapy (RET) philosophy 164
Record keeping 176
Recovery
 daily schedule 437
 five S's 429
 inventory 403
 plan 404
 renewing recovery plan 405
Recovery stages 58–59, 395
 a choice 396, 397, 450–451
 preparing individuals, couples and family
  166–168
 stages 53
Refusal skills
 targeted behaviors 230–231, 463
Relapse 271, 278
 autopsy 61
 coping with emergency 459
 coping with a lapse 457, 458
 interrupting 449
 prevention 272–275, 443–447, 490
  decision tree 277
 process 62
 reviewing personal risk 486–487
 symptoms 482, 483–485
 urge to use 455, 456

Relapse *(continued)*
  warning signs
    behavioral 272
    early 486
    internal 272
Relationship addiction 386
Relaxation
  deep breathing 469
  monitoring 470
Relaxing without substances 466–467
Residential treatment 195
Resistance 158
Responsibility 473–474
Retention times 33–34
Rohypnol 32
Route of admission 12

S

Screening, Geriatric 318, 320–321
Sedative, hypnotics, anxiolytics 20–21, 203
Self-acceptance 639
Self-care 231, 465
Self-confidence 512–513
Self-control 471
Self-esteem and mentoring 618–619
Self-help programs
  alternatives 159
  role 157–158
Self-honesty 553
Self-monitoring 433
Sensitivity to diversity 165, 306, 332–333,
    344–345, 353
Sequential treatment 162
Setting priorities 565
Sexual addiction 388
Shyness 249
Signs of unhealthy relationship 635
Situational confidence questionnaire (SCQ) 84
Skill building resources (refer to index) 375–662
Skill acquisition 253
Slip 222, 278
Social skills training 254
Social support
  developing and utilizing 491–492
  how to build 493–494
  interfering factors 498–489
  maintaining 495–497
Sociocultural environment 19
Solution focused therapy 219
  decreasing treatment dropout 223
  motivational strategies 222
  potential problems 221
  role of family 223
  stages 242–245
Special populations 289–361
  adolescent 303–315
  adults molested as children 342–344

AIDS-HIV 331–342
  court mandated 359–361
  geriatric 316–331
  women and minorities 353–359
Stages of dependence 53
  developmental stages 56–58
  patterns of use 55
  problematic behaviors/thoughts 54–55
Stages of recovery 53
Statistics, Geriatric 316
Steroids 31–32
Stimulants 29–31, 205–206
  medical treatment 235
Stinking thinking 477–478
Stop the rescuing 640
Substance
  alcohol interaction, Geriatric 331
  characteristics 11, 12, 13
  classification 19–32
    cannabinoids 22–23
    club drugs 32
    depressants 19–22
    hallucinogens 26–28
    opioids 23–26
    steroids 31–32
    stimulants 29–31
  common drugs of abuse 36–37
  information sheets
    alcohol 655
    cannabis 657
    cns depressants 656
    cns stimulants 660
    hallucinogens 659
    narcotics 658
    steroids 661
  retention times 33–34
  substances of abuse 33
  summary 594
Substance abuse 3
  causal factors 41–43, 54
  consequences 337
  continuing behaviors 5
  definition 6
  lifetime trends 44–46
  30 day prevalence 47–50
  parent checklist 596, 595
  pattern factors 3
  risk factors 376
  role of relationships 500
  self-diagnosing 383, 384–385
  symptoms 34–35
Substance abuse problem checklist (SAPC) 84
Substance dependence 3
  causal factors 41–43
  definition 7
  family dynamics 390
  family illness 389

family recovery needs 391–392
models 40–41
six cardinal signs 378
specifiers 7
symptoms 66, 379
Substances of abuse 33
Substance, set, setting 6, 66
Surviving the holiday blues 476
Surviving the loss of a relationship 510
Synergistic 13

T

Taking inventory 426
Time line follow back assessment method
    (TLFBAM) 85
The 12 steps 154
The 12 traditions 155
The Johnson individualized treatment plan
    178–179
The Johnson ITP-short form 177
The obsessive compulsive drinking Scale
    (OCDS) 85
Theoretical orientation 157
Therapeutic ratio 12
Therapist guidelines 165
Therapy 158
Time management 568
TWEAK 86
Twelve steps and dual diagnosis 529–543
Treatment concerns 163
Treatment
    assessment and referral 209–210
    contract 182
    course 170
    diagram 208
    geriatric considerations 323
    goals 163, 220, 326–327
        adolescent 303–315
        AIDS-HIV 337–338, 342
        women 346

individualized plan 174
obstacles to change 172–173
personal vulnerability 172
prioritization 169
review 209–210
rules 182
Treatment guidelines 153
Treatment models
    behavior modification 228
    cognitive restructuring 227
    dynamic cognitive-behavioral model 233
    psychodynamic 231
Treatment plan
    basic format 180
    group 196
    intensive outpatient 193–194
    outpatient 192
    partial hospitalization 194
    residential 195
Twelve things to do for a loved one 630
Types of drug effects 13

U

Understanding craving 430
    coping 431
Understanding experience of significant
    other 628–629
Understanding grief 546
Understanding impact on children 263
Understanding role of thinking and relapse 479
Understanding treatment experience 181

V

Vulnerability
    underlying characteristics 172

W

Withdrawal
    lingering 454
    symptoms 131